Human Resource Management

Baker College Edition

Robert L. Mathis | John H. Jackson |
Stella M. Nkomo | Myron D. Fottler |
R. Bruce McAffe

CENGAGE
Learning·

Australia • Brazil • Japan • Korea • Mexico • Singapore • Spain • United Kingdom • United States

CENGAGE
Learning·

Human Resource Management:
Baker College Edition

Human Resource Management: Essential Perspectives, Sixth Edition
Dr. Robert L Mathis, Dr. John H. Jackson
© 2012, 2009 South-Western, Cengage Learning. All rights reserved.

Human Resource Management Applications, 7th Edition
Stella M. Nkomo, Myron D. Fottler, R. Bruce McAfee
© 2011, 2008, 2005, South-Western, Cengage Learning. All rights reserved.

Executive Editors:
 Maureen Staudt
 Michael Stranz

Business Etiquette
Carol Bennet
© 2008, 2006 South-Western, Cengage Learning. All rights reserved.

Senior Project Development Manager:
 Linda deStefano

Marketing Specialist:
 Courtney Sheldon

Senior Production/
Manufacturing Manager:
 Donna M. Brown

Production Editorial Manager:
 Kim Fry

Sr. Rights Acquisition Account Manager:
 Todd Osborne

For product information and technology assistance, contact us at
Cengage Learning Customer & Sales Support, 1-800-354-9706

For permission to use material from this text or product,
submit all requests online at **cengage.com/permissions**
Further permissions questions can be emailed to
permissionrequest@cengage.com

This book contains select works from existing Cengage Learning resources and was produced by Cengage Learning Custom Solutions for collegiate use. As such, those adopting and/or contributing to this work are responsible for editorial content accuracy, continuity and completeness.

Compilation © 2012 Cengage Learning

ISBN-13: 978-1-285-12910-5

ISBN-10: 1-285-12910-5

Cengage Learning
5191 Natorp Boulevard
Mason, Ohio 45040
USA

Cengage Learning is a leading provider of customized learning solutions with office locations around the globe, including Singapore, the United Kingdom, Australia, Mexico, Brazil, and Japan. Locate your local office at:
international.cengage.com/region.
Cengage Learning products are represented in Canada by Nelson Education, Ltd.
For your lifelong learning solutions, visit **www.cengage.com /custom.**
Visit our corporate website at **www.cengage.com.**

Printed in the United States of America

Mathis, Jackson, Nkomo, Fottler, & McAffe, 2012

Brief Contents

Human Resource Management: Baker College Edition
Dr. Robert L Mathis, Dr. John H. Jackson | Stella M. Nkomo, Myron D. Fottler, R. Bruce McAfee | Carol Bennet

Entire text excerpted from:
Human Resource Management: Essential Perspectives, Sixth Edition
Dr. Robert L Mathis, Dr. John H. Jackson

Entire text excerpted from:
Human Resource Management Applications, 7th Edition
Stella M. Nkomo, Myron D. Fottler, R. Bruce McAfee

Entire module printed from:
Business Etiquette
Carol Bennet

Mathis., R.L., Jackson, J.H., Nkomo, S.M., Fottler. M.D., & McAffe, B. (2012) Human Resource Management, Mason, OH: Cengage Learning.

Mathis, Jackson, Nkomo, Fottler & McAffee, 2012

Mathis, R.L., Jackson, J.H., Nkomo, S.M., Fottler M.D., & McAffee, B. (2012). Human Resource Management, Mason, OH: Cengage Learning.

Dr. Robert L. Mathis

Dr. Robert L. Mathis is Professor Emeritus of Management at the University of Nebraska at Omaha (UNO). Born and raised in Texas, he received a BBA and MBA from Texas Tech University and a PhD in Management and Organization from the University of Colorado. At UNO he has received the University's "Excellence in Teaching" award.

Dr. Mathis has co-authored several books and published numerous articles covering a variety of topics during his career. Dr. Mathis also has held national offices in the Society for Human Resource Management (SHRM) and served as President of the Human Resource Certification Institute (HRCI). He also is certified as a Senior Professional in Human Resources (SPHR) by HRCI.

He has had extensive consulting experiences with organizations of all sizes and in a variety of areas. Firms assisted have been in the telecommunications, telemarketing, financial, manufacturing, retail, health care, and utility industries. He has extensive specialized consulting experience in establishing or revising compensation plans for small- and medium-sized firms. Internationally, Dr. Mathis has consulting and training experience with organizations in Australia, Lithuania, Romania, Moldova, and Taiwan.

Dr. John H. Jackson

Dr. John H. Jackson is Professor of Management at the University of Wyoming. Born in Alaska, he received his BBA and MBA from Texas Tech University. He worked in the telecommunications industry in human resources management for several years before completing his PhD in Management and Organization at the University of Colorado. During his academic career, Dr. Jackson has authored six other college texts and more than 50 articles and papers, including those appearing in *Academy of Management Review, Journal of Management, Human Resource Management,* and *Human Resources Planning.* He has consulted with a variety of organizations on HR and management development matters and served as an expert witness in a number of HR-related cases. At the University of Wyoming, he has served four terms as department head in the Department of Management and Marketing. Dr. Jackson received the university's highest teaching award and has been recognized for his work with two-way interactive television for MBA students. Two Wyoming governors have appointed him to the Wyoming Business Council and the Workforce Development Council. Dr. Jackson serves as president of Silverwood Ranches, Inc.

Preface

The importance of human resource issues for managers and organizations is evident every day. As indicated by frequent headlines and news media reports on downsizing, shortages of qualified workforce, employee discrimination, union activity, and other topics, the management of human resources is growing in importance in the United States and the world. Many individuals are affected by HR issues; consequently, they will benefit by becoming more knowledgeable about HR management and the nature of various activities. Every manager's HR actions can have major consequences for organizations.

This book has been prepared to provide an essential overview of HR management for students, HR practitioners, operating managers, and others in organizations. The positive reception of previous editions of *Human Resource Management: Essential Perspectives* confirmed the need for such a book. Consequently, we are pleased to provide an updated version. In addition, this book presents information in a way that is useful to various industry groups and professional organizations. Finally, this condensed view of HR management also addresses the interest in U.S. practices of HR management in other countries, making it a valuable resource for managers worldwide.

As authors, it is our belief that our book will continue to be a useful and understanding means for those desiring a concise discussion of the important issues and practices in HR management. It is our hope that it will contribute to more effective management of human resources in organizations.

Robert L. Mathis, PhD, SPHR
John H. Jackson, PhD

Brief Contents

Contents

HR's Role and Strategic Nature

HR—MEETING MANAGEMENT CHALLENGES

The role that HR plays in successful organizations is different today and can be a large part of an organization's success. Key issues include:

- Why HR has evolved from primarily an administrative function
- What are appropriate HR roles in Strategy Formulation
- How HR can measure its contributions to organizational success

Many resources affect an organization's performance. The people who are employed there are certainly a major contributor in some situations. Their talents, experience, reliability, expertise, and relationships affect the job they do and whether the organization succeeds or not. This chapter highlights how developing HR Frameworks for people to do their work successfully is important.

HUMAN RESOURCES AS ORGANIZATIONAL CORE COMPETENCY

As a field, human resource management is undergoing significant transformation. **Human resource (HR) management** is designing management systems to ensure that human talent is well used to accomplish organizational goals. Whether employees are in a big company with thousands of jobs or a small nonprofit agency, managing people in an organization is about more than simply administering a pay program, designing training, or avoiding lawsuits. If human resources are to be an important part of successfully competing in the marketplace, a different level of thinking about HR management is necessary.

The development and implementation of specific organizational strategies must be based on the areas of strength in an organization. Referred to as *core competencies*, those strengths are the foundation for creating a competitive advantage for an organization. A **core competency** is a unique capability that creates high value and differentiates an organization from its competition.

HR Functions

HR management can be thought of as seven interlinked functions taking place within organizations as Figure 1-1 shows. Additionally, external forces—legal, economic, technological, global, environmental, cultural/geographic, political, and social—significantly affect how HR functions are designed, managed, and changed. The functions can be grouped as follows:

- **Strategic HR Management:** As part of maintaining organizational competitiveness, *strategic planning for HR effectiveness* can be increased through the use of *HR metrics* and *HR technology*.

FIGURE 1-1 HR Management Functions

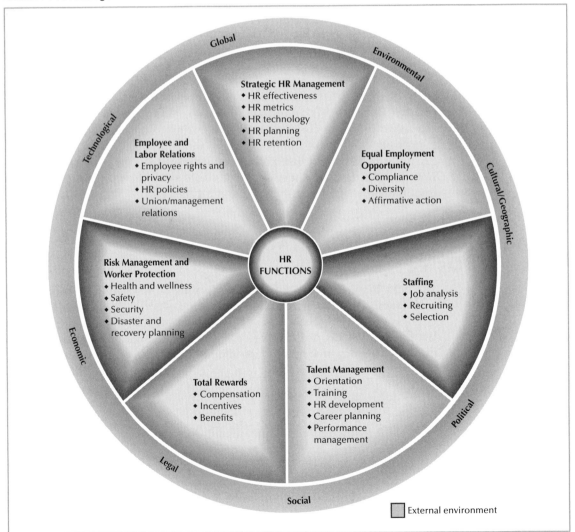

- **Equal Employment Opportunity:** *Compliance* with equal employment opportunity (EEO) laws and regulations affects all other HR activities.
- **Staffing:** The aim of staffing is to provide a sufficient supply of qualified individuals to fill jobs in an organization. *Workers, job design,* and *job analysis* lay the foundation for staffing by identifying what *people* do in their jobs. Through *HR planning,* managers anticipate the future supply and demand for employees and the nature of workforce issues, including the *retention* of employees. These factors are used when *recruiting* applicants for job openings. The *selection* process is concerned with choosing qualified individuals to fill those jobs.
- **Talent Management and Development:** Beginning with the *orientation* of new employees, talent management and development include different types of *training.* Also, *HR development* and *succession planning* of employees and managers is necessary to prepare for future challenges. *Career planning* identifies paths and activities for individual employees as they move within the organization. Assessing how well employees perform their jobs is the focus of *performance management.*
- **Total Rewards:** *Compensation* in the form of *pay, incentives,* and *benefits* rewards people for performing organizational work. To be competitive, employers develop and refine their basic *compensation* systems and may use *variable pay programs* such as incentive rewards. The rapid increase in the cost of *benefits,* especially health care benefits, will continue to be a major issue for most employers.
- **Risk Management and Worker Protection:** Employers must address various workplace risks to ensure protection of workers by meeting legal requirements and being more responsive to concerns for workplace *health* and *safety.* Also, workplace *security* has grown in importance along with *disaster and recovery planning.*
- **Employee and Labor Relations:** The relationship between managers and their employees must be handled legally and effectively. *Employer and employee rights* must be addressed. It is important to develop, communicate, and update *HR policies and procedures* so that managers and employees alike know what is expected. In some organizations, *union/management relations* must be addressed as well.

Organizational Culture and HR

The ability of an organization to use its human capital as a core competency depends in part on the organizational culture that is operating. **Organizational culture** consists of the shared values and beliefs that give members of an organization meaning and provide them with rules for behavior. The culture of an organization is seen in the norms of expected behaviors, values, philosophies, rituals, and symbols used by its employees, and it evolves over a period of time. Only if an organization has a history in which people have shared experiences for years does a culture stabilize. A relatively new firm, such as a business existing for less than 2 years, may not have developed a stabilized culture.

Competitive Advantage of Organizational Culture. Organizational culture should be seen as the "climate" of the organization that employees, managers, customers, and others experience. This culture affects service and quality, organizational productivity, and financial results. One facet of the culture of the organization, as viewed by the people in it, is that culture may affect the attraction and retention of competent employees.[1]

ORGANIZATIONAL PRODUCTIVITY

HR management can play a significant role in organizations by helping to create a culture that emphasizes effectiveness and productivity. In its most basic sense, **productivity** is a measure of the quantity and quality of work done, considering the cost of the resources used. Productivity can be a competitive advantage because when the costs to produce goods and services are lowered by effective processes, lower prices can be charged or more revenue made. Better productivity does not necessarily mean more output; perhaps fewer people (or less money or time) are used to produce the same amount.

One useful way of measuring the productivity of human resources is to consider **unit labor cost,** which is computed by dividing the average cost of workers by their average levels of output. Using unit labor costs, one can see that paying relatively high wages still can result in a firm being economically competitive if high productivity levels are achieved. Low unit labor costs can be a basis for a strategy focusing on human resources. Productivity and unit labor costs can be evaluated at the global, country, organizational, departmental, or individual level as part of various HR measurement metrics.

Productivity at the organizational level ultimately affects profitability and competitiveness in a for-profit organization and total costs in a not-for-profit organization. Perhaps of all the resources used for productivity in organizations, the ones often most closely scrutinized are the human resources. HR management efforts designed to enhance organizational productivity are as follows:

- *Organizational restructuring* involves eliminating layers of management and changing reporting relationships, as well as cutting staff through downsizing, layoffs, and early retirement buyout programs. That has become a concern in a number of industries as economic factors have changed.
- *Redesigning work* often involves having fewer employees who work longer hours and perform multiple job tasks. It may also involve replacing workers with capital equipment or making them more efficient by use of technology or new processes.
- *Aligning HR activities* means making HR efforts consistent with organizational efforts to improve productivity. This alignment includes ensuring that HR functions are not working against productivity.
- *Outsourcing analyses* involve HR in conducting cost-benefit analyses to justify outsourcing. Additional factors may include negotiating with outsourcing vendors, ensuring that contractors domestically and internationally are operating legally and appropriately, and linking organizational employees to the employees of the outsourcing firm.

Customer Service and Quality Linked to HR

Having managers and employees focus on customers contributes significantly to achieving organizational goals and maintaining competitive advantages. In most organizations, service quality is greatly influenced by individual employees who interact with customers. Employee job satisfaction also can be influenced by positive customer satisfaction. Customers often consider continuity of customer service representatives as important when making marketing and sales decisions.

Unfortunately, overall customer satisfaction with sales quality has declined in the United States and other countries. For example, the decline in customer satisfaction has affected many of the U.S. airlines. Even though some airlines have made efforts to improve services, customers continue to be rather skeptical of the improvements in the industry.[2]

Ethics and HR Management

Closely linked with the strategic role of HR is the way managers and HR professionals influence the ethics of people in organizations. How those ethics affect work and lives for individuals may aid in producing more positive work outcomes.

The need for great attention to ethics has grown in the past few years, as evidenced by the corporate scandals at numerous financial and investment firms in the United States and globally. These scandals illustrate that ethical lapses are not just symbolic; they affect numerous firms and employees. The expansion of the Internet has led to more publicity about ethical issues, including ethics in electronic job boards and postings. An increase in ethics issues has been identified by the Ethics Resource Center. One survey of 3,000 U.S. workers found that within a year, 52% had seen one incident of misconduct and 36% had observed two or more ethical violations. The survey also reported that almost 70% of the employers had done ethics training.[3]

The primary determinant of ethical behavior is organizational culture, which is the shared values and beliefs in an organization mentioned earlier. However, when the following four elements of ethics programs exist, ethical behavior is more likely to occur:

- A written code of ethics and standards of conduct
- Training on ethical behavior for all executives, managers, and employees
- Advice to employees on ethical situations they face, often made by HR
- Systems for confidential reporting of ethical misconduct or questionable behavior

Because people in organizations are making ethical decisions on a daily basis, HR management plays a key role as the "keeper and voice" of organizational ethics. All managers, including HR managers, must deal with ethical issues and be sensitive to how they interplay with HR activities. Figure 1-2 identifies some of the most frequent areas of ethical misconduct involving HR activities.

FIGURE 1-2 Examples of HR-Related Ethical Misconduct Activities

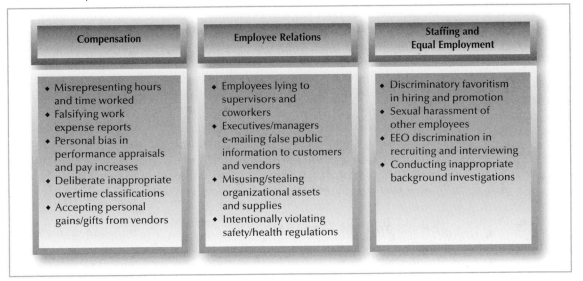

Compensation	Employee Relations	Staffing and Equal Employment
• Misrepresenting hours and time worked • Falsifying work expense reports • Personal bias in performance appraisals and pay increases • Deliberate inappropriate overtime classifications • Accepting personal gains/gifts from vendors	• Employees lying to supervisors and coworkers • Executives/managers e-mailing false public information to customers and vendors • Misusing/stealing organizational assets and supplies • Intentionally violating safety/health regulations	• Discriminatory favoritism in hiring and promotion • Sexual harassment of other employees • EEO discrimination in recruiting and interviewing • Conducting inappropriate background investigations

HR MANAGEMENT CHALLENGES

An overriding theme facing managers and organizations is to operate in a "cost-less" mode, which means continually looking for ways to reduce costs of all types—financial, operations, equipment, and labor. Pressures from global competitors have forced many U.S. firms to close facilities, use international outsourcing, adapt their management practices, increase productivity, and decrease labor costs to become more competitive. The growth of information technology, particularly that linked to the Internet, has influenced HR management as it handles the number, location, and required activities of employees.

These shifts have caused some organizations to reduce the number of employees, while at the same time scrambling to attract and retain employees with different capabilities than were previously needed. Responding to organizational cost pressures and restructurings, as well as the other HR challenges, has resulted in the transformation of HR management in organizations.

Economics and Job Changes

The shifts in the U.S. and global economy in the past years have changed the number and types of jobs present in the United States. The last recession affected many industries such as automotive and financial firms. In general, the United States has continued to have private- and public-sector jobs that are service economy in nature.

Further, projections of growth in some jobs and decline in others illustrate the shifts occurring in the U.S. economy. Most of the fastest-growing occupations percentage-wise are related to information technology and health care. The highest growth of jobs by percentage is in occupations that generally require more education and expertise training.

Workforce Availability and Quality Concerns. Various parts of the United States face significant workforce shortages that exist due to an inadequate supply of workers with the skills needed to perform the jobs being added. It may not be that there are too few people—only that there are too few with many of the skills being demanded. For instance, one survey of more than 2,000 employers found that the hardest jobs to fill are engineers, nurses, technicians, teachers, and sales representatives.[4]

Even though many Americans are graduating from high school and college, employers are concerned about the preparation and specific skills of new graduates. That is another reason why international outsourcing has grown. Unless major improvements are made to U.S. educational systems, U.S. employers will be unable to find enough qualified workers for the growing number of skilled jobs of all types. That is why talent management and development has become one of the most important issues emphasized by HR management.

Growth in Contingent Workforce. *Contingent workers* (temporary workers, independent contractors, leased employees, and part-timers) represent about one-fourth of the U.S. workforce. Many employers operate with a core group of regular employees who have critical skills, and then expand and shrink the workforce by using contingent workers.

The number of contingent workers has grown for many reasons. One reason is economics. Temporary workers are used to replace full-time employees, and many contingent workers are paid less and/or receive fewer benefits than regular employees. For instance, omitting contingent workers from health care benefits saves some firms 20% to 40% in labor costs.

Another reason for the increased use of contingent workers is that it may reduce legal liability for some employers. As more and more employment-related lawsuits have been filed, employers have become more wary about adding regular full-time employees. By using contract workers, including those in other countries, employers may reduce a number of legal issues regarding selection, discrimination, benefits, discipline, and termination.

Globalization of HR

The internationalization of business has proceeded at a rapid pace. Many U.S. firms, both large and small, receive a substantial portion of their profits and sales from other countries. Firms such as Coca-Cola, ExxonMobil, Microsoft, and General Electric derive half or more of total sales and profits from outside the United States. The reverse is also true. For example, Toyota, based in Japan, has grown its market share and its number of jobs in the United States and North America. Also, Toyota, Honda, Nissan, and other

Japanese automobile manufacturers, electronics firms, and suppliers have maintained operations in the United States, whereas Chrysler and General Motors have had to reduce major operations.

The globalization of business has shifted from trade and investment to the integration of global operations, management, and strategic alliances, which has significantly affected the management of human resources. Individuals from other countries are employees. There are three types of global workers: expatriate, host-country national, and third-country national.

An **expatriate** is a citizen of one country who is working in a second country and employed by an organization headquartered in the first country. Experienced expatriates can provide a pool of talent that can be tapped as the organization expands its operations more broadly into even more countries.

A **host-country national** is a citizen of one country who is working in that country and employed by an organization headquartered in a second country. Host-country nationals often know the culture, politics, laws, and business customs better than an outsider would.

A **third-country national** is a citizen of one country who is working in a second country and employed by an organization headquartered in a third country. For example, a U.S. citizen working for a British oil company as a manager in Norway is a third-county national. Staffing with third-country nationals shows a truly global approach.

When labor costs in the United States are compared with those in Germany and Korea, the differences are significant, as Figure 1-3 shows. As a result of these differences, many U.S. and European firms are moving jobs to lower-wage countries.

FIGURE 1-3 Hourly Compensation Costs for Manufacturing Production Workers

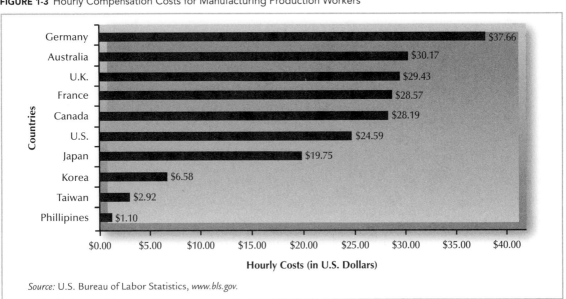

Source: U.S. Bureau of Labor Statistics, *www.bls.gov.*

Workforce Demographics and Diversity

The U.S. workforce has been changing dramatically. It is more diverse racially and ethnically, more women are in it than ever before, and the average age of its members is increasing. As a result of these demographic shifts, HR management in organizations has had to adapt to a more varied labor force both externally and internally. This growing diversity and aging of the workforce has raised employer concerns and means that HR is having to devote more time and effort to ensuring that nondiscriminatory policies and practices are followed.

HR Technology

Greater use of technology has led to organizational use of a *human resource management system (HRMS)*, which is an integrated system providing information used by HR management in decision making. This terminology emphasizes that making HR decisions, not just building databases and using technology, is the primary reason for compiling data in an information system.

The rapid expansion of HR technology serves two major purposes in organizations. One relates to administrative and operational efficiency, and the other to effectiveness. The most basic example is the automation of payroll and benefits activities. Beyond such basic applications, the use of Web-based information systems has allowed the HR unit in organizations to become more administratively efficient and communicate more quickly to employees.

The use of HR technology is also related to strategic HR planning. Having accessible data enables managerial decision making to be based to a greater degree on information rather than relying on managerial perceptions and intuition.

MANAGING HR IN ORGANIZATIONS

In a real sense, *every* manager in an organization is an HR manager. Sales managers, head nurses, drafting supervisors, college deans, and accounting supervisors all engage in HR management, and their effectiveness depends in part on the success of organizational HR systems. However, it is unrealistic to expect a nursing supervisor or an engineering manager to know about the nuances of equal employment regulations or how to design and administer a compensation and benefits system. For that reason, many organizations have people in an HR department who specialize in these activities, but HR in smaller organizations may be somewhat different.

In the United States and worldwide, small businesses employ more than 50% of all private-sector employees and generate new jobs each year.[5] In surveys over several years by the U.S. Small Business Association (SBA), the issues identified as significant concerns in small organizations were consistent: having sufficient numbers of qualified workers, the rapidly increasing costs of benefits, rising taxes, and compliance with government regulations. Notice these concerns have an HR focus, especially when governmental compliance with wage/hour, safety, equal employment, and other regulations are considered.

However, not every small organization is able to maintain an HR department. In a company with an owner and only three employees, the owner usually takes care of HR issues. As an organization grows, often a clerical employee is added to handle payroll, benefits, and required HR recordkeeping. If new employees are hired, supervisors and managers usually do the recruiting, selecting, and training. These HR activities reduce the time that supervisors and managers have to focus on operations, sales and marketing, accounting, and other business areas. Thus, for both small and large employers, numerous HR activities are being outsourced to specialized vendors. Typically, at around 100 employees, an organization will need to designate a person to specialize in HR management.

HR Management Roles

Several roles can be fulfilled by HR management. The nature and extent of these roles depend on both what upper management wants HR management to do and what competencies the HR staff have demonstrated. Three roles are typically identified for HR.

- *Administrative:* Focusing on clerical administration and recordkeeping, including essential legal paperwork and policy implementation.
- *Operational and employee advocate:* Managing most HR activities in line with the strategies and operations that have been identified by management and serving as employee "champion" for employee issues and concerns.
- *Strategic:* Helping to define the strategy relative to human capital and its contribution to organizational results.

HR Management Competencies and Careers

As HR management becomes more complex, greater demands are placed on individuals who make HR their career specialty. The transformation of HR toward being more strategic has implications for the competencies needed by HR professionals. Views of HR have changed over the years as the needed competencies and the results have changed. HR professionals at all levels need the following:

- Strategic knowledge and impact means
- Legal, administrative, and operational capabilities
- Technology knowledge and usage abilities

Senior HR leaders may need additional capabilities and competencies such as: (a) more business, strategic, HR, and organizational knowledge; (b) ability to lead changes; and (c) ethical behavior and results orientation/ performance. For a listing of some of the knowledge resources available in HR and their Internet addresses, see Appendix A.

HR and Strategy

The **strategy** an organization follows is its proposition for how to compete successfully and thereby survive and grow. Several different approaches to strategy formation exist. Many organizations have a relatively formal process for developing a written strategy encompassing a 5-year period with objectives and goals for each unit.

Strategic decisions relate to using resources in such a way that the organization can outperform its competitors. Organizations seek to achieve and maintain a competitive advantage in the marketplace by delivering high-quality products and services to their customers in a way that competitors cannot duplicate. Strategies might include revising existing products, acquiring new businesses, or developing new products or services using existing capabilities. Other strategic approaches might be to maintain a secure position with a single stable product (like WD-40) or to emphasize a constant stream of new products (like Apple). These are all viable strategies for different businesses, but the strategies chosen will determine the number, nature, and capabilities of people needed in the organization. Further, the people already in the organization may limit the strategies that might be successful.[6]

Regardless of which specific strategies are adopted for guiding an organization, having the right people in the right place at the right time will be critical to make the overall strategies work. If a strategy requires worker skills that are currently not available in the company, it will require time to find and hire people with those skills. Strategic HR management entails providing input into organizational strategic planning and developing specific HR initiatives to help achieve the organizational goals.

Although HR administrative and legally mandated tasks are important, strategic HR means adding value by improving the performance of the business. Some businesses are highly dependent on human capital for a competitive advantage; others are less so.

STRATEGIC PLANNING

Strategic planning is the process of defining an organizational strategy, or direction, and making decisions on allocating the resources of the organization (capital and people) to pursue this strategy. Successful organizations engage in this core business process on an ongoing basis. The plan serves as the roadmap that gives the organization direction and aligns resources. The process involves several sequential steps that focus on the future of the organization.

Figure 1-4 shows the strategic planning process for the organization. The planning process begins with an assessment of the current state of the business and the environmental forces that may be important during the planning cycle. Analysis of the strengths, weaknesses, opportunities, and threats (SWOT) is a typical starting point because it allows managers to consider both internal and external conditions.

FIGURE 1-4 Strategic Planning Process

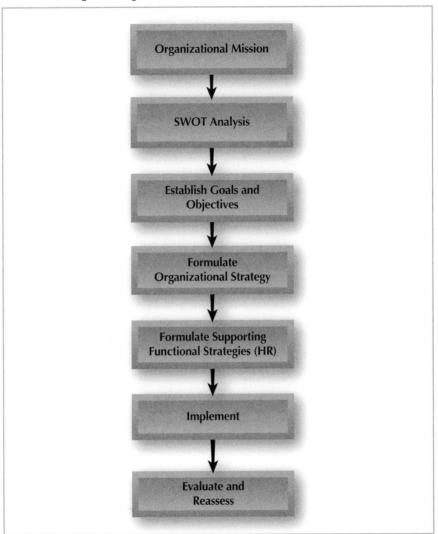

HR as Organizational Contributor

In organizations where there are identifiable core competencies related to people, HR practices can play a significant strategic role in organizational effectiveness. Effective management of talent provides managers with high-quality human resources to carry out the organizational strategies.

A wide array of data from both academics and consulting firms shows that HR practices really do make a significant difference to business outcomes. Some recognized HR best practices include:[7]

- *Incentive compensation:* Pay-for-performance systems that tie employee rewards directly to successful performance of job responsibilities

- *Training:* Talent development programs to ensure that all employees have the proper knowledge, skills, and abilities to perform their jobs and to grow with the organization
- *Employee participation:* Soliciting and using employee ideas and suggestions to give employees a sense of importance and value to the organization
- *Selectivity:* Setting stringent hiring standards to maintain a high level of quality when bringing employees into the organization
- *Flexible work arrangements:* Providing alternative work schedules to help employees balance their personal and professional lives

HR Effectiveness and Financial Performance

There are many different ways of measuring the financial contributions of HR and many challenges associated with doing so. Return on investment (ROI) is a common measure used by financial professionals to assess the value of an investment. For example, if a firm invests $20,000 for a supervisory training program, what does it gain in lower worker compensation costs, lower legal costs, higher employee productivity, and lower employee turnover? The benefits of HR programs are not always immediately visible, which is what makes measuring HR's impact such a challenge. However, efforts should be made to financially assess HR practices.

Strategy and Competition

Before the managers in an organization begin strategic determination, they study and assess the dynamics of the environment in which they operate to better understand how these conditions might affect their plans. This process of **environmental scanning** helps to pinpoint strengths, weaknesses, opportunities, and threats that the organization will face.

The quality and quantity of talent, the organizational culture, and the talent pipeline and leadership bench strength must be considered as well. The strengths and weaknesses of the organization represent factors within the organization that either create or destroy value. When assessing the internal environment, managers evaluate the quantity and quality of human resources, HR practices, and the organizational culture.

The strength of the talent pipeline is particularly important as the organization plans its future. Fulfilling strategic objectives is impossible without sufficient skills and talent. Leadership development and succession planning programs ensure that high-quality talent will be available to carry out the strategy. Effective development programs can reduce the high failure rate of people in leadership positions. Selecting individuals with the right talents and teaching them leadership skills can improve the quality of leaders and promote strategic success. **Succession planning** is the process of identifying a plan for the orderly replacement of key employees. The succession plan is the blueprint for managing the internal talent pipeline. Managers identify individuals who can fulfill new roles in the future and include them in the succession plan. This internal pool of talent is the reserve needed to meet the objectives in the strategic plan.

Competitors exist in both the product and labor markets. Competition in the product market determines the potential for the organization. If the organization is in a highly competitive industry (such as consumer electronics), strategies for growth rely heavily on innovation and driving down product costs. Competition in the labor market establishes the pricing for high-quality talent and determines the availability of workers. A detailed competitive analysis in both product and labor markets provides important information to managers regarding the possibility of meeting strategic objectives.

GLOBAL COMPETITIVENESS AND HR STRATEGY

The globalization of business has meant that more organizations now operate across borders with ties to foreign operations, international suppliers, vendors, employees, and other business partners. A global presence can range from importing and exporting to operating as a **multinational corporation (MNC)**. An MNC, sometimes called a "transnational corporation," is a corporation that has facilities and other assets in at least one country other than its home country. Because human resources are considered assets, the definition of MNC covers a large number of companies.

Having a global HR mindset means looking at HR issues from an international perspective, using ideas and resources throughout the world, and ensuring openness to other cultures and ideas. To effectively compete on an international scale, the organization needs expertise to administer all HR activities in a wide range of nations. Policies and practices should be established to address the unique demands for operating in a global context. For example, the organization may decide to standardize talent development and succession planning but permit local managers to establish compensation and labor relations policies. An ideal international approach strikes a balance between home-country and host-country policies that utilizes the best practices within the organization.

Globally-operating organizations must be aware of widely varying HR legal/regulatory systems due to politics, economic differences, and other factors. Emerging economies, in particular, pose major challenges to smooth operations and reliable conditions.

Offshoring

Competitive pressure to lower costs has resulted in many jobs being moved overseas in recent years. **Offshoring** is the relocation by a company of a business process or operation from one country to another. Firms offshore the production of goods as well as the delivery of services to lower-wage countries. Call centers in India are an example of business service offshoring to countries with well-educated, English-speaking workers. Product and software development projects are increasingly being offshored due to the loss of science and engineering talent in the United States. Predictions are that offshoring will increase in the future, and few firms have plans to return offshored jobs to the home country.

Global Staffing

Staffing for global operations includes a wide variety of alternatives. The optimal solution is to combine the expertise of local employees with the organization-specific knowledge of employees from the home country (headquarters). Some countries require that the organization employ a certain percentage of workers from the host country.

Leadership development is especially important for MNCs. It is becoming more important for individuals in top management positions to have international experience so that they understand the worldwide marketplace. Effective selection and development processes are needed to ensure that the right individuals are chosen for these roles. Leading across cultures requires specific skills, and organizations should provide formal training along with expatriate assignments to develop leaders who can achieve results in this demanding environment.

HR'S ROLE IN MERGERS AND ACQUISITIONS

The overall purpose of a merger or acquisition is to generate shareholder value by creating a more competitive, cost-efficient company by combining two existing companies. Strategic HRM can contribute to the success of mergers and acquisitions (M&As). Research has clearly shown that the majority of M&As fail to deliver on the expected financial, marketing, or product gains, with only about one-third of companies reporting that they achieved their goals.[8] A significant number of failed ventures can trace their roots to HR issues that were not properly addressed such as loss of key staff, culture clashes, and poor communication. To maximize the chances of a successful integration, HR should be involved before, during, and after the deal is completed.

To determine whether or not the two organizations should combine, a rigorous process of due diligence is conducted. **Due diligence** is a comprehensive assessment of all aspects of the business being acquired. Financial, sales and marketing, operations, and human resource staffs are all involved before the final decision is made to merge or acquire the company.

After the deal has been closed, the focus of HR activity switches to the orderly transition of basic HR processes such as payroll and benefits migration. The immediate concerns are often about basic services needed to run the operations. Frequent communication, employee hotlines, and guidance for managers all contribute to employee retention and loyalty during the chaotic early days of the transition. Early in the transition, managers focus on identifying key talent and establishing initiatives to retain these critical employees. Retention bonuses, special assignments, and enhanced severance can be used to keep key talent in place during the integration stage.

To realize the expected benefits of a merger, the months following the initial integration are critical. Culture changes started in the early days must be maintained. Practical issues regarding talent management and development along with combining compensation systems will solidify the new, united organization. Failure to effectively blend the workforces and move beyond the "us-and-them" mentality can lead to inferior business results, a loss of share-holder value, and the failure of the merger. Continued change efforts are needed to bring all employees to the "one organization" mentality.

STRATEGIES FOR MANAGING TALENT SUPPLY IMBALANCES

Organizations need to plan for both the quantity and quality of the workforce. Having sufficient workers with the right qualifications is essential to achieve the strategic plan. If the firm employs too many people for its needs, a talent surplus exists; if too few, a talent shortage. Because of the rapidly changing conditions, the organization may face a surplus in some parts of the business while facing a shortage in others.

Managing a Talent Surplus

A talent surplus can be managed within a strategic HR plan in a number of ways. The reasons for the surplus will guide the ultimate steps taken by the organization. If the workforce has the right qualifications but the sales revenue has fallen, the primary strategies would involve retaining workers while cutting costs. However, if the workforce is not appropriately trained for the jobs needed, the organization may lay off those employees who cannot perform the work. Managers may use various strategies in a progressive fashion to defer workforce reductions until absolutely necessary.

Reduction in Work Hours or Compensation.   In order to retain qualified employees, managers may institute reduced work hours on a temporary basis. Selected groups of employees may have their workweek reduced or all employees can be asked to take a day or week off without pay.

Across-the-board pay cuts can reduce labor costs while retaining skilled employees. It is important that pay cuts start at the very top of the organization so that employees do not bear all of the hardship. Uniform pay cuts can be felt as a shared sacrifice for the survival of the firm. Organizations may also reduce employee benefits, such as eliminating matching 401K contributions or raising employee health insurance premiums.

Attrition and Hiring Freezes.   Attrition occurs when individuals quit, die, or retire and are not replaced. By use of attrition, no one is cut out of a job, but those who remain must handle the same workload with fewer people. Unless turnover is high, attrition will eliminate only a relatively small number of employees in the short run, but it can be a viable alternative over a longer period of time. Therefore, employers may combine attrition with a freeze on hiring. Employees usually understand this approach better than they do other downsizing methods.

Voluntary Separation Programs.   Organizations can reduce the workforce while also minimizing legal risks if employees volunteer to leave. Often firms entice employees to volunteer by offering them additional severance, training, and benefits payments. Early retirement buyouts are widely used to encourage more senior workers to leave organizations early. These programs are viewed as a way to accomplish workforce reductions without resorting to layoffs.

Workforce Downsizing.   It has been given many names, including downsizing, rightsizing, and reduction in force (RIF), but it almost always means cutting employees. Layoffs on a broad scale have occurred with frightening regularity in recent years. Trimming underperforming units or employees as part of a plan that is based on sound organizational strategies may make sense. After a decade of many examples and studies, it is clear that downsizing has worked for some firms. However, it does not increase revenues; it is a short-term cost-cutting measure that can result in a long-term lack of talent. When companies cannibalize the human resources needed to change, restructure, or innovate, disruption follows for some time. Also, downsizing can hurt productivity by leaving "surviving" employees overburdened and demoralized.

Legal Considerations for Workforce Reductions

HR must be involved during workforce adjustments to ensure that the organization does not violate any of the nondiscrimination or other laws governing workforce reductions. Selection criteria for determining which employees will be laid off must comply with Title VII of the Civil Rights Act as well as the Age Discrimination in Employment Act and the Americans with Disabilities Act. A careful analysis and disparate impact review should be conducted before final decisions are made.

Under the federal Consolidated Omnibus Budget Reconciliation Act (COBRA), displaced workers can retain their group medical coverage for up to 18 months for themselves, and for up to 36 months for their dependents, if they pay the premiums themselves. Federal stimulus programs included enhanced COBRA coverage for displaced workers.

Employers must also comply with the Older Workers Benefit Protection Act (OWBPA) when implementing RIFs. The OWBPA requires employers to disclose the ages of both terminated and retained employees in layoff situations, and a waiver of rights to sue for age discrimination must meet certain requirements.

To provide employees with adequate notice of plant closings or mass layoffs, a federal law was passed, the Worker Adjustment and Retraining Notification (WARN) Act. This law requires private or commercial organizations that employ 100 or more full-time workers who have worked more than 6 months in the previous year to give a 60-day notice before implementing a layoff or facility closing that involves more than 50 people.

Managing a Talent Shortage

Managing a shortage of employees seems simple enough—simply hire more people. However, as mentioned earlier, there can be mismatches between the qualifications needed by employers and the skills possessed by workers. Companies can use a number of alternative tactics to manage a talent shortage:

- Use overtime
- Outsource work
- Implement alternate work arrangements
- Bring back recent retirees
- Use contingent workers
- Reduce turnover

The existing workers can work overtime to produce goods or services. This strategy can work on a short-term basis but is not a solution for a longer-term talent shortage. Workers may appreciate the extra hours and pay for awhile, but eventually fatigue sets in and productivity and quality may drop and injuries and absenteeism may increase. Reducing turnover of qualified employees should be an ongoing effort to maintain a talented workforce. Special attention may be required in times of talent shortages to hold on to skilled employees.

Alternate work arrangements, nontraditional schedules that provide flexibility to employees, include job sharing and telecommuting. These are creative solutions to attract and retain skilled employees who want flexibility. Employees are given more freedom in determining when and how they will perform their jobs. These arrangements are not costly to the organization but do require management support and planning to be effective. Retirees may be rehired on a part-time or temporary basis to fill talent gaps. The advantage is that these individuals are already trained and can be productive immediately. Care must be taken not to interfere with pension payments or other benefits tied to retirement.

The use of contingent employees, which are noncore employees who work at an organization on a temporary or as-needed basis, can provide short-term help. Professional employer organizations can lease employees to the firm, which is often a good solution for technical talent. Independent contractors can be hired on an as-needed basis to fill talent shortages. The use of independent contractors must be managed closely to ensure compliance with wage and hour, safety, and employee benefit statutes. When using contingent workers, special efforts are needed to assimilate them into the workforce and avoid an "us-and-them" mentality. Contingent workers fill an important need and managers can maximize their contributions through good employee relations practices.

Outsourcing involves transferring the management and/or routine performance of a business function to an external service provider. Organizations in the United States outsource a wide variety of noncore functions to reduce costs or to obtain skills and expertise not available in the organization.

TECHNOLOGY CHALLENGES

Technological advances have a major impact on organizations. New methods for communicating, processing information, and manufacturing have led to economic development around the globe. However, the improvements created by technology often mean that people and organizations must change in order to fully benefit from these advances.

Jobs have undergone major changes as a result of technology advances. In many cases, monotonous, repetitive operations have evolved into complex knowledge work that requires a new skill set. Work that previously was done by hand has been replaced by robotics and automation. Tool and die makers, once prized for their intricate, precision hand work, are now utilizing computer-aided design (CAD) and computer numerically controlled (CNC) software to complete their tasks. The skills needed in this work setting are very different from those of the past; communication, collaboration, technical ability, and adaptability are necessary for success in the future.

Technology has increased employee expectations regarding the speed and frequency of communication from managers. Employees are no longer content to wait for the monthly company newsletter or find out the latest news through formal channels. Company intranet portals can be a prime source of information for employees and should be used to inform employees about important events within the organization and the industry.

Facebook, LinkedIn, and other social networking sites allow employees to remain in constant contact with people inside and outside of the organization. Instant messages and cell-phone texting allow for real-time communication. The line between employees' personal and professional lives becomes blurred as these virtual communities are frequently accessed from the worksite. Potential litigation and damage to the organizational reputation and brand pose risks to the organization if access and content are not properly monitored.

However, monitoring employee actions and performance is much easier and less expensive due to technological advances. Transponders in semi-trailer trucks can record speed, mileage, and other operating data to evaluate driver performance. Video surveillance to reduce employee misconduct such as theft or cheating, or to track productivity is simple to implement. Computer use is routinely monitored.

The majority of organizations have e-mail use policies in place and monitor employee e-mail use. In general, the courts have supported employer monitoring, and there are few legal restrictions on employer action. Concerns about productivity and employee performance must be balanced with concerns for privacy and positive employee relations. Monitoring can lead to a lack of trust and may discourage creativity and the free exchange of ideas between employees.

MEASURING EFFECTIVENESS OF HR

A long-standing myth perpetuates the notion that one cannot really measure the value of HR practices. That myth has hurt HR's credibility because it suggests that either HR efforts do not add value or they are too far removed from business results to matter. That notion is, of course, untrue. HR, like all other functions, must be evaluated by considering the results of its actions and the value it adds to the organization. Unfortunately, the perceptions of managers and employees in many organizations are mixed because HR has not always measured and documented its contributions or communicated those results to executives, managers, and employees. Further, accounting practices treat expenditures on human capital and talent development as expenses rather than capital investments. This encourages a consumption attitude rather than a long-term investment strategy.

People-related costs are typically the largest controllable expense in organizations. Effective management of these costs can make the difference in the survival of the organization. Collecting and analyzing HR information can pinpoint waste and improper allocation of human resources. It is important that managers understand financial and operational measures that drive the business and relate HR decisions to key performance indicators (KPIs).

HR Metrics

HR metrics are specific measures tied to HR performance indicators. Metrics are typically used to assess the HR function and results within the organization over time. A metric can be developed using costs, quantity, quality, timeliness, and other designated goals. Metrics can be developed to track both HR's efficiency and effectiveness. A pioneer in developing HR measurements, Jac Fitz-Enz, has identified a wide range of HR metrics. A number of key HR metrics are shown in Figure 1-5.

Unlike financial reporting, there is no standard for the implementation and reporting of HR measures. Managers choose what and how to report to employees, investors, and other interested parties. This lack of consistency in HR reporting makes it difficult to evaluate an organization and to compare HR practices across organizations.[9]

Benchmarking is the process of comparing metrics of the business processes and outcomes to an industry standard or best practice. In other words, the organization compares itself to "best-in-class" organizations that demonstrate excellence for a specific process. Benchmarking is focused on external practices that the organization can use to improve its own processes and practices. When implementing benchmarking, managers should be careful to find organizations with similar contexts, cultures, operations, and size. Practices that would work effectively in an organization of 500 employees might not transfer very well to an organization with 5,000 employees.

HUMAN CAPITAL EFFECTIVENESS MEASURES

To fulfill its role as a strategic business partner, HR must quantify things that traditional accounting does not account for. Human resources may provide for both the biggest value and the biggest cost to organizations. Many of the HR metrics reflect people-related costs. Measuring the value is more challenging but equally important. Assessing the value of human resources demonstrates the importance of implementing effective HR practices to maintain a high-quality, engaged workforce.

FIGURE 1-5 Key HR Metrics

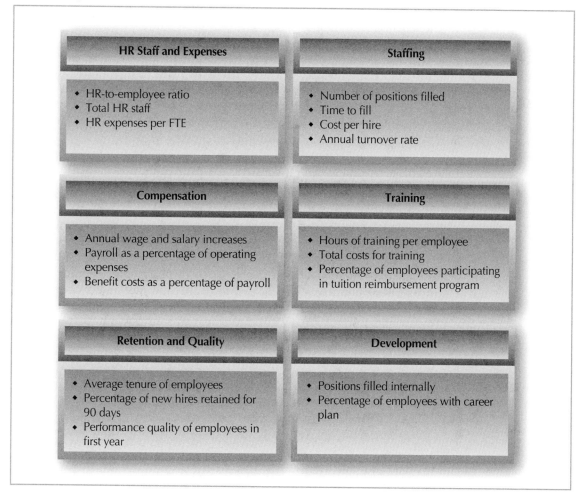

HR Staff and Expenses

- HR-to-employee ratio
- Total HR staff
- HR expenses per FTE

Staffing

- Number of positions filled
- Time to fill
- Cost per hire
- Annual turnover rate

Compensation

- Annual wage and salary increases
- Payroll as a percentage of operating expenses
- Benefit costs as a percentage of payroll

Training

- Hours of training per employee
- Total costs for training
- Percentage of employees participating in tuition reimbursement program

Retention and Quality

- Average tenure of employees
- Percentage of new hires retained for 90 days
- Performance quality of employees in first year

Development

- Positions filled internally
- Percentage of employees with career plan

Human capital refers to the collective value of the intellectual capital (competencies, knowledge, and skills) of the employees in the organization. This capital is the constantly renewable source of creativity and innovativeness in the organization but is not reflected in its financial statements.

Revenue per employee is a basic measure of human capital effectiveness. The formula is Revenue/Head Count (full-time employee equivalents). It is a measure of employee productivity and shows the sales revenue generated by each full-time employee. This measure is commonly used in government reporting (see Bureau of Labor Statistics, BLS) as well as by organizations to track productivity over time. If revenues increase but employee head count remains constant, productivity would increase.

A widely used financial measure that can be applied to measure the contribution and cost of HR activities is **return on investment (ROI)**, which is a calculation showing the value of investments in human resources. It can also be used to show how long it will take for the activities to pay for themselves. The following formula can be used to calculate the potential ROI for a new HR activity:

$$\text{ROI} = \frac{C}{A + B}$$

where:

A = Operating costs for a new or enhanced system for the time period
B = One-time cost of acquisition and implementation
C = Value of gains from productivity improvements for the time period

ROI is stressed because it is used in most other functions in an organization and is the "language" used by financial staff and top management. It allows managers to choose among various investment opportunities to determine the best use of funds.

Human capital value added (HCVA) is an adjusted operating profitability figure calculated by subtracting all operating expenses *except* for labor expenses from revenue and dividing by the total full-time head count. It shows the operating profit per full-time employee. Because labor is required to generate revenues, employment costs are added back into operating expense. The formula for HCVA is:

$$\frac{\text{Revenue} - \text{Operating Expense} - (\text{Compensation} + \text{Benefit Costs})}{\text{Full-Time Head Count}}$$

Human capital return on investment (HCROI) directly shows the amount of profit derived from investments in labor, the leverage on labor cost. The formula for HCROI uses the same adjusted operating profitability figure as for HCVA, but it is divided by the human capital cost:

$$\frac{\text{Revenue} - \text{Operating Expense} - (\text{Compensation} + \text{Benefit Costs})}{(\text{Compensation} + \text{Benefits Costs})}$$

Human economic value added (HEVA) shows the wealth created per employee. It shows how much more valuable the organization has become due to the investment in human capital. Wealth is the net operating profit of a firm after the cost of capital is deducted. Cost of capital is the minimum rate of return demanded by shareholders. When a company is making more than the cost of capital, it is creating wealth for shareholders. An HEVA approach requires that all policies, procedures, measures, and methods use cost of capital as a benchmark against which their return is judged. Human resource decisions can be subjected to the same analysis. The formula for HEVA is:

$$\frac{\text{Net Profit after Taxes} - \text{Cost of Capital}}{\text{Full-Time Head Count}}$$

Many financial measures can be tracked and reported to show the contribution human resources make to organizational results. Without such measures, it would be difficult to know what is going on in the organization, identify performance gaps, and provide feedback. Managers should require the same level of rigor in measuring HR practices as they do for other functions in the organization.[10]

Regardless of the time and effort placed on HR measurement and HR metrics, the most important consideration is that HR effectiveness and efficiency must be measured regularly for managers to know how HR is contributing to organizational success.

HR Audit

One general means for assessing HR is through an HR audit, which is similar to a financial audit. An **HR audit** is a formal research effort to assess the current state of HR practices in an organization. This audit is used to evaluate how well activities in each of the HR areas (staffing, compensation, health and safety, etc.) have been performed, so that management can identify areas for improvement. An HR audit often helps smaller organizations without a formal HR professional to identify issues associated with legal compliance, administrative processes and recordkeeping, employee retention, and other areas.

NOTES

1. Charles Rothrock and David Gregory, "How Corporate Culture Affects Organizational Value," *SHRM White Paper*, April 1, 2006, *www.shrm.org.*
2. Jenna McGregor, "When Service Means Survival," *BusinessWeek*, March 2, 2009, 26–33.
3. Ethics Resource Center, *www.ethics.org.*
4. "The Hardest Jobs to Fill in America," *Forbes*, June 4, 2009, *www.Forbes.com.*
5. *Small Business by the Numbers* and other reports from the U.S. Small Business Administration, *www.sba.gov.*
6. ". . . and HR Planning Is Less Formal," *Personnel Today*, February 27, 2007, 1–3; Sumita Ketkar and P. K. Sett, "HR Flexibility and Firm Performance: Analysis of a Multi-Level Causal Model," *International Journal of Human Resource Management*, 20 (2009), 1009–1038.
7. James Combs, Yongmei Liu, et al., "How Much Do High Performance Work Practices Matter? A Meta-Analysis of Their Effects on Organizational

Performance," *Personnel Psychology*, 59 (2006), 501–528; Jason Shaw, Brian Dineen, et al., "Employee-Organization Exchange Relationships, HRM Practices, and Quit Rates of Good and Poor Performers," *Academy of Management Journal*, 52 (2009), 1016–1033.
8. David Wentworth, "M&A Bounces Back: What Have We Learned?" *Institute for Corporate Productivity (i4cp) TrendWatcher*, No. 478, October 2, 2009; Harry Barkema and Mario Schijven, "Toward Unlocking the Full Potential of Acquisitions: The Role of Organizational Restructuring," *Academy of Management Journal*, 51 (2008), 696–722.
9. John Dooney, "SHRM Symposium on Human Capital Analytics," Society for Human Resource Management, 2007, *www.shrm.org.*
10. "Human Capital Strategy: Human Capital Measurement," November 30, 2007, *www.humancapitalstrategy.blogspot.com.*

INTERNET RESOURCES

Ethics & Policy Integration Centre—The Ethics & Policy Integration Centre is an online resource for ethical and policy issues. Visit the website at *www.ethicaledge.com.*

HRN Management Group—Information on strategic issues for HR, including news and success stories for key HR decision makers, is available by linking to the HRN Management Group website at *www.hronline.com.*

Society for Human Resource Management— The Society for Human Resource Management is the largest association devoted to Human Resource Management. Some of the most essential and comprehensive resources available for Human Resource professionals are contained within the SHRM website at *www.shrm.org.*

U.S. Department of Labor, Bureau of Labor Statistics—This website contains data on workforce composition and trends from the U.S. Department of Labor, Bureau of Labor Statistics. Visit the site at *www.stats.bls.gov.*

SUGGESTED READINGS

Rebecca M.J. Wells, "Outstanding Customer Satisfaction: The Key to a Talented Workforce?" *Academy of Management Perspectives*, August 2007, 87–89.

"Occupational Employment Projections to 2016," *Monthly Labor Review*, November 2007, *www.bls.gov.*

David Ulrich, Wayne Brockbank, et al., *HR Competencies: Mastery of the Intersection of People and Business* (Alexandria, VA: SHRM, 2008).

William Smith and Filiz Tabak, "Monitoring Employee Emails: Is There Any Room for Privacy?" *Academy of Management Perspectives*, November 2009, 33–48.

Equal Employment Opportunity and Diversity

HR—MEETING MANAGEMENT CHALLENGES

Equal employment opportunity and diversity of the workforce represent major issues for HR in most organizations. To explain why, this chapter considers:

- The legal underpinnings of EEO
- The controversy surrounding affirmative action
- Sources of increasing diversity

EEO remains one of an organization's challenges because of the amount of litigation associated with it. Yet the diversity in the workforce will increase in the years ahead, making it necessary to manage this part of the human resources function effectively.

EQUAL EMPLOYMENT OPPORTUNITY (EEO)

In the United States, using race, gender, disability, age, religion, and certain other characteristics as the basis for choosing among people at work is generally illegal. Doing so can also be quite expensive, as fines and back wages can be awarded as well as sizable lawsuit settlements. Inequality in the treatment of people with different backgrounds has been an issue for many years, but it was the Civil Rights Act of 1964 that started a legislative movement toward leveling the playing field in employment. Initially focus was on race, gender, and religion, but these characteristics were soon followed by age, pregnancy, and individuals with disabilities. Since then numerous Executive Orders, regulations, and interpretations by courts have affected the employer/employee relationship. Perhaps nothing has had the impact of Equal Employment Opportunity (EEO) on HR during the same period of time.

At the core of equal employment is the concept of discrimination. The word *discrimination* simply means "recognizing differences among items or people." For example, employers must discriminate (choose) among applicants for a job on the basis of job requirements and candidates' qualifications. However, when discrimination is based on race, gender, or some other factors, it is illegal and employers face problems. The following bases for protection have been identified by various federal, state, and/or local laws:

- Race, ethnic origin, color (including multiracial/ethnic backgrounds)
- Sex/gender (including pregnant women and also men in certain situations)
- Age (individuals over age 40)
- Individuals with disabilities (physical or mental)
- Military experience (military status employees and Vietnam-era veterans)
- Religion (special beliefs and practices)
- Marital status (some states)
- Sexual orientation (some states and cities)

These categories are composed of individuals who are members of a **protected category** under EEO laws and regulations.

Disparate Treatment

The first type of illegal discrimination occurs with employment-related situations in which either: (1) different standards are used to judge individuals, or (2) the same standard is used, but it is not related to the individuals' jobs. **Disparate treatment** occurs when members of one group are treated differently from others. For example, if female applicants must take a special skills test not given to male applicants, then disparate treatment may be occurring.[1]

Disparate Impact

Disparate impact occurs when members of a protected category are substantially underrepresented as a result of employment decisions that work to their disadvantage. The landmark case that established the importance of disparate impact as a legal foundation of EEO law is *Griggs v. Duke Power*, 1401 U.S. 424 (1971). The decision by the U.S. Supreme Court established two major points:

1. It is not enough to show a lack of discriminatory intent if the employment tool results in a disparate impact that discriminates against one group more than another or continues a past pattern of discrimination.
2. The employer has the burden of proving that an employment requirement is directly job related as a "business necessity." Consequently, the intelligence test and high school diploma requirements of Duke Power were ruled not to be related to the job.

This and a number of other decisions make it clear that employers must be able to document through statistical analyses that disparate treatment and disparate impact have not occurred.[2] Knowing how to perform these analyses is important in order for employers to follow appropriate equal employment guidelines.

FIGURE 2-1 EEO Concepts

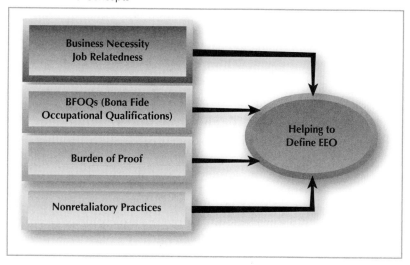

EQUAL EMPLOYMENT OPPORTUNITY CONCEPTS

Several basic EEO concepts have resulted from court decisions, laws, and regulatory actions. Four of these (see Figure 2-1) help clarify key EEO ideas.

Business Necessity and Job Relatedness. A **business necessity** is a practice necessary for safe and efficient organizational operations. Business necessity has been the subject of numerous court decisions. Educational requirements often are based on business necessity. However, an employer who requires a minimum level of education, such as a high school diploma, must be able to defend the requirement as essential to the performance of the job (job related), which may be difficult. For instance, equating a degree or diploma with the possession of math or reading abilities is considered questionable.

Bona Fide Occupational Qualification (BFOQ). Employers may discriminate on the basis of sex, religion, or national origin if the characteristic can be justified as a "bona fide occupational qualification reasonably necessary to the normal operation of the particular business or enterprise." Thus, a **bona fide occupational qualification (BFOQ)** is a characteristic providing a legitimate reason why an employer can exclude persons on otherwise illegal bases of consideration.

What constitutes a BFOQ has been subject to different interpretations in various courts. Legal uses of BFOQs have been found for hiring Asians to wait on customers in a Chinese restaurant or Catholics to serve in certain religious-based positions in Catholic churches.

Burden of Proof. Another legal issue that arises when discrimination is alleged is the determination of who has the **burden of proof,** which is what individuals who file suit against employers must prove to establish that illegal discrimination has occurred.

Based on the evolution of court decisions, current laws, and regulations the plaintiff charging discrimination must:

- be a *protected-category member,* and
- prove that *disparate impact* or *disparate treatment* existed.

Once a court rules that a preliminary case has been made, the burden of proof shifts to the employer. The employer then must show that the bases for making employment-related decisions were specifically job related and consistent with considerations of business necessity.

Nonretaliation. Employers are prohibited from retaliating against individuals who file discrimination charges. **Retaliation** occurs when employers take punitive actions against individuals who exercise their legal rights. For example, an employee who had reported harassment by a supervisor was fired, but the Supreme Court found that it is unlawful to discriminate against someone who has "made a charge, testified, assisted, or participated in any manner in an investigation, proceeding, or hearing."

To avoid charges of retaliation, the following actions are recommended for employers:

- Train supervisors on what retaliation is and what is not appropriate.
- Conduct a thorough internal investigation of any claims and document the results.
- Take appropriate action when any retaliation occurs.

RACE/ETHNIC/NATIONAL ORIGIN

The focus now shifts to equal employment laws and necessary considerations for managing HR in light of these laws. For a listing of all the major EEO laws and regulations, see Appendix B.

Civil Rights Act of 1964, Title VII

Although the very first civil rights act was passed in 1866, it was not until passage of the Civil Rights Act of 1964 that the keystone of antidiscrimination employment legislation was put into place. The Equal Employment Opportunity Commission (EEOC) was established to enforce the provisions of Title VII, the portion of the act that deals with employment.

Title VII of the Civil Rights Act states that it is illegal for an employer to:

1. *fail or refuse to hire or discharge any individual, or otherwise discriminate against any individual with respect to his compensation, terms, conditions, or privileges of employment because of such individual's race, color, religion, sex, or national origin, or*

2. *limit, segregate, or classify his employees or applicants for employment in any way that would deprive or tend to deprive any individual of employment opportunities or otherwise adversely affect his status as an employee because of such individual's race, color, religion, sex, or national origin.*

Title VII, as amended by the Equal Employment Opportunity Act of 1972, covers most employers in the United States. Any organization meeting one of the criteria in the following list is subject to rules and regulations that specific government agencies have established to administer the act:

- All private employers of 15 or more persons who are employed 20 or more weeks a year
- All educational institutions, public and private
- State and local governments
- Public and private employment agencies
- Labor unions with 15 or more members
- Joint labor/management committees for apprenticeships and training

Executive Orders 11246, 11375, and 11478

Numerous executive orders require that employers holding federal government contracts not discriminate on the basis of race, color, religion, national origin, or sex. An *Executive Order* is issued by the president of the United States to provide direction to government departments on a specific area. The Office of Federal Contract Compliance Programs (OFCCP) in the U.S. Department of Labor has responsibility for enforcing nondiscrimination in government contracts.

Executive Orders 11246, 11375, and 11478 are major federal EEO efforts for government contractors; many states have similar requirements for firms with state government contracts.

Civil Rights Act of 1991

The Civil Rights Act of 1991 requires employers to show that an employment practice is *job related for the position* and is consistent with *business necessity*. The act clarifies that the plaintiffs bringing the discrimination charges must identify the particular employer practice being challenged and must show only that protected-category status played *some role in their treatment*. One key provision of the 1991 act relates to how U.S. laws on EEO are applied globally.

Race and National Origin Issues

The original purpose of the Civil Rights Act of 1964 was to address race and national origin discrimination. This concern continues to be important today, and employers must be aware of potential HR issues that are based on race, national origin, and citizenship in order to take appropriate actions.

Employment discrimination can occur in numerous ways, from refusal to hire someone because of the person's race/ethnicity to the questions asked in a selection interview. For example, a trucking company settled a discrimination lawsuit by African American employees who were denied job assignments and promotions because of racial bias. In addition to paying a fine, the firm must report to the EEOC on promotions from part-time to full-time for dock worker jobs.

Sometimes racial discriminations can be more subtle. For example, some firms have tapped professional and social networking sites to fill open positions. However, networking sites exclude many people. According to one study, only 5% of LinkedIn users are black and 2% are Hispanic. This lack of access to these sites can easily be viewed as racial discrimination.[3]

Under federal law, discriminating against people because of skin color is just as illegal as discriminating because of race. For example, one might be guilty of color discrimination but not racial discrimination if one hired light-skinned African Americans over dark-skinned people.

Racial/Ethnic Harassment. The area of racial/ethnic harassment is such a concern that the EEOC has issued guidelines on it. It is recommended that employers adopt policies against harassment of any type, including ethnic jokes, vulgar epithets, racial slurs, and physical actions. The consequences of not enforcing these policies are seen in a case involving a small business employer that subjected Latinos to physical and verbal abuse. Hispanic males at the firm were subjected to derogatory jokes, verbal abuse, physical harm, and other humiliating experiences. Settling the case was expensive for the employer.

Contrast that case with another that shows the advantage of taking quick remedial action. An employee filed a lawsuit against an airline because coworkers told racist jokes and hung nooses in his workplace. The airline was able to show that each time any employee, including the plaintiff, reported problems, management conducted an investigation and took action against the offending employees. The court ruled for the employer in this case because the situation was managed properly.

Affirmative Action

Through **affirmative action,** employers are urged to hire groups of people based on their race, age, gender, or national origin to make up for historical discrimination. It is a requirement for federal government contractors to document the inclusion of women and racial minorities in the workforce. As part of those government regulations, covered employers must submit plans describing their attempts to narrow the gaps between the composition of their workforces and the composition of labor markets where they obtain employees. However, affirmative action has been the subject of numerous court cases and an ongoing political and social debate both in the United States and globally.

For example, a recent Supreme Court ruling held that race should *not* be used to the detriment of individuals who passed an examination and were qualified for promotions. In this case, the city of New Haven, Connecticut, threw out the results of a test for promotion where more white firefighters

FIGURE 2-2 The Debate about Affirmative Action

Arguments: Why Affirmative Action Is Needed

- Affirmative action is needed to overcome past injustices or eliminate the effects of those injustices.
- Affirmative action creates more equality for all persons, even if temporary injustice to some individuals may result.
- Raising the employment level of protected-class members will benefit U.S. society in the long run.
- Properly used, affirmative action does not discriminate against males or whites.
- Goals indicate progress is needed, not quotas.

Arguments: Why Affirmative Action Is Not Needed

- Affirmative action penalizes individuals (males and whites) even though they have not been guilty of practicing discrimination.
- It is no longer needed as an African American has been elected President.
- Affirmative action results in greater polarization and separatism along gender and racial lines.
- Affirmative action stigmatizes those it is designed to help.
- Goals become quotas and force employers to "play by the numbers."

passed than blacks or Hispanics. The city claimed it had to junk the tests because they would lead to an avalanche of lawsuits by black candidates who had not passed. The court said fear of litigation was no reason to rely on race to throw out the results.[4]

Supporters offer many reasons why affirmative action is important, while opponents argue firmly against it. Individuals can examine the points of both sides in the debate and compare them with their personal views of affirmative action. The authors of this text believe that whether one supports or opposes affirmative action, it is important to understand why its supporters believe that it is needed and why its opponents believe it should be discontinued. The reasons given most frequently by both sides are highlighted in Figure 2-2.

Managing Affirmative Action Requirements

Federal, state, and local regulations require many government contractors to compile affirmative action plans to report on the composition of their workforces. An **affirmative action plan (AAP)** is a formal document that an employer compiles annually for submission to enforcement agencies. Generally, contractors with at least 50 employees and $50,000 in government contracts annually must submit these plans. Courts have noted that any employer *may* have a *voluntary* AAP, although employers *must* have such a plan if they are government contractors. Some courts have ordered employers that are not government contractors to submit required AAPs because of past discriminatory practices and violations of laws.

The contents of an AAP and the policies flowing from it must be available for review by managers and supervisors within the organization. Plans vary in length; some are long and require extensive staff time to prepare.

Affirmative Action Plan Metrics.   A crucial but time-consuming part of an AAP is the analyses. The **availability analysis** identifies the number of protected-class members available to work in the appropriate labor markets for given jobs. This analysis can be developed with data from a state labor department, the U.S. Census Bureau, and other sources. The **utilization analysis** identifies the number of protected-class members employed in the organization and the types of jobs they hold.

Once all the data have been analyzed and compared, then *underutilization* statistics must be calculated by comparing the availability analysis with the utilization analysis. It is useful to think of this stage as a comparison of whether the internal workforce is a "representative sampling" of the available external labor force from which employees are hired.

Using the underutilization data, *goals* and *timetables* for reducing underutilization of protected-class individuals must then be identified. Actions that will be taken to recruit, hire, promote, and train more protected-class individuals are described. The AAP must be updated and reviewed each year to reflect changes in the utilization and availability of protected-category members. If the AAP is audited, the employer must be prepared to provide additional details and documentation.

SEX/GENDER DISCRIMINATION LAWS AND REGULATIONS

A number of laws and regulations address discrimination based on sex or gender. Historically, women experienced employment discrimination in a variety of ways. The inclusion of sex as a basis for protected-class status in Title VII of the 1964 Civil Rights Act has led to various areas of legal protection for women.

Pregnancy Discrimination

The Pregnancy Discrimination Act (PDA) of 1978 requires that any employer with 15 or more employees treat maternity leave the same as other personal or medical leaves. Closely related to the PDA is the Family and Medical Leave Act (FMLA) of 1993, which requires that individuals be given up to 12 weeks of family leave without pay and also requires that those taking family leave be allowed to return to jobs. The FMLA applies to both men and women.

Courts have generally ruled that the PDA requires employers to treat pregnant employees the same as nonpregnant employees with similar abilities or inabilities. Employers have been found to have acted properly when terminating a pregnant employee for excessive absenteeism due to pregnancy-related illnesses, because the employee was not treated differently from other employees with absenteeism problems.

Equal Pay and Pay Equity

The Equal Pay Act of 1963 requires employers to pay similar wage rates for similar work without regard to gender. A *common core of tasks* must be similar, but tasks performed only intermittently or infrequently do not make jobs different enough to justify significantly different wages. Differences in pay between men and women in the same jobs may be allowed because of:

1. Differences in seniority
2. Differences in performance
3. Differences in quality and/or quantity of production
4. Factors other than sex, such as skill, effort, and working conditions

Ledbetter v. Goodyear Tire & Rubber Co. was a significant U.S. Supreme Court decision on pay discrimination. Ledbetter, a female manager with Goodyear in Alabama, claimed that she was subjected to pay discrimination because she received lower pay during her career back to 1979, even though she did not file suit until 1998.[5] The decision examined this view and stated that the rights of workers to sue for previous years of paid discrimination are limited. However, in 2009 Congress passed the Lilly Ledbetter Fair Pay Act that canceled the Supreme Court ruling. The new law effectively eliminates the statute of limitations for employees to file pay discrimination claims.

Pay equity is the idea that pay for jobs requiring comparable levels of knowledge, skill, and ability should be similar, even if actual duties differ significantly. This theory has also been called *comparable worth* in earlier cases. Some state laws have mandated pay equity for public-sector employees. However, U.S. federal courts generally have ruled that the existence of pay differences between the different jobs held by women and men is not sufficient to prove that illegal discrimination has occurred.

A major reason for the development of the pay equity idea is the continuing gap between the earnings of women and men. For instance, in 1980, the average annual pay of full-time female workers was 60% of that of full-time male workers. By 2008, the reported rate of about 80% showed some progress but a continuing disparity. See Figure 2-3.

Sexual Harassment

The Equal Employment Opportunity Commission has issued guidelines designed to curtail sexual harassment. **Sexual harassment** refers to actions that are sexually directed, are unwanted, and subject the worker to adverse employment conditions or create a hostile work environment. Sexual

FIGURE 2-3 Female Annual Earnings as Percentage of Male Earnings

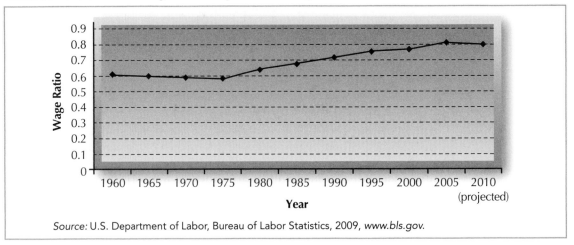

Source: U.S. Department of Labor, Bureau of Labor Statistics, 2009, *www.bls.gov.*

harassment can occur between a boss and a subordinate, among coworkers, and when nonemployees have business contacts with employees.

Most of the sexual harassment charges filed involve harassment of women by men. However, some sexual harassment cases have been filed by men against women managers and supervisors, and some have been filed by both men and women for same-sex harassment.

Managing Sex/Gender Issues

The influx of women into the workforce has had major social, economic, and organizational consequences. The percentage of women in the total U.S. civilian workforce has increased dramatically since 1950, to almost 50% today.

This growth in the number of women in the workforce has led to more sex/gender issues related to jobs and careers. A significant issue is related to biology (women bear children) and to tradition (women have a primary role in raising children). A major result of the increasing share of women in the workforce is that more women with children are working. According to the U.S. Bureau of Labor Statistics, about three-fourths of women aged 25–54 are in the workforce. Further, about half of all women currently working are single, separated, divorced, widowed, or otherwise single heads of households. Consequently, they are "primary" income earners, not co-income providers, and must balance family and work responsibilities. This responsibility may affect managers' perceptions of family/work conflict that may lead to promotability issues for women.

To guard against pay inequities that are considered illegal under the Equal Pay Act, employers should follow these guidelines:

- Include all benefits and other items that are part of remuneration to calculate total compensation for the most accurate overall picture.

- Make sure people know how the pay practices work.
- Base pay on the value of jobs and individual performance.
- Benchmark against local and national markets so that pay structures are competitive.
- Conduct frequent audits to ensure there are no gender-based inequities and that pay is fair internally.

The right to reassign women from hazardous jobs to ones that may be lower paying but less hazardous because of health-related concerns is another gender-related issue encountered by employers. Fears about higher health insurance costs and possible lawsuits involving such problems as birth defects caused by damage sustained during pregnancy have led some employers to institute reproductive and fetal protection policies. However, the U.S. Supreme Court has ruled that such policies are illegal. Also, having different job conditions for men and women is usually held to be discriminatory.

Jobs that pay well but are nontraditional jobs for women include: architects, computer programmers, software engineers, detectives, chefs, engineers, computer repair, construction, building inspectors, machinists, aircraft pilots, and firefighters.

Individuals with Differing Sexual Orientations

As if demographic diversity did not place enough pressure on managers and organizations, individuals in the workforce today have widely varying lifestyles that can have work-related consequences. Legislative efforts have been made to protect individuals with differing lifestyles or sexual orientations from employment discrimination, though at present only a few cities and states have passed such laws.

One visible issue that some employers have had to address is that of individuals who have had or are undergoing sex-change surgery and therapy. Federal court cases and the EEOC have ruled that sex discrimination under Title VII applies to a person's gender at birth. Thus, it does not apply to the new gender of those who have had gender-altering operations. Sexual orientation or sex-change issues that arise at work include the reactions of coworkers and managers and ensuring that such individuals are evaluated fairly and not discriminated against in work assignments, raises, training, or promotions.

Nepotism

Many employers have policies that restrict or prohibit **nepotism**, the practice of allowing relatives to work for the same employer. Other firms require only that relatives not work directly for or with each other or not be placed in positions where collusion or conflict could occur. The policies most frequently cover spouses, brothers, sisters, mothers, fathers, sons, and daughters. Generally, employer antinepotism policies have been upheld by courts, in spite of the concern that they tend to discriminate against women more than men (because women tend to be denied employment or to leave employers more often as a result of marriage to other employees).

Consensual Relationships and Romance at Work

When work-based friendships lead to romance and off-the-job sexual relationships, managers and employers face a dilemma: Should they "monitor" these relationships to protect the firm from potential legal complaints, thereby "meddling" in employees' private, off-the-job lives? Or do they simply ignore these relationships and the potential problems they present? These concerns are significant.

Most executives and HR professionals (as well as employees) agree that workplace romances are risky because they have great potential for causing conflict. They strongly agree that romance must not take place between a supervisor and a subordinate because potential sexual harassment issues could arise. Some employers have addressed the issue of workplace romances by establishing policies dealing with them.

Different actions may be appropriate if a relationship is clearly consensual than if it is forced by a supervisor–subordinate relationship. One consideration is the observation that consensual workplace romances can create hostile work environments for others in organizations.

Dealing with Sexual Harassment

Sexual harassment is a significant concern in many organizations and can occur in a variety of workplace relationships. As shown in Figure 2-4, individuals in many different roles can be sexual harassers. For example, third parties

FIGURE 2-4 Potential Sexual Harassers

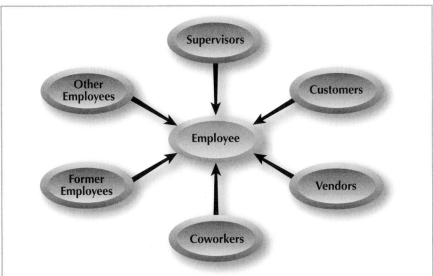

who are neither employers nor employees have been found to be harassers. Both customer service representatives and food servers have won sexual harassment complaints because their employers refused to protect them from regular sexual harassment by aggressive customers.

Most frequently, sexual harassment occurs when a male in a supervisory or managerial position harasses women within his "power structure." However, as noted earlier, women managers have been found guilty of sexually harassing male employees, and same-sex harassment also has occurred. Court decisions have held that a person's sexual orientation neither provides nor precludes a claim of sexual harassment under Title VII. It is enough that the harasser engaged in pervasive and unwelcome conduct of a sexual nature.

Types of Sexual Harassment

Two basic types of sexual harassment have been defined by EEOC regulations and a large number of court cases. The two types are different in nature and defined as follows:

1. **Quid pro quo** is harassment in which employment outcomes are linked to the individual granting sexual favors.
2. **Hostile environment** harassment exists when an individual's work performance or psychological well-being is unreasonably affected by intimidating or offensive working conditions.

In quid pro quo harassment, an employee may be promised a promotion, a special raise, or a desirable work assignment, but only if the employee grants some sexual favors to the supervisor. The second type, hostile environment harassment, may include actions such as commenting on appearance or attire, telling jokes that are suggestive or sexual in nature, allowing revealing photos and posters to be on display, or making continual requests to get together after work that can lead to the creation of a hostile work environment. Rude and discourteous behavior often is linked to sexual harassment.

As computer and Internet technology has spread, the number of electronic sexual harassment cases has grown. Sexual harassment is increasingly occurring via e-mails and Internet access systems. Cyber sexual harassment may occur when an employee forwards an e-mail joke with sexual content or accesses pornographic websites at work and then shares content with other employees. Cyber stalking, in which a person continually e-mails an employee requesting dates and sending personal messages, is growing as instant messaging expands.

Many employers have policies addressing the inappropriate use of e-mail, company computer systems, and electronic technology usage. Serious situations have led to employee terminations. Once a company disciplined more than 200 employees and fired 50 of them for having e-mailed pornographic images and other inappropriate materials using the company information system.

Many employers have equipped their computer systems with scanners that screen for inappropriate words and images. Offending employees receive warnings and/or disciplinary actions associated with "flagged" items.

Employer Responses to Sexual Harassment

Employers must be proactive to prevent sexual and other types of harassment. If the workplace culture fosters harassment, and if policies and practices do not inhibit harassment, an employer is wise to reevaluate and solve the problem before lawsuits follow.

Only if the employer can produce evidence of taking reasonable care to prohibit sexual harassment does the employer have the possibility of avoiding liability through an affirmative defense. Critical components of ensuring such reasonable care include the following:

- Establish a sexual harassment policy.
- Communicate the policy regularly.
- Train employees and managers on avoiding sexual harassment.
- Investigate and take action when complaints are voiced.

Harassment Likelihood

Research suggests that some people are more likely to be sexually harassed than others. For example, one study found that supervisors or women with more workplace authority are more likely to be harassed. Further research suggests that the likelihood of men to sexually harass, and the tolerance for sexual harassment by women vary across countries. Fundamental differences regarding power between men and women and a cultural support of sexual harassment lead to very different sexual harassment situations from country to country. According to this research, Canada, Denmark, Germany, The Netherlands, Sweden, and the United States are likely to have relatively *less* sexual harassment than countries like East Africa, Hong Kong, Indonesia, Malaysia, Mexico, Turkey, and Yugoslavia.[6]

AMERICANS WITH DISABILITIES ACT (ADA)

Organizations with 15 or more employees are covered by the provisions of the ADA, which are enforced by the EEOC. The act applies to private employers, employment agencies, and labor unions. State government employees are not covered by the ADA, which means that they cannot sue in federal courts for redress and damages. However, they may still bring suits under state laws in state courts.

Discrimination is prohibited against individuals with disabilities who can perform the **essential job functions**—the fundamental job duties—of the employment positions that those individuals hold or desire. These functions do not include marginal functions of the position.

For a qualified person with a disability, an employer must make a **reasonable accommodation**, which is a modification to a job or work environment that gives that individual an equal employment opportunity to perform. EEOC guidelines encourage employers and individuals to work together to determine what are appropriate reasonable accommodations, rather than employers alone making those judgments.

Reasonable accommodation is restricted to actions that do not place an undue hardship on an employer. An **undue hardship** is a significant difficulty or expense imposed on an employer in making an accommodation for individuals with disabilities. The ADA offers only general guidelines in determining when an accommodation becomes unreasonable and will place undue hardship on an employer.

Who Is Disabled?

As defined by the ADA, a **disabled person** is someone who has a physical or mental impairment that substantially limits that person in some major life activities, who has a record of such an impairment, or who is regarded as having such an impairment. Figure 2-5 shows the most frequent disabilities identified in ADA charges.

Mental Disabilities. A growing area of concern to employers under the ADA is individuals with mental disabilities. A mental illness is often more difficult to diagnose than a physical disability. Employers must be careful when considering "emotional" or "mental health" factors such as depression in employment-related decisions. They must not stereotype individuals with mental impairments or disabilities but must instead base their evaluations on sound medical information.

FIGURE 2-5 Most Frequent ADA Disabilities Cited

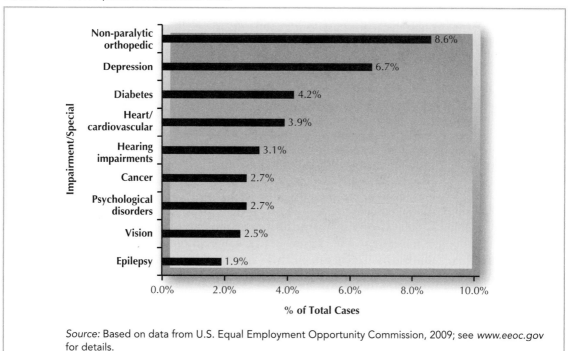

Source: Based on data from U.S. Equal Employment Opportunity Commission, 2009; see *www.eeoc.gov* for details.

Amendments to ADA (ADAAA). Congress passed amendments to the ADA, effective in 2009, that overruled several key cases and regulations. The effect was to *expand* the definition of disabled individuals to include anyone with a physical or mental impairment that substantially limits one or more major life activities without regard for the ameliorative effects of mitigating measures such as medication, prosthetics, hearing aids, and so on. Major life activities include, among others, walking, seeing, breathing, working, sleeping, concentrating, thinking, and communicating.

Genetic Bias Regulations

Related to medical disabilities is the emerging area of workplace genetic bias. As medical research has revealed the human genome, medical tests have been developed that can identify an individual's genetic markers for various diseases. Whether these tests should be used and how they are used can raise ethical issues.

Employers that use genetic screening tests do so for two primary reasons. Some use genetic testing to make workers aware of genetic problems that may exist so that medical treatments can begin. Others use genetic testing to terminate employees who may make extensive use of health insurance benefits and thus raise the benefits costs and utilization rates of the employer. A major company had to publicly apologize to employees for secretly testing to determine if they were genetically predisposed to carpal tunnel syndrome.

Genetic Information Nondiscrimination Act (GINA). Congress passed GINA to limit the use of information by health insurance plans. Employers are prohibited from collecting genetic information or making employment decisions based on genetic decisions. "Genetic information" includes genetic tests of the employee or family members and family medical history. It does not apply to "water cooler talk," or the inadvertent acquisition of information.

Managing Disabilities in the Workforce

At the heart of managing individuals with disabilities is for employers to make reasonable accommodations in several areas. First, architectural barriers should not prohibit disabled individuals' access to work areas or restrooms. Second, appropriate work tasks must be assigned. Satisfying this requirement may mean modifying jobs, work area layouts, or work schedules or providing special equipment.

Key to making reasonable accommodations is identifying the essential job functions and then determining which accommodations are reasonable so that the individual can perform the core job duties. Fortunately for employers, most accommodations needed are relatively inexpensive.

Recruiting and Selecting Individuals with Disabilities. Numerous employers have specifically targeted the recruitment and selection of individuals with disabilities. However, questions asked in the employment process should be job related.

One common selection test is a physical abilities test, which can be challenged as discriminatory based on the ADA. Such physical tests must be specifically job related, and not general. For example, having all applicants lift 50-pound weights, even though only some warehouse workers will have to lift that much, could be illegal. Also, rather than testing with barbells or other artificial weights, the employer should use the actual 50-pound boxes lifted in performing the specific jobs.

Employees Who Develop Disabilities.   For many employers, the impact of the ADA has been the greatest when handling employees who develop disabilities, not dealing with applicants who already have disabilities. As the workforce ages, it is likely that more employees will develop disabilities. For instance, a warehouse worker who suffers a serious leg injury while motorcycling away from work may request reasonable accommodation.

Employers must develop responses for handling accommodation requests from individuals who have been satisfactory employees without disabilities, but who now must be considered for accommodations if they are to be able to continue working. Handled inappropriately, these individuals are likely to file either ADA complaints with the EEOC or private lawsuits.

Employees sometimes can be shifted to other jobs where their disabilities do not affect them as much. For instance, the warehouse firm might be able to move the injured repair worker to a purchasing inventory job inside so that climbing and lifting are unnecessary. But the problem for employers is what to do with the next worker who develops problems if an alternative job is not available. Even if the accommodations are just for one employee, the reactions of coworkers must be considered.

Individuals with Mental Disabilities.   More ADA complaints are being filed by individuals who have or claim to have mental disabilities. The cases that have been filed have ranged from individuals with a medical history of paranoid schizophrenia or clinical depression to individuals who claim that job stress has affected their marriage or sex life. Regardless of the type of employees' claims, it is important that employers respond properly by obtaining medical verifications for claims of mental illnesses and considering accommodation requests for mental disabilities in the same manner as accommodation requests for physical disabilities.

Individuals with Life-Threatening Illnesses.   The U.S. Supreme Court has determined that individuals with life-threatening illnesses are covered by the ADA. Individuals with leukemia, cancer, or AIDS are all considered as having disabilities, and employers must respond to them appropriately or face charges of discrimination. Numerous individuals with life-threatening illnesses may intend to continue working, particularly if their illness is forecast to be multiyear in nature.

An additional requirement of the ADA is that all medical information be maintained in files separated from the general personnel files. The medical files must have identified security procedures, and limited access procedures must be identified.

Management Focus on ADAAA Adaptation.   After the changes made by ADAAA, less effort should be placed on determining whether an individual is indeed disabled—the individual probably is disabled. Rather, management should:

- Define essential functions in advance.
- Handle all requests for accommodation properly.
- Interact with the employee with good faith and documentation.
- Know and follow the reasonable accommodation rules.

OTHER AREAS OF POTENTIAL DISCRIMINATION

The populations of most developed countries—including Australia, Japan, most European countries, and the United States—are aging. These changes mean that as older workers with a lifetime of experiences and skills retire, HR faces significant challenges in replacing them with workers having the capabilities and work ethic that characterize many mature workers in the United States. Employment discrimination against individuals age 40 and older is prohibited by the Age Discrimination in Employment Act (ADEA).

Age Discrimination in Employment Act (ADEA)

The Age Discrimination in Employment Act (ADEA) of 1967, amended in 1978 and 1986, prohibits discrimination in terms, conditions, or privileges of employment against all individuals age 40 years or older working for employers having 20 or more workers. However, the U.S. Supreme Court has ruled that state employees may not sue state government employers in federal courts because the ADEA is a federal law. The impact of the ADEA is increasing as the U.S. workforce has been aging. Consequently, the number of age discrimination cases has been increasing, according to EEOC reports.

Older Workers Benefit Protection Act (OWBPA)

This law is an amendment to the ADEA and is aimed at protecting employees when they sign liability waivers for age discrimination in exchange for severance packages. To comply with the act, employees must be given complete accurate information on the available benefits. For example, an early retirement package that includes a waiver stating the employee will not sue for age discrimination if the employee takes the money for early retirement must include a written, clearly understood agreement to that effect.

The impact of the OWBPA is becoming more evident. Industries such as manufacturing and others offer early retirement buyouts to cut their workforces. For instance, Ford and General Motors offered large buyouts of which thousands of workers have taken advantage.

To counter significant staffing difficulties, some employers recruit older people to return to the workforce through the use of part-time and other scheduling options. During the past decade, the number of older workers holding part-time jobs has increased. It is likely that the number of older workers interested in working part-time will continue to grow.

A strategy used by employers to retain the talents of older workers is **phased retirement,** whereby employees gradually reduce their workloads and pay levels. This option is growing in use as a way to allow older workers with significant knowledge and experience to have more personal flexibility, while the organizations retain them for their valuable capabilities. Some firms also rehire their retirees as part-time workers, independent contractors, or consultants. Some provisions in the Pension Protection Act of 2006 allow pension distributions for employees who are reducing their work hours.

Religion and Spirituality in the Workplace

Title VII of the Civil Rights Act identifies discrimination on the basis of religion as illegal. The increasing religious diversity in the workforce has put greater emphasis on religious considerations in workplaces. However, religious schools and institutions can use religion as a bona fide occupational qualification for employment practices on a limited scale. Also, employers must make *reasonable accommodation* efforts regarding an employee's religious beliefs according to the U.S. Supreme Court.

Employers increasingly are having to balance the rights of employees with differing religious beliefs. One way to do that is to make reasonable accommodation for employees' religious beliefs when assigning and scheduling work, because many religions have differing days of worship and holidays. For example, some firms have established "holiday swapping pools," whereby Christian employees can work during Passover or Ramadan or Chinese New Year, and employees from other religions can work on Christmas. Other firms allow employees a set number of days off for holidays, without specifying the holidays in company personnel policies.

Immigration Reform and Control Acts (IRCA)

The United States has always had a significant number of immigrants who come to work in this country. The increasing number of immigrants who have entered illegally has led to extensive political, social, and employment-related debates. The existence of more foreign-born workers means that employers must comply with the provisions of the Immigration Reform and Control Acts (IRCA). Employers are required to obtain and inspect I-9 forms, and verify documents such as birth certificates, passports, visas, and work permits. They can be fined if they knowingly hire illegal aliens. E-verify is a federal government source that can be used for this verification. Federal contractors must use it to verify employees legal status.

Military Status and USERRA

The employment rights of military veterans and reservists have been addressed in several laws. The two most important laws are the Vietnam Era

Veterans Readjustment Assistance Act of 1974 and the Uniformed Services Employment and Reemployment Rights Act (USERRA) of 1994. Under the latter, employees are required to notify their employers of military service obligations. Employers must give employees serving in the military leaves of absence protections under the USERRA.

With the use of reserves and National Guard troops abroad, the provisions of USERRA have had more impact on employers. This act does not require employers to pay employees while they are on military leave, but many firms provide some compensation, often a differential. Many requirements regarding benefits, disabilities, and reemployment are covered in the act as well.

Sexual Orientation

Recent battles in a number of states and communities illustrate the depth of emotions that accompany discussions of "gay rights." Some states and cities have passed laws prohibiting discrimination based on sexual orientation or lifestyle. Even the issue of benefits coverage for "domestic partners," whether heterosexual or homosexual, has been the subject of state and city legislation. No federal laws of a similar nature have been passed. Whether gays and lesbians have any special rights under the equal protection amendment to the U.S. Constitution has not been decided by the U.S. Supreme Court.

Appearance and Weight Discrimination

Several EEO cases have been filed concerning the physical appearance of employees. Court decisions consistently have allowed employers to set dress codes as long as they are applied uniformly. For example, establishing a dress code for women but not for men has been ruled discriminatory. Also, employers should be cautious when enforcing dress standards for women employees who are members of certain religions that prescribe appropriate and inappropriate dress and appearance standards. Some individuals have brought cases of employment discrimination based on height or weight. The crucial factor that employers must consider is that any weight or height requirements must be related to the job, such as when excess weight would hamper an individual's job performance.

WORKFORCE COMPOSITION AND DIVERSITY

The existing U.S. workforce is changing, and projections indicate that more shifting will occur in the next few years.[7] To analyze the composition of workers and jobs in the United States, the U.S. Bureau of Labor Statistics (BLS) undertakes studies to identify current and future projected compositions. Because of economic shifts and their effects in different industries, some types of workers are scarce but in high demand, while others are available in excessive numbers.

A worker-related shift results from the U.S. workforce becoming more diverse. **Diversity** reflects the differences in human characteristics in an organization. The tangible indicators of diversity that employers must consider include the following:

- Race/ethnicity
- National origin/immigration
- Age/generational differences
- Gender—men and women
- Marital and family status
- Sexual orientation
- Disabilities
- Religion

Figure 2-6 shows various approaches to dealing with diversity.

The "business case" for diversity must be linked to key business goals and strategies and organizational results.[8] The business case for diversity includes the following:

- Diversity allows new talent and ideas from employees of different backgrounds, which can enhance organizational performance.
- Diversity helps recruiting and retention because protected-class individuals often prefer to work in organizations with coworkers of various demographics.
- Diversity allows for an increase of market share because customers can be attracted to purchase products and services with varied demographic marketing activities.
- Diversity can lead to lower costs because there may be fewer discrimination lawsuits.

FIGURE 2-6 Various Approaches to Diversity and Their Results

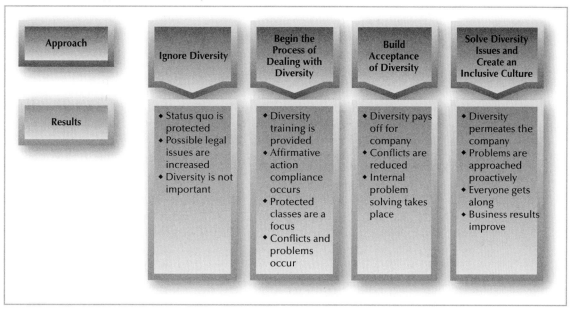

One concern with diversity programs is that they may be perceived as benefiting only certain groups of persons and not others. Diversity actions must be well thought out and address both the positive and negative aspects of such programs, given the workforce composition of many organizations.

Race and Ethnicity

Significant race and ethnic shifts in the U.S. population will occur in the next several decades. By the year 2050, racial/ethnic groups currently in the minority will likely make up more than 50% of the U.S. population. The Census Bureau says whites represent 67% of the population currently, but will be at approximately 48% in 2050. The Hispanic population will increase dramatically, to about 39% of the overall population, and will exceed the African American population. The Asian population will triple to about 9% by 2050.[9]

Another racial/ethnic factor is the growth in the number of immigrants to the United States and other developed countries. The United States has always had a significant number of immigrants who have come to work in this country. The increasing number of immigrants entering illegally has led to extensive political, social, and employment-related issues. In the United States, one concern is the large number of illegal immigrants hired to fill certain jobs at low cost, despite availability of unemployed U.S. workers.

Generational Differences

Much has been written about the expectations of individuals in different age groups and generations. For employers, these varied expectations present challenges, especially given economic, global, technology, and other changes in the workplace. Some common age/generational groups are labeled as follows:

- Matures (born before 1946)
- Baby boomers (born 1946–1964)
- Generation Xers (born 1965–1980)
- Generation Yers (millenials) (born 1981–2000)

As the economy and industries have changed, the aging of the U.S. workforce has become a significant concern. Workers over age 55 are delaying retirement more often, working more years, and/or looking for part-time work or phased retirement. Economic conditions are the predominant reasons why these workers are bypassing the "normal" retirement age of 65. As older and more experienced employees retire in the future, employers will face increasing gaps as they try to replace the experience and capabilities of baby boomers.

Generational differences in expectations are likely to add to challenges and conflicts in organizations. For instance, many baby boomers and matures are concerned about security and experience, while younger people have different concerns. Generation Yers are often seen as the "why" generation; they expect to be rewarded quickly, use more technology, and often ask more questions about why managers and organizations make the decisions they do.

Consider the dynamics of a mature manager directing Generation X and Y individuals, or Generation X managers supervising older, more experienced baby boomers as well as generation Y employees. However, stereotyping these individuals by generations may not reflect how actual individuals view their jobs and produce organizational results.

Gender Diversity

Women are becoming a greater percentage of workers in the U.S. workforce; they comprise more than 46% of the total employed individuals. However, men average more work time daily than do women.[10] Interestingly, as the economic and labor market has been shifting, the job fields dominated by men have been hit harder than those consisting mostly of women. Male workers are more heavily represented in manufacturing, farming, and other "male-dominated" industries, so male employees have been impacted more severely by the market shifts than women employees with their higher rates of participation in industries such as health care and education.

From this follows some of the gender issues that occur in organizations. First, women overall have lower average pay than men due to the nature of their jobs and work hours. Second, in most industries and countries, women make up a much smaller percentage of senior executives and managers in many organizations and occupations. Over the past decade more women have become managers, but women comprise less of senior level executive and board members than their numbers would suggest. Some of the wage gap between men and women is due to the greater family/home responsibilities that females have to meet.

Both women and men also are increasingly facing the need to aid older family members, as matures and baby boomers encounter health disabilities and other problems.

DIVERSITY TRAINING

Traditional diversity training has a number of different goals. One prevalent goal is to minimize discrimination and harassment lawsuits. Other goals focus on improving acceptance and understanding of people with different backgrounds, experiences, capabilities, and lifestyles.

Components of Traditional Diversity Training

Approaches to diversity training vary, but often include at least three components. *Legal awareness* is the first and most common component. Here, the training focuses on the legal implications of discrimination. A limited approach to diversity training stops with these legal "do's and don'ts."

By introducing *cultural awareness*, trainers hope to build greater understanding of the differences among people. Cultural awareness training helps all participants to see and accept the differences in people with widely varying cultural backgrounds.

The third component of diversity training—*sensitivity training*—is more difficult. The aim here is to "sensitize" people to the differences among them and how their words and behaviors are seen by others. Some diversity training includes exercises containing examples of harassment and other behaviors.

Mixed Results for Diversity Training

The effects of diversity training are viewed as mixed by both organizations and participants. A limited number of studies have been done on the effectiveness of diversity training. There is some concern that the programs may be interesting or entertaining, but may not produce longer-term changes in people's attitudes and behaviors toward others with characteristics different from their own.

Some argue that traditional diversity training more often than not has failed, pointing out that it does not reduce discrimination and harassment complaints. Rather than reducing conflict, in a number of situations diversity training has heightened hostility and conflicts. In some firms, it has produced divisive effects, and has not taught the behaviors needed for employees to work well together in a diverse workplace.[11]

This last point, focusing on behaviors, seems to hold the most promise for making diversity training more effective. For instance, dealing with cultural diversity as part of training efforts for sales representatives and managers has produced positive results. Teaching appropriate behaviors and skills in relationships with others is more likely to produce satisfactory results than focusing just on attitudes and beliefs among diverse employees.

The negative consequences of diversity training may manifest themselves broadly in a backlash against all diversity efforts. This backlash takes two main forms. First, and somewhat surprisingly, the individuals in protected groups, such as women and members of racial minorities, sometimes see the diversity efforts as inadequate and nothing but "corporate public relations." Thus, it appears that by establishing diversity programs, employers can raise the expectation levels of protected-group individuals, but the programs may not meeting the expectations.

On the other side, a number of individuals who are not in protected groups, primarily white males, believe that the emphasis on diversity sets them up as scapegoats for societal problems. Sometimes white males show hostility and anger at diversity efforts. Diversity programs are widely perceived as benefiting only women and racial minorities and taking away opportunities for men and nonminorities. This resentment and hostility is usually directed at affirmative action programs that employers have instituted.[12]

Trainers emphasize that the key to avoiding backlash in diversity efforts is to stress that people can believe whatever they wish, but at work their values are less important than their *behaviors*. Dealing with diversity is not about what people can and cannot *say*; it is about being *respectful* to others.

NOTES

1. Margaret M. Pinkham, "Employers Should Take Care When Making Decisions about Caregivers," *Employee Relations Law Journal*, Summer 2008, 35–40.

2. Anne Lindberg, "Disparate Impact or Disparate Treatment: Either Way Leads to Court," *Trend Watcher*, July 10, 2009, 1–5.

3. Fay Hansen, "Discriminatory Twist in Networking Sites Puts Recruiters in Peril," *Work Force Management*, September 2009, 1–5.

4. C. Tuna, N. Koppel, and M. Sanserino, "Job-Test Ruling Cheers Employers," *The Wall Street Journal*, July 1, 2009, B1; Adam Liptak, "Justices Find Bias Against Whites," *The Denver Post*, June 30, 2009, 1A.

5. Allen Smith, "Pay Bias Figures Prominently in New Supreme Court Forum," *HR News*, September 26, 2009, *www.shrm.org/hrnews*.

6. Harsh Luther and Uipan Luther, "A Theoretical Framework Explaining Cross-Cultural Sexual Harassment: Integrating Hofsteds and Schwartz," *Journal of Labor Research*, Winter 2007, 169–188.

7. "Employment Projections" *U.S. Bureau of Labor Statistics, www.bls.gov.*

8. Bill Leonard, "Diversity Initiatives Must Grow from Key Business Goals," *SHRMOnLine*, April 29, 2009, *www.shrm.org/hrdisciplines*; Ellen F. Curtis and Janice L. Dreachslin, "Integrative Literature Review: Diverse Management Interventions and Organizational Performance," *Human Resource Development Review*, 7 (2008), 107–134.

9. "An Older and More Diverse Nation by Mid-Century," *U.S. Census Bureau News*, August 14, 2008, *www.census.gov.*

10. *American Time Use Survey*, U.S. Department of Labor, 2008, *www.bls.gov/tus/#news.*

11. Susan Awbrey, "The Dynamics of Vertical and Horizontal Diversity in Organization and Society," *Human Resource Development Review*, 6 (2007), 7–32.

12. Carol Kulik, et al., "The Rich Get Richer: Predicting Participation in Voluntary Diversity Training," *Journal of Organizational Behavior*, Volume 28 (2007), 753–769.

INTERNET RESOURCES

Equal Employment Opportunity Commission— This website provides information on the EEOC. It includes details on employment discrimination facts, enforcement statistics, and technical assistance programs. Visit the site at *www.eeoc.gov.*

The Affirmative Action and Diversity Project—A resource for opinions surrounding the issues of affirmative action and its cultural and economic aspects can be found at *http://aad.english.ucsb.edu.*

Administration on Aging—This government website provides information on aging and age discrimination from government agencies, associations, and organizations. Visit the site at *www.aoa.gov.*

American Institute for Managing Diversity—The nation's leading nonprofit think tank dedicated to promoting and furthering the field of diversity management can be found at *www.aimd.org.*

SUGGESTED READINGS

"Discrimination Charges on the Rise," *Benefit News.com Employee Benefit News*, September 15, 2007, 82; Sam Hananei, "Federal Job Discrimination Complaints Hit Record," *Yahoo! News*, March 11, 2009, 1–2.

Andrew Slobodien and Katie O'Brien, "The ADA Amendments Act of 2008 and How It Will Change the Workplace," *Employee Relations Law Journal*, Winter 2008, 32–39.

Eileen Kelly, "Accommodating Religious Expression in the Workplace," *Employer Responsibility and Rights Journal*, 20 (2008), 45–56.

Frank Giancola, "The Generation Gap: More Myth than Reality," *Human Resource Planning*, 29 (2006), 32; Susan A. Murphy, *Leading a Multigenerational Workforce* (Washington, DC: AARP, 2007).

Individuals/HR Planning/Job Analysis

HR—MEETING MANAGEMENT CHALLENGES

Understanding how and why employees react to their jobs is a part of Human Resources, as is planning for the number of employees that will be needed. Job analysis helps identify what people are doing in their job and provides a way to initiate job descriptions. Issues include:

- Understanding jobs and the people who do them
- How HR can deal with turnover and retention
- Identifying skills that jobs require and the tasks involved

The common theme of the interaction between people and their jobs is covered in this chapter. Designing systems to keep or retain more people makes sense. Planning to avoid "surprises" in the number of employees that will be needed is basic to good HR management. And finally job analysis keeps the system current and jobs under appropriate scrutiny as things change.

INDIVIDUAL ORGANIZATIONAL RELATIONS

Relationships between individuals and their employers can vary widely from favorable to unfavorable. The individual's performance is a major part of whether the employer wants the individual to stay or go. Competent employees who are satisfied with their employers, who know what is expected, and who have less turnover potential are assets to the organization. But just as individuals in an organization can be a competitive advantage, they can also be a liability. When few employees are satisfied with their jobs, when people are constantly leaving, and when the employees who do remain work ineffectively, the organization faces a *competitive disadvantage* from its employees.

Psychological Contract

A concept that has been useful in discussing individuals' relationships with their employers is that of a **psychological contract**, which refers to the unwritten expectations employees and employers have about the nature of their work relationships. The psychological contract can create either a positive or negative relationship between an employer and an individual. It is best on trust and commitment that leads to meeting both the employer's and employee's expectations and needs.

Unwritten psychological contracts between employers and employees encompass expectations about both tangible items (e.g., wages, benefits, employee productivity, and attendance) and intangible items (e.g., loyalty, fair treatment, and job security). Employers may attempt to detail their expectations through handbooks and policy manuals, but those materials are only part of the total "contractual" relationship.

Traditionally, employees expected to exchange their efforts and capabilities for secure jobs that offered competitive pay, a solid range of benefits, and career progression within an organization, among other factors. But as some organizations have changed in economic terms, they have had to address various organizational crises by downsizing and eliminating workers who had given long and loyal service. Consequently, in these firms, remaining employees may question whether they should remain loyal to and stay with their employers. The psychological contract has changed.

A psychological contract may include these expectations:

Employers Provide

- Competitive compensation and benefits
- Flexibility to balance work and home life
- Career development opportunities

Employees Contribute

- Continuous skill improvement and increased productivity
- Reasonable time with the organization
- Extra efforts and results when needed

Individual Employee Performance and Motivation

The idea of a psychological contract between the individual employee and the organization helps clarify why people might stay or leave a job. But for an employer to *want* to keep an employee, that person must be performing well.

The three major factors that affect how a given individual performs are illustrated in Figure 3-1. They are: (1) individual ability to do the work, (2) effort expended, and (3) organizational support. The relationship of those factors is widely acknowledged in management literature as follows:

$$\text{Performance } (P) = \text{Ability } (A) \times \text{Effort } (E) \times \text{Support } (S)$$

Individual performance is enhanced to the degree that all three components are present with an individual employee, and diminished if any of these factors is reduced or absent. For instance, if several production workers have the abilities to do their jobs and work hard, but the organization provides outmoded equipment or the management style of supervisors causes negative reactions by the workers, the lack of organizational support may reduce individual performance.

FIGURE 3-1 Components of Individual Performance

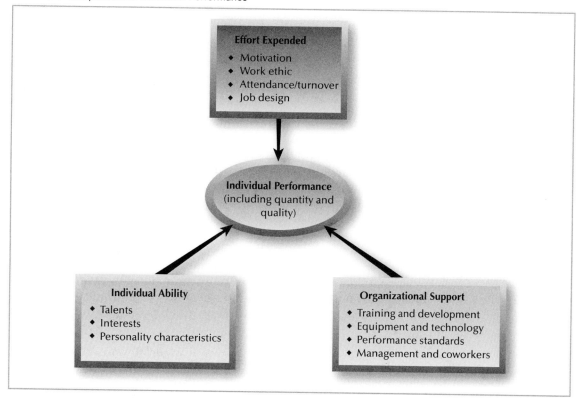

An example of how this performance equation can work in a positive way is seen in the link between individual motivation and organizational support in the form of coworkers. The motivation of poor-performing employees can sometimes be improved when these employees work more intensely with a group of better-performing workers. The link between individual motivation and organizational support has important HR management implications.

The desire within a person causing that person to act is called **motivation**. People usually act to reach a goal, which means that motivation is a goal-directed drive that seldom occurs in a void. The words *need, want, desire,* and *drive* are all similar to *motive,* from which the word *motivation* is derived. Approaches to understanding motivation vary because different theorists have developed their own views and models. Each approach has contributed to the understanding of human motivation, and details on different approaches can be found in various organizational behavior textbooks.

Motivation is complex and individualized, and managerial strategies and tactics must be broad-based to address the motivation concerns of individuals at work. Factors that can inhibit motivation and work performance include a worker's capacities and determination to get work done regardless of difficulties. For instance, with a poor-performing employee, managers must determine whether inadequate individual behavior is due to employee deficiencies, inconsistent reward policies, or low desire for the rewards offered.

Job Satisfaction

In its most basic sense, **job satisfaction** is a positive emotional state resulting from evaluating one's job experiences. Job *dissatisfaction* occurs when one's expectations are not met. For example, if an employee expects clean and safe working conditions, that employee is likely to be dissatisfied if the workplace is dirty and dangerous.

Dimensions of job satisfaction frequently mentioned include worker relationships, pay and benefits, performance recognition, and communications with managers and executives. Sometimes job satisfaction is called *morale.* Frequently cited reasons for decline in morale include more demanding and stressful work, fewer relationships with management, and less confidence in compensation and other rewards.[1]

The degree to which employees believe in and accept organizational goals and want to remain with the organization is called **organizational commitment**. Job satisfaction influences organizational commitment, which in turn affects employee retention and turnover.

A related idea is *employee engagement,* which is the extent to which an employee feels linked to organizational success. Surveys have shown that levels of employee engagement range from 15% to 45% for highly engaged workers, and 5% to 20% for disengaged ones.[2]

Engaged employees may be seen as "loyal" employees who are more than just satisfied with their jobs; they are pleased with the relationships with their employers. In changing labor markets, employers find that turnover of key people occurs more frequently when employee loyalty is low.

EMPLOYEE TURNOVER

Turnover occurs when employees leave an organization and have to be replaced. Many organizations have found that turnover is a costly problem. For instance, health care firms experienced over 30% turnover annually in one state. Just in registered nurse jobs, the turnover cost in the state was more than $125 million per year, with individual nurse turnover costs being $32,000 per person.[3]

The extent to which employers face high turnover rates and costs varies by organization and industry. For higher-level executives and professionals, turnover costs can run as much as two times the departing employees' annual salaries, and rates often are linked to executive job expectations and needed skills changes. In many service industries, the turnover rates and costs are frequently very high. In the retail industry, turnover in some companies averages more than 100% a year for part-time workers and around 75% a year for full-time workers. In the U.S. supermarkets, fast-food restaurants, and other retail service industry firms spend billions of dollars each year to deal with worker turnover.

Types of Employee Turnover

Turnover is classified in a number of ways. One classification uses the following categories, although the two types are not mutually exclusive:

- **Involuntary Turnover**

  Employees are terminated for poor performance or work rule violations

- **Voluntary Turnover**

  Employees leave by choice

Involuntary turnover is triggered at all levels by employers terminating workers due to organizational policies and work rule violations, excessive absenteeism, performance standards that are not met by employees, and other issues. Voluntary turnover too can be caused by many factors, some of which are not employer controlled. Common voluntary turnover causes include job dissatisfaction, pay and benefits levels, supervision, geography, and personal/family reasons. Career opportunities in other firms, when employees receive unsolicited contacts, may lead to turnover for individuals, especially those in highly specialized jobs such as IT. Voluntary turnover may increase with the size of the organization, most likely because larger firms are less effective in preventing turnover and have more employees who are inclined to move.

Another view of turnover classifies it based on whether it is good or bad for the organization:

- **Functional Turnover**

  Lower-performing or disruptive employees leave

- **Dysfunctional Turnover**

  Key individuals and high performers leave at critical times

Not all turnover is negative for organizations; on the contrary, functional turnover represents a positive change. Some workforce losses are desirable, especially if those who leave are lower-performing, less reliable, and/or disruptive individuals. Of course, dysfunctional turnover also occurs. That happens when key individuals leave, often at crucial times. For example, a software project leader who leaves in the middle of a system upgrade in order to take a promotion at another firm could cause the system upgrade timeline to slip due to the difficulty of replacing the employee and could also lead other software specialists in the firm to seek out and accept jobs at competitive firms.

Employees quit for many reasons, only some of which can be controlled by the organization, so another classification uses the following terms to describe types of turnover:

- **Uncontrollable Turnover**

  Employees leave for reasons outside the control of the employer

- **Controllable Turnover**

  Employees leave for reasons that could be influenced by the employer

Some examples of reasons for turnover the employer cannot control include: (1) the employee moves out of the geographic area, (2) the employee decides to stay home with young children or an elder relative, (3) the employee's spouse is transferred, and (4) the employee is a student worker who graduates from college. Even though some turnover is inevitable, employers recognize that reducing turnover saves money, and that they must address the turnover that is controllable. Organizations are better able to keep employees if they deal with the concerns of those employees that might lead to the controllable turnover.

Hiring new workers while laying off others is called **churn**. This practice raises a paradox in which employers complain about not being able to find skilled workers while they are laying off others. As organizations face economic and financial problems that result in layoffs, the remaining employees are more likely to consider jobs at other firms. In this situation, turnover is more likely to occur, and efforts are needed to keep existing employees. HR actions such as information sharing, opportunities for more training/learning, and emphasis on job significance can be helpful in lowering turnover intentions of individuals.

Measuring Employee Turnover

The U.S. Department of Labor estimates that the cost of replacing an employee ranges from one-half to five times the person's annual salary. The turnover rate for an organization can be computed as a monthly or yearly cost. The following formula, in which *separations* means departures from the organization, is widely used:

$$\frac{\text{Number of employee separations during the year}}{\text{Toral number of employees at midyear}} \times 100$$

Common turnover rates range from almost 0% to more than 100% a year and vary among industries. As a part of HR management systems, turnover data can be gathered and analyzed in a number of different ways, including the following categories:

- Job and job level
- Department, unit, and location
- Reason for leaving
- Length of service

- Demographic characteristics
- Education and training
- Knowledge, skills, and abilities
- Performance ratings/levels

Two examples illustrate why detailed analyses of turnover are important. A manufacturing organization had a companywide turnover rate that was not severe, but most of the turnover occurred within one department. That imbalance indicated that some specific actions on training supervisors and revising pay levels were needed to resolve problems in that unit. In a different organization, a global shipping/delivery firm found ways to reduce turnover of sales and service employees. The actions of that firm reduced its turnover, which contributed to an annual savings of more than $18 million in direct and indirect costs. In both of these examples, the targeted turnover rates declined as a result of employer actions taken in response to the turnover analyses that were done.

Areas to be included in calculating detailed turnover costs include the following:

- *Separation costs:* HR staff and supervisory time, pay rates to prevent separations, exit interview time, unemployment expenses, legal fees for separations challenged, accrued vacation expenditures, continued health benefits, and others
- *Vacancy costs:* Temporary help, contract and consulting firm usage, existing employee overtime, and other costs until the person is replaced
- *Replacement costs:* Recruiting and advertising expenses, search fees, HR interviewer and staff time and salaries, employee referral fees, relocation and moving costs, supervisor and managerial time and salaries, employment testing costs, reference checking fees, preemployment medical expenses, relocation costs, and others
- *Training costs:* Paid orientation time, training staff time and pay, costs of training materials, supervisor and manager time and salaries, coworker "coaching" time and pay, and others
- *Hidden/indirect costs:* Costs that are not obvious, such as reduced productivity, decreased customer service, additional unexpected employee turnover, missed project deadlines, and others

RETENTION OF HUMAN RESOURCES

Retaining employees is part of HR staffing and planning efforts. Turnover, as the opposite of retention, often has been seen as a routine HR matter requiring records and reports. However, what was once a bothersome detail has become a substantial HR issue for many employers. Organizations are being forced to study why employees leave and why they stay. Sometimes an individual in the HR area is assigned to specifically focus on retention to ensure that it receives high priority.

Myths and Realities about Retention

Keeping good employees is a challenge that all organizations share and that becomes even more difficult as labor markets change. Unfortunately, some myths have arisen about what it takes to retain employees. Some of the most prevalent myths and realities are as follows:

1. *Money is the main reason people leave.* Money certainly is a vital HR tool, and if people feel they are being paid inadequately, they may be more likely to leave. But if they are paid close to the competitive level they expect, other parts of the job become more important.
2. *Hiring has little to do with retention.* This is not true. Recruiting and selecting the people who fit the jobs and who are less likely to leave in the first place, and then orienting them to the company, can greatly increase retention. It is important to select for retention.

3. *If you train people, you are only training them for another employer.* Developing skills in employees may indeed make them more marketable, but it also tends to improve retention. When an employer provides employees with training and development assistance, job satisfaction may increase and employees are more likely to stay, particularly if they see more future opportunities internally.

4. *Do not be concerned about retention during organizational change.* That is exactly the time to worry about retention. Although some people's jobs may have to be cut because of economic organizational factors, the remaining employees that the company would like to keep may have the most opportunity and reason to leave voluntarily. For example, during a merger or acquisition, most workers are concerned about job security and their employer's future. If they do not feel a part of the new organization early on, many may leave or evaluate alternatives.

5. *If solid performers want to leave, the company cannot hold them.* Employees are best viewed as "free agents," who indeed can leave when they want. The key to keeping solidly performing employees is to create an environment in which they want to stay and grow.

Drivers of Retention

Because both people and jobs are so varied, managers and HR professionals need to realize that individuals may remain or leave their employment for both job-related and personal reasons. For instance, if employees choose to leave an organization for family reasons (e.g., because a spouse is transferring or to raise children), there may be a limited number of actions the employer can take to keep them on the job. However, there are significant actions that an employer can take to retain employees in many other circumstances. Figure 3-2 illustrates some of these "drivers" of retention, or areas in which employers can take action to strengthen the possibility of keeping employees.

Retention Assessment and Metrics

To ensure that appropriate actions are taken to enhance retention, management decisions require data and analyses rather than subjective impressions, anecdotes of selected individual situations, or panic reactions to the loss of key people.

The analysis of turnover data is an attempt to get at the cause of retention problems. Analysis should recognize that turnover is a symptom of other factors that may be causing problems. When the causes are treated, the symptoms can go away.

Some of the first areas to consider when analyzing data for retention include the work, pay/benefits, supervision, and management systems. Common methods of obtaining useful perspectives are employee surveys, exit interviews, and first-year turnover evaluations.

Retention evaluation is part of the broader organizational HR planning and staffing roles. The determination of the correct supply of human

FIGURE 3-2 Drivers of Retention

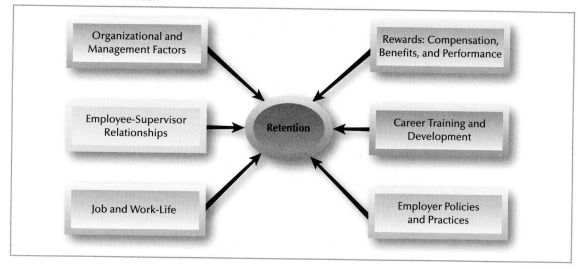

resources in a company is made by Human Resource planning and is covered next.

HUMAN RESOURCE PLANNING

Human resource planning is the process of analyzing and identifying the need for and availability of human resources so that the organization can meet its objectives. The focus of HR planning is to ensure the organization has the *right number of human resources,* with the *right capabilities,* at the *right times,* and in the *right places.* In HR planning, an organization must consider the availability and allocation of people to jobs over long periods of time, not just for the next month or even the next year.

Additionally, as part of the analyses, HR plans can include several approaches. Actions may include shifting employees to other jobs in the organization, laying off employees or otherwise cutting back the number of employees, retraining present employees, and/or increasing the number of employees in certain areas. Factors to consider include the current employees' knowledge, skills, and abilities and the expected vacancies resulting from retirements, promotions, transfers, and discharges. To do this, HR planning requires efforts by HR professionals working with executives and managers.

Organizational Size and HR Planning

The need for HR planning in larger organizations is especially important. For example, in a review, the U.S. government's Corps of Engineers, with a workforce of 35,000, was found to have an outdated strategic HR plan. Also, it had not done an organization-wide needs analysis for current and future workforce.

If adjustments to foreseeable changes were not made, people or even entire divisions could be working at cross-purposes with the rest of the organization.[4]

In a smaller business, even though the owner/manager knows on a daily basis what is happening and what should be done, planning is still important. One difficult area for HR planning in small businesses is family matters and succession. Particular difficulties arise when a growing business is passed from one generation to another, resulting in a mix of family and nonfamily employees.

HR Planning Process

The steps in the HR planning process are shown in Figure 3-3. Notice that the process begins with considering the organizational strategic planning objectives. Then the possible *available workforce* must be evaluated by identifying both the external and internal workforce.

Once those assessments are complete, forecasts must be developed to identify both the demand for and supply of human resources. Management then formulates HR staffing plans and actions to address imbalances, both short-term and long-term. One means of developing and measuring HR planning

FIGURE 3-3 HR Planning Process

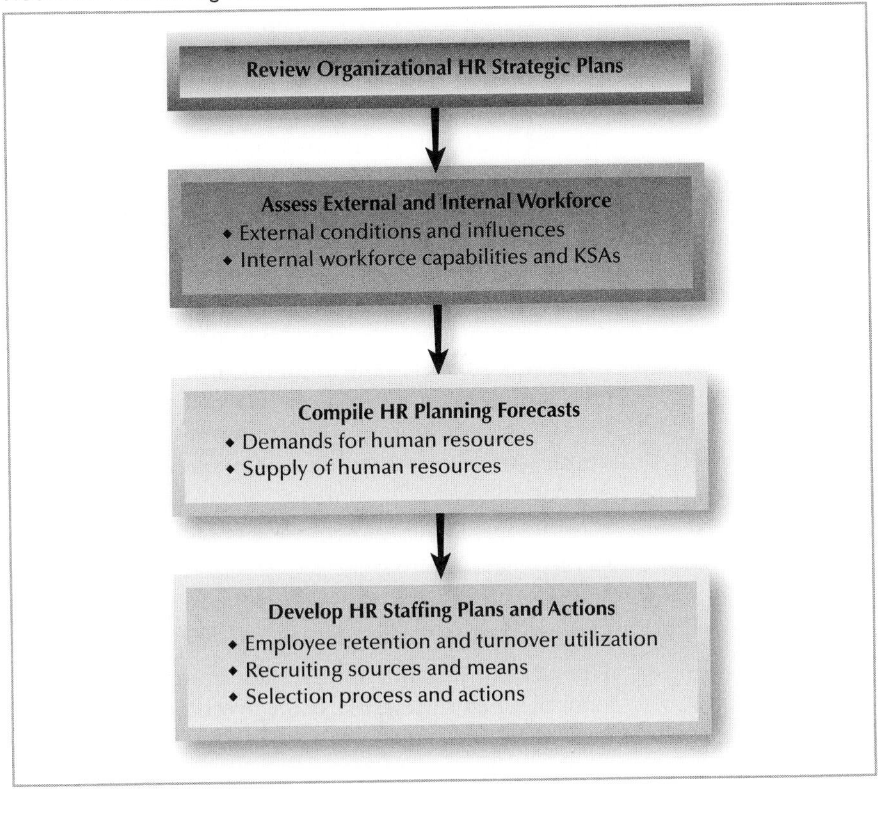

Review Organizational HR Strategic Plans

Assess External and Internal Workforce
- External conditions and influences
- Internal workforce capabilities and KSAs

Compile HR Planning Forecasts
- Demands for human resources
- Supply of human resources

Develop HR Staffing Plans and Actions
- Employee retention and turnover utilization
- Recruiting sources and means
- Selection process and actions

is use of a team of subject matter experts (SMEs) to increase the validity and reliability of the HR planning results. Specific strategies may be developed to fill vacancies or deal with surplus employees. For example, a strategy might be to fill 50% of expected vacancies by training employees in lower-level jobs and promoting them into more advanced anticipated openings.

Finally, HR plans are developed to provide specific direction for employee recruiting, selection, and retention. The most telling evidence of successful HR planning is a consistent alignment of the availabilities and capabilities of human resources with the needs of the organization over shorter or longer periods of time.

Assessing the External Workforce

The first stage of HR planning is to *examine organization objectives and plans.* If a network technology firm plans to double its number of client accounts from 100 to 200 in a 3-year period, that firm also must identify how many and what types of new employees will be needed to staff the expanded services, locations, and facilities. Several common external factors to be considered are highlighted next.

Economic and Governmental Factors

The general cycles of economic recession and economic boom in different businesses affect HR planning. Factors such as interest rates, inflation, and economic decline or growth affect the availability of workers and should figure into organizational and HR plans and objectives. There is a considerable difference between finding qualified applicants in a 4% unemployment market and in a 9% unemployment market. As the unemployment rate rises, the number of qualified people looking for work increases, often making it easier to fill some jobs.

A broad array of government regulations affects the labor supply and therefore HR planning. As a result, HR planning must be done by individuals who understand the legal requirements of various government regulations. In the United States and other countries, tax legislation at local, state, and federal levels affects HR planning. Elimination or expansion of tax benefits for job-training expenses might alter some job-training activities associated with workforce expansions. In summary, an organization must consider a wide variety of government policies, regulations, and laws during the HR planning process.

Competitive Evaluations

When making HR plans, employers must consider a number of geographic and competitive concerns. The *net migration* into a particular region is important. For example, in the past decade, the populations of some U.S. cities in the South, Southwest, and West have grown rapidly and have provided sources of labor. However, areas in the Northeast and Midwest have experienced declining populations.

Direct competitors are another important external force in HR planning. Failure to consider the competitive labor market and to offer pay scales and benefits competitive with those of organizations in the same general industry and geographic location may cost a company dearly in the long run.

Finally, the impact of *international competition* must be considered as part of environmental scanning. Global competition for labor intensifies as global competitors shift jobs and workers around the world, as illustrated by the outsourcing of jobs from the United States to countries with cheaper labor.

Changing Workforce Considerations

As mentioned in the previous chapter, significant changes in the workforce, both in the United States and globally, must be considered when doing external assessments for HR planning. Shifts in the composition of the workforce, combined with the use of different work patterns, have created workplaces and organizations that are notably different from those of a decade ago.

Many organizations face major concerns about having sufficient workers with the necessary capabilities. When scanning the potential and future workforce, it is important to consider a number of variables, including:

- Aging of the workforce
- Growing diversity of workers
- Female workers and work-life balancing concerns
- Availability of contingent workers
- Outsourcing possibilities

ASSESSING THE INTERNAL WORKFORCE

Analyzing the jobs that will need to be done and the capabilities of people who are currently available in the organization to do them is the next part of HR planning. The needs of the organization must be compared against the labor supply available both inside and outside the organization.

The starting point for evaluating internal workforce strengths and weaknesses is an audit of the jobs being done in the organization. A comprehensive analysis of all current jobs provides a basis for forecasting what jobs will need to be done in the future. Much of the data in the audit should be available from existing staffing and organizational databases. The following questions may be some key ones addressed during the internal assessment:

- What jobs exist now and how essential is each job?
- How many individuals are performing each job?
- What are the reporting relationships of jobs?
- What are the vital KSAs needed in the jobs?
- What jobs will be needed to implement future organizational strategies?
- What are the characteristics of those anticipated jobs?

FORECASTING HR SUPPLY AND DEMAND

The information gathered from scanning the external environment and assessing internal strengths and weaknesses is used to predict HR supply and demand in light of organizational objectives and strategies. **Forecasting** uses information from the past and the present to identify expected future conditions. Projections for the future are, of course, subject to error. Fortunately, experienced people usually are able to forecast with enough accuracy to positively affect long-range organizational planning.

The demand for employees can be calculated for an entire organization and/or for individual units in the organization. For example, a forecast might indicate that a firm needs 125 new employees next year, or that it needs 25 new people in sales and customer service, 45 in production, 20 in accounting and information systems, 2 in HR, and 33 in the warehouse. The unit breakdown obviously allows HR planners to better pinpoint the specific skills needed than does the aggregate method.

Once human resources needs have been forecast, then availability of qualified individuals must be identified. Forecasting availability considers both *external* and *internal* supplies. Although the internal supply may be somewhat easier to calculate, it is important to calculate the external supply as accurately as possible.

Estimating internal supply considers the number of external hires and the employees who move from their current jobs into others through promotions, lateral moves, and terminations. It also considers that the internal supply is influenced by training and development programs, transfer and promotion policies, and retirement policies, among other factors. In forecasting the internal supply, data from the replacement charts and succession planning efforts are used to project potential personnel changes, identify possible backup candidates, and keep track of attrition (resignations, retirements, etc.) for each department in an organization. Next we will consider how HR can help design the jobs those employees will do.

JOB DESIGN

Job design refers to organizing tasks, duties, responsibilities, and other elements into a productive unit of work. Identifying the components of a given job is an integral part of job design. Job design receives attention for three major reasons:

- Job design can influence *performance* in certain jobs, especially those where employee motivation can make a substantial difference.
- Job design can affect *job satisfaction*. Because people are more satisfied with certain job elements than others, identifying what makes a "good" job becomes critical. Reduced turnover and absenteeism also can be linked to effective job design.

FIGURE 3-4 Some Characteristics of People and Jobs

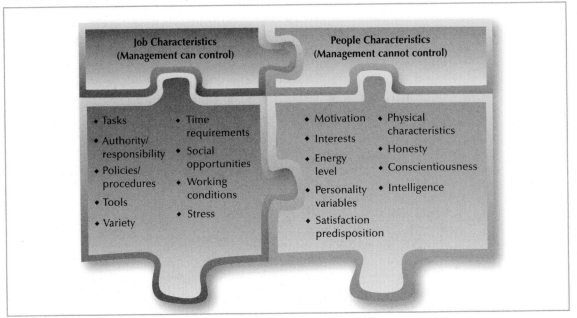

- Job design can impact both *physical* and *mental health*. Problems that may require assistance such as hearing loss, backache, leg pain, stress, high blood pressure, and even heart disease sometimes can be traced directly to job design.

Managers play a significant role in job design because often they are the people who establish jobs and their design components. They must make sure that job expectations are clear, that decision-making responsibilities and the accountability of workers are clarified, and that interactions with other jobs are integrated and appropriate.

The nature and characteristics of both jobs and people should be considered when job design is done. As Figure 3-4 indicates, managers can influence or control job characteristics, but usually not people characteristics.

Person-Job Fit

Not everyone would enjoy being an HR manager, an engineer, a nurse, or a drill-press operator. But some people like and do well at each of these jobs. The **person-job fit** is a simple but important concept of matching characteristics of people with characteristics of jobs. An employer can try to make a "round" person fit a "square" job, but it is hard to successfully reshape people. By redesigning jobs, the person-job fit may sometimes be improved more easily. For example, bank tellers talk to people all day; an individual who would rather not talk to others all day may do better in a job that does not require so much interaction because that part of the bank teller job probably cannot be changed. Different people will consider some jobs "good" and others "bad." As a result, people will fit different kinds of work.

Common Approaches to Job Design

One approach for designing or redesigning jobs is to simplify the job tasks and responsibilities. Job simplification may be appropriate for jobs that are to be staffed with entry-level employees. However, making jobs too simple may result in boring jobs that appeal to few people, causing high turnover. Several other approaches also have been used as part of job design.

Job Enlargement and Job Enrichment.   Attempts to alleviate some of the problems encountered in excessive job simplification fall under the general headings of job enlargement and job enrichment. **Job enlargement** involves broadening the scope of a job by expanding the number of different tasks to be performed. **Job enrichment** is increasing the depth of a job by adding responsibility for planning, organizing, controlling, or evaluating the job.

Job Rotation.   One technique that can break the monotony of an otherwise simple routine job is **job rotation**, which is the process of shifting a person from job to job. There are several advantages to job rotation with one being that it develops an employee's capabilities for doing several different jobs. Clear policies that identify for employees the nature and expectations of job rotations are more likely to make job rotation work.[5]

Job Sharing.   Another alternative used is **job sharing**, in which two employees perform the work of one full-time job. For instance, a hospital allows two radiological technicians to fill one job, and each individual works every other week. Such arrangements are beneficial for employees who may not want or be able to work full-time because of family, school, or other reasons. The keys to successful job sharing are that both "job sharers" must work effectively together and each must be competent in meeting the job requirements.

Using Worker Teams.   Typically, a job is thought of as something done by one person. However, where appropriate, jobs may be designed for teams to take advantage of the increased productivity and commitment that can follow such a change. Organizations can assign jobs to teams of employees instead of just individuals. Some firms have gone as far as dropping such terms as *workers* and *employees*, replacing them with *teammates, crew members, associates,* and other titles that emphasize teamwork.

The use of work teams has been a popular form of job redesign in the last decade. Improved productivity, increased employee involvement, greater coworker trust, more widespread employee learning, and greater employee use of knowledge diversity are among the potential benefits.[6] In a transition to work teams, efforts are necessary to define the areas of work, scope of authority, and goals of the teams. Also, teams must recognize and address dissent, conflict, and other problems.

JOBS AND WORK SCHEDULING

Considerations that can affect job design for both employers and employees are how the work is to be done, the time during which work is scheduled, and the location of employees when working. One factor changing how and when work is done is technology, including the creation of telework for some people.

Individuals who may be working at home or at other places illustrate **telework**, which means that employees work via electronic, telecommunications, and Internet means. The use of technology for telework is expected to grow, with almost 70% of private-sector respondents predicting more usage of IT resources in telework.[7] Some employers are allowing employees to *telecommute* one or more days a week. Telecommuting allows employees to work from home when bad weather or widespread health issues (e.g., pandemic flu) prevents them from coming to office facilities.

Alternative Work Schedule

Different types of work schedules have been developed for employees in different occupations and areas. The traditional U.S. work schedule of 8 hours a day, 5 days a week, is in transition. Workers in various occupations may work less or more than 8 hours at a workplace, and may have additional work at home.

The work schedules associated with jobs vary. Some jobs must be performed during "normal" daily work hours and on weekdays, while others require employees to work nights, weekends, and extended hours. Hours worked vary globally as well. There are significant differences in the hours worked in different countries. Given the global nature of many organizations, HR must adjust to different locations because of the international variations. Organizations are using many different work scheduling arrangements, based on industry demands, workforce needs, and other organizational factors. These different types include shift work and the compressed workweek.

Shift Work.   A common work schedule design is *shift work*. Many organizations need 24-hour coverage and therefore may schedule three 8-hour shifts per day. Most of these employers provide some form of additional pay, called a *shift differential*, for working the evening or night shifts. Some types of shift work have been known to cause difficulties for some employees personally, such as weariness, irritability, lack of motivation, and illness.[8] Nevertheless, some employers must have 24-hour, 7-day coverage, so shift work is likely to continue to be an option.

Compressed Workweek.   One type of work schedule design is the **compressed workweek**, in which a full week's work is accomplished in fewer than five 8-hour days. Compression usually results in more work hours each day and fewer workdays each week, such as four 10-hour days, a 3-day week, or 12-hour shifts. One survey in chemical industry plants found that 96% of the workers who shifted to 12-hour schedules did not wish to return to 8-hour schedules.[9] However, 12-hour schedules have led to sleep difficulties, fatigue, and an increased number of injuries.

Flexible Work Schedules. Flexible work schedules allow organizations to make better use of workers by matching work demands to work hours. One type of scheduling is **flextime**, in which employees work a set number of hours a day but vary the starting and ending times. In some industries, flextime allows more employees to be available at peak times when more customers and clients are present. The flexibility has aided in recruiting and retaining key staff members.

Work-Life Balancing

For many employees throughout the world, balancing their work and personal lives is a significant concern. Work-life balance is one of the top concerns in most countries.

Thousands of employees, both in large global firms like IBM and Hewlett-Packard and in many smaller firms, have flexible work schedules and/or use technology to work from locations away from the workplace as a way to help balance work and personal lives. Health care firms frequently allow employees to adjust their work schedules in order to address personal, family, health, and other issues.

JOB ANALYSIS

While job design attempts to develop jobs that fit effectively into the flow of the organizational work, the more narrow focus of job analysis centers on using a formal system to gather data about what people are doing in their jobs. A basic building block of HR management, **job analysis**, is a systematic way of gathering and analyzing information about the content, context, and human requirements of jobs. Most other functions in HR are based on and affected by job analysis.

An overview of job analysis is shown in Figure 3-5. The value of job analysis begins as the information is compiled into *job descriptions* and *job specifications* for use in virtually all HR activities.

Purposes of Job Analysis

Job analysis has grown in importance as the workforce and jobs have changed. To be effective, HR planning, recruiting, and selection all should be based on job requirements and the capabilities of individuals identified by job analysis. In EEO matters, accurate details on job requirements are needed, as the credentials in job descriptions can affect court decisions.[10] Additionally, compensation, training, and employee performance appraisals all should be based on the specific identified needs of the jobs. Job analysis also is useful in identifying job factors and duties that may contribute to workplace health/safety and employee/labor relations issues.

FIGURE 3-5 Job Analysis in Perspective

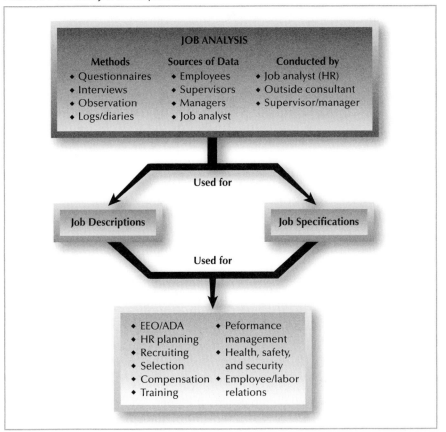

Task-Based Job Analysis

Task-based job analysis is the most common form and focuses on the tasks, duties, and responsibilities performed in a job. A **task** is a distinct, identifiable work activity composed of motions, whereas a **duty** is a larger work segment composed of several tasks that are performed by an individual. Because both tasks and duties describe activities, it is not always easy or necessary to distinguish between the two. For example, if one of the employment supervisor's duties is to interview applicants, one task associated with that duty would be asking job-related questions. **Responsibilities** are obligations to perform certain tasks and duties. Task-based job analysis seeks to identify all the tasks, duties, and responsibilities that are part of a job.

Competency-Based Job Analysis

Unlike the traditional task-based approach to analyzing jobs, the competency approach considers how knowledge and skills are used. **Competencies** are individual capabilities that can be linked to performance by individuals or teams.

The concept of competencies varies widely from organization to organization. The term *technical competencies* is often used to refer to specific knowledge and skills of employees. For example, the following have been identified as *behavioral competencies*:

- Customer focus
- Team orientation
- Technical expertise
- Results orientation
- Communication effectiveness

- Leadership
- Conflict resolution
- Innovation
- Adaptability
- Decisiveness

IMPLEMENTING JOB ANALYSIS

Prior to the job analysis process itself is the planning done to gather data from managers and employees. Probably the most important consideration is to identify the objectives of the job analysis, which might be as simple as updating job descriptions or as comprehensive as revising the compensation programs in the organization. Whatever the purpose identified, the effort needs the support of top management.

Preparing for and Introducing the Job Analysis

Preparation for job analysis includes identification of the jobs to be analyzed. Next reviewing organization charts, existing job descriptions, previous job analysis information, and other resources is part of the planning. This phase also identifies those who will be involved in conducting the job analysis and the methods to be used. A key part is identifying and communicating the process to appropriate managers, affected employees, and others.

Conducting the Job Analysis

If questionnaires are used, it is often helpful to have employees return them to supervisors or managers for review before giving them back to those conducting the job analysis. Questionnaires should be accompanied by a letter explaining the process and instructions for completing and returning them. If interviews are used, they may occur after the return of the questionnaires to clarify more details. Once data from job analyses are compiled, the information should be sorted by job, organizational unit, and job family.

Developing Job Descriptions and Job Specifications

At the fourth stage, the job analysts draft job descriptions and job specifications. Generally, organizations find that having managers and employees write job descriptions is not recommended for several reasons. First, it reduces consistency in format and details, both of which are important given the legal consequences of job descriptions. Second, managers and employees vary in their writing skills so they may write the job descriptions and job specifications to reflect what they do and what their personal qualifications are, not what the job requires. However, completed drafts should be reviewed with managers and supervisors, and then employees, before they are finalized.

Maintaining and Updating Job Descriptions and Job Specifications

Once job descriptions and specifications have been completed and reviewed by all appropriate individuals, a system must be developed for keeping them current and posted on a firm's intranet source. One effective way to ensure that appropriate reviews occur is to use current job descriptions and job specifications as part of other HR activities. For example, each time a vacancy occurs, the job description and specifications should be reviewed and revised as necessary *before* recruiting and selection efforts begin. Similarly, in some organizations, managers and employees review job descriptions during performance appraisal interviews.

Questionnaires

The questionnaire is a widely used method of gathering data on jobs. A survey instrument is developed and given to employees and managers to complete. The typical job questionnaire often covers the areas shown in Figure 3-6.

The questionnaire method offers a major advantage in that information on a large number of jobs can be collected inexpensively in a relatively short period of time. However, the questionnaire method assumes that employees can accurately analyze and communicate information about their jobs. Using interviewing and observation in combination with the questionnaire method allows analysts to clarify and verify the information gathered in questionnaires.

FIGURE 3-6 Typical Areas Covered in a Job Analysis Questionnaire

Duties and Percentage of Time Spent on Each	Contact with Other People
• Regular duties • Special duties performed less frequently	• Internal contacts • External contacts
Supervision	**Physical Dimensions**
• Supervision given to others • Supervision received from others	• Physical demands • Working conditions
Decisions Made	**Jobholder Characteristics**
• Records and reports prepared • Materials and equipment used • Financial/budget responsibilities	• Knowledge • Skills • Abilities • Training needed

Job Analysis and O*Net

A variety of resources related to job analysis are available from the U.S. Department of Labor (DOL). The resources have been developed and used over many years by various entities. *Functional job analysis* uses a competency approach to job analysis. A functional definition of what is done in a job can be generated by examining the three components of *data, people,* and *things.* The levels of these components traditionally have been used to identify and compare important elements of more than 120 jobs in the *Dictionary of Occupational Titles (DOT).* But O*Net is now the main DOL resource available and provides employers with a wide range of useful items.

Although not specifically a job analysis, O*Net is a database compiled by the U.S. Department of Labor to provide basic occupational data that cover more than 800 occupations based on the Standard Occupational Classification (SOC) developed by the government. O*Net also provides extensive links to additional resources on workplace issues.

Legal Aspects of Job Analysis

EEO legal compliance must focus on the jobs that individuals perform. The Uniform Guidelines on Employee Selection Procedures make it clear that HR requirements must be tied to specific job-related factors if employers are to defend their actions as a business necessity. This approach has direct impact on job descriptions and persons with disabilities who may apply for those jobs.

One result of the ADA is increased emphasis by employers on conducting job analyses, as well as developing and maintaining current and accurate job descriptions and job specifications. The ADA requires that organizations identify the *essential job functions*, which are the fundamental duties of a job. These do not include the marginal duties. The three major considerations used in determining essential functions and marginal functions are as follows:

- Percentage of time spent on tasks
- Frequency of tasks done
- Importance of tasks performed

Job analysis also should identify the *physical demands* of jobs. For example, the important physical skills and capabilities used on the job of nursing representative could include being able to hear well enough to aid clients and doctors. However, hearing might be less essential for a heavy equipment operator in a quarry.

Typically, job analysis identifies the percentage of time spent on each duty in a job. This information helps determine whether someone should be classified as exempt or nonexempt under the wage/hour laws.

JOB DESCRIPTIONS AND JOB SPECIFICATIONS

The output from analysis of a job is used to develop a job description and its job specifications. Together, these two documents summarize job analysis information in a readable format and provide the basis for defensible

FIGURE 3-7 Sample Job Description

Identification Section
Position Title: Customer Service Supervisor
Department: Marketing/Customer Service
Reports To: Marketing Director

EEOC Class: O/M
FLSA Status: Exempt

General Summary
Supervises, coordinates, and assigns work of employees to ensure customer
service department goals and customer needs are met.

Essential Job Functions
1. Supervises the work of Customer Service Representatives to enhance performance by
   coordinating duties, advising on issues or problems, and checking work. (55%)
2. Provides Customer Service training for company employees in all departments. (15%)
3. Creates and reviews reports for service orders for new and existing customers. (10%)
4. Performs employee performance evaluations, training, and discipline. (10%)
5. Follows up with customer complaints and issues and provides resolutions. (10%)
6. Conducts other duties as needed by guided by Marketing Director and executives.

Knowledge, Skills, and Abilities
- Knowledge of company products, services, policies, and procedures.
- Knowledge of marketing and customer programs, data, and results.
- Knowledge of supervisory requirements and practices.
- Skill in completing multiple tasks at once.
- Skill in identifying and resolving customer problems.
- Skill in oral and written communication, including Spanish communications.
- Skill in coaching, training, and performance evaluating employees.
- Skill in operating office and technological equipment and software.
- Ability to communicate professionally with coworkers, customers and vendors.
- Ability to work independently and meet managerial goals.
- Ability to follow oral and written instructions.
- Ability to organize daily activities of self and others and to work as a team player.

Education and Experience
Bachelor's degree in business or marketing, plus 3–5 years of industry experience. Supervisory, marketing,
and customer service experience helpful.

Physical Requirements	Percentage of Work Time Spent on Activity			
	0–24%	25–49%	50–74%	75–100%
Seeing: Must be able to see well enough to read reports.				X
Hearing: Must be able to hear well enough to communicate with customers, vendors, and employees.				X
Standing/Walking: Must be able to move about department			X	
Climbing/Stooping/Kneeling: Must be able stoop or kneel to pick up paper products or directories.	X		X	
Lifting/Pulling/Pushing: Must be able to lift up to 50 pounds.	X			
Fingering/Grasping/Feeling: Must be able to type and use technical sources.				X

Working Conditions: Normal working conditions absent extreme factors.

Note: *The statements herein are intended to describe the general nature and level of work being performed, but are not to be seen as a complete list of responsibilities, duties, and skills required of personnel so classified. Also, they do not establish a contract for employment and are subject to change at the discretion of the employer.*

job-related actions. They also identify individual jobs for employees by providing documentation from management.

In most cases, the job description and job specifications are combined into one document that contains several sections. A **job description** identifies the tasks, duties, and responsibilities of a job. It describes what is done, why it is done, where it is done, and, briefly, how it is done.

While the job description describes activities to be done, the **job specifications** list the knowledge, skills, and abilities (KSAs) an individual needs to perform a job satisfactorily. KSAs include education, experience, work skill requirements, personal abilities, and mental and physical requirements. Accurate job specifications identify what KSAs a person needs to do the job, not necessarily the current employee's qualifications.

Performance standards flow directly from a job description and indicate what the job accomplishes and how performance is measured in key areas of the job description. If employees know what is expected and how performance is to be measured, they have a much better chance of performing satisfactorily. Unfortunately, performance standards are often not developed as supplemental items from job descriptions. Even if performance standards have been identified and matched to job descriptions, they must be communicated to employees if the job descriptions are to be effective HR tools. Figure 3-7 shows a job description.

NOTES

1. For a more detailed review of job satisfaction factors, see "2009 Employee Job Satisfaction: Understanding the Factors That Make Work Gratifying," *SHRM Research*, 2009, *www.shrm.org*; Daniel C. Ganseter, "Measurement Challenges for Studying Work-Related Stressors and Strains," *Human Resource Management Review*, 18 (2008), 259–270.

2. Frank Giancola, "Employee Engagement: What You Need to Know," *Workspan*, October 2007, 55–59.

3. "Estimating Turnover Costs," *www.keepemployees.com*.

4. "Corps of Engineers Needs to Update Its Workforce Planning . . .," *Human Capital*, U.S. Government Accountability Office, May 2008, *www.goa.gov*.

5. Margaret Fiester, "Job Rotation, Total Rewards, Measuring Value," *HR Magazine*, August 2008, 33.

6. Ramon Rico, et al., "Team Implicit Coordination Processes," *Academy of Management Review*, 33 (2008), 163–184.

7. Rita Zeidner, "Telework Influencing Technology Investments," *HR Magazine*, July 2008, 22.

8. "Extended Unusual Work Shifts," *U.S. Occupational Safety & Health Administration*, September 7, 2005, *www.osha.gov*.

9. Martin Moore-Ede, et al., "Advantages and Disadvantages of Twelve-Hour Shifts, A Balanced Perspective," 2007, *www.ciridian.com*.

10. *Lamb v. Boeing Co.*, No. 5-18431 (4th Cir., Jan. 11, 2007).

INTERNET RESOURCES

Loyalty Research Center—This research center provides employee loyalty/employee engagement research and consulting services. Visit their site at *www.loyaltyresearch.com*.

Human Resource Planning Society—Information and resources on building a strategic HR plan are available at *www.hrps.org*.

Team Building, Inc.—This website provides information for team building services and team building training products. Visit the site at *www. teambuildinginc.com*.

Job Analysis.net—A resource for conducting a job analysis, including different types of methods, legal issues, questionnaires, and job descriptions, can be found at *www.jobanalysis.net*.

SUGGESTED READINGS

Arne L. Kallenberg, "The Mismatched Worker: When People Don't Fit Their Jobs," *Academy of Management Perspectives*, February 2008, 24–40.

Piers Steel and Cornelius König, "Integrating Theories of Motivation," *Academy of Management Review*, 31 (2006), 889–913.

Terrance M. McMenamin, "A Time to Work: Recent Trends in Shift Work and Flexible Schedules," *Monthly Labor Review*, December 2007, 3–14.

For details, go to the website listed in the boxed feature, as well as *www.dol.gov* and *www.onetcenter.org*. The value of O*Net is identified in various publications, including Max Maller, *The Manager's Guide to HR*, Chapter 1 (Alexandria, VA: SHRM, 2009).

Staffing: Recruiting and Selection

HR—MEETING MANAGEMENT CHALLENGES

Finding and choosing the right people for a job remains one of the most important HR issues. Considerations include:

- How best to locate good candidates
- Selecting good employees is more than just interviewing
- Poor background investigation can get you sued

Keeping a flow of good employees coming into the organization is a challenge. Recruiting and selection will always be needed as a certain amount of turnover will always occur. The key to success is approaching the recruiting and selection properly.

STAFFING

The staffing process used by an employer, based on HR planning and retention as key components, includes successful recruiting and selection efforts.

Recruiting is the process of generating a pool of qualified applicants for organizational jobs. If the number of available candidates equals the number of people to be hired, no real selection is required—the organization must either leave some openings unfilled or take all the candidates. One survey of employers in slow labor markets found that almost half of the hiring managers cited less qualified applicants as the biggest recruiting and hiring challenge.[1] It is important to view recruiting broadly as a key part of staffing, and not just as a collection of administrative and operational activities.

RECRUITING

Although recruiting can be expensive, an offsetting concept that must be considered is the *cost of unfilled jobs.* For example, consider a company in which three operations-related jobs are vacant. Assume these three vacancies cost the company $300 for each business day the jobs remain vacant. If the jobs are not filled for four months, the cost of this failure to recruit in a timely fashion will be about $26,000.

Although cost is certainly an issue, and some employers are quite concerned about cost per hire as well as the cost of vacancies, *quality* might be an important trade-off. For example, if an organizational strategy focuses on quality as a competitive advantage, a company might choose to hire only from the top 15% of candidates for critical jobs, and from the top 30% of candidates for all other positions. Though this approach may raise the cost per hire, it will improve workforce quality.

Labor Markets

Because recruiting takes place in different labor markets that can vary a great deal, learning some basics about labor markets aids in understanding recruiting. **Labor markets** are the external supply pool from which employers attract employees. To understand where recruiting takes place, one can think of the sources of employees as a funnel, in which the broad scope of labor markets narrows progressively to the point of selection and job offers, as Figure 4-1 shows. Of course, if the selected candidates reject the offers, then HR staff members must move back up the funnel to the applicant pool for other candidates, and in extreme cases may need to reopen the recruiting process.

When the unemployment rate is high in a given market, many people are looking for jobs. When the unemployment rate is low, there are fewer applicants. Unemployment rates vary with business cycles and present very different challenges for recruiting at different times. For instance, in some U.S. states, when many automobile plants closed and workers were laid off, manufacturers in other industries and even retailers experienced a significant increase in their numbers of job applicants, making recruiting easier and larger applicant pools a fact.

Different Labor Markets

The supply of workers in various labor markets differs substantially and affects staffing. Organizations recruit in a number of different labor markets, including industry-specific markets and occupational, educational and technical, and geographic markets.

FIGURE 4-1 Labor Market Components

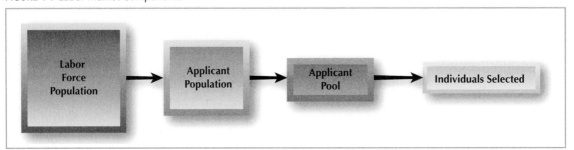

Labor markets can be classified by industry and occupation. For example, the biggest increases in U.S. jobs until the year 2016 are going to be in the positions of registered nurses, retail sales and customer service representatives, home health aides, and post-secondary teachers.[2] These data illustrate that recruiting will be more difficult in filling these jobs during the next few years. Trucking and welding jobs are also expected to present significant recruiting difficulties.

Another way to look at labor markets is by considering the educational and technical qualifications that define the people being recruited. Employers may need individuals with specific licenses, certifications, or educational backgrounds. An example of a tight labor market is that of business professors with PhDs, who are forecast to be in short supply in the next few years due to the retirement of baby boomers from faculty positions. Other examples of shortages in specific labor markets include certified auto mechanics, heating and air-conditioning technicians, and network-certified computer specialists.

A common way to classify labor markets is based on geographic location. Markets can be local, area or regional, national, or international. Local and area labor markets vary significantly in terms of workforce availability and quality, and changes in a geographic labor market may force changes in recruiting efforts. For instance, if a new major employer locates in a regional labor market, other existing area employers may see a decline in their numbers of applicants.

Employers in the United States are tapping global labor markets when necessary and expanding export work to overseas labor markets when doing so is advantageous. Firms in different industries are expanding in India, China, Indonesia, Romania, Poland, and other countries.

STRATEGIC RECRUITING DECISIONS

Recruiting efforts may be viewed as either continuous or intensive. *Continuous* efforts to recruit offer the advantage of keeping the employer in the recruiting market. For example, with college recruiting, some organizations may find it advantageous to have a recruiter on a given campus each year. Employers that visit a campus only occasionally are less likely to build a following at that school over time.

Intensive recruiting may take the form of a vigorous recruiting campaign aimed at hiring a given number of employees, usually within a short period of time.

Employment "Branding" and Image

The "employment brand" or image of an organization is the view of it held by both employees and outsiders. Organizations that are seen as desirable employers are better able to attract qualified applicants than are those with poor reputations. For example, one firm had good pay and benefits, but its work demands were seen as excessive, and frequent downsizings had resulted in some terminations and transfers. The result was high turnover and fewer applicants interested in employment at the company. That firm had a poor brand or image as an employer.

Organization-Based versus Outsourced Recruiting

A basic decision is whether the recruiting will be done by the employer or out-sourced to someone else. This decision need not be focused on an "either-or" situation entirely. In most organizations, HR staff members handle many of the recruiting efforts. However, because recruiting can be a time-consuming process and HR staff and other managers in organizations have many other responsibilities, outsourcing is a way to decrease the number of staff needed for recruiting and free some of their time for other responsibilities.

Professional Employer Organizations and Employee Leasing

A specific type of outsourcing uses professional employer organizations (PEOs) and employee leasing. The employee leasing process is simple: An employer signs an agreement with the PEO, after which the staff is hired by the leasing firm and leased back to the company for a fee. In turn, the leasing firm writes the paychecks, pays taxes, prepares and implements HR policies, and keeps all the required records for the employer.

One advantage of leasing companies for employees is that they may receive better benefits than they otherwise would get in many of the small businesses that use leasing firms. But all this service comes at a cost to employers. Leasing companies often charge employers between 4% and 6% of employees' monthly salaries. Thus, while leasing may save employers money on benefits and HR administration, it also may increase total payroll costs.

Regular versus Flexible Staffing

Another strategic decision affects whether recruiting will be done to fill staff-ing needs with regular full-time or part-time employees. Decisions as to which should be recruited hinge on whether to seek regular employees or to use more flexible approaches, which might include temporaries or independent contractors. A number of employers have decided that the cost of keeping a regular workforce has become excessive and is growing worse due to eco-nomic, competitive, and governmental considerations. However, not just money is at issue. The large number of employment regulations also con-strains the employment relationship, making many employers reluctant to hire new regular full-time employees.

Temporary Workers.   Employers who use temporary employees can hire their own temporary staff members or contract with agencies supplying tem-porary workers on a rate-per-day or rate-per-week basis. Originally developed to provide clerical and office workers to employers, temporary workers in pro-fessional, technical, and even managerial jobs are becoming more common. The importance of using temporary workers is illustrated through the use of computer technology by an educational publisher. The publisher utilized an automated employment, recruiting, and screening system to obtain sufficient temporary workers for its firm. That employer obtained sufficient qualified workers which resulted in a return on its hiring investment of $6 for every $1 of cost.[3]

Independent Contractors. Some firms employ independent contractors as workers who perform specific services on a contract basis. These workers must be truly independent as determined by regulations used by the U.S. Internal Revenue Service and the U.S. Department of Labor. Independent contractors are used in a number of areas, including building maintenance, security, advertising, and others. One major reason for the use of independent contractors is that some employers experience significant savings because benefits are not provided to those individuals.

EEO and Recruiting Efforts

Recruiting as a key employment-related activity is subject to various considerations, especially equal employment laws and regulations. As part of legal compliance in the recruiting process, organizations must work to reduce external disparate impact, or underrepresentation of protected-class members compared to the labor markets utilized by the employer. If disparate impact exists, then the employer may need to make special efforts to persuade protected-class individuals to apply for jobs. For employers with affirmative action plans (AAPs), special ways to reduce disparate impact can be identified as goals listed in those plans. Also, many employers that emphasize internal recruiting should take actions to obtain protected-class applicants externally if disparate impact exists in the current workforce.

Realistic Job Previews

Providing a balanced view of the advantages, demands, expectations, and challenges in an organization or a job may help attract employees with more realistic expectations and reduce the number of employees who quit a few months after being hired because the "reality" they discover does not match what they expected. Thus, recruiting efforts can benefit from *realistic job previews*.

Recruiting Source Choices: Internal versus External

Most employers combine the use of internal and external recruiting sources. Both promoting from within the organization (internal recruitment) and hiring from outside the organization (external recruitment) come with advantages and disadvantages.

Organizations that face rapidly changing competitive environments and conditions may need to place a heavier emphasis on external sources in addition to developing internal sources. A possible strategy might be to promote from within if a qualified applicant exists and to go to external sources if not.

However, for organizations existing in environments that change slowly, emphasis on promotion from within may be more suitable. Once the various recruiting policy decisions have been addressed, the actual recruiting methods can be identified and used for both internal and external recruiting.

INTERNET RECRUITING

Numerous Internet job boards, such as Monster and Yahoo! HotJobs, provide places for employers to post jobs or search for candidates. Job boards offer access to numerous candidates. Some Internet locations allow recruiters to search one website, such as MyJobHunter.com, to obtain search links to many other major job sites. Applicants can also use these websites to do one match and then send résumés to all jobs in which they are interested. However, a number of the individuals accessing these sites are "job lookers" who are not serious about changing jobs, but are checking out compensation levels and job availability in their areas of interest. Despite such concerns, HR recruiters find general job boards useful for generating applicant responses.

Many professional associations have employment sections at their websites. As illustration, for HR jobs, see the Society for Human Resource Management site, *www.shrm.org*, or WorldatWork, *www.worldatwork.org*. The SHRM organization has established a Job Posting Center that numerous recruiters and employers can use to post a wide range of industry openings. A number of private corporations maintain specialized career or industry websites to focus on IT, telecommunications, engineering, medicine, and other areas.

Despite the popularity of job boards and association job sites, many employers have learned that their own websites can be most effective and efficient when recruiting candidates. The most successful of these websites are created by experienced firms and take extensive actions to guide job seekers to the employer. Employers include employment and career information on their websites under headings such as "Employment" or "Careers." This is the place where recruiting (both internal and external) is often conducted. On many of these sites, job seekers are encouraged to e-mail résumés or complete online applications.

Recruiting and Internet Social Networking

The Internet has led to social networking of individuals on blogs, twitters, and a range of websites. Many people initially use the social media more than job board sites.[4] Internet connections often include people who work together as well as past personal contacts and friends.

The informal use of the Web presents some interesting recruiting advantages and disadvantages for both employers and employees. Social networking sites allow job seekers to connect with employees of potential hirers. For instance, some sites include posts on what it is like to work for a boss, and job hunters can contact the posters and ask questions. An example is LinkedIn, which has a job-search engine that allows people to search for contacts who work for employers with posted job openings.

Legal Issues in Internet Recruiting

With Internet recruiting expanding, new and different concerns have arisen. Several of these issues have ethical and moral as well as legal implications. The following examples illustrate some of these concerns:

- When companies use screening software to avoid looking at the thousands of résumés they receive, are rejections really based on the qualifications needed for the job?
- How can a person's protected-category and other information be collected and analyzed for reports?
- Are too many individuals in protected categories being excluded from the later phases of the Internet recruiting process?
- Which applicants really want jobs? If someone has accessed a job board and sent an e-mail asking an employer about a job opening, does the person actually want to be an applicant?
- What are the implications of Internet recruiting in terms of confidentiality and privacy?

Employment lawyers are issuing warnings to employers about remarks and other characteristics posted on LinkedIn, Facebook, and Twitter. According to one survey of employers, about three-fourths of hiring managers in various-sized companies checked persons' credentials on LinkedIn, about half used Facebook, and approximately one-fourth used Twitter.[5] Some of the concerns raised have included postings of confidential details about an employee's termination, racial/ethnic background, or gender and the making of discriminatory comments. All of these actions could lead to wrongful termination or discrimination lawsuits. Thus, because Internet usage has both advantages and disadvantages for recruiting, legal advice should be obtained, and HR employment-related policies, training, and enforcement should include such advice.

Advantages of Internet Recruiting

Employers have found a number of advantages to using Internet recruiting. A primary one is that many employers have saved money using Internet recruiting versus other recruiting methods such as newspaper advertising, employment agencies, and search firms, all of which can cost substantially more.

Another major advantage is that a very large pool of applicants can be generated using Internet recruiting. Individuals may view an employer more positively and obtain more useful information, which can result in more individual applications.

Internet recruiting also can save time. Applicants can respond quickly to job postings by sending electronic responses, rather than using "snail mail."

A good website and useful Internet resources also can help recruiters reach "passive" job seekers—those who have a good job and are not really looking to change jobs but who might consider it if a better opportunity were presented. These individuals often do not list themselves on job boards, but they might visit a company website for other reasons and check out the careers or employment section.

Disadvantages of Internet Recruiting

The positive things associated with Internet recruiting come with a number of disadvantages. Because of broader exposure, Internet recruiting often creates additional work for HR staff members and others internally. More online job postings must be sent; many more résumés must be reviewed; more e-mails, blogs, and twitters need to be dealt with; and expensive specialized software may be needed to track the increased number of applicants resulting from Internet recruiting efforts.

As noted, many individuals who access Internet recruiting sources are browsers who may submit résumés just to see what happens, but they are not actively looking for new jobs.

EXTERNAL RECRUITING

Even when the overall unemployment rate increases, some jobs and/or employers still face recruiting challenges. Regardless of the methods used, external recruiting involves some common advantages and disadvantages. Some of the prominent traditional and evolving recruiting methods are highlighted next.

Media Sources

Media sources such as newspapers, magazines, television, radio, and billboards typically have been widely used in external recruiting. Some firms have sent direct mail using purchased lists of individuals in certain fields or industries. Internet usage has led to media sources being available online, including postings, ads, videos, webinars, and many other expanding media services. In some cities and towns, newspaper ads are still very prominent, though they may trigger job searchers to go to an Internet source for more details.

Competitive Recruiting Sources

Other sources for recruiting include professional and trade associations, trade publications, and competitors. Many professional societies and trade associations publish newsletters or magazines and have websites containing job ads. Such sources may be useful for recruiting the specialized professionals needed in an industry.

Some employers have extended recruiting to customers. Retailers such as Wal-Mart and Best Buy have had aggressive programs to recruit customers to become employees in stores. While in the store, customers at these firms can pick up applications, apply online using kiosks, and even schedule interviews with managers or HR staff members. Other firms have included employment announcements when sending out customer bills or newsletters.

Employment Agencies

Employment agencies, both public and private, are a recruiting source. Every state in the United States has its own state-sponsored employment agency. These agencies operate branch offices in cities throughout the states and do not charge fees to applicants or employers. They also have websites that potential applicants can use without having to go to the offices.

Private employment agencies operate in most cities. For a fee collected from either the employee or the employer, these agencies do some preliminary screening and put employers in touch with applicants. Private employment agencies differ considerably in the levels of service, costs, policies, and types of applicants they provide.

Labor Unions

Labor unions may be a useful source of certain types of workers. For example, in electrical and construction industries, unions traditionally have supplied workers to employers. A labor pool is generally available through a union, and workers can be dispatched from the hiring hall to particular jobs to meet the needs of employers.

In some instances, labor unions can control or influence recruiting and staffing activity. An organization with a strong union may have less flexibility than a nonunion company in deciding who will be hired and where those people will be placed. Unions can benefit employers through apprenticeship and cooperative staffing programs, as they do in the building and printing industries.

Job Fairs

Employers in various labor markets needing to fill a large number of jobs quickly have used job fairs and special recruiting events. Job fairs have been held by economic development entities, employer and HR associations, and other community groups to help bring employers and potential job candidates together. For instance, the SHRM chapter in a midwestern metropolitan area annually sponsors a job fair at which 75 to 100 employers can meet applicants. Publicity in the city draws several hundred potential recruits for different types of jobs.

Educational Institutions and Recruiting

College and university students are a significant external source of entry-level professional and technical employees. Most universities maintain career placement offices in which employers and applicants can meet. A number of considerations affect an employer's selection of colleges and universities at which to conduct interviews.

Because college/university recruiting can be expensive and require significant time and effort, employers need to determine whether both current and future jobs require persons with college degrees in specific fields. A number of factors determine success in college recruiting. Some employers actively build continuing relationships with individual faculty members and career staff at designated colleges and universities. Maintaining a presence on campus by providing guest speakers to classes and student groups increases the contacts for an employer. Employers with a continuing presence and support on a campus are more likely to see positive college recruiting results.

High schools and vocational/technical schools may be valuable sources of new employees for some organizations. Many schools have a centralized guidance or placement office. Participating in career days and giving company tours to school groups are ways of maintaining good contact with school sources. Cooperative programs, in which students work part-time and receive some school credits, also may be useful in generating qualified future applicants for full-time positions.

INTERNAL RECRUITING

Filling openings internally may add motivation for employees to stay and grow in the organization rather than pursuing career opportunities elsewhere. The most common internal recruiting methods include: organizational databases, job postings, promotions and transfers, current-employee referrals, and re-recruiting of former employees and applicants. Some of the common advantages and disadvantages of internal recruiting are highlighted in Figure 4-2.

FIGURE 4-2 Advantages and Disadvantages of Internal Recruiting

ADVANTAGES	DISADVANTAGES
• The morale of a promotee is usually high. • The firm can better assess a candidate's abilities due to prior work actions. • Recruiting costs are lower for some jobs. • The process is a motivator for good performances by employees. • The process can aid succession planning, future promotions, and career development. • The firm may have to hire only at the entry level and then move employees up based on experience and performance.	• "Inbreeding" of employees may result in a less diverse workforce, as well as a lack of new ideas. • Those persons not promoted may experience morale problems. • Employees may engage in "political" infighting for promotions. • A development program often is needed to transfer employees into supervisory and management jobs. • Some managers may resist having employees promoted into their departments.

Internal Databases and Recruiting

HR information systems allow HR staff to maintain background and knowledge, skills, and abilities (KSA) information on existing employees. As openings arise, HR can access databases by entering job requirements and then get a listing of current employees meeting those requirements. Employment software can sort employee data by occupational fields, education, areas of career interests, previous work histories, and other variables. For instance, if a firm has an opening for someone with an MBA and marketing experience, the key words *MBA* and *marketing* can be entered in a search field, and the program displays a list of all current employees with these two items identified in their employee profiles.

The advantage of such databases is that they can be linked to other HR activities. Opportunities for career development and advancement are a major reason why individuals stay at or leave their employers. With employee databases, internal opportunities for individuals can be identified. Employee profiles are continually updated to include such items as additional training and education completed, special projects handled, and career plans and desires noted during performance appraisals and career mentoring discussions.

RECRUITING EVALUATION

To determine how effective various recruiting sources and methods have been, it is important to evaluate recruiting efforts. But in a survey, a majority of HR executives identified that their firms were not getting sufficient metrics on the quality of hires and how well the new hires fit into the organizations.[6]

To evaluate recruiting, organizations can see how their recruiting efforts compare with past patterns and with the recruiting performance of other organizations. Measures of recruiting effectiveness can be used to see whether sufficient numbers of targeted population groups are being attracted.

Information about job performance, absenteeism, cost of training, and turnover by recruiting source also helps adjust future recruiting efforts. For example, some companies find that recruiting at certain colleges or universities furnishes stable, high performers, whereas recruiting at other schools provides employees who are more prone to leave the organization. General metrics for evaluating recruiting include quantity and quality of applicants.

Quantity of Applicants

Because the goal of a good recruiting program is to generate a large pool of applicants from which to choose, quantity is a natural place to begin evaluation. The basic measure here considers whether the quantity of recruits is sufficient to fill job vacancies. A related question is: Does recruiting at this source provide enough qualified applicants with an appropriate mix of protected-category individuals?

Quality of Applicants

In addition to quantity, a key issue is whether or not the qualifications of the applicant pool are sufficient to fill the job openings. Do the applicants meet job specifications, and do they perform the jobs well after hire? What is the failure rate for new hires for each recruiter? Measures that can be used include items such as performance appraisal scores, months until promotion, production quantity, and sales volume for each hire.

Recruiting Satisfaction

The satisfaction of two groups is useful in evaluating recruiting. Certainly the views of managers with openings to fill are important, because they are "customers" in a very real sense. But the applicants (those hired and those not hired) also are an important part of the process and can provide useful input.

Managers can respond to questions about the quality of the applicant pool, the recruiter's service, the timeliness of the process, and any problems that they see. Applicants might provide input on how they were treated, their perceptions of the company, and the length of the recruiting process and other aspects.

Time Required to Fill Openings

Looking at the length of time it takes to fill openings is a common means of evaluating recruiting efforts. If openings are not filled quickly with qualified candidates, the work and productivity of the organization are likely to suffer. If it takes 45 days to fill vacant positions, managers who need those employees will be unhappy. As noted earlier, unfilled positions have an associated cost.

Evaluating the Cost of Recruiting

Different formulas can be used to evaluate recruiting costs. The calculation most often used to measure such costs is to divide total recruiting expenses for the year by the number of hires for the year:

$$\frac{\text{Recruiting expenses}}{\text{Number of recruits hired}}$$

The problem with this approach is accurately identifying what details should be included in the recruiting expenses. Should expenses for testing, background checks, relocations, or signing bonuses be included, or are they more properly excluded?

INCREASING RECRUITING EFFECTIVENESS

Evaluation of recruiting should be used to make recruiting activities more effective. Some common activities can help effectiveness are:

- *Résumé mining*—a software approach to getting the best résumés for a fit from a big database

- *Applicant tracking*—an approach that takes an applicant all the way from a job listing to performance appraisal results
- *Employer career website*—a convenient recruiting place on an employer's website where applicants can see what jobs are available and apply
- *Internal mobility*—a system that tracks prospects in the company and matches them with jobs as they come open
- *Realistic job previews*—a process that persons can use to get details on the employer and the jobs
- *Responsive recruitment*—whereby applicants receive timely responses

Another key way to increase recruiting effectiveness rests with the recruiters themselves. Those involved in the recruiting process can either turn off recruits or create excitement. For instance, recruiters who emphasize positive aspects about the jobs and their employers can enhance recruiting effectiveness. Thus, it is important that recruiters communicate well with applicants and treat them fairly and professionally.

SELECTION AND PLACEMENT

Some would argue that picking the right people for the jobs that need to be done is the most important part of human resource management. Certainly for a business that depends on good people and good performance for the organization to succeed, its importance is very high. For an organization that is failing, improvement may need to come from many different sources, but it is difficult to imagine appropriate changes coming without some new competent people to carry out those changes. In athletic organizations that are not doing well, it is the selection of new coaches and players that creates improvements, if any are to come, and the continued selection of good athletes and coaches that allows ongoing success.

Selection is the process of choosing individuals with the correct qualifications needed to fill jobs in an organization. Without these qualified employees, an organization is far less likely to succeed. A useful perspective on selection and placement comes from two HR observations that underscore the importance of effective staffing:

- "*Hire hard, manage easy.*" The investment of time and effort in selecting the right people for jobs will make managing them as employees much less difficult because many problems are eliminated.
- "*Good training will not make up for bad selection.*" When people without the appropriate aptitudes are selected, employers will have difficulty training them to do those jobs that they do not fit.

Placement

The ultimate purpose of selection is **placement**, or fitting a person to the right job. Placement of human resources should be seen primarily as a matching process. How well an employee is matched to a job can affect the amount and quality of the employee's work, as well as the training and operating costs required to prepare the individual for work life. Further, employee morale is an issue because good fit encourages individuals to be positive about their jobs and what they accomplish.[7]

Selection and placement activities typically focus on applicants' knowledge, skills, and abilities (KSAs), but they should also focus on the degree to which job candidates generally match the situations experienced both on the job and in the company. Psychologists label this *person-environment fit*. In HR it is usually called **person/job fit**. Fit is related not only to satisfaction with work but also to commitment to a company and to quitting intentions.

Lack of fit between KSAs and job requirements can be classified as a "mismatch." A mismatch results from poor pairing of a person's needs, interests, abilities, personality, and expectations with characteristics of the job, rewards, and the organization in which the job is located. Five mismatch situations are:[8]

- Skills/job qualifications
- Geography/job location
- Time/amount of work
- Earnings/expectations
- Work/family

Criteria, Predictors, and Job Performance

Regardless of whether an employer uses specific KSAs or a more general approach, effective selection of employees involves using selection criteria and predictors of these criteria. At the heart of an effective selection system must be the knowledge of what constitutes good job performance. When one knows what good performance looks like on a particular job, the next step is to identify what it takes for the employee to achieve successful performance. These are called selection criteria. A **selection criterion** is a characteristic that a person must possess to successfully perform work. Figure 4-3 shows that ability, motivation, intelligence, conscientiousness, appropriate risk, and permanence might be selection criteria for many jobs. Selection criteria that might be more specific to managerial jobs include "leading and deciding," "supporting and cooperating," "organizing and executing," and "enterprising and performing."

To determine whether candidates might possess certain selection criteria (such as ability and motivation), employers try to identify **predictors of selection criteria** that are measurable or visible indicators of those positive characteristics (or criteria). For example, as Figure 4-3 indicates, three good predictors of "permanence" might be individual interests, salary requirements, and tenure on previous jobs. If a candidate possesses appropriate amounts of any or all of these predictors, it might be assumed that the person would stay on the job longer than someone without those predictors.

The information gathered about an applicant through predictors should focus on the likelihood that the individual will execute the job competently once hired. Predictors can be identified through many formats such as application forms, tests, interviews, education requirements, and years of experience, but such factors should be used only if they are found to be valid predictors of specific job performance. Using invalid predictors can result in selecting the "wrong" candidate and rejecting the "right" one.

FIGURE 4-3 Job Performance, Selection Criteria, and Predictors

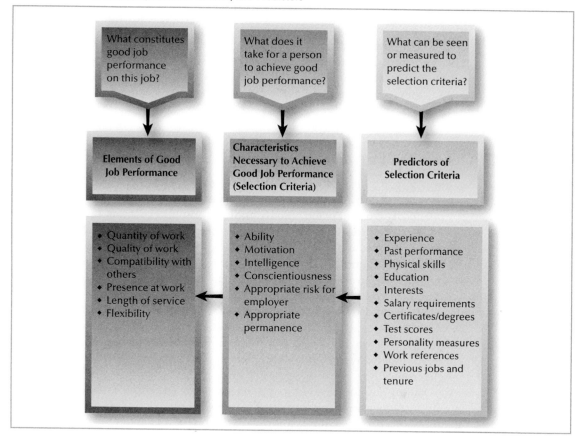

Combining Predictors

If an employer chooses to use only one predictor, such as a pencil-and-paper test, to select the individuals to be hired, the decision becomes straightforward. If the test is valid and encompasses a major dimension of a job, and an applicant does well on the test, then that person should be given a job offer. When an employer uses several predictors such as "three years of experience," "possesses a college degree," and "acceptable aptitude test score," job applicants are evaluated on all of these requirements and the multiple predictors must be combined in some way. Two approaches for combining predictors are:

- *Multiple hurdles:* A minimum cutoff is set on each predictor, and each minimum level must be "passed." For example, to be hired, a candidate for a sales representative job must achieve a minimum education level, a certain score on a sales aptitude test, and a minimum score on a structured interview.

- *Compensatory approach:* Scores from individual predictors are added and combined into an overall score, thereby allowing a higher score on one predictor to offset, or compensate for, a lower score on another. The combined index takes into consideration performance on all predictors. For example, when admitting students into graduate business programs, a higher overall score on an admissions test might offset a lower undergraduate grade point average.

THE SELECTION PROCESS

Most organizations take a series of consistent steps to process and select applicants for jobs. Company size, job characteristics, the number of people needed, the use of electronic technology, and other factors cause variations on the basic process. Selection can take place in a day or over a much longer period of time, and certain phases of the process may be omitted or the order changed, depending on the employer. If the applicant is processed in one day, the employer usually checks references after selection. Figure 4-4 shows steps in a typical selection process.

Individuals wanting employment can indicate interest in a number of ways. Traditionally, individuals have submitted résumés by mail or fax, or applied in person at an employer's location. But with the growth in Internet recruiting, many individuals complete applications online or submit résumés electronically.

Many employers conduct preemployment screening to determine if applicants meet the minimum qualifications for open jobs before they have the applicants fill out an application. When a job posting generates 1,000 or more applications, which is not unusual with large companies or in difficult economic times, responding to each would be a full-time job. Electronic screening can speed up the process. This may take several forms: disqualification questions; screening questions to get at KSAs and experience; valid assessment tests; and background, drug, and financial screening. Some of the assessments might include auditions for the job that are based on simulations of specific job-related tasks.

Some employers do not use preemployment screening prior to having applicants fill out an application form. Instead, the first step is to have every interested individual complete an application first. These completed application forms then become the basis for prescreening information.

Application forms, which are used universally, can take on different formats. Properly prepared, the application form serves four purposes:

1. It is a record of the applicant's desire to obtain a position.
2. It provides the interviewer with a profile of the applicant that can be used during the interview.
3. It is a basic employee record for applicants who are hired.
4. It can be used for research on the effectiveness of the selection process.

FIGURE 4-4 Selection Process Flowchart

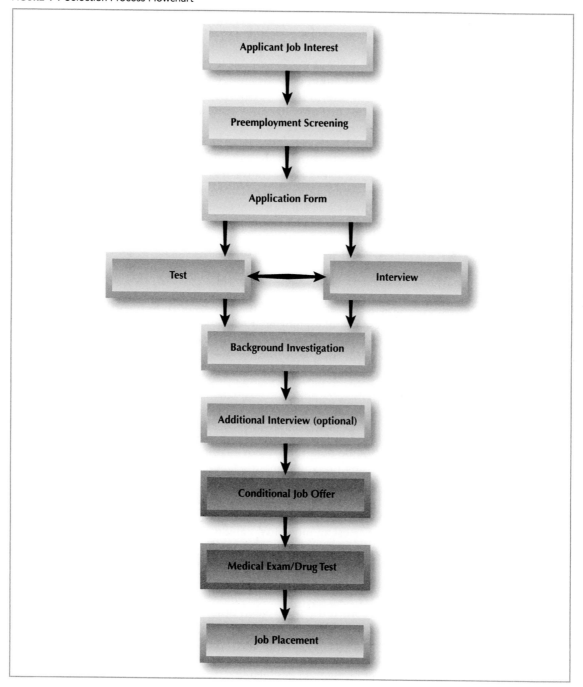

Appendix C shows a sample application form, and Appendix D shows commonly asked illegal inquires. Businesses are required to review and record identity documents, such as Social Security cards, passports, and visas, and to determine if they appear to be genuine. It is illegal to knowingly hire employees who are not in the country legally. The consequences for offending businesses are high; penalties range from $375 to $16,000 per incident and 6 months in prison. If HR personnel know they are working with fraudulent documents, corporate liability exists, and seizure of assets and criminal liability for top management can occur.

A government program called E-Verify is run by the Department of Homeland Security to help with this process. The use of E-Verify is mandatory for government contractors or subcontractors.

An employer should have a policy to comply with immigration requirements and to avoid knowingly hiring or retaining illegal workers. I-9s should be completed, updated, and audited.

Selection Testing

Many different kinds of tests can be used to help select qualified employees. Literacy tests, skill-based tests, personality tests, and honesty tests are used to assess various individual factors that are important for the work to be performed. These useful employment tests allow companies to predict which applicants will be the most successful before being hired.

However, selection tests must be evaluated extensively before being utilized as a recruiting tool. The development of the test items should be linked to a thorough job analysis. Also, initial testing of the items should include an evaluation by knowledge experts, and statistical and validity assessments of the items should be conducted. Furthermore, adequate security of the testing instruments should be coordinated, and the monetary value of these tests to the firm should be determined. For example, Gerber Products Company was found to be using preemployment selection tests for entry-level positions that did not have sufficient evidence of validity. The tests were negatively impacting minority applicants. Gerber paid 1,912 minority and female applicants $900,000 in back pay and interest.[9]

Tests that assess an individual's ability to perform in a specific manner are grouped as ability tests. These are sometimes further differentiated into *aptitude tests* and *achievement tests*. **Cognitive ability tests** measure an individual's thinking, memory, reasoning, verbal, and mathematical abilities. Tests such as these can be used to determine applicants' basic knowledge of terminology and concepts, word fluency, spatial orientation, comprehension and retention span, general and mental ability, and conceptual reasoning. The Wonderlic Personnel Test and the General Aptitude Test Battery (GATB) are two widely used tests of this type. Managers need to ensure that these tests assess cognitive abilities that are job related.

Physical ability tests measure an individual's abilities such as strength, endurance, and muscular movement. At an electric utility, line workers regularly must lift and carry equipment, climb ladders, and perform other physical tasks; therefore, testing of applicants' mobility, strength, and other physical.

Different skill-based tests can be used, including **psychomotor tests**, which measure a person's dexterity, hand–eye coordination, arm–hand steadiness, and other factors. Tests such as the MacQuarie Test for Mechanical Ability can measure manual dexterity for assembly-line workers and others using psychomotor skills regularly.

Many organizations use situational tests, or **work sample tests**, which require an applicant to perform a simulated task that is a specified part of the target job. Requiring an applicant for an administrative assistant's job to type a business letter as quickly as possible would be one such test.

Situational judgment tests are designed to measure a person's judgment in work settings. The candidate is given a situation and a list of possible solutions to the problem. The candidate then has to make judgments about how to deal with the situation. Situational judgment tests are a form of job simulation.

Personality Tests

Personality is a unique blend of individual characteristics that can affect how people interact with their work environment. Many organizations use various personality tests that assess the degree to which candidates' attributes match specific job criteria. For instance, a sporting goods chain offers job applicants a Web-based test. The test evaluates their personal tendencies, and test scores are used to categorize individuals for the hiring decision. Many types of personality tests are available, including the Minnesota Multiphasic Personality Inventory (MMPI) and the Myers-Briggs test.

Personality testing for selection flourished during the 1950s and large companies—such as Sears, Standard Oil, and Procter and Gamble—used such testing extensively. But in the 1960s researchers concluded that personality is not a good predictor for selection, and the use of these tests dropped drastically. In the 1990s, interest in research on personality as a selection tool resurfaced and vendors began selling personality-oriented selection tests. But a seminal research article appearing in *Personnel Psychology* concluded that personality explains so little about actual job outcomes that we should think very carefully about using it *at all* for employment decisions.[10]

Honesty/Integrity Tests

Companies are utilizing different tests to assess the honesty and integrity of applicants and employees. Employers use these tests as a screening mechanism to prevent the hiring of unethical employees, to reduce the frequency of lying and theft on the job, and to communicate to applicants and employees alike that dishonesty will not be tolerated. Honesty/integrity tests can be valid as broad screening devices for organizations if used properly.

However, these instruments have limitations. For instance, socially desirable responding is a key concern; some questions can be considered overly invasive, insulting, and not job related; sometimes "false positives" are generated (or an honest person is scored as "dishonest"); and test scores might be affected by individual demographic factors such as gender and race.

Polygraphs. The polygraph, more generally and incorrectly referred to as the "lie detector," is a mechanical device that measures a person's galvanic skin response, heart rate, and breathing rate. As a result of concerns about polygraph validity, Congress passed the Employee Polygraph Protection Act, which prohibits the use of polygraphs for preemployment screening purposes by most employers. The act does allow employers to use polygraphs as part of internal investigations of thefts or losses. But in those situations, the polygraph test should be taken voluntarily, and the employee should be allowed to end the test at any time.

SELECTION INTERVIEWING

Selection interviewing of job applicants is done both to obtain additional information and to clarify information gathered throughout the selection process. Interviews are commonly conducted at two levels: first, as an initial screening interview to determine if the person has met minimum qualifications, and then later, as an in-depth interview with HR staff members and/or operating managers to determine if the person will fit into the designated work area. Before the in-depth interview, information from all available sources is pooled so that the interviewers can reconcile conflicting information that may have emerged from tests, application forms, and references.

Interviewing for selection is imperfect and should be focused on gathering valid information that has not been gained in other ways. Because selection interviewing is imperfect, the focus must be on techniques that minimize errors and provide the best information.

Structured Interviews

A **structured interview** uses a set of standardized questions asked of all applicants so that comparisons can be made more easily. This type of interview allows an interviewer to prepare job-related questions in advance and then complete a standardized interviewee evaluation form that provides documentation indicating why one applicant was selected over another.

The structured interview is useful in the initial screening process because many applicants can be effectively evaluated and compared. However, the structured interview does not have to be rigid. The predetermined questions should be asked in a logical manner but should not be read word for word. The applicants should be allowed adequate opportunity to explain their answers, and interviewers should probe with additional questions until they fully understand the responses. This process can make the structured interview more reliable and valid than other interview approaches.

Less-Structured Interviews

Some interviews are done unplanned and are not structured at all. Such interviewing techniques may be appropriate for fact finding, or for counseling interviews. However, they are not best for selection interviewing. These interviews may be conducted by operating managers or supervisors who have had little interview training. An *unstructured interview* occurs when the interviewer improvises by asking questions that are not predetermined. A *semistructured interview* is a guided conversation in which broad questions are asked and new questions arise as a result of the discussion. For example: What would you do differently if you could start over again?

Who Conducts Interviews?

Job interviews can be conducted by an individual, by several individuals sequentially, or by panels or teams. For some jobs, such as entry-level jobs requiring lesser skills, applicants might be interviewed solely by a human resource professional. For other jobs, employers screen applicants by using multiple interviews, beginning with a human resource professional and followed by the appropriate supervisors and managers. Then a selection decision is made collectively. Managers need to ensure that multiple interviews are not redundant.

Other interview formats are also utilized. In a **panel interview**, several interviewers meet with the candidate at the same time so that the same responses are heard. Panel interviews may be combined with individual interviews. However, without proper planning, an unstructured interview can result, and applicants are frequently uncomfortable with the group interview format.

Effective Interviewing

Many people think that the ability to interview is an innate talent, but this contention is difficult to support. Just being personable and liking to talk is no guarantee that someone will be an effective interviewer. Interviewing skills are developed through training. To make interviewing more effective, interviewers should a) Plan the interview; b) Control the interview; and c) use effective questioning techniques.

Some types of questions to avoid in selection interviews include yes/no questions, obvious questions, questions that rarely produce a true answer, leading questions, illegal questions, and questions that are not job-related. Appendix E lists questions that are commonly used in selection interviews.

Problems in the Interview.   Operating managers and supervisors are more likely than HR personnel to use poor interviewing techniques because they do not interview often or lack training. Several problems include:

- *Snap judgments:* Some interviewers decide whether an applicant is suitable within the first two to four minutes of the interview, and spend the rest of the time looking for evidence to support their judgment.
- *Negative emphasis:* When evaluating suitability, unfavorable information about an applicant is often emphasized more than favorable information.
- *Halo effect:* The *halo effect* occurs when an interviewer allows a positive characteristic, such as agreeableness, to overshadow other evidence.

The phrase *devil's horns* describes the reverse of the halo effect; this occurs when a negative characteristic, such as inappropriate dress, overshadows other traits.

- *Biases and stereotyping:* "Similarity" bias occurs when interviewers favor or select people that they believe to be like themselves based on a variety of personal factors. Interviewers also should avoid any personal tendencies to stereotype individuals because of demographic characteristics and differences. For instance, age disparities may be a concern as younger executives are interviewing more senior personnel. Additionally, applicants' ethnic names and accents can negatively impact personal evaluations, and older workers are sometimes less likely to get interviewed and hired than are younger applicants.
- *Cultural noise:* Interviewers must learn to recognize and handle cultural noise, which stems from what applicants believe is socially acceptable rather than what is factual.

BACKGROUND INVESTIGATIONS

Failure to check the backgrounds of people who are hired can lead to embarrassment and legal liability. Hiring workers who commit violent acts on the job is one example. While laws vary from state to state, for jobs in certain industries, such as those that provide services to children, vulnerable adults, security, in-home services, and financial services, background checks are mandated in some states. Nationally background checks are required for people with commercial drivers' licenses who drive tractor-trailer rigs and buses interstate.

Lawyers say that an employer's liability hinges on how well it investigates an applicant's background. Consequently, details provided on the application form should be investigated extensively, and these efforts should be documented.

Negligent hiring occurs when an employer fails to check an employee's background and the employee later injures someone on the job. There is a potential negligent hiring problem when an employer hires an unfit employee, a background check is weak, or an employer does not research potential risk factors that would prevent the positive hire decision. Similarly, **negligent retention** occurs when an employer becomes aware that an employee may be unfit for employment but continues to employ the person, and the person injures someone.

Medical Examinations and Inquiries

Medical information on applicants may be used to determine their physical and mental capabilities for performing jobs. Physical standards for jobs should be realistic, justifiable, and linked to job requirements. Even though workers with disabilities can competently perform many jobs, they sometimes may be rejected because of their physical or mental limitations.

The ADA prohibits the use of preemployment medical exams, except for drug tests, until a job has been conditionally offered. Also, the ADA prohibits a company from rejecting an individual because of a disability and from asking job applicants any question related to current or past medical history until a conditional job offer has been made. Once a conditional offer of employment has been made, then some organizations ask the applicant to complete a preemployment health checklist or the employer pays for a physical examination of the applicant. It should be made clear that the applicant who has been offered the job is not "hired" until successful completion of the physical inquiry.

Drug testing may be conducted as part of a medical exam, or it may be done separately. Use of drug testing as part of the selection process has increased in the past few years. If drug tests are used, employers should remember that their accuracy varies according to the type of test used, the item tested, and the quality of the laboratory where the test samples are sent. Because of the potential impact of prescription drugs on test results, applicants should complete a detailed questionnaire on this matter before the testing. If an individual tests positive for drug use, then an independent medical laboratory should administer a second, more detailed analysis. Whether urine, blood, saliva, or hair samples are used, the process of obtaining, labeling, and transferring the samples to the testing lab should be outlined clearly and definite policies and procedures should be established.

References

References provided by the candidate are of very limited predictive value. Would someone knowingly pick a reference who would speak poorly of them? Of course not. Previous supervisors and employers may provide a better prediction. Good questions to ask previous supervisors or employers include:

- Dates of employment
- Position held
- What were the job duties?

- What strengths/weaknesses did you observe?
- Were there any problems?
- Would you rehire?

Work-related references from previous employers and supervisors provide a valuable snapshot of a candidate's background and characteristics. Telephoning references is common.

Making the Job Offer

The final step of the selection process is offering someone employment. Job offers are often extended over the telephone. Many companies then formalize the offer in a letter that is sent to the applicant. It is important that the offer document be reviewed by legal counsel and that the terms and conditions of employment be clearly identified. Care should be taken to avoid vague, general statements and promises about bonuses, work schedules, or other matters that might change later. These documents should also provide for the individual to sign an acceptance of the offer and return it to the employer, who should place it in the individual's personnel files.

Selecting for "Soft Skills"

Selection in its "scientific" form is about finding valid predictors of what will be needed on a job and picking people who score high on those predictors. These "hard skills" include cognitive skills, education, and technical skills. But these skills may not predict the difference between adequate and outstanding performance. Some argue that "soft skills" provide an important part of the ability to do a job successfully. What are "soft skills"? They are noncognitive abilities that are complementary to outstanding job performance. Examples might include:

Empathy	Leadership
Openness	Integrity
Cooperation	Ethical behavior
Interpersonal style	Effort
Conscientiousness	Emotional intelligence

But selection for soft skills is haphazard. Unlike hard skills, these skills may have to be inferred from past behaviors or from an interview.[11] Tests may be available to help with some soft skills, but the basic process presented in this chapter still must apply. First, identify KSAs, competencies, and job functions through job analysis. Next, decide how those will be identified in an applicant (tests, interviews, experience, etc.). Then use structured behavioral interviewing done by trained interviewers incorporating competency-focused questions. Finally, choose those applicants who are strong in the areas necessary to do the job.

NOTES

1. Rick Be, "Employment Doldrums May Be Easing, Survey Notes," *Workforce Management Online*, August 25, 2009, *www.workforce.com*.

2. U.S. Bureau of Labor Statistics, *www.bls.gov*.

3. Justin Lahart, "Employers Shed Fewer Temp Workers," *The Wall Street Journal*, September 5–6, 2009, A2; Patrick Buckley, et al., "The Use of Automated Employment Recruiting and Screening System for Temporary Professional Employees," *Human Resource Management*, 43 (2004), 233–241.

4. Dan Schaubel, "Skip Job Boards and Use Social Media Instead," *BusinessWeek Online*, July 29, 2009, 14.

5. Tresa Baidas, "Lawyers Warn Employers Against Giving Glowing Reviews on LinkedIn," *National Law Journal*, July 6, 2009, *www.nlj.com*.

6. Stephanie Overman, "Staffing Management: Measure What Matters," *Staffing Management*, October 1, 2008, *www.shrm.org*.

7. Melanie Wanzek, "On Second Thought," *Sunday World Herald*, May 10, 2009, CR1.

8. Arne Kalleberg, "The Mismatched Worker: When People Don't Fit Their Jobs," *Academy of Management Perspectives*, February 2008, 24–40.

9. "Gerber Agrees to Pay $900,000 to Minorities and Females for Hiring Discrimination," *Ceridian Abstracts*, August 26, 2009, *www.hrcompliance. ceridian.com*, 1.

10. Frederick Morgeson, et al., "Reconsidering the Use of Personality Tests in Personnel Selection Contexts," *Personnel Psychology*, 60, 2007, 683–729.

11. Charles Handler, "Dear Workforce . . .," *www.workforce.com*.

INTERNET RESOURCES

JobWeb—For a special report about labor markets and jobs outlook, visit *www.jobweb.com.*

Arbita—This consulting firm provides resources on recruiting-related topics, including a collection of articles and white papers. Visit the website at *www.arbita.net.*

HR-Guide.com—This website offers links to HR websites relating to selection and staffing resources, including information on methods, best practices, tests, and software programs. Visit the site at *www.hr-guide.com.*

UniformGuidelines.com—For a free resource on the use of selection procedures and tests to ensure compliance with federal laws, visit this website at *www.uniformguidelines.com.*

SUGGESTED READINGS

Steven D. Maurer and Yupin Liu, "Developing Effective E-Recruiting Websites: Insights for Managers from Marketers," *Business Horizons*, 50 (2007), 305–314.

Fay Hansen, "Sourcing Disappears as Applications Pile Up for Overwhelmed Recruiters," *Workforce Management Online*, July 23, 2009, *www.workforce.com.*

V. O'Connell, "Test for Dwindling Retail Jobs Spawns a Culture of Cheating," *The Wall Street Journal*, January 7, 2009, A1.

Joann Lublin, "For Job Hunters the Big Interview Is Getting Bigger," *The Wall Street Journal*, June 3, 2008, D1.

Training and Talent Management

HR—MEETING MANAGEMENT CHALLENGES

Improving the performance of employees in an organization frequently means training and managing the talent. Current issues include:

- Designing effective training programs
- Identifying and developing the talent
- Dealing with career issues

Competitive pressures require employees that have current knowledge, ideas, and skills. Employees have to be able to adapt to the changes that inevitably will come for the organization. Talent management is concerned with identifying and developing key human resources. It is a topic currently in vogue.

TRAINING AND HR

Competition forces business organizations to change and adapt to compete successfully. Changes in the way things must be done require training or re-training employees and managers. In this sense, training is an ongoing process for most organizations. Organizations in the United States spend more than $126 billion annually on training and development, or more than $1,000 per employee on average.[1]

Training is the process whereby people acquire capabilities to perform jobs. Training provides employees with specific, identifiable knowledge and skills for use in their present jobs. Organizational training may include teaching of "hard" skills, such as teaching sales representatives how to use intranet resources, a branch manager how to review an income statement, or a machinist apprentice how to set up a drill press. "Soft" skills are critical in many instances and can be taught as well. These skills may include communicating, mentoring, managing a meeting, and working as part of a team.

What kinds of activities usually require training? The most common training topics include, among others, safety, customer service, computer skills, quality initiatives, dealing with sexual harassment, and communication.[2] Further, documented benefits of well-done training include (for both individuals and teams) enhanced skills, greater ability to adapt and innovate,

FIGURE 5-1 Types of Training

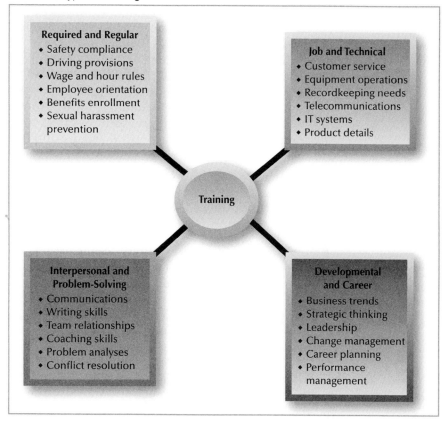

better self-management, and performance improvement. For organizations, research has shown that training brings improvements in effectiveness and productivity, more profitability and reduced costs, improved quality, and increased social capitol.

Training can be designed to meet a number of objectives and can be classified in various ways. Figure 5-1 shows some common groupings.

Strategic Training

Training is used strategically to help the organization accomplish its goals. For example, if sales increases are a critical part of the company's strategy, appropriate training would identify what is causing lower sales and target training to respond as part of a solution.

Strategic training can have numerous organizational benefits. It requires HR and training professionals to get intimately involved with the business and to partner with operating managers to help solve their problems, thus making significant contributions to organizational results. Additionally, a strategic training mind-set reduces the likelihood of thinking that training alone can solve most employee or organizational problems. It is not uncommon for operating managers and trainers to react to most important performance problems by saying, "I need a training program on *X*." With a strategic focus, the organization is more likely to assess whether training actually can address the most important performance issues and what besides training is needed. Training cannot fix all organizational problems.

The nature of technological innovation and change is such that if employees are not trained all the time, they may fall behind and the company could become less competitive. For example, consider the telecommunications industry today compared with ten years ago, with all the new technologies and the accompanying competitive shifts. Without continual training, organizations may not have staff members with the knowledge, skills, and abilities (KSAs) needed to compete effectively.

Training also can affect organizational competitiveness by aiding in the retention of employees. One reason why many individuals stay or leave organizations is career training and development opportunities. Employers that invest in training and developing their employees may enhance retention efforts.

Training as a Revenue Source.   Some organizations have identified that training can be a source of business revenue. For instance, Microsoft, Ceridian, Cisco, Hewlett-Packard, and other technology firms bundle customer training with products and services they sell. Also, manufacturers of industrial equipment offer customers training on machine upgrades and new features. Customers of many of these firms pay for additional training either by course, by participant, or as part of equipment or software purchases.

Integration of Performance with Training.   Job performance, training, and employee learning must be integrated to be effective, and HR plays a role in this integration. Organizations find that training experiences that use real business problems to advance employee learning are better than more traditional approaches. Rather than separating the training experience from the context of actual job performance, trainers incorporate everyday business issues as learning examples, thus increasing the realism of training exercises and scenarios. For example, as part of management training at General Electric, managers are given actual business problems to solve, and they must present their solutions to the business leaders in the firm. Using real situations for practice is yet another way of merging the lines between training, learning, and job performance.

TRAINING FOR GLOBAL STRATEGIES

For a global firm, the most brilliant strategies ever devised will not work unless the company has well-trained employees throughout the world to carry them out. A global look at training is important as firms establish and expand operations worldwide. For U.S. employers, the challenge has increased. According to a report, the number of U.S. job skills certifications declined 18% in one year, while there was a 47% increase in similar certifications in India. The conclusion of the study was that U.S. firms may not remain innovative and strategic leaders much longer, due to the decline in specialized skilled and technical workers.[3] Add this problem to the number of global employees with international assignments, and training clearly must be seen as part of global strategic success.

PLANNING FOR TRAINING

Whether global or national in scope, training benefits from careful planning before it is done. Planning includes looking at the "big picture" in which the training takes place as well as specifics for the design of a particular training effort. For example, the needs for skills have changed over time and things like adaptability, problem solving, and professionalism have increased in value in some firms. Planning to design training to include changes such as these makes for a more effective training program.

Another training planning issue for some companies is knowledge retention for the firm. When retirees leave, they take everything they have learned during a career. Perhaps a retiree is the only one in the company who knows how to operate a piece of machinery or mix a chemical solution. In some areas technology changes so fast that even young people leaving a company may take with them information that cannot easily be replicated. Companies are responding to this knowledge retention need in various ways, including identifying critical employees, having existing critical employees train and mentor others, producing how-to videotapes, and keeping former employees on call for a period of time after their departure.

Training plans allow organizations to identify what is needed for employee performance *before* training begins so that a fit between training and strategic issues is made. Effective training efforts consider the following questions:

- Is there really a need for the training?
- Who needs to be trained?
- Who will do the training?
- What form will the training take?
- How will knowledge be transferred to the job?
- How will the training be evaluated?

Orientation: Planning for New Employees

A good example of one kind of training that requires planning is orientation. Also called "onboarding," orientation is the most important and widely conducted type of regular training done for new employees. **Orientation**, which is the planned introduction of new employees to their jobs, coworkers, and the organization, is offered by most employers. It requires cooperation between individuals in the HR unit and operating managers and supervisors. In a small organization without an HR department, the new employee's supervisor or manager usually assumes most of the responsibility for orientation. In large organizations, managers and supervisors, as well as the HR department, generally work as a team to orient new employees. Unfortunately, without good planning, new employee orientation sessions can come across as boring, irrelevant, and a waste of time to both new employees and their department supervisors and managers.

Among the decisions to be made during planning are what to present and also, equally important, *when* to present it. Too much information on the first day leads to perceptions of ineffective onboarding. Several shorter sessions over a longer period of time, bringing in information as it is needed, are more effective. Effective orientation achieves several key purposes:

- Establishes a favorable employee impression of the organization and the job
- Provides organization and job information
- Enhances interpersonal acceptance by coworkers
- Accelerates socialization and integration of the new employee into the organization
- Ensures that employee performance and productivity begin more quickly

One way of expanding the efficiency of orientation is to use electronic resources. A number of employers place general employee orientation information on company intranets or corporate websites. New employees log on and go through much of the general material on organizational history, structure, products and services, mission, and other background, instead of sitting in a classroom where the information is delivered in person or by videotape. Specific questions and concerns can be addressed by HR staff and others after employees have reviewed the Web-based information. Successfully integrating new hires is important, and measuring the degree of success allows the orientation program to be managed.

A Training System

The way in which a firm plans, organizes, and structures its training affects the way employees experience the training, which in turn influences the effectiveness of the training. Effective training requires the use of a systematic training process. Figure 5-2 shows the four phases of a systematic

FIGURE 5-2 Systematic Training Process

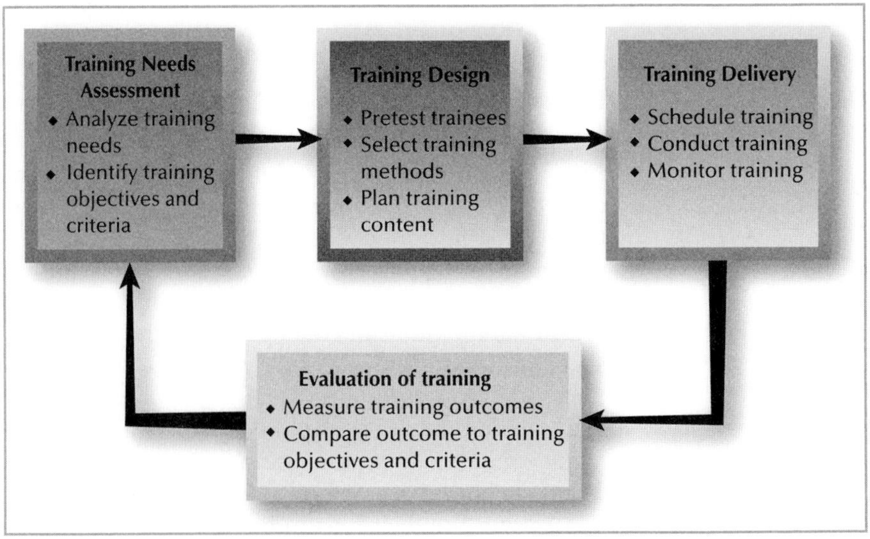

approach: assessment, design, delivery, and evaluation. Using such a process reduces the likelihood that unplanned, uncoordinated, and haphazard training efforts will occur. A discussion of the training process follows.

TRAINING NEEDS ASSESSMENT

Assessing organizational training needs is the diagnostic phase of a training plan. This assessment considers issues of employee and organizational performance to determine if training can help. Needs assessment measures the competencies of a company, a group, or an individual as they relate to what is required. It is necessary to find out what is happening and what should be happening before deciding if training will help, and if it will help, what kind is needed.

The first step in training needs assessment is analyzing what training might be necessary. There are three sources used to analyze training needs.

Organizational analysis comes from various operational measures of organizational performance. Departments or areas with high turnover, customer complaints, high grievance rates, high absenteeism, low performance, and other deficiencies can be pinpointed. Following identification of such problems, training objectives can be developed if training is a solution. During organizational analysis, focus groups of managers can be used to evaluate changes and performance that might require training.

The second way of analyzing training needs is to review *the jobs involved and the tasks performed* in those jobs. By comparing the requirements of jobs with the KSAs of employees, training needs can be identified. For example, at a manufacturing firm, analysis identified the tasks performed by engineers who served as technical instructors for other employees. By listing the tasks required of a technical instructor, management established a program to teach specific instructional skills; thus, the engineers were able to become more successful instructors.

The third means of diagnosing training needs focuses on *individuals and how they perform their jobs.* The following sources are examples that are useful for individual analysis:

- Performance appraisals
- Skill tests
- Individual assessment tests
- Records of critical incidents
- Assessment center exercises
- Questionnaires and surveys
- Job knowledge tools
- Internet input

Once training requirements have been identified using needs analyses, training objectives and priorities can be established by a "gap analysis," which indicates the distance between where an organization is with its employee capabilities and where it needs to be. Training objectives and priorities are then determined to close the gap.

TRAINING DESIGN

Once training objectives have been determined, training design can start. Whether job-specific or broader in nature, training must be designed to address the specific objectives. Effective training design considers the learners, instructional strategies, and how best to get the training from class to the job.

Working in organizations should be a continual learning process. Different approaches are possible because learning is a complex psychological process.

Learner Characteristics

For training to be successful, learners must be ready and able to learn. Learner readiness means that individuals have the ability to learn, which many people certainly have. However, individuals also must have the motivation to learn, have self-efficacy, see value in learning, and have a learning style that fits the training.

Learners must possess basic skills, such as fundamental reading and math proficiency, and sufficient cognitive abilities. Companies may discover that some workers lack the requisite skills to comprehend their training. Some have found that a significant number of job applicants and current employees lack the reading, writing, and math skills needed to learn the jobs.

A person's desire to learn training content, referred to as "motivation to learn," is influenced by multiple factors. For example, differences in gender and ethnicity and the resulting experiences may affect the motivation of adult learners. The student's motivational level also may be influenced by the instructor's motivation and ability, friends' encouragement to do well, classmates' motivational levels, the physical classroom environment, and the training methods used.

Learners must possess **self-efficacy**, which refers to people's belief that they can successfully learn the training program content. For learners to be ready for and receptive to the training content, they must feel that it is possible for them to learn it. As an example, some college students' levels of self-efficacy diminish in math or statistics courses when they do not feel able to grasp the material.

Training that is viewed as useful is more likely to be tried on the job. Perceived utility or value of training is effected by a need to improve, the likelihood that training will lead to improvement, and the practicality of the training for use on the job. Learners must perceive a close relationship between the training and things they want for it to be successful.

People learn in different ways. For example, *auditory* learners learn best by listening to someone else tell them about the training content. *Tactile* learners must "get their hands on" the training resources and use them. *Visual* learners think in pictures and figures and need to see the purpose and process of the training. Trainers who address all these styles by using multiple training methods can design more effective training.

Instructional Strategies

An important part of designing training is to select the right mix of strategies to fit the learners' characteristics. Practice/feedback, overlearning, behavioral modeling, error-based examples, and reinforcement/immediate confirmation are some of the prominent strategies available in designing the training experience.

For some kinds of training, it is important that learners practice what they have learned and get feedback on how they have done so they can improve. **Active practice** occurs when trainees perform job-related tasks and duties during training. It is more effective than simply reading or passively listening.

Overlearning is repeated practice even after a learner has mastered the performance. It may be best used to instill "muscle memory" for a physical activity in order to reduce the amount of thinking necessary and make responses automatic. But overlearning also produces improvement in learner retention.

The most elementary way in which people learn—and one of the best—is through **behavioral modeling**, or copying someone else's behavior. The use of behavioral modeling is particularly appropriate for skill training in which the trainees must use both knowledge and practice. For example, a new supervisor can receive training and mentoring on how to handle disciplinary discussions with employees by observing as the HR director or department manager deals with such problems.

The error-based examples method involves sharing with learners what can go wrong when they do not use the training properly. A good example is sharing with pilots what can happen when they are not aware of a situation they and their aircraft are entering. Situational awareness training that includes error-based examples has been shown to improve air crew situational awareness.[4]

The concept of **reinforcement** is based on the *law of effect*, which states that people tend to repeat responses that give them some type of positive reward and to avoid actions associated with negative consequences. Positively reinforcing correct learned responses while providing negative consequences at some point for wrong responses can change behavior. Closely related is an instructional strategy called **immediate confirmation**, which is based on the idea that people learn best if reinforcement and feedback are given as soon as possible after training.

Transfer of Training

Finally, trainers should design training for the highest possible transfer from the class to the job. Transfer occurs when trainees actually use on the job what knowledge and information they learned in training. The amount of training that effectively gets transferred to the job is estimated to be relatively low, given all the time and money spent on training. It is thought that many employees apply training to their jobs immediately after training, but among those who do not use the training immediately, the likelihood of it being used decreases over time.

TRAINING DELIVERY

Once training has been designed, the actual delivery of training can begin. Regardless of the type of training done, a number of approaches and methods can be used to deliver it. The growth of training technology continues to expand the available choices, as Figure 5-3 shows.

Whatever the approach used, a variety of considerations must be balanced when selecting training delivery methods. The common variables considered are:

- Nature of training
- Subject matter
- Number of trainees
- Individual versus team
- Self-paced versus guided
- Training resources/costs
- E-learning versus traditional learning
- Geographic locations
- Time allotted
- Completion timeline

Internal Training

Internal training generally applies very specifically to the organization and its jobs. It is popular because it saves the cost of sending employees away for training and often avoids the cost of outside trainers. Skills-based technical training is usually conducted inside organizations. Training materials can be created internally as well. Due to rapid changes in technology, the building and updating of technical skills may become crucial internal training needs. Basic technical skills training is also being mandated by federal regulations in areas where the Occupational Safety and Health Administration (OSHA), the Environmental Protection Agency (EPA), and other agencies have jurisdiction. Three types of internal delivery options will be discussed here: informal training, on-the-job training (OJT), and cross training.

FIGURE 5-3 Training Delivery Options

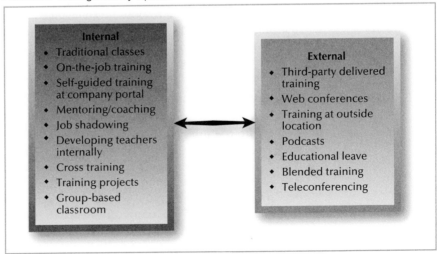

FIGURE 5-4 Stages for On-the-Job Training

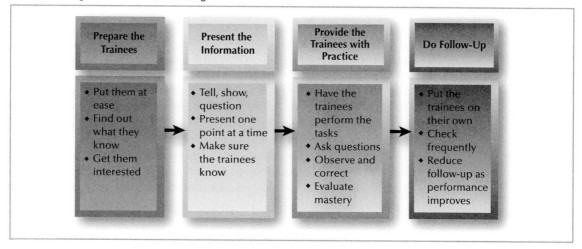

One internal source of training is **informal training**, which occurs through interactions and feedback among employees. Much of what employees know about their jobs they learn informally from asking questions and getting advice from other employees and their supervisors, rather than from formal training programs.

The most common type of training at all levels in an organization is *on-the-job training (OJT)* because it is flexible and relevant to what employees do. Well-planned and well-executed OJT can be very effective. Based on a guided form of training known as job instruction training (JIT), OJT is most effective if a logical progression of stages is used, as shown in Figure 5-4. In contrast with informal training, which often occurs spontaneously, OJT should be planned. The supervisor or manager conducting the training must be able to both teach and show the employees what to do.

However, OJT has some problems. Often, those doing the training may have no experience in training, no time to do it, or no desire to participate in it. Under such conditions, learners essentially are on their own, and training likely will not be effective.

Cross training occurs when people are trained to do more than one job— theirs and someone else's. For the employer, the advantages of cross training are flexibility and development. However, although cross training is attractive to the employer, it is not always appreciated by employees, who often feel that it requires them to do more work for the same pay. To counteract such responses and to make it more appealing to employees, learning "bonuses" can be awarded for successfully completing cross training.

External Training

External training, or training that takes place outside the employing organization, is used extensively by organizations of all sizes. Large organizations use external training if they lack the capability to train people internally or when many people need to be trained quickly. External training may be the best option for training in smaller firms due to limitations in the size of their training staffs and in the number of employees who need various types of specialized training.

Federal, state, and local governments provide a wide range of external training assistance and funding. The Workforce Investment Act (WIA) provides states with block grant programs that target adult education, disadvantaged youth, and family literacy. Employers hiring and training individuals who meet the WIA criteria receive tax credits and other assistance for 6 months or more, depending on the program regulations.

Some employers pay for additional formal education for their employees. Typically, the employee pays for a course that applies to a college degree and is reimbursed upon successful completion of the course. The amounts paid by the employer are considered nontaxable income for the employee up to amounts set by federal laws.

E-Learning: Online Training

E-learning is use of the Internet or an organizational intranet to conduct training online. E-learning is popular with employers. The major advantages are cost savings and access to more employees. Estimates are that corporate training conducted through learning technology will increase in the next few years. Almost 30% of learning hours today are totally technology based, according to one report, and e-learning is preferred by workers under the age of 30.[5]

However, e-learning is advancing gradually, not explosively. It has found favor as part of a "blended" solution that combines it with other forms of learning. By itself, e-learning is not rated among the top effective training practices by training professionals.

Many large employers use interactive two-way television to present classes. The medium allows an instructor in one place to see and respond to a "class" in any number of other locations. With a fully configured system, employees can take courses from anywhere in the world.

Computer-based training involves a wide array of multimedia technologies—including sound, motion (video and animation), graphics, and hypertext—to tap multiple learner senses. Computer-supported simulations within e-learning can replicate the psychological and behavioral requirements of a task, often in addition to providing some amount of physical resemblance to the trainee's work environment.

Virtual reality is also used to create an artificial environment for trainees so that they can participate in the training. Gaming is a possible e-learning tool.

A blended learning approach can use e-learning for building knowledge of certain basics, a Web-based virtual classroom for building skills, and significant in-person traditional instructor-led training sessions and courses. Use of such blended learning provides greater flexibility in the use of multiple training means and enhances the appeal of training activities to different types of employees.

TRAINING EVALUATION

Evaluation of training compares the post-training results to the pre-training objectives of managers, trainers, and trainees. Too often, training is conducted with little thought of measuring and evaluating it later to see how well it worked. Because training is both time consuming and costly, it should be evaluated.

Cost–benefit analysis and return-on-investment (ROI) analysis are commonly used to measure training results, as are various benchmarking approaches.

Cost–Benefit Analysis

Training results can be examined through **cost–benefit analysis**, which is comparison of costs and benefits associated with training. There are four stages in calculating training costs and benefits:

1. *Determine training costs.* Consider direct costs such as design, trainer fees, materials, facilities, and other administration activities.
2. *Identify potential savings results.* Consider employee retention, better customer service, fewer work errors, quicker equipment production, and other productivity factors.
3. *Compute potential savings.* Gather data on the performance results and assign dollar costs to each of them.
4. *Conduct costs and savings benefits comparisons.* Evaluate the costs per participant, the savings per participant, and how the costs and benefits relate to business performance numbers.

Return-on-Investment Analysis and Benchmarking

In organizations, training is often expected to produce an ROI. Still, too often, training is justified because someone liked it, rather than on the basis of resource accountability. ROI simply divides the return produced because of the training by the cost (or investment) of the training.

In addition to evaluating training internally, some organizations use benchmark measures to compare it with training done in other organizations. To do benchmarking, HR professionals gather data on training in their organization and compare them with data on training at other organizations in the same industry and in companies of a similar size. Comparison data are available through the American Society for Training and Development and its Benchmarking Service. This service has training-related data from more than 1,000 participating employers who complete detailed questionnaires annually. Training also can be benchmarked against data from the American Productivity & Quality Center and the Saratoga Institute.

TALENT MANAGEMENT

The need for talent management is brought on by a demographic landscape dominated by the impending retirement of experienced baby boomers, a shortage of young people entering the workforce in western Europe and a decline in the 35–44 age group in the United States. Issues are further complicated by the number of high school graduates who lack writing and verbal communication skills, as well as a work ethic, and the number of college graduates who are weak in writing, leadership, critical thinking, and creativity skills.[6] Where will the successful workforce of the future come from?

The idea that human capital can be a source of competitive advantage for some organizations is gaining ground, but most organizations are not designed or managed to optimize talent performance. Choices for dealing successfully with talent needs are to: (1) emphasize stability in employment and develop talent internally, (2) develop agility as an organization and buy talent as needed, or (3) use some combination of 1 and 2. So the nature of the business and the environment in which it operates to some extent define appropriate strategies for talent management.

Talent management has other characteristics that make it challenging as well. A major one is the nature of "talent" or people. For example, a "deep bench" of talent can be thought of as inventory. But unlike boxes full of empty bottles, talent does not always stay on the shelf until needed—it walks out the door for better opportunities. The shelf life of promising managers and specialists is short if they do not have opportunities where they are currently.

Talent Management "Systems"

Talent management seems to lend itself to the use of various software-based systems that purport to integrate all the pieces of talent management into one manageable whole. For example, one company used a talent management system in:

- Documenting new employee orientations and the onboarding training, regardless of how and where it was done.
- Tracking classroom training and certifications completed by all store employees.
- Automating registration of participants for training and development activities.
- Reporting on completions of training certifications for store employees.
- Compiling and reporting the training and development history of individuals for use with career planning and development.

However, according to one survey, although many companies are planning to use talent management technology, about half still use a manual approach.[7]

Scope of Talent Management

As talent management has evolved, a variety of approaches, ideas, and tools have come along. Some of the most prominent follow.

Target Jobs.   The first issue is to identify the types of jobs that will be the focus of talent management efforts. In some organizations, talent management focuses on the CEO and other executive jobs, rather than more broadly.

Other organizations target senior management jobs, mid-level managers, and other key jobs. However, those groups only represent about one-third of the total workforce, which raises the question of whether talent management efforts would be more useful if they were more widely implemented.

High-Potential Individuals.   Some organizations focus talent management efforts primarily on "high-potential" individuals, often referred to as "high-pos." Attracting, retaining, and developing high-pos have become the emphases for some talent management efforts. Some firms classify individuals as being in the top 10% and then set limits on the number of people who can participate in intensive talent management efforts. Other organizations view talent management more broadly. Targeting primarily high-pos may lead to many other employees seeing their career opportunities as being limited.

Competency Models.   What does a person who is ready to be moved up look like? What competencies should the person have? Competency models show knowledge, skills, and abilities (KSAs) for various jobs. An employer must ask, what talent do we need to achieve this? The answer can be found in a competency model. Competency models help to identify talent gaps. Some companies maintain libraries of competency models. These libraries create a clear path for talent planning. Competency models might be created for executives, managers, supervisors, salespeople, technical professionals, and others.

Talent Pools.   Talent pools are a way to reduce the risk that the company may not need a certain specialty after developing it. The idea is to avoid developing for a narrow specialized job and instead develop a group or pool of talented people with broad general competencies that could fit a wide range of jobs. Once developed, they can be allocated to specific vacancies. Just-in-time training and coaching can make the fit work.

Career Tracks.   Career tracks include a series of steps that one follows to become ready to move up. For example, a potential branch manager in a bank might take rotational assignments in customer sales, teller supervisor, credit cards, and other positions before being considered ready to handle the branch manager's job.

Assessment.   Assessment most often involves tests of one sort or another. Tests for IQ, personality, aptitude, and other factors are used. A portfolio of tests to help predict a person's potential for a job is called an "assessment center."

Development Risk Sharing.   The employer always runs the risk in developing talent that an employee who has been developed will leave with the valuable skills gained through development. An alternative to this risk is to have promising employees volunteer for development on their own time. Executive MBA programs that can be attended on evenings or weekends, extra projects outside a person's current assignment, volunteer projects with nonprofit organizations, and other paths can be used. The employer might contribute through tuition reimbursement or some selected time away from the job, but the risk is at least partly shared by the employee.

SUCCESSION PLANNING

The basis for dealing successfully with staffing "surprises" is succession planning. When a sudden loss of a manager occurs, the void is a serious problem. At that point it is too late to begin to develop a replacement. "Bench strength" and the leadership "pipeline" are metaphors for ways to prevent the void by having replacements ready.

However, succession planning involves more than simply replacement planning. Replacement planning usually develops a list of replacements for given positions. Succession planning must include a well-designed employee development system to reach its potential. It is the process of identifying a plan for the orderly replacement of key employees.

Whether in small or large firms, succession planning is linked to strategic planning through the process shown in Figure 5-5. The process consists of first defining positions that are critical to the strategy, and then making certain top management is involved personally with mentoring, coaching, and talent identification. It may be appropriate to tie some level of reward to executive success in the process. The next step is to assess the talent available in the organization and determine which have the potential, which are ready now for promotion, and which need additional development. The development practices can vary but should be aimed at specific needs in specific individuals. Finally, evaluating the success of the process is important, and appropriate measures are necessary to do so.

All the work involved in the succession planning process should result in two products: (1) identification of potential emergency replacements for critical positions and (2) other successors who will be ready with some additional development. The development necessary should be made clear to the people involved, along with a plan for getting the development.

Benefits of Formal Succession Planning

Employers are doing succession planning formally and informally. As companies become larger, the benefits of formal succession planning become greater. For larger companies, formal planning is recommended. Even government organizations can benefit from formal succession planning. Key benefits include:

- Having a supply of talented employees to fill future key openings
- Providing career paths and plans for employees, which aids in employee retention and performance motivation
- Continually reviewing the need for individuals as organizational changes occur more frequently
- Enhancing the organizational "brand" and reputation of the company as a desirable place to work

FIGURE 5-5 Succession Planning Process

INTEGRATE WITH STRATEGY
- What competencies will be needed?
- Which jobs will be critical?
- How should critical positions be filled?
- Will international assignments be needed?

INVOLVE TOP MANAGEMENT
- Is the CEO personally involved?
- Are top executives mentoring/coaching?
- Are there authority and accountability for succession goals?

ASSESS KEY TALENT
- Does this person have the competencies?
- What competencies are missing?
- Are assessments/performance evaluations/etc. valid?
- Is a results orientation used to identify high positions?
- Are individuals and career goals/interests compatible?

FOLLOW DEVELOPMENT PRACTICES
- How can missing competencies be developed?
- Are there opportunities for those in higher positions to interact with executives/board members?
- Can talent pools be created for job pools?
- What are the rewards to subordinate development?
- Are high position/successors to be told?

MONITOR/EVALUATE
- Are multiple metrics used?
- Are positions filled internally?
- Is the process viewed favorably?

CAREERS AND CAREER PLANNING

A **career** is the series of work-related positions a person occupies throughout his or her life. People pursue careers to satisfy their individual needs. Careers are an important part of talent management, but individuals and organizations view careers in distinctly different ways. Changes in employer approaches to planning for replacement managers based upon a less predictable business environment have put much of the responsibility for a career on the shoulders of individual employees.

However, companies have found that the lack of a career development plan leaves them vulnerable to turnover, and hiring from outside can have drawbacks.[8] When a company attempts to manage careers internally, there may be a typical career path that is identified for employees.

Organization-Centered Career Planning

Careers today are different than they were in the past, and managing them puts a premium on career development by both employers and employees. Effective career planning considers both organization-centered and individual-centered perspectives.

Organization-centered career planning frequently focuses on identifying career paths that provide for the logical progression of people between jobs in an organization. Individuals follow these paths as they advance in organizational units. For example, the right person might enter the sales department as a sales representative, then be promoted to account director, to district sales manager, and finally to vice president of sales.

The systems that an employer uses should be planned and managed to guide managers in developing employees' careers. The career path, or "map," is created and should be shared with the individual employee.

Employees need to know their strengths and weaknesses, and they often discover those through company-sponsored assessments. Then, career paths to develop the weak areas and fine-tune the strengths are developed.

Career paths represent employees' movements through opportunities over time. Although most career paths are thought of as leading upward, good opportunities also exist in cross-functional or horizontal directions.

As noted earlier, not everyone views a career the same way. Further, the way people view their careers depends on the stage of the career. Some research suggests that if employers expect employees to invest more of their personal resources of time and effort in career self-management, they may find it causes conflict with efforts to balance work and life off the job. People may feel they cannot invest great amounts of time beyond their job in career management and have a satisfactory work-life balance as well.[9] This seems especially true for younger employees.

Individual-Centered Career Planning

Organizational changes have altered career plans for many people. Individuals have had to face "career transitions"—in other words they have had to find new jobs. These transitions have identified the importance of **individual-centered career planning**, which focuses on an individual's responsibility for his or her career rather than on organizational needs.

For individuals to successfully manage their own careers, they should perform several activities. Three key activities are:

- *Do self-assessment*
- *Get feedback on reality*
- *Set career goals*

The typical career for individuals today includes more positions, transitions, and organizations—more so than in the past, when employees were less mobile and organizations were more stable as long-term employers. But there are general patterns in people's lives that affect their careers.

Theorists in adult development describe the first half of life as the young adult's quest for competence and for a way to make a mark in the world. According to this view, a person attains happiness during this time primarily through achievement and the acquisition of capabilities.

The second half of life is different. Once the adult starts to measure time from the expected end of life rather than from the beginning, the need for competence and acquisition changes to the need for integrity, values, and well-being. For many people, internal values take precedence over external scorecards or accomplishments such as wealth and job title status.

Early Career Issues.   Early career needs include finding interests, developing capabilities, and exploring jobs. Some organizations do a better job than others of providing those opportunities. Work-at-home programs, mentoring, performance bonuses, time with top executives, extensive training, hiring interns, reimbursement for more education, and rich 401(K) plans are some of the things employers are doing to make jobs more attractive for early career employees.

Career Plateaus.   Those who do not change jobs may face another problem: career plateaus. Many workers define career success in terms of upward mobility. As the opportunities to move up decrease, some employers try to convince employees they can find job satisfaction in lateral movement. Such moves can be reasonable if employees learn new skills that increase individual marketability in case of future layoffs, termination, or organizational restructurings.

An attempt to solve this problem, a **dual-career ladder**, is a system that allows a person to advance up either a management or a technical/professional ladder. Dual-career ladders are now used at many firms, most commonly in technology-driven industries such as pharmaceuticals, chemicals, computers, and electronics. For instance, a telecommunications firm created a dual-career ladder in its IT department to reward talented technical people who do not want to move into management. Different tracks, each with attractive job titles and pay opportunities, are provided. Some health care organizations are using "master" titles for senior experienced specialists such as radiologists and neonatal nurses who do not want to be managers. The masters often are mentors and trainers for younger specialists. Unfortunately, the technical/professional ladder may be viewed as "second-class citizenship" within some organizations.

Retirement Issues. Whether retirement comes at age 50 or age 70, it can require a major adjustment for many people. Some areas of adjustment faced by many retirees include self-direction, a need to belong, sources of achievement, personal space, and goals. To help address concerns over these issues, as well as anxieties about finances, some employers offer preretirement planning seminars for employees.

Women and Careers

According to the U.S. Bureau of Labor Statistics, the percentage of women in the workforce has more than doubled since 1970, and will reach almost 50% in the decade following 2010. Women are found in all occupations and jobs, but their careers may have a different element than those of men. Women give birth to children, and in most societies they are also primarily responsible for taking care of their children. The effect of this biology and sociology is that women's careers are often interrupted for childbirth and child rearing.[10]

Work, Family, and Careers. The career approach for women frequently is to work hard before children arrive, plateau or step off the career track when children are younger, and go back to career-focused jobs that allow flexibility when they are older. This approach is referred to as sequencing. But some women who sequence are concerned that the job market will not welcome them when they return, or that the time away will hurt their advancement chances. And indeed, many women's careers are stifled due to their career interruptions.

Glass Ceiling. Another concern specifically affecting women is the "glass ceiling." This issue describes the situation in which women fail to progress into top and senior management positions. Nationally, women hold about half of managerial/professional positions but only 10% to 15% of corporate officer positions.[11] Some organizations provide leaves of absence, often under FMLA provisions, but take steps to keep women who are away from work involved in their companies. Some have used e-mentoring for women temporarily off their jobs. Other firms use "phased returns" whereby women employees return to work part-time and then gradually return to full-time schedules.

Dual-Career Couples

As the number of women in the workforce continues to increase, particularly in professional careers, so does the number of dual-career couples. The U.S. Bureau of Labor Statistics estimates that more than 80% of all couples are dual-career couples. Marriages in which both mates are managers, professionals, or technicians have doubled over the past two decades.[12] Problem areas for dual-career couples include family issues and job transfers that require relocations.

For dual-career couples with children, family issues may conflict with career progression. Thus, one partner's flexibility may depend on what is "best" for the family. Additionally, it is important that the career development problems of dual-career couples be recognized as early as possible. Whenever possible, having both partners involved in planning, even when one is not employed by the company, may enhance the success of such efforts.

Traditionally, employees accepted transfers as part of upward mobility in organizations. However, for some dual-career couples, the mobility required because of one partner's transfer often interferes with the other's career. In addition to having two careers, dual-career couples often have established support networks of coworkers, friends, and business contacts to cope with both their careers and their personal lives. Relocating one partner in a dual-career couple may mean upsetting this carefully constructed network for the other person or creating a "commuting" relationship.

DEVELOPING HUMAN RESOURCES

Development represents efforts to improve employees' abilities to handle a variety of assignments and to cultivate employees' capabilities beyond those required by the current job. Development can benefit both organizations and individuals. Employees and managers with appropriate experiences and abilities may enhance organizational competitiveness and the ability to adapt to a changing environment. In the development process, individuals' careers also may evolve and gain new or different focuses.

Development differs from training. It is possible to train people to answer customer service questions, drive a truck, enter data in a computer system, set up a drill press, or assemble a television. However, development in areas such as judgment, responsibility, decision making, and communication presents a bigger challenge. These areas may or may not develop through ordinary life experiences of individuals. A planned system of development experiences for all employees, not just managers, can help expand the overall level of capabilities in an organization.

Some important and common management capabilities that may require development include an action orientation, quality decision-making skills, ethical values, and technical skills. Abilities to build teams, develop subordinates, direct others, and deal with uncertainty are equally important but much less commonly developed capabilities for successful managers. For some tech specialties (tech support, database administration, network design, etc.), certain nontechnical abilities must be developed as well: ability to work under pressure, to work independently, to solve problems quickly, and to use past knowledge in a new situation.

Development Needs Analyses

Like employee training, employee development begins with analyses of the needs of both the organization and the individuals. Either the company or the individual can analyze what a given person needs to develop. The goal, of course, is to identify strengths and weaknesses. Methods that organizations use to assess development needs include assessment centers, psychological testing, and performance appraisals.

Assessment Centers.   Collections of instruments and exercises designed to diagnose individuals' development needs are referred to as **assessment centers**. Organizational leadership uses assessment centers for both developing and selecting managers. Many types of employers use assessment centers for a wide variety of jobs.

In a typical assessment-center experience, an individual spends two or three days away from the job performing many assessment activities. These activities might include role-playing, tests, cases, leaderless-group discussions, computer-based simulations, and peer evaluations. Frequently, they also include in-basket exercises, in which the individual handles typical work and management problems. For the most part, the exercises represent situations that require the use of individual skills and behaviors. During the exercises, several specially trained judges observe the participants.

Psychological Testing.   Psychological tests have been used for several years to determine employees' developmental potential and needs. Intelligence tests, verbal and mathematical reasoning tests, and personality tests are often given. Psychological testing can furnish useful information on individuals about such factors as motivation, reasoning abilities, leadership style, interpersonal response traits, and job preferences.

The biggest problem with psychological testing lies in interpretation, because untrained managers, supervisors, and workers usually cannot accurately interpret test results. After a professional scores the tests and reports the scores to someone in the organization, untrained managers may attach their own meanings to the results.

Performance Appraisals.   Well-done performance appraisals can be a source of development information. Performance data on productivity, employee relations, job knowledge, and other relevant dimensions can be gathered in such assessments. In this context, appraisals designed for development purposes, may be different and more useful in aiding individual employee development than appraisals designed strictly for administrative purposes.

HR DEVELOPMENT APPROACHES

Investing in human intellectual capital can occur on or off the job and in "learning organizations." Development becomes imperative as "knowledge work," such as research skills and specialized technology expertise, increases for almost all employers. But identifying the right mix of approaches for development needs requires analyses and planning.

Coaching

The oldest on-the-job development technique is coaching, which is the training and feedback given to employees by immediate supervisors. Coaching involves a continual process of learning by doing. For coaching to be effective, employees and their supervisors or managers must have a healthy and open relationship. Many firms conduct formal courses to improve the coaching skills of their managers and supervisors.

Committee Assignments

Assigning promising employees to important committees may broaden their experiences and help them understand the personalities, issues, and processes governing the organization. For instance, employees on a safety committee can gain a greater understanding of safety management, which would help them to become supervisors. They also may experience the problems involved in maintaining employee safety awareness. However, managers need to guard against committee assignments that turn into time-wasting activities.

Job Rotation

The process of moving a person from job to job is called **job rotation**. It is widely used as a development technique. For example, a promising young manager may spend 3 months in a plant, 3 months in corporate planning, and 3 months in purchasing. When properly handled, such job rotation fosters a greater understanding of the organization and aids with employee retention by making individuals more versatile, strengthening their skills, and reducing boredom.

Assistant Positions

Some firms create assistant positions, which are staff positions immediately under a manager (e.g., Assistant to HR Director). Through such jobs, trainees can work with outstanding managers they might not otherwise have met. Some organizations set up "junior boards of directors" or "management cabinets" to which trainees may be appointed. These assignments provide useful experiences if they present challenging or interesting tasks to trainees.

Classroom Courses and Seminars

Most off-the-job development programs include some classroom instruction. Most people are familiar with classroom training, which gives it the advantage of being widely accepted. But the lecture system sometimes used in classroom instruction encourages passive listening and reduced learner participation, which is a distinct disadvantage. Sometimes trainees have little opportunity to question, clarify, and discuss the lecture material. The effectiveness of classroom instruction depends on multiple factors: group size, trainees' abilities, instructors' capabilities and styles, and subject matter.

Sabbaticals and Leaves of Absence

A **sabbatical** is time off the job to develop and rejuvenate oneself. Some employers provide paid sabbaticals while others allow employees to take unpaid sabbaticals. Popular for many years in the academic world, sabbaticals have been adopted in the business community as well. Some firms give employees 3 to 6 months off with pay to work on "socially desirable" projects. Such projects have included leading training programs in urban ghettos, providing technical assistance in foreign countries, and participating in corporate volunteer programs to aid nonprofit organizations.

Corporate Universities and Career Development Centers

Large organizations may use corporate universities to develop managers and other employees. Corporate universities take various forms. Sometimes regarded as little more than fancy packaging for company training, they may not provide a degree, accreditation, or graduation in the traditional sense. A related alternative, partnerships between companies and traditional universities, can occur where the universities design and teach specific courses for employers.

MANAGEMENT DEVELOPMENT

Although development is important for all employees, it is essential for managers. Without appropriate development, managers may lack the capabilities to best deploy and manage resources (including employees) throughout the organization.

Experience plays a central role in management development. Indeed, experience often contributes more to the development of senior managers than does classroom training, because much of it occurs in varying circumstances on the job over time. Yet, in many organizations it is difficult to find managers for middle-level jobs. Some individuals refuse to take middle-management jobs, feeling that they are caught between upper management and supervisors. Similarly, not all companies take the time to develop their own senior-level managers. Instead, senior managers and executives often are hired from the outside. Figure 5-6 shows experience-based sources of managers' learning and lists some lessons important in effectively developing supervisors, middle managers, and senior-level executives.

A number of approaches are used to mold and enhance the experiences that managers need to be effective. The most widely used methods are supervisor development, leadership development, management modeling, management coaching, management mentoring, and executive education.

Problems with Management Development Efforts

Development efforts are subject to certain common mistakes and problems. Many of the management development problems in firms have resulted from

FIGURE 5-6 Management Lessons Learned from Job Experience

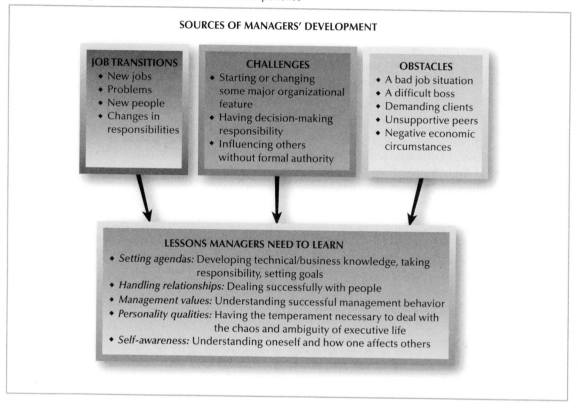

SOURCES OF MANAGERS' DEVELOPMENT

JOB TRANSITIONS
- New jobs
- Problems
- New people
- Changes in responsibilities

CHALLENGES
- Starting or changing some major organizational feature
- Having decision-making responsibility
- Influencing others without formal authority

OBSTACLES
- A bad job situation
- A difficult boss
- Demanding clients
- Unsupportive peers
- Negative economic circumstances

LESSONS MANAGERS NEED TO LEARN
- *Setting agendas:* Developing technical/business knowledge, taking responsibility, setting goals
- *Handling relationships:* Dealing successfully with people
- *Management values:* Understanding successful management behavior
- *Personality qualities:* Having the temperament necessary to deal with the chaos and ambiguity of executive life
- *Self-awareness:* Understanding oneself and how one affects others

inadequate planning and a lack of coordination of development efforts. Common problems include the following:

- Failing to conduct adequate needs analysis
- Trying out fad programs or training methods
- Substituting training for selecting qualified individuals

Another common management problem is *encapsulated development*, which occurs when an individual learns new methods and ideas, but returns to a work unit that is still bound by old attitudes and methods. The development was "encapsulated" in the classroom and is essentially not used on the job. Consequently, in this situation, it is common for individuals who participate in development programs paid for by their employers to become discouraged and move to new employers that allow them to use their newly developed capabilities more effectively.

NOTES

1. Herman Aquinis and Kurt Kraiger, "Benefits of Training and Development for Individuals and Teams, Organizations and Society," *Annual Review of Psychology*, 60 (2009), 451–474.
2. Julie Bos, "Maximize Every Training Dollar," *Workforce Management*, November 17, 2008, 39.
3. J. J. Smith, "U.S. Workers Tech Skills Declined While India, Eastern Europe Grew," *SHRM Global HR News*, September 2006, *www.shrm.org/global*.
4. Simon Branbury, et al., "FASA: Development and Validation of a Novel Measure to Assess the Effectiveness of Commercial Airline Pilot Situation Awareness Training," *International Journal of Aviation Psychology*, 17 (2007), 131–152.
5. American Society of Training and Development, *www.astd.org*.
6. Mark Schoeff, Jr., "Skills of Recent High School Graduates Leave Employers Cold," *Workforce Management*, April 13, 2007, 1–2.
7. "Talent Management Continues to Go High Tech," *HR Focus*, October 2009, 8–9.
8. Edward Lawler III, "Choosing the Right Talent," *Workspan*, July 2008, 73–75.
9. Jane Sturges, "All in a Day's Work?" *Human Resource Management Journal*, 18 (2008), 132.
10. Sherry Sullivan and Lisa Mainiero, "Benchmarking Ideas for Fostering Family Friendly Workplaces," *Organizational Dynamics*, 36, 2007, 45–62.
11. Jessica Marquez, "Gender Discrimination Begins Much Earlier than Exec Levels, Report Shows," *Workforce Management*, May 12, 2009, 1–3.
12. Cathy Arnst, "Women Want Careers Just as Much as Men," *Business Week*, March 27, 2009, 1.

INTERNET RESOURCES

American Society for Training & Development—This website on training and development contains information on research, education, seminars, and conferences. Visit the site at *www.astd.org*.

Learnativity.com—For articles and other resources on adult learning, training, and evaluation, visit this website at *www.learnativity.com*.

Taleo Corporation—For a research library on talent management resources, including articles and interactive tools, visit the Taleo website at *www.taleo.com/resources/research*.

Career Planning—This website is a resource for individual career planning. Visit the site at *www.careerplanning.org*.

SUGGESTED READINGS

Julie Bos, "Top Trends in Training and Leadership Development," *Workforce Management*, November 19, 2007, 36.

Malcolm S. Knowles, Elwood F. Holton III, and Richard A. Swanson, *The Adult Learner*, 6th ed. (New York: Elsevier, 2005).

Edward Lawler, *Talent: Making People Your Competitive Advantage* (San Francisco: Jossey-Bass, 2008).

Peter Cappelli, "The Great Circle of Talent Management," *Human Resource Executive Online*, August 20, 2007, *www.hreonline.com*, 1–3; Peter Cappelli, "Talent Management Cycles: Part II," *Human Resource Executive Online*, September 17, 2007, *www.hreonline.com*, 1–3.

Performance

HR—MEETING MANAGEMENT CHALLENGES

An effective performance management system focuses on identifying, measuring, and dealing with employees performance. These issues are discussed in this chapter because effective performance-management systems can contribute to organizational results. Key aspects include:

- Why organizational strategies are linked to a performance management system
- Establishing a legally defensible and effective performance appraisal system
- How to address performance problems and concerns with individuals

Employers want employees who perform their jobs well. Performance management is used to identify, communicate, measure, and reward employees who do just that. Performance management system design is one of the key methods HR management uses to contribute to organizational performance.

THE NATURE OF PERFORMANCE MANAGEMENT

The performance management process starts by identifying the strategic goals an organization needs to accomplish to remain competitive and profitable. Managers then identify how they and their employees can help support organizational objectives by successfully completing work. In a sense, the sum of the work completed in all jobs should advance the strategic plan. By adopting a "big-picture" approach, managers can successfully combine individual efforts in a manner that provides practical measures of organizational effectiveness.

Effective Performance Management

Often performance management is confused with one of its key components—performance appraisal. **Performance management** is a series of activities designed to ensure that the organization gets the performance it needs from its employees. **Performance appraisal** is the process of determining how well employees do their jobs relative to a standard and communicating that information to them.

An effective performance management system should do the following:

- Make clear what the organization expects
- Provide performance information to employees
- Identify areas of success and needed development
- Document performance for personnel records

Performance management starts with the development and understanding of organizational strategy and then becomes a series of steps that involve identifying performance expectations, providing performance direction, encouraging employee participation, assessing job performance, and conducting the performance appraisal. As Figure 6-1 suggests, successful performance management is a circular process that requires a system of administrative tools that effectively structures the dialogue between managers and their employees, and the motivation to utilize the system in a productive way.

A successful performance management system allows managers to better prepare employees to tackle their work responsibilities by focusing on these activities.

Even well-intentioned employees do not always know what is expected or how to improve their performance, which also makes performance management necessary. Additionally, dismissal of a poorly performing employee may

FIGURE 6-1 Components of Performance Management

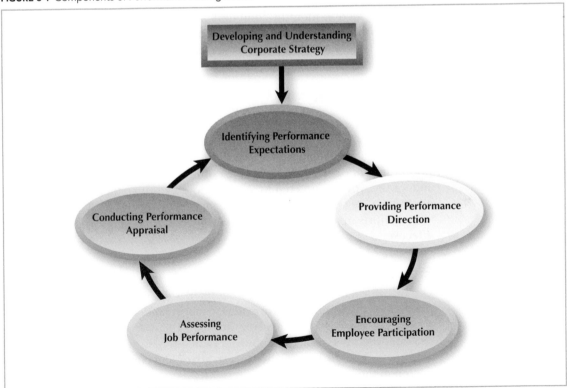

become necessary, and without evidence that the employee has been advised of performance issues, legal problems may result.

Performance management systems and appraisals are very common in the United States and some other countries. However, challenges can be experienced when performance management approaches are used in other countries where multinational organizations have operations, or when they are used with employees who have diverse cultural backgrounds with characteristics very different from those of an American background.

Performance-Focused Organizational Cultures

Organizational cultures vary on many dimensions, and one of these differences involves the degree to which performance is emphasized. Some corporate cultures are based on an *entitlement* approach, meaning that *adequate* performance and stability dominate the organization. Employee rewards vary little from person to person and are not based on individual performance differences. As a result, performance appraisal activities are seen as having few ties to performance and as being primarily a "bureaucratic exercise."

At the other end of the spectrum is a *performance-driven* organizational culture focused on results and contributions. In this context, performance appraisals link results to employee compensation and development. This approach is particularly important when evaluating CEO performance because companies want to hold top leaders accountable for corporate outcomes and motivate them to improve operational and financial results.[1]

It appears that where possible, a performance-based-pay culture is desirable. One study found that 33% of managers and 43% of nonmanagers felt their company was not doing enough about poor performers. The nonmanagers felt that failure to deal with poor performance was unfair to those who worked hard.[2] Additionally, performance-based pay can strengthen the link between employee and organizational goals, increase individual motivation, and augment worker retention, only if an organization develops sound performance plans.

IDENTIFYING AND MEASURING EMPLOYEE PERFORMANCE

Performance criteria vary from job to job, but the most common employee performance measures associated with many jobs include the following:

- Quantity of output
- Quality of output
- Timeliness of output
- Presence/attendance on the job
- Efficiency of work completed
- Effectiveness of work completed

Specific **job duties** are the most important elements in a given job. Duties are identified from job descriptions that contain the most important parts of individual jobs. They help to define what the organization pays employees to do. Therefore, the performance of individuals on important job duties should be measured and compared against appropriate standards, and the results should be communicated to the employee.

To complicate matters, multiple job duties are the rule rather than the exception in most jobs. An individual might demonstrate better performance on some duties than others, and some duties might be more important than others to the organization. Weights can be used to show the relative importance of several duties in one job.

Types of Performance Information

Managers can use three different types of information about employee performance, as Figure 6-2 shows. *Trait-based information* identifies a character trait of the employee—such as attitude, initiative, or creativity—and may or may not be job related.

Behavior-based information focuses on specific behaviors that lead to job success. A human resource director who institutes an "open-door policy" behaves in a manner that likely increases communication with employees. For example, salespeople might use different verbal persuasion strategies with customers because no one approach can be utilized successfully by all individuals.

Results-based information considers employee accomplishments. For jobs in which measurement is easy and obvious, a results-based approach works well. However, in this approach, that which is measured tends to be emphasized, which may leave out equally important but difficult-to-measure parts of work. For example, a car salesperson who gets paid *only* for sales may be unwilling to do paperwork and other work not directly related to selling cars.

Performance measures can be viewed as objective or subjective. The *objective measures* can be observed—for example, the number of cars sold or the

FIGURE 6-2 Types of Performance Information

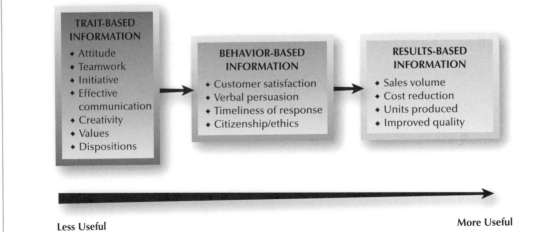

number of invoices processed can be counted. *Subjective measures* require judgment on the part of the evaluator and are more difficult to determine. One example of a subjective measure is a supervisor's ratings of an employee's "attitude," which cannot be seen directly. Consequently, both objective and subjective measures should be used carefully.

Relevance of Performance Criteria

Measuring performance requires focusing on the most important aspects of employees' jobs. For example, measuring the initiative of customer service representatives in an insurance claims center may be less relevant than measuring the number of calls the representatives handle properly. Likewise, evaluating how well a hotel manager is liked by peers is likely to be less relevant than evaluating the policies created by the manager to increase hotel profitability. These examples stress that the most important job criteria or duties should be identified in job descriptions and then conveyed to employees.

Performance Standards

Performance standards define the expected levels of employee performance. Sometimes they are labeled *benchmarks, goals,* or *targets*—depending on the approach taken. Realistic, measurable, clearly understood performance standards benefit both organizations and employees. In a sense, performance standards define what satisfactory job performance is, so performance standards should be established *before* work is performed.

Both numerical and nonnumerical standards can be established. Sales quotas and production output standards are familiar numerical performance standards. A standard of performance can also be based on nonnumerical criteria. Assessing whether someone has met a performance standard, especially a nonnumerical one, can be more difficult, but usually can be done.

Performance Metrics in Service Businesses

Measuring performance in service businesses is difficult, but the process is important. Measuring service performance is difficult because services are very individualized for customers, there is typically great variation in the services that can be offered, and service quality is somewhat subjective. Yet the performance of people in service jobs is commonly evaluated along with the basic productivity measure used in the industry. Some of the most useful sources of performance differences among managers in service businesses are:

- Regional differences in labor costs
- Service agreement differences
- Equipment/infrastructure differences
- Work volume

On an individual employee level, common measures are: cost per employee, incidents per employee per day, number of calls per product, cost per call, sources of demand for services, and service calls per day.

PERFORMANCE APPRAISALS

Performance appraisals are used to assess an employee's performance and provide a platform for feedback about past, current, and future performance expectations. Performance appraisal is variously called *employee rating, employee evaluation, performance review, performance evaluation,* or *results appraisal.*

Performance appraisals are widely used for administering wages and salaries, giving performance feedback, and identifying individual employee strengths and weaknesses. Most U.S. employers use performance appraisals for office, professional, technical, supervisory, middle management, and non-union production workers.

Indeed, performance appraisals be applied to a wide array of work-related questions, and by providing a road map for success, poor performance sometimes can be improved. Even after a positive appraisal, employees benefit if appraisals help them to determine how to improve job performance. In addition, even though an employer may not need a reason to terminate an employee, as a practical matter, appraisals can provide justification for such actions should that become necessary.

However, appraisal programs must be carefully developed to fully capitalize on the talents and efforts of employees. For instance, research has indicated that a gap often exists between actual job performance and the ratings of the work.[3] Poorly done performance appraisals lead to disappointing results for all concerned, and there is reason to believe that evaluations can cause bad feelings and damaged relationships if not managed well. Some believe that performance evaluations are an unnecessary part of work because of vague rating terms, self-interest, and/or deception on the part of rating managers. However, having no formal performance appraisal can weaken discipline and harm an employee's ability to improve.

Uses of Performance Appraisals

Organizations generally use performance appraisals in two potentially conflicting ways. One use is to provide a measure of performance for consideration in making pay or other administrative decisions about employees. This *administrative* role often creates stress for managers doing the appraisals and employees as well. The other use focuses on the *development* of individuals. In this role, the manager acts more as a counselor and coach than as a judge, a perspective that can change the overall tone of the appraisal process. The developmental performance appraisal emphasizes identifying current training and development needs, as well as planning employees' future opportunities and career directions. Figure 6-3 shows both uses for performance appraisals.

Administrative Uses of Appraisals.   Three administrative uses of appraisal impact managers and employees the most: (1) determining pay adjustments; (2) making job placement decisions on promotions, transfers, and demotions; and (3) choosing employee disciplinary actions up to and including termination of employment.

FIGURE 6-3 Uses for Performance Appraisals

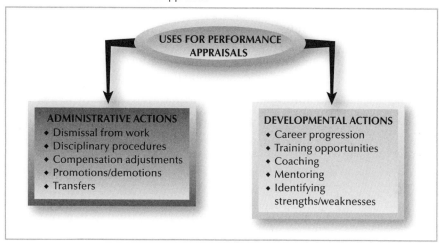

A performance appraisal system is often the link between additional pay and rewards that employees receive and their job performance. Performance-based compensation affirms the idea that pay raises are given for performance accomplishments rather than based on length of service (seniority) or granted automatically to all employees at the same percentage levels. In pay-for-performance compensation systems, historically supervisors and managers have evaluated the performance of individual employees and also made compensation recommendations for the same employees. If any part of the appraisal process fails, better-performing employees may not receive larger pay increases, and the result is perceived inequity in compensation.

U.S. workers say that they see little connection between their performance and the size of their pay increases due to flaws in performance appraisals. However, the use of such appraisals to determine pay is common.

Consequently, many people argue that performance appraisals and pay discussions should be done separately. Two major realities support this view. One is that employees often focus more on the pay received than on the developmental appraisal feedback. The other is that managers sometimes manipulate ratings to justify the pay they wish to give individuals or the amount the market or budget situation suggests should be given.[4] As a result, many employees view the appraisal process as a "game," because compensation increases have been predetermined before the appraisal.

To address these issues, numerous organizations have managers first conduct performance appraisals and discuss the results with employees, and then several weeks later hold a shorter meeting to discuss pay issues. To improve the administrative processes of performance appraisals, many employers have implemented software so that managers can prepare appraisals electronically. Firms are using such HR technology not only to administer appraisals but also to combine employee development and talent management into a package that is integrated.

Developmental Uses of Appraisals. For employees, a performance appraisal can be a primary source of information and feedback that builds their future development in an organization. By identifying employee strengths, weaknesses, potentials, and training needs through performance appraisal feedback, supervisors can inform employees about their progress, discuss areas in which additional training may be beneficial, and outline future developmental plans.

The manager's role in performance appraisal meetings parallels that of a coach, discussing good performance, explaining what improvements are needed, and showing employees how to improve. It is clear that employees do not always know where and how to improve, and managers should not expect improvement if they are unwilling to provide developmental feedback. Positive reinforcement for desired behaviors contributes to both individual and organizational growth. The purpose of the feedback is both to reinforce satisfactory employee performance and to address performance deficiencies. The developmental function of performance appraisal can also identify areas in which the employee might wish to grow.

Decisions about the Performance Appraisal Process

A number of decisions must be made when designing performance appraisal systems. Some important ones are identifying the type of appraisal system to use, the timing of appraisals, and who will conduct appraisals.

Informal versus Systematic Appraisal Processes. Performance appraisals can occur in two ways: informally and/or systematically. A supervisor conducts an *informal appraisal* whenever necessary. The day-to-day working relationship between a manager and an employee offers an opportunity for the employee's performance to be evaluated. A manager communicates this evaluation through conversation on the job, over coffee, or by on-the-spot discussion of a specific occurrence. Frequent informal feedback to employees can prevent "surprises" during a formal performance review. However, informal appraisal can become *too* informal. For example, a senior executive at a large firm so dreaded face-to-face evaluations that he delivered one manager's review while both sat in adjoining stalls in the men's room.

A *systematic appraisal* is used when the contact between a manager and employee is formal, and a system is in place to report managerial impressions and observations on employee performance. Systematic appraisals feature a regular time interval, which distinguishes them from informal appraisals. Both employees and managers know that performance will be reviewed on a regular basis, and they can plan for performance discussions.

Timing of Appraisals. Most companies require managers to conduct appraisals once or twice a year, most often annually. Employees commonly receive an appraisal 60 to 90 days after hiring, again at 6 months, and annually thereafter. *Probationary* or *introductory employees*, who are new and in a trial period, should be informally evaluated often—perhaps weekly for the first month, and monthly thereafter until the end of the introductory period. After that, annual reviews are typical. For employees in high demand, some employers use accelerated appraisals—every 6 months instead of every year. This is done to retain those employees so that more feedback can be given and pay raises may occur more often.

One way to separate the administrative and developmental uses of appraisals is to implement the following appraisal schedule: (1) First hold a performance review and discussion; (2) later hold a separate training, development, and objective-setting session; and (3) within two weeks, have a compensation adjustment discussion. Having three separate discussions provides both the employee and the manager with opportunities to focus on the administrative, developmental, and compensation issues. Using this framework is generally better than addressing all three areas in one discussion of an hour or less, once a year.

Legal Concerns and Performance Appraisals

Because appraisals are supposed to measure how well employees are doing their jobs, it may seem unnecessary to emphasize that performance appraisals must be job related. However, it is important for evaluations to adequately reflect the nature of work, and employees should have fair and nondiscriminatory performance appraisals. Companies need to have appraisal systems that satisfy the courts, as well as performance management needs.

WHO CONDUCTS APPRAISALS?

Performance appraisals can be conducted by anyone familiar with the performance of individual employees. Possible rating situations include the following:

- Supervisors rating their employees
- Employees rating their superiors
- Team members rating each other
- Employees rating themselves
- Outside sources rating employees
- A variety of parties providing multisource, or 360-degree, feedback

Supervisory Rating of Subordinates

The most widely used means of rating employees is based on the assumption that the immediate supervisor is the person most qualified to evaluate an employee's performance realistically and fairly. To help themselves provide accurate evaluations, some supervisors keep performance logs noting their employees' accomplishments so that they can reference these notes when rating performance. For instance, a sales manager might periodically observe a salesperson's interactions with clients so that constructive performance feedback

FIGURE 6-4 Traditional Performance Appraisal Process

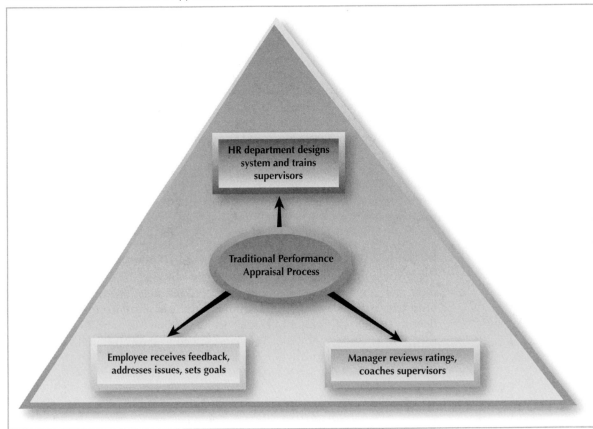

can be provided at a later date. Figure 6-4 shows the traditional review process by which supervisors conduct performance appraisals on employees.

Employee Rating of Managers

A number of organizations ask employees to rate the performance of their immediate managers. Having employees rate managers provides three primary advantages. First, in critical manager-employee relationships, employee ratings can be quite useful for identifying competent managers. The rating of leaders by combat soldiers is one example of such a use. Second, this type of rating program can help make a manager more responsive to employees. This advantage can quickly become a disadvantage if the manager focuses on being "nice" rather than on managing; people who are nice but have no other qualifications may not be good managers in many situations. Finally, employee appraisals can contribute to career development efforts for managers by identifying areas for growth.

A major disadvantage of having employees rate managers is the negative reaction many superiors have to being evaluated by employees. Also, the fear of reprisals may be too great for employees to give realistic ratings. This may prompt workers to rate their managers only on the way the managers treat them, not on critical job requirements. The problems associated with this appraisal approach limit its usefulness to certain situations, including managerial development and improvement efforts.

Team/Peer Rating

Having employees and team members rate each other is another type of appraisal with potential both to help and to hurt. Peer and team ratings are especially useful when supervisors do not have the opportunity to observe each employee's performance but other work group members do. One challenge of this approach is how to obtain ratings with virtual or global teams, in which the individuals work primarily through technology, not in person (i.e., an online college class). Another challenge is obtaining ratings from and for individuals who are on different special project teams throughout the year.

Some contend that any performance appraisal, including team/peer ratings, can negatively affect teamwork and participative management efforts. Although team members have good information on one another's performance, they may not choose to share it in the interest of sparing feelings. Despite the problems, team/peer performance ratings are probably inevitable, especially where work teams are used extensively.

Self-Rating

Self-appraisal works in certain situations. As a self-development tool, it requires employees to think about their strengths and weaknesses and set goals for improvement. Employees working in isolation or possessing unique skills may be particularly suited to self-ratings because they are the only ones qualified to rate themselves. Overall, the use of self-appraisals in organizations has increased.[5] However, employees may use quite different standards and not rate themselves in the same manner as supervisors.

Outsider Rating

People outside the immediate work group may be called in to conduct performance reviews. This field review approach can include someone from the HR department as a reviewer, or completely independent reviewers from outside the organization. Examples include a review team evaluating a college president or a panel of division managers evaluating a supervisor's potential for advancement in the organization. A disadvantage of this approach is that outsiders may not know the important demands within the work group or organization.

The customers or clients of an organization are good sources for outside appraisals. For sales and service jobs, customers may provide useful input on the performance behaviors of employees. For instance, many hospitality organizations such as restaurants and hotels use customer comments cards to gather feedback about the service provided by customer contact personnel, and this information is commonly used for job development purposes.

Multisource/360-Degree Feedback

The use of multisource rating, or 360-degree feedback, has grown in popularity in organizations. Multisource feedback recognizes that for many jobs, employee performance is multidimensional and crosses departmental, organizational, and even global boundaries. Therefore, information needs to be collected from many different sources to adequately and fairly evaluate an incumbent's performance in one of these jobs. The major purpose of 360-degree feedback is *not* to increase uniformity by soliciting like-minded views. Instead, it is designed to capture evaluations of the employee's different roles to provide richer feedback during an evaluation.

Significant administrative time and paperwork are required to request, obtain, and summarize feedback from multiple raters. Using electronic systems to summarize the information can greatly reduce the administrative demands of multisource ratings and increase the effectiveness (i.e., privacy and expediency) of the process.[6]

As originally designed and used, multisource feedback focuses on the use of appraisals for future development of individuals. Conflict resolution skills, decision-making abilities, team effectiveness, communication skills, managerial styles, and technical capabilities are just some of the developmental areas that can be examined. Even in a multisource system, the manager remains a focal point, both to receive the feedback initially and to follow up with the employee appropriately.

The popularity of 360-degree feedback systems has led to the results being used for compensation, promotion, termination, and other administrative decisions. A number of questions have arisen as multisource appraisals have become more common.

Evaluating Multisource Feedback. Research on multisource/360-degree feedback has revealed both positives and negatives. More variability than expected may be seen in the ratings given by the different sources. Thus, supervisor ratings must carry more weight than peer or subordinate input to resolve the differences. One concern is that those peers who rate poor-performing coworkers tend to inflate the ratings so that the peers themselves can get higher overall evaluation results.

Another concern is whether 360-degree appraisals improve the process or simply multiply the number of problems by the total number of raters. Also, some wonder whether multisource appraisals really create better decisions that offset the additional time and investment required. These issues appear to be less threatening when the 360-degree feedback is used *only for development*, so companies should consider using multisource feedback primarily as a developmental tool to enhance future job performance[7] while effectively reducing the use of multisource appraisals as an administrative tool.

TOOLS FOR APPRAISING PERFORMANCE

Performance can be appraised by a number of methods. Some employers use one method for all jobs and employees, some use different methods for different groups of employees, and others use a combination of methods. The following discussion highlights different tools that can be used and some of the advantages and disadvantages of each approach.

Category Scaling Methods

The simplest methods for appraising performance are category scaling methods, which require a manager to mark an employee's level of performance on a specific form divided into categories of performance. A *checklist* uses a list of statements or words from which raters check statements that are most representative of the characteristics and performance of employees. Often, a scale indicating perceived level of accomplishment on each statement is included, which becomes a type of graphic rating scale.

Graphic Rating Scales

The **graphic rating scale** allows the rater to mark an employee's performance on a continuum indicating low to high levels of a particular characteristic. Because of the straightforwardness of the process, graphic rating scales are commonly used in performance evaluations.[8] Figure 6-5 shows a sample appraisal form that combines graphic rating scales with essays. Three aspects of performance are appraised using graphic rating scales: *descriptive categories* (such as quantity of work, attendance, and dependability), *job duties* (taken from the job description), and *behavioral dimensions* (such as decision making, employee development, and communication effectiveness).

Concerns with Graphic Rating Scales. Graphic rating scales in many forms are widely used because they are easy to develop and provide a uniform set of criteria to equally evaluate the job performance of different employees. However, the use of scales can cause rater error because the form might not accurately reflect the relative importance of certain job characteristics, and some factors might need to be added to the ratings while others might need to be deleted. If they fit the person and the job, the scales work well. However, if they fit poorly, managers and employees who must use them frequently complain about "the rating form."

A key point must be emphasized. Regardless of the scales used, the focus should be on the job duties and responsibilities identified in job descriptions. The closer the link between the scales and what people actually do, as identified in current and complete job descriptions, the stronger the relationship between the ratings and the job, as viewed by employees and managers. Also, should the performance appraisal results be challenged by legal actions, the closer performance appraisals measure what people actually do, the more likely employers are to prevail in those legal situations.

Behavioral Rating Scales. In an attempt to overcome some of the concerns with graphic rating scales, employers may use behavioral rating scales designed to assess individual actions instead of personal attributes and characteristics. Different approaches are used, but all describe specific examples of employee job behaviors. In a behaviorally–anchored rating scale (BARS), these examples

FIGURE 6-5 Sample Performance Appraisal Form

Date sent: 4/19/11		**Return by:** 5/01/11	
Name: Joe Hernandez		**Job title:** Receiving Clerk	
Department: Receiving		**Supervisor:** Marian Williams	
Employment status (check one): Full-time __X__ Part-time _____		**Date of hire:** 5/12/02	

Rating period: From: 4/30/10 To: 4/30/11

Reason for appraisal (check one): Regular interval __X__   Introductory ____   Counseling only ____   Discharge ____

Using the following definitions, rate the performance as I, M, or E.

I—Performance is below job requirements and **improvement is needed.**

M—Performance **meets** job requirements and standards.

E—Performance **exceeds** job requirements and standards **most** of the time.

SPECIFIC JOB RESPONSIBILITIES: List the prinicipal activities from the job summary, rate the performance on each job duty by placing an X on the rating scale at the appropriate location, and make appropriate comments to explain the rating.

I ——————————————— M ——————————— E

Job Duty #1: Inventory receiving and checking

Explanation: _____

_____

I ——————————————— M ——————————— E

Job Duty #2: Accurate recordkeeping

Explanation: _____

_____

I ——————————————— M ——————————— E

Attendance (including absences and tardies):   Number of absences ____   Number of tardies ____

Explanation: _____

_____

Overall rating: In the box provided, place the letter—**I, M, or E**—that best describes the employee's overall performance.

Explanation: _____

_____

are "anchored" or measured against a scale of performance levels. When creating a BARS system, identifying important *job dimensions*, which are the most important performance factors in a job description, is done first. Short statements describe both desirable and undesirable behaviors (anchors).

Several problems are associated with the behavioral approaches. First, creating and maintaining behaviorally–anchored rating scales requires extensive time and effort. In addition, various appraisal forms are needed to accommodate different types of jobs in an organization. For instance, because nurses, dietitians, and admissions clerks in a hospital all have distinct job descriptions, a separate BARS form needs to be developed for each.

Comparative Methods

Comparative methods require that managers directly compare the performance levels of their employees against one another, and these comparisons can provide useful information for performance management. An example of this process would be an information systems supervisor comparing the performance of a programmer with that of other programmers. Comparative techniques include ranking and forced distribution.

Ranking.   The **ranking** method lists the individuals being rated from highest to lowest based on their performance levels and relative contributions.[9] One disadvantage of this process is that the sizes of the performance differences between employees are often not fully investigated or clearly indicated. For example, the performances of individuals ranked second and third may differ little, while the performances of those ranked third and fourth differ a great deal. This limitation can be mitigated to some extent by assigning points to indicate performance differences. Ranking also means someone must be last, which ignores the possibility that the last-ranked individual in one group might be equal to the top-ranked employee in a different group. Further, the ranking task becomes unwieldy if the group to be ranked is large.

Forced Distribution.   Forced distribution is a technique for distributing ratings that are generated with any of the other appraisal methods and comparing the ratings of people in a work group. With the **forced distribution** method, the ratings of employees' performance are distributed along a bell-shaped curve. For example, a medical clinic administrator ranking employees on a 5-point scale would have to rate 10% of the employees as a 1 ("unsatisfactory"), 20% as a 2 ("below expectations"), 40% as a 3 ("meets expectations"), 20% as a 4 ("above expectations"), and 10% as a 5 ("outstanding").

Forced distribution has been used in some form by an estimated 30% of all firms with performance appraisal systems. At General Electric, in the "20/70/10" program, managers identify the top 20% and reward them richly so that few will leave. The bottom 10% are given a chance to improve or leave. The forced distribution system is controversial because of both its advantages and its disadvantages, which are discussed next.

One reason why firms have mandated the use of forced distributions for appraisal ratings is to deal with "rater inflation." If employers do not require a forced distribution, performance appraisal ratings often do not match the normal distribution of a bell-shaped curve.

The use of a forced distribution system forces managers to identify high, average, and low performers. Thus, high performers can be rewarded and developed, while low performers can be "encouraged" to improve or leave.

But the forced distribution method suffers from several drawbacks. One problem is that a supervisor may resist placing any individual in the lowest (or the highest) group. Difficulties also arise when the rater must explain to an employee why the employee was placed in one group and others were placed in higher groups.

A number of actions are recommended to address these problems if a forced distribution system is to be used, including many that are similar to those for making other methods of appraisals more legal and effective[10]:

- Use specific, objective criteria and standards to evaluate employees.
- Involve employees in program development.
- Ensure that sufficient numbers of individuals are being rated, so that ranking profiles are relevant.
- Train managers, and review their ratings to ensure job relatedness (no favoritism).

Narrative Methods

Managers and HR specialists may be required to provide written or oral appraisal information. Some appraisal methods are entirely written, rather than relying on predetermined rating scales or ranking structures. Documentation and descriptive text are the basic components of the critical incident method and the essay method.

In the **critical incident** method, the manager keeps a written record of both highly favorable and unfavorable actions performed by an employee during the entire rating period. When a "critical incident" involving an employee occurs, the manager writes it down. For instance, when a sales clerk at a clothing store spends considerable time with a customer helping him purchase a new suit, a manager might document this exceptional service for later review during an annual evaluation. The critical incident method can be used with other methods to document the reasons why an employee was given a certain rating.

The **essay** method requires a manager to write a short essay describing each employee's performance during the rating period. Some "free-form" essays are without guidelines; others are more structured, using prepared questions that must be answered. The rater usually categorizes comments under a few general headings. The essay method allows the rater more flexibility than other methods do. As a result, appraisers often combine the essay with other methods.

The effectiveness of the essay approach often depends on a supervisor's writing skills. Some supervisors do not express themselves well in writing and as a result produce poor descriptions of employee performance, whereas others have excellent writing skills and can create highly positive impressions.

If well composed, essays can provide highly detailed and useful information about an employees' job performance.

Management by Objectives

Management by objectives (MBO) specifies the performance goals that an individual and manager identify together. Each manager sets objectives derived from the overall goals and objectives of the organization; however, MBO should not be a disguised means for a superior to dictate the objectives of individual managers or employees. Other names for MBO include *appraisal by results, target coaching, work planning and review, performance objective setting*, and *mutual goal setting.*

MBO Process.   Implementing a guided self-appraisal system using MBO is a four-stage process. The stages are as follows:

1. *Job review and agreement.*
2. *Development of performance standards.*
3. *Setting of objectives.*
4. *Continuing performance discussions.*

The MBO process seems to be most useful with managerial personnel or employees who have a fairly wide range of flexibility and control over their jobs. When imposed on a rigid and autocratic management system, MBO often has failed. Emphasizing penalties for not meeting objectives defeats the development and participative nature of MBO.

Combinations of Methods

No single appraisal method is best for all situations. Therefore, a performance measurement system that uses a combination of methods may be sensible in certain circumstances. Using combinations may offset some of the advantages and disadvantages of individual methods.

When managers can articulate what they want a performance appraisal system to accomplish, they can choose and mix methods to realize those advantages. For example, one combination might include a graphic rating scale of performance on major job criteria, a narrative for developmental needs, and an overall ranking of employees in a department. Different categories of employees (e.g., salaried exempt, salaried nonexempt, and maintenance) might require different combinations of methods.

TRAINING MANAGERS AND EMPLOYEES IN PERFORMANCE APPRAISAL

Court decisions on the legality of performance appraisals and research on appraisal effectiveness both stress the importance of training managers and employees on performance management and on conducting performance appraisals. Managers with positive views of the performance appraisal system are more likely to use the system effectively. Unfortunately, such training occurs only sporadically or not at all in many organizations.

For employees, performance appraisal training focuses on the purposes of appraisal, the appraisal process and timing, and how performance criteria and standards are linked to job duties and responsibilities. Some training also discusses how employees might rate their own performance and use that information in discussions with their supervisors and managers.

Most systems can be improved by training supervisors in how to do performance appraisals. The following list is not comprehensive, but it does identify some topics covered in appraisal training:

- Appraisal process and timing
- Performance criteria and job standards that should be considered
- How to communicate positive and negative feedback
- When and how to discuss training and development goals
- Conducting and discussing the compensation review
- How to avoid common rating errors

Rater Errors

There are many possible sources of error in the performance appraisal process. One of the major sources is the raters. Although completely eliminating errors is impossible, making raters aware of them through training is helpful.

Varying Standards. When appraising employees, a manager should avoid applying different standards and expectations to employees performing the same or similar jobs. Such problems often result from the use of ambiguous criteria and subjective weightings by supervisors.

Recency and Primacy Effects. The **recency effect** occurs when a rater gives greater weight to recent events when appraising an individual's performance. Examples include giving a student a course grade based only on the student's performance in the last week of class and giving a drill press operator a high rating even though the operator made the quota only in the last two weeks of the rating period. The opposite of the recency effect is the **primacy effect,** which occurs when a rater gives greater weight to information received first when appraising an individual's performance.

Central Tendency, Leniency, and Strictness Errors. A manager may develop a rating pattern. Appraisers who rate all employees within a narrow range in the middle of the scale (i.e., rate everyone as "average") commit a **central tendency error,** giving even outstanding and poor performers an "average" rating.

Rating patterns also may exhibit leniency or strictness. The **leniency error** occurs when ratings of all employees fall at the high end of the scale. The **strictness error** occurs when a manager uses only the lower part of the scale to rate employees. To avoid conflict, managers often rate employees higher than they should. This "ratings boost" is especially likely when no manager or HR representative reviews the completed appraisals.

Rater Bias.   When a rater's values or prejudices distort the rating, this is referred to as **rater bias.** Such bias may be unconscious or quite intentional. For example, a manager's dislike of certain ethnic groups may cause distortion in appraisal information for some people. Use of age, religion, seniority, sex, appearance, or other "classifications" also may skew appraisal ratings if the appraisal process is not properly designed. A review of appraisal ratings by higher-level managers may help correct this problem.

Halo and Horns Effects.   The **halo effect** occurs when a rater scores an employee high on all job criteria because of performance in one area. For example, if a worker has few absences, the supervisor might give the worker a high rating in all other areas of work, including quantity and quality of output, without really thinking about the employee's other characteristics separately. The opposite is the *horns effect*, which occurs when a low rating on one characteristic leads to an overall low rating.

Contrast Error.   Rating should be done using established standards. One problem is the **contrast error,** which is the tendency to rate people relative to one another rather than against performance standards. Although it may be appropriate to compare people at times, the performance rating usually should reflect comparison against performance standards, not against other people.

APPRAISAL FEEDBACK

After completing appraisals, managers need to communicate results in order to give employees a clear understanding of how they stand in the eyes of their immediate superiors and the organization. Organizations commonly require managers to discuss appraisals with employees. The appraisal feedback interview provides an opportunity to clear up any misunderstandings on both sides.

Appraisal Interview

The appraisal interview presents both an opportunity and a danger. It can be an emotional experience for the manager and the employee because the manager must communicate both praise and constructive criticism. A major concern for managers is how to emphasize the positive aspects of the employee's performance while still discussing ways to make needed improvements.[11]

Employees usually approach an appraisal interview with some concern. They may feel that discussions about performance are both personal and important to their continued job success. At the same time, they want to know how their managers feel about their performance. Figure 6-6 summarizes hints for an effective appraisal interview for supervisors and managers.

FIGURE 6-6 Appraisal Interview Hints for Appraisers

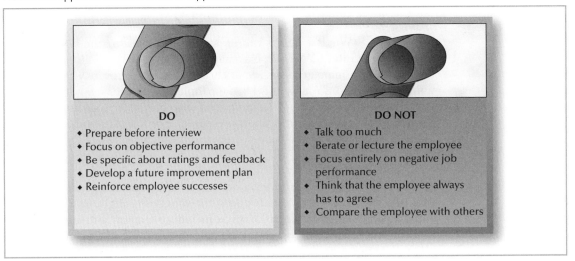

Feedback as a System

The three commonly recognized components of a feedback system are data, evaluation of that data, and some action based on the evaluation. *Data* are factual pieces of information regarding observed actions or consequences. Most often, data are facts that report what happened. Someone must evaluate the meaning or value of the data.

Evaluation is the way the feedback system reacts to the facts, and it requires performance standards. Managers might evaluate the same factual information differently than would customers (e.g., regarding merchandise exchange or credit decisions) or coworkers. Evaluation can be done by the person supplying the data, by a supervisor, or by a group.

For feedback to cause change, some decisions must be made regarding subsequent *action*. Regardless of the process used, the feedback components (data, evaluation, and action) are necessary parts of a successful performance appraisal feedback system.

Reactions of Managers

Managers who must complete appraisals of their employees often resist the appraisal process. Many feel that their role calls on them to assist, encourage, coach, and counsel employees to improve their performance. However, being a judge on the one hand and a coach and a counselor on the other hand may cause internal conflict and confusion for managers.

Knowing that appraisals may affect employees' future careers also may cause altered or biased ratings. This problem is even more likely when managers know that they will have to communicate and defend their ratings to the employees, their bosses, or HR specialists. Managers can easily avoid providing negative feedback to an employee in an appraisal interview and thus avoid unpleasantness in an interpersonal situation by making the employee's ratings positive. But avoidance helps no one. A manager owes an employee a well-done appraisal, no matter how difficult an employee is, or how difficult the conversation about performance might be.

Reactions of Appraised Employees

Employees may well see the appraisal process as a threat and feel that the only way for them to get a higher rating is for someone else to receive a low rating. This win-lose perception is encouraged by comparative methods of rating. Emphasis on the self-improvement and developmental aspects of appraisal appears to be the most effective way to reduce this reaction. However, in most cases, employees will view appraisals done well as what they are meant to be— constructive feedback.

Effective Performance Management

Regardless of the approach used, managers must understand the intended outcome of performance management.[11] When performance management is used to develop employees as resources, it usually works. When one key part of performance management, a performance appraisal, is used to punish employees, performance management is less effective.

Done well, performance management can lead to higher employee motivation and satisfaction. To be effective, a performance management system, including the performance appraisal processes, should be:

- Consistent with the strategic mission of the organization
- Beneficial as a development tool
- Useful as an administrative tool
- Legal and job related
- Viewed as generally fair by employees
- Effective in documenting employee performance

Many of these factors can be enhanced through the effective development of the performance management process. By making sure that raters understand how to consistently evaluate job performance, managers should be able to increase support for the performance management process throughout the organization.

NOTES

1. Patrick Shannon, Colleen O'Neill, Nanci R. Hibschman, and J. Carlos Rivero, "CEO Performance Evaluation: Getting It Right," *Perspective*, Mercer Human Resource Consulting, April 21, 2005.
2. "Survey: Failure to Deal with Poor Performers May Decrease Engagement of Other Employees," *Newsline*, June 22, 2006.
3. Kevin R. Murphy, "Explaining the Weak Relationship Between Job Performance and Ratings of Job Performance," *Industrial and Organizational Psychology*, 1, (2008), 148–160.
4. Samuel A. Culbert, "Get Rid of the Performance Review!" *The Wall Street Journal*, October 20, 2008, R4.

5. Adrienne Fox, "Curing What Ails Performance Reviews," *HR Magazine*, January 2009, 52–56.

6. Leanne Atwater, John F. Brett, and Atira Cherise Charles, "Multisource Feedback: Lessons Learned and Implications for Practice," *Human Resource Management*, 46 (2007), 285–307.

7. Leanne Atwater, John F. Brett, and Atira Cherise Charles, "Multisource Feedback: Lessons Learned and Implications for Practice," *Human Resource Management*, 46 (2007), 285–307; Anne Freedman, "Performance Management: Balancing Values, Results in Reviews," *Human Resource Executive*, August 2006, 62–63.

8. Leslie A. Weatherly, "Performance Management: Getting It Right from the Start," *SHRM Research Quarterly*, 2004.

9. Steve Scullen, Paul Bergey, and Lynda Aiman-Smith, "Forced Distribution Rating Systems and the Improvement of Workforce Potential," *Personnel Psychology*, 58 (2005), 1–31.

10. "A Positive Psychology Handbook for Entrepreneurs," *BusinessWeek, Small Biz*, February/March 2009, 47.

11. Aileen MacMillan, "Raising the Bar on Performance Management Practices to Optimize Performance Reviews and Goal Management," *HR.com*, April 2006, 2–12.

INTERNET RESOURCES

Free Management Library—This website is an integrated online library with resources for profit and nonprofit entities regarding performance management. Visit the site at *www.managementhelp.org*.

LegalWorkplace.Com—For valuable legal management information on performance issues and other HR topics, visit this resource center website at *www.ahipubs.com*.

Personnel Decisions International—This is a website for a firm specializing in the development of people utilizing many different development tools, including managing performance data. Visit the site at *www.personneldecisions.com*.

HR-Software.net—For links to numerous online performance appraisal software systems, visit this website at *www.hr-software.net*.

SUGGESTED READINGS

Herman Aguinis, *Performance Management* (Upper Saddle River, NJ: Pearson/Prentice Hall, 2007), 50–51.

Eric Harmon, Scott Hensel, and T. E. Lukes, "Measuring Performance in Services," *The McKinsey Quarterly*, February, 2006, 2–7.

Lisa Hartley, "Unified Talent Management and the Holy Grail," Best Practices in Performance Management, Special

Advertising Supplement to *Workforce Management* (Taleo), S5; Paul Loucks, "The Need for Web-Based Talent & Performance Management," *Workspan*, October 2007, 68–70.

Laura Roberts, et al., "How to Play to Your Strengths," *Harvard Business Review*, January 2005, 74–80; Peter Drucker, "Managing Oneself," *Harvard Business Review*, January 2005, 100–109.

Total Rewards and Compensation

HR—MEETING MANAGEMENT CHALLENGES

Compensation is always an issue with both management and employees. How can you have a "fair" compensation system? The following points are at the heart of compensation.

- Understand what the organization wants to accomplish with its pay
- Design a rational compensation system
- Comprehend executive compensation

Total rewards are the monetary and non-monetary rewards provided to employees to attract, motivate, and retain them. Critical to an effective rewards approach is the need to balance the interests and costs of the employers with the needs and expectations of employees. In some industries, such as financial services, health care, education, and hospitality, employee payroll and benefits comprise more than 60% of all operating costs. Although actual costs can be easily calculated, the value derived by employers and employees may prove more difficult to identify.

NATURE OF TOTAL REWARDS AND COMPENSATON

Because so many organizational funds are spent on employees, management should match total rewards systems and practices with what the organization is trying to accomplish. To do so, several decision points exist:

- Legal compliance with all appropriate laws and regulations
- Cost-effectiveness for the organization
- Internal, external, and individual equity for employees
- Performance enhancement for the organization
- Performance recognition and talent management for employees
- Enhanced recruitment, involvement, and retention of employees

Employers must balance their costs at a level that rewards employees sufficiently for their knowledge, skills, abilities, and performance accomplishments. During the past several years, total rewards have been a significant focus in HR, and different frameworks have been developed.

Types of Compensation

Rewards can be either intrinsic or extrinsic. *Intrinsic rewards* may include praise for completing a project or meeting performance objectives. Other psychological and social forms of compensation also reflect intrinsic type of rewards. *Extrinsic rewards* are tangible and take both monetary and nonmonetary forms. One tangible component of a compensation program is *direct compensation*, whereby the employer provides monetary rewards for work done and performance results achieved. *Base pay* and *variable pay* are the most common forms of direct compensation. The most common indirect compensation is employee *benefits*.

Base Pay.   The basic compensation that an employee receives, usually as a wage or a salary, is called **base pay.** Many organizations use two base pay categories, *hourly* and *salaried,* which are identified according to the way pay is distributed and the nature of the jobs. Hourly pay is the most common means and is based on time.

Employees paid hourly receive **wages,** which are payments calculated based on time worked. In contrast, people paid **salaries** receive the same payment each period regardless of the number of hours worked. Being paid a salary has typically carried higher status for employees than has being paid a wage. However, overtime may have to be paid to certain salaried employees as well as most wage earners as defined by federal and state laws.

Variable Pay.   Another type of direct pay is **variable pay,** which is compensation linked directly to individual, team, or organizational performance. The most common types of variable pay for most employees are bonuses and incentive program payments. Executives often receive longer-term rewards such as stock options.

Benefits.   Many organizations provide some rewards in an indirect manner. With indirect compensation, employees receive the tangible value of the rewards without receiving actual cash. A **benefit** is a reward—for instance, health insurance, vacation pay, or a retirement pension—given to an employee or a group of employees for organizational membership, regardless of performance. Often employees do not directly pay for all of the benefits they receive. Benefits are discussed in Chapter 8.

Compensation Philosophies

Two basic compensation philosophies lie on opposite ends of a continuum. At one end of the continuum is the *entitlement* philosophy; at the other end is the *performance* philosophy. Most compensation systems fall somewhere in between these two extremes.

The **entitlement philosophy** assumes that individuals who have worked another year are entitled to pay increases, with little regard for performance differences. Many traditional organizations that give automatic increases to their employees every year are practicing the entitlement philosophy. These automatic increases are often referred to as *cost-of-living raises*, even if they are not tied specifically to economic indicators. Further, most of those employees receive the same or nearly the same percentage increase each year.

A **pay-for-performance philosophy** requires that compensation changes reflect performance differences. Organizations operating under this philosophy do not guarantee additional or increased compensation simply for completing another year of organizational service. Instead, they structure pay and incentives to reflect performance differences among employees. Employees who perform satisfactorily maintain or advance their compensation levels more than marginal performers. The bonuses and incentives are based on individual, group, and/or organizational performance.

The total rewards approach reflects a more performance-oriented philosophy because it tends to place more value on individuals' performance, rather than just paying them based on having a job. When determining compensation, managers may also consider elements such as how much an employee knows or how competent an employee is. Some organizations use both compensation and variable pay programs as part of a total rewards approach for all levels of employees. Widespread use of various incentive plans, team bonuses, organizational gainsharing programs, and other designs links growth in compensation and variable pay to results.

Regularly communicating to employees and managers the compensation philosophy helps to reinforce the organizational commitment to it. A recent study found that communication of profit-sharing information increased knowledge, which influenced commitment and satisfaction. Communication also can enhance understanding and perceptions of pay policies, encouraging greater generalized pay satisfaction and career development.[1] Finally, establishing a dialogue with employees about total rewards enables them to be more involved with the development of pay systems that enhance talent and return on investment. A company's compensation philosophy can be used to develop individual talent in an organization.

HR Metrics and Compensation

Employers spend huge amounts of money for employee compensation. Just like any other area of cost, compensation expenditures should be evaluated to determine their effectiveness. Many measures can be used to do this.[2] Employee turnover/retention is one widely used factor. It assumes that compensation systems affect employees' decisions about staying with or leaving the organization. Other more specific measures are used as well, such as the ones shown in Figure 7-1.

The numbers for calculating appropriate measures are readily available to most HR professionals and chief financial officers, but such calculations are not made in many firms. Often the importance of using these numbers is not a priority for managers or CFOs. Ideally, compensation metrics should be computed each year, and then compared with metrics from past years to show how the rate of compensation changes compares with the rate of changes in the organization overall (revenues, expenses, etc.).

FIGURE 7-1 HR Metrics for Compensation

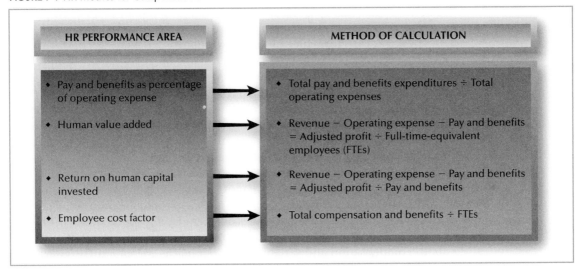

COMPENSATION SYSTEM DESIGN ISSUES

Depending on the compensation philosophies, strategies, and approaches identified for an organization, a number of decisions are made that affect the design of the compensation system. Some important ones are highlighted next.

Compensation Fairness and Equity

Most people in organizations work to gain money for their efforts. Whether employees receive base pay or variable pay, the extent to which they perceive their compensation to be fair often affects their performance, how they view their jobs, and their employers. This factor may lead to lower or higher turnover rates. Pay satisfaction also has been found to be linked to organizational-level performance outcomes.[3]

Equity.　The perceived fairness of what a person does (inputs) and what the person receives (outcomes) is called **equity**. Individuals judge equity in compensation by comparing their input (effort and performance) against the effort and performance of others and against the outcomes (the rewards received). These comparisons are personal and are based on individual perceptions, not just facts.

External Equity.　If an employer does not provide pay that employees view as equitable compared to other employees performing similar jobs in other organizations, that employer is likely to experience higher turnover. Another drawback is greater difficulty in recruiting qualified and high-demand individuals. By not being competitive, the employer is more likely to attract and retain individuals with less knowledge and fewer skills and abilities, resulting in lower overall organizational performance. Organizations track external equity by using pay surveys, which are discussed later in this chapter, and by looking at the compensation policies of competing employers.

Internal Equity in Compensation.   Internal equity means that employees receive compensation in relation to the knowledge, skills, and abilities (KSAs) they use in their jobs, as well as their responsibilities and accomplishments. Two key issues—procedural justice and distributive justice—relate to internal equity.

Procedural justice is the perceived fairness of the process and procedures used to make decisions about employees, including their pay. As it applies to compensation, the entire process of determining base pay for jobs, allocating pay increases, and measuring performance must be perceived as fair.

A related issue that must be considered is **distributive justice**, which is the perceived fairness in the distribution of outcomes. As one example, if a hardworking employee whose performance is outstanding receives the same across-the-board raise as an employee with attendance problems and mediocre performance, then inequity may be perceived.

To address concerns about both types of justice, some organizations establish compensation appeals procedures. Typically, employees are encouraged to contact the HR department after discussing their concerns with their immediate supervisors and managers.

Pay Secrecy.   Another equity issue concerns the degree of secrecy that organizations have regarding their pay systems. Pay information that may be kept secret in "closed" systems includes how much others make, what raises others have received, and even what pay grades and ranges exist in the organization.

Statistical Analysis.   The management of different fairness and equity issues requires managers to understand the various statistical methodologies that can be used to evaluate current compensation levels. For instance, HR professionals need to check how corporate pay programs compare to the compensation being offered by competing firms so that compensation can be adjusted to reflect the company's pay philosophy. HR professionals also must determine the degree to which compensation is distributed fairly within the organization based on such factors as job level, experience, training, and other human capital factors.

Market Competitiveness and Compensation

The market competitiveness of compensation has a significant impact on how equitably employees view compensation. Providing competitive compensation to employees, whether globally, domestically, or locally, is a concern for all employers. Some organizations establish specific policies about where they wish to be positioned in the labor market. These policies use a *quartile strategy*, as illustrated in Figure 7-2.

"Meet the Market" Strategy.   Most employers choose to position themselves in the *second quartile* (median), in the middle of the market, as identified by pay data from surveys of other employers' compensation plans. Choosing this level attempts to balance employer cost pressures and the need to attract

FIGURE 7-2 Compensation Quartile Strategies

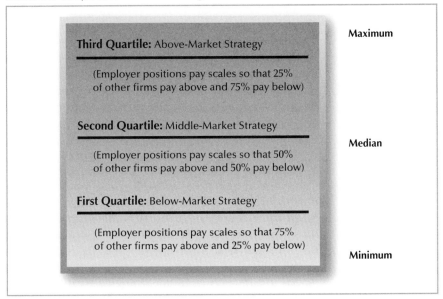

and retain employees, by providing mid-level compensation scales that "meet the market" for the employer's jobs.

"Lag the Market" Strategy.   An employer using a *first-quartile* strategy may choose to "lag the market" by paying below market levels, for several reasons. If the employer is experiencing a shortage of funds, it may be unable to pay more. Also, when an abundance of workers is available, particularly those with lower skills, a below-market approach can be used to attract sufficient workers at a lesser cost. Some employers hire illegal immigrants at below-market rates because of the large numbers of those individuals who want to work in the United States. The downside of this strategy is that it increases the likelihood of higher worker turnover. If the labor market supply tightens, then attracting and retaining workers becomes more difficult.

"Lead the Market" Strategy.   A *third-quartile* strategy uses an aggressive approach to "lead the market." This strategy generally enables a company to attract and retain sufficient workers with the required capabilities and to be more selective when hiring. Because it is a higher-cost approach, organizations often look for ways to increase the productivity of employees receiving above-market wages.

Selecting a Quartile.   The pay levels and pay structures used can affect organizational performance. Individual employee pay levels will vary around the quartile level, depending on experience, performance, and other individual factors. Deciding in which quartile to position pay structures is a function of a number of considerations. The financial resources available, competitive pressures, and the market availability of employees with different capabilities are external factors. For instance, some employers with extensive benefits programs or broad-based incentive programs may choose a first-quartile strategy so that their overall compensation costs and levels are not excessive.

Competency-Based Pay

The design of most compensation programs rewards employees for carrying out their tasks, duties, and responsibilities. The job requirements determine which employees have higher base rates. Employees receive more for doing jobs that require a greater variety of tasks, more knowledge and skills, greater physical effort, or more demanding working conditions. However, the design of some compensation programs emphasizes competencies rather than the tasks performed.

Competency-based pay rewards individuals for the capabilities they demonstrate and acquire. In knowledge-based pay (KBP) or skill-based pay (SBP) systems, employees start at a base level of pay and receive increases as they learn to do other jobs or gain additional skills and knowledge and thus become more valuable to the employer. For example, a printing firm operates two-color, four-color, and six-color presses. The more colors, the more skills required of the press operators. Under a KBP or SBP system, press operators increase their pay as they learn how to operate the more complex presses, even though sometimes they may be running only two-color jobs. A recent study determined that receiving SBP is related to learning and skill enhancement, which demonstrates that such compensation systems can be effective.[4]

When an organization moves to a competency-based system, considerable time must be spent identifying the required competencies for various jobs. Reliance on items such as college diplomas and degrees may need to change such that more emphasis is placed on demonstrated knowledge and competencies rather than degrees. *Progression* of employees must be possible, and employees must be paid appropriately for all their competencies. Any *limitations* on the numbers of people who can acquire more competencies should be clearly identified. *Training* in the appropriate competencies is particularly important. Also, a competency-based system needs to acknowledge or certify employees as they acquire certain competencies, and then to verify the maintenance of those competencies. In summary, use of a competency-based system requires significant investment of management time and commitment.

LEGAL CONSTRAINTS ON PAY SYSTEMS

Pay systems must comply with many government constraints. The important areas addressed by the laws include minimum-wage standards and hours of work. The following discussion examines the laws and regulations affecting base compensation.

Fair Labor Standards Act (FLSA)

The major federal law affecting compensation is the Fair Labor Standards Act (FLSA), which was originally passed in 1938. Compliance with FLSA provisions is enforced by the Wage and Hour Division of the U.S. Department of Labor. To meet FLSA requirements, employers must keep accurate time records and maintain those records for 3 years. Penalties for wage and hour violations often include awards of up to 2 years of back pay for affected current and former employees.

The provisions of both the original act and subsequent revisions focus on the following major areas:

- Establish a minimum wage.
- Discourage oppressive use of child labor.
- Encourage limits on the number of hours employees work per week, through overtime provisions (exempt and nonexempt statuses).

Minimum Wage. The FLSA sets a minimum wage to be paid to the broad spectrum of covered employees. The actual minimum wage can be changed only by congressional action. A lower minimum wage is set for "tipped" employees, such as restaurant servers, but their compensation must equal or exceed the minimum wage when average tips are included. Minimum-wage levels have sparked significant political discussions and legislative maneuvering at both the federal and state levels for the past decade. Consequently, a three-stage increase in the federal minimum wage occurred beginning in 2007 as part of the Fair Minimum Wage Act of 2007, which recently was set with the current minimum wage of $7.25 an hour. Note that if a state's minimum wage is higher, employers must meet the state level rather than the federal level.

Discussion also surrounds the payment of a "living wage" versus the minimum wage. A **living wage** involves earnings that are supposed to meet the basic needs of an individual working for an organization, including food, clothing, and shelter. In the United States, many cities have passed local living-wage legislation.

Child Labor Provisions. The child labor provisions of the FLSA set the minimum age for employment with unlimited hours at 16 years. For hazardous occupations, the minimum is 18 years of age. Individuals 14 to 15 years old may work outside school hours with certain limitations. Many employers require age certificates for employees because the FLSA makes the employer responsible for determining an individual's age. A representative of a state labor department, a state education department, or a local school district generally issues such certificates.

Exempt and Nonexempt Statuses. Under the FLSA, employees are classified as exempt or nonexempt. **Exempt employees** hold positions for which employers are not required to pay overtime. **Nonexempt employees** must be paid overtime. The current FLSA regulations used to identify whether or not a job qualifies for exempt status classifies exempt jobs into five categories:

- Executive
- Administrative
- Professional (learned or creative)
- Computer employees
- Outside sales

FIGURE 7-3 Determining Exempt Status under the FLSA

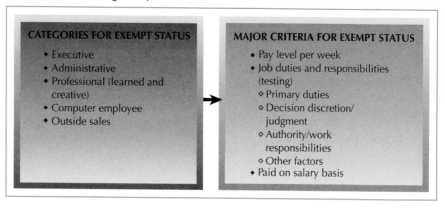

As Figure 7-3 indicates, the regulations identify several factors to be considered in exempt status: salaried pay levels per week, duties and responsibilities, and other criteria that must exist for jobs to be categorized as exempt. To review the details for each exemption, go to the U.S. Department of Labor's website at www.dol.gov.

The FLSA does not require employers to pay overtime for *salaried exempt* jobs, although some organizations have implemented policies to pay a straight rate for extensive hours of overtime. For instance, some electric utilities pay first-line supervisors extra using a special rate for hours worked over 50 a week during storm emergencies. A number of salaried exempt professionals in various IT jobs also receive additional compensation for working extensively more than 40 hours per week.

Overtime.   The FLSA establishes overtime pay requirements. Its provisions set overtime pay at one and one-half times the regular pay rate for all hours over 40 a week, except for employees who are not covered by the FLSA. Overtime provisions do not apply to farm workers, who also have a lower minimum-wage schedule.

The workweek is defined as a consecutive period of 168 hours (24 hours × 7 days) and does not have to be a calendar week. If they wish to do so, hospitals and nursing homes are allowed to use a 14-day period instead of a 7-day week, as long as overtime is paid for hours worked beyond 8 in a day or 80 in a 14-day period. No daily number of hours requiring overtime is set, except for special provisions relating to hospitals and other specially designated organizations. Thus, if a manufacturing firm operates on a 4-day/10-hour schedule, no overtime pay is required by the act.

The most difficult part is distinguishing who is and is not exempt. Some recent costly settlements have prompted more white-collar workers to sue for overtime pay. Retail managers, reporters, sales reps, personal bankers, engineers, computer programmers, and claims adjusters have won in some cases, as being nonexempt workers.

Common Overtime Issues. For individuals who are nonexempt, employers must consider a number of issues. These include the following:

- *Compensatory time off:* "Comp" hours are given to public-sector nonexempt employees in lieu of payment for extra time worked at the rate of one and one-half times the number of hours over 40 that are worked in a week. Comp time is currently not available in the private sector and cannot be legally offered to employees working for private for-profit organizations.
- *Incentives for nonexempt employees:* Employers must add the amount of direct work-related incentives to a person's base pay. Then overtime pay should be calculated as one and one-half times the higher (adjusted) rate of pay.
- *Training time:* Time spent in training must be counted as time worked by nonexempt employees unless it is outside regular work hours, not directly job-related, or falls under various other aspects. College degree programs may not be affected by these provisions.
- *Travel time:* Travel time must be counted as work time if it occurs during normal work hours, even on nonworking days, unless the nonexempt person is a passenger in a car, bus, train, airplane, or other similar mode of transportation. The complex clarifications regarding travel regulations affecting overtime should be reviewed by HR specialists to ensure compliance.

Independent Contractor Regulations

The growing use of contingent workers by many organizations has focused attention on another group of legal regulations—those identifying the criteria that independent contractors must meet. For an employer, classifying someone as an independent contractor rather than an employee offers a major advantage. The employer does not have to pay Social Security, unemployment, or workers' compensation costs. These additional payroll levies may add 10% or more to the costs of hiring the individual as an employee. Most federal and state entities rely on the criteria for independent contractor status identified by the Internal Revenue Service (IRS). However, the misclassification of employees as independent contractors is becoming an increasingly significant legal concern for organizations.[5]

Behavioral Control. Some key differences between an employee and an independent contractor have been identified by the IRS. The first set of factors consists of behavioral control factors, which indicate the extent to which an employer can control what a worker does and how a worker performs. One key area includes *business instructions given to the worker,* such as where and when to work, in what sequences, and with what tools and equipment, as well as how to purchase supplies and services. The other area is *business training given to the worker,* such as when someone must be trained to perform in a specific manner, rather than accomplishing results.

Financial Control. This set of factors focuses on the extent to which an employer can control the business facets of a worker's job. Considerations include how many *unreimbursed business expenses* a worker has and what investments a worker makes independently to do the job. Other financial factors include whether a worker *provides services to other firms*, how the *business pays the worker*, and if the worker can make a *profit or loss*.

Relationship-Type Factors. A number of other items can help clarify whether a relationship is truly independent or not, such as having *written contracts* and the *extent of services provided*. Also, if the employer *provides benefits*, such as insurance or pensions, it is more likely that the person is an employee, and not an independent contractor. For additional details, go to www.irs.gov.

Acts Affecting Government Contractors

Several compensation-related acts apply to firms having contracts with the U.S. government. The Davis-Bacon Act of 1931 affects compensation paid by firms engaged in federal construction projects valued at over $2,000. It deals only with federal construction projects and requires that the "prevailing" wage be paid on all such projects. The *prevailing wage* is determined by a formula that considers the rate paid for a job by a majority of the employers in the appropriate geographic area.

Two other acts require firms with federal supply or service contracts exceeding $10,000 to pay a prevailing wage. Both the Walsh-Healy Public Contracts Act and the McNamara-O'Hara Service Contract Act apply only to those who are working directly on a federal government contract or who substantially affect its performance.

Lilly Ledbetter Fair Pay Act

As a result of limited time allowed under law for claiming pay discrimination based on sex, religion, color, disability, and other protected characteristics, the Lilly Ledbetter Fair Pay Act was signed by President Obama in January 2009. Before the law was passed, individuals had to submit complaints of pay discrimination to the EEOC within a 180- or 300-day window, which was based on the state where the person was employed. This new legislation effectively negates any statute of limitations for filing a complaint, so claims of pay discrimination can now be made at any time after the alleged misconduct.[6]

DEVELOPMENT OF A BASE PAY SYSTEM

A base compensation system is developed using current job descriptions and job specifications. These information sources are used when *valuing jobs* and analyzing *pay surveys*—activities that are designed to ensure that the pay system is both internally equitable and externally competitive. The data compiled in these two activities are used to design *pay structures*, including *pay grades* and minimum-to-maximum *pay ranges*. After pay structures are established, individual jobs must be placed in the appropriate pay grades and employees' pay must be adjusted according to length of service and performance. Finally, the pay system must be monitored and updated.

Employers want their employees to perceive their pay levels as appropriate in relation to pay for jobs performed by others inside the organization. Frequently, employees and managers make comments such as "This job is more important than that job in another department, so why are the two jobs paid about the same?" Two general approaches for valuing jobs are available: job evaluation and market pricing. Both approaches are used to determine the values of jobs in relation to other jobs in an organization, and they are discussed next.

Valuing Jobs with Job Evaluation Methods

Job evaluation is a formal, systematic means to identify the relative worth of jobs within an organization. Several job evaluation methods are available for use by employers of different sizes.

Point Method.   The most widely used job evaluation method, the point method, looks at compensable factors in a group of similar jobs and places weights, or *points*, on them. A **compensable factor** identifies a job value commonly present throughout a group of jobs. Compensable factors are derived from job analysis and reflect the nature of different types of work performed in the organization.

The point method is the most popular because it is relatively simple to use and it considers the components of a job rather than the total job. However, point systems have been criticized for reinforcing traditional organizational structures and job rigidity. Although not perfect, the point method of job evaluation is generally better than the ranking and classification methods because it quantifies job elements.

Legal Issues and Job Evaluation.   Because job evaluation affects the employment relationship, specifically the pay of individuals, some legal issues are of concern. Critics have charged that traditional job evaluation programs place less weight on knowledge, skills, and working conditions for many female-dominated jobs in office and clerical areas than on the same factors for male-dominated jobs in craft and manufacturing areas. Employers counter that because they base their pay rates heavily on external equity comparisons in the labor market, they are simply reflecting rates the "market economy" sets for jobs and workers, rather than discriminating on the basis of gender.

Valuing Jobs Using Market Pricing

Some employers have scaled back their use of "internal valuation" through traditional job evaluation methods. They have instead switched to **market pricing**, which uses market pay data to identify the relative value of jobs based on what other employers pay for similar jobs. Jobs are arranged in groups tied directly to similar survey data amounts.

Key to market pricing is identifying relevant market pay data for jobs that are good "matches" with the employer's jobs, geographic considerations, and company strategies and philosophies about desired market competitiveness levels. That is why some firms have used market pricing as part of strategic decisions in order to ensure market competitiveness of their compensation levels and practices.

Advantages of Market Pricing.   The primary advantage cited for the use of market pricing is that it closely ties organizational pay levels to what is actually occurring in the market, without being distorted by "internal" job evaluation. An additional advantage of market pricing is that it allows an employer to communicate to employees that the compensation system is truly "market linked," rather than sometimes being distorted by internal issues. Employees often see a compensation system that was developed using market pricing as having "face validity" and as being more objective than a compensation system that was developed using the traditional job evaluation methods.

Disadvantages of Market Pricing.   The foremost disadvantage of market pricing is that for numerous jobs, pay survey data are limited or may not be gathered in methodologically sound ways. A closely related problem is that the responsibilities of a specific job in a company may be somewhat different from those of the "matching" job identified in the survey.[7]

Finally, tying pay levels to market data can lead to wide fluctuations based on market conditions. For evidence of this, one has only to look back at the extremes of the IT job market during the past decade, when pay levels varied significantly. For these and other types of jobs, the debate over the use of job evaluation versus market pricing is likely to continue because both approaches have pluses and minuses associated with them.

Pay Surveys

A **pay survey** is a collection of data on compensation rates for workers performing similar jobs in other organizations. Both job evaluation and market pricing are tied to surveys of the pay that other organizations provide for similar jobs.

Because jobs may vary widely in an organization, it is particularly important to identify **benchmark jobs**—ones that are found in many other organizations. Often these jobs are performed by individuals who have similar duties that require similar KSAs. For example, benchmark jobs commonly used in clerical/office situations are accounts payable processor, customer service representative, and receptionist. Benchmark jobs are used because they provide "anchors" against which individual jobs can be compared. An employer may obtain surveys conducted by other organizations, access Internet data, or conduct its own survey. Many different surveys are available from a variety of sources.

Internet-Based Pay Surveys.   HR professionals can access a wide range of pay survey data online. In many cases, pay survey questionnaires are distributed electronically rather than as printed copies, and HR staff members complete the questionnaires electronically. It is anticipated that during the next 5 years, most pay surveys will be conducted using electronic, Web-based technology.

The Internet provides a large number of pay survey sources and data. However, use of these sources requires caution because their accuracy and completeness may not be verifiable or may not be applicable to individual firms and employees.

Using Pay Surveys. The proper use of pay surveys requires evaluating a number of factors to determine if the data are relevant and valid. The following questions should be answered for each survey:

- *Participants:* Does the survey cover a realistic sample of the employers with whom the organization competes for employees?
- *Broad-based:* Does the survey include data from employers of different sizes, industries, and locales?
- *Timeliness:* How current are the data (determined by the date the survey was conducted)?
- *Methodology:* How established is the survey, and how qualified are those who conducted it?
- *Job matches:* Does the survey contain job summaries so that appropriate matches to job descriptions can be made?

PAY STRUCTURES

Once job valuations and pay survey data are gathered, pay structures can be developed. Data from the valuation of jobs and the pay surveys may lead to the establishment of several different pay structures for different job families, rather than just one structure for all jobs. A **job family** is a group of jobs having common organizational characteristics. Organizations can have a number of different job families. Examples of some common pay structures based on different job families include: (1) hourly and salaried; (2) office, plant, technical, professional, and managerial; and (3) clerical, IT, professional, supervisory, management, and executive. The nature, culture, and structure of the organization are considerations for determining how many and which pay structures to have.

Pay Grades

In the process of establishing a pay structure, organizations use **pay grades** to group individual jobs having approximately the same job worth. Although no set rules govern the establishment of pay grades, some overall suggestions can be useful. Generally, 11 to 17 grades are used in small and medium-sized companies, such as companies with fewer than 500 to 1,000 employees. Two methods are commonly used to establish pay grades: job evaluation data and use of job market banding.

Setting Pay Grades Using Job Evaluation Points. One approach to determining pay grades uses job evaluation points or other data generated from the traditional job evaluation methods discussed earlier in the chapter. This process ties pay survey information to job evaluation data by plotting a **market line** that shows the relationship between job value as determined by job evaluation points and job value as determined by pay survey rates.

Setting Pay Grades Using Market Banding. Closely linked to the use of market pricing to value jobs, **market banding** groups jobs into pay grades based on similar market survey amounts. The midpoint of the survey average is used to develop pay range minimums and maximums, the methods of which are discussed later in this chapter.

Pay Ranges

Once pay grades are determined, the pay range for each pay grade must be established. Using the market line as a starting point, the employer can determine minimum and maximum pay levels for each pay grade by making the market line the midpoint line of the new pay structure (see Figure 7-4). For example, in a particular pay grade, the maximum value may be 20% above the midpoint located on the market line, and the minimum value may be 20% below it. Once pay grades and ranges have been computed, then the current pay of employees must be compared with the draft ranges. A number of employers are reducing the number of pay grades and expanding pay ranges by broadbanding.

Broadbanding. The practice of using fewer pay grades with much broader ranges than in traditional compensation systems is called **broadbanding.** Combining many grades into these broadbands is designed to encourage horizontal movement and therefore more skill acquisition. About one-quarter of all employers in one survey are using broadbanding.[8] The main advantage of broadbanding is that it is more consistent with the flattening of organizational levels and the growing use of jobs that are multidimensional. The primary reasons for using broadbanding are: (1) to create more flexible organizations, (2) to encourage competency development, and (3) to emphasize career development.

Individual Pay

Once managers have determined pay ranges, they can set the pay for specific individuals. Setting a range for each pay grade gives flexibility by allowing individuals to progress within a grade instead of having to move to a new grade each time they receive a raise. A pay range also allows managers to reward the better-performing employees while maintaining the integrity of the pay system. Regardless of how well a pay structure is constructed, there usually are a few individuals whose pay is lower than the minimum or higher than the maximum due to past pay practices and different levels of experience and performance. Two types of such employees are discussed next.

FIGURE 7-4 Example of Pay Grades and Pay Ranges

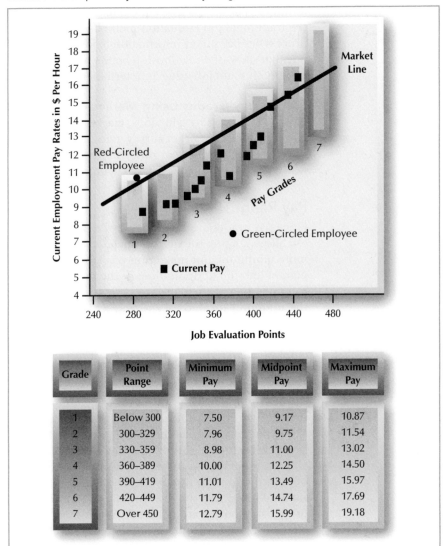

Grade	Point Range	Minimum Pay	Midpoint Pay	Maximum Pay
1	Below 300	7.50	9.17	10.87
2	300–329	7.96	9.75	11.54
3	330–359	8.98	11.00	13.02
4	360–389	10.00	12.25	14.50
5	390–419	11.01	13.49	15.97
6	420–449	11.79	14.74	17.69
7	Over 450	12.79	15.99	19.18

Red-Circled Employees. A **red-circled employee** is an incumbent who is paid above the range set for the job. For example, assume that an employee's current pay is $11.92 an hour, but the pay range for that person's pay grade is $7.96 to $11.54 an hour. The person would be red-circled. Management would try over a year or so to bring the employee's rate into grade.

Several approaches can be used to bring a red-circled person's pay into line. Although the fastest way would be to cut the employee's pay, that approach is not recommended and is seldom used. Instead, the employee's pay may be frozen until the pay range can be adjusted upward to get the employee's pay rate back into the grade. Another approach is to give the employee a small lump-sum payment but not adjust the pay rate when others are given raises.

Green-Circled Employees.   An individual whose pay is below the range set for a job is a **green-circled employee**. Promotion is a major contributor to this situation. Generally, it is recommended that the green-circled individual receive fairly rapid pay increases to reach the pay grade minimum. More frequent increases can be used if the minimum is a large amount above the incumbent's current pay.

Pay Compression.   One major problem many employers face is **pay compression,** which occurs when the pay differences among individuals with different levels of experience and performance become small. Pay compression occurs for a number of reasons, but the major one involves situations in which labor market pay levels increase more rapidly than current employees' pay adjustments.

In response to shortages of particular job skills in a highly competitive labor market, managers may occasionally have to pay higher amounts to hire people with those scarce skills. For example, suppose the job of specialized information systems analyst is identified as a $48,000 to $68,000 salary range in one company, but qualified individuals are in short supply and other employers are paying $70,000. To fill the job, the firm likely will have to pay the higher rate. Suppose also that several good analysts who have been with the firm for several years started at $55,000 and have received 4% increases each year. These current employees may still be making less than the $70,000 paid to attract and retain new analysts with less experience from outside. Making certain that pay rates for company jobs are market-based and pay raises are based on performance-based reviews are ways to mitigate salary compression.[9]

DETERMINING PAY INCREASES

Decisions about pay increases are often critical ones in the relationships between employees, their managers, and the organization. Individuals express expectations about their pay and about how much of an increase is "fair," especially in comparison with the increases received by other employees. This is why HR professionals must be actively involved in the communication of pay increases to help manage perceptions of any changes made to employees' compensation.

Pay increases can be determined in several ways: performance, seniority, cost-of-living adjustments, across-the-board increases, and lump-sum increases. These methods can be used separately or in combination.

Performance-Based Increases

As mentioned earlier, some employers have shifted to more pay-for-performance philosophies and strategies. Consequently, they have adopted the following means to provide employees with performance-based increases.

Targeting High Performers. This approach focuses on providing the top-performing employees with significantly higher pay raises. Some organizations target the top 10% of employees for significantly greater increases while providing more standard increases to the remaining satisfactory performers.

The primary reason for having such significant differentials focuses on rewarding and retaining the critical high-performing individuals.[10] Key to rewarding exceptional performers is identifying how much their accomplishments have been above the normal work expectations. The more "standard" increases for the average performers are usually aligned with labor market pay adjustments, so that those individuals are kept competitive. The lower performers are given less because of their performance issues, which "encourages" them to leave their organizations.

Pay Adjustment Matrix. A system for integrating appraisal ratings and pay changes must be developed and applied equally. Often, this integration is done through the development of a *pay adjustment matrix*, or *salary guide chart*. Use of pay adjustment matrices bases adjustments in part on a person's **compa-ratio**, which is the pay level divided by the midpoint of the pay range. To illustrate, the following is an example of the compa-ratio for an employee called *J*:

$$\text{Employee } J = \frac{\$13.35 \text{ (current pay)}}{\$15.00 \text{ (midpoint)}} \times 100 = 89 \text{ (Compa-ratio)}$$

Salary guide charts reflect a person's upward movement in an organization. That movement often depends on the person's performance, as rated in an appraisal, and on the person's position in the pay range, which has some relation to experience as well. A person's placement on the chart determines what pay raise the person should receive. According to the chart shown in Figure 7-5, if employee *J* is rated as exceeding expectations (3) with a compa-ratio of 89, that person is eligible for a raise of 7% to 9%.

Two interesting elements of the sample matrix illustrate the emphasis on paying for performance. First, individuals whose performance is below expectations receive small to no raises. This approach sends a strong signal that poor performers will not continue to receive increases just by completing another year of service. Second, as employees move up the pay range, they must exhibit higher performance to obtain the same percentage raise as those lower in the range performing at the "meets performance expectations" level (see Figure 7-5). This approach is taken because the firm is paying above the market midpoint but receiving only satisfactory performance rather than above-market performance. Charts can be constructed to reflect the specific pay-for-performance policies and philosophy in an organization.

Standardized Pay Adjustments

Several different methods are used to provide standardized pay increases to employees. The most common ones are discussed next.

FIGURE 7-5 Pay Adjustment Matrix

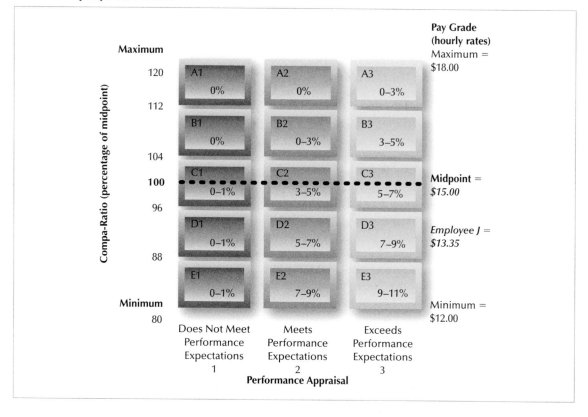

Seniority. The time spent in an organization or on a particular job, called **seniority,** can be used as the basis for pay increases. Many employers have policies that require a person to be employed for a certain length of time before being eligible for pay increases. Pay adjustments based on seniority often are set as automatic steps once a person has been employed the required length of time, although performance must be at least satisfactory in many nonunion systems.

Cost-of-Living Adjustments. A common pay-raise practice is the use of a *cost-of-living adjustment (COLA)*. Often, these adjustments are tied to changes in the Consumer Price Index (CPI) or some other general economic measure. However, numerous studies have revealed that the CPI overstates the actual cost of living, and, as stated previously, COLA increases do little to recognize employees for their relative contributions to the organization.

Across-the-Board Increases. Unfortunately, some employers give across-the-board raises and call them *merit raises,* which they are not. Usually the percentage raise is based on standard market percentage changes or financial budgeting determinations not specifically linked to the COLA. If all employees get the same percentage pay increase, it is legitimately viewed as having little to do with merit or good performance. For this reason, employers should reserve the term *merit* for any amount above the standard raise, and they should state clearly which amount is for performance and which amount is the "automatic" portion.

Lump-Sum Increases.   Most employees who receive pay increases, either for merit or for seniority, receive an increase in the amount of their regular monthly or weekly paycheck. For example, an employee who makes $12.00 an hour and then receives a 3% increase will move to $12.36 an hour.

In contrast, a **lump-sum increase (LSI)** is a one-time payment of all or part of a yearly pay increase. The pure LSI approach does not increase the base pay. Therefore, in the example of a person making $12.00 an hour, if an LSI of 3% is granted, the person receives a lump sum of $748.80 ($0.36 an hour $\times$ 2,080 working hours in the year). However, the base rate remains at $12.00 an hour, which slows down the progression of the base wages.

An LSI plan offers advantages and disadvantages. The major advantage of an LSI plan is that it heightens employees' awareness of what their performance levels "merited." Another advantage is that the firm can use LSIs to slow down the increase of base pay and thus reduce or avoid the compounding effect on succeeding raises. One disadvantage of LSI plans is that workers who take a lump-sum payment may become discouraged because their base pay has not changed. Unions generally resist LSI programs because of their impact on pensions and benefits, unless the total amount used in those computations includes the LSI.

EXECUTIVE COMPENSATION

Most organizations administer compensation for executives somewhat differently than compensation for other employees. An executive typically is someone in the top two levels of an organization, such as chief executive officer (CEO), president, senior vice president, chief operating officer, executive vice president, chief financial officer, or senior HR Executive. At the heart of most executive compensation plans is the idea that executives should be rewarded if the organization grows in profitability and value over a period of years.

Elements of Executive Compensation

Because many executives are in high tax brackets, their compensation often is provided in ways that offer significant tax savings, which means that their total compensation packages may be more significant than just their base pay. Thus, executives often are interested in current compensation and the mix of items in the total package.

Executive Salaries and Benefits.   Salaries of executives vary by the type of job, size of organization, the industry, and other factors. In some organizations, particularly nonprofits, salaries often make up 90% or more of total compensation. In contrast, in large corporations, salaries may constitute less than half of the total package. Survey data on executive salaries are often reviewed by boards of directors to ensure that their organizations are competitive.

Many executives are covered by *regular benefits plans* that are also available to nonexecutive employees, including traditional retirement, health insurance, and vacation plans. In addition, executives may receive *supplemental benefits* that other employees do not receive such as corporate-owned life insurance, company-paid financial planning, and estate-planning. *Deferred compensation* is another way of helping executives with tax liabilities caused by incentive compensation plans.

Executive Perquisites (Perks). In addition to the regular benefits received by all employees, perquisites often are received by executives. **Perquisites (Perks)** are special benefits—usually noncash items. Perks also can offer substantial tax savings because some of them are not taxed as income. Some commonly used executive perks are company cars, health club and country club memberships, first-class air travel, use of private jets, stress counseling, and chauffeur services.

Annual and Long-Term Executive Incentives and Bonuses. Annual incentives and bonuses for senior managers and executives can be determined in several ways. One way is to use a discretionary system whereby the CEO and the board of directors decide bonuses; the absence of formal, measurable targets detracts significantly from this approach. Another way is to tie bonuses to specific measures, such as return on investment, earnings per share, and net profits before taxes.

Executive performance-based incentives tie executive compensation to the long-term growth and success of the organization. However, whether these incentives really emphasize the long term or merely represent a series of short-term rewards is controversial. Short-term rewards based on quarterly or annual performance may not result in the kind of long-run-oriented decisions necessary for the company to perform well over many years. As would be expected, the total amount of pay-for-performance incentives varies by management level, with CEOs receiving significantly more than subsidiary or other senior managers.

A *stock option* gives individuals the right to buy stock in a company, usually at an advantageous price. Various types of stock option plans are the most widely used executive incentive. Despite the prevalence of such plans, research has found little relationship between providing CEOs with stock options and subsequent firm performance. The two items may not be closely linked in some firms.

"Reasonableness" of Executive Compensation

The notion of providing monetary incentives that are tied to improved performance results makes sense to most people. However, in the United States, there is an ongoing debate about whether executive compensation, especially that of CEOs, is truly linked to performance. Given the astronomical amounts of some executive compensation packages, this concern is justified.

The reasonableness of executive compensation is often justified by comparison to compensation market surveys, but these surveys usually provide a range of compensation data that requires interpretation. Some useful questions that have been suggested for determining whether executive pay is "reasonable" include the following:

- Would another company hire this person as an executive?
- How does the executive's compensation compare with that for executives in similar companies in the industry?
- Is the executive's pay consistent with pay for other employees within the company?
- What would an investor pay for the level of performance of the executive?

Link between Executive Compensation and Corporate Performance. Of all the executive compensation issues that have been raised, the one that is discussed most frequently is whether executive compensation levels, especially for CEOs, are sufficiently linked to organizational performance. Board members of some organizations have viewed CEO compensation as not being as closely linked to performance as needed, resulting in CEO total compensation being seen as too high.[11]

The most important reason for giving pay as incentives is that it is thought to be effective in motivating employees and increasing corporate performance and stock values. Another common reason for using variable compensation is related to the ability to attract and keep employees. These reasons apply to executives as well as to other employees. But in order for compensation based on these reasons to be effective, executive compensation packages must be linked to performance.

One key aspect in evaluating this topic is the performance measures used. In many settings, financial measures such as return on equity, return to shareholders, earnings per share, and net income before taxes are used to measure performance. However, a number of firms also incorporate nonfinancial organizational measures of performance when determining executive bonuses and incentives. Customer satisfaction, employee satisfaction, market share, productivity, and quality are other areas measured for executive performance rewards.

Measurement of executive performance varies from one employer to another. Some executive compensation packages use a short-term focus of one year, which may lead to large rewards for executive performance in a given year even though corporate performance over a multiyear period is mediocre, especially if the yearly measures are not carefully chosen.

A number of other executive compensation issues and concerns exist. Figure 7-6 highlights some of the criticisms and counterarguments in regard to executive compensation.

FIGURE 7-6 Common Executive Compensation Criticisms

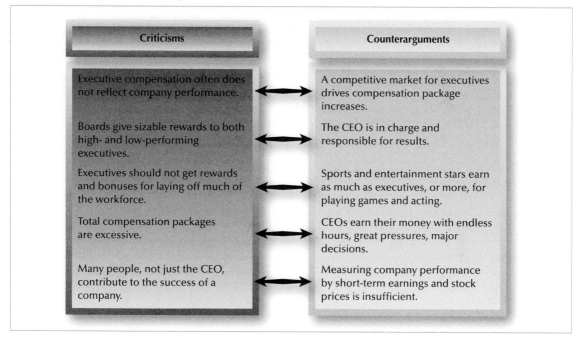

Executive Compensation and Boards of Directors. In most organizations, the board of directors is the major policy-setting entity and must approve executive compensation packages. Corporate directors receive compensation for board and committee meetings and other activities.[12] The **compensation committee** usually is a subgroup of the board of directors that is composed of directors who are not officers of the firm. A compensation committee generally makes recommendations to the board of directors on overall pay policies, salaries for top officers, supplemental compensation such as stock options and bonuses, and additional perquisites for executives.

One major concern voiced by many critics is that the base pay and bonuses of CEOs are often set by the members of board compensation committees, many of whom are CEOs or executives of other companies with similar compensation packages. Also, the compensation advisors and consultants to the CEOs often collect large fees, and critics charge that those fees distort the objectivity of the advice given.

To counter criticism, some corporations have changed the composition of the compensation committees by taking actions such as prohibiting "insider" company officers from serving on them. Also, some firms have empowered the compensation committees to hire and pay compensation consultants without involving executive management. Finally, better disclosure can provide the board with a fuller picture of a chief's entire compensation package.

NOTES

1. "Pay Communication: A Reality Check," *Workspan*, October 2008, 52–59; Terry Satterfield, "Pay Satisfaction: A Practical Approach to a Challenging Issue," *Workspan*, August 2008, 47–50.

2. For examples, see Dow Scott, Dennis Morajda, and Thomas D. McMillien, "Evaluating Pay Program Effectiveness," *WorldatWork Journal*, Second Quarter 2006, 50–59.

3. S. C. Currell, et al., "Pay Satisfaction and Organizational Outcomes," *Personnel Psychology*, 58 (2005), 613–640.

4. Erich C. Dierdorff and Eric A. Surface, "If You Pay for Skills, Will They Learn? Skill Change and Maintenance Under a Skill-Based Pay System," *Journal of Management*, 34 (2008), 721–743.

5. Thomas R. Bundy, "Worker Misclassification: The Next Big Legal Concern?" *Employee Relations Law Journal*, 33 (2007), 18–26.

6. Bill Leonard, "President Signs Wage Bias Law," *HR Magazine*, March 2009, 13; Towers Perrin, "New Law Makes Companies More Vulnerable to Complaints of Pay Discrimination," *www.towersperrin.com*.

7. Charles H. Fay and Madhura Tare, "Market Pricing Concerns," *WorldatWork Journal*, Second Quarter 2007, 61–69.

8. Mercer Human Resource Consulting, *2006 Compensation Planning Survey* (New York: Mercer Corporation, 2006).

9. Linda Ulrich, "Money Talks: Identifying, Preventing, and Alleviating Systematic Salary Compression Issues," *Workspan*, November 2008, 42–46.

10. Jessica Marquez, "Raising the Performance Bar," *Workforce Management*, April 24, 2006, 31–32.

11. Steven N. Kaplan, "Are U.S. CEOs Overpaid?" *Academy of Management Perspectives*, May 2008, 5–20; Edward Lawler III and David Finegold, "CEO Compensation: What Board Members Think," *WorldatWork Journal*, Third Quarter, 2007, 38–47.

12. "Compensation for Corporate Directors Rose Modestly in 2008," *Towers-Perrin Monitor*, October, 2009, *www.towersperrin.com*.

INTERNET RESOURCES

WorldatWork—This website provides information on products and services as well as research on compensation and benefits. Visit the site at *www.worldatwork.org*.

Compensation Resources, Inc.—Specialty services such as developing, designing, and implementing compensation plans are provided by this consulting firm. Visit its website at *www.compensationresources.com*.

Institute of Management and Administration (IOMA)—For information on salary sources that are reviewed by the IOMA, visit the website at *www.ioma.com*.

National Compensation Survey (NCS)—This website provides comprehensive measures of occupational wages, employment cost trends, and benefit incidence and detailed plan provisions. Visit the site at *www.bls.gov/ncs/home.htm*.

SUGGESTED READINGS

Laura Sejen, "Merging Reward and Talent Management to Strengthen Company Performance," *Workspan*, January 2009, 66–69.

For additional details on different methods, see *Job Evaluation: Methods to the Process* (Scottsdale, AZ: WorldatWork), 2005, 159 pp.

Peter Acker and John Cummings, "What in the World Is Happening with Long-Term Incentives?" *Workspan*, September 2008, 64–68.

Xiamoneg Zhang, et al., "CEOs on the Edge: Earnings Manipulation and Stock-Based Incentives," *Academy of Management Journal*, 51 (2008), 241–258.

Variable Pay and Benefits

HR—MEETING MANAGEMENT CHALLENGES

Variable pay and benefits offer employers opportunities to increase productivity and retention respectively. The opportunities presented by incentives and benefits will be present only if employers understand how they can work and their drawbacks. It is important to consider the following:

- Individual, group, and organization incentives can increase motivation
- Sales compensation provides opportunities to increase sales
- Benefits can be designed to fit the company's strategy

Tying pay to performance holds a promise that employers and employees both find attractive. For employees it can mean more pay and for employers it can mean more output per employee and therefore more productivity. Incentive pay must be tied to performance to be successful. Employers often fill the role of major provider of benefits for citizens. Although federal regulations require U.S. employers to provide certain benefits, U.S. employers voluntarily provide many others.

VARIABLE PAY: INCENTIVES FOR PERFORMANCE

Variable pay is compensation linked to individual, group/team, and/or organizational performance. Variable pay plans attempt to provide tangible rewards, traditionally known as *incentives,* to employees for performance beyond normal expectations. The philosophical foundation of incentives rests on several basic assumptions:

- Some jobs contribute more to organizational success than others.
- Some people perform better and are more productive than others.
- Employees who perform better should receive more compensation.
- Many employees' total compensation should be tied directly to performance and results.

Incentives can take many forms. For example, they can include simple praise, "recognition and reward" programs that award trips and merchandise, bonuses for performance accomplishments, and rewards for successful results for the company. A variety of possibilities exist, but a successful plan will include a combination of different types of incentives.

Developing Successful Pay-for-Performance Plans

Employers adopt variable pay or incentive plans for a number of reasons. Key reasons that many employers adopt these plans are as follows:

- Link strategic business goals and employee performance
- Enhance organizational results and reward employees financially for their contributions
- Recognize different levels of employee performance through different rewards
- Achieve HR objectives, such as increasing retention, reducing turnover, recognizing training, and rewarding safety

As economic conditions have changed in industries and among employers, the use of variable pay incentives has changed as well. Under variable pay programs, employees can have a greater sharing of the gains or declines in organizational performance results.

Variable pay plans can be considered successful if they meet the objectives the organization had for them when they were initiated and if they work with the organizational culture and the financial resources of the organization. Both financial and nonfinancial rewards for performance are important in pay-for-performance plans. The manner in which targets are set and measured is important.[1] Three elements that affect the success of variable pay systems are discussed next. These are highlighted in Figure 8-1.

Does the Plan Fit the Organization? The success of any incentive pay program relies on its consistency with the culture of the organization. When it comes to variable pay-for-performance plans, one size does not fit all. A plan that has worked well for one company will not necessarily work well for

FIGURE 8-1 Effective Variable Pay Plans

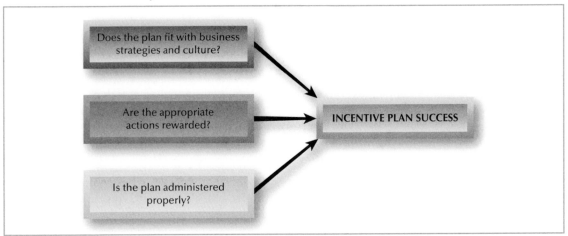

another. For an incentive plan to work, it must be linked to the objectives of the organization, its financial resources, and its desired performance results.

Does the Plan Reward Appropriate Actions? Variable pay systems should be tied as much as possible to desired performance. Employees must see a direct relationship between their efforts and their financial and nonfinancial rewards. Because people tend to produce what is measured and rewarded, organizations must make sure that what is being rewarded is clearly linked to what is needed. Linking pay to performance may not always be appropriate. For instance, if the output cannot be measured objectively, management may not be able to correctly reward the higher performers with more pay. Managers may not even be able to accurately identify the higher performers. For example, in an office where tasks are to provide permits for building renovations, individual contributions may not be identifiable or appropriate.

Is the Plan Administered Properly? A variable pay plan may be complex or simple, but it will be successful only if employees understand what they have to do to be rewarded. The more complicated a plan is the more difficult it will be to communicate it meaningfully to employees. Experts generally recommend that a variable pay plan include several performance criteria. But having multiple areas of focus should not overly complicate the calculations necessary for employees to determine their own incentive amounts. Managers also need to be able to explain clearly what future performance targets need to be met and what the rewards will be.

Metrics for Variable Pay Plans

Firms in the United States are spending significant amounts on variable pay plans as incentives. For instance, according to one survey, incentive expenditures in one year totaled $46 billion. Interestingly, more than $30 billion was paid on incentive merchandise and about $13 billion was spent on travel incentives. With such incentive expenditures increasing each year, it is crucial that the results of variable pay plans be measured to determine the success of the programs.[2]

Various metrics can be used, depending on the nature of the plan and the goals set for it. Figure 8-2 shows some examples of different metrics that

FIGURE 8-2 Metric Options for Variable Pay Plans

ORGANIZATIONAL PERFORMANCE	SALES PROGRAMS	HR RELATED
• Actual change vs. planned change • Revenue growth • Return on investment • Average employee productivity change	• Increase in market share • Customer acquisition rate • Growth of existing customer sales • Customer satisfaction	• Employee satisfaction • Turnover costs • Absenteeism cost • Workers' comp claims • Accident rates

can be used to evaluate variable play plans. Regardless of the variable pay plan, employers should gather and evaluate data to determine if the expenditures are justified by increased organizational operating performance. If the measures and analyses show positive results, the nature of the plan is truly a pay-for-performance one. If not, the plan should be changed to one that is more likely to be successful.

Successes and Failures of Variable Pay Plans

Even though variable pay has grown in popularity, some attempts at incentives have succeeded while others have not. Incentives *do* work, but they are not a panacea because their success depends on multiple factors.[3] The positive view that many employers have of variable pay is not shared by all workers. If individuals see incentives as desirable, they are likely to put forth the extra effort to attain the performance objectives that trigger the incentive payouts. But not all employees believe that they are rewarded when doing a good job, and not all employees are motivated by their employers' incentive plans.

Given the complexity of these plans, the following factors can contribute to the success of incentive plans:

- Develop clear, understandable plans that are continually communicated.
- Use realistic performance measures.
- Keep the plans current and linked to organizational objectives.
- Clearly link performance results to payouts that truly recognize performance differences.
- Identify variable pay incentives separately from base pay.

Three Categories of Variable Pay

The incentives offered in variable pay plans can be classified into three categories: individual, group/team, and organizational. There are advantages and disadvantages to each.

Individual incentives are given to reward the effort and performance of individuals. Some common means of providing individual variable pay are piece-rate systems, sales commissions, and individual bonuses. Others include special recognition rewards such as trips or merchandise.

When an organization rewards an entire group/team for its performance, cooperation among the members may increase. The most common *group/ team incentives* are gainsharing or goalsharing plans, in which the employees on a team that meets certain goals, as measured against performance targets, share in the gains.

Organizational incentives reward people according to the performance results of the entire organization. These programs often share some of the financial gains made by the firm with employees through payments calculated as a percentage of the employees' base pay. The most prevalent forms of organization-wide incentives are profit-sharing plans and employee stock plans.

Figure 8-3 shows some of the programs that fall under each type of incentive pay plan. These programs are discussed next.

FIGURE 8-3 Categories of Variable Pay Plans

INDIVIDUAL INCENTIVES

Individual incentive systems tie personal effort to additional rewards. Conditions necessary for the use of individual incentive plans are as follows:

- Individual performance must be identified.
- Individual competitiveness must be desirable.
- Individualism must be stressed in the organizational culture.

Piece-Rate Systems

The most basic individual incentive systems are piece-rate systems. Under **straight piece-rate system,** wages are determined by multiplying the number of units produced (such as garments sewn or service calls handled) by the piece rate for one unit. Because the cost is the same for each unit, the wage for each employee is easy to figure, and labor costs can be accurately predicted.

A *differential piece-rate system* pays employees one piece-rate wage for units produced up to a standard output and a higher piece-rate wage for units produced over the standard. Managers often determine the quotas or standards by using time and motion studies.

Bonuses

Individual employees may receive additional compensation in the form of a **bonus,** which is a one-time payment that does not become part of the employee's base pay. Individual bonuses are used at all levels in some firms and are the most popular short-term incentive plan.

A bonus can recognize performance by an employee, a team, or the organization as a whole. When performance results are good, bonuses go up. When performance results are not met, bonuses go down. Most employers base part of an employee's bonus on individual performance and part on company results, as appropriate. Numerous CEOs receive bonuses based on specific results. A unique type of bonus used is a "spot" bonus, so called because it can be awarded at any time. Spot bonuses are given for a number of reasons, perhaps for extra time worked, extra efforts, or an especially demanding project. Often, spot bonuses are given in cash, although some firms provide managers with gift cards, travel vouchers, or other noncash rewards. The keys to successful use of spot bonuses are to keep the amounts reasonable and to provide them only for exceptional performance accomplishments.

GROUP/TEAM INCENTIVES

The use of groups/teams in organizations has implications for incentive compensation. Although the use of groups/teams has increased substantially in the past few years, the question of how to compensate their members equitably remains a significant challenge.

Team incentives can take the form of either cash bonuses for the team or items other than money, such as merchandise or trips. But group incentive situations may place social pressure on members of the group. Everyone in the group succeeds or fails. Therefore, some argue that team incentives should be given to team members equally, although not everyone agrees.

Design of Group/Team Incentive Plans

In designing group/team incentive plans, organizations must consider a number of issues. The main concerns are how and when to distribute the incentives, and who will make decisions about the incentive amounts.

Several decisions about how to distribute and allocate group/team rewards must be made. The two primary ways for distributing those rewards are as follows:

1. *Same-size reward for each member:* All members receive the same payout, regardless of job level, current pay, seniority, or individual performance differences.

2. *Different-size reward for each member:* Employers vary individual rewards depending on such factors as contribution to group/team results, current pay, years of experience, and skill levels of jobs performed.

Generally, more organizations use the first approach. The combination of equal team member award payouts and individual pay differences rewards performance by making the group/team incentive equal while also recognizing that individual differences exist and are important to many employees. The size of the group/team incentive can be determined either by using a percentage of base pay for the individuals or the group/team as a whole, or by offering a specific dollar amount.

To reinforce the effectiveness of working together, some group/team incentive programs allow members to make decisions about how to allocate the rewards to individuals. In some situations, members vote; in some, a group/team leader decides. In other situations, the incentive "pot" is divided equally, thus avoiding conflict and recognizing that all members contributed to the team results. However, many companies have found group/team members unwilling to make decisions about coworkers' incentives.

Types of Group/Team Incentives

Group/team reward systems use various ways of compensating individuals. The components include individual wages and salaries in addition to the other rewards. Most organizations that use group/team incentives continue to pay individuals based either on the jobs performed or the individuals' competencies and capabilities. The two most common types of group/team incentives are team results and gainsharing.

Group/Team Results. Pay plans for groups/teams may reward all members equally on the basis of group output, cost savings, or quality improvement. The design of most group/team incentives is based on a "self-funding" principle. That means the money to be used as incentive rewards is obtained through improvement of organizational or group results, and can be structured as either a group or company-wide incentive.

Gainsharing. The system of sharing with employees greater-than-expected gains in profits and/or productivity is **gainsharing.** Also called *teamsharing* or *goalsharing*, the focus is to increase "discretionary efforts," which are the difference between the maximum amount of effort a person can exert and the minimum amount of effort that person needs to exert to keep from being fired.

To develop and implement a gainsharing or goalsharing plan, management must identify the ways in which increased productivity, quality, and financial performance can occur and decide how some of the resulting gains should be shared with employees. Measures such as labor costs, overtime hours, and quality benchmarks often are used. Both organizational measures and departmental measures may be targeted, with the weights for gainsharing split between the two categories.

ORGANIZATIONAL INCENTIVES

An organizational incentive system compensates all employees according to how well the organization as a whole performs during the year. The basic concept behind organizational incentive plans is that overall results depend on organization-wide efforts and cooperation. The purpose of these plans is to produce better results by rewarding cooperation throughout the organization. For example, conflict between marketing and production can be overcome if management uses an incentive system that emphasizes organization-wide profit and productivity. To be effective, an organizational incentive program should include everyone from nonexempt employees to managers and executives. Two common organizational incentive systems are profit sharing and employee stock plans.

Profit Sharing

As the name implies, **profit sharing** distributes some portion of organizational profits to employees. One research study found that profit-sharing plans in small firms can help to enhance employee commitment and increase job-related performances of individuals.[4] The primary objectives of profit-sharing plans can include the following:

- Increase productivity and organizational performance
- Attract or retain employees
- Improve product/service quality
- Enhance employee morale

Typically, the percentage of the profits distributed to employees is set by the end of the year before distribution, although both timing and payment levels are considerations. In some profit-sharing plans, employees receive portions of the profits at the end of the year; in others, the profits are deferred, placed in a fund, and made available to employees on retirement or on their departure from the organization.

Drawbacks of Profit-Sharing Plans. When used throughout an organization, including with lower-level workers, profit-sharing plans can have some drawbacks. First, employees must trust that management will disclose accurate financial and profit information. Second, profits may vary a great deal from year to year, resulting in windfalls or losses beyond the employees' control. Third, payoffs are generally far removed by time from employees' efforts; therefore, higher rewards may not be obviously linked to better performance.

Employee Stock Plans

Two types of organizational incentive plans use stock ownership in the organization to reward employees. The goal of these plans is to get employees to think and act like "owners."

A **stock option plan** gives employees the right to purchase a fixed number of shares of company stock at a specified exercise price for a limited period of time. If the market price of the stock exceeds the exercise price, employees can then exercise the option and buy the stock. The number of firms giving stock options to nonexecutives has declined in recent years, primarily due to changing laws and accounting regulations.

Employee Stock Ownership Plans. Firms in many industries have an **employee stock ownership plan (ESOP),** which is designed to give employees significant stock ownership in their employers.

Establishing an ESOP creates several advantages. The major one is that the firm can receive favorable tax treatment on the earnings earmarked for use in the ESOP. Another is that an ESOP gives employees a "piece of the action" so that they can share in the growth and profitability of their firm. Employee ownership may motivate employees to be more productive and focused on organizational performance.

SALES COMPENSATION

The compensation paid to employees involved with sales and marketing is partly or entirely tied to individual sales performance. Salespeople who sell more products and services receive more total compensation than those who sell less. Sales incentives are perhaps the most widely used individual incentives. The intent is to stimulate more effort from salespeople so they earn more money.

Types of Sales Compensation Plans

Sales compensation plans can be of several general types, depending on the degree to which total compensation includes some variable pay tied to sales performance. A look at three general types of sales compensation and some challenges to sales compensation follows.

Salary Only.   Some companies pay salespeople only a salary. The *salary-only approach* is useful when an organization emphasizes serving and retaining existing accounts over generating new sales and accounts. This approach is frequently used to protect the income of new sales representatives for a period of time while they are building up their clientele. Generally, the employer extends the salary-only approach for new sales representatives to no more than six months, at which point it implements one of the other systems discussed below.

Straight Commission.   A widely used individual incentive system in sales jobs is the **commission,** which is compensation computed as a percentage of sales in units or dollars. Commissions are integrated into the pay given to sales workers in three common ways: straight commission, salary-plus-commission, and bonuses.

In the *straight commission system,* a sales representative receives a percentage of the value of the sales the person has made. Consider a sales representative working for a consumer products company who receives no compensation if that person makes no sales, but who receives a percentage of the total amount of all sales revenues that person has generated. The advantage of this system is that it requires the sales representative to sell in order to earn. The disadvantage is that it offers no security for the sales staff.

To offset this insecurity, some employers use a **draw** system, in which sales representatives can draw advance payments against future commissions. The amounts drawn are then deducted from future commission checks.

Salary-Plus-Commission or Bonuses.   The form of sales compensation used most frequently is the *salary-plus-commission,* which combines the stability of a salary with the performance aspect of a commission. A common split is 80–20% or 70–30% salary to commission, although the split varies by industry and can be based on numerous other factors. Some organizations pay salespeople salaries and then offer bonuses that are a percentage of the base pay, tied to how well each employee meets various sales targets or other criteria. A related method is using *lump-sum bonuses,* which may lead to salespeople working more intensively to get more sales results than the package approach.

Sales Compensation Challenges

Sales incentives work well, especially when they are tied to the broad strategic initiatives of the organization and its specific marketing and sales strategies. However, as economic and competitive changes have occurred, employers in many industries have faced challenges in their sales. Firms can analyze more thoroughly their sales compensation costs, assess how the sales pay is increasing or decreasing performance efforts by employees, and then evaluate the extent to which the sales and profit goals are being met.

Effectiveness of Sales Incentive Plans.   So many organizations have sales incentive plans that it would be logical to think those plans are effective. However, many sales compensation plans are not seen as effective by either salespeople or managers and executives. One problem that can occur is constantly making too many changes in sales incentives, resulting in confusion by many people. Frequent changes reduce the effectiveness of plans and create problems with the sales representatives and managers. HR professionals may be involved in designing, revising, and communicating sales incentive plans, as well as responding to the complaints and concerns of sales representatives.

EMPLOYEE BENEFITS

An employer may provide benefits to workers for being part of the organization. A **benefit** is an indirect reward given to an employee or group of employees for organizational membership. Benefits often include retirement plans, vacations with pay, health insurance, educational assistance, and many more programs.

Benefits are costly for the typical U.S. employer, averaging from 30% to 40% of payroll expenses. In highly unionized manufacturing and utility industries, they may be over 70% of payroll. The costs of benefits are increasing, sometimes faster than inflationary rates, causing some organizations to require employees to help pay for these benefits.

Benefits and HR Strategy

In the United States, a challenge for employers is how to best manage the balancing act between the growing costs of benefits and the use of those benefits in accomplishing organizational goals. For instance, organizations can choose to compete for or retain employees by providing different levels of base compensation, variable pay, and benefits. Indeed, when a lagging economy causes organizations to downsize or cut various programs, some companies have remained focused on benefits, exploring new benefits options and adopting a more comprehensive approach to compensation management. This is why benefits should be looked at as a vital part of the total rewards "package" when determining organizational strategies regarding compensation.

It is important that benefits be used to help create and maintain competitive advantages. Benefits should not be viewed entirely as cost factors because they can positively affect HR efforts. Given the intense competition for competent workers, companies should consider investing in benefits packages that are attractive for those employees.

Employers may offer benefits to aid recruiting and retention, impact organizational performance, and meet legal requirements. Also, some employers see benefits as reinforcing the company philosophy of social and corporate citizenship. Employers that provide good benefits are viewed more positively within a community and the industry by customers, civic leaders, current employees, and workers in other firms. Conversely, employers who are seen as skimping on benefits, cutting benefits, or taking advantage of workers may be viewed more negatively.

The primary reasons executives see for offering benefits is to attract and retain talent and meet responsibilities to employees. According to a survey by an international consulting firm, 48% of executives see benefits as extremely important to a company's competitive effectiveness and another 41% saw benefits as somewhat important.[5]

A major advantage of benefits is that they generally are not taxed as income to employees. For this reason, benefits represent a somewhat more valuable reward to employees than an equivalent cash payment. This feature makes benefits a desirable form of compensation to employees if they understand the value provided by the benefits.

Benefits Plan Design

Benefits plans can provide flexibility and choices for employees, or they can be standardized for all employees. Increasingly, employers are finding that providing employees with some choices and flexibility allow individuals to tailor their benefits to their own situations. However, the more choices available, the higher the administrative demands placed on organizations. A number of key decisions are part of benefits design:

- How much total compensation, including benefits, can be provided?
- What part of the total compensation of individuals should benefits constitute?
- Which employees should be provided which benefits?
- What expense levels are acceptable for each benefit offered?
- What is being received by the organization in return for each benefit?
- How flexible should the package of benefits be?

Part-Time Employee Benefits.   Another key design issue is whether or not to provide benefits coverage to part-time employees. Many employers do not provide part-time employee benefits, except some time-off leave benefits.

Part-time employees who do receive benefits usually do so in proportion to the percentage of full-time work they provide.

Flexible Benefits.   As mentioned, as part of both benefits design and administration, many employers offer employees choices for benefits. A **flexible benefits plan** allows employees to select the benefits they prefer from groups of benefits established by the employer. Sometimes called a *flex plan* or *cafeteria plan*, these plans have a variety of "dishes," or benefits, available so that each employee can select an individual combination of benefits within some overall limits.

Because many flexible plans have become so complex, they require more administrative time and information systems to track the different choices made by employees. Despite the disadvantages, flex plans will likely continue to grow in popularity.

HR and Benefits Administration.   With the myriad of benefits, it is easy to see why many organizations must make coordinated efforts to administer benefits programs. Benefits administration responsibilities can be split between HR specialists and operating managers. HR specialists play the more significant role, but managers must assume responsibility for some of the communication aspects of benefits administration. One significant trend affecting HR is that outsourcing of benefits administration may be necessary.

HR Technology and Benefits

The spread of HR technology, particularly Internet-based systems, has significantly changed the benefits administration time and activities for HR staff members. Internet and computer-based systems are being used to communicate benefits information, conduct employee benefits surveys, and facilitate benefits administration. Recent research shows that these systems can decrease expenses, increase positive communication, and effectively connect people across many different HR functions, including benefits management.[6]

Information technology allows employees to change their benefits choices, track their benefits balances, and submit questions to HR staff members and external benefits providers. Some systems provide prepackaged connections with benefits providers so that information technology requirements are minimized. Use of online benefits enrollment has increased significantly. The greatest use has been to allow employees to sign up for, change, or update their benefits choices through Web-based systems.

Benefits Measurement

The significant costs associated with benefits require that analyses be conducted to determine the payoffs for the benefits. With the wide range of benefits that are offered, numerous HR metrics can be used such as the following:

- Benefits as a percentage of payroll (pattern over a multiyear period)
- Benefits expenditures per full-time-equivalent (FTE) employee

- Benefits costs by employee group (full-time vs. part-time, union vs. nonunion, management, professional, technical, office, etc.)
- Benefits administration costs (including staff time multiplied by the staff pay and benefits costs per hour)
- Health care benefits costs per participating employee

Metrics are used to measure the return on the expenditures for various benefits programs provided by employers. Some common benefits that employers track using HR metrics are workers' compensation, wellness programs, prescription drug costs, leave time, tuition aid, and disability insurance. The point is that both benefits expenditures generally, and costs for individual benefits specifically, need to be measured and evaluated as part of strategic benefits management.

Benefits Cost Control

Because benefits expenditures have risen significantly in the past few years, particularly for health care, employers are focusing more attention on measuring and controlling benefits costs, even reducing or dropping benefits offered to employees.

Another common means of benefits cost control is cost sharing, which refers to having employees pay for more of their benefits costs. This is commonly used for health insurance costs. Three other means of health insurance cost control are using wellness programs, adding employee health education efforts, and changing prescription drug programs.

Benefits Communication

Benefits communication and satisfaction of employees with their benefits are linked. For instance, employees often do not fully understand their health benefits, a situation that can cause individual dissatisfaction. Consequently, many employers should consider developing special benefits communication systems to inform employees about the monetary value of the benefits they provide. Employers can use various means, including videos, CDs, emails, electronic alerts, newsletters, and employee meetings. All these efforts are done to ensure that employees are knowledgeable about their benefits. Some of the important information to be communicated includes the value of the plans offered, why changes have to be made, and the fundamental financial costs of the plans. The Employee Retirement Income Security Act (ERISA) also requires sponsors of health programs to write a *summary plan description* that details the rights and benefits associated with particular plans, and these documents must be easy to understand.[7]

Benefits Statements.   Some employers give individual employees a "personal statement of benefits" that translates benefits into dollar amounts. Increasingly, firms are using the Internet to provide statements, with estimates that 60% of employers are doing so.[8] These statements often are used as part of a total rewards education and communication effort. The Employee

Retirement Income Security Act (ERISA) also requires that employees receive an annual pension-reporting statement, which also can be included in the personal benefits statement.

TYPES OF BENEFITS

A wide range of benefits are offered by employers. Some are mandated by laws and government regulations, while others are offered voluntarily by employers as part of their HR strategies.

Government-Mandated Benefits

There are many mandated benefits that employers in the United States must provide to employees by law. Social Security (federal) and unemployment insurance (state) are funded through a tax paid by the employer based on the employee's compensation. Workers' compensation laws exist in all states. In addition, under the Family and Medical Leave Act (FMLA), employers must offer unpaid leave to employees with certain medical or family difficulties. Other mandated benefits are funded in part by taxes, through Social Security. The Consolidated Omnibus Budget Reconciliation Act (COBRA) mandates that an employer continue to provide health care coverage—albeit paid for by the employees—for a time after employees leave the organization. The Health Insurance Portability and Accountability Act (HIPAA) requires that most employees be able to obtain coverage if they were previously covered in a health plan and provides privacy rights for medical records.

A major reason for additional mandated benefits proposals is that federal and state governments would like to shift many of the social costs for health care and other expenditures to employers. This shift would relieve some of the budgetary pressures facing government entities that otherwise might have to raise taxes and/or cut spending.

The federal plan for universal health care benefits for individuals has been passed, but given the complexity of the bill and uncertainty over how it will work, it is unclear exactly how such coverage will impact organizations, sponsors of health benefits, and health care providers. Additional mandated benefits have been proposed for many other areas but not adopted are as follows:

- Child-care assistance
- Pension plan coverage that can be transferred by workers who change jobs
- Core benefits for part-time employees working at least 500 hours a year
- Paid time off for family leave
- Paid time off for pregnancy and child bearing

Voluntary Benefits

Employers voluntarily offer other types of benefits to help them compete for and retain employees. By offering additional benefits, organizations are assuming a need to provide greater security and benefits support to workers

FIGURE 8-4 Types of Benefits

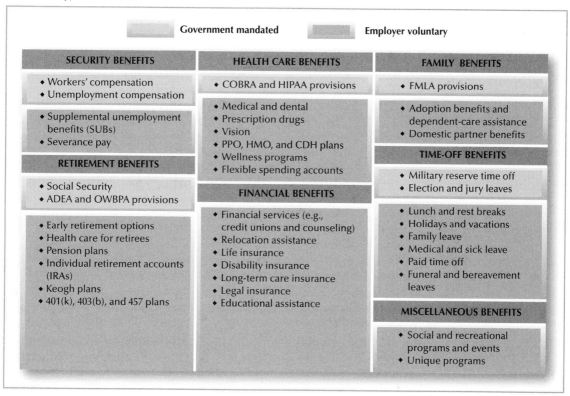

with widely varied personal circumstances. In addition, as jobs become more flexible and varied, both workers and employers recognize that choices among benefits are necessary, as evidenced by the growth in flexible benefits and cafeteria benefit plans. Figure 8-4 lists seven types of mandated and voluntary benefits. The following sections describe them by type.

SECURITY BENEFITS

A number of benefits provide employee security. These benefits include some mandated by laws and others offered by employers voluntarily. The primary benefits found in most organizations include workers' compensation, unemployment compensation, and severance pay.

Workers' Compensation

Workers' compensation provides benefits to persons who are injured on the job. State laws require most employers to supply workers' compensation coverage by purchasing insurance from a private carrier or state insurance fund or by providing self-insurance. Government employees in the United States are covered under the Federal Employees Compensation Act, administered by the U.S. Department of Labor. The workers' compensation system requires employers to give cash benefits, medical care, and rehabilitation services to employees for injuries or illnesses occurring within the scope of their employment. In exchange, employees give up the right to pursue legal actions and awards.

Unemployment Compensation

Another benefit required by law is unemployment compensation, established as part of the Social Security Act of 1935. Because each U.S. state operates its own unemployment compensation system, provisions differ significantly from state to state. The tax is paid to state and federal unemployment compensation funds. The percentage paid by individual employers is based on "experience rates," which reflect the number of claims filed by workers who leave.

An employee who is out of work and is actively looking for employment normally receives up to 26 weeks of pay, at the rate of 50% to 80% of normal pay. Most employees are eligible. However, workers fired for misconduct or those not actively seeking employment generally are ineligible.

Severance Pay

As a security benefit, **severance pay** is voluntarily offered by employers to individuals whose jobs are eliminated or who leave by mutual agreement with their employers. Employer severance pay provisions often provide severance payments corresponding to an employee's level within the organization and the person's years of employment. The Worker Adjustment and Retraining Notification Act (WARN) of 1988 requires that many employers give 60 days' notice if a mass layoff or facility closing is to occur. The act does not require employers to give severance pay.

HEALTH CARE BENEFITS

Employers provide a variety of health care and medical benefits, usually through insurance coverage. The most common plans cover medical, dental, prescription drug, and vision care expenses for employees and their dependents.

Increases in Health Benefits Costs

For several decades, the costs of health care have escalated at rates well above those of inflation and changes in workers' earnings. For instance, the reduction in the number of obstetricians caused by litigation fears and the price of malpractice insurance has increased costs due to higher premiums and diagnostic testing. In addition, the costs of health care have increased by two percentage points over increases in the GDP across many developed nations for close to 50 years. As a result of large increases such as these, many employers find that dealing with health care benefits is time consuming and expensive.

Uninsured Workers. Some of the health benefits cost pressures are due to health care providers having to cover the costs for the rising number of individuals in the United States without health insurance coverage. A number of uninsured workers are illegal immigrants; others work for employers that do not provide benefits. The costs are shifted to those with health insurance paid for by employers, making this a high-profile political issue that has driven attention to health care reform.

Retirees' Health Benefits Costs. Another group whose benefits costs are rising is retirees whose former employers still provide health benefits coverage. To control retiree health benefits costs, some firms are cutting their benefits or requiring retirees to pay higher rates for health benefits. Approximately 75% of employers in one survey have increased health insurance premiums in recent years. Many of the retirees worked for their employers for 20, 30, or more years, yet the reward for their long service increasingly is a reduction in health care benefits. As a result, many individuals are delaying retirement until age 65 so that Medicare coverage can be secured.

Controlling Health Care Benefits Costs

Employers offering health care benefits are taking a number of approaches to controlling their costs. The most prominent ones are changing copayments and employee contributions, using managed care, switching to mini-medical plans or consumer-driven health plans, and increasing health preventive and wellness efforts.

Changing Copayments and Employee Contributions. The **copayment** strategy requires employees to pay a portion of the cost of insurance premiums, medical care, and prescription drugs. Requiring new or higher copayments and employee contributions is the most prevalent cost-control strategy identified by many employers surveyed.

These changes are facing significant resistance by employees, especially those who have had *first-dollar coverage*. With this type of coverage, all expenses, from the first dollar of health care costs, are paid by the employee's insurance. Experts claim that when first-dollar coverage is included in a basic health plan, many employees see a doctor for even minor illnesses, which results in an escalation of the benefits costs.

Using Managed Care. Several other types of programs attempt to reduce health care costs paid by employers. **Managed care** consists of approaches that monitor and reduce medical costs through restrictions and market system alternatives. Managed care plans emphasize primary and preventive care, the use of specific providers who will charge lower prices, restrictions on certain kinds of treatment, and prices negotiated with hospitals and physicians.

The most prominent managed care approach is the **preferred provider organization (PPO),** a health care provider that contracts with an employer or an employer group to supply health care services to employees at a competitive rate. Employees have the freedom to go to other providers if they want to pay the differences in costs. *Point-of-service plans* are somewhat similar, offering financial incentives to encourage employees to use designated medical providers.

Another managed care approach is a **health maintenance organization (HMO),** which provides services for a fixed period on a prepaid basis. The HMO emphasizes both prevention and correction. An employer contracts with an HMO and its staff of physicians and medical personnel to furnish complete medical care, except for hospitalization. The employer pays a flat rate per enrolled employee or per enrolled family. The covered individuals may then go to the HMO for health care as often as needed.

Mini-Medical Plans. Another type of plan that has grown in usage in the past few years is the *mini-medical plan.* This type of plan provides limited health benefits coverage for employees. In the past, these plans have been used more with part-time and lower wage level employees. But more employers are using these plans for full-time employees of all types. A typical mini-medical plan limits the number of doctor visits paid per year to fewer than 10, covers only certain prescription drugs, provides very limited hospital coverage, and caps total annual health benefits costs at $10,000 or less.

Consumer-Driven Health Plans

Some employers are turning to employee-focused health benefits plans. The most prominent is a **consumer-driven health (CDH) plan,** which provides employer financial contributions to employees to help cover their health-related expenses. A growing number of employers have switched to CDH plans, and others are actively considering switching to these plans. CDH plans are being offered by both large and small businesses and that more workers are signing up for them.

In these plans, which are also called *defined-contribution health plans,* an employer places a set amount into each employee's "account" and identifies a number of health care alternatives that are available. Then individual employees select from those health care alternatives and pay for part of the costs from their accounts.

There are two advantages to such plans for employers. One is that more of the increases in health care benefits costs are shifted to employees, because the employer contributions need not increase as fast as health care costs. Second, the focus of controlling health care usage falls on employees, who may have to choose when to use and not use health care benefits.

Health Savings Accounts. Often **Health savings accounts (HSAs)** are combined with high-deductible insurance to cut employer costs. Such insurance is defined as plans that have between $1,150 and $5,800 in deductibles for individuals, and between $2,300 and $11,600 in deductibles for families.[9] Other components of an HSA include the following:

- Both employees and employers can make contributions to an account.
- Individual employees can set aside pretax amounts for medical care into an HSA.

- Unused amounts in an individual's account can be rolled over annually for future health expenses.
- Incentives are included to encourage employees to spend less on health expenses.
- Contributions must be uniform for all employees enrolled in HSA accounts unless they are based on a cafeteria program.

Health Care Preventive and Wellness Efforts

Preventive and wellness efforts can occur in a variety of ways. Many employers offer programs to educate employees about health care costs and how to reduce them. Newsletters, formal classes, and many other approaches are all designed to help employees understand why health care costs are increasing and what they can do to control them. Many employers have programs that offer financial incentives to improve health habits. These wellness programs reward employees who stop smoking, lose weight, and participate in exercise programs, among other activities.

HIPAA Provisions.   The Health Insurance Portability and Accountability Act (HIPAA) of 1996 allows employees to switch their health insurance plans when they change employers, and to get new health coverage with the new company regardless of preexisting health conditions. The legislation also prohibits group insurance plans from dropping coverage for a sick employee and requires them to make individual coverage available to people who leave group plans.

One of the greatest impacts of HIPAA comes from its provisions regarding the privacy of employee medical records. These provisions require employers to provide privacy notices to employees.

RETIREMENT BENEFITS

The aging of the workforce in many countries is affecting retirement planning for individuals and retirement plan costs for employers and governments. In the United States, the number of citizens at least 55 years or older has increased significantly in recent years, and older citizens currently constitute a large portion of the population. Simultaneously, the age of retirement has declined, as it has been doing for decades. With more people retiring earlier and living longer, retirement benefits are becoming a greater concern for employers, employees, and retired employees.

Unfortunately, most U.S. citizens have inadequate savings and retirement benefits for funding their retirements. According to a study by the Employee Benefit Research Institute, almost 70% of individuals over age 55 have inadequately saved for retirement.[10] These individuals are heavily dependent on employer-provided retirement benefits. But many employers with fewer than 100 workers do not offer retirement benefits. Also, the economic downturn caused a reduction in the value of worker retirement accounts and contributions, leading many older employees to continue with their employment. Some individuals are relying solely on Social Security payments, which were not designed to provide full retirement income.

Social Security

The Social Security Act of 1935, with its later amendments, established a system providing *old-age, survivor's, disability*, and *retirement* benefits. Administered by the federal government through the Social Security Administration, this program provides benefits to previously employed individuals. Employees and employers share in the cost of Social Security through a tax on employees' wages or salaries.

Pension Plans

A **pension plan** is a retirement program established and funded by the employer and employees. Organizations are not required to offer pension plans to employees, and fewer than half of U.S. workers are covered by them. Small firms offer pension plans less often than do large ones.

Defined-Benefit Pension Plans. A "traditional" pension plan, in which the employer makes the contributions and the employee will get a defined amount each month upon retirement, is no longer the norm in the private sector. Through a **defined-benefit plan,** employees are promised a pension amount based on age and service. The employees' contributions are based on actuarial calculations on the *benefits* to be received by the employees after retirement and the *methods* used to determine such benefits. A defined-benefit plan gives employees greater assurance of benefits and greater predictability in the amount of benefits that will be available for retirement. Defined-benefit plans are often preferred by workers with longer service, as well as by small business owners.

Defined-Contribution Pension Plans. In a **defined-contribution plan,** the employer makes an annual payment to an employee's pension account. The key to this plan is the *contribution rate;* employee retirement benefits depend on fixed contributions and employee earnings levels. Profit-sharing plans, employee stock ownership plans (ESOPs), and 401(k) plans are common defined-contribution plans. Because these plans hinge on the investment returns on the previous contributions, the returns can vary according to profitability or other factors. Therefore, employees' retirement benefits are somewhat less secure and predictable. But because of their structure, these plans are sometimes preferred by younger, shorter-service employees.

Cash Balance Pension Plans. Some employers have changed traditional pension plans to hybrids based on ideas from both defined-benefit and defined-contribution plans. One such plan is a **cash balance plan,** in which retirement benefits are based on an accumulation of annual company contributions, expressed as a percentage of pay, plus interest credited each year. With these plans, retirement benefits accumulate at the same annual rate until an employee retires. Because cash balance plans spread funding across a worker's entire career, these plans work better for mobile younger workers.

Pension Plan Concepts

Pension plans can be either contributory or noncontributory. In a **contributory plan,** money for pension benefits is paid in by both employees and the employer. In a **noncontributory plan,** the employer provides all the funds for pension benefits. As expected, the noncontributory plans are generally preferred by employees and labor unions.

Certain rights are attached to employee pension plans. Various laws and provisions have been passed to address the right of employees to receive benefits from their pension plans. Called **vesting,** this right assures employees of a certain pension, provided they work a minimum number of years.

Individual Retirement Options

The availability of several retirement benefit options makes the pension area more complex. The most prominent options are individual retirement accounts (IRAs) and 401(k), 403(b), 457, and Keogh plans. These plans may be available in addition to company-provided pension plans and usually are contributory plans.

The **401(k) plan** gets its name from section 401(k) of the federal tax code. This plan is an agreement in which a percentage of an employee's pay is withheld and invested in a tax-deferred account. Many employers match employee 401(k) contributions, up to a percentage of the employee's pay. As a result, a significant number of employees contribute to 401(k) plans. The use of 401(k) plans and of the assets in them has grown significantly in the past few years. Employers frequently have programs to encourage employees to contribute to 401(k) plans.

Employee Retirement Income Security Act

The widespread criticism of many pension plans led to passage of the Employee Retirement Income Security Act (ERISA) in 1974. The purpose of this law is to regulate private pension plans so that employees who put money into them or depend on a pension for retirement funds actually receive the money when they retire.

ERISA essentially requires many companies to offer retirement plans to all employees if they offer retirement plans to any employees. Accrued benefits must be given to employees when they retire or leave. The act also sets minimum funding requirements, and plans not meeting those requirements are subject to financial penalties imposed by the IRS. Additional regulations require that employers pay plan termination insurance to ensure payment of employee pensions should the employers go out of business. To spread out the costs of administration and overhead, some employers use plans funded by multiple employers.

Retiree Benefits and Legal Requirements

Some employers choose to offer retiree health benefits that may be paid for by the retirees, the company, or both. The costs of such coverage have risen dramatically. To ensure that firms adequately reflect the liabilities for retiree health benefits, the Financial Accounting Standards Board issued Rule 106, which requires employers to establish accounting reserves for funding retiree health care benefits. For instance, one problem with retiree pension benefits is that a number of firms are facing unfunded pension liabilities.

Pension Protection Act of 2006.   The Pension Protection Act of 2006 has numerous reporting requirements that must be met by employers. These requirements make employers disclose the assets and liabilities of pension plans. The act also requires that employers increase funding to cover unfunded liabilities they face. Many of the provisions focus specifically on the liabilities created by defined-benefit plans that employers must cover.

FINANCIAL BENEFITS

Employers may offer workers a wide range of special benefits that provide financial support to employees. Figure 8-5 illustrates some common financial benefits. Employers find that such benefits can be useful in attracting and retaining employees. Workers like receiving these benefits, which often are not taxed as income.

Insurance Benefits

In addition to health-related insurance, some employers provide other types of insurance. These benefits offer major advantages for employees because many employers pay some or all of the costs. Even when employers do not pay any of the costs, employees still benefit because of the lower rates available through

FIGURE 8-5 Common Types of Financial Benefits

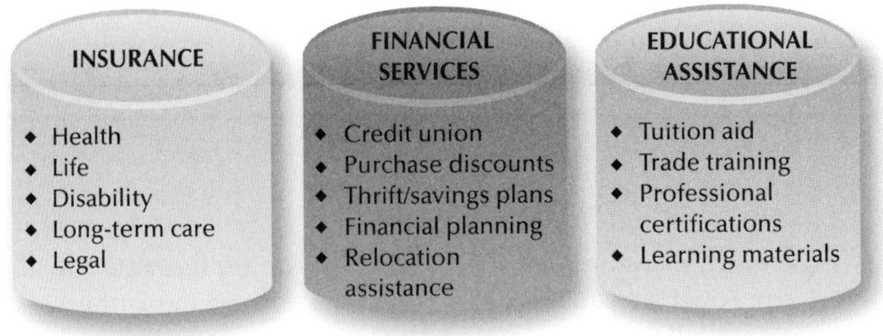

INSURANCE	FINANCIAL SERVICES	EDUCATIONAL ASSISTANCE
◆ Health	◆ Credit union	◆ Tuition aid
◆ Life	◆ Purchase discounts	◆ Trade training
◆ Disability	◆ Thrift/savings plans	◆ Professional
◆ Long-term care	◆ Financial planning	certifications
◆ Legal	◆ Relocation assistance	◆ Learning materials

group programs. The most common types of insurance benefits are life insurance, disability insurance, long-term care insurance, and legal insurance.

Financial Services

Financial benefits include a wide variety of items. A *credit union* sponsored by the employer provides saving and lending services for employees. *Purchase discounts* allow employees to buy goods or services from their employers at reduced rates. For example, a furniture manufacturer may allow employees to buy furniture at wholesale cost plus 10%, or a bank may offer employees use of a safe deposit box and free checking. Employee *thrift plans, savings plans,* or *stock investment plans* of different types may be available.

Financial planning and counseling are especially valuable services for executives, many of whom may need information on investments and tax shelters, as well as comprehensive financial counseling, because of their higher levels of compensation.

Educational Assistance

Another benefit that saves financial resources of employees comes in the form of educational assistance and tuition aid, which pays some or all of the costs associated with formal education courses and degree programs. Often the costs of books and laboratory materials are covered. Unless the education paid for by the employer meets certain conditions, the cost of educational aid must be counted as taxable income by employees.

FAMILY-ORIENTED BENEFITS

Balancing family and work demands presents a major challenge to many workers at all levels of organizations. Therefore, employers have established a variety of family-oriented benefits. Since 1993, employers also have been required to provide certain benefits to comply with the Family and Medical Leave Act (FMLA).

Family and Medical Leave Act

The FMLA covers all federal, state, and private employers with 50 or more employees who live within 75 miles of the workplace. Only employees who have worked at least 12 months and 1,250 hours in the previous year are eligible for leave under the FMLA. The law requires that employers allow eligible employees to take a total of 12 weeks' leave during any 12-month period for one or more of three situations:

- Birth, adoption, or foster care placement of a child
- Caring for a spouse, a child, or a parent with a serious health condition
- Serious health condition of the employee

A **serious health condition** is one requiring in-patient, hospital, hospice, or residential medical care or continuing physician care, or problems that exist beyond three days including treatment provided. An employer may require an employee to provide a certificate from a doctor verifying such an illness. The FMLA provides a number of guidelines regarding employee leaves:

- Employees taking family and medical leave must be able to return to the same job or a job of equivalent status or pay.
- Health benefits must be continued during the leave at the same level and conditions. If, for a reason other than serious health problems, the employee does not return to work, the employer may collect the employer-paid portion of the premiums from the nonreturning employee.
- The leave may be taken intermittently rather than in one block, subject to employee and employer agreements, when birth, adoption, or foster child care is the cause. For serious health conditions, employer approval is not necessary.
- Employees can be required to use all paid-up vacation and personal leave before taking unpaid leave.
- Employees are required to give 30-day notice, where practical.

Some provisions associated with the FMLA started January 16, 2009, expanding coverage for some employees and revising specific criteria of the regulations. One of the most noteworthy revisions to the FMLA involves providing 26 weeks of leave to individuals providing care to injured family members who served in the military.

Family-Care Benefits

Family issues are growing in importance for many organizations and for many workers. Many employers provide maternity and paternity benefits to employees who give birth. Some firms also provide adoption benefits.

Balancing work and family responsibilities is a major challenge for many workers. Some employers are addressing the child-care issue in the following ways:

- Providing referral services to help parents locate child-care providers
- Establishing discounts at day-care centers, which may be subsidized by the employer
- Arranging with hospitals to offer sick-child programs partially paid for by the employer
- Developing after-school programs for older school-age children, often in conjunction with local public and private school systems
- Offering on-site child-care centers

Another family issue of importance is caring for elderly relatives. An increasing number of organizations are offering benefits that help employees more effectively balance their work and elder-care responsibilities. Besides time off provided by the FMLA, some of these benefits include subsidies for elder-care expenses, referrals to elder-care providers, and elder-care assistance for emergencies.[11]

Measuring the Effectiveness of Family Benefits

Employers that have provided child-care and other family-friendly assistance have found the programs beneficial for several reasons. The greatest advantage is in aiding employee retention.[12] Employees are more likely to stay with employers who aid them with work-life balancing. Child-care benefits can produce significant savings, primarily due to decreased employee absenteeism and turnover. Analyses of elder-care costs-benefits show similar results. To determine such metrics, costs for recruiting, training, turnover, and lost productivity often are included.

Benefits for Domestic Partners

As lifestyles change in the United States, employers are being confronted with requests for benefits from employees who are not married but have close personal relationships with others. The terms often used to refer to individuals with such arrangements are *domestic partners* and *spousal equivalents*. The employees who are submitting these requests are: (1) unmarried employees who are living with individuals of the opposite sex and (2) gay and lesbian employees who have partners.

TIME-OFF AND OTHER BENEFITS

Time-off benefits represent a significant portion of total benefits costs. Employers give employees paid time off for a variety of circumstances. Paid lunch breaks and rest periods, holidays, and vacations are common.

Holiday and Vacation Pay

Most employers provide pay for a variety of holidays. In the United States, employers commonly offer 10 to 12 holidays annually. Employers in many other countries are required to provide a significantly higher number of holidays, approaching 20 to 30 days in some cases. In both the United States and other countries, the number of holidays offered can vary depending on state/provincial laws and union contracts.

Paid vacations are a common benefit. Employers often use graduated vacation-time scales based on employees' lengths of service. Some organizations have a "use it or lose it" policy whereby accrued vacation time cannot be carried over from year to year. Some employers have policies to "buy back" unused vacation time. Other employers, such as banks, may have policies requiring employees to take a minimum number of vacation days off in a row. Regardless of the vacation policies used, employees are often required to work the day before and the day after vacation time off.

Leaves of Absence

Employers grant *leaves of absence*, taken as time off with or without pay, for a variety of reasons. All the leaves discussed here add to employer costs even if unpaid. That is because the missing employee's work must be covered, either by other employees working additionally or by temporary employees working under contract.

Leaves are given for a variety of purposes. Some, such as *military leave, election leave*, and *jury leave*, are required by various state and federal laws. *Funeral leave* or *bereavement leave* is another common type of leave offered.

Medical and *sick leave* are closely related. Many employers allow employees to miss a limited number of days because of illness without losing pay. More than 50% of all U.S. workers receive paid sick leave. But U.S. employers do not provide paid sick leave to as many workers percentagewise as do the employers in other developed countries. Some employers allow employees to accumulate unused sick leave, which may be used in case of catastrophic illnesses. Others pay their employees for unused sick leave.

Paid-Time-Off Plans

A growing number of employers have made use of a **paid-time-off (PTO) plan,** which combines all sick leave, vacation time, and holidays into a total number of hours or days that employees can take off with pay. Many of those employers have found PTO plans to be more effective than other means of reducing absenteeism and in having time off scheduled more efficiently. Other advantages cited by employers with PTO plans are ease of administration and as an aid for recruiting and retention and for increasing employee understanding and use of leave policies.

NOTES

1. Bruce Ellig, "What Pay for Performance Should Measure," *WorldatWork Journal*, Second Quarter, 2008, 64–75.

2. Leo Jakobson, "$46 Billion Spent on Incentives," *Incentive*, November 2007, 27–28.

3. Patricia K. Zinghelm and Jay R. Schuster, "Revisiting Effective Incentive Design," *WorldatWork Journal*, First Quarter, 2005, 50–58.

4. A. Bayo-Moriones and M. Larraa-Kintana, "Profit-Sharing Plans and Affective Commitment," *Human Resource Management*, March–April 2009, 207–226.

5. "An Executive Perspective on Employee Benefits," *McKinsey Quarterly Survey*, April 2006, 1, *www .mckinseyquarterly.com;* "Incorporate 'Employer of Choice' Goals into Strategic, Benefits Planning," *Best Practices in HR*, September 22, 2006, 3.

6. Thomas W. Gainey and Brian S. Klaas, "The Use and Impact of e-HR: A Survey of HR Professionals," *People and Strategy*, 31 (2008) , 50–55.

7. Robert Whiddon, "Ranking Health Plans on Satisfaction," *Employee Benefits News*, June 15, 2008;

Dennis Ackley, "Communication: The Key to Putting the Benefit Back in Benefits," *Workspan*, February 2006, 31–34; Betty Sosnin, "What's in Your Summary Plan Description?" *HR Magazine*, August 2007, 63–70.

8. Jill Elswick, "Loaded Statements: Web-Based Total Compensation Statements Keep Employees in the Know," *BenefitNews.com*, May 2005, *www .benefitnews.com.*

9. Christine Keller and Christopher E. Condeluci, "Tax Relief and Health Care Act Should Prompt Re-examination of HSAs," *SHRM HR Legal Report*, July–August 2007, 1–8.

10. *EBRI 2010 Retirement Confidence Study*, *www .ebri.org.*

11. Stephanie Armour, "Juggling Work, Care for Aging Parent: Some Companies Help Their Workers," *USA Today*, June 26, 2007, 3B.

12. Reagan Baughman, Daniela DiNardi, and Douglas Holtz-Eakin, "Productivity and Wage Effects of 'Family Friendly' Fringe Benefits," *International Journal of Manpower*, 24 (2003), 247.

INTERNET RESOURCES

HR-Guide.com—This website discusses incentives and gainsharing in detail. Visit the site at *www.hr-guide.com.*

MyStockOptions.com—For tools to communicate with, educate, and train employees about stock options, visit this website at *www.mystockoptions.com.*

BenefitNews.Com—This website is a resource for surveys, archived articles, and the latest trends and information regarding employee benefits. Visit the site at *www.benefitnews.com.*

Work-Life and Human Capital Solutions—This website provides organizations with information and resources for employees on work and family issues such as child care and elder care. Visit the site at *www.workfamily.com.*

SUGGESTED READINGS

M. J. Gibbs, et al., "Performance Measure Properties and Incentive System Design," *Industrial Relations*, 48 (2009), 237–264.

Bonnie Schindler, "Understanding Private Company Incentive Pay Practices," *Workspan*, March 2008, 43–48; Dan Kleinman, "Getting Our Bonus Expectations Right," *Workspan*, July 2009, 75–76.

For an overview and details, see Jerry S. Rosenbloom, *The Handbook of Employee Benefits: Design, Funding, and Administration*, 6th ed. (New York: McGraw-Hill, 2005).

"An Employee's Guide to Health Benefits under COBRA: The Consolidation Omnibus Budget Reconciliation Act of 1986," U.S. Department of Labor Manual, Employee Benefits Security Administration, *www.dol.gov.*

Risk Management and Employee Relations

HR—MEETING MANAGEMENT CHALLENGES

Employer protection activities help manage risks and maintain a safe and healthy work environment. This chapter highlights the factors affecting risk management in organizations as well as those affecting of employee relations. Key issues are:

- Ensuring that worker health, safety, and security are consistently addressed
- Having employee relations, rights and responsibilities addressed by HR policies and practices
- Controlling and measuring employee absenteeism as well as using discipline appropriately

Components of risk management are workplace safety, employee health and wellness, and workplace and worker security. The employment relationship is a reciprocal one in which both employer and employee have contractual rights as well as responsibilities. Employers must address such issues as privacy, use of electronic communications, absenteeism, and discipline.

RISK MANAGEMENT, HEALTH, SAFETY, AND SECURITY

In the United States and most developed nations, the concept of using prevention and control to minimize or eliminate a wide range of risks in workplaces has been expanding. **Risk management** involves responsibilities to consider physical, human, and financial factors to protect organizational and individual interests.[1] Its scope can range from workplace safety and health to disaster preparation. A well-done HR risk management program can affect the bottom line through direct savings in workers' compensation costs, civil liability damages, and litigation expenses, as well as by increasing the likelihood of winning bids and government contracts.

The first emphasis in HR risk management in most organizations is health, safety, and security. The terms *health, safety,* and *security* are closely related. The broader and somewhat more nebulous term is **health,** which refers to a general state of physical, mental, and emotional well-being. A healthy person is free from illness, injury, or mental and emotional problems that impair normal human activity. Health management practices in organizations strive to maintain employees' overall well-being.

Typically, **safety** refers to a condition in which the physical well-being of people is protected. The main purpose of effective safety programs in organizations is to prevent work-related injuries and accidents. The purpose of **security** is protecting employees and organizational facilities. With the growth of workplace violence and other risk management issues, security has become a concern for employers and employees alike.

Current State of Health, Safety, and Security

In a recent year in the United States, about 4 million nonfatal injuries and illnesses occurred at work. That was down from previous years. Specific rates vary depending on the industry, type of job, and other factors. The number of workplace injuries also varies by employer size, with smaller employers having more injuries per employee.

While injury accidents in general are down, injuries resulting in disabilities among American workers are growing. The problem seems to be related partly to unhealthy lifestyles. The aging workforce also is a factor. Older workers have lower frequencies of disability, but when they are out of work due to injuries, it is usually for a longer period of time.

To reduce risk of lawsuits, a number of companies have turned to employment practices liability insurance (EPLI), mandatory arbitration, and internal conflict resolution programs. EPLI can provide some protection from employment-related lawsuits, but generally it is available only if employment practices, policies, recordkeeping, past claims, training, complaints, and problems pass muster. Mandatory arbitration requires all employees to agree, as a condition of employment, that they will participate in arbitration rather than instituting a lawsuit to settle any employment differences.

LEGAL REQUIREMENTS FOR SAFETY AND HEALTH

Employers must comply with a variety of federal and state laws when developing and maintaining healthy, safe, and secure workforces and working environments. Three major legal areas are workers' compensation legislation, the Americans with Disabilities Act, and child labor laws.

Workers' Compensation

Workers' compensation laws in some form are on the books in all states today. Under these laws, employers contribute to an insurance fund to compensate employees for injuries received while on the job. Premiums paid reflect the accident rates of the employers, with employers that have higher incident rates being assessed higher premiums. These laws usually provide payments to replace wages for injured workers, depending on the amount of lost time and the wage level. They also provide payments to cover medical bills and for retraining if a worker cannot go back to the current job. Most state laws also set a maximum weekly amount for determining workers' comp benefits.

One aspect of workers' compensation coverage relates to the use of telecommuting by employees. In most situations, while working at home for employers, individuals are covered under workers' compensation laws. Therefore, if an employee is injured while doing employer-related work at home, the employer likely is liable for the injury.

Workers' compensation costs have become a major issue for many employers. These costs usually represent from 2% to 10% of payroll for most employers. The major contributors to increases have been higher medical costs and litigation expenses.[2] However, the frequency of workers' compensation claims for lost time has decreased some in all industry groups.

The Family and Medical Leave Act (FMLA) affects workers' compensation as well. Because the FMLA allows eligible employees to take up to 12 weeks of leave for their serious health conditions, injured employees may ask to use that leave time in addition to the leave time allowed under workers' comp, even if it is unpaid. Some employers have policies that state that FMLA leave runs concurrently with any workers' comp leave.

Americans with Disabilities Act and Safety Issues

Employers sometimes try to return injured workers to light-duty work to reduce workers' compensation costs. However, under the Americans with Disabilities Act (ADA), when making accommodations for injured employees through light-duty work, employers may undercut what are really essential job functions. Also, making such accommodations for injured employees for a period of time may require employers to make similar accommodations for job applicants with disabilities. Health and safety recordkeeping practices have been affected by an ADA provision that requires all medical-related information to be maintained separately from all other confidential files.

Child Labor Laws

Safety concerns are reflected in restrictions affecting younger workers, especially those under the age of 18. Child labor laws, found in section XII of the Fair Labor Standards Act (FLSA), set the minimum age for most employment at 16 years. For "hazardous" occupations, 18 years is the minimum. Figure 9-1 lists 17 occupations that the federal government considers hazardous for children who work while attending school.

In addition to complying with workers' compensation, ADA, and child labor laws, most employers must comply with the Occupational Safety and Health Act of 1970. This act has had a tremendous impact on the workplace. The act is administered by the Occupational Safety and Health Administration.

OCCUPATIONAL SAFETY AND HEALTH ACT

The Occupational Safety and Health Act of 1970 was passed "to assure so far as possible every working man or woman in the Nation safe and healthful working conditions and to preserve our human resources." Every employer

FIGURE 9-1 Selected Child Labor Hazardous Occupations (minimum age: 18 years)

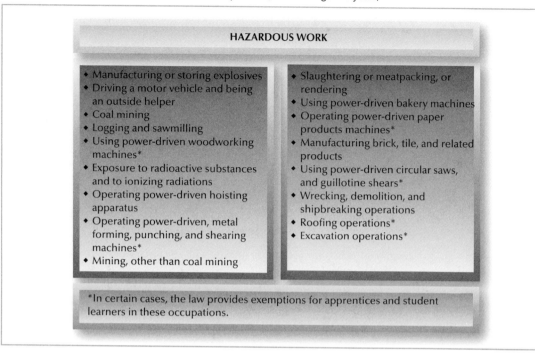

HAZARDOUS WORK

- Manufacturing or storing explosives
- Driving a motor vehicle and being an outside helper
- Coal mining
- Logging and sawmilling
- Using power-driven woodworking machines*
- Exposure to radioactive substances and to ionizing radiations
- Operating power-driven hoisting apparatus
- Operating power-driven, metal forming, punching, and shearing machines*
- Mining, other than coal mining

- Slaughtering or meatpacking, or rendering
- Using power-driven bakery machines
- Operating power-driven paper products machines*
- Manufacturing brick, tile, and related products
- Using power-driven circular saws, and guillotine shears*
- Wrecking, demolition, and shipbreaking operations
- Roofing operations*
- Excavation operations*

*In certain cases, the law provides exemptions for apprentices and student learners in these occupations.

that is engaged in commerce and has one or more employees is covered by the act. Farmers having fewer than 10 employees are exempt. Employers in specific industries, such as coal mining, are covered under other health and safety acts. Federal, state, and local governments are covered by separate statutes and provisions.

The Occupational Safety and Health Act of 1970 established the Occupational Safety and Health Administration, known as OSHA, to administer its provisions. By making employers and employees more aware of safety and health considerations, OSHA has significantly affected organizations. OSHA regulations appear to have contributed to reductions in the number of accidents and injuries in some cases. But in other industries, OSHA has had little or no effect.

OSHA Enforcement Standards

To implement OSHA regulations, specific standards were established to regulate equipment and working environments. Two provisions have been recognized as key to employers' responsibility to comply with OSHA. These are as follows:

- *General duty*: The act requires that the employer has a "general duty" to provide safe and healthy working conditions, even in areas where OSHA standards have not been set.[3] Employers who know or reasonably should know of unsafe or unhealthy conditions can be cited for violating the general duty clause.

- *Notification and posters*: Employers are required to inform their employees of safety and health standards established by OSHA. Also, OSHA posters must be displayed in prominent locations in workplaces.

OSHA Recordkeeping Requirements

Employers are generally required to maintain a detailed annual record of the various types of injuries, accidents, and fatalities for inspection by OSHA representatives and for submission to the agency. OSHA guidelines state that facilities whose accident records are below the national average rarely need inspecting. But those with high "days away from work scores" may get letters from OSHA and perhaps an inspection.

Four types of injuries or illnesses are defined by the Occupational Safety and Health Act. They are as follows:

- *Injury- or illness-related deaths*: fatalities at workplaces or caused by work-related actions
- *Lost-time or disability injuries*: job-related injuries or disabling occurrences that cause an employee to miss regularly scheduled work on the day following the accident
- *Medical care injuries*: injuries that require treatment by a physician but do not cause an employee to miss a regularly scheduled work turn
- *Minor injuries*: injuries that require first aid treatment and do not cause an employee to miss the next regularly scheduled work turn

OSHA Inspections

The Occupational Safety and Health Act provides for on-the-spot inspections by OSHA representatives, called compliance officers or inspectors. In *Marshall v. Barlow's, Inc.*, the U.S. Supreme Court held that safety inspectors must produce a search warrant if an employer refuses to allow an inspector into the plant voluntarily. The Court also ruled that an inspector does not have to show probable cause to obtain a search warrant. A warrant can be obtained easily if a search is part of a general enforcement plan.[4]

When an OSHA compliance officer arrives, managers should ask to see the inspector's credentials. Next, the HR representative for the employer should insist on an opening conference with the compliance officer. The compliance officer may request that a union representative, an employee, and a company representative be present while the inspection is conducted.

OSHA has been criticized on several fronts. Because the agency has so many worksites to inspect, employers have only a relatively small chance of being inspected. Some suggest that employers pay little attention to OSHA enforcement efforts for this reason. Employers, especially smaller ones, continue to complain about the complexity of complying with OSHA standards and the costs associated with penalties and with making changes required to remedy problem areas.

SAFETY MANAGEMENT

Well-designed and well-managed safety programs can pay dividends in reduced accidents and associated costs, such as workers' compensation and possible fines. Further, accidents and other safety concerns usually decline as a result of management efforts that emphasize safety. Often, the difference between high-performing firms with good occupational safety records and other firms is that the former have effective safety management programs. Both HR and operating managers must be involved in coordinating health, safety, and security efforts. Successful safety management includes several components highlighted next.

Organizational Commitment and a Safety Culture

At the heart of safety management is an organizational commitment to a comprehensive safety effort that should be coordinated at the top level of management and include all members of the organization. Three approaches are used by employers in managing safety. Figure 9-2 shows the organizational, engineering, and individual approaches and their components. Successful programs may use all three in dealing with safety issues.

Safety Policies, Discipline, and Recordkeeping

Designing safety policies and rules and disciplining violators are important components of safety efforts. Frequently reinforcing the need for safe behavior

FIGURE 9-2 Approaches to Effective Safety Management

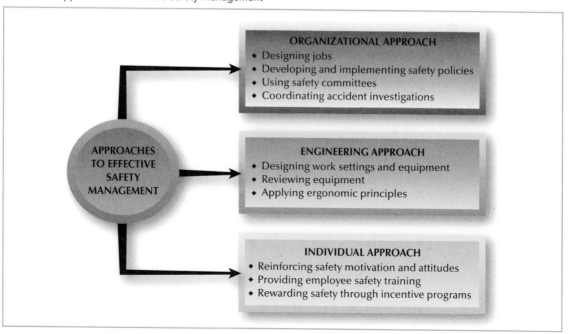

and frequently supplying feedback on positive safety practices are also effective ways of improving worker safety. Such safety-conscious efforts must involve employees, supervisors, managers, safety specialists, and HR staff members.

For policies about safety to be effective, good recordkeeping about accidents, causes, and other details is necessary. Without records, an employer cannot track its safety performance, compare benchmarks against other employers, and may not realize the extent of its safety problems.

Safety Training and Communication

Good safety training reduces accidents, and can be done in various ways. Regular training sessions with supervisors, managers, and employees are often coordinated by HR staff members. Communication of safety procedures, reasons why accidents occurred, and what to do in an emergency is part of that training. Without effective communication, training is insufficient. To reinforce safety training, continuous communication to develop safety consciousness is necessary.

Safety Committees

Employees frequently participate in safety planning through safety committees, often composed of workers from a variety of levels and departments. A safety committee generally meets at regularly scheduled times, has specific responsibilities for conducting safety reviews, and makes recommendations for changes necessary to avoid future accidents. Usually, at least one member of the committee comes from the HR department.

Inspection, Investigation, and Evaluation

It is not necessary to wait for an OSHA inspector to check the work area for safety hazards. Inspections may be done regularly by a safety committee or by a company safety coordinator. Problem areas should be addressed immediately to keep work productivity at the highest possible levels. OSHA inspects organizations with above-average rates of lost workdays more frequently. When accidents occur, they should be investigated by the employer's safety committee or safety coordinator.

The phases of accident investigation are in Figure 9-3. While identifying why an accident occurred is useful, taking steps to prevent similar accidents from occurring is even more important.

FIGURE 9-3 Phases of Accident Investigation

Measuring Safety Efforts

Organizations should monitor and evaluate their safety efforts. Just as organizational accounting records are audited, a firm's safety efforts should be audited periodically as well. Accident and injury statistics should be compared with previous accident patterns to identify any significant changes. This analysis should be designed to measure progress in safety management.

Safety efforts can be measured. Some common ones are workers' compensation costs per injury/illness; percentage of injuries/illnesses by department, work shifts, and job categories; and incident rate comparisons with industry and benchmark targets. Regardless of the specific measures used, it is critical to be able to track and evaluate safety management efforts using relevant HR metrics.

EMPLOYEE HEALTH

Employee health problems are varied—and somewhat inevitable. They can range from minor illnesses such as colds to serious illnesses related to the jobs performed. Employers face a variety of workplace health issues, some of which are discussed next.

Substance Abuse

Use of illicit substances or misuse of controlled substances, alcohol, or other drugs is called **substance abuse.** The millions of substance abusers in the workforce cost global employers billions of dollars annually, although recently there has been a decline in illegal drug use by employees. Most companies have a drug-screening policy that focuses on preemployment testing.

A company should have a written policy covering alcohol and drugs and the possession of illegal drugs at work. Such a policy should prohibit employees from coming to work under the influence of alcohol or drugs. The policy should be communicated in writing, and each employee should sign off and understand that failure to take a test can lead to adverse inference.[5]

Employers' concerns about substance abuse stem from the ways it alters work behaviors, causing increased tardiness, increased absenteeism, a slower work pace, a higher rate of mistakes, and less time spent at the work station. It can also cause an increase in withdrawal (physical and psychological) and antagonistic behaviors, which may lead to workplace violence. Alcohol testing and drug testing are used by many employers, especially following an accident or some other reasonable cause. Some employers also use random testing programs.

Types of Drug Tests.   There are several different types of tests for drug use: urinalysis, radioimmunoassay of hair, surface swiping, and fitness-for-duty testing. The innovative fitness-for-duty tests can be used alone or in conjunction with drug testing. These tests can distinguish individuals under the influence of alcohol or prescription drugs to the extent that their abilities to perform their jobs are impaired. Some firms use fitness-for-duty tests to detect work performance safety problems before putting a person behind dangerous equipment.

Handling Substance Abuse Cases. The Americans with Disabilities Act (ADA) affects how management can handle substance abuse cases. Current users of *illegal* drugs are specifically excluded from the definition of *disabled* under the act. However, those addicted to *legal* substances (e.g., alcohol and prescription drugs) are considered disabled under the ADA. Also, recovering substance abusers are considered disabled under the ADA.

To encourage employees to seek help for their substance abuse problems, a *firm-choice option* is usually recommended and has been endorsed legally. In this procedure, a supervisor or a manager confronts the employee privately about unsatisfactory work-related behaviors.

Emotional/Mental Health

Many individuals are facing work, family, and personal life pressures. A variety of emotional/mental health issues arise at work that must be addressed by employers. It is important to note that emotional/mental illnesses such as schizophrenia and depression are considered disabilities under the ADA.

Depression is another common emotional/mental health concern. The effects of depression are seen at all organizational levels, from warehouses and accounting offices to executive suites. Employees who appear to be depressed are guided to employee assistance programs and helped with obtaining medical treatment.

Health and Older Employees

The graying of the workforce has been mentioned previously, but there are implications for health and safety. All signs point to an abundance of older workers, as many are showing signs of working beyond age 65. As noted earlier, there is a diminishing pool of successful younger workers to replace them. Data show that older workers have fewer injuries, but are out of work longer when they do, and these injuries cost more to fix.

Health Promotion

Employers concerned about maintaining a healthy workforce must move beyond simply providing healthy working conditions and begin promoting employee health and wellness in other ways. **Health promotion** is a supportive approach of facilitating and encouraging healthy actions and lifestyles among employees. Health promotion efforts can range from providing information and increasing employee awareness of health issues to creating an organizational culture supportive of employee health enhancements.

Wellness programs are designed to maintain or improve employee health before problems arise by encouraging self-directed lifestyle changes. Programs emphasize healthy lifestyles and environment, including reduced cholesterol and heart disease risks and individualized exercise programs and follow-up. These programs use information and subtle psychology to motivate people to live healthier lifestyles. They typically focus on exercise, nutrition, sleep, stress, and life balance.

Employee Assistance Programs. One method organizations use as a broad-based response to health issues is an **employee assistance program (EAP),** which provides counseling and other help to employees having emotional, physical, or other personal problems. In such a program, an employer typically contracts with a counseling agency for the service. Employees who have problems may then contact the agency, either voluntarily or by employer referral, for assistance with a broad range of problems. Counseling costs are paid for by the employer, either in total or up to a preestablished limit. Done well, EAPs can help reduce health care and other costs.

SECURITY CONCERNS AT WORK

Traditionally, when employers have addressed worker health and safety, they have been concerned about reducing workplace accidents, improving safety practices, and reducing health hazards at work. However, in the past decade, providing security for employees has become important. Notice that virtually all of the areas discussed in the following text have significant HR implications. Heading the list of security concerns is workplace violence.

Workplace Violence

Workplace violence is an attack directed at someone at work or on duty. For example, physical assault, threats, harassment, intimidation, and bullying all qualify. There are a number of warning signs and characteristics of a potentially violent person at work. Individuals who have committed the most violent acts have had a relatively common profile. A profound humiliation or rejection, the end of a marriage, the loss of a lawsuit, termination from a job, or other sources of stress may make a difficult employee turn violent. Too often violence that begins at home with family or "friends" can spill over to the workplace. Also, many abused women report being harassed frequently at work, by telephone or in person, by abusing partners.

Dealing with Workplace Violence. The increase in workplace violence has led many employers to develop policies and practices for trying to prevent and respond to workplace violence. Policies can identify how workplace violence is to be dealt with in conjunction with disciplinary actions and referrals to EAPs. Training of managers is important, as well as creating a *violence response team,* composed of security personnel, key managers, HR staff members, and selected employees.

Security Management

A comprehensive approach to security management is needed to address a wide range of issues, including workplace violence. HR managers may have responsibility for security programs or may work closely with security managers or consultants.

Security Audit.   In a **security audit,** HR staff conduct a comprehensive review of organizational security. Sometimes called a *vulnerability analysis,* such an audit uses managers inside the organization (e.g., the HR manager and the facilities manager) and outsiders (e.g., security consultants, police officers, fire officials, and computer security experts) to assess security issues.

Typically, a security audit begins with a survey of the area around the facility. Such factors as lighting in parking lots, traffic flow, location of emergency response services, crime in the surrounding neighborhood, and the layout of the buildings and grounds are evaluated.

Controlled Access.   A key part of security involves controlling access to the physical facilities of the organization. Many workplace homicides occur during robberies. Therefore, employees who are most vulnerable, such as taxi drivers and convenience store clerks, can be provided bulletproof partitions and restricted access areas.

Controlling computer access may be an important part of securing IT resources. Coordination with information technology resources to change passwords, access codes, and otherwise protect company information may be important.

Employee Screening and Selection.   A key facet of providing security is screening job applicants. HR management is somewhat limited by legal constraints on what can be done with the use of psychological tests and checking of references. However, firms that do not screen employees adequately may be subject to liability if an employee commits crimes later.

DISASTER PREPARATION AND RECOVERY PLANNING

During the past several years, a number of significant disasters have occurred. Some have been natural disasters, such as hurricanes, major snowstorms, flooding in various states, tornadoes, and forest fires. There also has been concern about terrorism, and some firms have been damaged by fires and explosions. All of these situations have led to HR management having an expanded role in disaster planning.

Disaster Planning

For disaster planning to occur properly, three components must be addressed by HR, as shown in Figure 9-4. Imagine that a hurricane destroys the work

FIGURE 9-4 Disaster Planning Components

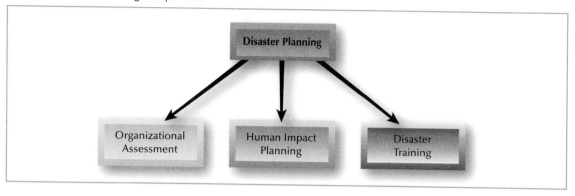

facility where employees work, as well as many of the employees' homes. Or picture an explosion or terrorist attack that prohibits workers from getting to their workplaces. Such situations illustrate why each of the components has human dimensions to be addressed.

Organizational Assessment. Organizational assessment includes establishing a disaster planning team, often composed of representatives from HR, security, information technology, operations, and other areas. The purpose of this team is to conduct an organizational assessment of how various disasters might affect the organization and its employees. Then a disaster recovery plan is developed to identify how the organization will respond to different situations.

Human Impact Planning. A number of areas are part of human impact planning, including items such as having backup databases for numerous company details, along with employee contact information. Who will take responsibilities for various duties and how these efforts will be coordinated must be identified.

Disaster Training. All of the planning efforts may be wasted if managers and employees are not trained on what to do when disasters occur. This training covers a wide range of topics, including the following: first aid/CPR, hazardous materials containment, disaster escape means, employer contact methods, and organizational restoration efforts.

But training is not sufficient without conducting exercises or simulations for managers and employees to use the training. Regular tests to ensure that information technology and databases are security accessible outside of the main location should occur. Testing responses if a workplace violence attack occurs may identify additional activities needed in an organization. Training must be a continuing consideration and must reflect updated disaster planning efforts.[6]

Disaster Planning for Disease

One issue during the past few years has been the spread of various kinds of viruses and flu throughout the world. The global nature of business travel has increased the likelihood of the spread of a deadly virus. Two key issues are whether to evacuate expatriate employees from locations where flu occurs and how to protect local employees if the flu symptoms occur in their area.

EMPLOYER AND EMPLOYEE RIGHTS AND RESPONSIBILITIES

Four interrelated HR issues are considered part of this topic: *employee rights, HR policies, absenteeism,* and *discipline.* Employees come to work with some rights, but many more are granted or constrained by the HR policies and rules an employer sets. For example, such rules include policies on absenteeism. Further, discipline used against those who fail to follow policies and rules has both employee and employer rights dimensions.

Rights generally do not exist in the abstract. Instead, **rights** are powers, privileges, or interests granted by law, nature, or tradition. **Statutory rights** are the result of specific laws or statutes passed by federal, state, or local governments. Various federal, state, and local laws have granted employees certain rights at work, such as equal employment opportunity, collective bargaining, and workplace safety. These laws and their interpretations also have been the subjects of a considerable number of court cases because employers also have rights.

Rights are offset by **responsibilities,** which are obligations to perform certain tasks and duties. Employment is a reciprocal relationship in that both the employer and the employee have rights and obligations. The reciprocal nature of rights and responsibilities suggests that both parties to an employment relationship should regard the other as having rights and should treat the other with respect.

Employment Contracts

When individuals become employees, they will encounter both employment rights and responsibilities. Employment rights and responsibilities can be spelled out formally in written employment contracts or in employer handbooks and policies disseminated to employees. Contracts can formalize the employment relationship.

Traditionally, employment contracts have been used mostly for executives and senior managers, but the use of employment contracts is filtering down in the organization to include highly specialized professional and technical employees who have scarce skills. An **employment contract** is a formal agreement that outlines the details of employment. Depending on the organization and individuals involved, employment agreements may contain a number of provisions.

Employment contracts may include **noncompete agreements,** which prohibit individuals who leave an organization from working with an employer in the same line of business for a specified period of time. A noncompete agreement may be presented as a separate contract or as a clause in an employment contract. Though primarily used with newly hired employees, some firms have required existing employees to sign noncompete agreements.

Implied Contracts

The idea that a contract (even an implied or unwritten one) exists between individuals and their employers affects the employment relationship. The rights and responsibilities of the employee may be spelled out in a job description, in an employment contract, in HR policies, or in a handbook, but often they are not. The rights and responsibilities of the employee may exist *only* as unwritten employer expectations about what is acceptable behavior or performance on the part of the employee. When the employer fails to follow up on the implied promises, the employee may pursue remedies in court.

RIGHTS AFFECTING THE EMPLOYMENT RELATIONSHIP

As employees have increasingly regarded themselves as free agents in the workplace and as the power of unions has changed in the United States, the struggle between individual employee and employer "rights" has become heightened. Employers frequently do not fare well in court in employee "rights" cases. Several concepts from law and psychology influence the employment relationship: employment-at-will, wrongful or constructive discharge, just cause, due process, and distributive and procedural justice.

Employment-at-Will

Employment-at-will (EAW) is a common-law doctrine stating that employers have the right to hire, fire, demote, or promote whomever they choose, unless there is a law or a contract to the contrary. Conversely, employees can quit whenever they want and go to another job under the same terms. An employment-at-will statement in an employee handbook usually contains wording such as the following:

> *This handbook is not a contract, express or implied, guaranteeing employment for any specific duration. Although we hope that your employment relationship with us will be long term, either you or the Employer may terminate this relationship at any time, for any reason, with or without cause or notice.*

Wrongful Discharge. Employers who run afoul of EAW restrictions may be guilty of **wrongful discharge,** which is the termination of an individual's employment for reasons that are illegal or improper. Employers should take several precautions to reduce wrongful-discharge liabilities. Having a well-written employee handbook, training managers, and maintaining adequate documentation are key.

Some state courts have recognized certain nonstatutory grounds for wrongful-discharge suits. Additionally, courts generally have held that unionized workers cannot pursue EAW actions as at-will employees because they are covered by the grievance arbitration process. As EAW has changed in interpretations and more wrongful-discharge lawsuits have been brought, employers have become more concerned about legal liability issues.[7]

Closely related to wrongful discharge is **constructive discharge,** which is deliberately making conditions intolerable to get an employee to quit. Under normal circumstances, an employee who resigns rather than being dismissed cannot later collect damages for violation of legal rights. An exception to this rule occurs when the courts find that the working conditions were made so intolerable as to *force* a reasonable employee to resign. Then, the resignation is considered a discharge.

Just Cause and Due Process

Just cause is reasonable justification for taking employment-related action. The need for a "good reason" for disciplinary actions such as dismissal usually can be found in union contracts, but not in at-will situations. The United States has different just-cause rules than do some other countries. Even though definitions of *just cause* vary, the overall concern is fairness. To be viewed by others as *just*, the disciplinary action must be justified by the facts in the individual case.

Due process, like just cause, is about fairness. Due process is the requirement that the employer use a fair process to determine if there has been employee wrongdoing and that the employee have an opportunity to explain and defend his or her actions. Figure 9-5 shows some factors to be considered when combining an evaluation of just cause and due process. How HR managers address these factors determines whether the courts perceive employers' actions as fair.

FIGURE 9-5 Criteria for Evaluating Just Cause and Due Process

JUST-CAUSE DETERMINANTS
- Was the employee warned of the consequences of the conduct?
- Was the employer's rule reasonable?
- Did management investigate before disciplining?
- Was the investigation fair and impartial?
- Was there evidence of guilt?
- Were the rules and penalties applied evenhandedly?
- Was the penalty reasonable, given the offense?

DUE PROCESS CONSIDERATIONS
- How have precedents been handled?
- Is a complaint process available?
- Was the complaint process used?
- Was retaliation used against the employee?
- Was the decision based on facts?
- Were the actions and processes viewed as fair by outside entities?

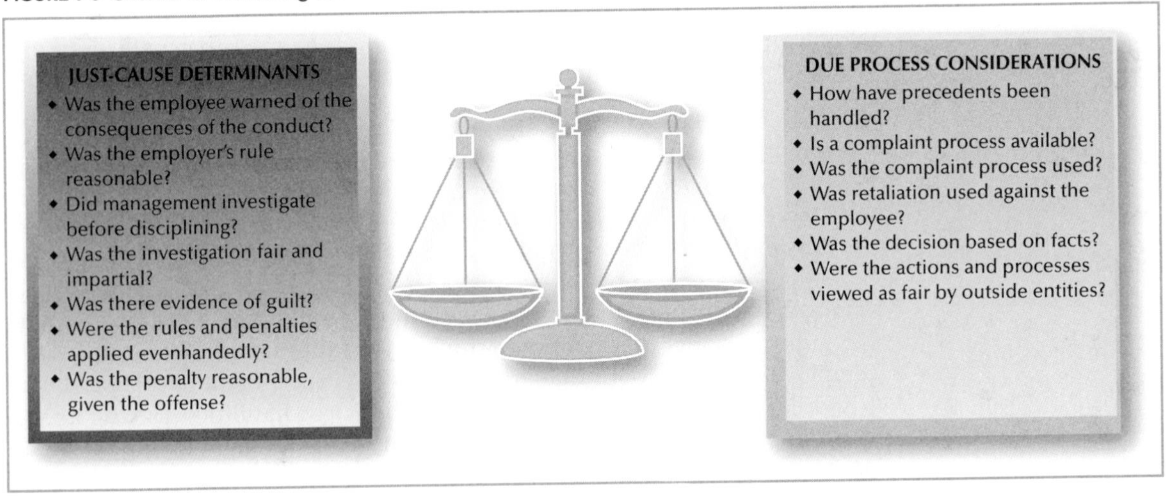

Work-Related Alternative Dispute Resolution

Disputes between management and employees over different work issues are normal and inevitable, but how the parties resolve their disputes can become important. Formal grievance procedures and lawsuits provide two resolution methods. However, more and more companies are looking to alternative means of ensuring that due process occurs in cases involving employee rights. Dissatisfaction with the expenses and delays that are common in the court system when lawsuits are filed explains the growth in alternative dispute resolution (ADR) methods such as arbitration, peer review panels, and ombuds.

Arbitration is a process that uses a neutral third party to make a decision, thereby eliminating the necessity of using the court system. Some firms use *compulsory arbitration*, which requires employees to sign a preemployment agreement stating that all disputes will be submitted to arbitration, and that employees waive their rights to pursue legal action until the completion of the arbitration process. Requiring arbitration as a condition of employment is legal. However, in some situations, exceptions have been noted, so a legal check of compulsory arbitration as part of ADR should be done before adopting the practice.

Some employers allow their employees to appeal disciplinary actions to an internal committee of employees. This panel reviews the actions and makes recommendations or decisions. **Peer review panels** use fellow employees and a few managers to resolve employment disputes. Panel members are specially trained volunteers who sign confidentiality agreements, after which the company empowers them to hear appeals.

Some organizations ensure process fairness through **ombuds**—individuals outside the normal chain of command who act as independent problem solvers for both management and employees. Ombuds address employees' complaints and operate with a high degree of confidentiality.

MANAGING INDIVIDUAL EMPLOYEE AND EMPLOYER RIGHTS ISSUES

Employees who join organizations in the United States bring with them certain rights, including *freedom of speech, due process,* and *protection against unreasonable search and seizure.* Although the U.S. Constitution grants these and other rights to citizens, over the years, laws and court decisions have identified limits on them in the workplace.

Employers have legitimate rights and needs to ensure that employees are doing their jobs and working in a secure environment, while employees expect their rights, both at work and away from work, to be protected. The **right to privacy** is defined in legal terms as an individual's freedom from unauthorized and unreasonable intrusion into personal affairs.

The dramatic increase in Internet communications, twitters, specialized computers, and telecommunications systems is transforming many workplaces. The use of technology items by employers to monitor employee actions is amplifying concerns that the privacy rights of employees are being threatened.

Privacy Rights and Employee Records

As a result of concerns about protecting individual privacy rights in the United States, the Privacy Act of 1974 was passed. It includes provisions affecting HR recordkeeping systems.

Employee Medical Records.   Recordkeeping and retention practices have been affected by the Americans with Disabilities Act (ADA). As interpreted by attorneys and HR practitioners, the Act requires that all medical-related information be maintained separately from all other confidential files.

Additionally, it is important that specific access restrictions and security procedures for employee records be established. These restrictions and procedures are designed to protect the privacy of employees and to protect employers from potential liability for improper disclosure of personal information. For instance, security breaches can occur through employer records regarding an employee's Social Security data, home address, and family details, especially by electronic means.[8]

A legal regulation called the Data Protection Act requires employers to keep personnel records up-to-date and to keep only the details that are needed. Personnel files and records usually should be maintained for three years. However, different types of records should be maintained for shorter or longer periods of time based on various legal and regulatory standards.

Electronic Records.   Another concern is how electronic records are maintained and secured, given the changes in software, e-mail, and other technology. Employers should establish electronic records policies to ensure legal compliance and to avoid violating individuals' personal rights.

Employees' Free Speech Rights

The right of individuals to freedom of speech is protected by the U.S. Constitution. However, that freedom is *not* an unrestricted one in the workplace. Three areas in which employees' freedom of speech has collided with employers' restrictions are controversial views, whistle blowing, and use of the Internet and other technology.

Questions of free speech arise over the right of employees to advocate controversial viewpoints at work. Employers must follow due process procedures and demonstrate that disciplinary actions taken against employees can be justified by job-related reasons.

Individuals who report real or perceived wrongs committed by their employers are called **whistle blowers.** The reasons why people report actions that they question vary and often are individual in nature. However, whistle blowers are less likely to lose their jobs in public employment than in private employment because most civil service systems follow rules protecting whistle blowers. A 2009 U.S. federal amendment said that for private employers to receive federal stimulus funding, they must have the same whistle-blowing regulations as the federal government.[9] However, no comprehensive whistle-blowing law fully protects the right to free speech of both public and private employees.

Technology and Employer/Employee Issues

The growth of technology use by employers and employees is constantly creating new issues to be addressed. Such technology usages as twitters, wikis, social networking, and blogs require attention by employers. Employers have a right to monitor what is said and transmitted through their network and voicemail systems, despite employees' concerns about free speech. Advances in information and telecommunications technology have become a major employer issue regarding employee and workplace privacy. There are recommended actions for employers to take when monitoring technology. Employers should monitor only for business purposes and strictly enforce the policy.

Given all the time and effort spent on technology through both work and personal actions, it is important for HR professionals to provide guidance to executives, managers, and employees. Some areas in which HR policies need to be made can include the following:

- Establishing security for voicemail system
- Communicating that the employer will attempt to monitor security, but it may not be totally guaranteed
- Restricting the use of employee records to a few individuals

Many employers have developed and disseminated electronic communications policies. Figure 9-6 depicts recommended employer actions, beginning with the development of these policies.

FIGURE 9-6 Recommended Employer Actions Regarding Electronic Communications

Employee Rights and Personal Behavior Issues

Another area to which employers must give attention is employee personal behavior. Personal behavior on or off the job could be an issue. For example, if an employer investigates off-the-job charges of illegal behavior, an invasion-of-privacy claim might result. On the other hand, failure to do due diligence could jeopardize disciplinary actions that should be taken by employers.

Employers may decide to review unusual behavior by employees both on and off the job. Organizations and HR also must deal with actions such as employees or managers being inappropriately angry, insulting, or extremely rude to customers, suppliers, or employees at different levels. Employers have put limits on employees' dress and appearance in some situations, including items such as visible tattoos, certain clothing and accessories, and body piercings.

BALANCING EMPLOYER SECURITY AND EMPLOYEE RIGHTS

Balancing employer and employee rights is difficult. On one side, employers have a legitimate need to ensure that employees are performing their jobs properly in a secure environment. On the other side, employees expect the rights that they have both at work and away from work to be protected.

Workplace Monitoring

In the United States, the right of protection from unreasonable search and seizure protects an individual against activities of the government only. Thus, employees of private-sector employers can be monitored, observed, and searched at work by representatives of the employer. Several court decisions have reaffirmed the principle that both private-sector and government employers may search desks, files, lockers, and computer files without search warrants if they believe that work rules have been violated.

Numerous employers have installed video surveillance systems in workplaces. Some employers use these systems to ensure employee security, such as in parking lots, garages, and dimly lit exterior areas. Other employers have installed them on retail sales floors and in production areas, parts and inventory rooms, and lobbies.

Employee activity may be monitored to measure performance, ensure performance quality and customer service, check for theft, or enforce company rules or laws. The common concerns in a monitored workplace usually center not on whether monitoring should be used, but on how it should be conducted, how the information should be used, and how feedback should be communicated to employees.

Employer Investigations

Another area of concern regarding employee rights involves workplace investigations. The U.S. Constitution protects public-sector employees in the areas of due process, search and seizure, and privacy at work, but private-sector employees are not protected. Whether on or off the job, unethical or illegal employee behavior can be a serious problem for organizations. Employee misconduct may include illegal drug use, falsification of documents, misuse of company funds, disclosure of organizational secrets, workplace violence, employee harassment, and theft.

Substance Abuse and Drug Testing

Employee substance abuse and drug testing have received a great deal of attention. Concern about substance abuse at work is appropriate, given that absenteeism, accident/damage rates, and theft/fraud are higher for workers using illegal substances or misusing legal substances such as drugs and alcohol.

The U.S. Supreme Court has ruled that certain drug-testing plans do not violate the Constitution. Private-employer programs are governed mainly by state laws, which can be a confusing hodgepodge. The Drug-Free Workplace Act of 1988 requires government contractors to take steps to eliminate employee drug use.

Drug Testing and Employee Rights.   Unless federal, state, or local law prohibits testing, employers have a right to require applicants or employees to submit to a drug test. Preemployment drug testing is widely used. When employers conduct drug testing of current employees, they generally use one of three policies: (1) random testing of everyone at periodic intervals, (2) testing only in cases of probable cause, or (3) testing after accidents.

From a policy standpoint, it is most appropriate to test for drugs when the following conditions exist:

- Job-related consequences of the abuse are severe enough that they outweigh privacy concerns.
- Accurate test procedures are available.
- Written consent of the employee is obtained.
- Results are treated confidentially, as are any medical records.
- Employer offers a complete drug program, including an employee assistance program.

HR POLICIES, PROCEDURES, AND RULES

HR policies, procedures, and rules greatly affect employee rights (just discussed) and discipline (discussed next). Where there is a choice among actions, policies act as general guidelines that help focus those organizational actions. **Policies** are general in nature, whereas procedures and rules are specific to the situation. The important role of all three requires that they be reviewed regularly.

Procedures provide customary methods of handling activities and are more specific than policies. For example, a policy may state that employees will be given vacations according to years of service, and a procedure establishes a specific method for authorizing vacation time without disrupting work.

Rules are specific guidelines that regulate and restrict the behavior of individuals. They are similar to procedures in that they guide action and typically allow no discretion in their application. Rules reflect a management decision that action be taken—or not taken—in a given situation, and they provide more specific behavioral guidelines than do policies.[10]

Employee Handbooks.   An employee handbook can be an essential tool for communicating information about workplace culture, benefits, attendance, pay practices, safety issues, and discipline. The handbooks are sometimes written in a formal legalistic fashion, but need not be. Handbooks may contain many different areas, but some policies commonly covered in them include:

- At-will prerogatives
- Harassment
- Electronic communication
- Pay and benefits
- Discipline
- Hours worked

To communicate and discuss HR information, a growing number of firms are distributing employee handbooks electronically using an intranet, which enables employees to access policies in employee handbooks at any time. It also allows changes in policies to be made electronically rather than distributed as paper copies.

EMPLOYEE ABSENTEEISM

One major application of HR policies and practices by employers relates to employees who are absent from their work and job responsibilities. **Absenteeism** is any failure by an employee to report for work as scheduled or to stay at work when scheduled. Being absent from work may seem like a normal matter to an employee. But if a manager needs 12 people in a unit to get the work done, and 4 of the 12 are absent much of the time, the work of the unit will decrease or additional workers will have to be hired to provide results.

Types of Absenteeism

Employees can be absent from work or tardy for several reasons. Clearly, some absenteeism is inevitable because of illness, death in the family, and other personal reasons. Though absences such as those that are health related are unavoidable and understandable, they can be very costly. Many employers have sick leave policies that allow employees a certain number of paid days each year for those types of *involuntary* absences. However, much absenteeism is avoidable, or *voluntary*.

One problem is that a number of employees see no real concern about being absent or late to work because they feel that they are "entitled" to some absenteeism. In many firms, a relatively small number of individuals are responsible for a large share of the total absenteeism in the organization. Sometimes work-related stress and strain can lead to absenteeism.[11]

Regardless of the reason, employers need to know if someone is going to be absent. Various organizations have developed different means for employees to report their absences. Regardless of the method used, employers need to have a clear policy on how the employee should notify the employer when an absence occurs.

Controlling Absenteeism

Voluntary absenteeism is better controlled if managers understand its causes clearly. Once they do, they can use a variety of approaches to reduce it. Organizational policies on absenteeism should be stated clearly in an employee handbook and emphasized by supervisors and managers.

There are a number of methods that employers can use to address absenteeism. The disciplinary approach is the most widely used. Other methods include positive reinforcement and paid-time-off programs.

HR Metrics: Measuring Absenteeism.
A major step in reducing the expense of absenteeism is to decide how the organization is going to record absences and what calculations are necessary to maintain and benchmark their rates. Controlling or reducing absenteeism must begin with continuous monitoring of the absenteeism statistics in work units. Such monitoring helps managers pinpoint employees who are frequently absent and departments that have excessive absenteeism. Various methods of measuring or computing absenteeism exist. One formula suggested by the U.S. Department of Labor is as follows:

$$\frac{\text{Number of person-days lost through job absence during period}}{(\text{Average number of employees}) \times (\text{Number of workdays})} \times 100$$

The absenteeism rate also can be based on number of hours instead of number of days.

One set of metrics that can be calculated is the rate of absenteeism, which can be based on annual, monthly, quarterly, or other periods of time. Other useful measures of absenteeism might include:

- *Incidence rate*: The number of absences per 100 employees each day
- *Inactivity rate*: The percentage of time lost to absenteeism
- *Severity rate*: The average time lost per absent employee during a specified period of time (a month or a year)

EMPLOYEE DISCIPLINE

The earlier discussion about employee rights provides an appropriate introduction to the topic of employee discipline, because employee rights often are a key issue in disciplinary cases. **Discipline** is a form of training that enforces organizational rules. Those most often affected by the discipline systems are problem employees. Common disciplinary issues caused by problem employees include absenteeism, tardiness, productivity deficiencies, alcoholism, and insubordination.

Training supervisors and managers on when and how discipline should be used is crucial. Employees see disciplinary action as more fair when given by trained supervisors who base their responses on procedural justice than when discipline is done by untrained supervisors.[12]

Approaches to Discipline

The disciplinary system can be viewed as an application of behavior modification to a problem or unproductive employee. The best discipline is clearly self-discipline. Most people can be counted on to do their jobs effectively when they understand what is required at work. But for some people, the prospect of external discipline helps their self-discipline. One approach is positive discipline.

Positive Discipline Approach. The positive discipline approach builds on the philosophy that violations are actions that usually can be corrected constructively without penalty. In this approach, managers focus on using fact finding and guidance to encourage desirable behaviors, rather than using penalties to discourage undesirable behaviors.

Progressive Discipline Approach. Progressive discipline incorporates steps that become progressively more stringent and are designed to change the employee's inappropriate behavior. Figure 9-7 shows a typical progressive

FIGURE 9-7 Progressive Discipline Process

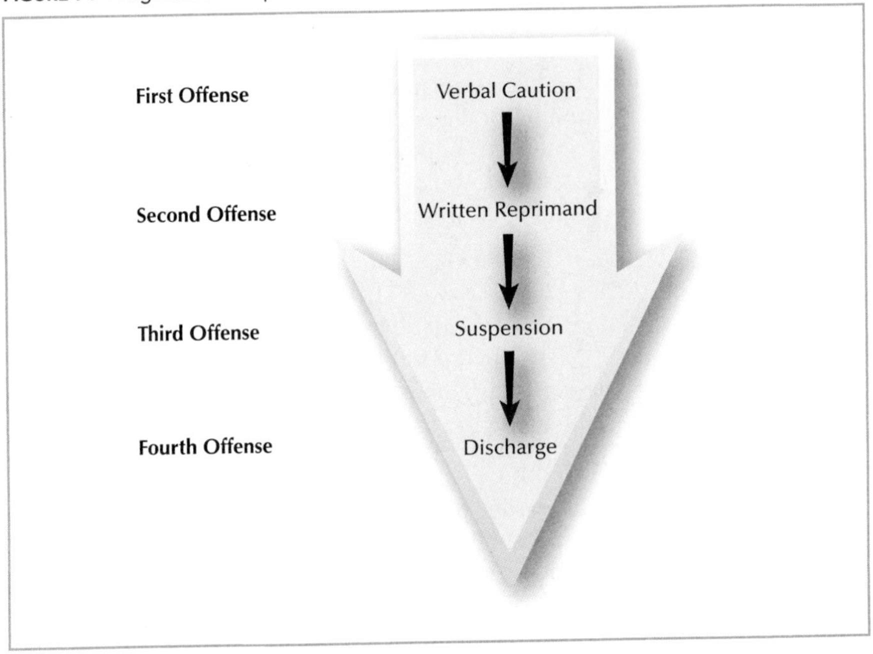

First Offense — Verbal Caution

Second Offense — Written Reprimand

Third Offense — Suspension

Fourth Offense — Discharge

discipline process; most progressive discipline procedures use verbal and written reprimands and suspension before resorting to dismissal.

Discharge: The Final Disciplinary Step. The final stage in the disciplinary process may be called *discharge, firing, dismissal,* or *termination,* among other terms. Regardless of the word used, **discharge** is when an employee is removed from a job at an employer. Both the positive and the progressive approaches to discipline clearly provide employees with warnings about the seriousness of their performance problems before dismissal occurs.

From a legal standpoint, terminating workers because they do not keep their own promises is likely to appear equitable and defensible in many courts, but nevertheless, it is important for the employer to consistently document reasons for termination and to follow appropriate HR processes discussed earlier.

NOTES

1. G. Leters, et al., "Towards a Balanced Approach in Risk Identification," *Engineering Management Journal,* Winter 2007, 3–9.

2. David Nevmark, et al., "The Impact of Provider Choice on Worker's Compensation Costs and Outcomes," *Industrial and Labor Relations Review,* 60 (2007), 121–141.

3. Bill Leonard, "OSHA Issues Final Rule on Personal Protective Equipment," *HR News,* November 19, 2007, *www.shrm.org,* 1.

4. *Marshall v. Barlow's, Inc.,* 98 S. Ct. 1816 (1978).

5. Nancy Delogv, "Essential Elements of a Drug-Free Workplace Program," *Professional Safety,* November 2007, 48–51.

6. Dian-Yan Liou and Chin-Huang Lin, "Human Resources Planning on Terrorism and Crises in the Asia Pacific Region," *Human Resource Management,* Spring 2008, 49–72.

7. Edward C. Tomlinson and William N. Bockanic, "Avoiding Liability for Wrongful Termination," *Employee Responsibilities and Rights Journal,* 21 (2009), 77–88.

8. Jared Shelly, "Hazardous Leaks," *Human Resource Executive,* September 2, 2009, 34–36.

9. Jessica Marquez, "Firms Getting Stimulus Face Tougher Whistle-Blower Law," *Workforce Management,* April 6, 2009, 4.

10. David W. Lehmon and Rangaraj Ramanujam, "Selectivity in Organizational Rule Violations," *Academy of Management Review,* 34 (2009), 643–657.

11. W. Darr and G. Johns, "Work Strain, Health, and Absenteeism," *Journal of Occupational Health Psychology* 13 (2008), 292–318.

12. Leanne E. Atwater, et al., "The Delivery of Workplace Discipline: Lessons Learned," *Organizational Dynamics,* 36 (2007), 392–403.

INTERNET RESOURCES

WorkersCompensation.com—This is a national website providing workers' compensation news and information for employers, employees, insurers, and medical providers. Visit the site at *www.workerscompensation.com.*

Occupational Safety & Health Administration—Access to OHSA regulations for compliance, newsroom, and much more can be found at the OSHA home page by visiting the website at *www.osha.gov.*

Human Resources Law Cases—This website provides information on workplace issues such as employment contracts and other issues. Visit the site at *www.hrlawindex.com.*

SHRM Policy Handbooks—This website contains sample policies, procedures, and handbooks collected by the Society for Human Resource Management. Visit the website at *www.shrm.org,* and click on Templates and Tools.

SUGGESTED READINGS

Donna Scimia, "A Common Sense Approach to Reducing Liability in Today's Workplace," *Employee Relations Law Journal,* Autumn 2007, 23–29.

Michael Burke, et al., "Relative Effectiveness of Worker Safety and Health Training Methods," *American Journal of Public Health,* 96, (2006) 315–325.

Lawrence P. Postol, "Drafting Noncompete Agreements for All 50 States," *Employee Relations Law Journal,* 33 (2007), 65–73.

Barry A. Friedman and Lisa J. Reed, "Workplace Privacy: Employee Relations and Legal Implications of Monitoring E-mail Use," *Employee Responsibilities Rights Journal,* 19 (2007), 75–83.

Union/Management Relations

HR—MEETING MANAGEMENT CHALLENGES

Even though union membership has been changing in the United States, labor relations must be considered an important part of HR. The future of employer-union relations may be evolving as political and work environments change. Key issues are:

- Why the state of unions in the United States has been changing
- How a number of legal requirements affect employer HR policies and practices
- When to resolve employee complaints and grievances

The changing nature of unions and unionization efforts will be interesting to observe during the next decade. Even though fewer workers have chosen to be union members than in the past, employers and HR professionals still need to have an understanding of the system of laws, regulations, court decisions, and administrative rulings related to unions. This is important because unions remain an alternative for employees in the event of poor HR management.

UNIONS: EMPLOYEE AND MANAGEMENT PERSPECTIVES

A **union** is a formal association of workers that promotes the interests of its members through collective action. The very existence of unions depends upon laws and legal action. An economic look at labor unions reveals "two faces." The "good face" emphasizes the fact that unions give members a "voice" to express dissatisfactions to management that likely would not be expressed otherwise. Some increases in productivity and an increase in earnings for members are typically associated with unionizing. The "bad face" emphasizes the negative effects that union wages have on allocation of resources, profitability, and productivity when the substantial compensation gains are considered.[1] But unions clearly have a place in the scheme of things, as they provide a balance to the unchallenged decision-making power of management where needed.

Exactly how economic and workforce changes affect employers and unions will be factors in the future of the labor/management relationship. Even though fewer workers have chosen to be union members in recent years than in the past, employers and HR professionals still need to understand the system of laws, regulations, court decisions, and administrative rulings related to. With this legal foundation, unions remain a strong alternative for employees in the event of poor HR management.

Unions did not seem to have a bright future in the 1930s when the National Labor Relations Act (NLRA) was passed, giving unions a legal right to exist. But they grew to represent about 36% of the workforce in the 1950s, only to see their strength in the private sector drop to less than 8% recently. However, in the public sector, union strength grew until recently.

In the United States, unions follow the goals of increasing compensation, improving working conditions, and influencing workplace rules. When a union is present, working conditions, pay, and work rules are determined through collective bargaining and designated in formal contracts. Part of understanding the current state of unionization in the United States is knowing why employees join unions and why employers resist unionization.

Why Employees Unionize

Whether a union targets a group of employees or the employees request union assistance, the union must win support from the employees to become their legal representative. Over the years employees have joined unions for two general reasons: (1) they are dissatisfied with how they are treated by their employers, and (2) they believe that unions can improve their work situations. If employees do not receive what they perceive as fair treatment from their employers, they may turn to unions for help in obtaining what they believe is equitable.[2] As Figure 10-1 shows, the major factors that can trigger unionization are issues of compensation, working conditions, management style, and employee treatment.

Why Employers Resist Unions

Employers usually would rather not have to deal with unions because doing so constrains what managers can and cannot do in a number of areas. Further, union workers receive higher wages and benefits than do nonunion workers. In turn, unions sometimes can be associated with higher productivity, although management must find labor-saving ways of doing work to offset the higher labor costs. Some employers pursue a strategy of good relations with unions, while others choose an aggressive, adversarial approach.

HR Responsibilities and Unionization.   To prevent unionization, as well as to work effectively with unions already representing employees, both HR professionals and operating managers must be attentive and responsive to employees. The pattern of dealing with unionization varies among organizations. In some organizations, operating management handles labor relations and HR has limited involvement. In other organizations, the HR unit takes primary responsibility for resisting unionization or dealing with unionized employees.

FIGURE 10-1 Factors Leading to Employee Unionization

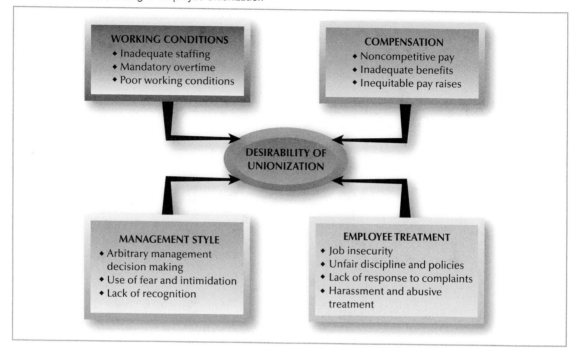

Unions Globally

Globalization, which causes economic competition among workers, companies, and nations around the world, is here to stay. The ability of a country to create jobs and attract investments can be affected by the favorability of union arrangements and labor laws. Changes in information technology have also decreased union bargaining power relative to management bargaining power. However, labor unions and labor movements have not been weakened in all cases, despite such pressures. Different laws and traditions have produced very different arrangements in different countries.

Laws that make it easier and cheaper to hire and fire employees may reduce unemployment. But in many countries, such laws cause discomfort because of the great inequality they create in the balance of power in the employer–employee relationship. As the world economy becomes more integrated, unions worldwide are facing changes from the pressures.

UNION MEMBERSHIP IN THE UNITED STATES

The statistics on union membership tell a disheartening story for organized labor in the United States during the past several decades. As shown in Figure 10-2, unions represented more than 30% of the workforce from 1945

FIGURE 10-2 Union Membership as a Percentage of the U.S. Civilian Workforce

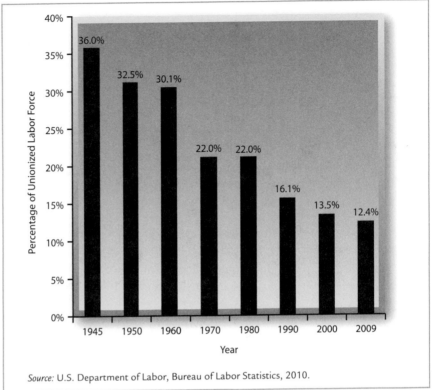

Source: U.S. Department of Labor, Bureau of Labor Statistics, 2010.

to 1960. But by 2009, unions in the United States represented only 12.4% of all civilian workers and 7.4% of the private-sector workforce. In fact, for the first time, the number of union workers employed by the government outnumbered union members in the private sector. Local, state, and federal union workers made up 51.5% (7.9 million) of all union members while private-sector union members dropped to 7.4 million.[3] The actual number of members has declined in most years even though more people are employed than previously.

But within those averages, some unions have prospered. In the past several years, certain unions have organized thousands of janitors, health care workers, cleaners, and other low-paid workers using publicity, pickets, boycotts, and strikes.

Reasons for U.S. Union Membership Decline

Several general trends have contributed to the decline of U.S. union membership, including deregulation, foreign competition, a larger number of people looking for jobs, and a general perception by firms that dealing with unions is expensive compared with nonunion alternatives. Management at many employers has taken a much more activist stance against unions than during the previous years of union growth, and economic downturns also have had negative impacts. Therefore, unions may no longer be seen as necessary for many workers, even though those workers enjoy the results of past union efforts to influence legislation that has been a benefit to them.

During the past decade, job growth in the United States has been the greatest in states located in the South, the Southwest, and the Rocky Mountains. Most of these states have little tradition of unions, more "employer-friendly" laws, and relatively small percentages of unionized workers. Much of the decline of union membership can be attributed to the shift in U.S. jobs from industries such as manufacturing, construction, and mining to service industries. There is a small percentage of union members in wholesale/retail industries and financial services, the sectors in which many new jobs have been added, whereas the number of industrial jobs continues to shrink.

One area that has led to union membership decline is the retirement of many union members in older manufacturing firms. Extremely high retiree pensions and health benefits costs have led some employers to face demands for cuts in benefits for both current and retired union employees. They also have led to employers reducing the number of current plants and workers, and unions attempting to maintain benefits costs and job security for remaining workers. In summary, private-sector union membership is primarily concentrated in the shrinking part of the economy, and unions are not making significant inroads into the fastest-growing segments in the U.S. economy.

Workforce Changes. Many of the workforce changes discussed in earlier chapters have contributed to the decrease in union representation of the labor force. The decline in many blue-collar jobs in manufacturing has been especially significant. Many white-collar workers see unions as resistant to change and not in touch with the concerns of the more educated workers in technical and professional jobs. In addition, many white-collar workers exhibit attitudes and preferences quite different from those held by blue-collar union members, and they tend to view unions as primarily blue-collar oriented.

Public-Sector Unionism

Unions have had significant success with public-sector employees. The government sector (federal, state, and local) is the most highly unionized part of the U.S. workforce, with more than 40% of government workers represented by unions. Local government workers have the highest unionization percentage of any group in the U.S. workforce. Although unions in the federal government hold the same basic philosophy as unions in the private sector, they do differ somewhat. Previous laws and executive orders have established methods of labor/management relations that consider the special circumstances present in the federal government.

Union Targets for Membership Growth

The continuing losses have led to disagreements among unions about how to fight the decline. Rather than remaining a part of the traditional AFL-CIO labor organization, seven unions split into a new group in 2005. Calling itself Change to Win (CtW), this association has a goal of taking a more aggressive approach to adding union members and affecting U.S. political legislation.

To attempt to counteract the overall decline in membership, unions are focusing on a number of industries and types of workers. One reason why Change to Win split off from the AFL-CIO was to target more effectively the addition of members in the retail, hospitality, home health care, and other service industries.

Historical Evolution of U.S. Unions

The union movement in the United States has existed in one form or another for more than two centuries. During this time, the nature of unions has evolved because of legal and political changes. The union movement in the United States began with early collective efforts by workers to address job concerns and counteract management power. As early as 1794, shoemakers organized a union, picketed, and conducted strikes. In those days, unions in the United States received very little support from the courts. In 1806, when the shoemakers' union struck for higher wages, a Philadelphia court found union members guilty of engaging in a "criminal conspiracy" to raise wages.

The *American Federation of Labor (AFL)* united a number of independent national unions in 1886. Its aims were to organize skilled craft workers and to emphasize economic issues and working conditions. As industrialization increased in the United States, many factories used semiskilled and unskilled workers. However, it was not until the *Congress of Industrial Organizations (CIO)* was founded in 1938 that a labor union organization focused on semiskilled and unskilled workers. Years later, the AFL and the CIO merged to become the AFL-CIO. That federation is the major organization coordinating union efforts in the United States today despite the split described previously.

Union Structure

Labor in the United States is represented by many different unions. Regardless of size and geographic scope, two basic types of unions have developed over time. In a **craft union,** members do one type of work, often using specialized skills and training. Examples are the International Association of Bridge, Structural, Ornamental and Reinforcing Iron Workers, and the American Federation of Television and Radio Artists. An **industrial union** includes many persons working in the same industry or company, regardless of jobs held. The United Food and Commercial Workers, the United Auto Workers, and the American Federation of State, County, and Municipal Employees are examples of industrial unions.

AFL-CIO Federation.   Labor organizations have developed complex organizational structures with multiple levels. The broadest level is the **federation,**

which is a group of autonomous unions. A federation allows individual unions to work together and present a more unified front to the public, legislators, and members. The most prominent federation in the United States is the AFL-CIO, which is a confederation of unions currently representing about 10 million workers.

Change to Win. The establishment of Change to Win (CtW) in 2005 meant that seven unions with about 6 million members left the AFL-CIO. The primary reason for the split was a division between different unions about how to stop the decline in union membership, as well as some internal organizational leadership and political issues.[4] Prominent unions in the CtW are the Teamsters, the Service Employees International Union, and the United Food and Commercial Workers.

National and International Unions. National and international unions are not governed by a federation even if they are affiliated with it. They collect dues and have their own boards, specialized publications, and separate constitutions and bylaws.

Like companies, unions find strength in size. In the past several years, about 40 mergers of unions have occurred, and a number of other unions have considered merging. For smaller unions, these mergers provide financial and union-organizing resources, and larger unions can add new members to cover managerial and administrative costs without spending funds to organize nonunion workers to become members.

Local Unions. Local unions typically have business agents and union stewards. A **business agent** is a full-time union official who operates the union office and assists union members. The agent runs the local headquarters, helps negotiate contracts with management, and becomes involved in attempts to unionize employees in other organizations. A **union steward** is an employee who is elected to serve as the first-line representative of unionized workers. Stewards address grievances with supervisors and generally represent employees at the worksite.

U.S. LABOR LAWS

The right to organize workers and engage in collective bargaining offers little value if workers cannot freely exercise it. Management has consistently developed practices to prevent unions from organizing employees. Over a period of many years, the federal government has taken action both to hamper unions and to protect them. Beginning in the late 1800s, federal and state legislation related to unionization was passed. The two most prominent acts are discussed next.

The Railway Labor Act (RLA) of 1926 represented a shift in government regulation of unions. The result of a joint effort between railroad management and unions to reduce transportation strikes, this act gave railroad employees "the right to organize and bargain collectively through representatives of their own choosing." In 1936, airlines and their employees were added to those covered by the RLA. In 1932, Congress passed the Norris-LaGuardia Act, which guaranteed workers some rights to organize and restricted the issuance of court injunctions in labor disputes.

The economic crises of the early 1930s and the continuing restrictions on workers' ability to organize into unions led to the passage of landmark labor legislation, the Wagner Act, in 1935. Later acts reflected other pressures and issues that required legislative attention. Three acts passed over a period of almost 25 years constitute the U.S. labor law foundation: (1) the Wagner Act, (2) the Taft-Hartley Act, and (3) the Landrum-Griffin Act. Each act was passed to focus on some facet of the relations between unions and management. Figure 10-3 indicates the primary focus of each act. Two other pieces of legislation, the Civil Service Reform Act and the Postal Reorganization Act, have affected union/management relations in the federal government.

Wagner Act (National Labor Relations Act)

The National Labor Relations Act, more commonly referred to as the Wagner Act, was an outgrowth of the Great Depression. With employers having to close or cut back their operations, workers were left with little job security. Unions stepped in to provide a feeling of solidarity and strength for many workers. The Wagner Act declared, in effect, that the official policy of the U.S. government was to encourage collective bargaining. Specifically, it established the right of workers to organize unhampered by management interference through unfair labor practices.

Unfair Labor Practices.   To protect union rights, the Wagner Act prohibited employers from using unfair labor practices. Five of those practices were identified as follows:

- Interfering with, restraining, or coercing employees in the exercise of their right to organize or to bargain collectively

FIGURE 10-3 Major National Labor Laws

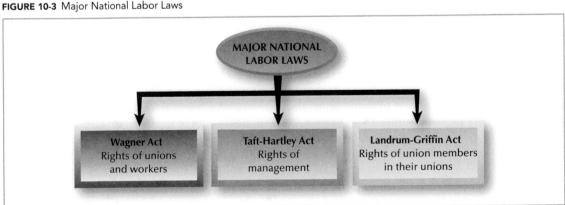

- Dominating or interfering with the formation or administration of any labor organization
- Encouraging or discouraging membership in any labor organization by discriminating with regard to hiring, tenure, or conditions of employment
- Discharging or otherwise discriminating against an employee because the employee filed charges or gave testimony under the act
- Refusing to bargain collectively with representatives of the employees

National Labor Relations Board.   The Wagner Act established the National Labor Relations Board as an independent entity to enforce the provisions of the act. The NLRB administers all provisions of the Wagner Act and of subsequent labor relations acts. The primary functions of the NLRB include conducting unionization elections, investigating complaints by employers or unions through its fact-finding process, issuing opinions on its findings, and prosecuting violations in court. The five members of the NLRB are appointed by the President of the United States and confirmed by the U.S. Senate.

Taft-Hartley Act (Labor Management Relations Act)

The passage in 1947 of the Labor Management Relations Act, better known as the Taft-Hartley Act, was accomplished as a means to offset the pro-union Wagner Act by limiting union abuses. It was considered to be pro-management and became the second of the major labor laws.

The new law amended or qualified in some respect all the major provisions of the Wagner Act and established an entirely new code of conduct for unions. The Taft-Hartley Act allows the President of the United States to declare that a strike presents a national emergency. A national emergency strike is one that would impact an industry or a major part of it in such a way that the national economy would be significantly affected. The act allows the U.S. President to declare an 80-day "cooling off" period during which union and management continue negotiations. Only after that period can a strike occur if settlements have not been reached.

Right-to-Work Provision.   One specific provision of the Taft-Hartley Act, section 14(b), deserves special explanation. This section allows states to pass laws that restrict compulsory union membership. Accordingly, several states have passed **right-to-work laws,** which prohibit requiring employees to join unions as a condition of obtaining or continuing employment. The laws were so named because they allow a person the right to work without having to join a union. The states that have enacted these laws are shown in Figure 10-4.

Landrum-Griffin Act (Labor Management Reporting and Disclosure Act)

The third of the major labor laws in the United States, the Landrum-Griffin Act, was passed in 1959. Because a union is supposed to be a democratic

FIGURE 10-4 Right-to-Work States

institution in which union members freely vote on and elect officers and approve labor contracts, the Landrum-Griffin Act was passed in part to ensure that the federal government protects the democratic rights of the members. Under the Landrum-Griffin Act, unions are required to establish bylaws, make financial reports, and provide union members with a bill of rights. The law appointed the U.S. Secretary of Labor to act as a watchdog of union conduct.

In a few instances, union officers have attempted to maintain their jobs by physically harassing or attacking individuals who have tried to oust them from office. In other cases, union officials have "milked" pension fund monies for their own use. Such instances are not typical of most unions, but illustrate the need for legislative oversight to protect individual union members.[5]

Civil Service Reform and Postal Reorganization Acts

Passed as part of the Civil Service Reform Act of 1978, the Federal Service Labor Management Relations statute made major changes in how the federal government deals with unions. The act also identified areas subject to bargaining and established the Federal Labor Relations Authority (FLRA) as an independent agency similar to the NLRB. The FLRA, a three-member body, was given the authority to oversee and administer union/management relations in the federal government and to investigate unfair practices in union organizing efforts.

In a somewhat related area, the Postal Reorganization Act of 1970 established the U.S. Postal Service as an independent entity. Part of the 1970 act prohibited postal workers from striking and established a dispute resolution process for them to follow.

Proposed Legislation

Other laws have been proposed, but at this writing none of them has been passed. One such law would bar companies from replacing workers who go on strike, which means that a union could in effect close a business down because strikers could not be replaced. Replacement workers or "scabs" have allowed companies to defeat union strikes in some cases in the past.

Another proposed law, the "Employee Free Choice Act," would allow unions to sign up workers and become recognized without an election. This approach goes against the U.S. tradition in which negotiated contracts must be agreed to by both parties. The proposed legislation has spawned considerable concern among businesses. Several large employers have resorted to direct actions in opposition to the EFCA.[6]

THE UNIONIZATON PROCESS

The typical union organizing process may begin in one of two primary ways: (1) a union targeting an industry or a company, or (2) employees requesting union representation. In the first case, the local or national union identifies a firm or an industry in which it believes unionization can succeed. The logic for targeting is that if the union succeeds in one firm or a portion of the industry, then many other workers in the industry will be more willing to consider unionizing. In the second case, the impetus for union organizing occurs when individual workers at an employer contact a union and express a desire to unionize. The employees themselves—or the union—may then begin to campaign to win support among the other employees.

Organizing Campaign

Like other entities seeking members, a union usually mounts an organized campaign to persuade individuals to join. As would be expected, employers respond to unionization efforts by taking various types of opposing actions.

Employers' Union Prevention Efforts.
Management representatives may use various tactics to defeat a unionization effort. Such tactics often begin when union publicity appears or during the distribution of authorization cards. Some employers such as Con Agra, Coca-Cola, and Wal-Mart hire

consultants who specialize in combating unionization efforts. Using these "union busters," as they are called by unions, appears to enhance employers' chances of winning the representation election. Union prevention efforts that may be conducted by consultants or done by management and outside labor attorneys include:[7]

- Holding mandatory employee meetings
- Distributing antiunion leaflets at work and mailing antiunion letters to employees' homes
- Providing and using antiunion videos, e-mails, and other electronic communications

Employers may make strategic decisions and take aggressive steps to remain nonunion. Such a choice is perfectly rational, but may require some specific HR policies and philosophies.

Unions' Organizing Efforts.   The organizing and negotiating successes of unions are tied to the economy and economic trends. The persuasion efforts by unions can take many forms, including personally contacting employees outside work, mailing materials to employees' homes, inviting employees to attend special meetings away from the company, and publicizing the advantages of union membership. Brochures and leaflets can be given to employees as they leave work, mailed to their homes, or even attached to their vehicles, as long as the union complies with the rules established by laws and the NLRB. The purpose of all this publicity is to encourage employees to sign authorization cards. To encourage individuals to become involved in unionization efforts, unions have adopted electronic means, such as establishing websites where interested workers can read about benefits of unionization. However, an employer can prohibit workers from using its e-mail system for union business.[8]

Authorization Cards

A **union authorization card** is signed by employees to designate a union as their collective bargaining agent. At least 30% of the employees in the targeted group must sign authorization cards before an election can be called.

Union advocates have lobbied for changing laws so that elections are not needed if more than 50% of the eligible employees sign authorization cards. As mentioned earlier, the proposed Employee Free Choice Act would eliminate the secret ballot for electing union representation and make it so that the union would automatically represent all workers if more than 50% of the employees signed authorization cards.

However, the fact that an employee signs an authorization card does not necessarily mean that the employee is in favor of a union. It means only that the employee is willing to put the union question to a vote. Employees who do not want a union might sign authorization cards because they want management to know they are disgruntled or because they want to avoid upsetting coworkers who are advocating unionization.

Representation Election

An election to determine if a union will represent the employees is supervised by the NLRB for private-sector organizations and by other legal bodies for public-sector organizations. If two unions are attempting to represent employees, the employees will have three choices: union A, union B, and no union.

Bargaining Unit.   Before any election, the appropriate bargaining unit must be determined. A **bargaining unit** is composed of all employees eligible to select a single union to represent and bargain collectively for them. If management and the union do not agree on who is and who is not included in the unit, the regional office of the NLRB must make the determination. Employees who constitute a bargaining unit have mutual interests in the following areas:

- Wages, hours, and working conditions
- Traditional industry groupings for bargaining purposes
- Physical location and amount of interaction and working relationships between employee groups
- Supervision by similar levels of management

Supervisors and Union Ineligibility.   Provisions of the National Labor Relations Act exclude supervisors from voting for or joining unions. As a result, supervisors cannot be included in bargaining units for unionization purposes, except in industries covered by the Railway Labor Act. A major case decided by the U.S. Supreme Court found that charge nurses with RN degrees were supervisors because they exercised independent judgment. This case and others have provided employers and unions with some guidance about who should be considered supervisors and thus excluded from bargaining units.[9]

Election Unfair Labor Practices.   Employers and unions engage in a number of activities before an election. Both the Wagner Act and the Taft-Hartley Act place restrictions on these activities. Once unionizing efforts begin, all activities must conform to the requirements established by applicable labor laws. Both management and the union must adhere to those requirements, or the results of the effort can be appealed to the NLRB and overturned.

Election Process.   If an election is held, the union needs to receive only a majority of the votes. For example, if a group of 200 employees is the identified bargaining unit, and only 50 people vote, only 26 (50% of those voting plus 1) need to vote yes for the union to be named as the representative of all 200 employees. Typically, the smaller the number of employees in the bargaining unit, the higher the likelihood that the union will win.

If either side believes that the other side used unfair labor practices, the election results can be appealed to the NLRB. If the NLRB finds evidence of unfair practices, it can order a new election. If no unfair practices were used and the union obtains a majority in the election, the union then petitions the NLRB for certification.

Certification and Decertification

Official certification of a union as the legal representative for designated private-sector employees is given by the NLRB, or for public-sector employees by an equivalent body. Once certified, the union attempts to negotiate a contract with the employer. The employer *must* bargain; refusing to bargain with a certified union constitutes an unfair labor practice.

When employees no longer wish to be represented by the union, they can use **decertification,** which is a process whereby a union is removed as the representative of a group of employees. Employees attempting to oust a union must obtain decertification authorization cards signed by at least 30% of the employees in the bargaining unit before an election may be called. If a majority of those voting in the election want to remove the union, the decertification effort succeeds.

Contract Negotiation (Collective Bargaining)

Collective bargaining, the last step in unionization, is the process whereby representatives of management and workers negotiate over wages, hours, and other terms and conditions of employment. This give-and-take process between representatives of the two organizations attempts to establish conditions beneficial to both. It is also a relationship based on relative power.

COLLECTIVE BARGAINING ISSUES

A number of issues can be addressed during collective bargaining. Although not often listed as such in the contract, management rights and union security are two important issues subject to collective bargaining. These leave issues common to collective bargaining.

Management Rights

Virtually all labor contracts include **management rights,** which are rights reserved so that the employer can manage, direct, and control its business. By including such a provision, management attempts to preserve its unilateral right to make changes in areas not identified in a labor contract. A typical provision might read as follows:

> *The employer retains all rights to manage, direct, and control its business in all particulars, except as such rights are expressly and specifically modified by the terms of this or any subsequent agreement.*

Union Security

A major concern of union representatives when bargaining is the negotiation of **union security provisions,** which are contract clauses to help the union obtain and retain members. One type of union security clause in labor contracts is the *no-layoff policy*, or *job security guarantee*. Such a provision is especially important to many union workers because of all the mergers, downsizings, and job reductions taking place in many industrial, textile, and manufacturing firms. However, for these very reasons, management is often unwilling to consider this type of provision.

Union Dues Issues.   A common union security provision is the *dues check-off* clause, which provides for the automatic deduction of union dues from the payroll checks of union members. The dues checkoff provision makes it much easier for the union to collect its funds, and without it, the union must collect dues by billing each member separately.

However, federal court cases have been filed that restrict unions from using such checkoff clauses for contributions to political and congressional candidates. A U.S. Supreme Court case supported the constitutionality of state laws that require labor unions to get written consent before using nonmember fees for political purposes. The Court noted that Washington, like many other states, allows public-sector unions to levy fees on nonmember employees, as well as "agency shop" agreements. But it held that under such arrangements, the union must obtain express authorization from the nonmembers to use their agency fees for election-related purposes.[10]

Types of Required Union Membership.   Another form of union security provision is *requiring union membership* of all employees, subject to state right-to-work laws. Closed shops require union membership to get a job, and are illegal except in limited situations within the construction industry. But other types of arrangements can be developed.

Classification of Bargaining Issues

The NLRB has defined collective bargaining issues in three ways. The categories it has used are mandatory, permissive, and illegal.

Issues identified specifically by labor laws or court decisions as subject to bargaining are **mandatory issues.** If either party demands that issues in this category be subject to bargaining, then that must occur. Generally, mandatory issues relate to wages, benefits, nature of jobs, and other work-related subjects. Mandatory subjects for bargaining include the following:

- Discharge of employees
- Grievances
- Work schedules
- Union security and dues checkoff
- Retirement and pension coverage
- Vacations and time off
- Rest and lunch break rules
- Safety rules
- Profit-sharing plans
- Required physical exam

Issues that are not mandatory and that relate to certain jobs are **permissive issues.** For example, the following issues can be bargained over if both parties agree: benefits for retired employees, product prices for employees, and performance bonds.

A final category, **illegal issues,** includes those issues that would require either party to take illegal action. Examples would be giving preference to union members when hiring employees or demanding a closed-shop provision in the contract. If one side wants to bargain over an illegal issue, the other side can refuse.

COLLECTIVE BARGAINING PROCESS

The collective bargaining process involved in negotiating a contract consists of a number of stages: preparation and initial demands, negotiations, settlement or impasse, and strikes and lockouts. Throughout the process, management and labor deal with the specifics of their relationship.

Preparation and Initial Demands

Both labor and management representatives spend considerable time preparing for negotiations. Employer and industry data concerning wages, benefits, working conditions, management and union rights, productivity, and absenteeism are gathered. If the organization argues that it cannot afford to pay what the union is asking, the employer's financial situation and accompanying data become relevant to the process. However, the union must request such information before the employer is obligated to provide it. Typical bargaining includes initial proposals of expectations by both sides. The amount of rancor or calmness exhibited may set the tone for future negotiations between the parties.

Core Bargaining Issues.   The primary focus of bargaining for both union and management is on the core areas of wages, benefits, and working hours and conditions. The importance of this emphasis is seen in several ways.

Union wages and benefits generally are higher in unionized firms than in nonunionized firms. In a recent year, median earnings for union members were $908/week compared with the nonunion amount of $710/week. The additional $198/week represents almost $10,000/year more for each union members' wages over nonunion wages. This labor cost difference is one reason management resists unions.

Continuing Negotiations

After taking initial positions, each side attempts to determine what the other side values highly so that the best bargain can be struck. Provisions in federal law require that both employers and union bargaining representatives negotiate in good faith. In good-faith negotiations, the parties agree to send negotiators who can bargain and make decisions, rather than people who do not have the authority to commit either group to a decision. To be more effective, meetings between the parties should be conducted professionally and address issues, rather than being confrontational. Refusing to bargain, scheduling meetings at absurdly inconvenient hours, and using other conflicting tactics may lead to employers or unions filing complaints with the NLRB.

Settlement and Contract Agreement

After reaching an initial agreement, the bargaining parties usually return to their respective constituencies to determine if the informal agreement is acceptable. A particularly crucial stage is **ratification** of the labor agreement, which occurs when union members vote to accept the terms of a negotiated labor agreement. Before ratification, the union negotiating team explains the agreement to the union members and presents it for a vote. If the members approve the agreement, it is then formalized into a contract. Figure 10-5 lists the typical items in a labor agreement.

Bargaining Impasse

Regardless of the structure of the bargaining process, labor and management do not always reach agreement on the issues. If they reach an impasse, then the disputes can be taken to conciliation, mediation, or arbitration.

Conciliation and Mediation. When an impasse occurs, an outside party such as the Federal Mediation and Conciliation Service may help the two deadlocked parties to continue negotiations and arrive at a solution. In **conciliation,** the third party assists union and management negotiators to reach a voluntary settlement, but makes no proposals for solutions. In **mediation,** the third party may suggest ideas for solutions to help the negotiators reach a settlement.

FIGURE 10-5 Typical Items in a Labor Agreement

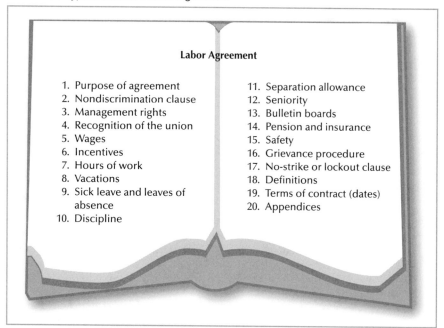

Labor Agreement

1. Purpose of agreement
2. Nondiscrimination clause
3. Management rights
4. Recognition of the union
5. Wages
6. Incentives
7. Hours of work
8. Vacations
9. Sick leave and leaves of absence
10. Discipline
11. Separation allowance
12. Seniority
13. Bulletin boards
14. Pension and insurance
15. Safety
16. Grievance procedure
17. No-strike or lockout clause
18. Definitions
19. Terms of contract (dates)
20. Appendices

In conciliation and mediation, the third party does not attempt to impose a solution. Sometimes fact finding helps to clarify the issues of disagreement as an intermediate step between mediation and arbitration.

Arbitration.   In **arbitration,** a neutral third party makes a decision. Arbitration can be conducted by an individual or a panel of individuals. "Interest" arbitration attempts to solve bargaining impasses, primarily in the public sector. This type of arbitration is not frequently used in the private sector because companies generally do not want an outside party making decisions about their rights, wages, benefits, and other issues. However, grievance or "rights" arbitration is used extensively in the private sector. Fortunately, in many situations, agreements are reached through negotiations without the need for arbitration. When disagreements continue, strikes or lockouts may occur.

Strikes and Lockouts

If a deadlock cannot be resolved, an employer may revert to a lockout—or a union may revert to a strike. During a **strike,** union members refuse to work in order to put pressure on an employer. Often, the striking union members picket or demonstrate against the employer outside the place of business by carrying placards and signs.

In a **lockout,** management shuts down company operations to prevent union members from working. This action may avert possible damage or sabotage to company facilities or injury to employees who continue to work. It also gives management leverage in negotiations. As a result of the decline in union power, work stoppages due to strikes and lockouts are relatively rare. In a recent year, a limited number of strikes or lockouts occurred nationally, and they were all settled quickly.

UNION/MANAGEMENT COOPERATION

The adversarial relationship that naturally exists between unions and management may lead to strikes and lockouts. However, as noted, such conflicts currently are relatively rare. Even more encouraging is the recognition on the part of some union leaders and employer representatives that cooperation between management and labor unions offers a useful route if organizations are to compete effectively in a global economy.

During the past decade, numerous firms have engaged in organizational and workplace restructuring in response to competitive pressures in their industries. Restructurings have had significant effects, such as lost jobs, changed work rules, and altered job responsibilities. When restructurings occur, unions can take different approaches, ranging from resistance to cooperation.

Employee Involvement Programs

It seems somewhat illogical to suggest that union/management cooperation or involving employees in making suggestions and decisions could be bad, and yet some decisions by the NLRB appear to have done just that. Some historical perspective is required to understand the issues that surrounded the decisions.

In the 1930s, when the Wagner Act was written, certain employers would form sham "company unions," coercing workers into joining them to keep legitimate unions from organizing the employees. As a result, the Wagner Act contained prohibitions against employer-dominated labor organizations. These prohibitions were enforced, and company unions disappeared. But the use of employee involvement programs in organizations today has raised new concerns along these lines.

Because of the Wagner Act, some employee involvement programs may be illegal, according to an NLRB decision dealing with Electromation, an Elkhart, Indiana, firm. Electromation used teams of employees to solicit other employees' views about such issues as wages and working conditions. The NLRB labeled these teams "labor organizations," in line with requirements of the Wagner Act. It further found that the teams were "dominated" by management, which had formed them, set their goals, and decided how they would operate. The results of this and other decisions have forced many employers to rethink and restructure their employee involvement efforts.

Federal court decisions have upheld the NLRB position in some cases and reversed it in others. One key to decisions allowing employee involvement committees and programs seems to be that these entities should not deal directly with traditional collective bargaining issues such as wages, hours, and working conditions. Other keys are that the committees should be composed primarily of workers and that they have broad authority to make operational suggestions and decisions.

Unions and Employee Ownership

Unions in some situations have encouraged workers to become partial or complete owners of the companies that employ them. These efforts were spurred by concerns that firms were preparing to shut down, merge, or be bought out. Such results were likely to cut the number of union jobs and workers.

Unions have been active in helping members put together employee stock ownership plans to purchase all or part of some firms.[11] Such programs have been successful in some situations but have caused problems in others. Some in the labor movement fear that such programs may undermine union support by creating a closer identification with the concerns and goals of employers, instead of "union solidarity."

GRIEVANCE MANAGEMENT

Unions know that employee dissatisfaction is a potential source of trouble for employers, whether it is expressed or not. Hidden dissatisfaction grows and creates reactions that may be completely out of proportion to the original concerns. Therefore, it is important that dissatisfaction be given an outlet. A **complaint,** which is merely an indication of employee dissatisfaction, is one outlet. If an employee is represented by a union, and the employee says, "I should have received the job transfer because I have more seniority, which is what the union contract states," and she submits it in writing, then that complaint becomes a grievance. A **grievance** is a complaint formally stated in writing.

Management should be concerned with both complaints and grievances, because both indicate potential problems within the workforce. Without a grievance procedure, management may be unable to respond to employee concerns because managers are unaware of them. Therefore, a formal grievance procedure provides a valuable communication tool for organizations, whether a union is present or not.

The typical division of responsibilities between the HR unit and operating managers for handling grievances is shown in Figure 10-6. These responsibilities vary considerably from one organization to another, even between unionized firms.

Grievance Procedures

Grievance procedures are formal channels of communication designed to resolve grievances as soon as possible after problems arise. First-line supervisors are usually closest to a problem. However, these supervisors are concerned with many other matters besides one employee's grievance, and may even be the subject of an employee's grievance. To receive the appropriate attention, grievances go through a specific process for resolution.[12]

Union Representation in Grievance Procedures. A unionized employee generally has a right to union representation if the employee is being questioned by management and if discipline may result. If these so-called *Weingarten rights* (named after the court case that established them) are violated and the employee is dismissed, the employee usually will be reinstated with back pay. Employers are not required to allow nonunion workers to have coworkers present in grievance procedure meetings. However, employers may voluntarily allow such presence.

FIGURE 10-6 Typical Division of HR Responsibilities: Grievance Management

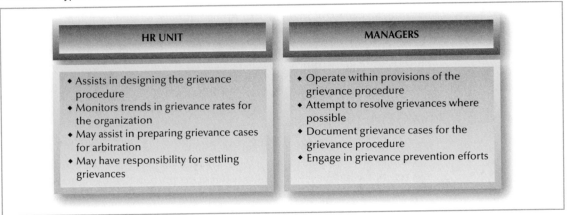

HR UNIT	MANAGERS
• Assists in designing the grievance procedure • Monitors trends in grievance rates for the organization • May assist in preparing grievance cases for arbitration • May have responsibility for settling grievances	• Operate within provisions of the grievance procedure • Attempt to resolve grievances where possible • Document grievance cases for the grievance procedure • Engage in grievance prevention efforts

Steps in a Grievance Procedure

Grievance procedures can vary in the steps included. A typical grievance procedure consists of the following steps:

1. The employee discusses the grievance with the union steward (the representative of the union on the job) and the supervisor.

2. The union steward discusses the grievance with the supervisor's manager and/or the HR manager.

3. A committee of union officers discusses the grievance with appropriate company managers.

4. The representative of the national union discusses the grievance with designated company executives or the corporate industrial relations officer.

5. If the grievance is not solved at this stage, it goes to arbitration. An impartial third party may ultimately dispose of the grievance.

Grievance arbitration is a means by which a third party settles disputes arising from different interpretations of a labor contract. This process should not be confused with contract or issues arbitration, discussed earlier, in which arbitration is used to determine how a contract will be written. The U.S. Supreme Court has ruled that grievance arbitration decisions issued under labor contract provisions are enforceable and generally may not go to court to be changed. Grievance arbitration includes more than 50 topic areas, with discipline and discharge, safety and health, and security issues being most prevalent.

NOTES

1. Barry Hirsh, "Sluggish Institutions in a Dynamic World: Can Unions and Industrial Competition Coexist?" *Journal of Economic Perspectives*, 22 (2008), 153–176.

2. Steven Abraham, et al., "The Relationship Among Union Membership, Facets of Satisfaction and Intent to Leave," *Employee Responsibilities and Rights Journal*, 20 (2008), 1–11.

3. "More Union Workers Now in Government," *The Denver Post*, January 23, 2010, 6B.

4. Gary Chaison, "The AFL-CIO Split: Does It Really Matter?" *Journal of Labor Research*, Spring 2007, 301–311.

5. Bill Leonard, "Court Upholds Union Reporting Requirements," *HR Magazine*, July 2008, 24.

6. Ann Zimmerman and Kris Maher, "Wal-Mart Warns of Democrat Win," *The Wall Street Journal*, August 1, 2008, W1.

7. For example, Jackson Lewis, a law firm with 29 offices nationwide, represents management exclusively; see *www.jacksonlewis.com*.

8. Rita Zeidner, "NLRB: Unions Not Guaranteed Use of Company E-Mail," *HR News*, December 28, 2007, *www.shrm.org*, 1.

9. Leigh Tyson and W. Jonathan Martin, "NLRB Clarifies When an Employee Is a 'Supervisor,'" *Ceridian Abstracts*, *www.hrcompliance.ceridian.com*.

10. Joanne Deschenaux, "High Court Upholds Limits on Use of Non Member's Union Fees," *Workplace Law Library—Labor Relations*, June 15, 2007.

11. Jacquelyn Yates, "Unions and Employee Ownership: A Road to Economic Recovery," *Industrial Relations*, 45 (2006), 709.

12. Annette Cox, et al., "Applying Union Mobilization Theory to Explain Gendered Collective Grievances," *Journal of Industrial Relations*, 49, (2007), 717–738.

INTERNET RESOURCES

Cornell Global Labor Institute—This website provides information and projects on union efforts to strengthen the response to globalization challenges. Visit the site at *www.ilr .cornell.edu/ globallaborinstitute.*

AFL-CIO—The AFL-CIO home page provides union movement information. Visit the website at *www.aflcio.org.*

National Labor Relations Board—For information on workplace rights and other issues, visit the NLRB website at *www.nlrb.gov.*

LaborNet—This website describes unions, news, legislation, and upcoming union events. Visit the site at *www.labornet.org.*

Federal Mediation & Conciliation Service—This service organization provides services and resources to promote stable labor and management relationships. Visit the website at *www.fmcs.gov.*

SUGGESTED READINGS

John Schmitt, et al., "Unions and Upward Mobility for Low Wage Workers," *Journal of Labor and Society,* 11 (2008), 337–348.

Lyle Scruggs and Peter Lange, "Where Have All the Members Gone? Globalization, Institutions and Union Density," *Journal of Politics,* 64 (2008), 126–153.

Lawrence Nurse and Dwayne Devonish, "Grievance Management and Its Links to Workplace Justice," *Employee Relations,* 29, (2007), 89–109.

Matthew Frankiewicz, "How to Win Your Arbitration Case Before It Even Starts," *Labor Law Journal,* 2009, 115–120.

Appendix A

Internet Resources

HR-RELATED INTERNET LINKS

Academy of Management
www.aom.pace.edu
American Arbitration Association
www.adr.org
American Federation of Labor/Congress of
Industrial Organizations (AFL-CIO)
www.aflcio.org
American Institute for Managing Diversity
www.aimd.org
American Payroll Association
www.americanpayroll.org
American Psychological Association
www.apa.org
American Society for Industrial Security
www.asisonline.org
American Society for Training and Development
www.astd.org
Australian Human Resource Institute
www.ahri.com.au
Chartered Institute of Personnel and
Development (UK)
www.cipd.co.uk
CPR International Institute for Conflict
Prevention & Resolution
www.cpradr.org
Employee Benefit Research Institute
www.ebri.org
Foundation for Enterprise Development
www.fed.org
Hong Kong Institute of Human Resource
Management
www.hkihrm.org

Human Resource Certification Institute
www.hrci.org
International Association for Human Resource
Information Management
www.ihrim.org
International Association of Industrial Accident
Boards and Commissions
www.iaiabc.org
International Foundation of Employee
Benefit Plans (IFEBP)
www.ifebp.org
International Institute of Human Resource
Management
www.iihrm.org
International Personnel Assessment Council
www.ipacweb.org
International Personnel Management Association
www.ipma-hr.org
Labor and Employment Relations Association
www.lera.uiuc.edu
National Center for Employee Ownership
www.nceo.org
National Health Information Resource Center
www.nhirc.org
Social Media Policies
www.socialmediagovernance.com
Society for Human Resource Management
www.shrm.org
Union Resource Network
www.unions.org
World at Work
www.worldatwork.org

SELECTED GOVERNMENT INTERNET LINKS

Bureau of Labor Statistics
   www.stats.bls.gov
Census Bureau
   www.census.gov
Department of Labor
   www.dol.gov
Employment and Training Administration
   www.doleta.gov
Equal Employment Opportunity Commission
   www.eeoc.gov
FedStats
   www.fedstats.gov
National Institute of Environmental Health
   Sciences
   www.niehs.nih.gov
National Institute for Occupational Safety and
   Health (NIOSH)
   www.cdc.gov/niosh

National Labor Relations Board
   www.nlrb.gov
Occupational Safety and Health Administration
   www.osha.gov
Office of Personnel Management
   www.opm.gov
Pension and Welfare Benefits Administration
   www.dol.gov/ebsa
Pension Benefit Guaranty Corporation
   www.pbgc.gov
Small Business Administration
   www.sba.gov
Social Security Administration
   www.ssa.gov
U.S. House of Representatives
   www.house.gov
U.S. Senate
   www.senate.gov

Major Federal Equal Employment Opportunity Laws and Regulations

Act	Year	Key Provisions
Broad-Based Discrimination		
Title VII, Civil Rights Act of 1964	1964	Prohibits discrimination in employment on basis of race, color, religion, sex, or national origin
Executive Orders 11246 and 11375	1965 1967	Require federal contractors and subcontractors to eliminate employment discrimination and prior discrimination through affirmative action
Executive Order 11478	1969	Prohibits discrimination in the U.S. Postal Service and in the various government agencies on the basis of race, color, religion, sex, national origin, handicap, or age
Vietnam Era Veterans' Readjustment Assistance Act	1974	Prohibits discriminations against Vietnam-era veterans by federal contractors and the U.S. government and requires affirmative action
Civil Rights Act of 1991	1991	Overturns several past Supreme Court decisions and changes damage claims provisions
Congressional Accountability Act	1995	Extends EEO and Civil Rights Act provisions to U.S. congressional staff
Race/National Origin Discrimination		
Immigration Reform and Control Act	1986 1990 1996	Establishes penalties for employers who knowingly hire illegal aliens; prohibits employment discrimination on the basis of national origin or citizenship
Gender/Sex Discrimination		
Equal Pay Act	1963	Requires equal pay for men and women performing substantially the same work
Pregnancy Discrimination Act	1978	Prohibits discrimination against women affected by pregnancy, childbirth, or related medical conditions; requires that they be treated as all other employees for employment-related purposes, including benefits

(Continued)

Act	Year	Key Provisions
Age Discrimination		
Age Discrimination in Employment Act (as amended in 1978 and 1986)	1967	Prohibits discrimination against persons over age 40 and restricts mandatory retirement requirements, except where age is a bona fide occupational qualification
Older Workers Benefit Protection Act of 1990	1990	Prohibits age-based discrimination in early retirement and other benefits plans
Disability Discrimination		
Vocational Rehabilitation Act and Rehabilitation Act of 1974	1973 1974	Prohibit employers with federal contracts over $2,500 from discriminating against individuals with disabilities
Americans with Disabilities Act	1990	Requires employer accommodations for individuals with disabilities

Appendix C

Sample Application Form

Application for Employment
An Equal Opportunity Employer*

Today's Date _____

PERSONAL INFORMATION

Please Print or Type

Name (Last) (First) (Full middle name)	Social Security number

Current address City State Zip code	Phone number ( )

What position are you applying for?	Date available for employment?	E-mail address

Are you willing to relocate? ☐ Yes ☐ No	Are you willing to travel if required? ☐ Yes ☐ No	Any restrictions on hours, weekends, or overtime? If yes, explain.

Have you ever been employed by this Company or any of its subsidiaries before? ☐ Yes ☐ No	Indicate location and dates

Can you, after employment, submit verification of your legal right to work in the United States? ☐ Yes ☐ No	Have you ever been convicted of a felony? ☐ Yes ☐ No	*Convictions will not automatically disqualify job candidates. The seriousness of the crime and the date of conviction will be considered.*

PERFORMANCE OF JOB FUNCTIONS

Are you able to perform all the functions of the job for which you are applying, with or without accommodation?

☐ Yes, without accommodation   ☐ Yes, with accommodation   ☐ No

If you indicated you can perform all the functions with an accommodation, please explain how you would perform the tasks and with what accommodation.

EDUCATION

School level	School name and address	No. of years attended	Did you graduate?	Course of study
High school				
Vo-tech, business, or trade school				
College				
Graduate school				

PERSONAL DRIVING RECORD

This section is to be completed ONLY if the operation of a motor vehicle will be required in the course of the applicant's employment.

How long have you been a licensed driver?	Driver's license number	Expiration date	Issuing State

List any other state(s) in which you have had a driver's license(s) in the past:

Within the past five years, have you had a vehicle accident? ☐ Yes ☐ No	Been convicted of reckless or drunken driving? If yes, give dates: ☐ Yes ☐ No	Been cited for moving violations? If yes, give dates: ☐ Yes ☐ No

Has your driver's license ever been revoked or suspended? If yes, explain: ☐ Yes ☐ No	Is your driver's license restricted? If yes, explain: ☐ Yes ☐ No

*We are an Equal Opportunity Employer. We do not discriminate on the basis of race, religion, color, gender, age, national origin, or disability.

Guidelines to Lawful and Unlawful Preemployment Inquiries

Subject of Inquiry	It May Not Be Discriminatory to Inquire about . . .	It May Be Discriminatory to Inquire about . . .
1. **Name**	a. Whether applicant has ever worked under a different name	a. The original name of applicant whose name has been legally changed b. The ethnic association of applicant's name
2. **Age**	a. If applicant is over the age of 18 b. If applicant is under the age of 18 or 21 if that information is job related (e.g., for selling liquor in a retail store)	a. Date of birth b. Date of high school graduation
3. **Residence**	a. Applicant's place of residence b. Alternative contact information	a. Previous addresses b. Birthplace of applicant or applicant's parents c. Length lived at current and previous addresses
4. **Race or Color**		a. Applicant's race or color of applicant's skin
5. **National Origin and Ancestry**		a. Applicant's lineage, ancestry, national origin, parentage, or nationality b. Nationality of applicant's parents or spouse
6. **Sex and Family Composition**		a. Sex of applicant b. Marital status of applicant c. Dependents of applicants or child-care arrangements d. Whom to contact in case of emergency
7. **Creed or Religion**		a. Applicant's religious affiliation b. Applicant's church, parish, mosque, or synagogue c. Holidays observed by applicant
8. **Citizenship**	a. Whether the applicant is a U.S. citizen or has a current permit/visa to work in the United States	a. Whether applicant is a citizen of a country other than the United States b. Date of citizenship

(*Continued*)

Subject of Inquiry	It May Not Be Discriminatory to Inquire about . . .	It May Be Discriminatory to Inquire about . . .
9. **Language**	a. Language applicant speaks and/or writes fluently, if job related	a. Applicant's native tongue b. Language used at home
10. **References**	a. Names of persons willing to provide professional and/or character references for applicant b. Previous work contacts	a. Name of applicant's religious leader b. Political affiliation and contacts
11. **Relatives**	a. Names of relatives already employed by the employer	a. Name and/or address of any relative of applicant b. Whom to contact in case of emergency
12. **Organizations**	a. Applicant's membership in any professional, service, or trade organization	a. All clubs or social organizations to which applicant belongs
13. **Arrest Record and Convictions**	a. Convictions, if related to job performance (disclaimer should accompany)	a. Number and kinds of arrests b. Convictions, unless related to job requirements and performance
14. **Photographs**		a. Photographs with application, with résumé, or before hiring
15. **Height and Weight**		a. Any inquiry into height and weight of applicant, except where a BFOQ exists
16. **Physical Limitations**	a. Whether applicant has the ability to perform job-related functions with or without accommodation	a. The nature or severity of an illness or physical condition b. Whether applicant has ever filed a workers' compensation claim c. Any recent or past operations, treatments, or surgeries and dates
17. **Education**	a. Training applicant has received, if related to the job b. Highest level of education applicant has attained, if validated that having certain educational background (e.g., high school diploma or college degree) is needed to perform the specific job	a. Date of high school graduation
18. **Military**	a. Branch of the military applicant served in and ranks attained b. Type of education or training received in military	a. Military discharge details b. Military service records
19. **Financial Status**		a. Applicant's debts or assets b. Garnishments

Appendix E

Questions Commonly Asked in Selection Interviews

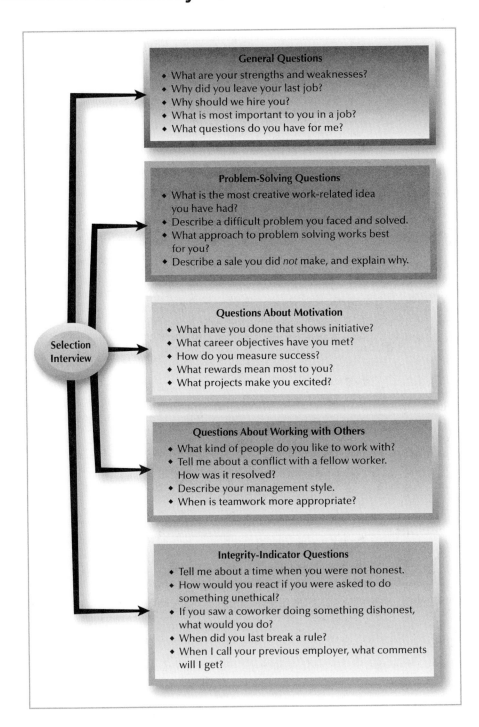

Selection Interview

General Questions
- What are your strengths and weaknesses?
- Why did you leave your last job?
- Why should we hire you?
- What is most important to you in a job?
- What questions do you have for me?

Problem-Solving Questions
- What is the most creative work-related idea you have had?
- Describe a difficult problem you faced and solved.
- What approach to problem solving works best for you?
- Describe a sale you did *not* make, and explain why.

Questions About Motivation
- What have you done that shows initiative?
- What career objectives have you met?
- How do you measure success?
- What rewards mean most to you?
- What projects make you excited?

Questions About Working with Others
- What kind of people do you like to work with?
- Tell me about a conflict with a fellow worker. How was it resolved?
- Describe your management style.
- When is teamwork more appropriate?

Integrity-Indicator Questions
- Tell me about a time when you were not honest.
- How would you react if you were asked to do something unethical?
- If you saw a coworker doing something dishonest, what would you do?
- When did you last break a rule?
- When I call your previous employer, what comments will I get?

Glossary

A

absenteeism Any failure by an employee to report for work as scheduled or to stay at work when scheduled.

active practice Performance of job-related tasks and duties by trainees during training.

adverse selection Situation in which *only* higher-risk employees select and use certain benefits.

affirmative action The hiring of groups of people based on their race, age, gender, or national origin.

affirmative action plan (AAP) A document reporting on the composition of an employer's workforce, required for federal contractors.

alternate work arrangements Nontraditional schedules that provide flexibility to employees.

arbitration Process that uses a neutral third party to make a decision.

assessment centers Collections of instruments and exercises designed to diagnose individuals' development needs.

attitude survey A survey that focuses on employees' feelings and beliefs about their jobs and the organization.

availability analysis Identifies the number of protected-class members available to work in the appropriate labor markets for given jobs.

B

balanced scorecard A framework used to report a diverse set of performance measures.

bargaining unit Employees eligible to select a single union to represent and bargain collectively for them.

base pay Basic compensation that an employee receives, usually as a wage or salary.

behavior modeling Copying someone else's behavior.

benchmark jobs Jobs found in many organizations that can be used for the purposes of comparison.

benchmarking Comparing the business results to industry standards.

benefit An indirect reward given to an employee or group of employees as part of membership in the organization.

bona fide occupational qualification (BFOQ) Characteristic providing a legitimate reason why an employer can exclude persons on otherwise illegal bases of consideration.

bonus One-time payment that does not become part of the employee's base pay.

broadbanding Practice of using fewer pay grades with much broader ranges than in traditional compensation systems.

burden of proof What individuals who file suit against employers must prove in order to establish that illegal discrimination has occurred.

business agent A full-time union official who operates the union office and assists union members.

business necessity A practice necessary for safe and efficient organizational operations.

C

career Series of work-related positions a person occupies throughout life.

career paths Represent employees' movements through opportunities over time.

cash balance plan Retirement program in which benefits are based on an accumulation of annual company contributions plus interest credited each year.

central tendency error Occurs when a rater gives all employees a score within a narrow range in the middle of the scale.

churn Hiring new workers while laying off others.

cognitive ability tests Tests that measure an individual's thinking, memory, reasoning, verbal, and mathematical abilities.

collective bargaining Process whereby representatives of management and workers negotiate over wages, hours, and other terms and conditions of employment.

commission Compensation computed as a percentage of sales in units or dollars.

compa-ratio Pay level divided by the midpoint of the pay range.

compensable factor Job value commonly present throughout a group of jobs within an organization.

competencies Individual capabilities that can be linked to enhanced performance by individuals or teams.

competency-based pay Rewards individuals for the capabilities they demonstrate and acquire.

complaint Indication of employee dissatisfaction.

compressed workweek A workweek in which a full week's work is accomplished in fewer than five 8-hour days.

conciliation Process by which a third party assists union and management negotiators to reach a voluntary settlement.

constructive discharge Process of deliberately making conditions intolerable to get an employee to quit.

consumer-driven health (CDH) plan Health plan that provides employer financial contributions to employees to help cover their own health-related expenses.

contingent worker Someone who is not an employee, but a temporary or part-time worker for a specific period of time and type of work.

contrast error Tendency to rate people relative to others rather than against performance standards.

contributory plan Pension plan in which the money for pension benefits is paid by both employees and the employer.

copayment Strategy of requiring employees to pay a portion of the cost of insurance premiums, medical care, and prescription drugs.

core competency A unique capability that creates high value and differentiates an organization from its competition.

cost-benefit analysis Comparison of costs and benefits associated with training.

craft union Union whose members do one type of work, often using specialized skills and training.

critical incident method The manager keeps a written record of both highly favorable and unfavorable actions performed by an employee during the entire rating period.

cross training Training people to do more than one job.

cumulative trauma disorders (CTDs) Muscle and skeletal injuries that occur when workers repetitively use the same muscles to perform tasks.

D

decertification Process whereby a union is removed as the representative of a group of employees.

defined-benefit plan Retirement program in which employees are promised a pension amount based on age and service.

defined-contribution pension plan Retirement program in which the employer makes an annual payment to an employee's pension account.

development Efforts to improve employees' abilities to handle a variety of assignments and to cultivate employees' capabilities beyond those required by the current job.

disabled person Someone who has a physical or mental impairment that substantially limits life activities, who has a record of such an impairment, or who is regarded as having such an impairment.

discharge When an employee is removed from a job at an employer.

discipline Form of training that enforces organizational rules.

disparate impact Occurs when members of a protected category are substantially underrepresented as a result of employment decisions that work to their disadvantage.

disparate treatment Occurs when members of a group are treated differently from others.

diversity Differences in human characteristics and composition in an organization.

draw Amount advanced against, and repaid from, future commissions earned by the employee.

dual-career ladder System that allows a person to advance up either a management or a technical/professional ladder.

due diligence A comprehensive assessment of all aspects of the business being acquired.

due process Requirement that the employer use a fair process to determine employee wrongdoing and that the employee have an opportunity to explain and defend his or her actions.

duty Work segment composed of several tasks that are performed by an individual.

E

electronic human resource management systems (e-HRM) The planning, implementation, and application of information technology to perform HR activities.

employee assistance program (EAP) Program that provides counseling and other help to employees having emotional, physical, or other personal problems.

employee stock ownership plan (ESOP) Plan designed to give employees significant stock ownership in their employers.

employment-at-will (EAW) Common-law doctrine stating that employers have the right to hire, fire, demote, or promote whomever they choose, unless there is a law or contract to the contrary.

employment contract Formal agreement that outlines the details of employment.

entitlement philosophy Assumes that individuals who have worked another year are entitled to pay increases, with little regard for performance differences.

environmental scanning The assessment of internal and external environmental conditions that affect the organization.

equity Perceived fairness between what a person does and what the person receives.

ergonomics Study and design of the work environment to address physical demands placed on individuals.

essay method The manager writes a short essay describing each employee's performance during the rating period.

exempt employees Employees who are not paid overtime.

expatriate A citizen of one country who is working in a second country and employed by an organization headquartered in the first country.

F

401(k) plan Agreement in which a percentage of an employee's pay is withheld and invested in a tax-deferred account.

federation Group of autonomous unions.

flexible benefits plan Program that allows employees to select the benefits they prefer from groups of benefits established by the employer.

flexible spending accounts Benefits plans that allow employees to contribute pretax dollars to fund certain additional benefits.

flextime Scheduling arrangement in which employees work a set number of hours a day but vary starting and ending times.

forced distribution Performance appraisal method in which ratings of employees' performance levels are distributed along a bell-shaped curve.

forecasting Using information from the past and the present to identify expected future conditions.

G

gainsharing System of sharing with employees greater-than-expected gains in profits and/or productivity.

graphic rating scale Scale that allows the rater to mark an employee's performance on a continuum.

green-circled employee Incumbent who is paid below the range set for a job.

grievance Complaint formally stated in writing.

grievance arbitration Means by which a third party settles disputes arising from different interpretations of a labor contract.

grievance procedures Formal channels of communication used to resolve grievances.

H

Halo effect Occurs when a rater scores an employee high on all job criteria because of performance in one area.

health General state of physical, mental, and emotional well-being.

health maintenance organization (HMO) Plan that provides services for a fixed period on a prepaid basis.

health promotion Supportive approach of facilitating and encouraging healthy actions and lifestyles among employees.

health reimbursement arrangement (HRA) Health plan in which the employer sets aside money in a health reimbursement account to help employees pay for qualified medical expenses.

health savings accounts (HSAs) High-deductible health plans with federal tax advantages.

host-country national A citizen of one country who is working in that country and employed by an organization headquartered in a second country.

hostile environment Sexual harassment in which an individual's work performance or psychological well-being is unreasonably affected by intimidating or offensive working conditions.

HR audit A formal research effort to assess the current state of HR practices.

HR metrics Specific measures tied to HR performance indicators.

human capital return on investment (HCROI) Directly shows the operating profit derived from investments in human capital.

human capital value added (HCVA) Calculated by subtracting all operating expenses *except* for labor expenses from revenue and dividing by the total full-time head count.

human economic value added (HEVA) Wealth created per employee.

human resource (HR) management Designing management systems to ensure that human talent is used effectively and efficiently to accomplish organizational goals.

human resource planning Process of analyzing and identifying the need for and availability of human resources so that the organization can meet its objectives.

I

illegal issues Collective bargaining issues that would require either party to take illegal action.

immediate confirmation Based on the idea that people learn best if reinforcement and feedback are given as soon as possible after training.

individual-centered career planning Career planning that focuses on an individual's responsibility for a career rather than on organizational needs.

industrial union Union that includes many persons working in the same industry or company, regardless of jobs held.

informal training Training that occurs through interactions and feedback among employees.

J

job analysis Systematic way of gathering and analyzing information about the content, context, and human requirements of jobs.

job description Identification of the tasks, duties, and responsibilities of a job.

job design Organizing tasks, duties, responsibilities, and other elements into a productive unit of work.

job duties Important elements in a given job.

job enlargement Broadening the scope of a job by expanding the number of different tasks to be performed.

job enrichment Increasing the depth of a job by adding responsibility for planning, organizing, controlling, or evaluating the job.

job evaluation Formal, systematic means to identify the relative worth of jobs within an organization.

job family Group of jobs having common organizational characteristics.

job rotation Process of shifting a person from job to job.

job satisfaction A positive emotional state resulting from evaluating one's job experiences.

job sharing Scheduling arrangement in which two employees perform the work of one full-time job.

job specifications The knowledge, skills, and abilities (KSAs) an individual needs to perform a job satisfactorily.

L

labor markets External supply pool from which organizations attract employees.

leniency error Occurs when ratings of all employees fall at the high end of the scale.

living wage Earnings that are supposed to meet the basic needs of an individual working for an organization.

lockout Shutdown of company operations undertaken by management to prevent union members from working.

lump-sum increase (LSI) One-time payment of all or part of a yearly pay increase.

M

managed care Approaches that monitor and reduce medical costs through restrictions and market system alternatives.

management by objectives (MBO) Performance appraisal method that specifies the performance goals that an individual and manager identify together.

management rights Rights reserved so that the employer can manage, direct, and control its business.

mandatory issues Collective bargaining issues identified specifically by labor laws or court decisions as subject to bargaining.

market banding Grouping jobs into pay grades based on similar market survey amounts.

market line Graph line that shows the relationship between job value as determined by job evaluation points and job value as determined by pay survey rates.

market pricing Use of market pay data to identify the relative value of jobs based on what other employers pay for similar jobs.

mediation Process by which a third party helps the negotiators reach a settlement.

motivation The desire within a person causing that person to act.

multinational corporation (MNC) A corporation that has facilities and other assets in at least one country other than its home country.

N

negligent hiring Occurs when an employer fails to check an employee's background and the employee injures someone on the job.

negligent retention Occurs when an employer becomes aware that an employee may be unfit for work but continues to employ the person, and the person injures someone.

nepotism Practice of allowing relatives to work for the same employer.

noncompete agreements Agreements that prohibit individuals who leave an organization from working with an employer in the same line of business for a specified period of time.

noncontributory plan Pension plan in which all the funds for pension benefits are provided by the employer.

nonexempt employees Employees who must be paid overtime.

O

offshoring The relocation by a company of a business process or operation from one country to another.

ombuds Individuals outside the normal chain of command who act as problem solvers for both management and employees.

open shop Firm in which workers are not required to join or pay dues to a union.

organizational commitment The degree to which employees believe in and accept organizational goals and desire to remain with the organization.

organizational culture The shared values and beliefs in an organization.

organizational mission The core reason for the existence of the organization and what makes it unique.

organization-centered career planning Career planning that focuses on identifying career paths that provide for the logical progression of people between jobs in an organization.

orientation Planned introduction of new employees to their jobs, coworkers, and the organization.

outsourcing Transferring the management and performance of a business function to an external service provider.

P

paid-time-off (PTO) plan Plan that combines all sick leave, vacation time, and holidays into a total number of hours or days that employees can take off with pay.

panel interview Interview in which several interviewers meet with candidate at the same time.

pay compression Occurs when the pay differences among individuals with different levels of experience and performance become small.

pay grades Groupings of individual jobs having approximately the same job worth.

pay survey Collection of data on compensation rates for workers performing similar jobs in other organizations.

pay-for-performance philosophy Requires that compensation changes reflect performance differences.

Peer review panels A committee of employees and managers whole resolve employment disputes when employees appeal disciplinary actions.

pension plan Retirement program established and funded by the employer and employees.

performance appraisal Process of determining how well employees do their jobs relative to a standard and communicating that information to them.

performance management Series of activities designed to ensure that the organization gets the performance it needs from its employees.

performance standards Indicators of what the job accomplishes and how performance is measured in key areas of the job description.

permissive issues Collective bargaining issues that are not mandatory and that relate to certain jobs.

perquisites (perks) Special benefits—usually noncash items—for executives.

person/job fit Matching the KSAs of individuals with the characteristics of jobs.

phased retirement Approach in which employees gradually reduce their workloads and pay levels.

physical ability tests Tests that measure an individual's abilities such as strength, endurance, and muscular movement.

placement Fitting a person to the right job.

policies General guidelines that focus organizational actions.

portability A pension plan feature that allows employees to move their pension benefits from one employer to another.

predictors of selection criteria Measurable or visible indicators of selection criteria.

preferred provider organization (PPO) A health care provider that contracts with an employer or an employer group to supply health care services to employees at a competitive rate.

primacy effect Occurs when a rater gives greater weight to information received first when appraising an individual's performance.

procedures Customary methods of handling activities.

productivity Measure of the quantity and quality of work done, considering the cost of the resources used.

profit sharing System to distribute a portion of the profits of an organization to employees.

protected category A group identified for protection under EEO laws and regulations.

psychological contract The unwritten expectations employees and employers have about the nature of their work relationships.

psychomotor tests Tests that measure dexterity, hand—eye coordination, arm—hand steadiness, and other factors.

Q

quid pro quo Sexual harassment in which employment outcomes are linked to the individual granting sexual favors.

R

ranking Performance appraisal method in which all employees are listed from highest to lowest in performance.

rater bias Occurs when a rater's values or prejudices distort the rating.

ratification Process by which union members vote to accept the terms of a negotiated labor agreement.

reasonable accommodation A modification to a job or work environment that gives a qualified individual an equal employment opportunity to perform.

recency effect Occurs when a rater gives greater weight to recent events when appraising an individual's performance.

recruiting Process of generating a pool of qualified applicants for organizational jobs.

red-circled employee Incumbent who is paid above the range set for a job.

reinforcement Based on the idea that people tend to repeat responses that give them some type of positive reward and avoid actions associated with negative consequences.

responsibilities Obligations to perform certain tasks and duties.

retaliation Punitive actions taken by employers against individuals who exercise their legal rights.

return on investment (ROI) Calculation showing the value of an investment.

right to privacy An individual's freedom from unauthorized and unreasonable intrusion into personal affairs.

rights Powers, privileges, or interests that belong to a person by law, nature, or tradition.

right-to-work laws State laws that prohibit requiring employees to join unions as a condition of obtaining or continuing employment.

risk management Involves responsibilities to consider physical, human, and financial factors to protect organizational and individual interests.

rules Specific guidelines that regulate and restrict the behavior of individuals.

S

sabbatical Time off the job to develop and rejuvenate oneself.

safety Condition in which the physical well-being of people is protected.

salaries Consistent payments made each period regardless of the number of hours worked.

salting Practice in which unions hire and pay people to apply for jobs at certain companies to begin organizing efforts.

security Protection of employees and organizational facilities.

security audit Comprehensive review of organizational security.

selection The process of choosing individuals with the correct qualifications needed to fill jobs in an organization.

selection criterion Characteristic that a person must possess to successfully perform work.

self-efficacy People's belief that they can successfully learn the training program content.

seniority Time spent in an organization or on a particular job.

serious health condition Health condition requiring in-patient, hospital, hospice, or residential medical care or continuing physician care.

severance pay Security benefit voluntarily offered by employers to individuals whose jobs are eliminated or who leave by mutual agreement with their employers.

sexual harassment Actions that are sexually directed, are unwanted, and subject the worker to adverse employment conditions or create a hostile work environment.

situational judgment tests Tests that measure a person's judgment in work settings.

statutory rights Rights based on laws or statutes passed by federal, state, or local governments.

stock option plan Plan that gives employees the right to purchase a fixed number of shares of company stock at a specified price for a limited period of time.

straight piece-rate system Pay system in which wages are determined by multiplying the number of units produced by the piece rate for one unit.

strategic planning The process of defining organizational strategy and allocating resources toward its achievement.

strategy An organization's proposition for how to compete successfully and thereby survive and grow.

stress interview Interview designed to create anxiety and put pressure on applicants to see how they respond.

strictness error Occurs when ratings of all employees fall at the low end of the scale.

strike Work stoppage in which union members refuse to work in order to put pressure on an employer.

structured interview Interview that uses a set of standardized questions asked of all applicants.

substance abuse Use of illicit substances or misuse of controlled substances, alcohol, or other drugs.

succession planning The process of identifying a plan for the orderly replacement of key employees.

T

task Distinct, identifiable work activity composed of motions.

team interview Interview in which applicants are interviewed by the team members with whom they will work.

telework Employees work with technology via electronic, telecommunications, and Internet means.

third-country national A citizen of one country who is working in a second country and employed by an organization headquartered in a third country.

total rewards Monetary and nonmonetary rewards provided by companies to attract, motivate, and retain employees.

training Process whereby people acquire capabilities to perform jobs.

turnover The process in which employees leave an organization and have to be replaced.

U

undue hardship Significant difficulty or expense imposed on an employer in making an accommodation for individuals with disabilities.

union Formal association of workers that promotes the interests of its members through collective action.

union authorization card Card signed by employees to designate a union as their collective bargaining agent.

union security provisions Contract clauses to help the union obtain and retain members.

union steward Employee elected to serve as the first-line representative of unionized workers.

unit labor cost Computed by dividing the average cost of workers by their average levels of output.

utilization analysis Identifies the number of protected-class members employed in the organization and the types of jobs they hold.

utilization review Audit of services and costs billed by health care providers.

V

variable pay Compensation linked to individual, group/team, and/or organizational performance.

vesting Right of employees to receive certain benefits from their pension plans.

W

wages Payments calculated directly from the amount of time worked by employees.

well pay Extra pay for not taking sick leave.

wellness programs Programs designed to maintain or improve employee health before problems arise.

whistle blowers Individuals who report real or perceived wrongs committed by their employers.

work sample tests Tests that require an applicant to perform a simulated task that is a specified part of the target job.

workers' compensation Security benefits provided to persons injured on the job.

wrongful discharge Termination of an individual's employment for reasons that are illegal or improper.

Index

Preface

The purpose of this book is to provide a single source of cases, exercises, incidents, and skill builders to supplement the basic text in human resource management. These materials offer a fresh approach to students based on dynamic, real-life organizational events, confronting both human resource managers and line managers who often implement human resource programs and policies. This book's contents are uniquely designed to increase analytical problem-solving skills and may be used in basic courses at the undergraduate and graduate levels. Topics range from traditional applications of human resource management theory to the more controversial issues of cultural awareness, telecommuting and Web 2.0 technologies, the financial impact of human resources, phased retirement, alcohol and drug abuse on the job, new federal legislation on discrimination issues, employment-at-will, work and family, and the human resource aspects of merger activities. The settings cover a wide variety of organizations with an emphasis on the growing service sector.

This book offers opportunities for learning experiences in its six major sections: (1) Human Resource Management in Perspective: Environment and Legal Issues; (2) Meeting Human Resource Requirements: Job Analysis/Design, Planning, Recruitment, and Selection; (3) Developing Effectiveness in Human Resources: Training, Career Development, and Performance Appraisal; (4) Implementing Compensation and Security: Compensation, Incentives, Benefits, and Safety and Health; (5) Enhancing Employee Relations: Discipline, Motivation, and Labor Relations; (6) International HR and Term Project. Each of these sections, except Part 6, contains cases, exercises, incidents, and skill builders.

Most cases are based on actual events occurring in private- and public-sector organizations. All names have been changed. The first two cases in the introductory section are designed to act as pre- and post-measures of the students' knowledge of human resource management. That is, the two cases in Part 1 can be used at the beginning of the course to pique interest in the material or at the end to test how much students have learned. The student becomes the decision maker in these classroom-tested cases. Questions are provided at the end of each case and incident to guide discussion, and/or the instructor may ask students to use the case analysis model suggested by the authors on the book's Web site.

The exercises include opportunities for students to simulate the human resource work environment through role playing, identifying and solving human resource problems, completing in-baskets, and applying human resource management theories. The role plays and in-basket exercises require students to act just as they might in a real management situation. Virtually all of the exercises can be completed within 45 minutes and all contain a set of detailed procedures to follow.

The incidents are mini-cases composed of critical human resource management events and are designed to help students develop problem-solving skills. They are intended to raise questions around issues that do not have definitive answers and may be used to stimulate class discussions or to introduce students to human resource management topics.

Skill builders are short, individual assignments that can be completed by students outside of class. The skill builders develop the specific technical skills needed by human resource professionals and line managers to effectively manage human resources.

The final item in this book—the Term Project—provides instructions for a group project and/or term assignment to enhance the learning of human resource management. This project is designed to be challenging and comprehensive by requiring students to draw upon material learned throughout the course.

The instructor's manual includes an analysis of the cases and incidents, solutions to the exercises and skill builders, and alternative approaches for using and presenting the materials in the book.

New to This Edition

Responding to the requests and recommendations of instructors, students, and HR professionals, the authors have included a number of new items in this edition:

- Exercise 3: Developing Environmentally Friendly HR Policies at City University
- Incident 7: Human Resource Information Systems Data Breach
- Case 11: Investigating a Sexual Harassment Case
- Case 39: The Use of Social Media in Employee Recruitment and Selection
- Exercise 44: Selecting from Imperfect Applicants
- Exercise 68: Executive Bonuses and Incentives
- Exercise 78: Domestic Partner Benefits
- Case 89: Violence at Work
- Exercise 91: Developing an Employee Dress Code
- Incident 92: Facebook Posting: I Hate My Stupid Boss
- Case 104: Outsourcing Jobs to India
- Case 106: A Clash of Cultures in the Workplace: German Managers in South Africa

In addition to numerous updates and revisions, the authors have significantly updated the data, scenarios, and information presented in the following:

- Exercise 5: Scanning the Contemporary Work Environment: Shifting Demographics
- Incident 10: The Cultural Diversity Training Program
- Exercise 16: The Older Worker Questionnaire
- Exercise 17: Is This Unlawful Discrimination?
- Exercise 18: What Is Sexual Harassment?
- Exercise 20: Group Debate Project
- Exercise 31: Work and Family Issues
- Skill Builder 33: Phased Retirement Options
- Exercise 40: Evaluating the Recruiting Function
- Exercise 55: Design and Evaluation of Training Programs
- Exercise 61: EvalSim—A Performance Evaluation Exercise
- Case 65: The Overpaid Bank Tellers
- Exercise 70: WageSim—A Compensation Administration Exercise
- Skill Builder 74: You Be the Judge: Is This Job Exempt?
- Case 77: Controlling Employee Benefit Costs

- Incident 84: The Medical Leave Problem (FMLA)
- Term Project 107: Human Resource System or Subsystem Evaluation

Acknowledgments

Many people have assisted in making this book possible. We are grateful to the following case contributors: Myron Glassman, J. Stewart Black, Gerald Calvasina, Susan Corriher, Diana Deadrick, Yvonne du Plessis, J. Kline Harrison, Sam Holliday, Hank Hummel, Ronald Karren, Margaret Foegen Karsten, Arno F. Knapper, Steve Maurer, M. Susan Taylor, and James Wimbush. Special thanks to Juanita Craig, Ralph Pederson, Jim Bavis, David Abernethy, Diane Marie Eckland, Rusty Rainey, and other friends who shared with us their professional knowledge and experiences in human resource management for developing materials for the book.

The authors wish to acknowledge the contribution of the reviewers of the previous edition of this book. They are:

- Dr. Tina C. Elacqua, LeTourneau University
- Cheryl Crozier Garcia, Ph.D., SPHR, GPHR, Hawaii Pacific University
- Karen Jacobs, LeTourneau University
- Dr. Kimberlee Keef, University of Memphis
- Joe Mosca, Monmouth University
- Elizabeth E. Regimbal, Cardinal Stritch University
- Stacy Rogers, SPHR, CPRW, Sullivan University
- Romila Singh, Ph.D, University of Wisconsin–Milwaukee
- Thomas Tudor, University of Arkansas at Little Rock

Stella Nkomo would like to thank the Faculty of Economic and Management Sciences at the University of Pretoria for its support in the revision of this edition. She also wants to thank her research assistant Anna-Marie Nieuwoudt for her assistance. She also appreciates the steadfast support of her husband, Mokubung, and her son, Sebenza.

Myron Fottler would like to thank his wife, Carol, for her assistance and input into the current and all previous editions of this book. Her contributions were particularly important in the development of several cases and incidents based on her own experiences and those of friends and relatives. He is also extremely grateful to Megan McLendon, Whitney Windham, and Sarah Cox, who have done a tremendous job preparing new materials and editing old materials for this seventh edition of our book.

Bruce McAfee would like to thank the College of Business and Public Administration at Old Dominion University for their support. He also appreciates the support of his wife, Chris, and his son, Ethan.

This book would have been impossible without the outstanding work of the people at South-Western/Cengage Learning.

Finally, we would like to thank our students for their invaluable suggestions for revising and clarifying the materials in this book.

Stella M. Nkomo

Myron D. Fottler

R. Bruce McAfee

CORRELATION TABLE

TOPIC	CASES	EXERCISES	INCIDENTS	SKILL BUILDERS
Adverse Impact	12,38			
Affirmative Action	12	20		24
Application Blanks		43		48
Arbitration		101		
Benefits	76,77	31,78,79,80	81,82,83,84,97	
Career Development	51,53			
Collective Bargaining	99	100		
Compensation	1,65,66,67,99	68,69,70,71,72,78	73	74,75
Cultural Awareness		106		
Disabilities		19	21,45	
Discipline	1,20,88,89,90	91,101	47,92,93,94,95	
Disaster Preparation			85	
Discrimination	8,12,38,60	16,17,18,19	9,10,21,22,23, 45,93	24
Diversity Issues	8	20	9,10	
Dress Policy		91	93	
Ethics	1,13	64,71,72	45,81	
Employment at will	15			
Executive Perks		68,80		
Exit Interviews			46	
FLSA				74
FMLA			84	
Family Issues		31	84	
Health/Safety	52,77,85	86	81,84,87	
HR Challenges		4		
HR Data Breach			7	
HR Environment/Policies		3,5		
HR Forecasting				32
HR Functions	2	6,29		
HR Strategy	1,2,26	4,40		
HR Structure	2			
HR Trends		5		
Incentives	66,67,76	68,69,80	73	
Immigrants	14	20		
International HR	8,103,104,105	20,106	9	
Interviewing		41,42,43,49	46	50
Internet Blog			92	
Job Analysis	38	30		49,58
Job Descriptions		30		49,58

Labor Relations	98,99	100,101		102
Layoffs/Downsizing	25	28,29	96	
Management Development	51,53	54		
Mentoring	53			
Mergers		4	97	
Motivation	66		96,97	
NLRA		100		102
Nepotism			47	
Orientation	52		57	
Outsourcing	104	29		
Pay Inversion		72		
Performance Appraisal	25,59,60	61,62,63,64		
Privacy Issues	14,39,88,90		92	
Promotion	1,12,51			
Recruiting	34,35,36	40		49
References		43		
Retirement			81	33
Safety/Health	52,77,85	86	81,84,87	
Selection	14,34,35,36,37, 38,39,103,105	41,42,43,44	9,22,45,47	48,49,50
Self Appraisal	59		84	
Seniority			21	
Sexual Harassment	11	18		
Sexual Orientation		78	23	
Social Networking	39	92		
Substance Abuse	88		94	
Surveys of Employees	8			
Telecommuting		20		49
Termination	88	20,28,100,101		
Testing	37,38,88	43	94	50
Training	52,53,105	55,56,106	10,57	58
Turnover/Retention	66	6	46	
Unfair Labor Practices	98,99			
Union Organizing	98			102
Utilization Analysis				24
Violence At Work	89			
Wage Structures				75
Wage Surveys	65			
Whistle Blowing	13			
Work Schedules	27			

Contents

1

Human Resource Management in Perspective: Environment and Legal Issues

1 CASE

The New Director of Human Resources

Mount Ridge Engineering Systems designs, builds, and operates standardized, coal-fired utility plants in Kentucky. These small generating plants (35 megawatts and 55 megawatts) are built adjacent to an industrial plant that utilizes steam in its operations. Mount Ridge sells the steam to the industrial plant and electricity to the local utility. Under federal regulations, utilities are required to purchase this independently produced power if it is cost competitive. When Garrett Levinson founded the company, he firmly believed that the future of electric generation in the United States would depend upon coal as the primary fuel and standardization as a method of cost control and efficiency. This new technology, known as "cogeneration," is rapidly coming of age as many companies turn to these systems as a way to cut energy costs. Mount Ridge's very efficient plants have allowed it to pursue a cost leadership business strategy.

When the firm was formed four years ago, Joyce Newcombe was hired as director of human resources. Newcombe had recently graduated with an MBA from a large university in the Southeast. At the time of its establishment, the company had four employees in addition to Newcombe: the president and founder, a senior vice president of operations, a vice president for administration, and a vice president of cost and estimation. From the start, Mount Ridge had both the financing and plans to build seven plants over the next five- to eight-year period. Joyce Newcombe was hired to develop all of the necessary human resource programs, plans, and policies needed to staff the plants once they became operational. She explained, "When I was hired, all we had was a dream and a plan. I had an office with a desk, chair, and telephone. I literally had to develop an entire human resource system." During the first year, Newcombe developed benefit packages for both corporate and plant personnel, an employee handbook, job descriptions, a salary program, a supervisor's manual, and other basic personnel policies. In less than three years, the company built five plants. The size of the workforce grew from 5 to 39 people at corporate headquarters and from 0 to 183 employees in the plants (see Exhibit 1.1 for the company's organizational structure).

The company became remarkably successful in a short period of time. Newcombe was promoted to vice president. In addition to having two plants currently under construction in the state, Mount Ridge plans to build an additional two to three plants in the Northeast. The demand for cogeneration plants is strong in New Jersey, Connecticut, Maine, and Massachusetts, where state energy regulators are concerned about high electricity prices. Forecasts indicate that the company will grow to a total of nine plants and approximately 650 corporate and plant employees over the next two to three years.

The company faced a dilemma with regard to determining benefits and salaries for its employees. These had to be competitive, but not so high as to attract workers from Mount Ridge's "customers"—its industrial hosts and the local utility. In addition, since profits were to be reinvested into the business to finance future plant expansion, a profit-sharing plan was not feasible. Another important goal of the company was to remain nonunion by offering

EXHIBIT 1.1 *Organization Structure*

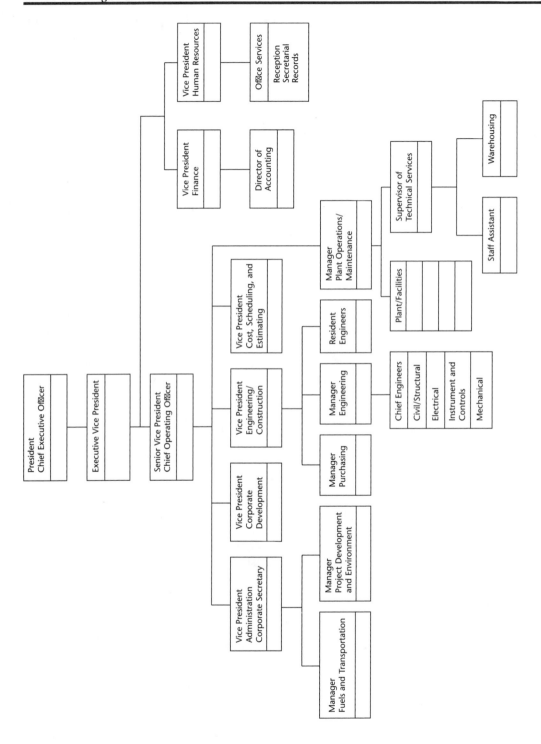

employees a good quality of work life and attractive benefits. Balancing these two goals was often difficult. Low-cost production was critical to Mount Ridge's competitive position. The importance of these goals is reflected in the words of President Levinson: "Mount Ridge places great value on its relationship with our industrial and utility clients. Our internal employee relationship has an equally important role in order to maintain an enjoyable and productive workforce for the future. Management believes that companies that are good to their employees reap the benefits in terms of increased productivity and loyalty." As part of an effort to build this philosophy into its human resource programs, employee appreciation dinners are held annually at each of the five plants. The president and other corporate officers attend each of the dinners given throughout the state. These dinners have been well-received by employees.

PLANT OPERATIONS

Most of Mount Ridge's plants are scattered throughout the state. Each plant employs approximately 45 workers. The typical plant structure is shown in Exhibit 1.2. Each plant is run by a plant superintendent who reports directly to the manager of plant operations and maintenance. While personnel operations are generally centralized at corporate headquarters, the plant superintendent and shift supervisor of each plant are largely responsible for the day-to-day administration of personnel policies. Newcombe admits, "One of our biggest problems has been getting management—especially plant management—to understand the legal and governmental regulations affecting human resource procedures." Although Newcombe developed a detailed employee handbook and supervisor's manual, over the years there have been situations where supervisors have not followed company policy. Newcombe recounted one such incident that occurred in one of the older plants during her third year with the company.

THE TERMINATION

One of the first plants built was the Edison plant. It is located in a medium-sized rural community in the eastern region of Kentucky and employs 45 workers. Bud Johnson, who started at the plant as a laborer, worked his way into a position as an auxiliary operator. An auxiliary operator is responsible for assisting the control room operator and the equipment operator in the basic operations and maintenance of the plant's generating system. In the two years that Johnson was in this position, he learned quickly and knew a good deal about the equipment operator's job. On many occasions, Johnson was asked to fill in when the equipment operator was absent or when there was a problem that no one else could handle. One day Johnson approached the plant superintendent, Larry Braxton, about a promotion to equipment operator:

Johnson: Larry, you know I can handle the equipment operator position, and I'd like to be considered for a promotion.

Braxton: That's not the point. We all know you are capable, but we just don't have any openings right now. Besides, the job qualifications require that you spend sufficient time as an auxiliary operator before moving up to an equipment operator. Just sit tight.

Johnson: Well, I hope some openings will come up soon. I really would like to make more money, and I know that I am qualified. You know I can learn quickly. Look at how fast I moved up from being a laborer.

After this conversation, Johnson was again called on several times to help out with the equipment operator's job and to explain the readings and gauges to Wilma Barker, one of the

EXHIBIT 1.2 *Typical Plant Structure*

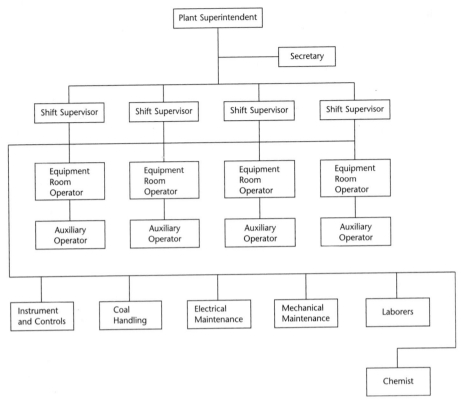

1 Plant Superintendent

1 Secretary

1 Chemist

1 Instrument and Controls

4 Shift Supervisors

8 Equipment Room Operators

16 Auxiliary Operators

2 Electrical Maintenance

2 Mechanical Maintenance

3 Coal Handlers

6 Laborers

      1 Assigned to Electrical Maintenance

      1 Assigned to Mechanical Maintenance

      2 Assigned to Coal Handling

      2 Assigned to Plant Clean Up

45 Total Plant Staff

equipment room operators. When Johnson did not receive a pay increase or promotion after his annual evaluation, he met with Braxton and told him that he was dissatisfied with his pay and felt that because he often performed the equipment operator's job, he ought to be paid at that rate instead of his present rate as an auxiliary operator. Braxton told him he would have to remain at the pay of an auxiliary operator and that he should be satisfied with that for the time being. Johnson became quite upset and stormed out of Braxton's office. The next day, Johnson did not report to work and did not call in to report his absence.

Company policy stated that when an employee is absent and fails to notify his or her supervisor, the employee may be terminated. When Johnson returned to work the following day, he told Braxton that he had decided to quit his job because he was very dissatisfied with his pay. Johnson was asked to sign a termination notice form required by company policy and was told by Braxton that he would receive a copy of the form in the mail.

A week later, Newcombe received a phone call from Johnson. Johnson told her that the reason given on the copy of the termination form he had just received in the mail was incorrect (see Exhibit 1.3). He had not left to take another job but had left because he was dissatisfied with his pay and lack of promotion at the plant. He explained that he had spoken with the plant superintendent about this several times. Johnson told Newcombe that he wanted his personnel records to be corrected and that he had been asked by Braxton to sign a blank form. He alleged that Braxton had added the incorrect reason after he had signed the form. Johnson also stated that he thought the Department of Labor would have something to say about this whole incident.

QUESTIONS

1. Discuss the relationship between corporate human resources structure and operations at the plant level. What impact, if any, did that relationship have on the situation described by Newcombe?

2. How should Newcombe have handled this situation?

3. What, if any, disciplinary action should have been taken against the plant superintendent (Braxton) at the time of the incident?

4. If Johnson's allegations were true, what are the legal ramifications of Braxton's behavior?

5. Describe Mount Ridge's business strategy. What is the relationship between its business strategy and its human resource practices?

6. What strategic human resource issues will Newcombe likely face as the company expands to the Northeast? How might this expansion affect the structure of the organization and its human resource department?

EXHIBIT *1.3 Termination Form for Bud Johnson*

NOTICE OF TERMINATION
This form MUST BE completed for EVERY termination

DEPARTMENT USE ONLY

REASON FOR TERMINATION	PAYROLL DEPARTMENT

1. SOCIAL SECURITY NUMBER

`1 2 3` — `0 9` — `7 6 2 5`

Johnson   Bud   O.
2. NAME   Last   First   Middle

348 Bismark Street
3. MAILING ADDRESS   Number   Street

Mount Ridge, Kentucky
City   State   Zip

587-6089
4. HOME PHONE

Auxiliary Operator
5. JOB TITLE

6. Termination date	Last day worked
11/1/06	10/31/06

7. Recommended for other employment	8. Replacement Required
Yes ☐ No ☒	Yes ☒ No ☐

9. Immediate Supervisor   Phone

Larry Braxton

10. Plant Location

Edison

11. Sex   M ☒   F ☐

12. Ethnic Background

REASON FOR TERMINATION

13. LAY-OFF — No replacement required ☐

14. DISCHARGE
   ☐ Absenteeism (give dates)
   ☐ Not qualified (explain)
   ☐ Other (explain)

15. VOLUNTARY QUIT
   ☐ Leave of absence granted
     (ending . . . .)
   ☐ Dissatisfied pay
     (overtime, rate, etc.)
   ☐ Dissatisfied distance to work
     (miles . . . .)
   ☒ To take another job
     (employer, rate)
   ☐ Leaving town
   ☐ Dissatisfied working conditions
     (explain)
   ☐ Other (explain)

16. EXPLANATION (Use additional sheet if necessary)

PAYROLL DEPARTMENT

17. EMPLOYEE number _____
18. HIRE DATE _____
19. RATE _____
20. HOURLY ☐   SALARIED ☐

                Days $

Regular pay thru _____ _____
Vacation _____ _____
Severance _____ _____
Pay in lieu of notice
Deductions:
   W/H (Federal & State)   (_____)
   FICA   (_____)
   Other, i.e., Insurance   (_____)
           TOTAL $ _____

EMPLOYMENT OFFICE

Larry Braxton
23. Plant supervisor

Bud Johnson
24. Employee signature

_____, SIGNATURE ACKNOWLEDGES RECEIPT OF THIS NOTICE
        Date

SUPERVISOR'S REPORT OF TERMINATION

WERE WRITTEN WARNING NOTICES OR PERFORMANCE EVALUATION GIVEN?
   ☐ YES (ATTACH COPIES)   ☐ NO

WHAT WAS EMPLOYEE'S REACTION TO COUNSEL, WARNING NOTICES, OR PERFORMANCE EVALUATION?

REASON FOR TERMINATION. (UNEMPLOYMENT INSURANCE CLAIMS ARE A MAJOR COST TO THE COMPANY. WHEN FACTUAL INFORMATION IS LACKING, THE STATE EMPLOYMENT DEVELOPMENT DEPARTMENT GENERALLY FAVORS THE EMPLOYEE'S CLAIM—EVEN THOUGH IT MAY NOT BE MERITED. THEREFORE, THE EXACT REASONS FOR TERMINATION ARE EXTREMELY IMPORTANT. IN ADDITION, THIS INFORMATION CAN BE ESSENTIAL FOR THE RESOLUTION OF UNFAIR LABOR PRACTICE AND EQUAL EMPLOYMENT CASES.)

The Human Resource Function of Harrison Brothers Corporation

COMPANY HISTORY

Harrison Brothers Corporation was founded in upstate New York on September 15, 1898, by Aubrey and William Harrison. Harrison Brothers is a multi-line traditional department store that carries mainly men's, women's, and children's clothing. In recent years, the store has expanded to include household furnishings and other items for the home. The long-term goal of the company is to become the leading chain of department stores in the Northeast, selling moderate- to higher-priced merchandise to middle-class, fashion-conscious customers. Harrison Brothers is one of the largest privately owned retail stores in the United States. A majority of its twenty stores are located in the Northeast. Its largest store is located in a major urban center and has 950 employees. The company is highly decentralized and maintains a very small corporate office.

INDUSTRY CHALLENGES

Traditional department stores like Harrison Brothers are beginning to experience the effects of a number of changes in the retail industry. Not long ago, major department stores succeeded by being all things to all customers. However, today's customer is looking for both value and specialization. Superstores and giant discounters are also popping up. At the same time, the industry faces the challenge of keeping a well-trained, highly motivated sales staff and management team. James Harrison, CEO of Harrison Brothers, describes the company's strategic challenges for the next five years: "We can no longer continue to do the same old things that gave us a reputation for fair value. We must reposition ourselves—floor to floor—offering exciting brand names, excellent sales help, and frequent sales. We need a sales staff that knows the merchandise and understands customer preferences. Buying expertise is also critical because fashions and consumer tastes never stay the same. We have five strategic goals:

1. Convert non-selling space into revenue-generating selling space.
2. Build up underdeveloped merchandise categories.
3. Invest aggressively in private brands like Polo, Nautica, and Tommy Hilfiger.
4. Reduce costs through the use of advanced computer systems to project sales and manage inventory.
5. Improve productivity of sales associates, buyers, and department heads."

James Harrison took over the business after earning an MBA at a prestigious business school in the Northeast. Unlike previous family members, he wanted to take a much more deliberate approach to charting the future of Harrison Brothers. To do this, he hired a consultant to assist in assessing the company's strengths and weaknesses. Harrison felt the employee quality and performance would be one of the keys to the future. As part of his analysis, the consultant sought to learn more about the human resource function within Harrison Brothers. He decided to interview a few of the human resource and other key managers at the store level. Both groups were also asked to complete a questionnaire of their perceptions of the responsibilities of the human resource function (see Exhibit 1.4).

EXHIBIT 1.4 *Results of Questionnaire Completed by HR*

Managers and Non-HR Managers[a]

HR Responsibilities	HR Managers	Store Managers
Staffing	4.5	4.5
Training and Development	3.5	4.5
Performance Management	4.5	4.0
Compensation	3.0	3.5
Safety	2.5	2.5
Knowledge of Business	2.0	4.5
Managing Change	2.0	4.5

[a]Respondents were given a list of human resource responsibilities and asked to rate their importance to store performance using a scale of 1 (not very important) to 5 (very important). The responses were aggregated for all stores. The numbers in the table represent the mean ratings for each item. The questionnaire was completed by all the human resource managers and store managers at each store.

THE WESTPARK STORE*

Brenda McCain has been the human resource manager at the Westpark store for the past four years. Prior to her employment at Harrison Brothers, Brenda had several years of experience in retail stores and came to Harrison Brothers after being a buyer at one of its major competitors. McCain has a degree in fashion merchandising from a college in New Jersey. Currently, there are 950 employees at the Westpark store. The staff includes salespeople, sales support employees (dock, marking room, clerical, and accounting), maintenance, security, and management. The human resource department consists of five people (see Exhibit 1.5). During the peak holiday season, a number of people are hired as floating sales staff. These temporary workers may number close to 100.

THE HUMAN RESOURCE MANAGER'S JOB

McCain talked about the human resource department's areas of responsibility: "Our business has really grown in the last two years. We are carrying more specialty and designer clothing lines and have added items we hope will appeal to moderate- to high-income customers. When I came here four years ago, I found too many of the human resource operations being performed by the operations manager, Pat Hartlake, and one of the department heads, Rich Jenkins. Since that time, I have attempted to set up procedures and policies to assure proper staffing of the store. I spend most of my time just managing the human resource department. I think it is important to keep abreast of the performance of workers, and I like to observe their work habits regularly. I also spend a good deal of time on selecting applicants for the sales and support jobs. There is heavy turnover on the sales floor in our business, and the average salesperson at Harrison Brothers is either part-time, an older employee, or one who is 'in-between jobs'—if a better job came along, they would snap it up immediately. For example, of the 119 part-time people hired in the last four months, 65 have left."

McCain went on to explain their selection procedures: "The main sources of our applicants are newspaper ads and word-of-mouth by present or past employees. We select people based on how well they do in the interview. Right now, I conduct about 25 to 30 interviews a week and perhaps more during the holiday rush. I have enough experience in

*The interview at the Westpark store reflects what the consultant heard throughout the company.

EXHIBIT 1.5 *Harrison Brothers Organization Chart*

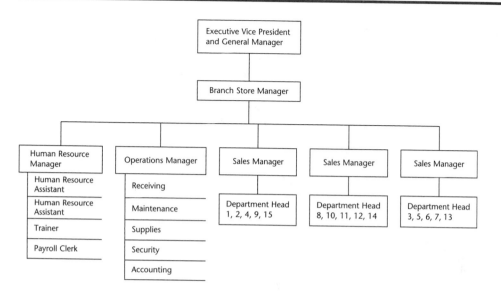

Department Identification

1. Children's (boys, girls, infants)	9. Cosmetics
2. Shoes	10. Domestics
3. Dresses	11. China/etc.
4. Men's	12. Housewares
5. Women's coats	13. Fine jewelry
6. Fashion accessories	14. Sporting goods
7. Intimate apparel	15. Toys
8. Furniture/Carpet/Bedding	

(Each department head supervises several sales clerks.)

retail to know what it takes to be a good salesperson. We place a lot of weight on their motivation, personality, and drive. Little or no useful information is gained from high school or college records or references. I do check their application forms for an indication of job stability, though.

"The training of new salespeople occurs every two weeks and every week during the holiday season. Now and then we get some employees who cannot effectively complete the cash register training. Our trainer, Joanne Flynn, tries to expose them to selling techniques and how to properly interact with customers. Although we have a trainer, I do spend a good deal of time with her and will help out if the training classes are too large.

"When I came here, discipline was a continual bone of contention between the employees and supervisors. Employees felt the present procedures were inconsistently enforced and applied. Each supervisor was administering punishment depending on his or her own interpretation of the problem. Now, I am totally responsible for all disciplinary actions. I discuss the alleged wrongful act with the employee's supervisor to assess the magnitude of the act. I then talk with the employee before deciding upon the appropriate consequences. In this way, we have better consistency in the application of disciplinary rules. Any employee who receives three disciplinary actions is eligible for dismissal.

"While we hire our salespeople at the minimum wage, we do perform an annual evaluation of their performance to determine merit increases. We use sales productivity as the major criterion. Performance is evaluated on average sales per hour. For example, say an employee works in an eight percent department. The hourly quota would be calculated by dividing the hourly wage by the percent level. This determines how much the sales clerk would have to sell to break even. For any sales above that level, the clerk receives a commission. At evaluation time, if the clerk's sales per hour are above the breakeven point, the new hourly wage is determined by multiplying the sales per hour by the percent level. For example, assume that a salesperson works in an eight percent department and earns $8 per hour. The employee would have to sell $100 per hour to break even. Any sales above that level would receive a commission. If sales at evaluation time were actually $150 per hour, hourly pay would increase to $12 per hour (150 times .08). We have had moderate success with this system, although I'm not sure how much it helps us to retain good employees.

"For our sales support staff, we have supervisors basically evaluate the employee's quality and quantity of work. Last year, though, we incorporated a form of employee development into the evaluation process. Supervisors are required to discuss the employees' career opportunities and professional development with them. I initiated this as a form of career planning and hopefully as a way to keep good employees. Unfortunately, supervisors have been slack in doing the assessment. They seem to be more anxious to get the performance evaluation completed. Several employees came to me to say they had not received a 'professional assessment' since the program was instituted.

"There is a lot more we need to do here in human resources, but we are somewhat constrained by cost considerations and the realities of the retail industry. The turnover in the sales areas gives me little free time to develop new programs and ideas."

INTERVIEW WITH THE STORE MANAGER

Jennifer Daft recently joined Harrison Brothers after being recruited from a major specialty retailer. Jennifer had a number of years of experience in management and retail. During the interview, she talked about her perceptions of the human resource department in her store. "I think they are too internally focused most of the time. Brenda and the rest of her staff seem to be struggling to keep up with the day-to-day activities. I don't know if they are understaffed or not. Our store has experienced very high turnover. With the new strategic direction of our company, however, I need human resources to be more of a key player. It's not hard to get the merchandise we want to sell, but we need people who know how to merchandise it and how to sell it to customers. There are a lot of changes going on in the company. It's not going to be a smooth ride for a while. We're all going to have to learn how to do things differently and better to stay competitive. Our human resource people are no exception."

INTERVIEW WITH THE OPERATIONS MANAGER

Pat Hartlake, the operations manager, talked about interactions with the human resource department: "I have a good working relationship with the human resource department, but it took some time to develop that relationship. McCain has a good understanding of the retail business, and I am impressed with her knowledge of store operations. They have been somewhat slow in filling the vacant sales positions, and they don't always respond as quickly as they should. They seem terribly understaffed and overworked most of the time.

"Let me give you an example of what I mean. A few weeks ago, I was faced with an employee situation that was evolving to the point where I felt termination was necessary. I went to the Human Resource Department to discuss the case to be sure I had covered all bases. With all of the laws today, one needs to be careful in making decisions. They never seem to be able to produce answers to questions without hedging. I had to wait almost two weeks before I got any help from them. In the meantime, the situation with the employee continued to deteriorate. I can understand their reluctance to terminate sales staff because of the difficulty in recruiting new people. In a way, however, the old system seemed to be a lot less complicated. Department managers knew how to handle situations that came up in their departments. Don't get me wrong! I know that as we continue to grow we're probably going to need an even larger human resource department."

QUESTIONS

1. How does McCain view her role as human resource manager?
2. What is Harrison Brothers' business strategy?
3. What is the structure and staffing of the human resources department?
4. Analyze the data in Exhibit 1.4. What are its implications?
5. Given the organization's size and strategic goals, evaluate the development of the human resource function at Harrison Brothers. What problems do you see? How could its major human resource functions be improved?

Developing Environmentally Friendly HR Policies at City University

I. OBJECTIVES

    A. To understand the critical role HR can play in an organization's green initiatives to ensure and support sustainability goals.

    B. To identify environmentally friendly HR policies and initiatives within the key HR functions.

II. OUT-OF-CLASS PREPARATION TIME: 1 hour

III. IN-CLASS TIME SUGGESTED: 45 minutes

IV. PROCEDURES

    A. Read the entire exercise before class. Students may want to conduct some research before class on environmental responsibility and sustainability. They can also visit the following Web sites:

        www.carbonfootprint.com

        www.greenatwork.com

    B. The class should be divided into groups of four. The groups should be given 20 minutes to brainstorm ideas for green initiatives that fall within HR's responsibility. Each group should complete Form 1.1.

    C. The instructor should then ask each group to present their list to the rest of the class. After the first group shares its list, the rest of the groups should only add things that are new or different.

    D. If time permits, the entire class should discuss the following questions: 1) What is HR's role in building a greener organization? 2) What are the potential benefits in terms of attracting and retaining talent? 3) How should Andrea proceed in order to develop an overall strategy for "greening" the HR function at the university?

BACKGROUND

Alice Vanderbilt has been the Director of Human Resources at City University for the past five years. The sprawling state university is located about 15 miles north of the city center in a bustling suburb known for its rolling hills and plentiful trees. The campus itself is quite beautiful with lots of green areas and ponds. Two major thoroughfares are within close proximity. The student enrollment was 17,000 six years ago but has grown to 20,000 students. The University has many degree programs but has gained a reputation for excellent engineering programs. Recently the university built a research complex that houses a number of research projects focusing on innovation in environmental engineering.

A majority of its 20,000 students commute from the various towns and communities daily to attend day and evening classes. Only about 30 percent of the students live on campus. International students represent less than 5 percent of the student population. There are 1,300 faculty and staff. During the week, the campus is a hub of activity. Most of the in-state residential students drive home for the weekend and return on Monday morning or late Sunday evening. Despite the growth of the city over the years, there is no public transport system except for a light rail trolley system that mainly services the city center with a few routes to key suburbs south of the city. There is no line running to the university. Thus, most of the City University's staff members drive to work in their own cars. Most students also have their own cars since many students work part-time. Parking demands continue to outstrip available space. Last year, the campus paved over one of the green areas to make space for an additionally 1,500 cars. A new 4-story parking deck is also under construction.

Three months ago, Dr. Jeanette Marshall was installed as the 20th president of the University. Dr. Marshall has already embarked on a number of initiatives since taking office. At a management planning session two weeks ago, she announced a new initiative, Green Leadership for a Sustainable Campus. At the session, she shared her vision for greening the campus: I want City University to become "the most green-friendly university in the country."

At the session the following objectives were developed:

- To create an environmental culture where everyone is committed to protecting the environment.

- To leverage the University's knowledge and expertise to "green" the campus.

- To encourage positive environmental behavior in staff.

- To implement and encourage green practices for the entire campus.

- To reward best practice in "greening" the campus.

- To partner with the local community on green projects of mutual interest.

Each manager was given the assignment to identify green initiatives and policies for their area of responsibility. All managers were expected to have a draft proposal completed within the next two months for review and discussion by the larger group. Since the planning session, Alice had been giving a lot of thought to what she could propose. Alice also believed she needed to first come up with some basic ideas for green initiatives and would then work toward an overall HR strategy for greening the workplace. She admitted to herself that she had really not thought about HR implications of environmental sustainability. Yes, recycling was obvious but what else can be achieved through the HR function?

HR Functional Area	Possible Green Initiatives and Policies	Potential Benefit(s)
Recruitment and Staffing		
Orientation		
Compensation and Benefits		
Work Practices and Policies		
Performance Management		
Reward Systems		
Employee Cafeteria		
Employee Communications		

4 EXERCISE

Human Resource Challenges during Mergers

I. OBJECTIVES

A. To sensitize you to the actual and potential human resource challenges facing organizations contemplating or implementing a merger.

B. To familiarize you with various human resource strategies and tactics for managing a successful merger process.

II. OUT-OF-CLASS PREPARATION TIME: 30 minutes

III. IN-CLASS TIME SUGGESTED: 50 minutes

IV. INSTRUCTIONS

A. In groups of three to five students, read the "Situation," below as well as the merger challenges listed on Form 1.2.

B. Each group will be assigned one or more of the merger challenges listed in Form 1.2. Search the Web sites outlined in the Internet Skill Builder in Part 1, the Internet sites listed below, or other sites to identify one or more human resource strategies and tactics to address each of your assigned merger challenges.

C. One person from each group will present the strategies and tactics developed to address their assigned merger challenges together with the group's assessment of the highest priorities. Each group should also identify which of the challenges and strategies/tactics for addressing each will be most crucial for implementing a successful merger.

Useful Web sites for this research include the following:

http://www.workforceonline.com/

http://www.hrmgt.com/

http://www.hrworld.com

http://www.pohly.com/admin7.shtml

SITUATION

Katherine Montgomery is the Director of Human Resources for a faith-based hospital in the Southwest. In addition to a BS in Nursing, she also has an MA in Human Resources Management and has been active in her local Society for Human Resources Management. Recently, Katherine has heard rumors that her hospital may be in merger discussions with the academic medical center in the same city. The academic medical center is larger in terms of beds (804 versus 658 beds), total revenue, staff, and external research grants. In addition, the medical center is state-associated and many employees are either union members or have civil service job protection. Katherine's hospital is private, not-for-profit, and has no labor union representation. Based on a private communication with her human resources counterpart in the academic medical center, she is aware that neither of them has been involved in merger negotiations or planning.

Today, the city newspaper reported that the two institutions were taking part in merger talks and the expectation was that a final merger agreement would be signed within three months. Katherine is upset because she knows that most mergers fail primarily due to poor communications and incompatible corporate cultures. She is also saddened that her department was not included in the initial merger negotiations since she is well aware of the literature on merger challenges and has detailed knowledge of one healthcare merger failure in another city. She also strongly believes that the greater the degree to which the human resources department is involved in the merger process, the greater the likelihood of merger success.

As she contemplates her course of action, she lists the human resource challenges both organizations would face before, during, and after the merger. These appear in Form 1.2.

Until now, she has not had to consider which human resource strategies and tactics would be most appropriate for addressing each of the challenges she has identified in Form 1.2. She has called Professor Martin Smith in the Department of Management at the local university and asked if he or some of his graduate students could assist her in completing Form 1.2. With that input, she then intends to schedule an appointment to speak with her CEO in order to indicate how her department could assist in the merger process. Specifically, she plans to present him with a human resource plan for successfully integrating the two hospitals based on Form 1.2.

Potential Challenge/Problem	Appropriate Strategies/Tactics
1. Rumors, misinformation, and inadequate information	
2. Conflicting corporate cultures	
3. Existing state government civil services rules and union contracts	
4. Neither organization fully aware of the skills, knowledge, and abilities of the other's management or staff	
5. Likely staff reconfiguration, reassignments, and layoffs	
6. Determination of which human resources practices to retain	
7. Management of staff morale and stress levels	
8. Turnover of valued employees	
9. Unclear job assignments and reporting relationships	
10. Lack of understanding of new policies and procedures	
11. Overall strategy to market her department's role and potential value to the CEO.	

Indicate Highest Priority Concerns: _____

5 EXERCISE

Scanning the Contemporary Work Environment: Shifting Demographics

I. OBJECTIVES

The purpose of this exercise is to help you understand the potential influence of trends and changes in the external environment on the design and implementation of human resource management practices.

II. OUT-OF-CLASS PREPARATION TIME: None

III. IN-CLASS TIME SUGGESTED: 20–30 minutes

IV. PROCEDURES

A. This exercise should be done in groups of four to five students.

B. After completion of the exercise, each group will present its ideas to the rest of the class.

C. Listed below are some of the major predictions about changes or trends in the labor/ employment environment that will take place. Read each trend and list some ideas about the impact of these trends on the major human resource management functions: staffing and placement, training and development, salary administration, performance evaluation, job design, promotions, and career planning. That is, what human resource issues will organizations face because of these changes?

Trend   **Impact on HRM**

1. Increasing government regulation of health care

2. Aging of the workforce

3. Increase in outsourcing, offshoring, and employee leasing

4. Increasing diversity of the American labor force (e.g., women and minorities in the labor force)

5. Multigenerational workforce

6. Increasing use of social networks

7. Increasing number of foreign-born employees

8. Global warming and growing environmental awareness

9. Labor shortages at all skill levels

10. Threat of stagnant economic growth in United States and globally

Suggested Internet Resources

U.S. Department of Labor	http://www.dol.gov
EEOC	http://www.eeoc.gov
Society for Human Resource Management	http://www.shrm.org
Conference Board	http://www.conference-board.org
OSHA	http://www.osha.gov
U.S. Census Bureau	http://www.census.gov
United Nations	http://www.un.org
International Labor Office	http://www.ilo.org

6   EXERCISE

*Evaluating the Financial Impact of Human Resource Management
Activities: Reducing the Cost of Turnover*

I. OBJECTIVES

A. To provide you with practice in analyzing data and drawing conclusions regarding managerial implications.

B. To make you aware of the potential costs of controllable, dysfunctional turnover and its impact on net income or profit.

C. To make you aware of the potential benefits of human resource management activities to an organization's "bottom line."

II. OUT-OF-CLASS PREPARATION TIME: 2 hours

III. IN-CLASS TIME SUGGESTED: 45 minutes

IV. PROCEDURES

Read the entire exercise, including the "Background" on the Charlotte Health System and the three exhibits. Using the data in the exhibits, do the calculations (on your own, prior to class) requested on Form 1.3. Then, assemble groups of three to five students during the class period and discuss each of the questions. At the end of the class period, have a spokesperson for each group discuss the group's answers and rationale with the entire class.

BACKGROUND

The healthcare industry has undergone dramatic change and restructuring during the decade of the 1990s and early 2000s. Mergers, consolidations, and downsizing have become the norm as organizations struggled to provide more cost-effective, high-quality services demanded by managed-care organizations and corporate employers. A major response to these pressures has been the development of "integrated delivery systems," which typically combine multiple units of hospitals, physician practices, outpatient facilities, long-term care facilities, and insurance.

The goal of these systems is to provide "seamless" care through internal referrals, a common electronic medical record, common policies and procedures, etc. However, the reality has been somewhat less than a total success. Among the problems identified have been differences in values and incentives between the organizational units, lack of top management knowledge of some of the units acquired, and inability to "integrate" the different units clinically and managerially.

The Charlotte (North Carolina) Health System was developed from a base of a public hospital to which various delivery sites were added after Harry Majors became CEO 15 years ago. Since his arrival, Majors and his executive team have created the dominant health system in North Carolina. Despite this success, the system continues to be under pressure from employers and managed-care organizations to further reduce its costs and document both clinical quality and cost-effectiveness.

Almost four years ago, Majors and the board of directors decided that the time had come to "professionalize" the human resource function since the organizations they had purchased or aligned with exhibited varying degrees of sophistication and vastly different policies and procedures. Betty Williams was recruited from another health system as the new VP for Human Resources. Williams came to her job after completion of an MA degree in Human Resources Management from the University of Alabama and 16 years of experience in the

	Department Budget per Year			
Budget Cost	One	Two	Three	Four
Salaries and Benefits	$110,000	$233,000	$288,000	$324,000
Equipment and Supplies	24,000	39,000	48,000	57,000
Communications	41,000	62,000	73,000	81,000
Totals	$175,000	$334,000	$409,000	$462,000

field. During the three years she has been at Charlotte Health System, she has hired three new HRM staffpersons in recruitment, employee benefits, and compensation.

H.R. COST JUSTIFICATION

As the Board has considered how to reduce the cost of service delivery in the system, the corporate office in general, and the Human Resources Department in particular, have come under increased scrutiny. Williams has been told she needed to justify the additional budget allocation to her department over the past three years. Exhibit 1.6 shows her department's budget for year one (the year prior to her arrival) as well as the three years since her arrival. The board has calculated the "extra" costs of the Human Resources Department over the past three years (using year one as the base) to be $680,000. The largest percentage cost increases were in "salaries and benefits" and in "equipment and supplies." Most of the latter increases were the result of upgrades in computer hardware and software.

The Board has scheduled a meeting for next Monday. One of the agenda items is to examine the costs of the Human Resource Management Department with the possibility of a budget cut for next year. Williams has been asked to make a presentation to justify her budget and how expansion of her department has contributed to the system's "bottom line." She has considered a number of changes she made which she believes have improved overall system performance. Among these were the development of system career ladders to increase employee retention, in-house management training programs to improve management competence, development of "model" staffing ratios to reduce employee stress and burnout, quarterly performance reviews to increase employee feedback, absenteeism incentive programs, and initiation of an annual employee survey to identify problem areas.

After some discussion with her staff, Williams decided that it would be easier to "document" the benefits of increased employee retention. Exhibit 1.7 shows the employee

EXHIBIT 1.7 *Annual Turnover Rate by Category for Years One through Four*

	Percent Turnover per Year			
Personnel Categories	One	Two	Three	Four
Executive ($n = 127$)[+]	12.8	11.5	9.2	8.3
Physician ($n = 367$)	18.1	17.6	17.9	15.6
Other Professional ($n = 615$)	22.6	22.1	18.3	15.6
Nonprofessional ($n = 804$)	29.0	26.3	27.1	24.3
Totals[++] ($n = 19.3$)	23.8	22.3	21.3	18.8

[+]*n is the average number of employees in each category over the four-year period.*
[++]*This is the weighted average turnover rate for all four categories for each of the four years.*

Turnover Costs	All Categories[+]	Personnel Category			
		Executive	Physician	Other Professional	Nonprofessional
	($n = 1913$)	($n = 127$)	($n = 367$)	($n = 615$)	($n = 804$)
Separation Costs:					
Exit Interviews	50.73	62.50	73.00	51.00	38.50
Administrative Costs	119.27	127.00	132.50	116.00	114.50
Separation Pay	348.01	2,254.00	1,034.00	—	—
	518.01	2,443.50	1,239.50	167.00	153.00
Replacement Costs:					
Job Advertisements	1,346.49	1,805.00	2,416.50	1,127.50	953.00
Pre-Employment Administration	353.28	405.00	416.50	386.50	291.00
Entrance Interviews	324.86	486.00	724.50	284.00	148.00
Assessment Testing	271.69	382.50	695.00	214.50	105.00
Staff Time	249.00	417.50	522.00	212.00	126.00
Travel/Moving Expenses	293.68	1,215.50	1,110.50	—	—
Processing New Employees	87.50	87.50	87.50	87.50	87.50
Medical Examinations	175.00	175.00	175.00	175.00	175.00
	3,101.50	4,974.00	6,147.50	2,487.00	1,855.50
Training Costs					
Informational Literature	80.00	80.00	80.00	80.00	80.00
Formal Training	147.53	340.00	516.50	35.00	35.00
On-the-Job Training	68.15	—	—	212.00	159.50
	295.68	420.00	596.50	327.00	274.50
Reduced Productivity during Learning Period	3,133.37	4,000.00	6,500.00	3,452.00	1,215.50
Total	$7,048.56	$11,837.50	$14,483.50	$6,433.00	$3,528.50

[+]*weighted average*

turnover by category for year one (the year before Williams's arrival) as well as for each of the following three years since her arrival. These data show a decline in turnover for all four personal categories over the four-year period.

Williams and her staff have calculated the average cost of turnover per employee by personnel category and these calculations are shown in Exhibit 1.8. Most of these calculations can be documented from personnel records. The exception is the "reduced productivity during the learning period." For these calculations, the staff calculated the average monthly productivity for a small sub-sample of the individuals who left and compared it to the average monthly productivity of those who replaced them during their first three months. They then calculated the dollar cost of this lost productivity for a one-year period.

Their assumption is that the lower productivity continues at the same level for a 12-month period and then disappears. More realistically, the lower productivity probably declines over time but continues for longer than a 12-month period. However, they feel their method of calculation is a good approximation of reality since their overestimation of the productivity loss is offset by the shorter time period of their calculations.

Exhibit 1.8 shows that the total cost for each individual who leaves the Charlotte Health System averages $7,049 but this varies from a high of $14,484 for physicians to a low of $3,644 for nonprofessional employees. These costs are divided into separation costs, replacement costs, training costs, and costs of reduced productivity (for the new employee) during the (assumed) one-year learning period.

QUESTIONS

1. Are the calculated benefits of reduced turnover sufficient to justify the $680,000 in increased costs associated with the expansion of the Human Resource Management Department? Would your answer be the same if "reduced productivity during the learning period" was excluded from the analysis?

2. In addition to improved employee retention, what are some other areas of potential economic benefit to the organization from having a Human Resource Department? What calculations would you do to prove such benefits?

Personnel Category	**Savings in Year**			**Total Savings**
	Two	**Three**	**Four**	
Executive				
Physician				
Other Professional				
Nonprofessional				
All Categories	_____	_____	_____	_____

Calculation of Savings or Loss:

1. Total Incremental Savings from Higher Employee Retention
   for all Personnel Categories for Years 2, 3, and 4.

2. Total Incremental Costs of the Human Resource Management   −$680,000
   Department Budget for Years 2, 3, and 4.

Net Savings or Loss   _____

Benefit/Cost Ratio (1) ÷ (2)   _____

Human Resource Information Systems Data Breach

Sweets, Inc., a candy manufacturer, is finalizing the implementation of a comprehensive human resource information data system covering its 400-plus employees. It has been working on the system for two years and hopes to finish it within the next few months. This system will eliminate virtually all of the paper forms used by the Human Resource Department. The firm has been transferring all of the information contained on these forms to its computer. When the process is complete, the firm will be able to store, analyze, retrieve, and distribute most of its HR information.

Shortly, the company will be able to post job openings on the Internet and retrieve incoming job applications. It will know what skills and abilities all of its employees possess and what training each has received. It will be able to access performance appraisal information on all employees to determine job performance levels and necessary training. The firm will be able to examine pay and benefit information to determine individual and aggregate compensation levels. It will also be able to easily prepare various documents such as Form EEO–1. All of this information will be available with just a few key strokes.

Until yesterday everything had gone smoothly. Then, a major problem developed that turned everything upside down. A laptop computer containing sensitive data went missing from one of the HR offices. Was it stolen? Did someone borrow it to work on at home? Was it just moved to another office? No one knew for sure and a frantic search began, but it was without success.

The human resource director decided he had better call the company president and the head of computer operations to explain what had happened. The president wanted to know immediately what information was stored on the computer and how this information could be retrieved by others, assuming it was stolen. The HR director stated that he was not sure if the laptop had been stolen, but that employee compensation information was probably on the computer, including each person's name, address, telephone number, and social security number. The confidential information was password protected, so the average citizen could not retrieve it, but an experienced hacker might be able to do so. All three executives were aware of recent incidents in which sensitive computer data had been compromised at many large corporations and that these corporations had issued warnings to those affected. The question that needed to be addressed was what action Sweets, Inc. should take given its present situation.

QUESTIONS

1. What action do you recommend that Sweets, Inc. take now? Explain your reasoning.

2. What steps can the firm take to prevent this problem from occurring in the future?

3. What additional information needs to be gathered before any decisions are made or action taken?

Diversity Issues

8   CASE

▬▬▬▬ *Managing Diversity: Johnson Chemical International*

Jeff Rice, vice president of corporate human resources at Johnson Chemical International, was very anxious about the meeting he was about to have with John Henderson (CEO), Gary Polaski (secretary and general counsel), Steven Hong (vice president of operations, Haverford plant), and Matt Beale (vice president of public affairs and communications). The last two days had been quite tense in the company ever since an e-mail (see Exhibit 1.9) was sent throughout the company's Haverford plant.

Johnson Chemical International is one of the world's leading manufacturers of specialty chemical products. The company was founded in 1902 by Herman Johnson, who was an MIT-trained chemist. Over the years, Johnson Chemical has built a reputation for producing high-quality products developed through cutting-edge technology and research. As a privately held corporation, Johnson Chemical does not report sales or earning figures. It has plants and operations in 30 countries and manufacturing facilities in 10 countries (Argentina, Canada, Kenya, Indonesia, Greece, United Kingdom, Japan, Taiwan, Malaysia, and Brazil). Johnson Chemical employs more than 14,500 people worldwide with its headquarters located in Chicago. Employment in the United States is about one-half of its total workforce worldwide, with a majority of those employees in the Chicago area. Because of its need for highly trained scientists and technicians, the company recruits a substantial number of employees with training in the science and engineering fields.

The U.S. manufacturing operations are conducted at the Haverford plant, about 15 miles outside of Chicago. The state-of-the-art plant is about three million square feet and is one of the most modern chemical manufacturing facilities in the world. The facility also has state-of-the-art laboratories and houses the company's research division. In addition to its hourly employees, the company employs a large number of R&D employees consisting of scientists, technicians, and engineers. Because of its need for highly trained technical employees, the company conducts extensive recruiting at the major colleges and universities with outstanding science and engineering programs. A majority of Johnson Chemical's top management has come from the technical ranks of the company. Its current CEO, John Henderson, is a chemical engineer and the former president of international operations.

THE MEETING

John Henderson: Come on in, Jeff. Good morning, folks. I want to thank you for meeting with me this morning. We have a major problem on our hands. A crude e-mail has sent a tidal wave through the company. It's already hit the press. We've had several calls from the media asking for us to comment on what has happened. Matt, how are we handling the calls?

Matt Beale: John, I have issued a press release that basically states that Johnson Chemical does not tolerate any form of racist or sexist jokes and the individual responsible will be dealt

EXHIBIT 1.9 *The E-Mail Message*

The e-mail message

Morning Puzzle: Do you recognize these acronyms?

UFO
IBB
NAACP

Answer: UFO = Ugly ------- Orientals; IBB = Itty bitty breasts; and NAACP = -------, apes, alligators, coons and possums

---

with appropriately. Our information systems folks are trying to determine the origins of the e-mail.

Gary Polaski: John, don't worry. We are on firm legal grounds if we fire the individual or individuals responsible for using the company e-mail to send racist and sexist jokes. I think we should take very strong action when we find out who is responsible.

Steven Hong: Well, we better do something fast because it is certainly affecting plant operations. People aren't working but are busy talking about the e-mail. I'm afraid that it really has taken people off track for the time. It also seems to be unleashing some grievances that our women and minority employees have about their treatment in the company. The men and white employees seem to be worried that they're going to all be blamed for the e-mail or, even worse, that they agree with the sentiments in that e-mail. John, I'm worried about the impact of this on employee morale.

Jeff Rice: John, since the e-mail I have had several women and minority employees, especially the African-American employees, come to my office to talk about problems and other incidents in the company. To be honest, it has caught me off guard. We have an excellent equal opportunity/affirmative action program in place and have made some strides in hiring women and minorities in the last five years (see Exhibit 1.10). I am wondering if we've really done enough.

John Henderson: I'm not sure what you mean, Jeff. Our company has enjoyed a good reputation as a leader in the industry when it comes to equal employment opportunity. How could this happen?

Jeff Rice: Well, I was thinking about this last night. You know, John, in the last few years we have begun to have a more diverse group of employees after years of being a company with

EXHIBIT 1.10 *Employment Trends*

There has been a 10 percent increase in employee growth at the Haverford Plant.

The percent of women employees has increased from 10 to 15 percent.

The percent of African-American employees has remained at 6 percent.

The percent of Asian employees has increased from 5 to 10 percent.

Plant turnover averages 2 percent, but is ten times higher for women and African Americans.

The percent of women in management/supervisory positions increased from 2 to 2.7 percent.

The percent of African Americans in management/supervisory positions increased from 1.5 to 2.0 percent.

The percent of Asians in management/supervisory positions increased from 2 to 3.5 percent.

There has been an 8 percent increase in minority scientists (most of that represents Asians).

The percentage of women scientists has grown by 2 percent.

The highest ranking woman in the company is Meredith Jensen, vice president and deputy counsel.

The highest ranking African-American manager is vice president for equal opportunity and employee relations.

The highest ranking Asian manager is vice president, plant operations.

---

primarily white male employees. Perhaps, it was only a matter of time before these tensions emerged.

John Henderson: Well, we're going to have to get a handle on the issues. Jeff, I want you and your staff to find out what the issues are and give me a report on your findings in 60 days. After we review your report, we'll have to determine what we need to do. Get whatever help you need from consultants. I expect a negative media backlash on this thing, and we're going to have to show that we are a company prepared to deal with tough issues. I have prepared a companywide message that will be sent to all employees this afternoon (see Exhibit 1.11).

RICE'S REPORT

Two months after the meeting, Jeffrey Rice sent John Henderson and the rest of the executive staff a 20-page confidential report of his findings. Excerpts from his report are contained in Exhibits 1.12–1.18. With the assistance of a consulting firm, Rice organized focus groups with African-American employees, women employees, Asian employees, and white male

EXHIBIT 1.11 *Letter to Employees from John Henderson, CEO*

Dear Johnson Employees:

By now, you have heard about the e-mail that was sent through the company's computer system that contained offensive comments. I want to be very clear: We will not tolerate behavior that makes our work environment uncomfortable and hostile for others. The telling of racist, sexist, or offensive comments is not appropriate behavior at Johnson Chemical. It is disrespectful of fellow employees. Using company e-mail to perpetuate offensive views of others violates company policy. Rest assured that we will see that those responsible for sending the e-mail are duly disciplined.

I am counting on you to respect your fellow employees and to commit to ensuring a working climate that is tolerant of our diversity.

John Henderson

John Henderson

---

employees. Focus groups were recruited on a volunteer basis and were facilitated by the consultants to assure confidentiality and candidness (see Exhibit 1.12). The topics covered in the focus groups are shown in Exhibit 1.13. The views expressed by each group are summarized in Exhibits 1.14–1.17. In addition to the focus groups, an employee attitude survey was also administered to all plant employees. The results of the survey are shown in Exhibit 1.18.

QUESTIONS

1. Evaluate Johnson Chemical's actions in dealing with the e-mail.

2. Examine the data contained in Exhibits 1.10 and 1.12–1.17. What seem to be the most significant diversity issues at Johnson Chemical?

3. What is the cost of these problems to the organization? What will happen if they are not addressed?

4. Where and how do these issues need to be dealt with?

5. What support, skills, and training do managers need to deal with these issues?

6. What human resource management systems or policies need to be examined and possibly modified?

As you know, we continue to be committed to having an equal opportunity work climate at Johnson Chemical. In an effort to achieve this goal, we invite you to participate in a focus group to help us collect data around issues of diversity. The focus groups will be organized so that we bring together different categories of employee groups over the next two months.

To assure confidentiality and anonymity, the actual discussion sessions will be facilitated by an outside consultant group we have contracted to assist us in our efforts. Discussion will focus on your experiences and thoughts on topics related to our human resource policies and systems, and equal opportunity work climate.

I hope you will be willing to participate in one of the focus groups. Thank you in advance for your help. If you have any questions, please call my office. I'll be happy to provide additional information.

Sincerely,

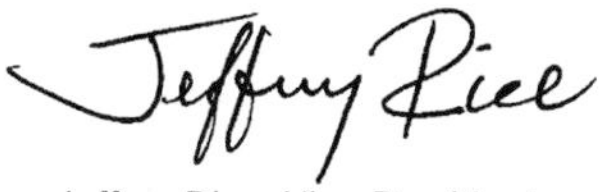

Jeffrey Rice

Jeffrey Rice, Vice President
Corporate Human Resources

EXHIBIT 1.13 *Focus Group Discussion Areas*

1. Comment on your experience and view of the following areas of the company:

   A. Recruitment and hiring: sources of recruits; selection criteria; orientation of new employees

   B. Promotion: fairness of rating system; adequacy of opportunity

   C. Training and career development: access to training; selection of trainees; adequacy of and availability of career development counseling

   D. Performance management: pros and cons of the performance appraisal process; supervisor feedback

   E. Benefits: adequacy; administration of benefits

   F. Affirmative action program: effectiveness of target of opportunity efforts; attitudes toward

   G. Treatment: personal experiences of bias or barriers because of one's race, ethnicity or gender, or other areas

Recruitment of African-Americans scientists and engineers is inadequate.

African-Americans have to be "more qualified" than other groups to get a job in the company.

African-American students from historically black schools participate in summer intern programs but are rarely hired as full-time employees.

African-Americans employees do not have access to the same training and development opportunities as white employees. Selection for training and development rests with supervisors. This allows supervisors with negative views of the potential of African-Americans to control who gets access to training.

The promotion system is driven by potential ratings given by supervisors, and African-Americans are disproportionately given low potential ratings for promotability.

White supervisors are not comfortable working with African-American employees, and many do not know how to give helpful performance feedback.

Most of the African-American employees are pigeonholed into staff positions in management.

African-Americans can't break into the "informal network," and are excluded from many social activities.

Because there were so few African-Americans in higher level positions, there are no mentors and role models.

African-Americans are stereotyped as being non-technical, lazy, and not suitable for management.

Racial slurs and jokes are often heard on the plant floor.

There is the "rule of three"—no three African-American employees should be seen together in the cafeteria or other places. If so, majority group employees assume something is going on or ask, "Why are the African-American employees all eating together?"

Women are not treated as individuals but subjected to sex role stereotypes. They are viewed as emotional, non-technical, and subordinate. Women who display different behaviors (assertive, good technical skills) are characterized as "pushy or macho."

A myth persists that many of the women in the company don't need to work.

Many male supervisors don't know how to work with women as peers and, therefore, treat female subordinates in condescending ways.

Women are often made to feel that their ideas are inconsequential. They are cut off in meetings, especially when a woman is the only female in a group meeting.

There are too few women in management and supervisory positions.

None of the top women in the company are in line positions.

There are no women in senior management.

Women receive lower potential ratings than men in the company.

Women are excluded from the "old boys" network.

Women are always being tested with offensive sexual jokes or comments.

Affirmative action stigmatizes women and makes them look like victims rather than leaders.

Company benefits do not have programs to help women balance work and family.

Asian employees are stereotyped as having excellent technical skills but not having suitable skills for management.

Asian employees are not promoted because supervisors tend to give them low ratings on communication skills.

Asian employees are stigmatized by affirmative action and shouldn't be lumped with other minority groups in the company.

There are a very small number of Asian managers in the company relative to their numbers in the company.

Most employees are ignorant of the diversity among Asian employees (e.g., Chinese, Korean, Japanese, etc.).

White men are stereotyped as racist and sexist.

The company's affirmative action plan has lowered opportunities for white employees.

White supervisors have to be careful when managing minority employees.

African-American employees are hostile toward white supervisors.

The company's focus on equal employment opportunity doesn't include white men.

Women employees are overly sensitive; plant environments are tough.

EXHIBIT 1.18 *Results of Employee Survey: Percentage of Employees with Favorable Responses*

Question	All Employees	African-Americans	Asian	Women
My department is effectively managed.	75	57	74	60
People in my department have the skills and abilities to be an effective team.	85	79	82	78
I feel proud to work at Johnson Chemical.	75	60	70	61
I am satisfied with my opportunity to get a better job.	79	39	65	44
I like the work I do.	85	75	84	74
My manager gives me feedback that helps improve my performance.	52	38	51	35
My department has a climate that respects employee diversity.	65	49	60	48
My manager is sensitive to the relationship between my work life and my personal life.	61	58	59	49
My supervisor applies company policies and rules regardless of race, gender, etc.	77	54	65	55

9 INCIDENT

Too Much Diversity?

Bill Baldwin, president and founder of Baldwin Scientific Instruments, had just finished meeting with Tran, a Baldwin assembler of Vietnamese descent. Tran was very upset about the treatment that he and his Vietnamese co-workers had been receiving from their first-line Latino supervisors, a brother and sister who were originally from Peru. Tran had reported that the two supervisors did not respect any of the 10 Vietnamese assemblers, that they were intentionally mean and rude to them, and that they spoke negatively about them in Spanish behind their back. He pointed out that the assemblers are the key to the firm's success, and asked the president to take immediate action to restore the respect they deserved.

Baldwin was aware that distrust and friction existed between the Latinos and Vietnamese. Fortunately, there had never been any fights or even loud arguments. However, he noticed that during lunch both groups sat apart and spoke in their native languages. At the annual company summer picnic and Christmas party, both groups also sat separately, and, while cordial, were never very friendly toward one another. Baldwin realized that part of the problem might be that the Latinos were often in supervisory positions whereas the Vietnamese were mostly assemblers. This structure reflected the fact that the Latino supervisors had far more experience and length of service than the new Vietnamese employees did. Bill also realized that another part of the problem might be that the head of the assembly department, a non-immigrant Californian who supervised the brother and sister, was not an effective leader because he refused to address employee relations problems. He knew a lot about assembling instruments, but allowed problems to fester among the diverse workforce rather than solve them.

As Baldwin was pondering what should be done, the sales manager walked into the office and gleefully announced that another large order had just come in. Baldwin knew this would necessitate the hiring of five more skilled assemblers, and that advertisements in the southern California area newspapers would result in mostly Latino and Vietnamese applicants. He wondered what the firm's hiring policy should be, given that he did not want to create more problems.

QUESTIONS

1. If you were Bill Baldwin, what actions would you take in response to Tran's request?

2. What hiring policy should the firm follow?

3. Does the firm have too diverse a workforce?

The Cultural Diversity Training Program

Dr. Jennifer Barnes is an Assistant Professor of Organization Behavior and Human Resource Management of a major state university in the Southeast. Her university is located in a large city which is 61 percent black. In recent years, the university has aggressively recruited black faculty and graduate students. Specifically, the university has funded new faculty positions and graduate fellowships for minorities.

Recently Dr. Barnes read about a new university-sponsored cultural diversity training program that was required for all academic administrators/supervisors and offered to faculty and staff. Since Dr. Barnes teaches two human resource management courses, she decided to enroll in the one-day seminar in anticipation of utilizing the material in her own courses. She expected the program would cover the full range of workforce diversity including age, race, gender, ethnicity, physical abilities, and sexual orientation. She also thought there might be some discussion of the impact of parental status, religious beliefs, and dual-career couples. Finally, she expected to experience a high level of involvement in the process through the use of case studies, sensitivity training, incidents, and role playing.

When Dr. Barnes attended the program, she was quite disappointed. There was a series of lectures by seven different speakers, including one external consultant on cultural diversity and several university administrators. While the seminar coordinator told the participants she wanted their input and involvement, the speakers were scheduled for one-hour blocks and used most or all of their allotted time with their formal presentations. Throughout the day only seven comments or questions were asked by participants. In addition, the only concept of diversity discussed by the presenters was racial diversity.

Other types of workforce diversity were mentioned in passing by one presenter but were otherwise ignored. The emphasis for most of the presentations was on the changing workforce demographics and the consequent necessity for the university to be more open, accommodative, and responsive to black students, employees, or potential employees. One of the speakers noted that while blacks constitute 60 percent of the city's population and 30 percent of the area's population, only 15 percent of the students and 4 percent of the faculty are black. Moreover, only three percent of the academic administrators at the university are black. The unspoken assumption was that the participants (most of whom were white) harbored racial animosity toward blacks. Therefore, they needed to modify their attitudes and behavior in order to better recruit, retain, and relate to black employees or students.

Dr. Barnes felt that both the content and process of the seminar left much to be desired. After the seminar, she discussed her experience with her department chair. The chair agreed to discuss it with the Dean of the School of Business. After doing so, he reported that it had been decided at the highest levels of the university that "in our environment, diversity means black." She interpreted that comment to mean that the political "powers that be" in the university were only interested in the racial aspect of diversity. Consequently, she did not expect to see future changes in the diversity training program.

1. What is cultural diversity?

2. Why is cultural diversity an important issue for all organizations? What are the potential disadvantages of ignoring it as an issue? What steps should a proactive organization take to respond to this challenge?

3. Evaluate the content and training method used by the university in this training program. Do you have any suggestions for improvement? How might such changes be implemented?

The Legal and Regulatory Environment

11 CASE
Investigating a Sexual Harassment Case

I. OBJECTIVE

The purpose of this exercise is to help you understand the procedures for investigating an allegation of sexual harassment in the workplace.

II. OUT-OF-CLASS PREPARATION TIME: Read the material on sexual harassment in your textbook as well as the background below before class.

III. IN-CLASS TIME SUGGESTED: 20–30 minutes

IV. PROCEDURES

D. This exercise should be done in groups of four to five students.

E. Each group should read the scenario and the sexual harassment policy.

F. Each group must develop a sexual harassment investigation plan that details how they will go about determining if wrongdoing has occurred. After completion of the group discussion, each group will present its investigation plan to the rest of the class.

SCENARIO

James Tilden is the Human Resource Manager at SenGlas, Inc., which manufactures specialized glass for industrial use. The company has 300 employees and a management staff of seven including Tilden's position. SenGlas has been in business for over 50 years and has a well-established human resource department.

On Friday morning, the company's shipping coordinator, Mary Booth, came into Tilden's office quite agitated and said she was fed up. She wanted to file a formal complaint against one of her co-workers, Bob Simonsky, a fork-lift driver, for his harassing behavior toward her. Simonsky had been working with SenGlas for twenty years. Booth joined the company five years ago and had held administrative positions before getting promoted to her present position in the warehouse. Both of them worked on the second shift in the plant. She told Tilden that Simonsky was continuing to treat her in a very nasty manner because he didn't want to work with a woman. Booth said she had tried for a long time to ignore his actions toward her. However, she said his behavior toward her was getting out of hand and that she no longer looked forward to coming to work and was suffering from headaches every day. She claimed Simonsky's behavior created a hostile work environment for her and she could no longer bear it.

In her written complaint, Booth specifically alleged the following:

■ That Simonsky had made false accusations about her behavior toward another employee, Ginny Miller. Simonsky had told Miller that Booth was threatening to hurt her physically;

■ That Simonsky on more than one occasion had revved his fork-lift engine and drove straight toward her while laughing when she tried to give him orders about a delivery;

■ That he had slammed the metal forks of his fork-lift on the ground in an intimidating manner;

- That he continuously refused to take any directions from her about which shipping trucks to load or unload;

- That twice he had thrown a cigarette butt at her;

- That he would regularly tear up instructional notes she left for him;

- That Simonsky had told another worker, Henry Mueller, that "Booth had f----- with the wrong person and that when he got through with her not even Jesus Christ himself would be able to save her."

- That two other fork lift drivers, John Griffin and Henry Jackson, had overheard Simonsky say that women did not belong in the warehouse area and that he preferred working with men.

- That when she first started in the position as shipping coordinator that Simonsky had told her, "I hate that maggot. I should have killed her when I had the chance," referring to Sally Jenkins who held the shipping coordinator position before her.

Although Tilden had only joined the company six months ago, he had heard about Simonsky's bad temperament from many people in the company. On one occasion Simonsky had even been rude to him. Tilden asked Booth if she had reported the incidents to her supervisor. She indicated she had and her supervisor had told her he would speak to Simonsky. Tilden decided he had better review SenGlas' sexual harassment policy (see Exhibit 1.19) before investigating Booth's allegations.

EXHIBIT 1.19 *Excerpt from SenGlas's Sexual Harassment Policy*

SenGlas prohibits sexual harassment of its employees and applicants for employment by any employee or non-employee. Such conduct may result in disciplinary action up to and including discharge. This policy covers all SenGlas employees regardless of position held. The Company will not tolerate, condone, or allow sexual harassment, whether engaged in by fellow employees, supervisors, associates, clients, or other non-employees who conduct business with the Company. All SenGlas employees are entitled to work in an environment free from sexual harassment and a hostile or offensive working environment. We recognize sexual harassment as unlawful discrimination, similarly to conduct that belittles or demeans any individual on the basis of race, religion, national origin, sexual preference, age, disability, or other similar characteristics or circumstances.

According to federal law, sexual harassment is any behavior that includes unwelcome sexual advances, requests for sexual favors, making sexual or romantic advances toward an employee, and persisting despite the employee's rejection of the advances or other verbal or physical conduct of a sexual nature when:

- submission to, or rejection of, such conduct is used as the basis for promotions or other employment decisions;

- the conduct unreasonably interferes with an individual's job performance or creates an intimidating, hostile, or offensive work environment.

No manager or supervisor shall threaten or imply that an employee's refusal to submit to sexual advances will adversely affect that person's employment, compensation, advancement, assigned duties, or any other term or condition of employment or career development. Sexual joking, lewd pictures, and any conduct that tends to make employees of one gender "sex objects" are prohibited.

If an employee believes that he/she has been subject to sexual harassment or any unwanted sexual attention, he/she should:

- make their unease and/or disapproval directly and immediately known to the harasser;

- make a written record of the date, time, and nature of the incident(s) and the names of any witnesses; and

- report such complaints to their supervisor immediately. If the supervisor is the cause of the offending conduct, the employee may report this matter directly to the Human Resource Manager. All complaints will be promptly and thoroughly investigated. Such investigations will be completed within two weeks of the complaint. Confidentiality of reports and investigations of sexual harassment will be maintained to the greatest extent possible. Any manager, supervisor, or employee who, after appropriate investigation, is found to have engaged in sexual harassment of another employee will be subject to disciplinary action, up to and including termination of employment. The disciplinary process outlined in the SenGlas Disciplinary Policy (HR Handbook, page 15) will be applied.

If any party directly involved in a sexual harassment investigation is dissatisfied with the outcome or resolution, that individual has the right to appeal the decision. The dissatisfied party should submit his or her written comments to the Vice President of Operations at SenGlas who will review the matter.

SenGlas will not in any way retaliate against any individual who makes a report of sexual harassment nor permit any employee to do so. Retaliation is a serious violation of this sexual harassment policy as well as federal laws. All such violations should be reported immediately. Any person found to have retaliated against another individual for reporting sexual harassment will be subject to appropriate disciplinary action, up to and including termination.

Note: Sexual Harassment Complaint Forms are available on the Intranet.

Analyzing Promotion Data: Applying the 80% Rule

Thomas L. Rutherford, human resource director of Food Chain Supermarkets, Inc., was jolted by the conversation he just had with Walter Jackson, an employee in the company's distribution warehouse. Jackson had complained that black employees were being passed over for promotions in favor of white employees who had less experience and seniority. Jackson had gone on to explain that he had resigned his position in the meat department of the warehouse because, despite his experience and job performance, he felt he would not get promoted. He explained that he had been passed over for promotion three times since he started work with Food Chain Supermarkets.

After Jackson left his office, Rutherford immediately began to investigate his claims. He called in Mark Walters, his personnel assistant, and explained to him the conversation he'd just had with Jackson. "The last thing I want on my hands is a discrimination suit," Rutherford told Mark. "I want you to get some data on promotions that have occurred in the last couple of years in our warehouse operations. Also, while you're at it, get the same information for our stores. Also, here are the names of three black employees given to me by Jackson. Pull their files and try to get any facts on what happened with their promotion requests."

Mark replied, "I don't think it will be too difficult to pull together the information, Tom, now that we have finally gotten our personnel records centralized. But I'll probably have to talk with some of the department managers and supervisors also." Rutherford suggested that he also interview the three black employees. As Mark left his office, Rutherford began to think about the company's human resource practices and Jackson's allegations.

BACKGROUND

Food Chain Supermarkets, Inc. is a regional chain of supermarkets located in the Midwest. Additionally, the company operates a central warehouse, bakery, and its own transportation system. Its main office, distribution center (warehouse), and a dozen stores are located in Reed County. Presently, the company employs over 1,600 people in the county. According to recent census data, Reed County's labor force is about 22 percent black. The company has plans to refurbish its stores and to open four additional stores over the next two years. Rutherford was hired in anticipation of this growth to help better manage the company's personnel needs.

The distribution center has five departments: grocery, meat, frozen food, produce, and transportation. Each department has two shifts. The starting times of various employees on the same shifts are staggered. Both receiving and shipping functions are carried out at the warehouse. Order puller, order selector, order picker, and picker are synonymous terms for the same position. A warehouse crew leader is a working supervisor who not only assigns duties but also performs the same duties as subordinates. Management positions in the stores consist of assistant produce manager, produce manager, grocery manager trainee, relief grocery manager, deli manager, relief assistant manager, assistant manager, head cashier, and assistant head cashier.

Background information on some of the key people in this situation include:

Clifford Gemson: Clifford Gemson was hired as a produce clerk in June 2007. He had originally applied for a management position. He had three years of grocery store management experience including six months in produce management with another company. Gemson worked in two stores between June 2007 and April 2008. On several occasions,

Gemson asked his district manager (J. Perkins) and his store manager (C. Fagen) about promotion to vacant produce manager positions. The first vacancy was filled on October 8, 2007, by Bob Watkins, a white employee. Watkins, a produce clerk, had eighteen months of experience with us. Watkins, who had no management experience, was replaced by another white employee, Sheila Wilson, on November 8, 2007. Wilson was selected on the basis of her Food Chain Supermarket experience as a produce clerk and an assistant produce manager for six months. Gemson was not considered for either vacancy.

Roy Thompson: Roy Thompson was hired by Food Chain Supermarket at our warehouse on September 18, 2004 as a maintenance (sanitation) employee. His duties included forklift driving, sorting damaged food, and rebuilding pallets. His prior work experience included supervisory duties and self-employment. Thompson trained a white employee of Food Chain (Neal Marcy, hired May 12, 2007) who was promoted to crew leader of the maintenance (sanitation) department on June 16, 2007. Before Marcy was hired, Thompson asked his supervisor (E. Jones) for the crew leader job to which Marcy was promoted. Jones told Thompson that he would never be a crew leader as long as he was supervisor. Jones denies saying this. According to Thompson, his supervisors had repeatedly told him that he had both excellent attendance and performance. On August 15, 2008, a junior white employee, Earl Hanes (with less company experience than Thompson), was promoted to a sanitation crew leader for the same shift and in the same department that Thompson worked. According to Jones, Hanes was better qualified because of his previous work experience.

Leslie LeBlanc: Leslie LeBlanc was hired by Food Chain Supermarket on July 8, 2005 as a frozen food picker. Her next position was frozen food loader. LeBlanc was trained to act as a "fill-in" crew leader, and in fact did fill in as a crew leader until Ricky Anderson, a white employee, was hired. LeBlanc trained Anderson in the duties of a "fill-in" crew leader who then assumed LeBlanc's place as "fill-in" crew leader. Anderson was offered a full-time crew leader's position, which he refused. LeBlanc was never offered this job. LeBlanc had previously informed Food Chain Supermarket management of her prior experience as a shift leader at a textile mill.

Walter Jackson: Walter Jackson was employed by Food Chain Supermarket on April 14, 2004 at the warehouse in the meat department. (Milk, dairy products, and meat are in the same department.) Jackson's job duties prior to April 2008 included milk picking, unloading, and forklift driving. In the spring of 2008, a crew leader told Jackson that he was up for promotion to crew leader in the department. Terry Gibson, a white employee, received the job on June 7, 2008. Gibson was initially hired on January 11, 2004, resigned February 5, 2004, and was rehired November 3, 2004. Jackson had more company and departmental experience than Gibson. However, he was never considered for the position. Gibson's prior duties were solely picking meat and Jackson had supervised Gibson when Jackson served as "fill-in" crew leader prior to Gibson's promotion. The supervisor asserted that Gibson had broader departmental experience than Jackson. Since that time, two other employees in the meat department with less seniority and experience have been promoted over Jackson.

HUMAN RESOURCE PRACTICES

When Rutherford was hired four months ago, the president had explained that because of the physical dispersion of the stores, human resource policies were decentralized with a great deal of responsibility placed on the district managers. Promotion recommendations and decisions were made by supervisors of the different departments in the warehouse. In order to be promoted to a warehouse crew leader, an employee had to be on the same shift and in the same department as the opening. The factors utilized in promotion decisions at the warehouse were character, integrity, good sound morals, correct attitude, and initiative. The company felt that the supervisor was in the best position to judge whether or not an employee was promotable. There was no system for employees to apply for promotions. Written performance evaluations were limited to office employees, merchandisers, and store managers. At the retail stores, store supervisors made promotion recommendations to the district manager. Promotions were limited to persons recommended by the store managers. The district managers agreed with the store managers 90 to 95 percent of the time. The district manager decided who would be promoted, transferred, demoted, hired, or terminated for all positions up to the department head. Job vacancies were not routinely posted. Employees could be transferred from store to store as needed.

Rutherford recalled a conversation he recently had with one of the district managers, Joe Perkins: "We really don't need to post jobs since each district manager is usually aware of openings in his or her district and which employees are ready for promotion. Further, an employee doesn't have to ask in order to be considered for a promotion. Although we don't have a written evaluation system, the job performance of an employee is conveyed by word of mouth from one level of supervision to another."

TWO WEEKS LATER

Rutherford received the reports and data prepared by Mark on promotions within the warehouse and stores for the past two years (see Exhibit 1.20). Mark also prepared summaries of what had happened to Jackson and the other three black employees mentioned by Jackson. As Rutherford began reading through the report, he wondered what changes would be needed at Food Chain Supermarket in order to create equal opportunities for all employees. He never wanted to have another conversation like the one he had with Jackson two weeks earlier.

QUESTIONS

1. Analyze the table in Exhibit 1.20. What conclusions do you reach? Is there evidence of discrimination in promotion decisions?

2. Do you believe that Gemson, Thompson, LeBlanc, and Jackson were discriminated against?

3. What are some of the potential disadvantages of a "word of mouth" promotion system?

4. What should Rutherford do now?

5. What kinds of policies can the company design to better integrate minorities into management positions?

EXHIBIT 1.20 *Report on Promotion Rates*

TO: T. L. Rutherford, Director of Human Resources
FROM: Mark Walters, Human Resource Assistant
RE: Promotions

I have collected the data you requested on promotion rates at our warehouse and stores for the last two years (see table). I have also summarized what I learned about the Jackson situation and the other three promotion cases he mentioned.

| | | **Promotion Rates** | | | | | |
| | | **Total Employees** | | | **Total Promotions** | | **Promotion Rates** | |
Unit	**Year**	**White**	**Black**	**White**	**Black**	**White Rate**	**Black Rate**
Warehouse/Stores	2008	1,603	284	171	21	10.66%	7.39%
Warehouse/Stores	2007	1,414	291	122	27	8.62	9.27
Warehouse	2008	411	173	42	13	10.21	7.50
Warehouse	2007	223	192	18	21	8.07	10.90
Stores	2008	1,192	111	129	8	10.80	7.20
Stores	2007	1,191	99	104	6	8.73	6.10

Note: In 2008, blacks represented 5.8 percent of 137 store promotions and 9 percent of the work force.
In 2007, 94.6 percent of the managers were white and in 2006, 94.7 percent were white.

13 CASE

Blowing the Whistle: Accounting Practices at Glenfair Electronics

Bob Schein, vice president of human resources at Glenfair Electronics, sat at his desk thinking about the meeting he had just had with Anwar Patel, an accountant. He had listened intently to Patel describe what had transpired in the finance department during the last few weeks. Patel joined Glenfair after completing his degree in accounting five years ago. For the past three years, he had been preparing Glenfair's sales revenue reports. As a listed company, Glenfair was required by the Securities and Exchange Commission to issue public sales and profit forecasts. Glenfair Electronics had over 10,000 employees and a reputation for producing high-quality electronic components used in a number of manufacturing applications. The company had begun to experience a slowdown in product demand, and their share price had declined as well in the last year and a half.

Patel had told Schein that he had been instructed to use a different and more aggressive accounting method for forecasting and calculating projected sales revenue for the coming year. He believed that such an approach could mislead shareholders about Glenfair's likely future sales performance. The previous chief financial officer (CFO) had taken a rather conservative approach and did not stretch the boundaries of acceptable practices. Since the beginning of the year, however, Patel was working under a new CFO, John Beatty. Beatty had joined Glenfair earlier in the year after not obtaining a promotion to CFO at his previous company. Everyone perceived him to be smart and ambitious and it was clear that he was determined to make his mark at Glenfair. When Patel pointed out that the proposed accounting methods were very different from Glenfair's traditional practices for reporting sales revenue, he told Schein that Beatty had said, "Well, I am the new CFO, and I have a different view and approach." However, it was his next remark that disturbed Patel the most. According to Patel, Beatty went on to say, "Sales should turn around next quarter, and we are justified in reporting higher expected sales revenue in the coming months. Besides, Anwar, don't you want your Glenfair stock to do well?" Projected higher sales revenue could indeed burnish Glenfair's earnings outlook and probably help its stock price.

When Patel persisted in questioning the accounting methods, Beatty allegedly told him to do his job as instructed. Since that conversation, Patel felt that Beatty had become hostile toward him, and they no longer had a friendly relationship. Despite his fears, Patel felt he had to come to Schein for advice. Schein could see that Patel was worried about Beatty finding out about their meeting.

Schein was disturbed by what he had heard from Patel and sat at his desk thinking about what he should do as vice president of human resources.

QUESTIONS

1. If you were Schein, what would you do, if anything? Explain.

2. What should Schein do about Patel's claim that Beatty has become hostile toward him?

3. What rights and protections do whistle-blowers have in the workplace today?

14 CASE

▰▰▰▰▰ *LGA Industries: Employing Undocumented Immigrants*

David Martin was excited to start his new position as the manager of staffing, training, and development for LGA Industries, a carpet and rug manufacturer located in a mid-sized Texas town. LGA Industries had been producing well-known and high-quality carpets and rugs for the past 100 years. Over the years, its workforce had grown to just under 2,000 employees. Martin had just completed a master's degree in Human Resource Management from the University of Texas at El Paso. In the last few years, LGA Industries had found it increasingly difficult to locate and hire employees to meet the growing demand for its products. Their traditional sources of labor were drying up as many high school graduates left the small town to seek employment in places like Dallas and Houston. The pay for unskilled jobs was $8.50 per hour. Martin learned that 45 percent of hires in the last four years consisted of immigrants from Mexico and other Latin American countries. The Latino population of the town, which had been less than 5 percent in 1990, was now about 25 percent.

Martin's predecessor, who retired last month, had been with LGA Industries for 15 years. Martin was anxious to introduce some of the new and up-to-date HR practices he had been taught at the university. Within his first two months on the job, he was to fill five new plant positions. The company had received a large order that needed to be completed within the next six months. Given the increasing difficulty that LGA had finding employees for new positions, the company had begun using an employment agency. When Martin contacted the agency, they assured him they would have no problem sending him prospective applicants. When five candidates showed up at his office about a week later, Martin was quite impressed with how quickly the agency had responded. When he interviewed the candidates, he found it odd that they were not able to tell him much about their previous employment experience. Three of the candidates appeared to know only a few words of English. Martin decided to talk with the HR manager at LGA Industries about the candidates. He was surprised when the manager told him not too worry—the agency was quite reliable and had sent them good candidates in the past.

Martin was curious and decided to look at the files and records of previous hires. He was not able to locate the I-9 Forms for any of the newly hired Latino employees, nor could he find them on the HR database. Martin knew from his academic training and previous work experience that employers were required to complete an I-9 Form for all employees to verify eligibility for employment in the United States. When he asked the HR manager about the missing forms, Martin was told that the employment agency took care of them whenever they sourced candidates, and the forms were probably on file in their offices. About a week after the new employees were on board, Martin received an anonymous note in his inbox that read, "LGA Industries hires illegal immigrants." He showed the note to the HR manager who told him that he should not believe everything he reads and that LGA had little choice but to get labor wherever it could.

Martin was quite upset when he went home that evening. He suspected his new employer was hiring undocumented immigrant workers. The next morning he called the employment agency and asked for a copy of the I-9 Forms of the five employees they had just hired at LGA Industries. He was told that the forms were not ready and were usually kept at the agency.

Martin knew the Immigration Reform and Control Act (see Exhibit 1.21) required that if an employee does not have the proper documentation within three business days of his/her start date, the employer must terminate the employee. The next day his manager bluntly told him there was no need for him to worry or follow up with these new employees.

QUESTIONS

1. What factors appear to be affecting LGA Industries' staffing practices?

2. Who is responsible for meeting the requirements of the Immigration and Reform and Control Act with respect to the completion of I-9 forms?

3. If you were Martin, what would you do now?

Form I-9

The Immigration Reform and Control Act of 1986 (IRCA) made the knowing employment of unauthorized aliens illegal. Under IRCA, employers may hire only persons who may legally work in the U.S., i.e., citizens and nationals of the U.S. and aliens authorized to work in the U.S.

With the enactment of IRCA, the legal obligations of employers, hiring new employees have been greatly increased. Employers are required to verify the identity and eligibility for employment of all persons they hire after November 6, 1986. It is also unlawful for employers to knowingly hire a person who is not authorized to work in the U.S., or continue to employ such a person. Thus, IRCA requires employers to complete a Form I-9 for each new employee.

Employers may be held liable for an employee's failure to complete Section 1. The employee has three business days from the date of her or his hiring to provide the employer with the documentation of identity and work authorization needed to complete Section 2 of the I-9 Form ("three business days" requires an employer to count weekends and holidays as business days if the employer is open for business on those days). The employee must present original documents (not photocopies) that establish identity and employment eligibility. If an employee does not have the proper documentation within three business days of his or her start date, the employer must terminate the employee. However, if, within that time, the employee produces a receipt showing that he or she has applied for a work authorization or identification document, the employee must be given 90 days to produce the required documentation. The employer must complete Section 2 of the I-9 Form within three business days of the date an employee is hired. Employees must not be required to produce specific documents. The employer must accept the documents enumerated in the Form I-9 "Lists of Acceptable Documents" in any of the combinations indicated on the form.

On the other hand, demanding excessive documentation can also result in substantial fines. IRCA's anti-discrimination provisions prohibit employers of four or more employees from discriminating against certain protected individuals (including permanent residents, temporary residents, special agricultural workers, refugees, and asylees) with respect to hiring, discharging, recruiting, or referring for a fee.

I-9s must be retained for the duration of an employee's employment, plus one year, or for a minimum of three years from the date of hire, whichever is longer. Employers must keep a record of employees whose work authorizations will expire and re-verify the authorization to work of such employees prior to expiration.

Employer Obligations for Document Retention

Employers must retain the I-9 Form for every employee for the full duration of that individual's employment, with the exception of the individuals previously classified as exempt from the I-9 requirement. Additionally, every employer must keep each employee's I-9 form on file for either three years after the date of hire or for one year after employment is terminated, whichever is greater. Employers should accurately organize and maintain all I-9 records. The Department of Homeland Security and/or the Department of Labor may ask to review I-9 documentation. I-9 documents must be provided to these federal agencies upon request.

Offenses

Failure to properly complete an I-9.

Knowingly hiring, continuing to employ, or contacting to obtain the services of an unauthorized alien.

Providing or knowingly accepting false social security cards.

Pattern and practice of I-9 compliance failure.

Monetary Sanctions

Paperwork violations may result in fines from $100 and $1,100 for every individual for which a mistake is made.

Substantive violations may result in fines from $200 to $11,000 per unauthorized employee depending on whether it is the first offense or a repeat offense.

In 1996, Executive Order 12989 was passed, which imposes a one-year ban on federal contractors who knowingly hire unauthorized non-immigrant workers.

Criminal penalties including fines and imprisonment may also be imposed if there appears to be a deliberate pattern or practice of violations of these requirements or where a company knowingly hires ten or more non-immigrant workers who are illegally in the USA.

Source: Lurie, D. (March 2005). "The I-9 Form: Everything HR Professionals Need to Know About the I-9 Employment Verification Process." Society for Human Resource Management White Paper (www.shrm.org).
www.dol.gov/compliance accessed February 6, 2010.

The Broken Employment Contract?

Arthur Wayne was shocked as he walked out of Sara Bell's office. It was hard for him to understand what had just transpired. Bell, treasurer of EcoCare, a large health insurance company located in Michigan, had just told Wayne of the decision to terminate his employment and had requested his immediate resignation in return for a severance pay arrangement whereby he would continue to receive his salary for six months or until he found other employment. As he looked at the date on his watch calendar, May 7, Wayne realized that he had been hired exactly five years ago by Bell. Bell had told Wayne that EcoCare was not satisfied with his administration of the company car program and that, given the number of complaints about the program from other employees, it was in the best interest of the company to ask for his immediate resignation. Wayne, assistant to the treasurer, had been in charge of the program for the past year. During a meeting the day before with both Bell and the vice president of operations, George Findlay, he had been unable to explain why there were so many complaints about the program. One such complaint had involved the claim that someone had set back the odometers on several company cars while the vehicles were under Wayne's control.

After his termination, Wayne requested that the decision to ask for his resignation be reviewed by the company president and the chairperson of the board of trustees of EcoCare. Wayne felt that he had been wrongfully discharged and had been under the impression that he had a contract for continued employment as long as his performance was satisfactory. He further maintained that his supervisor had not properly followed the termination policies and procedures of EcoCare.

In preparation for the review, the president asked the director of human resources, Chris Miller, to investigate the facts of the situation and the events leading up to Wayne's termination.

HUMAN RESOURCE DEPARTMENT'S INVESTIGATION

In order to prepare its report for the president, the human resource department decided not only to review Wayne's personnel file but also to interview Wayne, Bell, and others involved in the case. Two weeks later, Miller prepared the following summary of what had been learned.

> After seven years with a local bank in Michigan, Arthur Wayne sought the assistance of an employment agency to obtain a job that would give him more opportunities for advancement. Wayne had graduated with a degree in Business Administration and had completed 15 hours toward his MBA in Finance. The employment agency referred him to our company. After several pre-employment interviews and a psychological test, Wayne was hired as an assistant to the company treasurer, Sara Bell. His duties primarily consisted of analyzing and preparing certain financial reports under the direction of Bell. Wayne came to us with excellent work experience and admirable references from his previous employers.

According to Wayne, he felt at the time of his employment that he had a contract with EcoCare that was partly oral (Bell's statements during the job interview) and partly written. Wayne told us that during his pre-employment interview with Bell, he had specifically asked about job security and was told that as long as he did his job, he could remain with the company until he reached retirement age. He further indicated that he had been told by Bell that if he came to EcoCare, he would not have to look for another job because she knew of no one ever being discharged. Wayne also told us that a copy of the Supervisory Manual was handed to him during his interview with Bell. He said he specifically recalled reading through the sections of the manual that pertained to discipline and termination procedures at that time (see the Appendix for relevant sections).

At the end of that interview Bell made Wayne a job offer, which he accepted. The Manual is given to all management employees as an aid in supervising persons in their charge and not as a declarative of the contract terms of an employee's hire. Our personnel policy has always been to discharge for just cause only, pursuant to the procedures described in the manual. These procedures apply to all EcoCare employees who have completed their probationary period.

During his five years as assistant to the treasurer, Wayne received above average performance ratings. Last year, he was given the responsibility of administering the company car program. In April of this year, employees began complaining to Bell and Findlay about Wayne's handling of the program. Wayne indicated that he'd had only a brief conversation with Bell about these complaints before the meeting of May 6.

We also spoke with Bell and Findlay about Wayne's employment and subsequent termination. According to Bell, she did tell Wayne during the interview that he would have a job as long as his performance was satisfactory. Bell told us that she made that statement based on her understanding of our company's policies and did not intend her statement as a promise of a permanent job.

Bell and Findlay report that Wayne was fired because of continued personality conflicts with other employees. They report that he was unable to work with other employees and that this was an important job requirement for anyone managing the company car program. After receiving numerous complaints about Wayne's handling of the program, they finally requested from him various reports and documents concerning the odometer discrepancies. Ultimately, they called a meeting with Wayne in an attempt to resolve the problems. During the May 6 meeting, Wayne was reported to have been defensive and insubordinate and unable to provide any satisfactory answers to their questions. At the conclusion of the meeting, they both felt that it would be in the best interest of the company if Wayne were asked to resign. Bell called Wayne into her office the next day and asked for his resignation.

APPENDIX

EXCERPTS FROM SUPERVISORY MANUAL

Section IV. Disciplinary Procedures
(Note: If the unacceptable behavior is repeated between six months and one year, the last disciplinary action will be applied. If the behavior is repeated after one year, it will be treated as a new occurrence for disciplinary purposes.)

A. All discipline shall be administered in a fair, consistent, and reasonable manner within EcoCare.

B. Whenever the work performance or personal behavior of an employee is below department standards, a series of progressive, corrective steps will be taken. Before any of these steps are undertaken, however, the employee shall be counseled about his or her performance discrepancy, what he or she must do to improve the performance, and the action the supervisor will take if the performance is not corrected.

C. Within our discipline system, discipline will be given only for cause. Furthermore, the disciplinary action should fit the problem it is intended to correct.

D. All disciplinary action should be duly documented and reported by the supervisor on Form 29B. The form also requires the employee's signature.

E. The following series of steps shall be followed in administering discipline within EcoCare:

1. Oral Warning: Supervisor should discuss the unacceptable behavior with the employee and document such by completing Section A of Form 29B and obtaining the employee's signature.

2. Written Warning: A written warning should be issued if the unacceptable behavior continues. The supervisor completes Section B of Form 29B and gives the employee the blue copy. The human resource department receives the canary copy.

3. Suspension: If the employee's behavior continues uncorrected, the employee shall be suspended for a given time without pay. Normally, suspension should not exceed five working days. Supervisors should consult with their immediate supervisor and the human resource department before implementing this action. The supervisor shall complete Section C of Form 29B and also include the date the employee should return to work.

4. Discharge: If the employee's behavior is not corrected, the employee shall be terminated. Due to the serious nature of termination, it is recommended that the supervisor review the case with both his or her immediate supervisor and the human resource department before discharging the employee. Examples of reasons for termination without prior corrective discipline are covered in Section V. Note, however, that in such cases the employee should first be suspended according to the following procedures:

Suspension Pending Discharge: (This paragraph applies to all proposed discharges except those which are a result of application of the normal disciplinary procedures.)

a. When an employee's misconduct warrants immediate discharge under Section V, the employee should be first suspended without pay.

b. At the time of suspension, the employee should be informed by the supervisor to leave the premises and that he or she will be notified if and when he or she is to return to work.

c. The supervisor should document the suspension by completing an Employee Discipline Report. The supervisor should consult with the Human Resource Department to determine the appropriate course of action.

Section V. Termination
(Reasons for Immediate Termination.)

1. Misconduct, such as fighting, gambling, or use of profane or abusive language toward others.

2. Furnishing proprietary company information to unauthorized agents or persons.

3. Refusal to obey direct orders from the immediate supervisor (insubordination).

4. Willful damage of company property.

5. Failure to notify supervisor or manager during three successive working days of absence.

6. Engaging in a business likely to conflict with the business of the company without prior permission.

7. Dishonesty, falsification of employee's own or other employee's time cards, company records, employment application, etc.

8. Illegal use or possession of alcohol, drugs, etc.

9. Reporting to work or engaging in company business under the influence of alcohol or drugs.

QUESTIONS

1. Did Wayne have an employment contract, either oral or written, with EcoCare? Why or why not?

2. What problems, if any, do you see with EcoCare's pre-employment process?

3. Can an employer's written human resource policies ever be construed as a contract between an employer and an employee?

4. Was Wayne terminated for just cause? Why or why not?

5. How can companies protect themselves against a claim of wrongful discharge?

16 EXERCISE

The Older Worker Questionnaire

I. OBJECTIVES

A. To familiarize you with typical stereotypes toward older workers and the managerial implications of these stereotypes.

B. To provide you with factual information regarding older workers.

II. OUT-OF-CLASS PREPARATION TIME: 10 minutes to complete the Older Worker Questionnaire

III. IN-CLASS TIME SUGGESTED: 20–30 minutes for group and class discussion of all items on the Older Worker Questionnaire

IV. PROCEDURES

Prior to the class meeting in which this exercise will be discussed, you should read any material on older workers assigned by your instructor and complete the Older Worker Questionnaire (see Exhibit 1.22).

At the start of the exercise, the class will be divided into groups of three to five by your instructor. Your group's task is to discuss each item on the questionnaire and arrive at a consensus regarding the correct answer (20-minute time limit). After all groups have finished, the instructor will present the correct answers along with an explanation. Each group should record these answers alongside the group's own answers and then compare the two to determine the number right and wrong.

EXHIBIT 1.22 *The Older Worker Questionnaire*

Mark the statements "T" for true or "F" for false.

——— 1. Younger workers tend to have higher job satisfaction than older ones.

——— 2. Employees aged 50–65 use on average about an equal amount of healthcare as those in their 30s and 40s.

——— 3. Employers value older workers' loyalty, work ethic, reliability, and experience.

——— 4. About 20 percent of the work force is over 55.

——— 5. Few individuals (less than 10 percent) plan to work after age 65.

——— 6. An important reason older workers retire is that they do not feel valued by the company.

——— 7. The typical unemployment rate for those over 55 has been about 6 percent since 1949.

——— 8. The average retired worker receives over $2,000 a month in Social Security benefits.

——— 9. Older workers generally require less light for performing a task than do younger workers.

———10. All workers are required to collect full Social Security benefits at age 65.

———11. Younger workers are more motivated to exceed expectations than older workers.

———12. Employers view older workers as more productive, at least as attractive in terms of employment, but as more costly than younger workers.

———13. Older employees usually take a longer period of time to learn something new than do younger workers.

———14. The Age Discrimination in Employment Act only applies to workers who are 59 or older.

———15. Younger workers miss more work due to injuries and illness than do older workers.

———16. Ninety percent of Americans over the age of 50 say they learn best by watching and listening.

———17. Older workers who were born between 1946 and 1964 are referred to as "baby boomers."

———18. Older employees tend to react more slowly than younger employees.

———19. Loyalty to a firm among workers over the age of 45 is strong.

———20. One's ability to taste and smell tends to improve with age.

17 EXERCISE

Is This Unlawful Discrimination?

I. OBJECTIVES

A. To help you understand the application of the six major federal laws that regulate equal rights in employment. These laws are Title VII of the Civil Rights Acts of 1964 as amended by the Equal Employment Opportunity Act of 1972, the Civil Rights Act of 1991, the Lilly Ledbetter Fair Pay Act of 2009, the Age Discrimination in Employment Act of 1967, the Vocational Rehabilitation Act of 1973, and the Americans with Disabilities Act of 1990.

B. To help you understand the court's interpretation of these laws.

C. To help you understand the legal definition of discrimination and the burden of proof placed on defendants and plaintiffs.

II. OUT-OF-CLASS PREPARATION TIME: 60 minutes

III. IN-CLASS TIME SUGGESTED: 45 minutes

IV. PROCEDURES

A. Read the exercise and review the major laws before class.

B. The class should be divided into groups of four.

C. Each group should read each of the incidents that follow and answer these questions:

1. What legal statute(s) apply in this case?

2. What issue(s) must the court decide in this case?

3. If you were the judge, how would you rule? Did the employer discriminate unlawfully? Why or why not?

1. Elaine Mobley worked as a social worker with the Virginia Health Department's child abuse program for two years. Mobley was a member of the nonsectarian Unitarian Universalist Church. During her first six months on the job, she divorced her husband of ten years. Her supervisor, a devout Baptist, encouraged her to discuss her marital problems with a Christian psychotherapist. On a number of occasions, the supervisor encouraged other employees in the department who were also Baptists to convert Mobley. Some employees held prayer meetings at her desk while others gave her the silent treatment. Their attempts to convert Mobley did not stop. At one point, the supervisor made her participate in a Christian puppet show. Another time she found a handwritten note on her desk from Jesus that read, "How can you speak of God and reject me? I love you and know all about you." Her attendance at work declined because there were days she did not want to face the stress in her work environment. Mobley filed a complaint with the director of the division stating that she was being constantly bombarded with efforts to convert her to a Baptist. Shortly thereafter, Mobley was fired from her job. Mobley filed a lawsuit claiming that she had been fired because of religious discrimination.

2. Edward Roberts, a black truck driver, applied in person for a tractor trailer truck driver position at a trucking company on March 31, 2005, in response to a newspaper ad. Roberts' application listed 22 months of prior experience as a road driver. He had an

additional 10 years of experience which he did not list on the application due to a lack of space on the form. Roberts was neither interviewed nor contacted by the company about the status of his application. In June 2005, Roberts saw an identical advertisement for tractor trailer truck drivers. Upon inquiry, Roberts learned that eight persons (all white) had been hired as truck drivers between April and June 2005. All of those hired had less than 22 months of driving experience. The company contended that Roberts was not hired because no opening existed when he applied. Roberts filed a discrimination complaint in District Court.

3. Thelma Jones had worked at a large public accounting firm for five years when the partners proposed her as a candidate for partnership. Of the 662 partners in the firm, seven were women. Of the 88 persons proposed that year, Jones was the only woman. Forty-seven were admitted to partnership, 21 were rejected, and 20, including Jones, were held for "reconsideration." Thirteen of the 32 partners who submitted comments on Jones's performance supported her candidacy, three recommended holding her application, eight stated that they had insufficient knowledge to comment, and eight recommended denial. While the partners praised her outstanding performance, both supporters and opponents of her candidacy indicated that she was sometimes overly aggressive, unduly harsh, difficult to work with, and impatient with staff. One partner described her as "macho." In a meeting with a senior partner about her candidacy, she was told that, to improve her chances for partnership, she should "walk more femininely, talk more femininely, dress more femininely, wear make-up, style her hair, and wear jewelry." When the partners refused to reconsider her candidacy the following year, she sued the firm, charging sex discrimination.

4. James McFadden was a transsexual who, while still biologically male, announced to his employer (East Coast Airlines) that he intended to dress and act as a woman in preparation for "surgical sex reassignment." Mr. McFadden was subsequently fired from his pilot's job for refusing to comply with its requirement that he continue to dress and act as a man. McFadden filed a lawsuit in District Court alleging that East Coast Airlines had conspired to discriminate against him on the basis of sex (now to be female) and that he was treated differently from other women employed by the airline.

5. Andrew Johnson, a black maintenance worker, was constantly referred to as "Chicken Little," "Chicken George," "Sparerib Kid," "Boy," and "Watermelon Man" by his white supervisor. These names were used not just during private conversations but in the presence of other workers. Despite several complaints to senior management, the name-calling persisted for several months. When management finally investigated Johnson's claims, the supervisor admitted the comments but argued that he was only kidding. The supervisor was instructed to stop both the name-calling and kidding. A fellow employee warned Johnson that his days were probably numbered because he had gone over the head of his supervisor. Shortly thereafter, Johnson was injured on the job. While he was at home recuperating, his supervisor called to say that he accepted his resignation. Johnson denied resigning and wrote asking for his job back. His request was denied. Johnson filed a lawsuit alleging that he had been a victim of harassment because of his race.

6. Paul Martin had worked 12 years for the Department of Transportation when he applied for a promotion to dispatcher. Martin scored 75 on an interview test. Betty Palmer, another candidate, scored 73 and got the job. Martin sued the county for reverse discrimination. The county said that both Martin and Palmer were qualified and that Palmer had gotten the

job as part of a voluntary affirmative action plan designed to achieve a work force that reflected the race and gender composition of the county. The county pointed out that none of 238 skilled craft worker jobs in the county were held by women.

7. Elnora Williams, a black female teacher with ten years of classroom experience and partial completion of her doctoral degree in education, applied for several vacant middle and secondary principalships in the Knox County school system. Each time she applied, she was told by the superintendent that "the school district believed that a 'male image' is necessary for a middle or secondary school principal." No females had occupied a principal position in the school district. Williams subsequently filed a lawsuit in District Court accusing the school system of discrimination.

8. Frank Poole had been teaching hearing-impaired students in the Jackson County schools for six years when he was hospitalized with *pneumocystis carinii* pneumonia and, subsequently, was diagnosed as having AIDS. Despite the county medical director's report that Poole's condition did not place his students or others in the school at any risk, the Department of Education reassigned Poole to an administrative position and barred him from teaching in the classroom. Poole filed suit, alleging that the Department discriminated against him on the basis of his disability (AIDS).

9. Lauren Hill worked in the plant of Hillbrook Manufacturing Company from 1979 until 1998. During much of this time, salaried employees were given raises or denied raises based on their supervisor's evaluation of their performance. In March 1998, six months before she was to take early retirement, Hill submitted a questionnaire to the EEOC alleging certain acts of sex discrimination, and in July she filed a formal EEOC charge. After taking early retirement in November 1998, Hill commenced a pay discrimination claim under Title VII of the Civil Rights Act and the Equal Pay Act. She alleged that at the time of retirement she was being paid significantly less than any of her male colleagues. Hill also said she had evidence that during the course of her employment with Hillbrook that several supervisors had given her poor evaluations because of her sex and that as a result of these evaluations her pay was not increased as much as it would have been if she had been evaluated fairly. Further, these pay decisions continued to affect her pay throughout her employment with Hillbrook. Therefore, she wanted to be compensated accordingly for the discrimination she had experienced during her employment with Hillbrook.

10. After working as a title clerk for Harrison and Sons Car Dealership for five years, Donna Skeen resigned. At 62 years of age, Donna had decided that she did not want to put up with the treatment she had received at the dealership. She had demanded an end to the teasing she experienced, but to no avail. In a suit she filed in District Court, Skeen alleged that the managers in the dealership referred to her as the "old lady with the sagging boobs." When she forgot something or made an error on a title, she was asked if she had Alzheimer's. If she complained about the temperature in the dealership, she was asked if she was suffering from hot flashes. The owner, Frank Harrison, said that there was lots of informal teasing in the dealership among employees and that Skeen often referred to herself as the "Grandma" of the staff.

11. Officials of a city government charged with discrimination signed a consent decree agreeing to an affirmative action plan with specific promotion and hiring goals for increasing the number of minority firefighters in the city's fire department. Four years later, when faced with severe budget problems, the city implemented a layoff plan aimed at protecting

minority employees who were recently hired. Jerome Atwood, a white firefighter, was laid off even though he had greater seniority than many of the minority firefighters who retained their jobs. Atwood filed a lawsuit charging reverse discrimination.

12. Herbert Fox worked as an office furniture salesman for 25 years with the same company. In his 25th year with the company, he went on leave for clinical depression. When it was time for him to return from leave, he told the company he could not return to work as scheduled. Subsequently, Fox and the company agreed upon a new date for return. However, Fox also requested that he be allowed to miss the first couple of morning sales meetings (a request prompted by the side effects of his antidepressant medicine) or to work on a part-time basis. His request was denied by the company, and they also told Fox that, because of increasing financial pressures, the company would be expecting 110 percent from him on his return to work. Fox did not report to work on the agreed-upon date and filed for disability benefits. The company subsequently terminated him. Fox filed a discrimination suit against the company alleging that the requirements attached to his return to work caused a relapse of his depression.

13. Lia Lee, a Laotian-American, worked for Federal and State Bank for over three years as teller. She had always received outstanding performance reviews from her supervisors. Consequently, when a position became available at the customer service desk that handled customer inquiries and problems, Lia applied for the position. She did not get the promotion. The bank argued that she was not promoted because she did not have sufficient English skills to calm irate customers. Lia Lee filed a lawsuit alleging that Federal and State Bank had overlooked her for a promotion because of her accent.

14. Margaret Reynolds, 5 feet 10 inches, 190 pounds, applied for a job as a fitness instructor teaching aerobics at Slendercise, Inc. She had always been very healthy and fit. She ate healthy foods, worked out five days a week, and could do all of the complicated aerobics steps and exercises. Slendercise, Inc. rejected Margaret's application to teach aerobics because of her size. Reynolds did not look anything like the svelte women on the company's Web site and promotional brochures. The company further argued that an aerobics instructor had to look leaner than the public and that people must believe Slendercise, Inc., will help them improve, not just maintain, their shape. Margaret filed a complaint with the Equal Employment Opportunity Commission alleging weight discrimination.

15. Abdul Mohammed, a Pakistani-American, was employed as a steelworker. As a devout Muslim, Mohammed was obligated to engage in daily prayer. Mohammed, along with five other Muslims working at the plant, asked management to provide a room where they could hold their daily prayers during lunch hour. The plant was located miles from the nearest mosque. Management told the employees that it did not have a room that could be used for such purposes. Consequently, Mohammed and his fellow Muslims were forced to recite their prayers in full view of other employees. Other employees ridiculed the Muslims during their daily prayers and called them derogatory names such as "camel jockey" and "raghead." After being humiliated on several occasions by taunts from other employees, Mohammed and his fellow Muslims once again asked management to provide them with a private space in which to pray. Management again denied their request. Shortly thereafter, Mohammed filed a case with the Equal Employment Opportunity Commission alleging religious harassment and ethnic discrimination.

18 EXERCISE

What Is Sexual Harassment?

I. OBJECTIVES

A. To familiarize you with the EEOC sexual harassment guidelines.

B. To teach you the meaning of these guidelines as they relate to the workplace.

C. To teach you the manager's and organization's role in preventing sexual harassment.

D. To show you the complexities involved in identifying sexual harassment in the workplace and in interpreting EEOC guidelines.

II. OUT-OF-CLASS PREPARATION TIME: 20 minutes to read the EEOC guidelines and complete the sexual harassment questionnaire

III. IN-CLASS TIME SUGGESTED: 45 minutes for group and class discussion of all items on the sexual harassment questionnaire

IV. PROCEDURES

Prior to the class meeting in which this exercise will be discussed, you should read the EEOC Guidelines on Discrimination Because of Sex (see Exhibit 1.23) and any other material related to sexual harassment assigned by your instructor. You also need to complete the 20-item sexual harassment questionnaire shown (Exhibit 1.24).

At the start of the exercise, the instructor will divide the class into groups of three to five students. Your group's task is to discuss each item on the questionnaire and arrive at a consensus regarding whether each item constitutes sexual harassment. More importantly, you need to develop a rationale for your answer (20-minute time limit). After all groups have finished, the class as a whole will discuss the questionnaire items. To facilitate discussion, groups will take turns presenting their analysis. For example, one group will present its analysis regarding Item 1, another group will present Item 2, another Item 3, and so on.

EXHIBIT 1.23 *Code of Federal Regulations [Revised as of July 1, 2006]*

GUIDELINES ON DISCRIMINATION BECAUSE OF SEX
Sec. 1604.11 Sexual harassment.

Harassment on the basis of sex is a violation of section 703 of title VII. Unwelcome sexual advances, requests for sexual favors, and other verbal or physical conduct of a sexual nature constitute sexual harassment when (1) submission to such conduct is made either explicitly or implicitly a term or condition of an individual's employment, (2) submission to or rejection of such conduct by an individual is used as the basis for employment decisions affecting such individual, or (3) such conduct has the purpose or effect of unreasonably interfering with an individual's work performance or creating an intimidating, hostile, or offensive working environment. The principles involved here continue to apply to race, color, religion, or national origin.

In determining whether alleged conduct constitutes sexual harassment, the Commission will look at the record as a whole and at the totality of the circumstances, such as the nature of the sexual advances and the context in which the alleged incidents occurred. The determination of the legality of a particular action will be made from the facts, on a case by case basis.

With respect to conduct between fellow employees, an employer is responsible for acts of sexual harassment in the workplace where the employer (or its agents or supervisory employees) knows or should have known of the conduct, unless it can show that it took immediate and appropriate corrective action.

Source: Equal Employment Opportunity Commission, 2010 Web site.

EXHIBIT 1.24 *Sexual Harassment Questionnaire*

Instructions: Read each situation and circle your answer.

Situation		Would it be Sexual Harassment?		
1.	Mr. (Ms.) X (Supervisor) posts cartoons on the bulletin board containing sexually related materials.	Yes	No	Uncertain
2.	Mr. (Ms.) X (Supervisor) constantly tells sexually-related jokes to female (male) subordinates.	Yes	No	Uncertain
3.	Mr. (Ms.) X (Supervisor) asks a female (male) subordinate for a date, which she (he) willingly accepts.	Yes	No	Uncertain
4.	Mr. (Ms.) X (Supervisor) pats or pinches a female (male) subordinate.	Yes	No	Uncertain
5.	Mr. (Ms.) X (Supervisor) terminates a female (male) subordinate for not complying with his (her) request for sexual favors. He (she) has recently given the subordinate a positive performance appraisal.	Yes	No	Uncertain
6.	Mr. (Ms.) X (Supervisor) sexually assaults a female (male) subordinate.	Yes	No	Uncertain
7.	Mr. (Ms.) X (Supervisor) denies a raise to a female (male) subordinate for failing to go out on a date.	Yes	No	Uncertain
8.	Mr. X (Supervisor) habitually calls all female employees "sweetie" or "honey."	Yes	No	Uncertain
9.	Mr. (Ms.) X (Supervisor) asks a female (male) employee how she (he) feels about sex education in schools.	Yes	No	Uncertain
10.	Mr. X (Supervisor) recommends that a female subordinate wear revealing attire at work.	Yes	No	Uncertain
11.	Mr. (Ms.) X (Supervisor) fails to promote a female (male) subordinate for not granting sexual favors.	Yes	No	Uncertain
12.	Mr. (Ms.) X (Supervisor) invites a female (male) subordinate to accompany him (her) on a two-day meeting in another city.	Yes	No	Uncertain
13.	Mr. X (Supervisor) leans and peers over the back of a female employee when she wears a low-cut dress.	Yes	No	Uncertain
14.	Mr. (Ms.) X (Supervisor) tells a female (male) job applicant that she (he) will not be hired unless she (he) agrees to grant sexual favors.	Yes	No	Uncertain
15.	Mr. (Ms.) X (Supervisor) invites a female (male) subordinate to meet him (her) at a bar that features female (male) exotic dancers.	Yes	No	Uncertain
16.	Mr. (Ms.) X (Supervisor) invites a female (male) subordinate to come over to his (her) apartment for a hot tub party.	Yes	No	Uncertain
17.	Male (female) workers whistle every time female (male) employees walk by their work area.	Yes	No	Uncertain
18.	A married female employee and a married male employee are having an affair.	Yes	No	Uncertain
19.	Male (female) employees repeatedly use vulgar language when talking to each other. Two female (male) employees often overhear what is said and find it offensive.	Yes	No	Uncertain
20.	A male (female) repair technician who works for another firm asks female (male) employees for dates whenever he (she) comes to repair equipment.	Yes	No	Uncertain

I. **OBJECTIVES**

A. To help you understand the application of the Americans with Disabilities Act (ADA).

B. To help you understand the court's interpretation of the ADA.

C. To help you understand the meaning of the terms "disability," "qualified individual," and "reasonable accommodation."

II. **OUT-OF-CLASS PREPARATION TIME:** 45 minutes

III. **IN-CLASS TIME SUGGESTED:** 45 minutes

IV. **PROCEDURES**

A. Read the exercise and review the Americans with Disabilities Act's definitions of "disability," "qualified individual," and "reasonable accommodation."

B. The class should be divided into groups of four.

C. Each group should read each of the case incidents that follow and answer these questions:

1. What issue(s) must the court decide in this case?

2. If you were a member of the jury, how would you vote? Did the employer discriminate unlawfully? Why or why not?

1. THE OVERWEIGHT HOSPITAL ATTENDANT

Betty Thomas applied for a position as an attendant for the mentally retarded in a residential facility operated by the Mental Health Retardation Hospital (MHRH). She had previously worked for MHRH in an identical position. She had an excellent work record and left employment with MHRH on good terms. When Thomas reapplied for the position she previously held, she stood 5 feet 2 inches tall and weighed 320 pounds. During her pre-employment physical, it was determined that although Thomas was morbidly obese, no limitations were found that affected her ability to do the job. MHRH refused to hire Thomas because of her obesity, claiming that her weight compromised her ability to evacuate patients in the event of an emergency and put Thomas at greater risk of developing serious ailments that might lead to higher absenteeism, as well as increasing MHRH's exposure to workers' compensation claims.

2. IS ATTENDANCE AT THE WORKPLACE AN ESSENTIAL JOB FUNCTION?

In 1996 Diane worked in the Edmond, Oklahoma Post Office and witnessed the murder of several of her co-workers. She was diagnosed by her doctor with post-traumatic stress disorder and subsequently left her job at the Post Office because working there aggravated her symptoms. In March 2009, while working as a service coordinator at Avaya Communications, Diane became aware of an altercation between two employees where one of the individuals, by the name of Lunsford, had previously threatened to "go postal." Lunsford was suspended from his job. Upon hearing of his return to work, Diane became physically ill and left work. Her current doctors confirmed that she suffered from post-traumatic stress disorder and was unable to work in an environment that she perceived to be unsafe. She eventually was placed on short-term disability leave. After being on short-term disability for two months, Diane requested that her employer either 1) relocate Lunsford, 2) allow her to work out of her home, or 3) allow her to transfer to another position in the Oklahoma City area.

After further investigation by the employer, Diane's requested accommodations were denied. One year later, her request for long-term disability benefits were also denied, and Diane was subsequently discharged because she was unable to return to work. The company maintained that Diane's job required her to be physically present and that her attendance at the job site was an essential function of her job. While her job description did not specifically state that attendance at the work site was an essential function, the company claimed that her presence was required for the appropriate supervision, training, and teamwork required of all coordinators, and that her requested accommodations were not reasonable.

3. THE ULTIMATUM

Joan, a warehouse worker, was diagnosed with carpal tunnel syndrome. She was subsequently assigned to reduced duties. However, the duties were later multiplied, increasing her arm and wrist pain. When Joan presented her employer with a doctor's note advising her to take a six-week leave of absence, the employer gave her an ultimatum—show up for work or lose her job. Joan decided to sue under the ADA, claiming her carpal tunnel syndrome was a disability worthy of accommodation.

4. THE FAINTING TECHNICIAN

Jane Flighty was fired after she fainted on the job because the company believed she was suffering from an unknown disability. After the fainting episode, she was sent to a physician. The physician's initial diagnosis was that Jane suffered from syncope, a loss of consciousness caused by a temporary deficiency of blood supply to the brain. Later, the physician determined that the employee was within normal limits and that there was no explanation for the fainting. The company discharged Jane without any further medical examination, concluding that she was a safety risk because she was likely to faint again.

5. THE GUN SLINGER

John Hitman was fired when he was caught carrying a gun into work. He was hospitalized following the incident and was diagnosed with a mental disorder. His attorney informed the company of his mental status and asked that they delay any decision about his employment status. The company fired John for his clear violation of company rules.

Contributed by Gerald E. Calvasina, Southern Utah University

Group Debate Project

I. OBJECTIVES

A. To help you understand both sides of controversial human resource management issues.

B. To allow you to apply human resource management concepts in understanding the policy implications of the issues.

II. OUT-OF-CLASS PREPARATION TIME: Equivalent to time required for students to complete a major term paper assignment.

III. IN-CLASS TIME SUGGESTED: 45 minutes

IV. PROCEDURES

A. Each debate will consist of two teams: an affirmative team that upholds the proposition and a negative team that opposes it. Debates can be scheduled throughout the semester to coincide with course content. For example, the comparable worth debate should be held after compensation is covered in the course. Alternatively, all debates could be held at the end of the term.

B. Students should be divided into groups of three or four depending on the number of debate topics to be covered during the semester. The number of debaters on each side should be equal and the time allowed for each side should be the same.

C. Each group should be assigned to either the affirmative or negative side of a topic.

D. Each team conducts research on its topic. Because of the current nature of the debate topics, you are encouraged to consult current periodicals (e.g., *Business Index, Business Periodicals Index,* and so on) in addition to academic journals and books. You may want to review the list of journals in the Skill Builders in Part 1.

E. Each team prepares a written paper (8–10 pages) analyzing both sides of the topic in addition to presenting its arguments. The paper should be divided into three major parts: Introduction, Discussion, and Conclusion. (See additional instructions that follow.)

F. The debate is held in class; the two sides present their arguments with the affirmative side opening and closing the debate.

G. A chairperson presides over the debate and keeps time.

H. The debating teams' presentations are evaluated by the rest of the class and by the instructor (see Form 1.4).

ADDITIONAL INSTRUCTIONS FOR DEBATE TEAMS

Structure of Classroom Debates

First Affirmative	6 minutes
First Negative	6 minutes
Second Affirmative	6 minutes
Second Negative	6 minutes
Rebuttals: Negative	5 minutes
Rebuttals: Affirmative	5 minutes
Audience Cross-Examination	10 minutes

TIPS ON ORAL PRESENTATION

1. All of the speeches in the debate, except the first affirmative speech, should be given extemporaneously by the debaters. They should not be read. Essentially, the debaters' comments must reflect what was presented in the previous speech.

2. The first affirmative speech should be used to build the affirmative case. The affirmative debaters should give an overview of the major arguments they will use to uphold the proposition.

3. The first negative speech must be presented with the content of the first affirmative speech in mind. The aim of the negative speech is to cast doubt on the affirmative's arguments. The second speeches on both sides attempt to elaborate and build arguments as needed.

4. The rebuttal should directly address the arguments made by the other side.

5. Two excellent sources on debating are: Ericson, J. M. 1987. *The Debater's Guide.* Carbondale, IL: Southern Illinois University and Freeley, A. J. & Steinberg, D. L. 2005. *Argumentation and Debate: Critical Thinking for Reasoned Decision Making.* Belmont, CA: Wadsworth.

SUGGESTED DEBATE PROPOSITIONS (YOUR INSTRUCTOR MAY ASSIGN OTHER TOPICS)

1. Resolved: That the Employee Free Choice Bill be passed by Congress to eliminate secret-ballot union representation elections in the workplace in favor of a card check process.

2. Resolved: That employment-at-will or termination-at-will should remain the basic doctrine governing employee dismissal and should not be subject to legislative control.

3. Resolved: That federal legislation should be passed to prohibit discrimination against homosexuals in the workplace.

4. Resolved: That employee diversity enhances organizational performance.

5. Resolved: That telecommuting enhances employee productivity and morale while reducing turnover.

6. Resolved: That employers should develop and enforce policies prohibiting dating between co-workers.

7. Resolved: That U.S. immigration laws should be changed to allow more immigration by technical specialists from emerging/developing countries.

8. Resolved: That the use of contingent workers is an effective and efficient means of staffing.

9. Resolved: Regulation of stock options and bonuses for high-level executives should be minimized in order to attract and retain high-level executives.

SUGGESTED PAPER FORMAT

Your written paper will follow a form known as a "full brief"—a comprehensive analysis of both sides of a given proposition, outlined logically, from which the debater can develop his or her case. Each team should have a minimum of 10 references (in most cases you will have many more). The paper will consist of three parts: Introduction, Discussion, and Conclusion.

Introduction:

  a. Statement of the proposition and your group's position.

  b. Why is the issue important?

  c. Origin and history of the issue—keep it brief.

  d. Outline the conflicting arguments—why is there a controversy?

Discussion: (This is the major section of your analysis.)

  a. Present arguments to support your position.

  b. Back up your arguments with sound reasoning and evidence.

Conclusion:

  a. Summarize the main points of the discussion—recapitulate your major points.

  b. End with an affirmation or denial of the proposition (depending on whether you have the affirmative or negative position).

Debate:

Use the following scale to write in a rating on each item below for each team.

1	2	3	4
POOR	FAIR	GOOD	SUPERIOR

	Affirmative Team	**Negative Team**
I. Analysis (Was the analysis reasonable, complete, and clear?)		
II. Reasoning and evidence (Were the arguments structured soundly based on research facts and examples? Were arguments logical?)		
III. Organization (Was each speech clearly and cogently organized so that you could follow the structure of the debate?)		
IV. Rebuttal (Were unsupported points and assertions challenged by the opposing team?)		
V. Delivery (Was each speech effectively presented? Consider voice inflection, eye contact, and tone.)		
VI. Questions (Did the team adequately answer audience questions?)		
VII. Overall team rating		

In my opinion, the most effective debating was done by the _____ team.

(Affirmative or Negative)

Comments for Affirmative Team:

Comments for Negative Team:

21 INCIDENT

Giving Up Seniority to Accommodate a Disabled Colleague

Jim Martin had been loading and unloading cargo for East Coast Airlines for five years. His job performance ratings had always been above average. One day, Martin injured his back on the job. Because of his injury, he could no longer perform his job as a cargo handler.

The human resource manager, Angela Fisher, suggested that he apply for a transfer to another job appropriate to his skills and qualifications that did not involve physical strain. Transfer requests were governed by East Coast Airlines' seniority policy. Everything being equal, employees with greater seniority were given preference for transfers. Martin requested a transfer to a vacant mailroom position. At the same time, Bryan Beckwith, an employee with greater seniority than Jim, also applied for the vacant position. A position in the mailroom was viewed by many employees as an attractive alternative to some of the other blue-collar positions such as cargo and baggage handling.

After reviewing the transfer requests of the two employees, Angela Fisher awarded the position to Beckwith who had greater seniority at East Coast Airlines than Martin. Her decision was based on East Coast Airlines' seniority policy. In desperation, Martin went to Beckwith and asked him to please withdraw his transfer bid, explaining that he had requested the transfer because of an injury. Martin was hoping that his colleague would understand his plight. Beckwith refused to withdraw his request. Martin went to Fisher and requested an exception to the seniority policy that would allow him, rather than Beckwith, to work in the mailroom. Martin argued that since he was disabled because of his work as a cargo handler, he should be given preference over Beckwith. Fisher said that company policy did not allow her to make any exceptions. Martin lost his job at East Coast Airlines because there were no other vacancies for which he qualified.

QUESTIONS

1. If you were Beckwith, would you have dropped your transfer request to help Martin?

2. Should Fisher have given Martin preference over Beckwith because of his disability? Does seniority override the "reasonable accommodation" as specified in the Americans with Disabilities Act?

"Beautyism" in the Workplace

Harold Hughes is a Professor of Management and Chair of the Department of Management in a College of Business Administration at a major university in the Southeast. Professor Hughes is 52 years old and has been divorced for the past eight years. During that time, he has dated several women for varying periods of time, but is not currently dating or in a relationship.

Recently, Professor Hughes' long-time administrative assistant (Helen Schully) retired from the University at age 60 after 25 years of service. He then put together a committee of three departmental members to assist him in selecting a new administrative assistant. These three committee members were Professors Don Hall and Mike Meyers as well as Pauline Nelson, the department's financial officer. The position was advertised internally within the university as well as externally in the local newspaper.

The committee met, developed a list of selection criteria with appropriate weights, reviewed thirteen applications, and selected four female applicants for interviews. These four were Melissa (a 47-year-old administrative assistant in a local insurance company), Sally (a 38-year-old secretary at the university), Carol (a 52-year-old administrative assistant at the university), and Diane (a 27-year-old secretary at a local bank). Melissa and Carol have BS degrees while Sally is studying for her BA degree at the university. Diane is a high school graduate with no college credits. A college degree (in hand or in process) and/or previous experience as an administrative assistant were two of the selection criteria the committee chose prior to the interviews.

Originally, the committee had selected only Melissa, Sally, and Carol for final interviews. However, Diane had personally brought her application by the office, met briefly with Harold to express her interest in the position, and had received his assurance she would be among those interviewed. He then informed the other committee members that he had added Diane to the group to be interviewed. During the interview process, the other three committee members noticed that Howard seemed quite "taken" with Diane even though (on paper) she seemed to have the least impressive credentials for the position. She was extremely attractive and recently divorced with a four-year-old son. The three other committee members all agreed that Carol seemed to have the education and all the skills, knowledge, and abilities the committee had previously identified (including knowledge of the university bureaucracy).

Despite their consensus, Harold said the person would be working for him, and that he "felt more comfortable with Diane." After the decision was made and Diane was offered and accepted the position, Professor Hall remarked to Professor Meyers "Harold must have been thinking with his ___!" Professor Meyers agreed but added that Diane was "hot" and would definitely "enhance the scenery around here." Pauline Nelson was upset because she felt Harold was sexist since he made the selection decision "based purely on physical attraction."

QUESTIONS

1. What is "beautyism"?

2. To what degree was "beautyism" a factor in this decision? How do you know?

3. Why and to what degree do more attractive male and female job applicants have an advantage in the interview process?

4. What can managers do to eliminate the "beautyism" bias during job interviews?

5. If "beautyism" is frequently used as an informal selection criterion for new employees, what strategies do you suggest to address this issue?

Sexual Orientation Incidents: Bootstrapping Discrimination

1. James Smith, an openly gay man, was employed as a postal worker in Farmingdale, New York for approximately 12 years. He repeatedly received satisfactory to excellent performance evaluations. Smith's sexual orientation was known to his co-workers, who repeatedly assaulted him with sexually derogatory comments and names. He was exposed to frequent threats, obscenities, and nasty letters that referred to his homosexuality. Notes were placed on the wall in the employees' bathroom with Smith's name and the name of celebrities who had died of AIDS. Pornographic photographs were taped to his work area, male dolls were placed in his vehicle, and copies of *Playgirl* magazine were sent to his home. After suffering a heart attack, Mr. Smith resigned from his position. He filed a lawsuit against the post office charging sex discrimination. Mr. Smith argued in his petition that the abuse he endured because of his sexual orientation was so severe that he ultimately suffered a heart attack.

2. John Ortega was employed for five years by Mexicana, Inc., which operates a chain of restaurants in Washington and Oregon. Ortega first worked as a host and then became a food server in one of the Washington restaurants. Throughout his employment with Mexicana, Ortega was subjected to a relentless campaign of insults, name calling, and vulgarities. Ortega had complained to his general manager and assistant manager of the restaurant where he worked, but the abuse did not cease. Male co-workers and one of his supervisors referred to Ortega as a "she" or "her" constantly. He was mocked for walking like a woman, holding a tray like a woman, and having effeminate gestures. Ortega was called sexually derogatory names, such as "faggot" and "female whore."

   Pranks were played on him as well. One such incident ended in a fight between Ortega and a co-worker. Ortega and the co-worker were then called into a meeting with Mexicana's human resources director. The director told Ortega to report any further harassment to the area manager, who would address the issue. The human resources director also promised to do spot checks herself over a two-week period to ensure that the harassment stopped. Mexicana had a clearly stated policy against harassment which stated: "An employee who believes that he or she has been harassed by a co-worker, supervisor, or anyone acting on behalf of the company should immediately report the facts of the incident to the Mexicana EEO officer at the corporate office or to the area manager responsible for the restaurant." The human resources director made one check and Ortega told her that conditions were improving. However, about two weeks later Ortega got into a heated argument with his assistant manager and walked off the job. He was subsequently fired for leaving work in the middle of a shift. A month later, Ortega filed a complaint with the EEOC. Thereafter, he initiated a lawsuit charging he was harassed because of his sex.

3. Delilah Deacon filed a lawsuit against her employer, Hairlocks Preferred in New York City, accusing them of unlawful discrimination because of her sex, sex stereotyping, and/ or sexual orientation. Delilah, a lesbian, was employed as a hair assistant at Hairlocks Preferred, a prestigious, high-end hair salon known for its innovative haircutting techniques. Delilah had wanted to move into one of the high-paying haircutting positions

after working as an assistant for several months. Hairlocks Preferred had a rigorous training program that had to be completed before anyone could advance to cutting clients' hair. Only about 10–15 percent of the total number of assistants at the salon completed the difficult and challenging training program. It took successful candidates at least two or three years to complete the training. In addition to its reputation for innovative haircuts, Hairlocks Preferred was known for hiring employees who embodied many different lifestyles and sexual orientations, including a female-to-male transsexual, an openly bisexual man, and both male and female gay employees. It was not uncommon for employees to engage in sexually charged banter in the workplace.

Deacon enrolled in the training program, but according to Hairlocks Preferred, her performance was erratic both in the training program and in her duties as a hair assistant. One of the senior stylists indicated that Deacon was frequently unavailable when needed to assist and that she had been rude to clients or rough with their hair. Other stylists complained she was hostile and disrespectful. Her performance in the basic cutting class was rated inadequate to advance to the next level. Deacon argued that her behavior was a result of the harassment she suffered because of her sexual orientation and gender. While she indicated she had not been at all reticent about her lesbianism while working at the salon, Deacon alleged that on several occasions the owner had told her that females rarely became hair stylists because clients preferred men. Deacon also charged that a range of derogatory comments were hurled at her while she worked at Hairlocks. She was often referred to as "Donald" instead of Delilah, called a "dyke," and was once told by a co-worker that she needed to have sex with a man. In her lawsuit, Deacon alleged the owner of Hairlocks, who was a pre-surgery male-to-female transsexual, informed her that she was being fired because of the way she looked and wore her hair. Hairlocks Preferred countered that she had been fired because of her poor performance.

QUESTIONS

1. What issue(s) must the court decide in each case? What laws, if any, have been violated?

2. If you were the judge, how would you rule? Why?

3. Sexual orientation in the workplace is an increasingly important HR issue. How should companies manage this issue?

24 SKILL BUILDER

Data Analysis for Affirmative Action Plans

I. OBJECTIVES

A. To enhance your understanding of how to prepare a utilization/availability analysis for Affirmative Action Plans.

B. To teach you the data analysis requirements under affirmative action guidelines.

II. TIME REQUIRED TO COMPLETE: Two to three hours

III. INSTRUCTIONS

You work for a manufacturing firm located in Charlotte, North Carolina, and your company has just been awarded its first federal contract of $250,000. This contract is to supply, over a two-year period, one of your major products to the Department of Defense. You have been asked by your boss, the plant manager, to perform the utilization/availability analyses required under Executive Order 11246 as input in developing an Affirmative Action Plan (AAP) for the Office of Federal Contract Compliance Programs (OFCCP).

You have reviewed the guidelines from the OFCCP on the requirements (see Exhibit 1.25). You have also pulled together labor market data in addition to compiling a detailed breakdown of the company's workforce by job category, sex, and race (see Exhibits 1.26, 1.27, 1.28, and 1.29).

REQUIRED

Using the relevant data, complete Form 1.5. You may need to generate additional forms for your use. It is easier to set this up in spreadsheet form. This is the first step toward developing an Affirmative Action Plan. Be sure to list any assumptions you make about the relevant labor market for each job category. Also be sure to indicate the job categories in which women and minorities are underutilized. Make any other recommendations you deem necessary to the plant manager.

EXHIBIT 1.25 *Summary of OFCCP/AAP Guidelines*

Definition

An affirmative action program is a management tool designed to ensure equal employment opportunity. A central premise underlying affirmative action is that over time and absent discrimination, a contractor's work-force will generally reflect the gender, racial, and ethnic profile of the labor pools from which the contractor recruits and selects. Affirmative action programs contain a diagnostic component, which includes a number of quantitative analyses designed to evaluate the composition of the workforce of the contractor and compare it to the composition of the relevant labor pools. Affirmative action programs also include action-oriented programs. If women and minorities are not being employed at a rate to be expected given their availability in the relevant labor pool, the contractor's affirmative action program includes specific practical steps designed to address this underutilization. Effective affirmative action programs also include internal auditing and reporting systems as a means of measuring the contractor's progress toward achieving the workforce that would be expected in the absence of discrimination.

Utilization Analysis

An AAP must contain a utilization analysis—a comparison of the percentages of women and minorities in each job category within the company (organizational profile or a workforce analysis) with the percentages available in the relevant labor market (availability analysis). An organizational profile is a depiction of the staffing pattern within an establishment. It is one method contractors can use to determine whether barriers to equal employment opportunity exist in their organizations. The profile provides an overview of the workforce at the establishment that may assist in identifying organizational units where women or minorities are underrepresented or concentrated.

The contractor must use either the organizational display or the workforce analysis as its organizational profile: An organizational display is a detailed graphical or tabular chart, text, spreadsheet, or similar presentation of the contractor's organizational structure. The organizational display must identify each organizational unit in the establishment, and show the relationship of each organizational unit to the other organizational units in the establishment. An organizational unit is any component that is part of the contractor's corporate structure. In a more traditional organization, an organizational unit might be a department, division, section, branch, group, or similar component. In a less traditional organization, an organizational unit might be a project team, job family, or similar component. The term includes an umbrella unit (such as a department) that contains a number of subordinate units, and it separately includes each of the subordinate units (such as sections or branches). For each organizational unit, the organizational display must indicate the following:

i. The name of the unit;

ii. The job title, gender, race, and ethnicity of the unit supervisor (if the unit has a supervisor);

iii. The total number of male and female incumbents; and

iv. The total number of male and female incumbents in each of the following groups: Black, Hispanic, Asians/Pacific Islander, and American Indians/Alaskan Native.

Alternatively, a company may use a workforce analysis approach. A workforce analysis is a listing of each job title as appears in applicable collective bargaining agreements or payroll records ranked from the lowest paid to the highest paid within each department or other similar organizational unit including departmental or unit supervision. For each job category, the total number of male and female incumbents in each of these groups (Black, Hispanic, Asian/Pacific Islander, and American Indians/Alaskan Native) is indicated (see Exhibit 1.29). An analysis of all major job groups and the extent to which minorities or women are underutilized is also requested. Underutilization is having fewer minorities or women in a particular job category than would reasonably be expected, according to their availability in the relevant labor market. Two factors must be considered in determining availability:

1. The percentage of minorities or women with requisite skills in the reasonable recruitment area, defined as the geographical area from which the contractor usually seeks or reasonably could seek workers to fill the positions in question; and

2. The percentage of minorities or women among those promotable, transferable, and trainable within the contractor's organization.

Based on Revised 41 C.F.R. Chapter 60, Office of Federal Contract Compliance Programs, Department of Labor. The new guidelines became effective in 2000.

EXHIBIT 1.26 *Workforce Analysis*

Job Categories	Overall Totals (Sums of Columns B thru K)	Number of Male Employees					Number of Female Employees				
		White (Not of Hispanic Origin)	Black (Not of Hispanic Origin)	Hispanic	Asian or Pacific Islander	American Indian or Alaskan Native	White (Not of Hispanic Origin)	Black (Not of Hispanic Origin)	Hispanic	Asian or Pacific Islander	American Indian or Alaskan Native
	A	B	C	D	E	F	G	H	I	J	K
Officials and managers*	154	138	2	0	0	0	13	1	0	0	0
Professionals	137	126	1	0	0	0	10	0	0	0	0
Technicians	76	61	2	1	1	0	6	2	0	3	0
Sales workers	77	65	4	0	0	0	7	1	0	0	0
Office and clerical	188	21	3	0	1	0	144	17	2	0	0
Craft workers (skilled)	150	120	15	1	2	0	9	3	0	0	0
Operatives (semiskilled)	294	200	58	2	10	2	16	4	0	2	0
Laborers (unskilled)	655	504	82	5	10	1	38	10	3	2	0
Service workers	89	17	49	5	1	2	2	9	2	0	2
TOTALS	1,820	1,252	216	14	25	5	245	47	7	7	2

*Includes supervisors

EXHIBIT 1.27 *Civilian Labor Force by Sex and Race, Charlotte, Gastonia, Rock Hill, NC-SC, SMSA, 2000*[1]

Sex and Race	Civilian Labor Force	Employed	Unemployed
Both Sexes			
TOTAL	514,796	489,574	25,222
White	417,540	400,260	17,280
Black	90,270	82,710	7,560
American Indian, Eskimo, and Aleut	1,093	1,048	45
Asian and Pacific Islander	2,193	2,066	127
Hispanic	3,700	3,490	210
Female			
TOTAL	233,298	220,545	12,753
White	184,190	175,420	8,770
Black	45,970	42,150	3,820
American Indian, Eskimo, and Aleut	495	467	28
Asian and Pacific Islander	993	938	55
Hispanic	1,650	1,570	80

[1] *Numbers are fictionalized based on North Carolina Census Data.*

EXHIBIT 1.28 *Occupations of the Civilian Labor Force by Sex and Race, 2000, Charlotte, Gastonia, Rock Hill, NC-SC SMSA[1]*

Occupation	Total[2]	Total White	Total Black	American Indian	Asians	Hispanic	White Not Hispanic	Black Not Hispanic	Total Minority
TOTAL									
All industries	447,254	364,832	78,955	1,348	1,837	3,165	362,595	78,302	84,659
Managerial and professional specialty	87,018	77,673	8,482	119	689	589	77,211	8,410	9,807
Technicians	10,077	8,557	1,415	20	80	53	8,517	1,407	1,561
Sales occupations	45,837	42,341	3,241	84	141	287	42,115	3,203	3,772
Administrative support, including clerical	72,927	62,762	9,857	115	173	387	62,438	9,814	10,489
Service workers	47,097	29,970	16,627	225	249	429	29,765	16,429	17,332
Farming, forestry, and fishing	5,483	4,301	1,103	53	19	26	4,282	1,103	1,201
Precision production and craft	59,987	51,716	7,830	282	130	477	51,341	7,757	8,646
Operators and fabricators	92,707	69,331	22,678	344	251	713	68,884	22,515	23,823
Handlers, equipment cleaners, helpers, and laborers	26,121	18,181	7,722	106	105	204	18,042	7,664	8,079

[1] *North Carolina portion only.*
[2] *Racial and ethnic group columns may not be additive to total due to "race or ethnic group not classified" in census response.*

EXHIBIT 1.29 *Occupations of the Female Civilian Labor Force by Sex and Race, 2000, Charlotte, Gastonia, Rock Hill, NC-SC SMSA[1]*

Occupation	Total[2]	Total White	Total Black	American Indian	Asians	Hispanic	Not Hispanic	Not Hispanic	Total Minority
TOTAL									
All industries	202,039	160,509	40,184	524	702	1,436	159,524	39,821	42,490
Managerial and professional specialty	36,447	30,864	5,346	48	167	260	30,682	5,290	5,765
Technicians	4,667	3,716	923	7	16	23	3,706	915	961
Sales occupations	20,006	17,652	2,211	53	71	170	17,524	2,181	2,482
Administrative support, including clerical	55,628	48,504	6,928	86	95	280	48,269	6,898	7,359
Service workers	28,122	17,269	10,557	134	143	261	17,159	10,425	10,963
Farming, forestry, and fishing	1,166	877	278	6	5	0	877	278	289
Precision production and craft	5,778	4,488	1,256	13	14	51	4,450	1,250	1,328
Operators and fabricators	43,556	32,601	10,588	169	165	344	32,375	10,503	11,181
Handlers, equipment cleaners, helpers, and laborers	6,669	4,538	2,097	9	26	47	4,507	2,081	2,162

[1] North Carolina portion only.
[2] Racial and ethnic group columns may not be additive to total due to "race or ethnic group not classified" in census response.

Job Category	Sex		Race				
	Male	**Female**	**White**	**Black**	**Hispanic**	**Asian**[1]	**American Indian**[2]
Number of employees							
Percentage of employees (utilization)							
Percent available							
Underutilized							

[1] *Asian/Pacific Islander*
[2] *American Indian/Alaskan Native*

Note: A table will be needed for each job category.

2

Meeting Human
Resource
Requirements:
Job Analysis/
Design, Planning,
Recruitment, and
Selection

25 CASE

Employee Layoffs at St. Mary's Hospital

St. Mary's Hospital is a medium-sized, 400-bed hospital in a northwestern city. It was established in 1908 by the Sisters of the Sacred Heart, an order of Catholic sisters. The facility has grown gradually over the years and is now the third largest hospital in the city. It is entirely nonunion and has never experienced an employee layoff since its inception.

Robert Barry has been the CEO of the hospital for 11 years. Eight years ago, he hired Sharon Osgood as director of Human Resources. Osgood has an MA in Human Resource Management and has been instrumental in formalizing the institution's human resources' policies and procedures.

Occupancy rates in the hospital had run between 76 and 82 percent from 1990 to 2002. However, since then, occupancy has fallen to 57 percent. This decline has been experienced throughout the industry and is the result of changing reimbursement policies, emphasis on outpatient services, increasing competition, and the financial meltdown of 2008–2010. The declining occupancy rate has affected this hospital's revenues to such an extent that it ran a deficit for the first time last year. The only response to these changes thus far has been a tightening of requirements for equipment or supply purchases.

At the most recent quarterly meeting of the Board of Directors, Barry presented the rather bleak financial picture. The projected deficit for the coming year was $3,865,000, unless some additional revenue sources were identified or some additional savings were found. The Board's recommendation, based on the immediate crisis and the need to generate short-term savings, was to lay off employees. They recommended that Barry consider laying off up to 10 percent of the hospital's employees with an emphasis on those in "nonessential" areas.

Barry responded that the hospital's employees had never been laid off in the history of the institution. Moreover, he viewed the employees as "family" and would have great difficulty implementing such a layoff. Nevertheless, since he had no realistic short-term alternative for closing the "revenue gap," Barry reluctantly agreed to implement a layoff policy that would be as fair as possible to all employees, provide a guarantee of reemployment for those laid off, and find additional revenue sources so that layoffs would be unnecessary in the future.

Barry then called Sharon Osgood into his office the next morning, shared his concerns, and asked her to prepare both a short-term plan to save $3 million over the next year through staff layoffs, as well as a long-term plan to avoid layoffs in the future. Osgood's concerns were that the layoffs themselves might be costly in terms of lost investment in some of the laid-off employees, higher turnover costs, lost efficiency, potential lawsuits, and lower morale. She was concerned that the criteria for the layoffs not only *be* equitable, but also *appear to be* equitable to the employees. She also wanted to make sure that those being laid off received "adequate" notice so they could make alternative plans or so the hospital could assist them with finding alternative employment. Since the hospital had no previous experience with employee layoffs and no union contract constraints, her feeling was that both seniority and job performance should be considered in determining who would be laid off.

Osgood knew the hospital's performance appraisal system was inadequate and needed to be revamped. While this task was high on her "to do" list, she also knew she had to move ahead with her recommendations on layoffs immediately. The present performance appraisal system uses a traditional checklist rating scale with a summary rating. Since there is no forced distribution, the average ratings of employees in different departments vary widely.

Exhibit 2.1 shows the summary ratings of employees in each department. Most supervisors across all departments rate many of their subordinates either "satisfactory" or "outstanding." Osgood has done a quick review of those employees whose overall ratings were "unsatisfactory" or "questionable." Most are employees with less than three years of seniority, whereas the "satisfactory" employees have worked an average of seven years for St. Mary's Hospital. Osgood is preparing to submit her recommendations to Barry and has come to you for advice. Exhibit 2.2 provides a summary of the distribution of employees and payroll expense by department for the most recent year.

QUESTIONS

1. Identify the major problem or problems at St. Mary's Hospital and the causes.

2. What are some alternatives for dealing with these problems? For example, is it possible to avoid employee layoffs through the use of attrition?

3. Develop a plan for implementing employee layoffs over the next year that will generate $3 million in savings. Give specific details concerning departments affected, the use of seniority versus merit, the amount of notice, and out-placement activities. What additional information (if any) will you need? Provide a rationale for each recommendation, together with reasons why other alternatives were not chosen.

4. What might be the effects of a layoff plan on "survivors" in terms of morale, job security, organizational commitment, productivity, and career planning? How could you avoid or minimize any potential problems in these areas?

5. What long-term solutions do you see for St. Mary's Hospital once it gets its cash flow problems under control and eliminates its deficit? What can it do to increase revenue so that future layoffs will not be necessary?

6. What difficulties exist in using performance as a criterion for layoffs? How can such difficulties be overcome?

EXHIBIT 2.1 *Percentage Distribution of Performance Appraisal Summary Ratings by Department at St. Mary's Hospital*

Department	Unsatisfactory: Needs to Improve Substantially	Questionable: Needs Some Improvement	Satisfactory: Meets Normal Expectations	Outstanding: Substantially Exceeds Norms
Nursing	6.4	6.4	54.2	33.0
Allied Health	5.7	6.2	47.8	40.3
Central Administration	2.7	3.1	67.5	26.7
Dietetics/Nutrition	2.1	6.2	68.3	23.4
Housekeeping/Maintenance	7.8	12.4	54.6	25.2
Medical Staff	1.1	6.2	63.8	28.9

EXHIBIT 2.2 *The Distribution of Employment and Payroll Expenditures at St. Mary's Hospital*

Department	Number of Employees	Payroll ($)	Annual Turnover Rates (%)*
Nursing	602	$15,050,000	12.2
Allied Health Departments	261	5,742,000	8.7
Central Administration	154	6,160,000	3.5
Dietetics/Nutrition	65	1,430,000	7.3
Housekeeping and Maintenance	36	540,000	8.4
Medical Staff	32	1,680,000	2.1
TOTAL	1,150	$30,602,000	9.5*

*Represents weighted average turnover for all employees.

Strategic Human Resource Management

The School of Business Administration at Old State University is one of 12 state-supported collegiate business schools in a midwestern state. It is located in a city with a population of 400,000 and a diversified industrial base. Old State University is the only state-supported institution in town. One small private college provides competition to the university's business school.

Recently, the university experienced leadership transition when Dr. George Barnes, dean of the College of Business Administration since 1988, retired. During his administration, enrollment increased from 1,792 undergraduates and 142 MBA students in the 1988–1989 academic year to 2,284 undergraduates and 233 MBA students in the most recent academic year.

Dean Barnes was well-liked by students, faculty, and the central administration of Old State University. However, he had not led the School of Business in any new directions and had basically concentrated on "doing the same things better." The "same things" meant an emphasis on traditional programs (accounting, marketing, finance, and so on), teaching undergraduate students in the age range of 18–22 in daytime programs, and teaching a small number of full-time MBA students. The latter have been mostly graduates of the school's undergraduate program who decided they were willing to spend two more years on campus to obtain the second degree.

Dean Barnes has also successful in upgrading the proportion of faculty with terminal degrees from 75 percent in 1988 to 90 percent in the most recent year. Exhibit 2.3 provides faculty and student enrollment data for the university for selected years during Barnes's tenure.

During the most recent academic year, the dean's search committee (consisting of faculty, students, alumni, central administration, and local business representatives) met frequently, screened over 100 applicants, and personally interviewed six. While the committee arrived at no consensus, the majority supported Jack Blake for the deanship. An offer was made and, after several weeks of negotiation, Blake accepted the deanship. His background consisted of an MBA from a prestigious Ivy League business school and executive leadership positions in a variety of U.S. corporations in marketing. He left the position of vice president of marketing at a Fortune 500 company to accept the deanship.

During the screening interviews with the search committee, Blake made it clear that if he were selected, the College of Business would be "moving in new directions and exploring new markets." Blake made it clear that he did not want to be a "paper pusher," but rather an innovator and entrepreneur. When pressed for specifics, he indicated he "would have to study the situation in more detail."

When the new dean arrived on campus in the fall, he immediately convened a Strategic Planning Committee to 1) evaluate the university's external environment, opportunities, threats, competitive advantages, and internal strengths and weaknesses, and 2) recommend a new long-term mission, goals, objectives, and programs. The committee consisted of two senior professors, the university's vice president for academic affairs, one graduate student, one undergraduate student, two prominent alumni, and two local business leaders.

The committee recommended that the school focus on the adult learner since demographic analysis suggested the age group 18–22 in the state was shrinking and would be a declining market over the next decade. Specific recommendations included 1) offering more

Academic Year	Faculty	Faculty with PhD	Student Enrollment		
			BS	MBA	Total
1988–1989	69	52	1,792	142	1,934
1995–1996	74	57	1,913	154	2,067
2000–2001	78	66	2,065	221	2,286
2006–2007	85	76	2,284	233	2,517
2010–2011	90	81	2,587	248	2,837

evening courses for both undergraduate and graduate students; 2) structuring the schedule so that both degrees could be earned entirely in the evening; 3) offering credit courses in some suburban locations; 4) offering requested noncredit practitioner courses at the school, at the employer's worksite, and in various underserved small cities around the state; 5) exploring possibilities of offering degree programs at these locations; 6) offering new MBA degree concentrations in such areas as management of the arts, healthcare management, and public sector management, and 7) offering a new "executive" MBA.

The new dean enthusiastically endorsed the report and distributed copies at the last faculty meeting of the fall semester. Several questions were raised, but it did not appear that serious opposition existed. However, at a following meeting of department chairs, the dean indicated that his top priority for the next academic year was to fill five vacant positions with new faculty who would be supportive of the new directions in which the school was moving. Specifically, he asked them to keep several criteria in mind while recruiting and selecting new faculty. These included previous managerial work experience, a willingness to teach night courses, a willingness to travel to other cities to offer coursework, an ability to work with management practitioners on continuing education training and special projects, and previous experience in teaching executives.

In addition, Dean Blake suggested that the chairs consider those criteria when evaluating the performance of existing faculty and recommending salary increases. Finally, he indicated that one of the faculty positions would be used to recruit a new assistant dean for external affairs who would become his link to the practitioner community. This person would be involved with helping practicing managers identify their needs, working with faculty to meet these needs, and negotiating contracts for these services.

When word of the dean's faculty recommendations spread through the rumor mill, the reaction was swift and negative. Many of the "old-guard" faculty felt they were hired primarily to teach full-time students on campus during the day. Consequently, they were threatened by the new evaluation criteria. They were also concerned that the dean was interjecting non-academic criteria into their departmental faculty recruitment processes and diverting resources to nonacademic activities. These faculty felt the inevitable result would be a declining quality of education in the school.

A group of these faculty has asked to meet with the dean to discuss his proposals. The dean is preparing a justification for both his strategy and his human resource management (faculty) recommendations.

1. How and why do strategic decisions affect human resource management policies? Can human resource policies or constraints ever affect strategy? Why or why not?

2. Identify the problem and causes of the problem in this case.

3. Evaluate Dean Blake's strategy and human resource policies. Did the strategy make sense in terms of the internal and external environment of the school? Do the human resource strategies support and reinforce the organizational strategy? Why or why not?

4. Evaluate the process by which Dean Blake implemented the strategic and human resources changes. Can you suggest any improvements?

5. How can resistance to his plans and strategies be overcome?

The Alternative Work Schedule

BACKGROUND

March 13 marked an important day in the history of Building Products, Inc. The planning committee was meeting to determine the work schedule for all of the production workers at its new plant. Attending the meeting was the human resource director, the plant manager, and the production manager. The plant was scheduled to open in a few months, and it was time to begin hiring new employees.

The committee knew that the new work schedule would need to meet specific parameters. First, the plant's production process would require that chemicals and materials be heated to high temperatures, so the plant would have to operate 24 hours a day, seven days a week, 363 days a year. On Christmas Day and the day before Christmas, the plant would shut down with only two employees needed—a production operator and a maintenance technician. Second, workers would not be able to take breaks all at one time. Rather, they would need to stagger the breaks and cover for each other. Third, having the standard 8-to-5 work schedule would not be possible, given the need for 24-hour coverage. Likewise, a work schedule that entails three shifts, each working eight-hour days would not work because coverage is needed seven days a week, and employees need time off to rest.

After much discussion, the human resources director suggested that the firm try a schedule that she had heard about at another firm. The schedule entailed dividing workers into four crews, with each crew working 12-hour shifts on either three or four consecutive days or nights. It also meant that employees would switch between day shifts and night shifts. More specifically, the schedule of rotation for one crew would be as follows:

4 night shifts—12 hours per night (7 PM to 7 AM)

2 days/nights off

3 day shifts—12 hours per day (7 AM to 7 PM)

2 days/nights off

3 night shifts—12 hours per night (7 PM to 7 AM)

2 days/nights off

4 day shifts—12 hours per day (7 AM to 7 PM)

8 days/nights off

Repeat sequence throughout this and future years

A typical schedule over a 28-day period for each of the four crews would be:

	Week 1	Week 2	Week 3	Week 4
Crew	S M T W T F S	S M T W T F S	S M T W T F S	S M T W T F S
A	O N N N O O D	D D D O O O O	O O O O N N N	N O O D D D O
B	N O O D D D O	O N N N O O D	D D D O O O O	O O O O N N N
C	O O O O N N N	N O O D D D O	O N N N O O D	D D D O O O O
D	D D D O O O O	O O O O N N N	N O O D D D O	O N N N O O D

Key: N night shift; O off work; D day shift

The human resources director noted that by dividing all of the workers into four crews, the schedules for the crews could be integrated in such a way that only one crew would be working, yet all hours could be covered (see schedule above). Each crew would consist of 17 production operators, two warehouse/forklift truck workers to take product off the line, and one production supervisor. Also, she suggested that overtime pay be granted to employees when they work more than 40 hours per week. An employee who works a 48-hour week would receive straight pay for 40 hours and time-and-one-half for eight more hours. This equates to 52 hours of straight pay. Thus, in the course of a 28-day period, employees would work shifts totaling 168 hours, but be paid for 176 hours. In addition, she recommended that employees who work over a holiday receive double pay for those hours, but that no additional overtime pay be provided for working Saturday or Sunday.

After hearing the human resources director's recommendations, the plant manager and the production manager sat quietly, trying to digest the plan. The schedule was completely unlike anything they had ever experienced, and it struck them as bizarre. They could not help but question whether the plan would actually work. They also wondered if there might not be a better production schedule.

QUESTIONS

1. What do you see as the strengths and weaknesses of the human resources director's work schedule from (a) the employees' perspective, and (b) the firm's perspective?

2. Would you recommend the firm use the new work schedule? Why?

3. What alternative work schedule could be used?

28 EXERCISE

Which Employee Should Be Terminated?

I. OBJECTIVES

  A. To make you aware of the difficulties involved in making termination decisions.

  B. To familiarize you with possible criteria a manager can use in making termination decisions.

  C. To give you practice in conducting termination interviews.

II. OUT-OF-CLASS PREPARATION TIME: 10 minutes to read exercise and decide which employee should be terminated

III. IN-CLASS TIME SUGGESTED: 40–50 minutes

IV. PROCEDURES

Either at the beginning of or before class, you should read the exercise and determine which title examiner should be terminated. This exercise requires that groups determine which company employee should be terminated. To start the exercise, the instructor will ask five students to play the role of title examiners. One will play the role of Rick Feinberg, another the role of Jeff Simon, and so on. These individuals will be asked to leave the classroom and prepare to play their roles. They should study carefully the material contained in this exercise and determine how to respond if, in fact, they are the one chosen to be terminated.

The instructor will divide the remaining students into groups of four to six. Each group should develop a list of criteria for layoffs/termination, and rank the title examiners from first to go to last to go. After the group has reached a consensus, it should select one spokesperson to communicate the decision to the title examiner who is to be terminated.

After all groups have finished performing the preceding tasks, the role play begins. One at a time, each group's spokesperson announces to the class which title examiner his or her group believes should be terminated. The instructor then brings that person into the room and asks him or her to sit down at the front of the class. The spokesperson sits down opposite the title examiner, tells that person that he or she is terminated, and gives the rationale behind the decision. The title examiner then responds in any realistic way that he or she deems appropriate. This process continues until all groups' spokespersons have had an opportunity to present their decision. A critique of the role plays and a discussion of the difficulties involved in terminating an employee should then follow.

SITUATION

The Stanton Title Insurance Company was founded in 1964 by Harvey Stanton to sell title insurance policies to buyers of real estate. The company works closely with a group of about 35 lawyers who, although they do not actually buy the title insurance policies, encourage their clients (the property purchasers) to do so. When the company was originally established, Stanton was its only employee. As company sales increased, new employees were hired, and now 23 individuals are working in various capacities for the firm. Stanton has always followed the policy of making all major decisions himself. This includes all personnel decisions such as determining who should be hired and how much they should be paid.

Title Examiner	Current Salary	Work Quality	Work Quantity	Knowledge of Job	Dependability	Cooperativeness
Rick Feinberg	$56,500	Excellent	Good	Excellent	Good	Poor
José Sanchez	$32,000	Good	Good	Fair	Excellent	Excellent
Kathy Wallace	$36,500	Good	Fair	Good	Fair	Excellent
Doris Matthews	$45,000	Poor	Good	Excellent	Good	Good
Anthony Pope	$50,200	Good	Poor	Excellent	Excellent	Excellent

Five of the employees work primarily on examining titles at local government offices. In recent weeks, Stanton has noticed that the workload of these five employees has declined considerably. In part, this is due to the recent election of three "no-growth" candidates to the city council. In addition, a competing firm has recently opened an office in town and is successfully taking away business. Stanton has reluctantly decided that he must terminate the employment of one of the title examiners. He simply cannot transfer one of them to a new position. His only question is, which one?

A summary of Harvey's evaluation of each title examiner is in Exhibit 2.4; a profile of each of the five title examiners appears below.

Rick Feinberg: 45 years old; white; married with three children; 20 years with the company; graduated from a community college; knows how to resolve difficult title policies due to his extensive experience; is difficult to get along with; antagonizes other employees at main office; hates to fill out company reports not related to title examination and refuses to do so on occasion; will not work overtime under any condition, which puts a burden on others.

José Sanchez: 23 years old; Latino; married; attending college; one year with the company; wife works at main office as a computer programmer; works very hard and is eager to learn; well-liked by all employees and is highly dependable; is never absent and will gladly work overtime to meet emergencies; with more experience, he should be an outstanding title examiner; is highly loyal and dedicated; moved recently to a new apartment across the street from the government office where he works.

Kathy Wallace: 24 years old; single; college degree; African-American; working on MBA at night; three years with company; well-liked by employees; very active in community affairs; capable of moving up to a top management position with the company; often misses work due to school and community activities.

Doris Matthews: 36 years old; married; white; attended community college but did not graduate; ten years with company; niece of Harvey Stanton; has had eye problems and headaches, which affected work quality this year and may continue to do so; has been very helpful in getting new business for the company; is well-known and highly respected by law firms.

Anthony Pope: 63 years old; white; 15 years with company; no college; hard working and well-liked by employees; three children in college; a solid, stable employee who is able to remain calm and solve problems in crisis situations; excellent at resolving conflicts between employees; well-known to local government officials; very slow but highly accurate worker.

■■■■■■ *Outsourcing the Human Resource Management Functions*

I. OBJECTIVES

A. To familiarize you with the potential costs and benefits of human resource management outsourcing.

B. To familiarize you with the degree to which various human resource management functions are being successfully outsourced.

II. OUT-OF-CLASS PREPARATION TIME: 50 minutes

III. IN-CLASS TIME SUGGESTED: 30 minutes

IV. INSTRUCTIONS

A. In groups of three to five students, read the "Situation" below, as well as Forms 2.1 and 2.2.

B. Each group will complete Forms 2.1 and 2.2, as well as Question 1. List as many outsourcing benefits and costs for both employers and employees as you can on Form 2.1. Put an X beside your group's assessment of the corporate benefits (Form 2.2) of outsourcing each HR function.

C. One person in each team will report the group's assessment and recommendations (Question 1) to the class.

SITUATION

Sharon Osmond is the vice president of human resources for Silicon Electronics, a small electronics company in the Silicon Valley area outside of San Francisco. She has been concerned that their patched-together human resource information system uses a software program so outdated that Peoplesoft will no longer support it. This morning she met Edward Cutter, the CEO of her company, in the parking lot as they were both coming to work.

Cutter told her of a conversation he had with a consultant from Hewitt Associates, Inc., a human resource management consulting company. The consultant said that when the entire human resource management function was outsourced to Hewitt, they had saved a company similar to his almost $400,000 in human resource management costs last year. The consultant also told Cutter that a number of blue-chip companies have joined the HR outsourcing bandwagon including AT&T, Motorola, American Express, and Prudential. Based on that conversation, Cutter then asked Osgood to do some research and let him know whether it made sense to consider outsourcing some or all of the current human resource management functions at Silicon Electronics to Hewitt or a similar firm.

Osgood was quite upset after the conversation because she knew her own position, as well as positions of her subordinates, might be in jeopardy. However, after recovering from her initial shock, she called Mary Gannon, her former professor of Human Resources Management at California State University, to solicit her input. Professor Gannon told Osgood she would get back to her in a week after giving this assignment to one of the student groups in her Human Resources Management class.

Your group has been given this assignment. Professor Gannon has asked your group to do the research necessary to complete Forms 2.1 and 2.2 and then answer the questions below.

QUESTIONS

1. Complete Forms 2.1 and 2.2 using information gathered from the various human resource Web sites listed throughout this book. Identify as many benefits and costs from both the employer and employee perspective as you can as a result of outsourcing the entire human resource function (Form 2.1). Also consider which human resource functions have the greatest potential to be outsourced based on what other companies are doing and why (Form 2.2). On the basis of these assessments, which of the three strategies should Osmond recommend to Cutter and why? Circle either a, b, or c and be prepared to explain your reasons based on Forms 2.1 and 2.2.

   a. Do not outsource any of the human resource functions.

   b. Outsource only the following human resource functions:_____

   c. Outsource all of the human resource functions.

Employer
Benefits
Costs

Employee
Benefits
Costs

The Potential Expected Corporate Benefits Associated with Outsourcing Specific Human Resource Functions

HR Functions	Potential Expected Benefits			
	Uncertain	Very Low	Moderate	Very High
1. Payroll and benefits				
2. Recruitment				
3. Selection				
4. Information technology				
5. Training				
6. Performance management				
7. All HR functions				

30 EXERCISE
Job Analysis: Writing Job Descriptions

I. **OBJECTIVES**

    A. To familiarize you with the job analysis process and with job descriptions.

    B. To give you practice writing job descriptions.

II. **OUT-OF-CLASS PREPARATION TIME:** 30 minutes

III. **IN-CLASS TIME SUGGESTED:** 45 minutes

IV. **PROCEDURES**

    A. Before beginning this exercise, you should (a) review carefully, if you have not already done so, the different methods organizations use to conduct job analyses, and (b) review the Job Analysis Questionnaire (Exhibit 2.5).

    B. Students should be divided into pairs. Each person should then interview his or her partner with reference to a job about which the partner is very familiar. Use the Job Analysis Questionnaire for the interview. The questionnaire can be used to help determine the major responsibilities and tasks of the job and the required knowledge, skills, abilities, and personal characteristics needed to perform the job.

    C. After each student has interviewed his or her partner, write a job description covering your partner's job. Remember to use action verbs when describing the employee's tasks, duties, and responsibilities. It is also important that specific duties be grouped and arranged in descending order of importance. The completed job description should follow the format shown in Exhibit 2.6. The completed job description should be shown to the partner to determine whether additional information is required or whether changes should be made. Your instructor may require that you turn in a final copy of the completed job description for the next class.

    D. If time permits, the entire class should discuss the various uses of job descriptions and the effectiveness of the interview as a method of job analysis.

EXHIBIT 2.5 *Job Analysis Questionnaire*

A. Job Responsibilities and Duties

1. Job title

2. Department title and/or division title

3. Title of immediate supervisor

4. Description of duties (Describe the duties in enough detail to provide a complete and accurate description of the work.)

    a. Provide a general overall summary of the purpose of your job.

    b. What are the major results or outputs of your job?

    c. Describe the duties and tasks you perform daily; weekly; monthly.

    d. Describe duties you perform irregularly.

5. List any machines, instruments, tools, equipment, materials, and work aids used in your job. Indicate percent of time used.

6. Describe the nature of your responsibility for nonhuman resources (money, machinery, equipment, and so on). What monetary loss can occur through an error?

7. What reports and records do you prepare as part of your job? When are they prepared?

8. What is the source of instructions for performing your job (e.g., oral or written specifications)?

9. Describe the nature and frequency of supervision received.

10. How is your work reviewed, checked, or verified?

B. Reporting Relationships

11. How many employees are directly under your supervision? What are their job titles?

12. Do you have full authority to hire, terminate, evaluate, and transfer employees under your supervision? Explain.

13. What contacts are required with other departments or persons other than your immediate department in performing your job? Describe the nature and extent of these contacts.

C. Working Conditions

14. Describe the working conditions present in the location and environment of your work such as cold/heat, noise, fumes, dust, and so on. Indicate frequency and degree of exposure.

15. Describe any dangers or hazards present in your job.

D. Job Qualifications (Be certain not to list the incumbent's qualifications, but what is required for performance by a new employee.)

16. Describe the kind of previous work experience necessary for satisfactory performance of this job.

17. What is the amount of experience required?

18. What kinds of knowledge, skills, and abilities (KSAs) are needed to perform the job?

19. What is the minimal level of education (grammar, high school, two-year college, four-year college, etc.) required?

20. Are any special physical skills and/or manual dexterity skills required to perform the job?

21. Are there any special certification, registration, license, or training requirements?

EXHIBIT 2.6 *Sample Job Description*

Job Title: Shift Supervisor

Position Purpose: The purpose of this position is to maintain a safe and efficient plant operation through directing the activities of the operation's personnel and providing a management support function for the plant superintendent.

Typical Job Duties:
1. Directs the activities of the operations personnel and coordinates the activities of the maintenance personnel.
2. Issues written communication to employees concerning personnel policies and operational concerns.
3. Administers a maintenance request program through collecting requests, scheduling, and recording maintenance activities.
4. Administers the plant tagging procedure.
5. Conducts the training and safety programs for shift employees.
6. Schedules shift assignments to reflect workload and vacation schedules.
7. Performs administrative tasks such as recording workers' time, maintaining records concerning operational activities, and updating written procedures.
8. Prepares annual budget for assigned plant area and maintains the inventory level on these items.
9. Appraises performance of shift employees annually.
10. Counsels employees on disciplinary problems and job-related performance.
11. Assumes plant superintendent's duties when assigned.

Physical Requirements: Walking and climbing stairs

Working Conditions: Good, some noise

Equipment and Machines Used: CRT, spectrometer, PH meter, conductivity meter

Reporting Relationships: The shift supervisor reports directly to the plant superintendent. The shift supervisor directs the control room operator, two or more utility operators, trainees, and other assigned personnel, and coordinates the activities of the maintenance personnel present on shift.

Qualifications:
   Education: Associate degree or equivalent training (e.g., management training classes) OR five (5) years of management experience.
   Related Experience: Minimum of three (3) years as a control room operator for a coal-fired boiler operation.

Job Knowledge/Skills Required:
1. Comprehensive understanding of plant systems.
2. Fundamental understanding of electrical systems and motor control centers.
3. Thorough knowledge of boiler chemistry.
4. Comprehension of flow, logic, and electrical prints.
5. Ability to perform elementary mathematical and algebraic calculations.
6. Communication and human relations skills.
7. Ability to operate CRT, spectrometer, PH meter, and conductivity meter.
8. Managerial skills.

━━━━━━━━━━ *Work and Family Issues*

I. **OBJECTIVES**

   A. To understand the conflicts that sometimes arises between the individual's work and family responsibilities.

   B. To analyze the advantages and disadvantages of alternative policies and programs that attempt to reconcile the sometimes conflicting demands of work and family.

II. **OUT-OF-CLASS PREPARATION TIME:** 1 hour

III. **IN-CLASS TIME SUGGESTED:** 45 minutes

IV. **PROCEDURES**

   A. Read the entire exercise before class. Students may want to conduct research on the topic prior to class.

   B. Develop a list of possible policies and programs for this company to better reconcile work and family life before class.

   C. Share your group's recommendations with the rest of the class.

      Form groups of three to five students, share your ideas with one another, and write out your group recommendations for policies and procedures to better reconcile employee work and family responsibilities on Form 2.3. Form 2.3 should also be used to provide details of your recommendations as well as a time frame for implementation. This time frame will depend upon how high a priority the group assigns to a particular recommendation and how much time will be required to work out the details of the proposal. In preparing your recommendations, consider the pros and cons of responding to the needs of nurses with small children without alienating other nurses who do not have small children.

   D. Present your group's recommendations to the instructor and to other class members.

BACKGROUND

Sunshine Health Services provides home healthcare services to a metropolitan area of 1.5 million in Florida. Patient visits are primarily based on referrals from physicians and health systems. The company currently offers services in eight different locations in the area and served 11,000 patients in their homes over the past year. Sunshine is a for-profit facility that generated revenues of $10,400,000 dollars and a net profit of $430,000 dollars in the most recent fiscal year. The company currently employs a total of 243 staff, of which 186 are nurses.

Most of the home visits are conducted by home health nurses. However, the nursing shortage has negatively impacted the company's ability to recruit and retain the number and quality of nurses needed to service the existing volume of patient visits, much less staff up for the four percent annual growth in patient visits per year expected through 2015.

Home health care has had a difficult time competing for new nursing graduates because pay rates are lower than those in hospitals. The 18 percent turnover rate of nurses at Sunshine exceeds the area nurse turnover rate of 12 percent. In addition to salary, some nurses prefer the hospital environment to home health care and others feel hospitals offer more "family friendly" benefits as compared to home health care. Currently Sunshine provides either part-time (20 hours per week) or full-time (40 hours per week) employment options. However, they do not offer any type of flex time.

The company has taken the position that the individual's family and work life are, and should be, separate. Both require time and effort, but should never interfere with each other. The company's philosophy has been that each individual has a responsibility to hire or otherwise provide child-care service or whatever other services are necessary for the proper functioning of the family. The company's responsibility has been only to provide part-time and full-time jobs for employees while serving customer needs.

Recently, that philosophy has been challenged by several employees who claim the company is insensitive to employees who have family responsibilities. In particular, they cite the lack of any child-care facilities and family-leave policies. They argue that uniform personnel policies applied rigidly to all employees (irrespective of their family situation) are inherently unfair. If the company really viewed their employees as family members, it would be more flexible in accommodating the employee's family responsibilities.

The company CEO, Renee Brent, recently read an article in *BusinessWeek* identifying the best companies for women. This article identified a number of family-oriented policies and programs followed by 24 leading companies. Among the most significant of these were modifications in the company culture, executive development to enhance sensitivity, subsidized babysitting, child care, sick-child care, telecommuting, on-site take-home meals, elder care, job sharing, mentorship programs, women on the Board, career development policies, family leave policies, maternity leave with partial pay, modified work and family benefits, flexible benefits, hiring a pluralistic workforce, job sharing, mentoring programs, and part-time professional and/or executive positions. Some of the 24 corporations identified in the *BusinessWeek* article were in health services.

A potential major source of nursing staff for the company is the large number of nurses in the area who are out of the labor force. While some of these have left the field permanently to pursue other opportunities, others have left the field on a temporary basis to raise children or for other reasons. If a substantial number of these nurses could be enticed back into the labor force through the development of attractive job options at Sunshine, the nurse staffing issue might be elevated. Such options would need to meet the needs of a largely female work force to help them balance their work and family responsibilities.

Policy or Program	Specific Details	Time Frame for Implementation*
1.		
2.		
3.		
4.		
5.		
6.		
7.		
8.		
9.		
10.		
11.		
12.		

*short-term within the next year; intermediate term one to two years; long-term more than two years.

Human Resource Forecasting Assignment

I. OBJECTIVES

A. To give you practice in forecasting an organization's human resource needs.

B. To familiarize you with some of the factors that affect an organization's future human resource needs (growth, automation, turnover).

C. To familiarize you with the complexities involved in making human resource forecasts.

D. To point out that all human resource forecasting is based on assumptions and that these assumptions are critical to the accuracy of the forecast. Incorrect assumptions lead to erroneous forecasts.

II. TIME REQUIRED TO COMPLETE: One to two hours

III. INSTRUCTIONS

You have been given the assignment of forecasting the human resource needs of the National Bank and Trust Company which currently employs approximately 1,100 people. The bank presently has 50 branch offices located throughout the metropolitan area, each of which employs approximately 14 individuals. The bank expects to add 38 branches during the next three years. Branches within the bank differ considerably in size, so the figures given represent averages.

During the past month, the bank has placed an order for 30 automated teller machines to be placed in its former branch offices. These machines are scheduled to be in operation December 31, one year from now. The bank has found that for each new machine purchased, one less teller is needed, on average. A breakdown of the bank's current staffing is shown in Table 2.1.

The bank has asked you to perform three human resource forecasting tasks. First, based on the assumptions given below, you are required to determine employee turnover for the main office, the former branches, and the new branches. Your boss would like to know this information for each of the next three years and for each of the major personnel categories (i.e., supervisors, tellers/clerical, and main office). Your job is to complete Table 2.2.

Second, your boss would like to know the number of new employees the bank will need to hire for each major personnel category for each of the next three years. Your job is to complete Table 2.3.

Table 2.1 *Present Staffing*

Total Employees	**1,100**
Number of Branches	50
Supervisors per Branch	4
Number of Supervisors	200
Tellers per Branch	10
Number of Tellers	500
Branch Employees	700
Main Office Employees	400

Table 2.1 *Turnover*

Employee Category	Year 1	Year 2	Year 3
Former Branch Supervisors			
Former Branch Tellers			
Main Office			
New Branch Supervisors			
New Branch Tellers			

Table 2.3 *Number of Employees to be Hired*

Employee Category	Year 1	Year 2	Year 3
Former Branch Supervisors			
Former Branch Tellers			
Main Office			
New Branch Supervisors			
New Branch Tellers			
Totals			

Table 2.4 *Year-End Employment*

Employee Category	Year 1	Year 2	Year 3
Former Branch Supervisors			
Former Branch Tellers			
Main Office			
New Branch Supervisors			
New Branch Tellers			
Totals			

Finally, your boss would like to know the total number of employees who will be working for the bank as of the end of each of the next three years. Your job is to complete Table 2.4.

In order to complete your assignment, your boss has told you to make a number of assumptions. They are:

A. You are making all projections in December for subsequent years ending December 31.

B. With regard to former branches, assume

1. The 50 former branches employ four supervisors and ten clerical personnel/tellers each.

2. On December 31 (one year hence), 30 teller machines are placed in operation and replace 30 tellers.

3. The bank does not terminate any employees because of the new teller machines. Rather, as tellers quit throughout the year, 30 are not replaced.

4. Turnover is 30 percent for tellers/clerical personnel, and 20 percent for supervisors.

C. With regard to new branches, assume

   1. New branches are added as follows: 10 in Year 1, 12 in Year 2, and 16 in Year 3.

   2. Each new branch employs 14 individuals (four supervisors and ten tellers/clerical).

   3. New branches are added evenly throughout the year. Thus, for the purpose of calculating turnover, on average, there are five new branches in Year 1 (50% 10); 16 in Year 2 [10 in Year 1 plus 6 (50% 12)]; and 30 in Year 3 [22 plus 8 (50% 16)].

   4. Turnover is 30 percent for tellers/clerical personnel, and 20 percent for supervisors.

D. With regard to the main office, assume that turnover will be 10 percent per year.

33 SKILL BUILDER

Phased Retirement Options

I. OBJECTIVES

A. To give you practice in using the Internet to generate information relevant to solving human resource problems.

B. To familiarize you with the various options to traditional employee retirement.

II. TIME REQUIRED TO COMPLETE: One to two hours

III. INSTRUCTIONS

Read the "Situation" below and then search the Internet for the following: 1) phased retirement options; 2) advantages or benefits of each option for employees and the employer; and 3) disadvantages or costs of each option.

Possible Web sites are:

http://www.magicnet.net/benefits.index.html

http://www.vcn.bc.ca/timework.worksite.htm

http://www.insword.com/newsletter/index.html

Then, fill in Form 2.4 by identifying three phased retirement options and provide at least one advantage and disadvantage for each of the three listed options. Be prepared to present your findings and recommendations to the class.

SITUATION

The Owens Engineering Company provides a full range of engineering services to a wide variety of governmental and private organizations in the Denver metropolitan area. Ron Owens, the company president, has become increasingly concerned about his company's demographics. Two-thirds of their 82 engineers range in age from 50 to 67 years old. The company's current retirement policy is to offer retirement to all employees who reach age 55 or more, with 25 or more years of service.

Within the next few years, Owens has determined that 42 percent of the engineers will be eligible for retirement, and based on past company data, 70 percent will retire within two years of their actual eligibility. This means he expects to lose 29 out of 82 engineers to retirement over the next four years. In addition, the "normal" annual turnover rate among engineers has been 8 percent. This would reduce the company's pool of engineers by another seven per year, or 28 over the next four years.

After discussing the situation with Susan Barber, the human resources manager, Owens concludes that most voluntary turnover is unavoidable. While the company provides competitive salaries and benefits for the Denver area, the local unemployment rate is relatively low (averaging 7.8 percent), and there are few unemployed engineers in the area. Future forecasts are for a continued tight labor market for engineers in Denver.

Owens and Barber determined that the best way to deal with their potential engineer shortage is to retain older engineers as they become eligible for retirement. This decision is not only based on the numbers, but also on the qualities and qualifications the company anticipates losing. For example, when four senior civil engineers retired during the past year, the company lost their contacts and influence, their knowledge of their customers, special

Option 1	
Advantages/Benefits to the Company	**Advantages/Benefits to the Employee**
1.	1.
2.	2.
3.	3.
Disadvantages/Costs to the Company	**Disadvantages/Costs to the Employee**
1.	1.
2.	2.
3.	3
Option 2	
Advantages/Benefits to the Company	**Advantages/Benefits to the Employee**
1.	1.
2.	2.
3.	3.
Disadvantages/Costs to the Company	**Disadvantages/Costs to the Employee**
1.	1
2.	2.
3.	3.
Option 3	
Advantages/Benefits to the Company	**Advantages/Benefits to the Employee**
1.	1.
2.	2
3.	3.
Disadvantages/Costs to the Company	**Disadvantages/Costs to the Employee**
1.	1.
2.	2.
3.	3.

requirements in the contract bidding process, and their knowledge about who to see and how to get things done internally.

Barber is a friend of your human resource management instructor this term. Your instructor has assigned your student team the term project of assisting Owens Engineering in assessing its options for retaining its older engineers.

Recruitment and Selection

34 CASE

Recruiting Recreational Vehicle Surveyors

Liberty Engineering Company is located in a large suburb of Cleveland, Ohio. The company was founded during the 1940s and does a considerable amount of drafting and design work for the major automotive companies and their suppliers. When sales in the auto industry are high, Liberty Engineering experiences a significant volume of work. However, when recessions hit the automotive marketplace, work at Liberty also sharply decreases.

In an attempt to stabilize revenues, the president of Liberty Engineering decided it would be prudent to diversify the company by bidding on government contracts. The company had little experience in these areas, but the president felt that this would not preclude it from bidding on contracts and obtaining them.

Within a six-month period, the company had bid on and lost two contracts. However, a third bid pertaining to the safety and use of recreational vehicles proved to be successful. The contract was for several hundred thousand dollars and was granted on a cost-plus basis. The government was interested in obtaining information regarding how people actually use recreational vehicles such as pick-up truck campers, motor homes, and various kinds of camping trailers. Ultimately, the purpose of the study was to determine what additional safety rules, if any, should be established relating to the manufacture and use of recreational vehicles. Among the pieces of information desired by the government were how much weight citizens place in their recreational vehicles, what kinds of trailer hitches are in use, whether recreational vehicles have proper suspension systems, and to what extent citizens are aware of the safety features of their recreational vehicles.

In Liberty Engineering's proposal to the government, the company stated that it would recruit, select, and train qualified individuals to survey over 1,000 recreational vehicles. The surveying would be done at three different sites: in the desert, at the seashore, and in the mountains. At a meeting with government officials, three locations were selected: Lake Mead, Nevada; Cape Hatteras, North Carolina; and Smoky Mountains National Park, Tennessee. Two other important decisions were also made at the meeting. First, to ensure consistency of data collection, all surveyors would be trained together at a campground at Smoky Mountains National Park. Second, the employees would then be divided and sent to their respective job sites. It was also decided that each survey crew would consist of one leader and four surveyors, and that two crews would be sent to each data collection site.

All responsibility for recruiting and training the 30 employees (6 leaders and 24 surveyors) fell upon the shoulders of Bob Getz, the new human resource director. Getz had worked as a designer for Liberty Engineering for 20 years before being transferred to human resources. At the same time that a project Getz had been working on for two years ended, the then-current human resource director resigned, so he was a logical choice. In addition, Getz was well-liked by most of Liberty's older employees and knew a great deal about the company's policies and procedures. Getz's major shortcoming was that he knew little about staffing activities.

Before recruiting potential job applicants, Getz knew that he would first need to develop a set of job descriptions for all 30 employees. Since crews would be doing essentially similar jobs, albeit at different locations, he needed only to develop job descriptions for each of four survey positions and that of the leader. Hence, he obtained the list of data that was to be collected on each vehicle, determined the tasks required to collect the data, and divided the tasks into four job positions. Getz realized that the job duties of each surveyor would ultimately need to be changed based on actual experience. Nonetheless, he sketched out the following job descriptions:

Surveyor I: Take pictures of recreational vehicle with a camera. Interview driver and record information received.

Surveyor II: Read and record scale weights for each recreational vehicle tire. Take tire pressures and measure tread depth. Record make, size, and air capacity of each tire.

Surveyor III: Unhook trailer hitch, if present, and record make of hitch, ball diameter, and whether levelers are present. Determine type of suspension on recreational vehicle and count number of leaf springs, if present.

Surveyor IV: Stop recreational vehicle as it enters campground, explain to driver the purpose of the study, ask the driver to participate in study. When survey of recreational vehicle is complete, discuss the findings with the driver.

The leader's responsibilities would be to plan daily work activities, motivate the employees to do the surveying, complete all forms, and do occasional troubleshooting.

With job descriptions in hand, Getz met with Norm Larson, vice president of Liberty Engineering Company, who was ultimately responsible for conducting the recreational vehicle surveys. During the meeting, Getz learned that all 30 employees were to meet at Smoky Mountains National Park on June 10. They were to be trained on the job for four days, and the company would provide them with lodging and food while they were there. All employees were to provide their own transportation to the park, to their subsequent job sites, and then back home. The company would pay them for travel time but would not provide any mileage allowance, lodging, or food. Upon arrival at the job site, employees would need to find accommodations for July and August, and would receive no lodging or food allowance from the company during their stay. Once work commenced at each job site, employees would be responsible for providing their own transportation to and from the campground.

All employees were to be paid $11.15 per hour. No vacation benefits, sick days, or other major benefits would be provided. The company would, however, provide benefits mandated by law such as Social Security and workers' compensation. No one under the age of 18 would be hired because of safety reasons.

After the meeting with Larson, Getz decided he should check with the campground management at the different job sites. He learned that most recreational vehicles leave campgrounds early in the morning and enter late in the afternoon. Few arrive or depart between 10 AM and 4 PM. In order to survey a maximum number of vehicles, crews would need to work from 6 AM to 11 AM and from 3 PM to 8 PM, a total of ten hours a day. Therefore, each crew could work a four-day-on and a four-day-off schedule. Getz was told that temperatures at Cape Hatteras would range between 65 and 95 degrees Fahrenheit, while at Lake Mead they would range between 85 and 115 degrees Fahrenheit. Neither of these locations would provide employees with any shade; hence, employees at these sites would need to work in the sun and wear uniforms, including hats. The Smoky Mountains National Park location would be cooler than the others and surveying could be done in shaded areas. When Getz asked the campground managers whether they knew of any people who would be interested in working on the survey project, their response was, "You've got to be kidding." The manager at Lake Mead campground flatly told Getz that he could not conceive of any person being willing to drive from Lake Mead to Tennessee and back under the conditions he outlined. He suggested that Getz put a want ad in the Cleveland newspaper.

After talking with the campground managers, Getz was quite depressed. He knew that he had to hire 30 employees within the next few weeks. He knew that six of them had to have sufficient leadership skills to get the job done while not antagonizing the employees so much that they would quit. He further realized that the 24 surveyors would have to enjoy the outdoors and be willing to tolerate extreme heat. He realized, too, that the ideal surveyor would be one who had above-average knowledge of auto mechanics, legible handwriting, reasonable communication skills, and an ability to work well with others under adverse conditions. What Getz did not know was how he could recruit and hire 30 people who fit this description.

QUESTIONS

1. If you were Bob Getz, how would you recruit the needed employees?

2. Evaluate the Lake Mead campground manager's suggestion that Getz recruit employees by placing a want ad in the Cleveland newspaper.

3. What should the firm do if they are unable to recruit sufficient employees for the job?

Recruiting and Selecting High-Level Managers through the Internet

Michael Jackson is the president and CEO of a small hotel corporation (Jackson Hotels, Inc.) which caters to high-end vacationers in resort communities. The company currently employs 2,144 staff members at its corporate headquarters in Palm Springs, CA and its other hotels in Scottsdale, AZ; Aspen, CO; Orlando, FL; Santa Fe, NM; Sea Island, GA; and Charleston, SC. Recently, the company underwent a strategic planning process. The plan envisions adding ten new locations and tripling its workforce over the next five years. The human resource challenge is to recruit experienced and high-quality managers for its corporate headquarters, recruit managers for new hotels, and manage existing and expansion hotels in a variety of managerial roles.

Up to the present, Jackson has relied on his contacts in the hotel industry to recommend candidates for these positions. Some have been hired and some have not, and many of those hired have not performed as well as Jackson had hoped and expected. During an informal discussion with Carol Cross, one of his hotel managers, Cross suggested most of the larger hotel chains now recruit their managers and other professionals through the Internet. She suggested that Internet recruitment might enhance both the quantity and quality of the applicant pool.

Jackson then asked his vice president of human resources, Shirley Gomez, to research online recruiting and make recommendations to him. She reported the following:

- Finding qualified and motivated employees was one of the top three business worries among small companies like his own.

- Almost all large companies and many small companies now provide online recruiting and some only accept online applications.

- Almost all applicants for professional and managerial positions now use the Internet.

- Another trend is the use of online prescreening tools to separate the qualified applicants from the unqualified.

- Some hotel chains are now tapping into skilled foreign labor through the Internet.

- There are more than 2,500 Web sites that contain job postings and among the most prominent generic Web sites are:

  http://www.monster.com
  http://www.careerpaths.com
  http://www.careerbuilder.com
  http://www.careermosaic.com
  http://www.hotjobs.com
  http://www.flipdog.com
  http://www.jobtrak.com
  http://www.spherion.com

- The latest generation of Web tools includes online job fairs in which companies can meet candidates in a virtual environment and can chat with them online.

- All approaches to online recruitment and selection seem to be cost effective relative to alternatives.

- The three main approaches to Internet recruiting are job boards (like the Web sites above), professional/career Web sites, which focus on particular occupations and professions, and employer Web sites.

Gomez has asked your professor of Human Resources Management (Dr. Martin Cannon) to help her formulate recommendations for Jackson. Dr. Cannon has asked your class to meet in small groups of two to four students each to address her questions and report to the class. These questions are outlined below.

QUESTIONS

1. What are the advantages and disadvantages of Internet recruitment and selection for a small, but expanding company like Jackson Hotels? How would you minimize the disadvantages?

2. Which of the above three approaches to online recruiting and selection (if any) makes the most sense in this case and why?

3. What prescreening hurdles would you impose in your Internet recruitment in order to pre-qualify a small number of truly qualified applicants? Why?

4. Based on your knowledge of other companies' Web sites, what information should Jackson Hotels provide to job applicants and what steps should follow Internet recruitment to identify the most qualified applicants?

36 CASE

Recruiting and Selecting Low-Level Workers among Seniors

Jackson Hotels, described previously in Case 35, also has a challenge in recruiting and selecting lower-level employees in their resort hotels for such jobs as desk clerk, night manager, reservations, maid service, food service, and maintenance. In many cases, the labor pool of qualified candidates found in larger cities is simply not available or adequate in or near resort communities.

Shirely Gomez, vice president for human resources, has determined that senior citizens might be the best recruitment option for Jackson Hotels given the high-income customers the hotel chain seeks to serve. Her rationale is they have a vast amount of experience, lower accident rates, lower absentee rates, and higher job satisfaction scores than younger workers. As a result of changing attitudes of both employers and employees as well as the increasing availability of seniors in resort areas, she noted that many other companies have begun to target seniors for recruitment. These organizations realize seniors usually have proven employment experience, job savvy, reliability, interpersonal skills, and commitment to the employer. She believes these qualities are important determinants of success in the hotel jobs she hopes to fill in the future. She is also aware that many seniors gravitate toward independent contracting, on-call work, and temporary assignments rather than full-time employment.

Gomez is concerned that some hotel chains have been successfully sued for failure to do adequate background checks on all new employees. In some cases, this failure resulted in the theft of personal property or worse. Consequently, she is aware that whatever processes of recruitment and selection she initiates will need to incorporate some type of background investigation. Up to the present, she has relied on local newspaper advertisements and applicant interviews with hotel managers to recruit and screen applicants. Results have been unsatisfactory thus far due to high turnover and mixed performance among the newly hired employees. She expects present recruitment approaches to be even more inadequate as the hotel chain expands over the next five years. She has asked your professor, Dr. Martin Cannon, to help her focus her recruitment and selection strategies for the years ahead. More specifically, she has asked him to help her answer the questions below. Dr. Cannon, in turn, has asked your class to form groups of two to four students each to discuss these questions and report to the class.

QUESTIONS

1. What recruitment sources do you recommend Jackson Hotels use to recruit seniors for the kinds of positions they are planning to utilize? Why?

2. What background investigations, if any, would you recommend to differentiate acceptable from unacceptable job candidates? Why?

3. What selection criteria and processes would you recommend to identify the best candidates? Why?

Selecting Patient Escorts

City Hospital is located in the heart of a large midwestern city. It is one of five major hospitals in the area and has recently built a small addition for treating well-known patients, such as professional football players, top company executives, and singing stars. Visiting or local celebrities always choose City Hospital if they need treatment.

City Hospital has about 1,200 hospital beds and employs 4,500 individuals, including about 40 patient escorts. The job of patient escort is a rather simple one, requiring only minimal training and no special physical talents. When patients need to be moved from one location to another, patient escorts are summoned to assist in the move. If the move is only a short distance, however, a nurse or orderly can move the patient. Of particular importance is the fact that patient escorts almost always take patients who are being discharged from their hospital room to the front door of the hospital. A wheelchair is always used, even if the patient is able to walk unassisted. Thus, the typical procedure is for the nurse to call for a patient escort. The escort then gets a wheelchair and goes to the patient's room, assists the patient into the wheelchair, picks up the patient's belongings, wheels the patient down to the hospital's front door or to his or her car in the parking lot, and returns to the work station.

The job of patient escort is critical to the hospital since the escort is always the last hospital representative the patient sees, and hence has a considerable influence on the patient's final perception of the hospital. Of approximately 40 escorts, about three-fourths are men and one-fourth are women. Most are high school graduates in their early twenties. Some, particularly those on the early morning shift, are attending college at night and working for the hospital to earn money to pay college expenses. Four of the escorts are older women who had previously served as hospital volunteers and then decided to become full-time employees instead. Turnover among patient escorts is quite high and has averaged 25 percent in recent years. In addition, upward mobility in the hospital is quite good, and as a result, another 25 percent of the escorts typically transfer to other jobs in the hospital each year. Thus, about half of the patient escorts need to be replaced annually.

The hospital follows a standard procedure when hiring patient escorts. When a vacancy occurs, the human resource department reviews the file of applications of individuals who have applied for the patient escort job. Usually the file contains at least 20 applications because the pay for the job is good, the work is undemanding, and few skills are required. The top two or three applicants are asked to come to the hospital for interviews. Typically, the applicants are interviewed first by the human resource department and then by the patient escort supervisor. The majority of those interviewed know some other employees of the hospital, so the only reference check is a call to these employees. Before being hired, applicants are required to take physical exams given by hospital doctors.

Every new escort attends an orientation program the first day on the job. This is conducted by a member of the hospital's human resource department. The program consists of a complete tour of the hospital; a review of all the hospital's HR policies, including a description of its promotion, compensation, and disciplinary policies; and a presentation of the hospital's mission and philosophy. During this orientation session, employees are told that the hospital's image in the community is of major importance and that all employees should strive to maintain and enhance this image through their conduct. After orientation, all patient escorts receive on-the-job training by their immediate supervisor.

During the last two years, the hospital has experienced a number of problems with patient escorts, which have had an adverse effect on the hospital's image. Several patients have complained to the hospital administration that they were treated rudely, or in some cases roughly, by one or more patient escorts. Some complained that they were ordered around or scolded by an escort during the discharge process. Others stated that their escorts were careless when wheeling them out of the hospital to their cars. One person reported that an escort carelessly tipped him over. All escorts are required to wear identification tags, but patients usually cannot remember the escort's name when lodging a complaint to the hospital. Additionally, the hospital usually has difficulty determining which escort served which patient because escorts often trade patients. Finally, even when the hospital can identify the offending escort, the employee can easily deny any wrongdoing. He or she often counters that patients are generally irritable as a result of their illness and, hence, are prone to complain at even the slightest provocation.

At the hospital administrator's request, the human resource manager asked the chief supervisor of patient escorts, the head of the staffing section within the human resource department, and the assistant human resource director to meet with her to review the entire procedure used to select patient escorts. It was hoped that a new procedure could be devised that would eliminate the hiring of rude, insulting, or careless patient escorts.

During the meeting, a number of suggestions were made as to how the selection procedure might be improved. Criticisms of the present system were also voiced. The chief supervisor of patient escorts argued that the problem with the hospital's present system is that the application form is void of any useful information. He stated that the questions that really give insights into the employee's personality are no longer on the application form. He suggested that applicants be asked about their hobbies, outside activities, and their personal likes and dislikes on the application form. He also suggested that each applicant be asked to submit three letters of recommendation from people who know the applicant well. He wanted these letters to focus on the prospective employee's personality, particularly the applicant's ability to remain friendly and polite at all times.

The assistant human resource director contended that the hospital's interviewing procedure should be modified. He observed that, during the typical interview, little attempt is made to determine how the applicant reacts under stress. He suggested that if applicants were asked four or five stress-producing questions, the hospital might be in a better position to judge their ability to work with irritable patients.

The head of the staffing section noted that patient escorts require little mental or physical talent and agreed that the crucial attribute escorts need is the ability to always be courteous and polite. He wondered whether an attitude test could be developed that would measure the applicant's predisposition toward being friendly, helpful, sensitive, and so on. He suggested that a job analysis could be done on the patient escort position to determine those attitudes that are critical to being a successful patient escort. When the job analysis was complete, questions could be developed that would measure these critical attributes. The test questions could be given to the hospital's present patient escorts to determine whether the test accurately distinguishes the best escorts from the worst. The head of the staffing section realized that many of the questions might need to be eliminated or changed, and if the test appeared to show promise, it would probably need to be revalidated in order to meet government requirements. He felt, however, that a well-designed test might be worth the effort and should at least be considered.

The meeting ended with all four participants agreeing that the suggestion of trying to develop an attitude test was probably the most promising. The assistant human resource director and chief supervisor of patient escorts stated that they would conduct a thorough job analysis covering the patient escort position and develop a list of attitudes that are critical to its success. A second meeting would then be scheduled to prepare the actual test questions.

QUESTIONS

1. Critique each of the alternative approaches suggested for solving the problem of selecting patient escorts at City Hospital.

2. Recommend a procedure for recruiting and hiring patient escorts.

3. Besides improving its selection procedures, what other actions could the hospital potentially take to improve the behavior of the patient escorts?

38 CASE

A Solution for Adverse Impact

A federal government agency was in need of assistance regarding its staffing practices. Recently, some of the job applicants had complained that the selection procedures for one of the entry-level law enforcement jobs were discriminatory. The personnel specialists, who had previously ignored this possibility, were now alerted to the potential problem of adverse impact against women and minorities.

Bob Santos was a personnel specialist for the agency and had been employed with the staffing division for almost three years. He kept up with the laws and regulations on discrimination and equal employment opportunity. About two months ago, he attended a training seminar on the Uniform Guidelines on Employee Selection Procedures. Upon returning to the agency, Santos decided that an evaluation of their current staffing practices was necessary because they were developed prior to the adoption of the Uniform Guidelines in 1978. These Guidelines were designed to provide a framework for determining the proper use of selection procedures. They indicated how organizations should evaluate their selection rates using the four-fifths rule, and also specified the standards that organizations should use to validate their procedures.

THE SELECTION PROCESS

The selection of entry-level agents for the law enforcement job involved a two-step, multiple-hurdle process. Applicants were first required to pass a cognitive ability test, a similar but somewhat easier test than the Scholastic Aptitude Test (SAT). The exam was made up of 25 verbal items and 25 quantitative items. A candidate was required to receive a passing score of 70 (35 of the items correct) in order to be eligible for the second step of the selection process, an interview. A three-member panel of supervisors asked each applicant questions on how they would deal with various hypothetical job situations. After an initial period of questions regarding the applicant's education and experience, the applicant was given a situation and then asked to respond to the situation. Typically, after each candidate's initial response, further questioning would ensue from the panel to determine the full response of the candidate. The interview would last about a half hour. At the end of the interview, the three interviewers would rate the candidate on ten dimensions, including attitude, motivation, communication, and so on. Candidates receiving high scores on most of the dimensions would pass the interview. After a physical examination and a security check, the candidate would be hired and asked to report to training.

THE DETERMINATION OF ADVERSE IMPACT

Santos knew that the guidelines required employers to make adverse impact determinations at least once a year. Although records had been kept, the agency had not calculated the selection rates over the past three years. Santos thought that it was long overdue and decided to have this done as soon as possible. A week later, the selection rates were tabulated. The data are presented in Exhibit 2.7.

After calculating the adverse impact for both the test and the interview, he decided that a discussion with the personnel psychologist in the agency would be necessary. A meeting was arranged between Santos, his supervisor and head of the staffing division, and the personnel

This case was prepared by Ronald J. Karren, Isenberg School of Management, University of Massachusetts.

EXHIBIT 2.7 *Tabulation of Selection Rates*

	Pass Rates for the Test		
Group	Number Who Took Test	Number Who Passed	Pass Rate %
Whites	282	134	47.5
Blacks	36	10	27.8
Hispanics	102	44	43.1
Asians	0	0	0
Native Americans	0	0	0
Men	385	170	44.2
Women	35	18	51.4
Total	420	188	44.8

	Pass Rates for the Interview		
Group	Number Who Interviewed	Number Who Passed	Pass Rate %
Whites	112	87	77.7
Blacks	8	5	62.5
Hispanics	40	22	55.0
Men	148	109	73.6
Women	12	5	41.7
Total	160	114	71.2

Note: The number interviewed for each group is less than the number who passed the test. The difference represents individuals who did not wish to continue through the second part of the selection process.

psychologist for the agency, Ron Burden. A discussion ensued regarding the validation requirements of the Uniform Guidelines. It was decided that the original job analysis was poorly done and that very little documentation had been retained by the agency. Although there was a task inventory, the major tasks or job duties had not been rated for importance, frequency, difficulty, and trainability. Burden pointed out that this documentation would be critical if they ever needed to defend the selection procedures in court. By the end of the meeting, the group decided that it would probably be a good idea to do another job analysis that was in accordance with the new Uniform Guidelines. Burden felt that the selection procedures would have to be modified to fit the results of the job analysis. He was asked to determine how the job analysis would be done, while Santos would coordinate the project in the field.

JOB ANALYSIS

The Uniform Guidelines recognize that there is not a single best way to analyze the job. Since there was little documentation available, Ron Burden had to decide on a method or technique that would generate from the agents and supervisors the important work responsibilities and the tasks associated with them. After much deliberation, he decided to use the critical-incident technique. Burden knew that if the agency wanted to continue using situational questions in the interview, the critical-incident job analysis technique readily lends itself to the development of this type of question. The method involves collecting reports of behaviors that are critical, in that they distinguished between successful and unsuccessful work performance. Instructions to the agents and supervisors were to include

1) the circumstances that preceded the incident, 2) the setting in which the incident occurred, 3) what the agent did that was effective or ineffective, and 4) the consequences of the incident.

Burden asked a sample of agents to develop three critical incidents and to indicate the task associated with each critical incident. Upon receipt of the critical incidents, Burden and Santos derived an inventory of work behaviors. This list of work behaviors was then sent back to the agents, and they were asked to rate the importance of the behavior, how frequently it was performed, and the amount of training that was required to learn that behavior.

When this information was collected, Burden and Santos generated a list of major job tasks or job duties. They assigned all the important work behaviors to their associated tasks. This list of tasks and work behaviors was then sent out to a group of supervisors who were asked to review the list. This same group of supervisors were also asked to meet for a two-day conference later in the month to determine the important knowledge, skills, abilities, and other characteristics (KSAOs) required to perform these work behaviors. Burden also planned for these experts to select the critical incidents to be used for the new interview.

SUPERVISORY CONFERENCE

At the conference, the supervisors were given the inventory of tasks and their corresponding work behaviors. They were asked to derive the KSAOs and then rate how important the skill or ability was for the performance of the work behaviors. The most important knowledge, skills, abilities, and other characteristics are shown in Exhibit 2.8.

The job experts were asked to evaluate the current staffing practices in light of this list of KSAOs. Burden, Santos, and the supervisors agreed that the content of the exam would have to be changed to reflect the first three KSAOs. Burden proposed a reading comprehension exam in which the content would be a small sample of the procedures, laws, and regulations that are taught at the training academy. Applicants would read a section and then answer questions regarding the laws and regulations taught in that section. This type of test has been called a "miniature training and evaluation test." All the parties agreed that this job-related procedure would be a good way of assessing the first three KSAOs.

The job experts wanted to retain the interview. Burden and Santos agreed as long as the following conditions were met:

1. All interview questions would have to be job-related.

2. Critical incidents from the job analysis would be selected to assess the last five KSAOs.

3. Sample answers to each critical incident would be determined in advance. Interviewee responses would be rated on a five-point scale defined explicitly in advance.

EXHIBIT 2.8 *KSAOs Derived from the Task/Behavior Inventory*

1. Knowledge of federal law
2. Knowledge of procedures and regulations
3. Reading and verbal comprehension
4. Ability to perform effectively in dangerous situations
5. Ability to communicate effectively
6. Skill in interpersonal relations
7. Judgment ability
8. Ability to solve problems quickly and effectively

4. The same scoring method would be used for each applicant. All procedures would be used consistently for each applicant so that all applicants had the same chance of being selected.

5. All interviewers would be required to attend a training session to learn how to administer and assess the structured interview.

The supervisors agreed to these conditions. However, they did not want the interview to be completely structured. They felt that the interview should begin with a few questions regarding the applicant's past education and experience. Burden and Santos agreed to this with the stipulation that this information should not bias the candidate's assessment and scoring at the end of the interview.

When Burden and Santos returned to the agency, they were happy about what had transpired at the supervisory conference. The question that remained was the type of validation to be used on the newly developed selection procedures. Burden felt that they should validate the selection procedures with a criterion-related validity strategy. They would collect the scores for both the interview and the test and later compare them to either success in training or their performance appraisal at the end of the first year. Since Burden was familiar with these procedures, he felt that this was a preferred strategy over a content validity strategy. On the other hand, Santos felt that a predictive validity study was too costly and unnecessary. Since their newly developed procedures were job-related, a content validity approach was sufficient. Instead of arguing over which type of validation strategy to use, they decided to discuss the matter with Santos's supervisor and meet again later in the week.

QUESTIONS

1. Is there any evidence of adverse impact against any race, sex, or ethnic groups?

2. If the total selection process for a job has no adverse impact, should the individual components of the selection process be evaluated for adverse impact?

3. Which type of validation would you use? Why? What are the differences between content and criterion-related validity studies?

4. Evaluate the job analysis procedures used in this case. Is it necessary to do such a thorough analysis?

5. If you are doing a criterion-related validity study, should your criterion be success in training or on-the-job performance?

The Use of Social Media for Employee Recruitment and Selection

Karen Johnston is a 55-year-old director of a small health planning agency in an urban area of the South. Her agency employs a total of 18 staff members, most of whom are female. As a graduate of the MBA program with a Healthcare concentration, she has been an active alumnus of that program at the local state university. She also serves as chairperson of the Community Advisory Board (CAB) for the program and has taken two student interns a year for her agency over the past eight years. The CAB advises the program faculty concerning curriculum, accreditation issues, internships, job placements, scholarships, etc.

Recently, Johnston was asked by the program's internship director to select one master's student intern for the upcoming fall semester and she agreed to do so. He then forwarded to her the resumes of three students for her consideration as he had done in the past. Previously, she had considered grade point average, previous work experience, and career goals in making her decision concerning who to interview and who to select for the internship.

This time she decided to also see if any of the internship candidates had posted profiles on social media Web sites such as Facebook, Twitter, or LinkedIn. To her surprise, all three (one male and two females) had posted profiles on at least one of these social media Web sites. Two of the three posted information regarding their student extracurricular activities, work activities, family, and friends. Karen found those to be helpful in helping her form a more complete picture of the internship applicant. However, the third profile posted on Facebook by one of the female applicants shocked her. She found semi-nude pictures, allusions to heavy drinking, and a comment that Lisa "was looking for a hot guy to bring out my wild side."

Johnston immediately called the internship coordinator and told him that she would like to interview the first two students and would select one for the internship. However, she told him that the third applicant should never have been allowed into the masters program and that he needed to have a long "heart-to-heart" talk with her if she was to have a future in the field of health services administration. She also suggested that this student might be counseled to seek employment in another field altogether. Then when the CAB met, Johnston described her experience to the faculty and executive board members. When the program director explained that faculty have little control over the personal lives of students, Johnston suggested that perhaps they need to counsel students concerning "professional behavior."

QUESTIONS

1. What lessons can you draw from this case regarding how students, employers, and faculty can use social media such as Facebook during the recruitment and selection process?

2. What policies, if any, should employers develop concerning the use of social media for various purposes, including employee recruitment and selection?

EXERCISE

▬▬▬▬▬ *Evaluating the Recruiting Function*

I. OBJECTIVES

   A. To make you aware of the necessity of evaluating the efficiency and effectiveness of various recruitment sources.

   B. To provide you with practice analyzing data, drawing conclusions, and planning a strategy to remedy identified problems or deficiencies.

   C. To make you aware of the linkages among staff turnover, recruitment sources, recruitment methods, and adequate staffing.

II. OUT-OF-CLASS PREPARATION TIME: 2 hours

III. IN-CLASS TIME SUGGESTED: 45 minutes

IV. PROCEDURES

   Read the entire exercise, including the background on St. Vincent's Hospital. Then, using the data provided in Exhibit 2.9, do the calculations on Form 2.5. A yield ratio is the number of applicants necessary to fill vacancies with qualified people. It is the relationship of applicant inputs to outputs at various decision points. For example, the yield ratio for all recruitment sources in Exhibit 2.9 shows that 273 nurse applicants were generated over the three-year period from 2007 to 2009. Since only 221 were classified as potentially qualified, the yield ratio is 273/221 or 1.24 to 1. The yield ratio for "potentially qualified" among "walk-ins" is 1.26 (53 ÷ 42). The average cost per nurse hired among "walk-ins" is $119.23 ($1,550 ÷ 13). Students should form groups of two to four students each and calculate the yield ratios for each recruitment source at each stage of the recruitment process on Form 2.5. These data show that the hospital needs to start with more than five times as many applicants as it needs to fill job openings and more than 13 times as many applicants as it hopes to have as above-average performers.

   Do the calculations for Form 2.5 on your own prior to class. Think about the implications of these data for future recruitment at the hospital. Then, look at Exhibit 2.10 in conjunction with the background description and think about the implications for the recruiting process. During the class period, form groups of three to five, which will act as a consulting team for the hospital. With your group, discuss and answer the questions at the end of this exercise. At the end of the class period, have a spokesperson for each group discuss the group's answers and rationale with the entire class.

BACKGROUND

   St. Vincent's Hospital is a 260-bed hospital in a northeastern city affiliated with the Roman Catholic Church. The administrator is Sister Claire, a 56-year-old member of the Daughters of Charity religious order. During the last decade, the hospital operated with a nursing staff of approximately 450 registered nurses and experienced a nursing turnover rate of about 25 percent per year. The turnover rate was average for the city during this time period. However, it has accelerated to an average of 35 percent over the past three years.

   These higher turnover rates have put additional pressure on the recruiting process to provide larger numbers of qualified candidates. However, Sam Barnett, director of human resources, has reported more difficulty locating qualified nurse candidates over the last three years. Barnett's office has prepared the recruitment data shown in Exhibit 2.9. The data show that 273 applicants (from all sources) had to be screened to produce 52 qualified candidates who accepted a job offer. One year later, 19 of these 52 had left the hospital. The last column shows the direct and indirect costs of recruitment by source, including clerical time, supervisor time, and direct costs, such as travel and postage. The human resource department has also conducted a telephone survey of all the nurses they could locate who did not accept a job offer from the hospital during the most recent three-year period. Reasons for such rejections are shown in Exhibit 2.10.

Sister Mary Louise, the 62-year-old director of nursing service, has conducted all off-site recruitment for many years. This includes attending both the local Nursing Job Fair and the State Nursing Association Annual Meeting. She has begun to feel burned out as a result of all her external recruiting and internal evaluation of candidates over the years.

At a recent meeting, she suggested that an outside group (your group) be brought in to analyze the recruiting process, identify problems and opportunities, and suggest improvements. Sister Mary Louise and Barnett readily agreed to an outside consultant because they are aware of current nursing shortages due to declining nursing school enrollments. St. Vincent's Hospital itself contributed to this enrollment decline by closing its own School of Nursing due to fewer applications and the high cost of operation.

EXHIBIT 2.9 *Data on Recruitment Sources for Registered Nurses at St. Vincent's Hospital, 2007–2009*

Recruitment Source	Number of Applicants	Potentially Qualified	Invitation for Interview	Qualified and Offered Job	Accepted Job	One-Year Survival	Above-Average Rating	Total Recruitment Costs
1. Internet applications	83	72	60	38	21	12	5	$1,145
2. Walk-ins	34	17	8	6	3	1	1	900
3. Employee referrals	13	12	7	5	4	3	2	400
4. Newspaper ads	24	16	8	4	2	1	0	750
5. Journal ads	19	18	10	8	4	2	2	450
6. Educational institutions								
Junior colleges	16	13	11	6	2	2	1	1,200
Hospital-based schools	8	8	3	2	1	0	0	800
University programs	24	24	16	14	10	8	7	1,300
7. Private employment agency	9	9	8	5	2	2	1	4,000
8. Public employment agency	8	4	2	1	1	0	0	600
9. Direct mail	15	14	4	3	1	0	0	450
10. Job fair	13	7	5	3	1	1	1	900
11. State Nursing Association meeting	7	7	4	3	0	0	0	1,150
Totals	273	221	146	98	52	33	20	$14,045

FORM 2.5 *Yield Ratios at Each Step in the Recruitment Process and Recruitment Cost per Nurse Hired, St. Vincent's Hospital, 2007–2009*

Recruitment Sources	Yield Rates						Average Cost Per Nurse Hired
	Potentially Qualified	Accepted Interview	Offered Job	Accepted Job	One-Year Survival	Above-Average Rating	
1. Internet applications							
2. Walk-ins							
3. Employee referrals							
4. Newspaper ads							
5. Journal ads							
6. Educational institutions							
Junior colleges							
Hospital-based schools							
University programs							
7. Private employment agency							
8. Public employment agency							
9. Direct mail							
10. Job fair							
11. State Nursing Association meeting							
Averages for all sources	1.24	1.87	2.79	5.25	8.27	13.65	

Reason	Number	Percent
Recruitment Processes		
Job attributes not communicated	2	4.3
Negative perception of recruiter	12	26.1
Negative perception of hospital	2	4.3
Lack of timely follow-up	13	28.3
Perceived lack of honesty in recruitment process	1	2.2
Negative information from recruiter	1	2.2
Job Attributes		
Location of hospital	3	6.5
Salary offer	2	4.3
Hours of work	2	4.3
Promotional opportunities	0	0.0
Fringe benefits	0	0.0
Working conditions	3	6.5
Perceived poor job "match"	5	10.9
Totals	46	100.0

Since recruitment of new nurses has begun to fall behind turnover of nurses employed at St. Vincent's Hospital, the vacancy rate has begun to increase. Five years ago, only 11 percent of staff nursing positions were unfilled. This percentage has now increased to 23 percent. One result has been an exhausting workload on the existing nursing staff. In addition to increased turnover, the symptoms of staff burnout (i.e., stress, conflict, absenteeism) are becoming more evident.

QUESTIONS

1. How would you evaluate the nurse recruiting strategy currently being used by St. Vincent's Hospital? Is the hospital using too few or too many recruiting sources? Why?

2. If you feel that the hospital is using too many recruitment sources, which ones would you eliminate and why?

3. What stage or stages in the recruitment process seem to be most amenable to improvements? What specific improvements would you suggest to decrease the yield ratios? Why?

41   EXERCISE

Selection Decisions

I. OBJECTIVES

A. To make you aware of the complex criteria often used to select candidates for administrative positions.

B. To help you develop skills in planning and implementing semi-structured interviews.

C. To give you practice in preparing for, participating in, or evaluating the selection interview.

II. OUT-OF-CLASS PREPARATION TIME: 2 hours

III. IN-CLASS TIME SUGGESTED: 45 minutes

IV. PROCEDURES

A. Read the entire exercise including the "Background," "Questions for the Semi-structured Interview," and the various forms. During the previous class period, the instructor should have selected eight students in the class to prepare for two in-class interviews in the following class period. The eight consists of four executive committee members, two applicants, and two observers (one for each interview). These eight will role play interviews of the two applicants or act as an observer for each interview.

B. Prior to class, the six interviewers or interviewees should prepare for their respective roles in the role playing exercise. Committee members should fill in the first two columns of Form 2.6 and the interviewer questions on Form 2.7 in pencil or on a separate sheet of paper. This will facilitate committee discussion, reduce the amount of class time needed for interview preparation, and save the forms themselves for the final list of criteria (Form 2.8) and interview questions (Form 2.7). Committee members should be prepared to play their roles (Form 2.7) as they would expect the described individuals to behave in real life. The observer for each group interview (two in total) read Form 2.8 in advance. Then, he or she should fill it out during the interview and be prepared to discuss it at the end of the class period.

The two applicants in each group should review their résumés in either Exhibit 2.11 or Exhibit 2.12 and be prepared to elaborate on any of the data in the résumé, as well as to provide supplementary information not on the résumé to the committee. An alternative to using two class members as job applicants is to use two individuals from outside the class.

C. During the class period, the four person interview committee should spend 10 to 15 minutes comparing notes and designing a final set of criteria and weighting system for Form 2.6 and interview questions for Form 2.7.

Neither the applicants nor the observers should be present during these discussions. When the committee is ready, the applicants should be called from outside the room one at a time. In the meantime, the applicants should be doing final preparations for their interviews, including consideration of how they will respond to hypothetical questions that may be asked.

Possible selection criteria the committee may want to consider are: previous experience as a hospital CEO, educational background, ability to "fit" into the organization in terms of personal views and goals, knowledge of Brookdale Hospital and its problems, ideas for solving the hospital's problems, interpersonal skills, communication skills, and administrative skills.

D. Each candidate is then interviewed for 10 to 15 minutes. After each interview, board members fill out the remainder of Form 2.6 including the rating of each candidate on each criterion, the total score for each, and any additional comments. The observer will take notes and make an evaluation on Form 2.8 during the interviews. At the conclusion of the two interviews, the committee will compare notes and make a decision concerning which candidate should be recommended for the position and why.

E. When the committee has finished the interview and assessment process, the instructor will ask each the committee and observers to report to the entire class in the following order: the committee decision and rationale, the performance of the two applicants, and each observer's report. Lessons learned concerning the selection interview process are then presented by both interviewers and interviewees. Depending on class size, this "wrap-up" phase should take 10 to 15 minutes.

BACKGROUND

Brookdale Hospital is a 420-bed proprietary (for-profit) hospital located in a large midwestern city. The hospital was originally founded by a group of local physicians in 1948. In 1982, they sold out to one of the national hospital chains and are now part of a large system of hospitals involving 49 hospitals with about 12,000 beds in 18 states (mostly in the Midwest). The corporation follows a policy of decentralization. Consequently, while corporate support services have been provided, the hospital has continued to operate with a great deal of autonomy.

Recently, the hospital has begun to experience declines in occupancy rates and increased annual deficits. John Rhodes has been the CEO for the past eight years. Two months ago, he suffered a stroke and, at the advice of his physician, has decided to retire at age 55. The board of trustees has appointed the associate administrator, Terry Bradford, as the acting administrator and CEO while a search for Rhodes's replacement is made. The executive committee of the board has advertised the position widely over the past six weeks in a variety of professional publications, including *The Wall Street Journal*.

As a result of the résumés generated through this recruitment process, the board has selected the two top candidates for the position: Terry Bradford and Chris Smith, an administrator of a small 60-bed hospital in a nearby city. Résumés for each are shown in Exhibits 2.11 and 2.12. The committee has also developed a job description for the position as shown in Exhibit 2.13.

The process for hiring a new CEO requires a formal vote by the entire board as well as concurrence by the president of the corporation. However, the latter two steps have always been formalities. The critical decision is the recommendation of the executive committee. This committee consists of the following four individuals: Sam Gordon, Amanda Simpson, Steve Bailey, and Jane Sears.

Gordon is a physician and the chief of the medical staff (salaried position), and has been with the hospital for 13 years. He is 58 years old and has a specialty in general surgery. He has been concerned about what he views as the eroding power of physicians' vis-à-vis administrators and outside regulators over the past few years. Consequently, he would like the

EXHIBIT 2.11 *Résumé 1*

TERRY A. BRADFORD
119 Brook Hollow Lane
Columbus, Ohio

Job Objective
To secure a position as chief executive officer for a large proprietary hospital in the Midwest.

Education

1982–1986:	Oberlin College, Oberlin, Ohio
	Major: Sociology
	Degree: BA, June 1986, *cum laude*, GPA 3.52
1992–1993:	Ohio State University, Columbus, Ohio
	Major: Business Administration
	Emphasis: Organization Behavior
	Degree: MBA, June 1993, GPA 3.86
	Member: Beta Gamma Sigma (national scholastic honorary in Business)
Other:	After completing my MBA, I took two additional graduate courses in accounting and one additional course in finance at Ohio State University.

Employment History

November 2006–Present:	Acting Administrator, Brookdale Hospital, Columbus, Ohio
February 1995–November 2006:	Associate Administrator; Brookdale Hospital, Columbus, Ohio Duties: liaison between the CEO and the medical staff, nursing staff, and other major hospital departments; represents administrator at various functions; strategic planning and marketing; reviews financial and occupancy data.
June 1988–February 1995:	Assistant Administrator; Oakland Hospital, Oakland, Ohio Duties: worked with the Administrator and Associate Administrator on a variety of administrative functions in finance, personnel, marketing, and public relations.
August 1986–June 1988:	Personnel Assistant; Bayview Municipal Hospital, Bayview,Ohio Duties: designed personnel appraisal form, conducted selection interviews, designed and taught courses for supervisors, and designed advertisements for positions.

Personal

Date of Birth:	September 6, 1964
Height:	5'8"; Weight: 150 lbs.
Marital Status:	Divorced, no children
Hobbies:	Music, travel, and swimming

committee to recommend someone who can work well with physicians, understand their needs, and generally support their desires to provide high-quality patient care.

Simpson is president of the city council and was selected for both the board and the executive committee because of her political contacts. Her goals are to make sure the hospital survives, keeps its costs under control, and continues to provide some care for indigents. Since Brookdale is one of the major hospitals in the city serving her constituents, Simpson naturally is concerned that the corporation may shut its doors due to the deficits it has been experiencing. She feels the hospital has to be more innovative in developing and marketing new services to offset the declines in inpatient services.

EXHIBIT 2.12 *Résumé 2*

CHRIS A. SMITH

Home Address	**Office Address**
2057 Hickory Street	Administrator
Tiffin, Ohio	Morningside Hospital
	204 Jefferson Street
	Tiffin, Ohio

Personal: Married, two children

Educational Background:
BS—Heidelberg College, Tiffin, Ohio (1987)
MBA—Cleveland State University, Cleveland, Ohio (1992)

Experience:

Morningside Hospital, Tiffin, Ohio	November 1991–Present
Administrator	June 2006–Present
Associate Administrator	June 1998–June 2006
Assistant Administrator	November 1991–June 1998
Eastside Hospital Financial Manager, Tiffin, Ohio	June 1988–November 1991
McLains Department Store Financial Manager, Tiffin, Ohio	January 1987–June 1988

Member: Rotary Club and First Baptist Church

Interests: Snow skiing and politics

Bailey is president and CEO of Applied Electronics, a very successful company that he founded 18 years ago. He admits he still does not know much about health care, but has been a member of the board for 12 years due to his entrepreneurial talents and his business contacts. His view is that the hospital needs to become more entrepreneurial and businesslike, and focus on services that are profitable. He also believes that the hospital has not done enough to raise funds through private philanthropy.

Sears is the president of a local bank. She has an MBA from the Wharton School and has been in banking for 22 years. Her major concern is the deteriorating financial position of the hospital. In her view, the new CEO should have excellent financial management skills as well as an ability to work well with physicians. She views the previous CEO (Rhodes) as deficient in these areas.

The committee has invited both Bradford and Smith to interview for the position of CEO. The outline for the selection process is shown on Form 2.6 and the form for questions to be developed by the committee is on Form 2.7.

QUESTIONS FOR THE SEMI-STRUCTURED INTERVIEW

In its purest form, a structured interview occurs when the interviewers bring to the interview a list of predetermined questions to ask the interviewee. The advantage is that the interviewers have previously discussed and agreed upon the relevant criteria. During the interview, all interviewers focus on these criteria. Weighting of these criteria is often used as well. This systematic process usually results in higher levels of consistency among interviewers than is the case with unstructured interviews.

EXHIBIT 2.13 *Job Description: Chief Executive Officer, Brookdale Hospital*

Description of Work

General Statement of Duties: Supervises and coordinates administrative work of a complex nature involving the entire hospital and all its components; represents the hospital to outside stakeholders.

Supervision Required: Implements policies developed by the board of directors.

Supervision Exercised: Plans, organizes, motivates, coordinates, and directs a staff of administrative and clerical personnel. Total direct supervision involves over 15 individuals.

Example of Duties

1. Initiates and coordinates activities related to long-range planning and marketing of the hospital's services.

2. Develops and enforces policies and procedures related to administrative functions.

3. Coordinates major staff services, including budget, personnel, medical services, nursing services, dietetics, and housekeeping.

4. Develops and compiles administrative reports as required by the board or external regulatory agencies.

5. Performs related work as required.

Required Knowledge, Skills, and Abilities

Extensive and broad knowledge of complex management systems (internal and external) in a healthcare environment. Skill and ability in planning, marketing, personnel management, and financial management. Ability to relate to external stakeholders, including the board of directors.

Qualifications for Appointment

Education: Graduation from a college or university with major coursework in business administration, public administration, or health administration.

Experience: Ten years or more of progressively responsible experience in administration or management.

However, structured interviews do not allow the interviewee to discuss a topic of his or her choice or to provide additional information on areas that require further explanation. An unstructured interview emphasizes creating a supportive climate and helping the interviewees discuss values, goals, objectives, and career plans.

A compromise that retains the benefits of a structured interview while also creating the openness of the unstructured interview is the semi-structured interview. Here, the interviewers not only develop a set of structured questions to evaluate the candidate based on the agreed-upon criteria, but also ask open-ended questions, such as "What are your long-term career goals?" and "Why is that important to you?"

Develop a list of up to ten questions to ask the two applicants and decide which committee members should ask which questions. Be sure to consider the criteria identified on Form 2.6 as well as some open-ended questions designed to learn more about the applicant. Write these questions on Form 2.7.

Criteria: Major Dimension of the CEO Job (based on the job description/ personal characteristics desired	Weight of the Criteria (1–5)	Job Applicant Rating on the Criteria (1–10)		Total Score (Weight × Rating)		Comments About Each
		Bradford	Smith	Bradford	Smith	
1.						
2.						
3.						
4.						
5.						
6.						
7.						
8.						
9.						
10.						
Total Scores						

1.

2.

3.

4.

5.

6.

7.

8.

9.

10.

---

*Develop interview questions that are not biased or illegal, but which relate to the performance dimensions developed in Form 2.6.

1. How well did the committee establish rapport with each applicant?

2. How well did each of the candidates respond to the committee's questions? What improvements would you suggest? Why?

3. Approximately what percentage of the 15-minute interview time was spent listening to the applicant and what percentage consisted of committee questions and/or comments? How appropriate was this breakdown?

4. Did the committee overemphasize negative information, ask illegal questions, show bias based on irrelevant factors, or otherwise treat either applicant unfairly?

5. Did the committee probe unclear areas, or did it allow short answers that did not provide necessary information?

6. What is your overall assessment of the success of the committee in eliciting relevant information for making this selection decision? Why?

7. How well did the questions asked of the interviewees reflect the criteria established in Form 2.6?

42 EXERCISE

Selection Interview Role Play

I. OBJECTIVES

A. To help you develop skills in conducting selection interviews.

B. To provide you with practice in applying the basic principles of effective interviewing.

II. OUT-OF-CLASS PREPARATION TIME: 30–90 minutes, depending on role played (Students who play the applicant will need to prepare a résumé.)

III. IN-CLASS TIME SUGGESTED: 45 minutes

IV. PROCEDURES

The class should be divided into groups of three: an interviewer, applicant, and observer. Roles should be assigned ahead of time so you will have time to prepare your role. This is especially important for those of you who will play the role of interviewee since you are to use your own résumé and qualifications during the role play. The interviewer should prepare a set of interview questions. Read the scenario that follows and the role description provided by the instructor. Participants should assume that the interview is taking place in a campus placement office. The role play begins when the applicant arrives for the interview, and ends when both individuals have accomplished their objectives. At the end of the role play, the interviewer completes the interviewer's report (Form 2.9) and shares it with the applicant. Next, the observer provides feedback on his or her observations to the group (Form 2.10). The group then identifies and discusses the hardest part of the interview from both the interviewer's point of view and the applicant's perspective. If time permits, the entire class then discusses the reliability and validity of the interview as a method of selecting applicants for jobs.

SCENARIO

The director of college recruiting for Duro Insurance Company is presently recruiting college students for its administrative trainee program. The one-year training program involves a combination of on-the-job and formal classroom training. Upon successful completion of the training, a candidate is assigned a position as assistant department supervisor.

Duro Insurance Company ranks in the top 15 percent of life insurance companies nationally with in-force insurance in excess of $6 billion. Duro markets all forms of insurance, bonds, and pension products on an individual and group basis. More recently, the company added diversified financial services, including discount brokerage services, real estate financing, and mutual funds. The company is divided into six major divisions: Employee Benefits, Commercial Insurance, Individual Life, Automobile, Homeowners, and Diversified Financial Services and functionally into several major operating departments: Sales, Underwriting, Administrative, Loss Prevention, Actuarial, Claims, Legal, Financial and Investments, Advertising and Public Relations, Personnel, and Research and Policy Development. Duro has over 25,000 employees and more than 300 field offices throughout the country. Management at each field office consists of a manager, several department heads, and their assistants. The company has enjoyed a pattern of steady growth and expansion over the years.

Job Description for Administrative Trainee

1. Handle day-to-day administration of field office, including direct supervision of office clerks.

2. Plan and oversee the use of space, furniture, and equipment on a continuing basis and recommend changes as necessary.

3. Supervise computer processing operations for issuing and servicing insurance policies, including claims.

4. Implement and maintain accounting and collection procedures. The trainee works closely with the department head in learning these duties.

Job Qualifications

1. BS/BA with business management background (knowledge of accounting desired).

2. Ability to communicate effectively.

3. Ability to handle detail.

4. Ability to plan and direct activities of subordinate personnel.

5. Demonstrated leadership potential.

6. Knowledge of computers and software packages including Microsoft Office.

Additional Job Data

1. The trainee position reports directly to a department head.

2. Expected career progression is to assistant department supervisor (1–2 years) and, with continued development, to department head (4–5 years after supervisory assignment).

3. The position requires relocation.

4. The company offers competitive salaries and benefits, including a tuition repayment plan and in-house career planning and development.

Applicant _____   Position _____

Date _____   Interviewer _____

Rate the applicant's background and behavior, taking into consideration the factors listed for each area. Circle a rating for each factor. Give an overall rating, also.

1. Presentation (appearance, manner, oral communication skills, interest, motivation):

Poor 1 2 3 4 5 Excellent

2. Education (major, intellectual abilities, academic achievement, knowledge of field):

Poor 1 2 3 4 5 Excellent

3. Work experience (related experience, skill and competence, job performance, interpersonal skills, leadership):

Poor 1 2 3 4 5 Excellent

4. Summarize candidate's strengths:

5. Summarize candidate's weaknesses:

6. Overall evaluation and recommendation:

Poor 1 2 3 4 5 Excellent

Recommendation: ( ) Invite for field visit   ( ) Do not invite

Comments:

1. What was the quality of the interaction between the interviewer and applicant?

2. What type of interview did the interviewer use (structured, semi-structured, or nonstructured)? How well did it work?

3. Were the questions job-related?

4. What did the interviewer do to put the applicant at ease?

5. Did the interviewer listen? Did the interviewer spend too much time talking?

6. Did the interviewer follow up on questions not completely answered?

7. Did the interviewer gain enough information to make a decision about the applicant?

8. General observations.

43 EXERCISE

Which Selection Procedure Is Most Effective?

I. OBJECTIVES

    A. To examine the strengths and weaknesses of four different methods for selecting new employees.

    B. To enhance your oral communication skills.

II. OUT-OF-CLASS PREPARATION TIME: 30 minutes to prepare for the debate

III. IN-CLASS TIME SUGGESTED: 50–75 minutes

IV. PROCEDURES

Your instructor will divide the class into five groups at the end of class prior to conducting this exercise. There will be four debating groups consisting of three to five members each and one or more groups of "judges" that consist of the remaining class members. Debaters will be assigned one of four positions and told to prepare to argue in favor of that position. Judges will be told to read the textbook chapter pages that cover those positions. The issue to be debated is: Which approach to selecting new employees is relatively most effective? The positions are: 1) the structured interview; 2) the unstructured interview; 3) ability and personality tests; and 4) reviewing applications and résumés, and talking to or getting letters from listed references.

    At the start of the next class, your instructor will announce that a four-way debate will be held. The judges' role in the debate is to "search for the truth." They are to listen to the different sides presented and then, after the debate is finished, to tell the class what they believe is the "correct" answer to the debate question, not who "won" the debate.

    The debate consists of two rounds. The purpose of Round One (15–20 minutes) is for each team to learn the position of the other debating teams. Hence, each team has up to five minutes to explain their position as comprehensively as possible. At the completion of Round One, the debating teams are given up to ten minutes to prepare criticisms of each of the other three teams for Round Two. During this intermission, judges are to discuss what they have heard and begin to formulate their own position.

    In Round Two (15–20 minutes), each debating team is given up to five minutes to criticize the position of each of the other teams. Unlike a traditional debate, teams are not allowed to rebut the criticisms made by others. They must simply listen to them. Round Two ends when Team Four has finished criticizing the position of the other three teams.

    After the debate has ended, the judges have five minutes to discuss the issue among themselves and to arrive at a consensus, if possible. The judging team(s) then explains its decision to the debaters.

44 EXERCISE

Selecting from Imperfect Applicants

I. OBJECTIVES

A. To make you aware of the difficulties involved in selecting from a group of applicants who are not well qualified.

B. To give you practice in making selection decisions.

C. To familiarize you with possible selection criteria.

II. OUT-OF-CLASS PREPARATION TIME: 10 minutes to read the exercise and determine which applicant should be hired

III. IN-CLASS TIME SUGGESTED: 30–45 minutes

IV. PROCEDURES

Either at the beginning of class or before, read the exercise and determine which of the three applicants should be hired. You must hire one of the three people, even though none are perfect candidates.

After each class member has individually determined which applicant should be hired, the instructor will divide the class into groups of three or four. Each group must then discuss each applicant and examine each person's strengths and weaknesses. Based on this analysis, applicants are to be ranked in terms of desirability. After all of the groups are finished with their analysis, a representative from each group will present the group's decision as to which applicant should be hired, the criteria used, and the reasoning behind the decision.

SITUATION

Buck Fleming operates a two-person saw mill in a small village in one of the northern states. The village has a population of about 60 during the winter months and about 800 during the summer months. It is located on a large lake, and has a general store, a bar, a volunteer fire department building, and a small post office. The nearest larger town is about 45 miles away and has a population of about 5,000.

After contracting with property owners, Fleming cuts trees on their property and takes the logs to his mill, saws them into boards, and then trucks them to buyers. If the trees are veneer quality, he does not cut them into boards himself but sells them to another mill. Fleming does not pay the property owner until after the logs have been sold, thereby minimizing his out-of-pocket expenses. Once logs arrive at his mill, they are run through a machine, aptly called a debarker, which removes the bark. Then, Fleming saws the logs into boards of various lengths and widths, moves then along a conveyor, and stacks them in piles to dry out. When the boards are dry, he loads them onto his truck and delivers them to buyers.

Fleming has had a difficult time hiring the one extra person he needs to run his operation. Most last only a short time and then quit. The job is quite dangerous, extremely dirty, and must be performed outside in the hot summer sun or in the cold, oftentimes snowy fall and spring. Little work gets done during the coldest winter months. Mosquitoes and black flies are another problem, particularly during May and June. Several years ago, an employee was working underneath a piece of heavy equipment when a log brace fell over, killing the man. Everyone in the area knew about this tragic accident, making it harder for Fleming to hire a new person.

Fleming wants to hire someone who could do all the jobs related to his operation, except running the saw that cuts the logs. He reserves this job for himself. He needs an employee who can drive a bulldozer to make a road to get to the trees, cut down trees either with a chain saw or a tree shearer, operate a skidder and a front-end loader, and drive a large logging truck. In addition, the person needs to be able to run the debarker, stack logs and boards, and help perform maintenance on all of the equipment. The employee will frequently come into contact with land owners when cutting trees on their property, so a good first impression is helpful, as well as a friendly personality. Fleming is willing to train someone to perform all of these operations if necessary, but would prefer someone who already has some of the needed skills. Fleming believes that the two most important selection criteria are the employee's ability to come to work on time every day and not to quit after a short time period.

The price of lumber increases during booms in the housing and remodeling business and decreases during a recession. Now, prices are low which makes it hard for Fleming to make a profit. As a result, he feels that he can only pay an employee $11.00 an hour with no benefits except those required by law. Fleming realizes that this is low, but it is the best he can offer until lumber prices rise. His most recent employee quit because he was offered a job that paid more, leaving Fleming in the position of needing a new helper now.

Fleming recently placed an advertisement in the local newspaper and received calls from three applicants. He then interviewed each and was not impressed with any of them. Nonetheless, he needs to hire one of them soon. The information on each applicant is given below. Some of this information he learned directly from the applicants, and some he obtained by talking with his friends who knew the applicants. In such a rural area, everyone knows almost everyone.

Chuck Maki

Chuck Maki is a polite, personable, nice-looking 22 year old who graduated from high school. He lives within one mile of the saw mill with his parents and knows the area and its people well, having lived here all of his life. Although Maki did not offer the information, Fleming knew that he had been in jail twice over the past three years for a total of about eight months. He was arrested for DUI and his license was suspended. While driving on a suspended license, Maki was arrested again. He has also been arrested for car theft and vandalism. When Fleming directly asked him about this, Maki replied that he knew he had a problem with liquor. In all instances he had gotten drunk and done "stupid things," but he has been sober for two weeks. Maki's driver's license is currently suspended but he hopes to get it back shortly. In the meantime, his parents will drive him to work or he can walk. Chuck has no prior logging experience, having worked as a bartender for a few years after graduating from high school. He is currently unemployed and is willing to start work immediately.

Bud Hoover

Bud Hoover is approximately 25 years old and has never finished high school. For the past month, he has lived in a trailer with three friends about 20 miles from the saw mill and is currently unemployed. He grew up in Kentucky and has worked in a variety of jobs, keeping most of them for less than six months. During the past three years, he had held five different jobs, all in different towns. He has had experience as a pizza delivery driver, a car washer, a tire changer, a dishwasher, and a yard maintenance employee. He has no knowledge of logging equipment, but says he likes working on trucks and other equipment. Hoover seems to be an incessant talker and is a heavy smoker. He has an older car for getting to work and can start work after he returns from a trip in two weeks.

JIM BRYCE

Jim Bryce is in his mid-thirties and has worked in the construction trade since dropping out of high school. He was laid off from his job in Florida five months ago due to a lack of work and has not found a new job since. Several years ago he fell off of a barn roof and hurt himself badly. Then, a year later he cut his hand with a miter saw, needing further hospitalization. Jim accumulated so many medical bills that he needed to declare bankruptcy. He wears his hair long, has several tattoos, and needs dental work. He lives about 35 miles from the mill, temporarily staying with his uncle, and has an old truck that needs repair. Jim loves to work outdoors, and the cold and heat do not bother him. He has a good knowledge of construction but not of logging, logging equipment, or the area. He is available for work immediately.

The Ethical Selection Dilemma at Integrity Motors

BACKGROUND

Integrity Motors has been retailing quality used cars and trucks for the past ten years. It is located in a large midwestern city, and has become the largest and most successful used car dealership in the region. Integrity Motors employs 11 full-time salespersons. Timmy Blackburn, the owner, wants to maintain a policy of having a lean, yet highly productive staff, which means that the employees have to be dependable, highly competent, and willing to work at a high level of productivity for long hours each day.

After ten years at Integrity Motors, the sales manager was resigning to start his own business. Blackburn felt he needed the same type of employee he had had in the position— someone who had considerable experience as a sales manager, was a good motivator, had good communication and management skills, was creative, and who would be committed to the dealership for many years. Although Blackburn felt it prudent to take the necessary time to carefully select a new sales manager, time was of the essence because the end of the year was approaching and the inventory needed to be drastically reduced.

Applications for the job started pouring in almost immediately. After a week, 45 applicants had expressed interest in the job, of which ten potentially suitable candidates were invited for interviews. A panel comprised of the office manager, Helen Smith; the service manager, Joe Washington; and Timmy Blackburn interviewed the ten applicants. Based on the interviews, it was clear that one candidate, Gladys Morrison, was outstanding compared to all other applicants. Morrison had recently moved to the area from a metropolitan city where she was a sales manager for 15 years. Everyone agreed that she was the perfect candidate. The next morning an offer would be extended to Morrison. Everyone left the meeting feeling satisfied that they had made an excellent choice.

A NEW DEVELOPMENT

The next morning when Blackburn arrived at the dealership he was met by Smith and Washington, who seemed troubled. Apparently, after the meeting the prior evening, Smith happened to meet an old friend at a convenience store. The friend told Smith she was four months pregnant and that, coincidentally, her new neighbor was also four months pregnant. To Smith's surprise, the pregnant neighbor was Gladys Morrison, the person to whom the dealership would extend a job offer the next morning. Smith said nothing to her friend about Morrison's employment inquiry or pending job offer, yet throughout the night, Smith pondered about the potential hire.

The next morning, as Smith shared this development with Blackburn and Washington before Gladys Morrison was contacted, all three discussed the potential consequences of hiring Morrison. Washington was astounded that Morrison had not informed them of her pregnancy. Blackburn quickly told him that legally she did not have to tell them, and furthermore, any employment decision could not be based on her pregnancy. Smith observed that though legally this was true, from a practical standpoint the dealership could not afford to be without a sales manager for an extended period of time. Blackburn, too, was concerned about her potential absence as well as her potential inability to work for long periods under intense pressure, especially when they needed to reduce inventory. Smith also reminded them that although Morrison was clearly the best applicant, there were at least nine other applicants who would be suitable sales managers.

1. What are the legal and ethical issues involved in this case? Was it ethical for Gladys Morrison to have applied for the position in the first place?

2. Should the owner hire Morrison or some other applicant? Should the information about the pregnancy be considered?

3. If Morrison is hired, how could Integrity Motors accommodate her pregnancy?

Contributed by James C. Wimbush, Indiana University

46 INCIDENT

The Exit Interviews and Employee Retention

William James has recently been hired as the director of human resources for an academic medical center located in the Northeast. While he was interviewing for the position, several administrators and physicians told him that employee morale, particularly among registered nurses, was extremely low. James later learned that the annual turnover rate of nurses at this facility has averaged 18.4 percent as compared to 11.6 percent in the metropolitan area over the past three years.

James was aware that all exiting employees are required to complete an exit interview questionnaire and interview prior to receiving their final paycheck. He then asked his assistant to pull the files for all exit interviews of departing nurses and prepare a summary of the major reasons for leaving and specific suggestions for how the facility could increase its retention of nurses.

When the results were compiled, James was disappointed. The utility of these data was very low. Most of the respondents indicated they were leaving for personal reasons, family responsibilities, or another job offer. Very few volunteered recommendations for how the facility could improve nurse retention even when asked directly on both the questionnaire and during the interview. The recommendation mentioned most frequently was better parking.

The prevailing opinion of individuals with whom James spoke was that departing employees are reluctant to discuss any sensitive issues or concerns for fear of alienating the interviewer or supervisor. He was told no one wanted to possibly jeopardize their recommendation to other employers due to anything they might say during the exit interview. Through his informal conversations with nurses and nurse supervisors, he knew there were many problems and concerns shared by many nurses including inadequate staffing, lack of respect and support from supervisors and top management, favoritism in salary increases and promotions, and high stress levels due to all of the above. Yet, he was unable to document these problems and others with the current exit interview data.

James is now attempting to determine the best methods of identifying employee problems and assessing employee reaction to the organization, its various components, and various human resource policies and programs. He is also interested in determining the factors which cause many of the long-tenured nurses to stay.

QUESTIONS

1. Discuss the nature and causes of the problem of nurse retention.

2. Should James attempt to improve the exit interview process? If so, how should this be done?

3. What other assessment alternatives should he consider using in addition to, or rather than, exit interviews in order to determine the underlying causes of turnover and enhance retention in the future?

4. How can James use the information generated about why nurses stay or leave to improve nurse retention?

47 INCIDENT

Nepotism

Though Ellen Arnold had been with the firm less than six weeks, she had already caused considerable problems for Jim Staples, Doris Nusbaum, and the architects. Staples was the office manager whose branch of a large architectural firm had 25 architects and 8 personal assistants. While he was in charge of the entire office, Nusbaum was in charge of the assistants who were not assigned to work for particular architects, but were assigned by Nusbaum to tasks on an as-needed basis.

Ellen Arnold had been brought to the office by her father, one of the firm's founders who worked at a different office. The father announced that he had hired his daughter to work for Nusbaum during this and future summer vacations from college. Unfortunately, Arnold had no skills whatsoever that related to the duties required. In addition, the office was fully staffed and did not need any additional help.

Nusbaum was irate when she learned that she was to find work for and supervise Arnold. She was particularly upset that Arnold was hired without the firm following the standard selection process and that Arnold was just "dumped on her doorstep." She told Staples, "Ellen has no knowledge of architecture whatsoever. I have no work for her. I don't want to have anything to do with her!"

On her first day of work, Arnold was shown her desk but was assigned no specific tasks. Within a few days, she introduced herself to all of the architects and started spending more and more time in their offices. Wanting to make a favorable impression on Arnold's father, the architects willingly talked with her at length. One of the young architects was particularly taken by her, and vice versa. She spent more time in his office than in any other office. Meanwhile, the other personal assistants were starting to complain about all of the attention that Arnold was receiving and that she was not doing her share of the administrative tasks. In addition, the architects were falling behind in their work. A vicious rumor was circulating that Arnold had a brother who also might be thrust upon the office. During all of this, Nusbaum refused to have anything to do with Arnold and reminded Staples that she was his problem.

QUESTIONS

1. What are the major problems in this case?

2. If you were Jim Staples, what steps would you take to solve the problems depicted in this case?

3. What are the advantages and disadvantages of having a "no nepotism" policy?

48 SKILL BUILDER

Evaluating Job Application Forms

I. OBJECTIVES

A. To familiarize you with the criteria for selecting questions to put on an application form.

B. To give you practice in evaluating the questions on an application blank.

II. TIME REQUIRED TO COMPLETE: 1 hour

III. INSTRUCTIONS

Review the application form that appears in Exhibit 2.14. This form is used by United Holy Radio Network for their administrative and clerical employees. You should thoroughly review the legal requirements for pre-employment inquiries and other relevant information on application forms found in your text. Use the guide below to evaluate the questions that appear on the application. Prepare a short write-up summarizing your findings and make specific recommendations for improving the questions.

QUESTIONS TO BE ASKED IN EVALUATING APPROPRIATENESS OF APPLICATION BLANK ITEMS

1. Is this question job-related?

2. Will answers to this question have an adverse impact in screening out members of protected groups (i.e., disqualify a significantly larger percentage of members of one particular group than of others)?

3. Is this question really needed to judge an applicant's qualifications and suitability for the job?

4. Does the question constitute an invasion of privacy?

5. Can the applicant's response to this question be verified?

EXHIBIT 2.14 *Job Application Form*

United Holy Radio Network Application for Employment

Name: _____

(Last)   (Middle initial)   (First)

                                                                    PHOTO

Street Address: _____

_____

(City)   (State)

Sex: **Male**   **Female**   **Age:**_____

Own home: Yes   No   How long?_____   Rent: Yes   No   How long?_____

Phone No. (____) _____

Marital Status: Married   Divorced   Never   Married   Widowed   (circle one)

If married indicate name of spouse: _____

Of what country are you a citizen?: _____

Indicate languages spoken fluently: _____

List all physical disabilities:_____

Religion: _____

Church membership: _____

Name of Minister: _____

How often do you attend church? _____

List church activities:_____

Do you smoke?:   Yes   No   Do you consume alcoholic beverages?:   Yes   No

Have you ever been arrested?:   Yes   No   Indicate offenses: _____

Military experience: _____ Type of discharge: _____

Education

High school name: _____ Date of graduation: _____

Business or technical school name: _____ Degree:_____

Attended: _____ Date of graduation:_____

Junior/community college name: _____ Degree: _____

Attended: _____ Date of graduation: _____

College name: _____ Degree: _____

Attended: _____ Date of graduation: _____

Work Experience

Name of employer: _____ Job title: _____ No. of years: _____

Reason for leaving: _____

Name of employer: _____ Job title: _____ No. of years: _____

Reason for leaving: _____

Name of employer: _____ Job title: _____ No. of years: _____

Reason for leaving: _____

I certify that all the information which I have given in this application is true, accurate, and complete. I understand that any misstatement or omission of a material fact may be a cause for dismissal.

Date: _____ Signature: _____

Source: Adapted from Robert D. Gatewood and Hubert S. Field, *Human Resource Selection* (New York: Dryden Press, 1987), p. 279.

Staffing for a Telecommuting Job

I. OBJECTIVES

A. To give you practice in revising a job description for a telecommuting job.

B. To enhance your understanding of how to prepare a staffing plan for a telecommuting job.

C. To familiarize you with some of the differences between staffing for telecommuting job environments versus staffing for traditional job (office) environments.

II. TIME REQUIRED TO COMPLETE: One to two hours

III. INSTRUCTIONS

A large pharmaceutical company located in the Northeast is one of the leading manufacturers of pharmaceuticals in the United States. Because of the intense competition in the industry and the heightened competition for highly skilled personnel, the company believes that quality-of-work-life (QWL) is a key factor for achieving a competitive advantage. In support of this belief, the company is considering the adoption of a telecommuting work arrangement for selected jobs.

The job of public relations specialist has been identified as an appropriate job for telecommuting because the job responsibilities are mostly information-related activities that require independent mental effort with no supervisory responsibilities. Exhibit 2.15 below contains the current job description for the public relations specialist, which reflects the primary job activities and qualifications for a full-time, in-office public relations specialist. There is currently only one job incumbent, and that person has resigned.

You have been asked to develop a plan for recruiting and hiring a replacement who will telecommute from home.

A. What method of job analysis do you recommend to determine the job requirements and job specifications for a telecommuting job? Is the method you recommend different from the method you would use if the job were performed in a traditional office environment?

B. What procedures do you recommend for recruiting and hiring a telecommuter? Are the procedures you recommend different from the procedures you would use if the job were performed in a traditional office environment?

C. What changes would you make to the job description in Exhibit 2.15 to reflect the telecommuting nature of the job?

D. What other recommendations would you make in order to ensure the successful implementation of a telecommuting work arrangement?

EXHIBIT 2.15 *Job Description*

Job Title: Public Relations Specialist

Department: Public Relations

Reports To: Director of Public Relations

General Summary: Serves as a writer on numerous firm publications; coordinates materials; writes, edits, and proofs articles, public relations publications, and advertising copy.

Essential Job Functions:
1. Writes, edits, and proofs public relations articles, newspaper copy, and human interest stories.
2. Writes advertising copy in conjunction with the marketing department.
3. Writes, edits, and coordinates printing and layout of company newsletter.
4. Meets with executives to determine public relations needs.
5. Meets with media officials and the public to publicize firm's accomplishments.
6. Attends informational meetings at the main office on an as-needed basis.
7. Gives presentations at meetings and other public events.
8. Performs other related duties as assigned by management.

Education and Experience Required: Degree in art/graphic design; demonstrated ability to use computer hardware/software; some experience in television or public speaking; considerable knowledge of journalism principles, English grammar and usage; demonstrated ability to write newspaper, news, and human interest articles, reports, brochures, and advertising copy; demonstrated ability to work and communicate effectively with others.

Contributed by Diana Deadrick, Old Dominion University

50 SKILL BUILDER

Test/Interview Validation

I. OBJECTIVES

    A. To enhance your understanding of the test/interview validation process.

    B. To give you experience in calculating the validity of a test.

    C. To give you experience in preparing a scatter diagram (optional).

II. TIME REQUIRED TO COMPLETE: 1 hour

III. INSTRUCTIONS

Assume you are the human resources director for a large hotel. During the hiring process, all job applicants are required to undergo an extensive interview with you or with one of your assistants. Each applicant is scored on how well they perform during the interview from 1 (very poorly) to 100 (highly effective). Several months ago, a testing organization met with you and told you that your selection process might be improved if you gave every applicant a general intelligence test, in addition to the interview. They suggested that you buy tests from them for $40 each and conduct a pilot study. So, you asked the 30 employees you hired most recently to take the test. The Pilot Study table shows the test and interview scores for these 30 employees. It also shows the overall score each employee received on his or her performance evaluation conducted by his or her supervisor.

Your task is to review the following two tables and answer the questions below:

1. Examine the correlation coefficients shown in the Study Statistics table. Should the firm use the test to hire future employees or is the interview alone sufficient? Explain your answer.

2. The validity coefficient between the general intelligence test score and the performance evaluation score is shown in the table. Use the formula below to verify that the calculation is correct. To assist you in making the calculation, the following formula is provided:

$$R \text{ (validity coefficient)} = \frac{N\Sigma XY - \Sigma X\Sigma Y}{\sqrt{N\Sigma X^2 - (\Sigma X)^2][N\Sigma Y^2 - (\Sigma Y)^2]}}$$

where N = number of subjects.

3. At the option of your instructor, prepare a scatter diagram showing the interview scores (X-axis) and the performance evaluation scores (Y-axis).

Study Statistics

General Intelligence Test Data		Interview Data		Combined Data	
Numerator	44470	Numerator	129170	Numerator	86820
X's	32264	X's	98684	X's	47205
Y's	400565	Y's	400565	Y's	400565
Denominator	113683	Denominator	198819.9	Denominator	137509
Correlation	0.39118	Correlation	0.649683	Correlation	0.6314

Pilot Study Data

Employee	Intelligence Test	Interview Score	Average Combined Score	Performance Evaluation Score
1	75	80	77.5	172
2	77	71	74	141
3	67	61	64	128
4	65	59	62	173
6	73	58	65.5	155
7	63	52	57.5	126
8	71	78	74.5	151
8	71	63	67	181
9	79	88	83.5	176
10	77	63	70	136
11	88	89	88.5	178
12	74	73	73.5	151
13	69	80	74.5	173
14	72	76	74	148
15	71	83	77	185
16	66	77	71.5	138
17	61	74	67.5	133
18	74	89	81.5	181
19	64	80	72	188
20	73	62	67.5	140
21	78	77	77.5	177
22	67	71	69	173
23	81	94	87.5	185
24	75	81	78	175
25	66	74	70	138
26	70	62	66	133
27	77	82	79.5	181
28	75	83	79	173
29	81	85	83	188
30	76	69	72.5	128
SUMS	2176	2234	2205	4805

Contributed by Steve Maurer, Old Dominion University

3

Developing
Effectiveness
in Human
Resources:
Training, Career
Development,
and Performance
Appraisal

Orientation/Training/Career Development

51 CASE

Career Development at Electronic Applications

Electronic Applications Corporation is a major producer of silicon chips for the computer industry. It is located southeast of San Francisco in an area of high technology firms. Since its founding in 1972, the company has grown rapidly in terms of sales and profits, thus enhancing its stock price many times over. Human resource policies, however, have tended to lag behind company growth. Emphasis has been on reactive policies to meet the regulatory requirements of external stakeholders such as the federal government. In short, human resources have not been a high priority.

Recently, Harold Sweeney has been hired as director of human resources for the company. Sweeney had previously served as assistant personnel director for a large "blue-chip" corporation in southern California. He accepted his present position not only because of an increase in pay and responsibility, but also because of what he termed "the challenge of bringing this company from a 1970s human resources mentality to one more compatible with the realities of the 2000s."

Sweeney has been on the job for four months and has been assessing the situation to determine the more significant human resource problems. One problem seems to have been the high turnover among electrical engineers who work in research and development and are the core of the research function. Prior to the 2008–2010 financial crisis, the turnover rate averaged about 30 percent per year over the past three years. As a result of the recent financial crisis, however, unemployment in Silicon Valley has increased to 9.7 percent. Most technology companies are not hiring at all or are only hiring individuals on a highly selective basis. The result is that most employees have decided to stay put in the short term, but will be looking to take advantage of more attractive opportunities elsewhere when and if the economy improves. Sweeney was aware of these intentions and wanted to take steps now to minimize future employee turnover.

In assessing the cause of the problem, Sweeney checked area wage surveys and found Electronic Applications paid 5 to 8 percent above the market for various categories of electrical engineers. Since the company did not have a formal exit interview system, he could not check out other possible explanations through that mechanism. However, through informal conversations with a large number of individuals, including the engineers themselves, he learned that many of the engineers felt "dead-ended" in the technical aspects of engineering. In particular, the research and development department had lost some of the younger engineers who had been considered to be on the "fast track." Most had gone to competitors in the local area.

One particular research and development employee who impressed Sweeney was Helen Morgan. Morgan is 29 years old, has a BS degree in Electrical Engineering from California Institute of Technology, and is studying for her MBA at the University of Santa Clara at night. Helen had been employed for seven years at Electronic Applications, three in an entry-level engineering position and four as a section chief. The latter promotion was the highest position in research and development other than the position of director of research and development.

Morgan claimed that "the company doesn't really care about its good people." In her view, the present director, Harry James, does not want to allow his "better people" to move up in the organization. He is more interested in keeping them in his own department so he can meet his own departmental goals without having to orient and train new employees. Morgan also claimed she was told she "has a bright future with the company" by both James and the former personnel director. Her performance appraisals have been uniformly excellent. She went on to criticize the company for using an appraisal form with no sections for dealing with employee development. Morgan recommended that steps be taken to remedy each of the problems she identified. Among these steps were helping employees identify future development opportunities, rewards for supervisors who successfully mentor subordinates, planning to identify future job opportunities, better communication of job opportunities, identification of career paths and career ladders, greater efforts to help employees achieve work/family life balance, childcare assistance, and telecommuting opportunities.

Sweeney checked out the information Morgan had provided him and found it to be accurate. Moreover, he heard through the "grapevine" that she is in line for an excellent position with a nearby competitor. Clearly, he has an even greater challenge than he had anticipated. He realizes he has an immediate problem concerning high turnover of certain key employees. In addition, Sweeney also has a series of interconnected problems associated with career development. However, he is not quite sure what steps to take and in what order.

QUESTIONS

1. Describe the nature and causes of the problem faced by Harold Sweeney.

2. What additional questions should Sweeney ask or what additional information is needed before proceeding toward a solution to this problem? Why?

3. What are the individual and organizational benefits of a formalized career development system?

4. If Sweeney decides to develop a formalized career development system at Electronic Applications, what components or types of services should be offered? Why?

5. Should the career development activities be integrated with other human resource management activities? If yes, which ones? Why?

6. What criteria should Sweeney consider to evaluate good candidates for promotion? What criteria could be used to evaluate the performance of supervisors in development of their subordinates?

The Safety Training Program

Houghton Refrigeration Company builds refrigerators for large appliance companies. It employs about 300 people, mostly assembly-line workers, and is located in a small rural town in Ohio. The company typically builds, on a contract basis, chest freezers and small bar refrigerators. On occasion, however, it also builds standard size refrigerators. The president of the company is a former engineer, as are most of the other executives. These individuals are very knowledgeable about engineering, but have received little training in the basic principles of management.

During the summer months, volume at the factory increases significantly, and the company needs to hire about 40 new employees to handle the heavy workload. Most of these new employees are college students who attend a small private college located about 15 minutes from the plant. Some high school students are hired as well.

When a new employee is hired, the company asks him or her to complete an application and then to show up at the plant gate ready for work. Employees receive no orientation. The worker is shown to a work station and, after a minimum amount of on-the-job training, the new employee is expected to start performing a job. Most of the jobs are quite simple; hence, the training is typically completed within ten minutes. The first-line supervisor usually shows the employee how to do a job once, then watches while the employee does the job once, leaves, and comes back about 20 minutes later to see how the employee is progressing. Typical jobs at the plant include screwing 14 screws into the sides of a freezer, placing a piece of insulation into the freezer lid, and handing out supplies from the tool room.

The company has had excellent experience with college students over the years. Much of the success can be attributed to the older workers coming to the aid of the new employees when difficulties arise. Most new employees are able to perform their jobs reasonably well after their on-the-job training is completed. However, when unexpected difficulties arise, they are usually not prepared for them and need assistance from others.

The older workers have been especially helpful to students working in the "press room." However, Joe Gleason, the first-line supervisor there, finds it amusing to belittle the college students whenever they make any mistakes. He relishes showing a student once how to use a press to bend a small piece of metal, then exclaims, "You're a hot-shot college student; now let's see you do it." He then watches impatiently while the student invariably makes a mistake and then jokingly announces for all to hear, "That's wrong! How did you ever get into college anyway? Try it again, dummy."

One summer, the company experienced a rash of injuries to its employees. Although most of the injuries were minor, the company felt it imperative to conduct a series of short training programs on safe material-handling techniques. The president of the company realized that OSHA requires firms to maintain a safe and healthy work environment, and that it is important that employees know how to lift objects safely. The major issue was who should conduct the training. The human resource director was a 64-year-old former engineer who was about to retire and was a poor speaker. The only other employee in the human resource department was a new 19-year-old secretary who knew nothing about proper handling techniques. Out of desperation, the president finally decided to ask Bill Young, the first-line supervisor of the "lid-line" to conduct the training. Young recently attended a training program himself on safety and was active in the American Red Cross. He reluctantly agreed to conduct the training. It was to be done on a departmental basis with small groups of 10 to 15 employees attending each session.

At the first of these training sessions, Young nervously stood up in front of 14 employees, many of whom were college students, and read his presentation in a monotone voice. His entire speech lasted about one minute and consisted of the following text:

> Statistics show that an average of 30 people injure their backs on the job each day in this state. None of us wants to become a statistic.
>
> The first thing that should be done before lifting an object is to look it over and decide whether you can handle it alone or if help is needed. Get help if there's any doubt as to whether the load is safely within your capacity.
>
> Next, look over the area where you're going to be carrying the object. Make sure it's clear of obstacles. You may have to do a little housekeeping before moving your load. After you have checked out the load and route you're going to travel, the following steps should be taken for your safety in lifting:
>
> 1. Get a good footing close to the load.
>
> 2. Place your feet 8 to 12 inches apart.
>
> 3. Bend your knees to grasp the load.
>
> 4. Bend your knees outward, straddling the load.
>
> 5. Get a firm grip.
>
> 6. Keep the load close to your body.
>
> 7. Lift gradually.
>
> Once you've lifted the load and moved it, you'll eventually have to set it down—so bend your legs again—and follow the lifting procedures in reverse. Make sure that your fingers clear the pinch points. And, finally, it's a good idea to set one corner down first.

After Bill's speech ended, the employees immediately returned to work. By the end of the day, however, everyone in the plant had heard about the training fiasco, and all, except the president, were laughing about it.

QUESTIONS

1. Evaluate the company's on-the-job training program. Should it be changed?

2. Should the company install an employee orientation program for new factory workers, or is one not necessary?

3. What changes should be made in the company's safety training program?

4. What other ways might a firm emphasize safety and curtail accidents, other than training?

53 CASE

The Mentoring Problem at Walnut Insurance

Tom Morrison, president of Walnut Insurance, was sitting at his desk reading a letter he had just received and thinking about a recent meeting with his vice presidents. He knew he had to make a decision regarding whether to implement a new mentoring program, but he did not know what that decision should be at the moment.

Walnut Insurance has been selling liability insurance to firms in one particular industry for over 50 years. Its specialized niche in the insurance industry has made it highly successful. It employs about 2,400 individuals who work in 12 regional offices throughout the United States and at its Midwestern headquarters.

Walnut Insurance has six senior male vice presidents who report directly to Morrison. Over the years, these individuals have traveled between the various regional offices, working primarily with the insurance sales representatives. The VPs perform numerous functions when visiting the regional offices. They go out on overnight sales trips with the representatives to learn about customer problems, assist agents with policy questions, and provide training; they evaluate agents to determine who has the potential to be promoted; they pass on the firm's values and culture, which places heavy emphasis on honesty and satisfying customer needs; they assist agents in interpreting company policies; and they determine what new policies need to be developed.

Over the years, these VPs have performed one other valuable service to new employees—they have informally mentored some of them. Typically, each VP would pick out five or six promising agents and take them under his wing. He would get to know the agents well, point out strengths and weaknesses, and help them develop plans for achieving management positions. Over the years, this approach has worked quite well.

However, in the last two years the firm hired over 50 new agents and almost two-thirds of them were women. These individuals were college graduates who majored in a variety of disciplines. They were hired based on their sales skills, initiative, self-confidence, assertiveness, and physical appearance. Previously, almost all of the new hires were men. Morrison believed that the present informal mentoring system might result in women being excluded, so he thought that a formal system should be considered.

Thus, at one of the firm's regular retreats, Morrison broached the subject with his VPs. He commended them for their willingness to mentor agents voluntarily in the past, noted that many of the regional managers were a product of this mentoring, explained his concerns regarding the need for female agents to receive equal mentoring treatment, and asked them if they thought the process should be formalized by assigning specific agents to specific VPs.

Morrison's suggestion went over like a lead balloon—not a single person liked the idea in the least. In fact, they strongly opposed it and told Morrison as tactfully as they could. One VP explained that he was an elder in the church and had strong religious convictions. He did not want to travel with female employees on overnight sales calls because it might tarnish his image among his evangelical friends. He had no problem working with female employees in regional offices and had done so for many years. But, he did not want to travel with them.

Three other VPs were opposed to the idea because they were fearful of sexual harassment suits being filed against them. They knew that Title VII of the Civil Rights Act states that it is unlawful to harass a person because of that person's sex and that sexual harassment is defined as unwelcome sexual advances, requests for sexual favors, and other verbal or physical harassment of a sexual nature. The also knew that the law states that harassment is illegal when it is so frequent that it creates a hostile or offensive work environment or results in an adverse employment decision. They noted that a recent insurance trade publication article described numerous cases in which managers in several other insurance firms had been charged with harassment. The article explained that the law is unclear in many ways and how even if one is innocent of a charge, one's career can be ruined. The VPs demanded to know how and whether the firm would stand behind them if charged with sexual harassment.

One other VP objected to the idea because he wanted free choice in selecting employees to mentor. He argued that only the best agents are deserving of mentoring and that it would be a waste of time to mentor everyone. He asked, "Why should we mentor someone who does not have the potential to become a manager?" Another VP objected because he knew that his wife would not approve of any plan that would require that he work closely with young female agents, particularly at night in faraway locations.

After hearing all of these objections, Morrison asked the VPs to give further thought to the issue. He restated that mentoring was critical to the firm's success and that it was important that women not be left out of the process.

In the week that followed, Tom had not heard anything more regarding the issue from any VP. However, he had received a letter from one wife (see Exhibit 3.1) and it was clear what she thought of the idea. Nonetheless, the final decision was his to make.

EXHIBIT 3.1 *Letter from a VP's Wife*

January 23, 20xx
1105 Edgewater Dr.
Sometown, USA

Mr. Tom Morrison
President, Walnut Insurance Company

Dear Tom,

I am writing to you regarding the new mentoring proposal that is being considered. My husband told me about it at dinner last week and I have been worried about it ever since.

As you may know, my husband and I have been married for 28 years and have raised three lovely children. We are dedicated to each other and have strong family values. We try to act as good role models to our children and to others.

To be honest, I am very concerned about what effects the new mentoring program might have on our marriage. My husband is faithful to me and I trust him with other women under typical circumstances. However, the new program involves special circumstances and I do not trust the women he might need to mentor. Some of these women may be so ambitious that they will stop at nothing to get promoted. They would not hesitate to destroy a marriage or my husband's career if they thought it would help them get ahead.

I would appreciate it if you would find a different alternative. Surely, some other approach would accomplish your goals.

Sincerely yours,

Joyce Butler

Joyce Butler

---

1. If you were Tom Morrison, would you implement a formal mentoring program at Walnut Insurance? If so, how would you address the VP's concerns?

2. What alternatives to a formal mentoring program are available to Morrison?

▨▨▨▨▨▨ *Management Development: The I-MBA Request*

Warren Vander, HR director, and Delane Beck, general manager at Nipigon Mining Products Corporation, were meeting to discuss an important request they had just received from Thomas Williams, a control engineer. Williams had a BS in Electrical Engineering from a well-known Western university and had been with the firm for eight years. He had read an advertisement in the local paper regarding a new I-MBA program offered by State University and wanted to know if the firm would pay the tuition. The two-year program would cost close to $50,000, is limited to 50 students, and requires that students take approximately 20 online classes and attend two one-week residency experiences. The advertisement stated that the program offers an integrated curriculum and focuses on leadership, strategic planning, marketing, management information systems, human resource administration, and production management. Since Williams's request was the first of its kind at the firm, any decision made would be precedent setting for employees who want to take classes offered through the Internet.

The meeting focused on a number of topics. First and foremost was the $50,000 price tag. Vander was somewhat shocked by the cost and wondered if there was not a cheaper alternative. He knew that many universities were now offering programs through the Internet and that they were not cheap, but he questioned why this program would cost so much. He wondered whether the firm should spend such a large sum on one person and whether Williams should be required to pay some, or most, of the cost. Vander noted that $50,000 would pay for a lot of classes for many employees at the nearby community college and that the firm could hire outside trainers to conduct a management development program at the company for that same amount. He reasoned that even if the firm needed to pay outsiders $2,000 per day, it could buy 25 days of management development training for up to 30 employees. He figured this might be more beneficial to the firm than spending a large sum on just one person.

Furthermore, Vander questioned whether the firm should spend such a large sum on Williams. He knew that Williams had been with the firm for eight years and had always received high performance ratings. He also knew that Williams held a critical position in the firm and was always on-call, meaning that if equipment failed at any time, the firm reserved the right to ask him to come to work above and beyond his normal work hours. This precluded Williams from taking regular classes at any university. While Williams was technically competent, he was also a "computer geek." He lacked strong interpersonal skills and tended to be arrogant and defensive. Vander also wondered whether Williams would remain with the company once he finished his degree. He worried that Williams would finish the program and then, with a new credential in hand, leave for a better opportunity elsewhere. By the same token, Vander was concerned with how Williams might react if the firm did not grant his request. Would he quit the firm and join one that would pay for an Internet-based program?

Beck was skeptical regarding the quality of the program and whether it was as rigorous and as educationally sound as a traditional one. She knew that the State University's College of Business had an excellent reputation, but this program was new and untested. She wondered if the program would be fraught with problems given that the faculty would be offering it for the first time. She also wondered if the program would sufficiently improve Williams's weak interpersonal skills to make him capable of being promoted to plant manager, to vice president of manufacturing, or to an even higher position. Beck noted that if Williams completed this program, he would have face-to-face contact with other students for just the two one-week residencies. She questioned whether this would be sufficient to improve his interpersonal skills. On the other hand, she reasoned that spending $50,000 to improve Williams's overall management skills might be worth it to the firm if he was capable of assuming ever-increasing responsibilities, even if the program did not vastly improve his interpersonal skills.

After discussing Williams's request for some time, Beck and Vander concluded that the firm had sufficient funds to pay for employees to complete I-MBA programs out of its training and development budget. They felt that under the right conditions, it might be beneficial for the firm to do so, given that it did not presently have any formalized management development programs. However, in order to be consistent, they would need to develop a comprehensive policy that would spell out criteria for determining whether the firm should grant I-learning requests. What they did not know was what those criteria should be and whether Williams's request should be granted in light of these criteria. They also did not know if there would be a better alternative for developing management skills.

QUESTIONS

1. What other management development approaches, other than the I-MBA program, could Nipigon Mining Products Corporation use to improve managerial skills?

2. What criteria should the firm use to determine if it will pay for employees to enroll in any degree program offered on the Internet, including an I-MBA program?

3. Should the firm grant Thomas Williams's request?

55 **EXERCISE**

Design and Evaluation of Training Programs

I. OBJECTIVES

A. To help you determine which training methods are most appropriate for achieving particular objectives.

B. To show you the linkages between training objectives, training methods, and training evaluation.

C. To help you learn how to identify and write training objectives.

D. To build skill in the evaluation of training programs.

II. OUT-OF-CLASS PREPARATION TIME: 1 hour

III. IN-CLASS TIME SUGGESTED: 45 minutes

IV. PROCEDURES

Prior to the class meeting in which this exercise will be discussed, read the entire exercise and use a pencil to complete Forms 3.1 and 3.2. Or you may use a separate sheet of paper. At the beginning of the class period, the instructor should divide the class into discussion groups of three to five students. Each group should begin by completing Form 3.1. If you are unfamiliar with any of the training methods listed, consult your textbook or ask your instructor.

Look at each training objective/outcome and then determine which training methods would be most appropriate for achieving each of the four training objectives on Form 3.1. Since each group member comes into the class period with his or her own ideas on which training method is most appropriate for achieving which objectives, there may be a need for some discussion and negotiation before a group consensus can emerge.

Put an "x" beside the method that seems most appropriate for achieving each objective or outcome. For example, if you believe that classroom instruction would be a good method of facilitating knowledge acquisition on the part of a training program participant, put an "x" in that space. Then, put an "x" wherever any particular training method seems appropriate for achieving particular training objectives or outcomes. For each of the four objectives or outcomes, you should have at least two, but no more than four, training methods that are identified as most appropriate.

Now, look at the data in Exhibit 3.2. These data are taken from a training needs analysis of executives and middle managers at Corporation X. The percent opposite each training need indicates the percentage of executives and middle managers citing each of the four top-rated training needs.

This company has had no previous formal training programs for its employees, and the newly hired director of employee development has asked your group to answer the following questions:

1. What training objectives and training needs do you select as the highest priority for future training (see Exhibit 3.2)?

2. What training methods should be used to meet this need and the related training objectives (see Form 3.1)?

	TRAINING OBJECTIVES					
Training Method	**Knowledge Acquisition**	**Attitude Change**	**Problem-Solving Skills**	**Interpersonal Skills**	**Participant Acceptance**	**Knowledge Retention**
Information Processing:						
Lecture (with questions)						
Conference (discussion)						
Sensitivity training						
Laboratory training						
Observation						
Closed-circuit TV						
Programmed instruction						
Correspondence courses						
Videos						
Reading lists						
Simulation:						
Cases						
Incidents						
Role playing						
Business games						
In-Basket exercises						
On-the-Job:						
Job rotation						
Committee assignments						
On-the-job coaching						
Feedback from performance appraisal						
Apprenticeships						

EXHIBIT 3.2 *Results of a Training Needs Assessment*

Survey of Executives and Middle Managers Top Four Areas of Executive and Middle Management Training

	Percentage citing need
Performance appraisal techniques	44
Strategic planning	38
Employee motivation	32
Marketing	27

FORM 3.2 *The Relationship between Training Objectives and Training Methods*
Occupational Group: Executives and Middle Managers Training Need:
_____ (Choose one of the needs identified in Exhibit 3.2.)

Training Objectives	Training Methods	Evaluation Methods
1.	1.	1.
2.	2.	2.
3.	3.	3.

3. What training evaluation method should be used to evaluate each training method or program?

Before answering the questions and completing Form 3.2, review the information in Form 3.1 and Exhibit 3.2. Select the priority training need for executive and middle managers for the coming year. Write that priority training need on Form 3.2.

Now, develop specific objectives for the training program or programs you are recommending. You may have up to three objectives and three training programs or methods. These will be listed on Form 3.2 as well. If your group selected strategic planning as one of the programs, then possible objectives might be increased knowledge about the process of strategic planning or successful development of a strategic plan for the corporation or the executive's department. Likewise, an objective for a performance appraisal program might be the design of an appropriate performance appraisal form and process for the individual middle manager's particular situation.

The final step is to determine the most appropriate method of evaluating the particular training program or programs. The four major methods of evaluation in order of their degree of complexity and difficulty are as follows:

1. Participant reaction—usually determined by a questionnaire immediately at the conclusion of the training program.

2. Learning—assessment of knowledge about or attitudes toward a particular subject, both before and after a training experience.

3. Behavioral change—changes in on-the-job behavior or performance as measured by performance appraisals, subordinate's perceptions, supervisor's perceptions, and/or individual productivity data.

4. Organizational effectiveness—decreases in departmental or organizational costs, turnover, absenteeism, and grievances, and increases in departmental or organizational sales, income, or productivity as compared to a control group of those not attending training.

QUESTIONS

1. Once you had determined the training need and training objectives, how did you determine which training method would be most appropriate?

2. Identify one or two training evaluation methods you recommended on Form 3.2. Why did you choose this evaluation method and what problems might you encounter in using it in a valid way?

3. What are the most effective training or educational methods to facilitate your own learning? Why?

56 EXERCISE
On-the-Job Training

I. OBJECTIVES

   A. To provide you with practice in conducting on-the-job training.

   B. To make you aware of the problems a supervisor may encounter when training employees.

II. OUT-OF-CLASS PREPARATION TIME: One to two hours

III. IN-CLASS TIME SUGGESTED: 45 minutes

IV. PROCEDURES

An important task for most supervisors is to instruct new employees on the methods and procedures necessary to perform various job tasks. Initially, the employee may be totally unfamiliar with a particular task. This places an additional burden on the manager to make his or her instructions as clear and precise as possible. In this exercise, you will be asked to train one or more members of the class on how to perform a task. After the training is complete, it will be critiqued.

Preparation for the training can be done individually or in groups of three to five members, at the instructor's option. If groups are used, the instructor will divide up the class during the class period prior to the one in which this exercise will be conducted. Each group will then meet outside of class to prepare for the training. Each individual or group should begin by selecting a task to teach one or more class members. For example, one of the following could be picked:

- How to lift heavy objects safely.

- How to fold a napkin like those in fancy restaurants.

- How to tie a special knot used by tree surgeons, Merchant Marine or Navy personnel.

- How to fix a dripping faucet.

- How to use a volt-ohm meter such as an electrician might use.

- How to use a Blackberry or other communication device.

- How to use a complex calculator.

- How to apply for a job online.

- How to set up a blog.

In selecting a task, pick one that is performed in industry, one that most class members do not already know how to perform, and one that is sufficiently complicated that trainees cannot perform instantly. Remember, you will have to provide all of the materials necessary to perform the task.

Finally, you must choose the best approach for conducting the training (lecture, demonstrations, and so on) and the steps that will be followed when conducting the training. If you are working in groups, a spokesperson (the one who will actually conduct the training for the group) should also be selected.

At the start of class, the instructor will select four or more groups/individuals to actually conduct on-the-job training. Depending upon the task, the instructor will also select one or more students to serve as trainees. At this point, the trainers will, one at a time, conduct training. This will be followed by a critique of each training session by all class members. Toward the end of class, those groups/individuals who did not actually conduct training during class will briefly explain how they would have conducted their training.

The Orientation Problem

Carol Burgess is a letter carrier and a part-time trainer of letter carriers for the U.S. Postal Service in a major city on the west coast. She trains all new letter carriers in her service area, which encompasses the northern half of her state. Over the past five years she has trained 318 new letter carriers. Typically, the training is offered prior to the new letter carrier's entry onto the job, although sometimes it occurs shortly thereafter.

The training program typically encompasses both the orientation of new employees to the U.S. Postal Service and the development of specific skills needed by the new letter carrier. The latter involves practice in casing mail (i.e., sorting) to appropriate locations of a case in preparation for delivery, reading maps, determining appropriate sequencing of delivery, and customer relations. The total training program takes three full days (one day of orientation and two days of skills training).

The orientation part of the training program encompasses both an orientation packet and a discussion of various Postal Service policies and procedures. The orientation packet typically includes information about employee benefits, holidays, copies of certain standard forms (i.e., IRS withholding forms), outline of emergency and accident procedures, key terms used in the U.S. Postal Service, copies of the health and life insurance options, and telephone numbers and locations of the personnel department and other important offices. In addition, an explanation of the U.S. Postal Service operation and purpose is provided. This explanation includes the training to be received, the letter carrier's duties and responsibilities, job standards and expected production levels, Postal Service rules and regulations, and the chain of command for reporting purposes are also provided. Burgess concludes her orientation with an offer of help and encouragement for the future.

The assumption built into the orientation is that it will be supplemented at the job site by the direct supervisor who will provide all the necessary information about the particular facility, the personnel at the facility, the area covered by the route or routes to which the new employee will be assigned, and the additional written information such as the employee handbook and the union contract. According to Postal Service policy, each new letter carrier should get three days of on-the-job training, of which one is paid for by the training division and two are charged to the supervisor's production. Burgess learned from subsequent conversations with her former trainees over the past five years that the orientation provided by the direct supervisor varied from practically nothing to fairly extensive. In some stations, the supervisor greeted the new employee, introduced the person to one other employee, and explained their own expectations regarding attendance, personal conduct, and productivity. Then, the employee was given an assignment and allowed to "sink or swim." Several supervisors were known in the Postal Service to be "SOBs." While 83 percent of new hires have survived their probationary 90-day period over the past three years, less than 20 percent survived in certain stations.

Last night Burgess received a telephone call from Edith Jones, one of her former trainees who finished training ten weeks ago. Jones is a single parent with two school-age children who had left her job as a secretary and taken the letter carrier job in order to make more money. Jones was in tears as she described her experience at her station. Her supervisor had given her no written materials, introduced her to only one other employee, and has shifted her from route to route over the ten weeks she has worked at the facility. No help or support of any kind has been offered, but the supervisor has continually berated her for the number of hours she has taken to case and deliver routes. She had tried to study maps during her days off in order to learn the various areas covered by various routes, but this only helped a little.

Each route had to be delivered in a particular order and it took time to learn the sequence. The other letter carriers were all stressed and working overtime themselves. Consequently, they ignored her and offered no assistance. Jones told Burgess that she was on the verge of quitting. Burgess told her to "hang in there because it does get easier with time."

As a result of all the complaints she had received from former trainees (some of whom survived the 90-day probationary period), Burgess decided to recommend to the area postmaster a program to train supervisors as to how to orient new letter carriers. However, she was not sure what specific items the supervisors should include in their new employee orientation and how to train them.

QUESTIONS

1. Describe the nature and causes of the U.S. Postal Service orientation problem in this case.

2. What types of orientation for new employees should direct supervisors provide at the work site?

3. What training methods should be used to train the supervisors, assuming approval of the proposal?

4. What written materials should the supervisor provide for new letter carriers in light of what Carol Burgess already provides?

5. In addition to the written materials discussed in the previous question, what else should the supervisor do to orient new letter carriers?

58 SKILL BUILDER

Identifying Training Needs through Task Analysis

I. OBJECTIVES

A. To introduce you to the process and purposes of assessing training needs.

B. To give you practice in determining training needs for a job.

II. TIME REQUIRED TO COMPLETE: 2 to 3 hours

III. INSTRUCTIONS

There are generally three analyses used to determine an organization's training needs: 1) organization analysis, 2) task or operations analysis, and 3) person analysis. This assignment allows you to perform a task analysis for a particular job by interviewing and observing a job holder. A task analysis involves systematic collection of data about a specific job. Its purpose is to determine what an employee should be taught to perform the job at the desired level. It generally includes a description of the major tasks of the job, standards of performance, how the tasks are to be performed to meet the standards, and the skills, knowledge, and abilities necessary. You will conduct the task analysis by following the steps described below:

Step 1: Select a job to analyze. You may choose a job currently held by a relative, friend, fellow student, etc. (If you completed "Exercise 30: Writing Job Descriptions" in Part 2, you may use that job.) Ask the job holder if you may interview him or her about the position and/or also observe him or her performing the job.

Step 2: Obtain a job description for the job you selected or prepare one by interviewing the job holder. The job description should describe in general terms the worker's major duties and responsibilities. For example, a job description for an accounts receivable clerk might include the following duties and responsibilities:

a. Invoice shipments to customers on a monthly basis.

b. Prepare journal vouchers at the end of the month to record cash receipts and sales by product lines.

When preparing the job description, be sure to include those things that are critical to performing the job satisfactorily, no matter how infrequently or briefly they occur, and the knowledge, skills, and abilities needed.

Step 3: This step involves identifying the tasks associated with performing each of the major duties of the job. You are to identify the overt, observable behaviors that are involved in performing the job. Arrange (if possible) to observe the worker performing his or her job and develop a list of the tasks involved. A task listing includes behavioral statements of how the job is to be performed. Using the example for the accounts receivable clerk, the tasks associated with invoicing customers might include:

a. Pull and review invoice master.

b. Extend and update invoice master.

c. Add correct discount and freight charges.

d. Make necessary amount of copies on copy machine.

When you complete this step, you should have a report that includes the title of the job, the major duties (responsibilities) of the job, the tasks associated with each duty/responsibility, and the knowledge and skills required of job incumbents.

Step 4: Once you have completed Steps 1–3, answer the following questions and include them in your report:

a. What training would benefit a person performing the job? If you had to design a training program for the job, what content areas would be needed, based on your analysis?

b. What training method would be best (on-the-job training, seminars, apprenticeships, vestibule, etc.)? Why?

Performance Appraisal

59 CASE

The Self-Appraisal Problem

Leroy Washington, human resource director at Engel Products, was faced with a problem that he had not experienced before and was uncertain how to proceed. The problem was related to the firm's self-evaluation appraisal process. This process requires supervisors to evaluate themselves by completing two forms. The first form, Responsibilities and Goal Accomplishments Self Evaluation Report (see Exhibit 3.3), requires that supervisors write down their primary job duties/responsibilities along with the objectives that they had agreed to accomplish during the past year. They are to evaluate themselves from 1 (Outstanding) to 4 (Unsatisfactory). They also need to write an overall performance summary. The second form, Career Development Self Evaluation Report (see Exhibit 3.4), is used for training and development purposes and asks supervisors to indicate their strengths, evaluate themselves in terms of ten criteria, and develop plans for improving their skills and knowledge. It also asks supervisors to explain their career interests by specifying what jobs they aspire to hold in the future. For each objective, they are required to specify the criteria they will use to judge whether the objective was met and a date by which the objective will be accomplished.

Washington's major problem was that one of the sales staff supervisors had not completed her self-evaluation on time. The firm had a policy that all supervisors were to be evaluated annually by their immediate manager. The policy stipulated that each supervisor was to complete a self-evaluation and turn it into his/her immediate manager by a specific date. Prior to seeing this self-evaluation, the manager would also complete an evaluation on the supervisor. The two would then meet, trade evaluations, compare the two documents, and discuss differences. The completed evaluations were then turned in to the HR director for review.

Unfortunately, Carol McCalmont had not turned in her evaluation by the deadline. Washington told McCalmont's manager, Janet Weber, that the deadline had passed and asked Weber to remind McCalmont to quickly turn in the self-evaluation. One week later, the self-evaluation had not been completed; McCalmont stated she was still working on it and would turn it in soon. Another week went by, and McCalmont still had not submitted the self-evaluation, so Washington told Weber to let McCalmont know that she would not receive a scheduled raise until the report was completed.

Two more weeks passed and nothing happened. Then, Washington received a file that contained a performance review for McCalmont, written by Weber. However, the file did not include McCalmont's required self-evaluation. Washington immediately called Weber to find out why McCalmont had not completed the report and why Weber had submitted her evaluation in the absence of a self-evaluation. Weber responded that she could only guess as to why McCalmont had not completed the report: the self-appraisal process was too time-consuming, and she did not want to admit that her performance was unsatisfactory in some areas. Weber added that she did not want to hold up McCalmont's raise any longer and that is

Instructions: List below your major job responsibilities and the objectives you set for yourself to accomplish during the past year. Then, rate yourself on each of these items as follows:

1—Outstanding—Your performance far exceeds this job requirement. You far exceeded this goal.

2—Commendable—Your performance exceeds this job requirement. You exceeded this goal.

3—Competent—Your performance met this job requirement. You met this goal.

4—Unsatisfactory—Your performance did not meet this job requirement. You did not meet this goal.

Job Responsibilities   *Rating*

1.
2.
3.
4.

List other job responsibilities and ratings on a separate page.

Goal Accomplishments (List Goals)   *Rating*

1.
2.
3.
4.

List other goals and ratings on a separate page.

PERFORMANCE SUMMARY (Using the space below write a summary of your job performance for the past year. Attach additional sheets if necessary.)

EXHIBIT 3.4 *Career Development Self-Evaluation Report*

PART A—STRENGTHS. Describe below your specific technical, interpersonal, managerial, and other job-related strengths.

PART B—DEVELOPMENTAL NEEDS. Indicate below the technical, interpersonal, managerial, or other job-related weaknesses you perceive in yourself.

PART C—IMPROVEMENT PLANS. State below what steps you plan to take to improve your weaknesses, including any training/education you would like the firm to offer to you.

PART D—SKILL EVALUATION. Evaluate yourself in terms of the ten skills listed below.

SKILL	Unsatisfactory	Competent	Commendable	Outstanding
1. Work quality	4	3	2	1
2. Technical skills	4	3	2	1
3. Productivity	4	3	2	1
4. Adaptability	4	3	2	1
5. Interpersonal skills	4	3	2	1
6. Planning skills	4	3	2	1
7. Initiative	4	3	2	1
8. Decision making	4	3	2	1
9. Analytical skills	4	3	2	1
10. Profit orientation	4	3	2	1

PART E—FUTURE JOB. Indicate what job or jobs you would like to hold in the future.

why she completed and submitted her evaluation. She believed that a small raise was warranted and that McCalmont's failure to complete a self-evaluation should not disqualify her from receiving the raise.

QUESTIONS

1. What action should Leroy Washington take in response to Carol McCalmont's and Janet Weber's actions? Should McCalmont be granted a raise even though she had not completed her self-evaluation?

2. Evaluate Engel Product's self-appraisal system. Should it be changed to make it more effective? Is it too time-consuming?

3. Should the firm eliminate the self-appraisal portion of its appraisal system?

60 CASE

Mills Paper Company: Performance Management or Age Discrimination?

Lance Amato, CFO for Mills Paper Company, sat at his desk dreading the upcoming meeting with John Carpenter, a general accountant with the company. He was going to notify Carpenter of his termination from the company. Although it was going to be a difficult meeting, Amato felt the company had no choice and had done everything possible to assist Carpenter in meeting the performance expectations that had been set for him. As he sat waiting for the meeting to begin, Amato reviewed Carpenter's performance record and history at Mills.

Carpenter had been hired by Mills Paper Company two years earlier. At the time, he was 56 years old and had come to Mills with considerable experience. When hired, Carpenter signed a written performance agreement, a patent and confidentiality agreement, and a standard ethics letter. Mills used a management by objectives performance appraisal system for its managerial staff. The expectations and objectives of positions were put into a performance agreement annually. Within one week of employment, Carpenter and his supervisor at the time, Henry Castagnera, had agreed upon the objectives and performance metrics for Carpenter's position. Carpenter signed the MBO agreement.

Carpenter's tenure at Mills Paper was marred by a number of poor performance appraisals and demotions. In the first quarter after he started work, Carpenter received a poor performance rating from his direct supervisor. At the time, several managers, including the president of Mills, expressed their disappointment and concern about Carpenter's performance as division controller (see Exhibit 3.5). However, the files indicated that despite the poor performance rating, Carpenter received a seven percent salary increase the first year of his employment.

Due to the reorganization of the company shortly thereafter, Carpenter was assigned to a different division and supervisor. His new supervisor, Bob Crane, had prepared a set of objectives for Carpenter. During a mid-year review, Crane rated his performance as "needs improvement." The review he submitted contained substantive comments to support the rating (see Exhibit 3.6). As part of the improvement plan Crane developed for Carpenter, it was agreed that his performance would be reviewed again in three months. Crane had noted the following in Carpenter's personnel file at that time, "There has not been positive action in order to improve, and in some areas we have even lost ground."

EXHIBIT 3.5 *Comments from John Carpenter's Performance Appraisal*

- Information furnished not consistently accurate
- Poor supervision of direct reports
- Accounting information not submitted on time
- Managers not satisfied with the financial guidance provided
- Paucity of key financial information available concerning manufacturing operations
- Slow response to requests for information

EXHIBIT 3.6 *Excerpts from Performance Appraisal Conducted by Bob Crane*

- Lack of solid response and follow through on specific requests for assistance

- Organization concerning financial aspects of strategy preparation and budgeting was not good

- No solid proposals given on how to improve the effectiveness of the accounting department

- Managers not satisfied with responses and state they were "wishy-washy"

- Very little improvement around routine reporting

- No initiative in putting together a better financial forecasting form

---

Crane made further suggestions for Carpenter's improvement that included meeting with general managers at Mills to help him understand their needs. He also charged Carpenter with developing and issuing a new forecasting form for use in the division. When Carpenter did not meet performance expectations, he was demoted by Crane to financial analyst with a change in title, reduced grade and responsibilities, but remained at the same pay. Once again, Carpenter was told his performance needed to improve.

Subsequent papers in the file showed Carpenter's performance did not improve or ever reach the level expected of someone with his background and skill. In a last ditch effort to manage Carpenter, Amato had given him the option of being demoted to a general accountant or being terminated for inability to perform his job. Carpenter chose to accept the second demotion with decrease in salary from $65,000 to $61,000. A set of performance objectives were developed for Carpenter in his new position. However, after two months it was clear that Carpenter was not able to meet the minimal targets that had been set for him. His financial reports continued to be of poor quality and were inaccurate. Finally, the decision was made to terminate Carpenter. As Amato reviewed Carpenter's file and the performance reviews, Amato wondered why they had not dismissed him earlier.

Amato looked up when he heard a knock on his door. It was Carpenter. After a rather formal greeting, he told Carpenter he was terminated for poor performance and would receive 21-weeks severance pay, payment for unused vacation time, and could also use the company's outplacement services. Carpenter reacted first with shock and then anger. He slammed the door as he left Amato's office. Two months later, Mills Paper Company was notified that Carpenter had filed a complaint with the local EEOC Office alleging age discrimination, unfair performance appraisal, and negligent and intentional infliction of emotional distress.

QUESTIONS

1. Evaluate Mills Paper Company's management of John Carpenter's performance. What are the strengths and weaknesses of their approach to performance appraisals (i.e., management by objectives)?

2. Do you agree or disagree with Lance Amato's observation that Carpenter should have been terminated earlier?

3. Review Exhibit 3.7, which lists employment laws relevant to performance appraisals. Do you think that Carpenter prevail in his charges against Mills? Why or why not? What are the elements of a legally defensible performance appraisal system?

EXHIBIT 3.7 *Legislation Relevant to Performance Appraisals*

LAW	PURPOSE	IMPLICATIONS FOR PERFORMANCE APPRAISALS
Title VII of Civil Rights Act of 1964	Outlaws discrimination based on race, color, sex, religion, or national origin.	Protection against performance appraisal policies and procedures and outcomes that are discriminatory; appraisal criteria must be job related and consistently applied.
Civil Rights Act of 1991 (CRA 1991)	Allows jury trials, compensatory and punitive damages in discrimination cases; alters burden of proof and other technical aspects of some cases.	Reduces plaintiff's burden of proving that particular practices of employer (e.g., performance appraisals, selection systems) caused discrimination; performance appraisal procedures should be well-documented; proper training should be provided to evaluators; consistent application of performance standards; there should be an appeal process for employees.
Equal Pay Act of 1963	Prohibits gender-based differences in pay for equal work, subject to limited exceptions.	Performance appraisal ratings results can be used to invoke and justify exceptions in performance bonuses (e.g., merit-based pay distinctions); men and women with similar performance ratings should receive similar bonuses.
Age Discrimination in Employment Act (ADEA) 1967	It is unlawful to discriminate against a person because of his/her age (40 or over) with respect to any term, condition or privilege of employment, including hiring, firing, promotion, performance evaluation, layoff, compensation, benefits, job assignments and training. The law applies to private employers, state, federal, and local governments as well as employment agencies and labor unions.	Provides protection against use of performance appraisal procedures and results to perpetrate age-based discrimination; evaluators should avoid stereotyping based on age and only use job-related performance criteria.
Americans with Disabilities Act (ADA) 1991	Prohibits employment discrimination based on disability.	Limits appraisal criteria to essential job functions and requires reasonable accommodation as to how performance is appraised.
At-will Employment	A doctrine of American law that defines an employment relationship in which any party can break the relationship with no liability, provided there was no express contract for a definite term governing the relationship and there is no collective bargaining agreement. Several states now recognize implied contracts that may be "implied" in human resource policies in employee handbooks or promises that were made at the time of employment.	Performance appraisal criteria and results must be job-related or based on the contract agreements (if there is a contract); termination cannot be based on unlawful discrimination; a company should follow its termination procedures as specified in company policies and handbooks.

EvalSim—A Performance Evaluation Exercise

I. OBJECTIVES

A. To familiarize you with some of the problems related to the use of performance appraisals and to provide alternative approaches for solving these problems.

B. To give you practice in making decisions and writing memos to employees regarding performance appraisal issues.

II. OUT-OF-CLASS PREPARATION TIME: 20 minutes to read exercise plus one hour to complete e-mail Items, either individually or with group members, and write responses

III. IN-CLASS TIME SUGGESTED: 45 minutes to discuss all e-mail Items

IV. PROCEDURES

This exercise can be done individually or in groups of three to five members, at the instructor's option. You are to begin by reading all of the material presented in this exercise. Assume that you are responsible for developing and maintaining the O'Leary Organization's performance appraisal system. You are to assume further that the items that follow were waiting in your e-mail when you arrived at work after a three-week vacation. First, you (or your team) are (is) to respond in writing to each employee who sent you an e-mail. Second, explain on a separate sheet of paper what additional actions you would take with reference to each item. For example, if you believe that you should gather additional information before making a final decision on an item, explain what information you would want. Or, if you believe that additional memos or discussions with someone in the company are needed, explain this. You (or your team) should bring both the memos and the "Additional Action" sheets to class. Be prepared to present and defend these materials during the class discussion.

SITUATION

The O'Leary Organization is a medium-sized organization with headquarters in the Midwest. You may assume that the organization is a manufacturing company, a hospital, an insurance company, a university, or virtually any other medium-sized organization with which you are familiar.

The training and development section consists of you or your team. In addition to conducting training, you have full responsibility for the organization's performance evaluation system. The O'Leary Organization's present performance appraisal system, which you are to assume you or your team designed, requires that all employees be evaluated by their supervisor on a periodic basis. All employees are evaluated at the end of a 90-day period (the initial employment period) and on a yearly basis thereafter. The performance appraisal form used by the organization is shown in Exhibit 3.8. Supervisors are required to complete this form for each of their employees at the appropriate time, discuss the evaluation with the employee, ask the employee to sign the form at the end of the evaluation interview, and return the completed form to the human resource department.

EXHIBIT 3.8 *The O'Leary Organization Performance Appraisal Form*

NAME	IDENTIFICATION NUMBER	
TITLE	DEPARTMENT	
TODAY'S DATE	APPRAISAL PERIOD	Annual
	FROM___ TO___	90 day

Part I Performance Rating

	1	2	3	4	5
Ability					
Attendance					
Attitude					
Appearance					
Conduct					
Initiative					
Work with Group					
Promotability					
Quantity of Work					
Quality of Work					
Overall Level of Performance					

1—Unsatisfactory 2—Below Average 3—Satisfactory 4—Good 5—Excellent

Part 2 Additional Questions: Answer the following on a separate sheet of paper.

1. List your major goals for the next year.
2. Describe additional training that you believe you need to achieve those goals.
3. State what you believe are your major strengths and weaknesses.
4. Do you have any additional comments or suggestions for improving your job performance or work environment?

Prepared by _____   Title _____
COMMENTS BY REVIEWED EMPLOYEE:

Employee's Signature _____   Date _____

(Employee signature does not indicate agreement, merely acknowledgment of this report.)

Item 1

To: HR Department
From: Tom Morrison, Accounting Department
RE: 90-Day Employee Evaluation

I just received my 90-day employee evaluation and received mostly 3s on it. My boss explained his evaluation to me by saying that I was making good progress on the job. He added that if I continue to show improvement, I will receive 4s and 5s like the more experienced employees do. Why am I being evaluated against older, more experienced workers? That doesn't seem right. I believe that considering my limited experience, I deserve "excellent" evaluations.

Item 2

To: HR Department
From: Paul Lands, Computer Center
RE: Performance Evaluation

Joe Meena and I started together at the O'Leary Organization two years ago. We are both in the Computer Center doing the same job, only he works one shift, and I work another. Two weeks ago, when we compared our performance evaluations, I discovered that he received all 5s whereas I received mostly 4s. The thing that irks me is that he and I both know we are doing an equally good job. His boss is just more lenient in his evaluation than is my boss. I don't think this whole system is fair, particularly since he may get promoted (based on his performance evaluation) before I do. Can't something be done about this?

Item 3

To: HR Department
From: Jill Best, Manager
RE: Performance Appraisal Form Question

I am a relatively new manager and am filling out the Performance Appraisal Form for the first time on one of my employees. I am not clear what some of the terms on the form mean. Specifically, I don't know what is meant by the term "conduct" or by the term "attitude." Would you please explain them to me?

Item 4

To: HR Department
From: Sue Peters, Supervisor
RE: Administering Employee Evaluations

I have recently received from your office a request to conduct evaluations this month on three of my employees. As you probably know, I was promoted to this supervisory position just one week ago as a result of the former supervisor's termination. I don't feel that I can presently conduct a fair evaluation of these employees. Do you want me to do them anyway?

Item 5

To: HR Department
From: Karen Blackwell, Supervisor
RE: Evaluation of Heather Morrison

This morning I conducted an evaluation interview with Heather Morrison. Although I had given her a 4 on initiative last year, I gave her a 2 in that category this year. When I told her this, she became very angry and said the evaluation should have been at least a 3 and probably a 4 again. I attempted to explain my evaluation to her, but she wouldn't listen. Instead, she continued to argue with me, but could not give me any concrete examples that would allow me to improve her rating on this category. If a situation like this comes up again, how should I handle it?

Item 6

To: HR Department
From: Howard Adams, Supervisor
RE: Necessity of Signing Evaluation Forms

Recently I conducted a performance evaluation interview with Harold Wallace. At the end of the interview, when I asked him to sign the appraisal form at the bottom, he refused. I asked him if the evaluation was accurate, and he said yes. I also explained to him that signing the form only represented an acknowledgment that he had been evaluated. He replied that he had nothing to gain from signing the form, and, therefore, why sign it? I don't know what I should do. Harold is somewhat of a problem and is often quite stubborn.

Item 7

To: HR Department
From: Margaret Windell, Purchasing
RE: Annual Performance Review

I have a rather troublesome question to ask you. I would ask it of my boss but she is currently in the hospital. For the last 23 years I have received an overall performance review, and my evaluations have all shown that I am an excellent employee. I am six years from retirement and, frankly, I have reached the point where performance evaluations aren't of any consequence to me. I know I am doing a good job. I know I won't get promoted or transferred, and I am at the top of my pay grade. So why should I continue to be evaluated formally?

Item 8

To: HR Department
From: Sarah Wade, Maintenance Engineer
RE: Employee Appraisal Form

When I was over in the HR Department yesterday looking at my file, I saw the appraisal form that was completed on me one month ago. I was shocked to see the following statement written on it under "Remarks": "Sarah has a very poor work attitude and doesn't appear willing to change it." My boss, Marilyn Turner, had also changed my evaluation on "attitude" from 4 to a 2. I am positive the negative statement was not on the evaluation form when I signed it. Needless to say, I want you to do something about this!

Item 9

To: HR Department
From: Chris Green, Supervisor
RE: Performance Evaluation of Bill Young

Next week, I must conduct a performance evaluation interview with Bill Young who works by himself in the evenings. While I was completing the evaluation form on him, I realized that it was impossible for me to evaluate him on one of the evaluation categories, "Work with Group." What should I do? I am afraid if I leave it blank it will affect his "Overall Level of Performance" score and hence, his chances of promotion.

Item 10

To: HR Department
From: Jeff Skala, Finance Department
RE: Confidentiality of Performance Evaluation

As you know, over the past year I have been experiencing a series of personal problems, all of which have adversely affected my job performance. These problems reflected themselves on my recent performance evaluation as my "marks" slipped from mostly 4s to mostly 2s. I can't disagree with my evaluation, but I don't think it was right for my boss, Helen Jackson, to tell two of my co-workers that she had given me a 1 on "Quality of Work." It seems to me that this type of information should be confidential since it is none of their business.

---

62 EXERCISE

Performance Appraisal Interview Role Play

I. OBJECTIVES

A. To allow you practice in conducting a performance appraisal interview.

B. To compare and contrast different approaches to the performance appraisal interview.

C. To help you develop sensitivity toward communication problems in performance appraisal interviews.

II. OUT-OF-CLASS PREPARATION TIME: 20–30 minutes

III. IN-CLASS TIME SUGGESTED: 45 minutes

IV. PROCEDURES

A. Read the exercise before coming to class.

B. Four students should be selected to participate in two different performance appraisal interviews (A and B). Two will play the role of the employee and two will play the role of the supervisor. Role assignments should be made in the prior class period or before class begins. The instructor will provide role sheets.

C. The persons playing the role of the employee should read "Employee's Role."

D. The person playing the role of supervisor A should read the "Supervisor Role A," and the person playing the role of supervisor B should read the "Supervisor Role B."

E. During the class period in which the role plays will occur, all role play participants should be taken outside of the classroom and given time to prepare their respective roles. All other members of the class are to observe the two different sets of interviews and record their observations on separate sheets of paper.

F. Supervisor A conducts a 10–15 minute appraisal interview with one of the employees in the front of the class. The other role play pair remains in the hall outside the classroom until their turn.

G. After the first role play is completed, the second role play pair enters the classroom and conducts its appraisal interview. The first role play team joins the rest of the class to observe the interview.

H. The entire class discusses both interviews.

SITUATION

Tri-City Health Services is a large non-profit center providing basic outpatient health services and health education programs to low-income families in the Southwest. The center employs over 40 physicians and nurses and more than 200 other workers in various staff positions. Pat Smith has been working as a junior assistant in the fund raising and grants department for the past two years and has worked on the children's health care program. Smith has done well in performing her job—all performance objectives have been met or surpassed for the year. However, this year she has been reprimanded on more than one occasion for spending too much time on the Internet. On one occasion Smith was supposed to be at a meeting, only to be found busy adding to her Facebook page. Company reports show that Smith's Internet usage is the highest of all staff in the department.

Each year on the anniversary date of the employee's hire, his or her supervisor must conduct a performance appraisal interview. Chris Jackson, the supervisor of Pat Smith, has completed the performance evaluation form shown in Exhibit 3.9 and is ready to discuss the evaluation with Smith.

INSTRUCTIONS FOR OBSERVERS

Your task is to evaluate two different sets of performance interviews. As you observe the interviews, consider the following:

1. How did the supervisor begin the interview? Was the purpose of the interview clearly stated?

2. What type of interview approach did the supervisor use? Who did most of the talking: the employee or the supervisor?

3. Did the supervisor learn how the employee feels about the job or about his or her performance?

4. Did both parties gain a clear understanding of the problem and its solution?

5. Were any specific action plans made to resolve the problem(s)?

6. Are there any ways in which the supervisor could improve the interview? How?

7. Which interview was most effective? Why?

EXHIBIT 3.9 *Performance Evaluation Form*

I. Rating Categories

Performance Dimensions	Performance Level	Points (Maximum = 5)
Quality of Work (The degree to which the employee's work is free of flaws)	*Excellent*	5
Quantity of Work (The total amount of acceptable work completed within time and resources available)	*Excellent*	5
Attendance (Includes absences and tardiness)	*Poor*	1
Cooperation (The degree to which the employee cooperates with and is respected by co-workers)	*Average*	3
Initiative and Self-Reliance (The degree to which the employee is independent and self-directed)	*Excellent*	5
Work Timeliness (The degree to which the employee exhibits skill in planning and scheduling activities; uses work time efficiently)	*Below Average*	2
Responsibility (The degree to which the employee is willing to accept responsibility for details in work)	*Above Average*	4
Total Points		25

II. Objectives and Goals

A. Did the employee set any specific work-related goals this performance period?
Yes (X)   No ( )

B. If yes, what were they?
To complete and implement a fund-raising program by April 1.
To obtain a 15 percent increase in federal grants by April 1.

C. To what extent were they met?
Employee met or exceeded both objectives. The fund-raising effort was very successful (over $25,000 was raised) and federal grants have been increased by 18 percent this year.

Overall evaluation of goal achievement? *Excellent*

III. Overall Evaluation of Employee Performance (support evaluation with comments)

The employee has done a fine job on performance objectives but continues to have a problem with tardiness. Based on this, the overall rating for the year is average (25 out of 35 points). I do not recommend the employee for a promotion at this time.

IV. Performance and Career Development

Instructions: This section should be discussed and completed during the appraisal interview with the employee.
1. What action could the employee take in the coming year to improve his/her performance?

2. What specific support is needed by the employee to improve his/her performance?

3. What kind of work or job does the employee want to be doing in the next two years? Five years?

4. What training and development would the employee benefit from in the coming year? Be specific.

V. Performance Goals for Coming Year

Instructions: The supervisor and employee must complete the table below and list the employee's goals and key performance indicators for the coming year:

Key Performance Area	Goals	Key Measures

Supervisor Signature   Date   Employee Signature   Date

63 EXERCISE

Which Performance Appraisal Format Is Most Effective?

I. **OBJECTIVES**

A. To examine the strengths and weaknesses of four different methods for appraising employees.

B. To enhance your oral communication skills.

II. **OUT-OF-CLASS PREPARATION TIME:** 30 minutes to prepare for the debate

III. **IN-CLASS TIME SUGGESTED:** 50–75 minutes

IV. **PROCEDURES**

Your instructor will divide the class into five groups in the class prior to conducting this exercise. There will be four debating groups consisting of three to five members each and one or more groups of judges that consist of the remaining class members. Debaters will be assigned one of four positions and told to prepare to argue in favor of that position. Judges will be told to read the textbook chapter pages that cover those positions. The issue to be debated is: Which approach to appraising employees is the most effective? The positions are: 1) trait appraisal instruments such as the graphic rating scale; 2) behavioral appraisal instruments such as the behaviorally anchored rating scale; 3) a ranking or forced distribution system; and 4) outcome appraisal instruments such as management by objectives.

At the start of the next class, your instructor will announce that a four-way debate will be held. The judges' role in the debate is to "search for the truth." They are to listen to all four sides presented and then, after the debate is over, tell the class what they believe is the correct answer to the debate question, not who won the debate.

The debate consists of two rounds. The purpose of Round One (15–20 minutes) is for each team to learn the position of the other debating teams. Hence, each team has up to five minutes to explain their position as comprehensively as possible. At the completion of Round One, the debating teams are given up to ten minutes to prepare criticisms of each of the other three teams for Round Two. During this intermission, judges are to discuss what they have heard and begin to formulate their own position.

In Round Two (15–20 minutes), each debating team is given up to five minutes to criticize the position of each of the other teams. Unlike a traditional debate, teams are not allowed to rebut the criticisms made by others. They must simply listen to them. Round Two ends when Team Four has finished criticizing the position of the other three teams.

After the debate has ended, the judges have five minutes to discuss the case with each other and arrive at a consensus, if possible. The judging team(s) then explains its decision to the debaters.

64 EXERCISE

Ethical Performance Appraisal Issues

I. **OBJECTIVES**

A. To make you aware that many performance appraisal decisions involve ethical issues.

B. To familiarize you with some of the many ethical performance appraisal issues.

C. To familiarize you with various criteria that can be used to determine if an action is ethical.

D. To make you aware of some of the reasons why a manager may be tempted to act unethically when evaluating subordinates.

II. **OUT-OF-CLASS PREPARATION TIME:** 15 minutes to read each of the situations presented and answer Question 1 below

III. **IN-CLASS TIME SUGGESTED:** 20–40 minutes

IV. **PROCEDURES**

At the start of class, the instructor will divide the class into teams of three to five students. Your group should discuss each of the situations below and answer the following questions in the space provided:

1. Is the manager in the case acting in an ethical manner? Yes or No? (Answer Y or N under the letter "E" below.)

2. Would your group act in the same manner as the manager? Yes or No? (Answer Y or N under the letter "G" below.)

After all groups have answered the questions above, the instructor will ask one or more of them to present their answers.

In trying to answer the first question, your group may want to consider some or all of the questions listed below that could be used to judge whether an act is ethical. You may also want to consider other criteria/questions provided by your instructor or suggested in the textbook.

A. Does the action involve intentional deception?

B. Does the action purposely benefit one party at the expense of another?

C. Is the action fair and just to all concerned?

D. Would you or the manager feel comfortable if the action were made public, or must it remain a secret?

E. Would you need to justify the action by telling yourself that you can get away with it or that you will not need to live with the decision's consequences? Would you recommend the action to others?

F. Will the action build goodwill and better relationships?

INSTRUCTIONS: Read each of the following scenarios and answer questions 1 and 2 above in the space provided with either a "Y" for Yes or an "N" for No.

E   G

_____ _____ 1. A supervisor has an employee who is an outspoken homosexual. The supervisor does not like homosexuals. As a result, the supervisor purposely rates him lower than deserved on his performance appraisal form.

_____ _____ 2. A firm has recently been charged with discriminating against minorities. The firm denies the charges but asks all supervisors to make sure they do not discriminate. In order to avoid any possible discrimination charge, a manager rates one poor performing minority employee higher than deserved on the performance appraisal form.

_____ _____ 3. A manager has a male subordinate who is married with three children. This employee is a known womanizer and has been spotted by several employees socializing with women other than his wife, including prostitutes. The supervisor does not believe this is appropriate and rates the employee lower than deserved on the performance appraisal form.

_____ _____ 4. A female employee who recently had a baby negotiated a change from full-time to part-time status with the HR department. Her supervisor, also a working mother, resents the fact that she is able to spend more time at home with her child. The supervisor rates her lower than deserved on the performance appraisal form in an attempt to force her to switch back to full-time status or to quit.

_____ _____ 5. A firm has a 360-degree performance appraisal system that includes asking all subordinates to rate and evaluate their boss. A manager wants to be promoted so he gives all employees higher performance evaluations than they deserve in hopes that they, in turn, will rate him higher.

_____ _____ 6. A manager realizes that an employee's attendance is so poor that she is likely to get terminated within the next few months. So, in order to build a more solid case against the employee and further justify the inevitable termination, the manager rates the subordinate lower than deserved on the performance appraisal form.

_____ _____ 7. A manager wants to get promoted in order to get a substantial raise. He believes that he will be judged, in part, in terms of how effective he has been at developing high-performing subordinates as evidenced by his subordinates' performance appraisal scores. In order to enhance his promotion chances, he rates his employees higher than deserved.

_____ _____ 8. A manager wants to give one particularly hard-working, reliable subordinate a big raise in order to keep her from accepting a job elsewhere. The manager does not want to have to replace this employee and train a new one. However, there is limited raise money available, and it is based on merit. So, he rates another employee lower than deserved, thereby reducing this person's raise, in order to be able to give the other a larger raise.

_____ _____ 9. A manager wants to get rid of a disliked subordinate, so she rates the employee lower than deserved in hopes that the employee will quit.

_____ _____ 10. A manager wants to help a subordinate who has become a friend to get a promotion, so she gives her a higher evaluation than deserved.

4

Implementing
Compensation
and Security:
Compensation,
Incentives,
Benefits, and
Safety and Health

Compensation

65 CASE

The Overpaid Bank Tellers

State Bank is located in a southwestern town of about 50,000 people. It is one of four banks in the area and has the reputation of being the most progressive. Russell Duncan has been the president of the bank for 15 years. Before coming to State Bank, he worked for a large Detroit bank for ten years. Duncan has implemented a number of changes that have earned him a great deal of respect and admiration from bank employees and townspeople alike. For example, in response to a growing number of Spanish-speaking people in the area, he hired Latinos and placed them in critical bank positions. He organized and staffed the city's only agricultural loan center to meet the needs of the area's farmers. In addition, he established the state's first "uniline" system for handling customers waiting in line for a teller.

Perhaps more than anything else, Duncan is known for establishing progressive human resource practices. He strongly believes that the bank's employees are its most important asset and continually searches for ways to increase both employee satisfaction and productivity. He feels that all employees should strive to continually improve their skills and abilities and, hence, he cross-trains employees and sends many of them to courses and conferences sponsored by banking groups such as the American Institute of Banking.

With regard to employee compensation, Duncan firmly believes that employees should be paid according to their contribution to organizational success. Ten years ago, he implemented a results-based pay system under which employees could earn raises from 0 to 8 percent each year, depending on their job performance. Raises are typically determined by the bank's HR committee during February and are granted to employees on March 1 of each year. Six years ago, in addition to granting employees merit raises, the bank also began giving cost-of-living raises. Duncan had been originally opposed to this idea but could determine no alternative.

One February, another bank in town conducted a wage survey to determine the average compensation of bank employees in the city. The management of State Bank received a copy of the wage survey and was surprised to learn that its 23 tellers, as a group, were being paid an average of $22 per week more than were tellers at other banks. The survey also showed that employees holding other positions in the bank (e.g., branch managers, loan officers, and file clerks) were being paid wages similar to those paid by other banks (see Exhibit 4.1).

After receiving the report, the HR committee of the bank met to determine what should be done regarding the tellers' raises. The committee knew that none of the tellers had been told how much their raises would be, but that they were all expecting both merit and cost-of-living raises. They also realized that, if other employees learned that the tellers were being overpaid, friction could develop and morale might suffer. The committee knew that it was costing the bank over $26,000 annually to pay the tellers. Finally, they knew that as a group the bank's tellers were highly competent, and they did not want to lose any of them.

Position	Bank 1	Bank 2	Bank 3	State Bank
Commercial Loan Officer	$78,600	$79,500	$77,900	$78,400
Consumer Loan Officer	59,200	54,700	55,760	59,000
Mortgage Loan Officer	57,100	55,900	59,500	57,200
Branch Manager	57,700	59,400	58,800	58,400
Assistant Branch Manager	40,800	40,400	40,600	40,300
New Accounts Officer	33,900	33,800	33,700	33,800
Officer Trainee	33,200	33,000	33,400	33,300

Average Weekly Earnings of Local Bank Tellers				
Tellers	$482	$479	$485	$504

QUESTIONS

1. If you were on the HR committee of State Bank, what decisions would you suggest regarding raises for the tellers?

2. How much faith should the HR committee place in the accuracy of the wage survey?

3. Critique State Bank's policy of giving merit raises that range from 0 to 8 percent, depending on job performance.

4. Critique the bank's policy of giving cost-of-living raises. Do you think that they should be eliminated?

66 CASE

Rewarding Volunteers

Northern University is a large university in a small college town in the Northwest. After several years of political pressure, internal conflicts, and negotiations, the university applied for, and was granted, an FCC license for a new public radio affiliate. The general goals of the station were to provide quality noncommercial alternative broadcasting with an emphasis on local and national news, jazz, and classical music. The station would have no paid commercials but would broadcast public service announcements and cultural events.

A short-term objective was to assemble and train a volunteer staff (mostly students and faculty) until funds could be provided for an all-professional staff of experienced board operators and program announcers. Exhibit 4.2 shows the organization structure of the radio station. The general manager, chief engineer, news director, administrative assistant, and program director were all full-time paid positions. All of the other positions were either part-time employees, part-time work-study students, or unpaid part-time volunteers. The latter were mostly university faculty and their spouses.

The students volunteered to get training and experience, which they hoped would propel them into careers in the media. Faculty volunteered either for the new experience or because they liked playing particular types of music. The others volunteered to help the station and to meet new people. Volunteers were trained and used as both announcers and in "behind the scenes" positions such as board operators. Many of the board operators were told they could become announcers in the future.

EXHIBIT 4.2 *Organizational Structure of the Station*

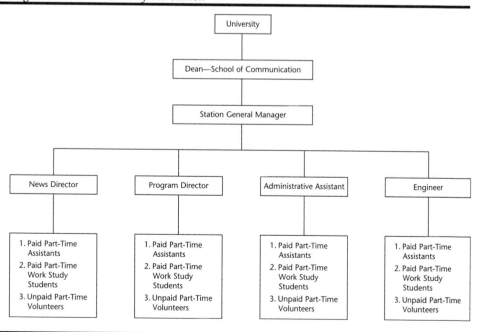

The program director's responsibilities included developing the on-air program schedule, which consisted of National Public Radio (NPR) standards such as "Morning Edition" and "All Things Considered" as well as jazz in the mornings and classical music in the afternoons. He also developed the volunteer training program (including both equipment operation and on-air announcing) and scheduled and supervised the volunteers and work-study students. The program director also did some on-air announcing and worked as the internal liaison, coordinating the various departments. He reported directly to the station general manager, who was responsible for all aspects of internal station management as well as developing and sustaining relationships with external constituencies.

PROBLEMS

The person hired initially as program director had a leadership style that did not fit well in a volunteer-oriented organization. Specifically, he was task-oriented and had few skills in managing others. This leadership style contributed to conflicts within the organization, and the program director left the organization by mutual consent after nine months on the job. The position of program director remained unfilled for nine months.

During that time period, the general manager and the administrative assistant split the work ordinarily done by the program director, including the recruitment, selection, training, and scheduling of the volunteers. However, none of these activities were ever institutionalized in terms of written policies and procedures. For example, there were no written job descriptions for volunteers explaining duties and responsibilities for particular positions. Nor was there any formal feedback system for evaluating volunteer performance and/or receiving volunteer input. Voluntary recruitment and opportunities for volunteer training were also reduced during this period.

After nine months a new program director was hired. She had previous experience as a program director at another public radio station and came highly recommended. Her initial statement was one of amazement at the high quality of announcing among the volunteers. In fact, she sent out a memorandum to that effect during her second week on the job. However, as time passed, more and more of the volunteer announcers were told by the program director that their services were no longer required as announcers. They were offered the opportunity to work behind the scenes as board operators with no on-air announcing. Most chose to simply quit.

When challenged by the volunteers, the new program director stated that there was too much voice variation among the volunteers and an all-professional sounding station needs more uniformity. Since there was no money to hire full-time professional announcers, the program director (as well as several other paid staff) began to do more of the on-air announcing. The program director herself was working more than 60 hours per week. No new volunteers were being trained. Most of the old volunteers had either quit or been demoted. The five still doing on-air announcing then requested a meeting with the general manager.

At the meeting, these volunteer announcers indicated their displeasure concerning the decisions of the program director. The volunteers indicated that they had contributed not only their time but also had made monetary contributions to the station and had encouraged others to do so. The general manager thanked the announcers for their contributions of time and money, but indicated he had given the program director control of the programming including personnel matters. They were still welcome to do volunteer work at the station and could continue announcing "for the time being." The volunteers were not happy with this response and promptly submitted their resignations.

The general manager now had a bigger problem on his hands. The paid staff were already spread too thin and stretched to the limit even before the latest volunteer resignations. The station was committed to 20 hours of programming each day. NPR daily programs and prerecorded tapes could not fill the entire programming gap since they also required staff time to produce. The station clearly was in a crisis situation.

QUESTIONS

1. Describe the fundamental problem in this case together with its causes.

2. What specific mistakes were made by (a) the general manager and (b) the program director?

3. Did you ever do unpaid volunteer work? What were your purposes/goals and to what degree did you achieve them?

4. What types of rewards are most appropriate for volunteers? To what degree were these provided to volunteers at the radio station?

5. What steps should the station general manager take now?

■■■■■■ *Evaluating Nontraditional Incentive Systems: Howe 2 Ski Stores*

Howe 2 Ski Stores is a chain of three ski and snowboarding shops located in the suburbs of a large eastern city. Maria Howe, a ski enthusiast and business school major, started the company ten years ago after her college graduation with financial backing from her family and several friends. From its inception, Howe 2 Ski Stores was intended to provide state-of-the-art equipment and clothing for skiers at all skill levels, from beginner to champion. It was to be staffed by employees who were themselves advanced skiers and could provide expert advice on the choice of clothing and equipment, and it was intended to have a quick response time that would permit the last-minute purchase of equipment and clothing prior to a ski trip.

Howe originally drew from a pool of skiing friends and fellow students to staff the stores and still prefers to hire part-time employees with skiing expertise who might leave in a year over more stable, full-time employees with less expertise and interest in the sport. Whether administrative staff, cashiers, clerks, or molders (employees who fit bindings to skis), employees were encouraged to keep up with the latest skiing equipment and trends, attend ski vendor shows, try out demo equipment, and give feedback on the store's inventory in order to help provide the highest quality, state-of-the-art equipment and advice for the customer.

Suggestion boxes were placed in the store and Howe herself regularly collected, read, and acted upon the suggestions made by the clerks and customers. She developed special advertising campaigns to build an image for the nearby slopes in order to increase the market. As the business grew, Howe even added a line of rental equipment in order to lower the costs and encourage people to try the sport.

Although profits grew irregularly due to weather effects and the faddish nature of the sport, Howe's efforts paid off in the long term, and within four years business had grown sufficiently to permit the opening of a second Howe 2 Ski Store in another suburb about ten miles from the first. In order to increase sales, about six years ago, Howe took a chance on the growing snowboarding market and the East Coast location and added a line of equipment for this sport. Snowboarding had caught on especially among Generation X and 75 percent of people who snowboard are under age 25. The move turned out to be a very good one. The snowboarding market increased by more than 300 percent in four years and continues to experience a slower but stable pattern of growth as snowboarding became a Winter Olympic sport in 1999. The snowboard market had also spawned a whole line of complementary accessories and apparel. Young snowboarders preferred a "hip hop" look of hooded flannel shirts and baggy pants. This market has enabled Howe to smooth out the number of sales occurring throughout the year.

Three years ago, Howe was able to open a third store, located within a 15-mile radius from the other two. Although managers have been hired to run each of the stores and the total number of employees has grown to 65, Howe's basic strategy has remained the same—high quality, state-of-the-art products, a knowledgeable staff, and quick response time. Profits from the stores have continued to grow, although at a slower rate. Competition from other ski stores has also increased noticeably within the last two years.

The threat of increased competition has been exacerbated by signs that employee productivity has begun to slide. Last year, there were eight occasions where expensive ski orders were not delivered in time for the customers' ski vacations. Although Howe used a variety of maneuvers to retain the customers' patronage (such as paying for the customers to rent equipment of equivalent quality, express-shipping the equipment to the customer as soon as it was delivered, and lowering the price of the equipment), the costs of these late orders were high. She realizes that word of these kinds of incidents could significantly damage the store's reputation for exceptional service. Furthermore, at least 15 percent of all ski orders were more than two days late, even though customers did not miss a trip or vacation as a result.

In an attempt to respond to these difficulties, Howe instituted a merit performance system for the molders (employees who fit the binding to skis). Although productivity seemed to increase for awhile, waves of discontent happened all over the stores. The molders felt that their merit ratings were inaccurate because the store managers could not observe them much of the time. Further, they argued that their performance would have been much higher had not other employees interrupted them with questions about appropriate bindings or failed to clearly identify the appropriate equipment on the sales tickets.

Other employees also complained because they were not given the opportunity for merit pay. The buyers, who visit ski shows, examine catalogs, and talk with sales representatives in order to decide on the inventory, argued that their work was essential for high sales figures and quality equipment. Sales clerks claimed that their in-depth familiarity with an extensive inventory and their sales skills were essential to increasing sales. They also noted their important role in negotiating a delivery date that the molders could meet. Similar arguments were made by the people in the credit office who arranged for short-term financing if necessary and the cashiers who verified costs and checked credit card approvals. Even the stockers noted that the store would be in a bad way if they did not locate the correct equipment in a warehouse full of inventory and deliver it in a timely manner to the molders.

Howe had to concede that the employees were correct on many of these points, so she suspended the merit plan at the end of the ski season and promised to reevaluate its fairness. Even more convincing were several indications that productivity problems were not limited to molder employees. Complaints about customer service increased 20 percent during the year. Several customers noted that they were allowed to stand, merchandise in hand, waiting for a clerk to help them, while clerks engaged in deep conversations among themselves. Younger college student employees were often found listening to music on their iPods. Although Howe mentioned these concerns to employees in the stores when she visited and asked the store managers to discuss them in staff meetings, the complaints from customers continued.

A record number of "as is" skis were sold at the end of the season sale because they were damaged in the warehouse, the store, or by the molders. The closing inventory revealed that 20 percent of the rental equipment had been lost or seriously damaged without resulting charges to the renters because records were poorly maintained. Regular checks of the suggestion boxes in the store revealed fewer and fewer comments. Employees just did not seem to notice these problems, or worse, did not seem to care.

Howe was very bothered by all these factors and felt they could not be attributed to the growth of the business alone. She knew it would be impossible to maintain her competitive position with these events occurring in her stores. At a recent Small Business Forum meeting, Howe heard the guest speaker, a university professor, suggest that employers consider a group of non-traditional incentive plans in order to increase employee motivation and involvement and reduce the costs of operating. For example, some companies were using time-off schemes, gainsharing, bonuses tied to new product knowledge, and contests and prizes. Howe decided to investigate these topics further to see whether they might be appropriate for her stores.

1. Given the background information about Howe 2 Ski Stores, discuss the feasibility of implementing lump sum bonuses, pay for knowledge, profit sharing, and gainsharing plans. What plan or plans would you recommend that Howe look at most closely and why?

2. Assuming that Howe decides that a gainsharing plan is feasible, what could be done to increase the likelihood of success?

3. What negative effects are likely to result from even the successful implementation of a gainsharing plan?

Contributed by M. Susan Taylor, University of Maryland and J. Kline Harrison, Wake Forest University

68 EXERCISE

Executive Bonuses and Incentives

I. OBJECTIVES

A. To help you understand the complexities involved in designing an executive compensation system that will reward performance in areas which are sustainable and result in long-term organizational success.

B. To demonstrate the necessity to balance financial and non-financial criteria for executive compensation in both the short term and long term.

II. OUT-OF-CLASS PREPARATION TIME: 1 hour

III. IN-CLASS TIME SUGGESTED: 1 hour

IV. PROCEDURES

1. Read the entire exercise including the Background information below before class. After reading the Background information in the case, review information in your text or on the Internet on the topics of "Executive Bonuses" and "Executive Incentives."

2. Then, form groups of three to five students in class and answer the questions on Form 4.1 regarding a possible new design for an executive compensation system at Internet Applications. Once these questions have been discussed by the group and a group consensus (or majority opinion) on each has been reached, write your answers on Form 4.1.

3. The groups should then complete Form 4.2, which is partially completed for you but leaves space for additional short-term and long-term criteria for executive compensation. As you consider your plan, be sure to evaluate incentives that (if goals are accomplished) will make the company and its products sustainable over the long term. Add additional criteria as you see fit. Then, indicate for each criterion you retain what percent of total compensation should be based on each and how each should be divided among short-term bonuses and long-term stock options.

4. After completing Forms 4.1 and 4.2, the group should inform the instructor. When all groups have finished steps two and three, each group should have a spokesperson orally summarize their recommendations, the rationale for them, and their potential downsides for the entire class.

BACKGROUND

Internet Applications is a medium-sized computer software company that has grown rapidly since its inception 20 years ago in a large Texas city. While the company has had its "ups and downs" over the 20-year period, it has grown to be one of the top 1,000 U.S. companies in terms of total revenues. The company is currently doing well financially with revenue and earnings growth per share each up approximately 10 percent over the past year. However, its stock price is still approximately 50 percent below its previous peak price of 48 dollars per share achieved 10 years earlier.

The board of directors consists of some local public officials as well as industry experts and financiers, many of whom are CEOs of other companies in Texas. The current CEO, Donald Tisdale, was appointed to the position three years ago. Recently, the board was shocked to see their company and the CEO highlighted in the annual *BusinessWeek* survey, which listed executives who did the least to earn their pay in the last year. Among the factors sighted was the lagging stock price, earnings that were still below those achieved four years earlier before the "financial crisis," and a board that continued to increase the CEO's total annual compensation despite the lagging earnings and stock price. As a result, the CEO's total compensation was approximately 580x that of the average employee in the company.

The board has based its short-term and long-term CEO compensation on the earnings of other CEOs in the metropolitan area and in the industry. They have also relied on an executive compensation consultant who indicated the CEO's total compensation was well within industry norms. As a result, the board was insulted by the *BusinessWeek* article and felt inclined to write a defense of their pay practices. However, one member suggested they seek some additional information before responding in a formal way.

The board asked their human resource vice president, Henrietta Peach, to make a recommendation concerning this issue. She suggested the director of compensation, Ellen Bennett, should conduct a study of executive compensation and make recommendations to the board. Bennett agreed and has asked your instructor to assist in her research and future recommendations. Your instructor has asked each team in the class for their analysis and recommendations as noted in Forms 4.1 and 4.2 in this case.

Your instructor has also shared with you the following information that he and Bennett have discovered in their research:

■ Executive compensation consists of five components with mean percentages in U.S. corporations as follows:

1. Big salary (35%)

2. Short-term incentives or bonuses (24%)

3. Long-term incentives or stock plans (31%)

4. Benefits (5%)

5. Perquisites (5%)

■ Greater use of both short-term and long-term executive bonuses and stock incentives among top and middle managers is associated with higher subsequent levels of profitability.

■ There is a high level of current pressure from the Securities and Exchange Commission (SEC) as well as some large pension programs (TIAA-CREF and CALPERS) to better link pay and performance among executives. Toward that end, they have proposed guidelines for executive compensation. These pension funds have described executive compensations in many of the companies in which they hold stock as "Heads I win, tails we flip again." As a result, they believe that excessive executive compensation dilutes stockholder equity and the returns of those who hold stock in the company. The problem is that in these companies executive pay is higher each year regardless of profitability, stock price, or meeting the needs of employees or customers.

■ The late Peter Drucker, 20 years ago, indicated that executive pay was "off the charts" at that time. He recommended that the CEO total compensation should be no more than 20x the pay of the average rank and file employee.

- Current practices for determining executive compensation use competitive benchmarking by a compensation committee within the board of directors that utilizes comparisons with similar companies in terms of size, sales, industry, geographic region, etc. They also tend to use executive compensation consultants who have been recommended by other companies. Some critics have claimed that these consultants may have a conflict of interest in that boards tend to hire and re-hire those who "rubber stamp" their particular compensation preferences.

- CEO compensation among U.S. corporations is approximately 400x that of the average worker in these companies. This ratio is much higher than the same ratio in other developed countries. In fact, U.S. top executives are the highest paid in the world. This has created a "trust gap," or a frame of mind, among employees that leads them to mistrust senior management intentions, doubt their competence, and resent their self-congratulatory pay. This issue has become salient when the same companies simultaneously engage in large-scale layoffs and downsizing. Research indicates that companies with higher pay differentials between executives and rank and file employees have lower levels of employee and customer satisfaction and declining market shares.

- Short-term incentives are usually given annually and may take the form of either cash or stock. Annual bonuses may also be based on achievement of specific objectives. Long-term incentives usually take the form of stock options used to link stockholder and executive incentives.

- Today the goal is to provide executive incentives that address the concerns of stockholders, employees, and customers. Companies that address all three stakeholders in their executive compensation tend to perform better in financial terms over the long run.

- Balanced score cards have been developed to provide a more comprehensive evaluation of the organization's performance, taking into account not only stock price and financial returns but also employee satisfaction, customer satisfaction, market share, measures of product or service quality, innovation and product leadership, and low levels of employee turnover. The alleged benefits of balanced score cards are that they allow executives to focus on not only short-term financial results but also on factors which build future economic and non-economic success.

1. What short-term (bonuses) and long-term (stock incentive plans) ideas for executive incentives do you suggest? Why?

   Bonuses:

   _____

   _____

   _____

   _____

   _____

   _____

   Stock Incentives:

   _____

   _____

   _____

   _____

   _____

   _____

2. What percentage of total executive compensation should be in the bonus category and what percent should be in the stock incentive category? Why?

   Short-Term Bonuses:

   _____

   _____

   Long-Term Stock Incentives:

   _____

   _____

   Why?: _____

   _____

   _____

   _____

3. How would you address the interest of stockholder, customers, and employees in your executive compensation plan?

   Stockholders:

   _____

   _____

   _____

   Employees:

   _____

   _____

   _____

Customers:

_____

_____

_____

4.   Do you approve of the following executive compensation reforms that have been suggested by critics and in Congress? (Yes or No)

■ Require stockholder approval for all executive pay packages. _____

■ Require a standard ratio between CEO total compensation and that of the average employee in the company. _____

■ Require compensation committees of the board of directors to be composed of "public members" (non-CEOs). _____

■ Require compensation committees to justify their pay recommendations in terms of some combination of increased employee satisfaction, customer satisfaction, product innovation, and market share. _____

Percentage of Compensation
Total (Incentives) (Bonuses)
(Company Stock)

Stockholders:

- Earnings Growth per Share
- Stock Price Increase per Share
- Cash Flow per Share
- Growth and Market Share

_____

_____

_____

Employees:

- Employee Retention
- Employee Satisfaction
- Percent of Employees Receiving Training
- and Development

_____

_____

_____

Customers:

- Measured Quality of Products
- Product Innovation
- Customer Satisfaction

_____

_____

_____

Benchmark Ratio of CEO Total Compensation to Average Employee Pay _____: 1

69 EXERCISE

Allocating Merit Raises

I. **OBJECTIVES**

    A. To make you aware of the difficulties involved in making merit raise decisions.

    B. To familiarize you with possible criteria a manager can use in making merit raise decisions.

II. **OUT-OF-CLASS PREPARATION TIME:** 10–20 minutes to read exercise and decide each professor's merit raise

III. **IN-CLASS TIME SUGGESTED:** 30–40 minutes

IV. **PROCEDURES**

Either at the beginning of or before coming to class, you should read the exercise and determine merit raises for each professor.

To start the exercise, the instructor will divide the class into groups of three to five students. Each group should develop a fair procedure that will be used to determine merit raises and then decide the dollar raise to be given to each professor. After each group finishes, one member will write the raise amounts on the board or overhead for all class members to see. Then, once all groups have disclosed their raises, a spokesperson for each group will explain the procedure used to determine their raises.

SITUATION

Small State University is located in the eastern part of the United States and has an enrollment of about 8,000 students. The College of Business has 40 full-time and more than 30 part-time faculty members. The college is divided into five departments: Management, Marketing, Finance and Accounting, Decision Sciences, and Information Technology. Faculty members in the Management Department are evaluated each year based on three primary criteria: 1) teaching, 2) research, and 3) service. Teaching performance is based on student course evaluations over a two-year period. Service to the university, college, profession, and community is also based on accomplishments over a two-year period. Research is based on the number of journal articles published over a three-year period. Teaching and research are considered more important than service to the university. In judging faculty performance, the department chair evaluates each professor in terms of four standards: Far Exceeds Standards, Exceeds Standards, Meets Standards, and Fails to Meet Standards. The results of this year's evaluations are shown in Exhibit 4.3.

Due to financial problems and cutbacks this year, Small State University has agreed to give raises totaling just $6,300 to the Management Department. Your task as department chair is to divide the $6,300 among the faculty members. Keep in mind that these raises will likely set a precedent for the future and that the professors will view the raises as a signal for what behavior and achievements are valued.

A profile of each of the professors is provided below.

Professor Houseman: 55 years old; 25 years with the university; teaches Principles of Management sections; teaches over 400 students per year; has written over 40 articles and given over 30 presentations since joining the college; wants a good raise to catch up with others.

EXHIBIT 4.3 *Department Chairs' Rating of Job Performance*

Professor	Current Salary	Teaching	Research	Service
Houseman	$92,000	Exceeds	Exceeds	Meets
Jones	$116,000	Exceeds	Far Exceeds	Exceeds
Ricks	$135,000	Meets	Meets	Far Exceeds
Matthews	$97,000	New Hire	New Hire	New Hire
Karas	$100,000	Far Exceeds	Exceeds	Meets
Franks	$90,000	Meets	Fails to Meet	Exceeds

Professor Jones: 49 years old; 10 years with the university; teaches Human Resource Management and Organizational Behavior; stepped down as department chair three years ago; teaches about 200 students a year; has written over 30 articles and two books since joining the college; recently received an $80,000 grant for the college from a local foundation, and wants a good raise as a reward for obtaining the grant.

Professor Ricks: 61 years old; 6 years with university; teaches Labor Relations and Organizational Development; stepped down as dean of the College of Business two years ago and took a $20,000 pay cut; teaches about 180 students per year; has written only two articles in the last six years due to administrative duties; very active in the community and serves on several charity boards; wants a good raise to make up for loss of $20,000.

Professor Matthews: 28 years old; new hire—only four months with the university; teaches Employee Relations and Compensation Management; just graduated with a PhD; will teach about 110 students this year. To be competitive in the job market, the college paid Professor Matthews $97,000 plus provided a reduced teaching load for two years and a $6,000 per year summer stipend; none of the other faculty received this when they were first hired or subsequently; had two minor publications while a doctoral student but none since joining the college; wants a good raise to pay student loans and furnish a new residence.

Professor Karas: 32 years old; 4 years with university; teaches International Business and Honors sections of Management Principles; teaches about 150 students per year; won Teacher of the Year Award this year; published 12 articles in last four years; has been interviewing for a new job at other universities and may leave if a good raise is not forthcoming.

Professor Franks: 64 years old; 18 years with university; teaches Principles of Management and Human Resource Management; teaches about 150 students per year; principal advisor for management-major students; has not written any articles during the last four years; plans on retiring within two–three years, and wants a good raise to enhance pension plan.

70 EXERCISE

WageSim—A Compensation Administration Exercise

I. OBJECTIVES

A. To familiarize you with some of the problems involved in building and maintaining a compensation system.

B. To provide you with alternative approaches for solving some typical compensation-related problems.

C. To give you practice in writing memos to employees regarding compensation issues.

D. To familiarize you with job evaluation procedures.

II. OUT-OF-CLASS PREPARATION TIME: 20 minutes to read exercise plus one hour to respond to the E-mail Items (either individually or in a group)

III. IN-CLASS TIME SUGGESTED: 45 minutes to discuss all E-mail Items

IV. PROCEDURES

This exercise can be done individually or in groups of three to five members, at the instructor's option. You are to begin by reading all of the material presented in this exercise. Assume that you are responsible for developing and maintaining the Mack Organization's wage and salary system. Assume further that the person who previously had these responsibilities has just quit and left you all of the E-mail Items that follow. First, you (or your team) are (is) to respond in writing to each employee who sent an e-mail. Second, explain on a separate sheet of paper what additional actions you would take with reference to each item. For example, if you believe that you should gather additional information before making a final decision on an item, explain what information you would need. Or, if you believe that additional memos or discussions with someone in the company are needed, explain this. You (or your team) should bring both the memos and the Additional Action sheets to class. Be prepared to present and defend these materials during the class discussion.

SITUATION

The Mack Organization is a large organization headquartered in the midwestern United States. It has offices located throughout the country and employs over 700 individuals. You may assume the organization is a chemical company, a manufacturing company, a bank, a insurance firm, or any large organization with which you are familiar.

The Mack Organization's human resource department includes a compensation administration section that consists of two individuals, one of whom is you (or your team). The company has several different wage structures, including one for executives and one for clerical personnel. For compensation purposes, all clerical employees are divided into five job classifications. The organization's current wage structure for clerical personnel is shown in Exhibit 4.4.

HOW SALARIES ARE DETERMINED

Employee salaries directly relate to the work they do and how well they do it. Two major factors work together to establish the salaries payable for various jobs—job evaluation and salary ranges.

EXHIBIT 4.4 *Mack Organization's Wage Structure for Clerical Personnel*

Job Title	Salary	Number of Employees
Office Services Aide	$25,259 minimum	40
	$33,262 maximum	
Office Services Assistant	$26,588 minimum	30
	$35,337 maximum	
Administrative Assistant	$30,041 minimum	20
	$39,604 maximum	
Senior Assistant	$34,628 minimum	40
	$45,083 maximum	
Executive Assistant	$43,364 minimum	20
	$54,794 maximum	

JOB EVALUATION

Job evaluation is a method of measuring the relative worth of each job in the organization compared to all the other jobs, based on an objective analysis of the duties and responsibilities of the position. The Mack Organization job evaluation is as follows: A description that defines the function of the job and lists the major duties performed is written for each job. Each description is then evaluated by a standing committee of employees from various areas of the organization who have a broad knowledge of the jobs that exist throughout the organization. Their evaluation is based on "yardsticks," including knowledge required, freedom of action, accountability, contacts with employees and customers, physical effort required, unusual working conditions, research responsibilities, and supervision or management responsibilities. Based on these yardsticks, the job is assigned a point value. By listing all positions according to their point value, the relative worth of each position is established.

GRADE LEVELS AND SALARY RANGES

Based on the total points received in a job evaluation, jobs are assigned to a grade level. Each grade has an entry or minimum salary and a maximum salary payable for the jobs in that grade; the amounts between the entry and maximum salary comprise the salary range for the grade.

Usually employees begin at the bottom of each salary grade. Employees are considered for a merit increase after six months of satisfactory service. After this, they may receive an annual merit increase upon completion of satisfactory service. There are a total of six possible merit increases. Cost-of-living increases are granted periodically by the organization to all employees.

E-mail Items

Item 1

To: Wage & Salary Division
From: Mary Wallace—Vice President
Re: Request for pay increase/promotion

This is to formally request your endorsement of my intent to promote Susan Anthony, an administrative assistant in my office, to the position of senior assistant. I realize a requirement for senior assistant is proficiency in Adobe InDesign (a desktop publishing program) and that Ms. Anthony is not yet proficient.

However, aside from this, Ms. Anthony possesses the necessary skills to perform all tasks in this office. Ms. Anthony has been with this office for five years and is a loyal and dedicated employee. I wholeheartedly encourage your endorsement of this recommendation and pay increase. A vacant senior assistant position is available in this office. Please advise as soon as possible.

Item 2

To: Wage and Salary Section
From: Kelly Actor
Re: Request for pay increase

I have been with this company for ten years. My present position with this company is senior assistant, at the maximum pay level. The Wispette Company has offered me a position that would give me a 9% increase in salary for similar duties. Since I do enjoy my work, I hate to leave. However, my financial obligations to my family leave me with no choice. My husband recently has been disabled, with no hope of employment for three years. As I mentioned, I have enjoyed my ten years with this company. My supervisor and I get along well. I have not missed any work during the ten years except for the two-week vacation during the summer. If you will match the Wispette Company's offer, I would prefer to stay with your company. I understand there is no opening for an executive assistant, which would be a comparable position. I need an answer soon.

Item 3

To: Wage and Salary Section
From: Jane Swenk, Supervisor
Re: Long-term employee wage dispute

M.O. Scott, an administrative assistant, expressed concern that her daughter, also an administrative assistant, was making an equal amount of money. M.O. has been employed for 28 years, her daughter for five. Merit raises are given yearly only for the first five years, and M.O. has not gotten one in 23 years. I don't think this policy is fair. M.O. should get something for her longer service. Please respond so I can explain the situation to her.

Item 4

To: Compensation Administration
From: HR Director
Re: Payroll budget for next month

Please prepare a payroll budget for next month for clerical employees. Make whatever assumptions you feel are necessary in doing your calculation. Just let me know what the assumptions are. Many thanks.

Item 5

To: Wage and Salary Section
From: Bob Franklin, Administrative Aide
Re: Pay inequity question

I was recently hired as an administrative assistant and received the minimum pay for this position. Why do some office service aides make more than I do? My duties and responsibilities are much greater than theirs.

Item 6

To: Compensation Section
From: Betty Dyer, Supervisor
Re: Pay for Tammy Tuff

Tammy Tuff is an excellent administrative assistant in my office. She does an outstanding job with all assignments and performs beyond standards for an administrative assistant in everything she does. She completes her assignments in half the time of other aides and voluntarily assumes extra duties after finishing her assignments. In addition to her outstanding performance, Ms. Tuff has improved morale in the office since she started nine months ago. She always has a smile on her face and brightens the day for co-workers with her pleasant disposition. Best of all, she makes others feel important, and this has carried over to their work. Everyone seems to take pride in their work; consequently, performance and productivity are up. Due to Tammy's influence, the turnover rate is zero, leaving her with no promotion potential in this office. Based on Tammy's excellent performance, skills that exceed the requirements of the job, and attitude that has improved morale, I feel that Tammy deserves to be paid as a senior assistant even though she is not one and there is no senior assistant vacancy.

Item 7

To: Wage & Salary
From: Chris Markley, Supervisor
Re: Pay question

I am relatively new to the position of senior assistant and was told that pay for my job is based on points. I thought it was based on job duties and performance. What do points have to do with it?

Item 8

To: W & S
From: McNamara, Department Manager
Re: Employee problem

Mary White, an office services aide, left two hours early yesterday, without permission, to attend a civil rights rally. Should she be paid for this time?

Item 9

To: Wage & Salary Section
From: Sue L. Ross, Supervisor
Re: Pay for Julie Tate

Julie Tate, senior assistant, has been temporarily assigned some of the duties of an executive assistant position. The position is temporarily vacant due to the executive secretary being gone for four weeks. Julie has been told by me that she may be assigned higher-level duties on occasion, but she is not satisfied. She insists that she deserves financial compensation for absorbing some duties of an executive assistant. None of the additional duties is too difficult for Julie to handle, and she actually does an excellent job on all assignments when she stops complaining about her unfair treatment. I am recommending that Julie be paid at the rate of an executive assistant position so that I can assign her higher-level duties whenever my executive assistant is on vacation or sick leave. This way Julie will not complain about the grade level of her work, and the flow of work in the office will proceed smoothly without disruption. Please respond to this recommendation.

Item 10

To: Wage and Salary Section
From: Doris Pope, Department Head
Re: Frances Brown, Administrative Aide

The administrative assistant in my department, Frances Brown, has decided she would like to work at home four days a week and in the office one day. Given her job duties, this will pose no problem for this office. However, I am not sure how this will affect her pay. Will it increase her pay or decrease it? Please advise.

Thanks.

71 EXERCISE

Ethical and Practical Compensation Dilemmas

I. OBJECTIVES

   A. To familiarize you with a variety of different compensation dilemmas and possible solutions to them.

   B. To make you aware that some compensation decisions involve ethical issues.

   C. To familiarize you with various criteria that can be used to distinguish between ethical and unethical behavior.

II. OUT-OF-CLASS PREPARATION TIME: 5 minutes to read all or some of the Ethical Compensation Dilemmas below, as assigned by your instructor

III. IN-CLASS TIME SUGGESTED: 20–75 minutes, depending on how many of the Dilemmas below are assigned by your instructor

IV. PROCEDURES

At the start of class, you will be divided into groups of three to five and assigned one or more of the following ten Compensation Dilemmas to analyze. Your group should answer the questions asked at the end of each Dilemma and be prepared to present your decisions. While answering these questions, your group may want to address the questions below. They are designed to help you determine if an issue involves ethical considerations.

1. Does the action involve intentional deception?

2. Does the action purposely benefit one party at the expense of another?

3. Is the action fair and just to all concerned? The Golden Rule not only dictates that we "do unto others as we would have them do unto us" but also commands that we treat others as we might wish to be treated.

4. Would the manager feel comfortable if the action were made public or must it remain a secret?

5. Are managers justifying the action by telling themselves that they can get away with it or that they will not need to live with the decision's consequences?

6. Would the decision maker recommend the action to other managers or firms?

7. Will the action build goodwill and better relationships?

In answering the questions, you also may also want to consider three different schools of thought regarding ethical decision making. The Utilitarian Approach argues that decision outcomes should result in the greatest good for the greatest number of people. The Moral Rights Approach holds that decisions should be consistent with fundamental rights and privileges as set forth in the Bill of Rights or some other document such as the United Nations' Declaration of Human Rights. The Justice Approach stresses that decisions should be equitable and follow the distributive justice and fairness principle. Some argue that the ideal decision occurs when it is supported by the ethical standards of all three ethical approaches.

After all groups have finished their analysis (ten minutes or less) of each Compensation Dilemma, the instructor will call on one or more groups to answer the questions presented. This will be followed by a class discussion of each Dilemma.

1. Based on an evaluation of the knowledge, skills, and abilities needed to do each job, a company has determined that two jobs (Job A and Job B) are equal. However, when the firm studies the labor market, it finds that applicants for Job A are plentiful whereas those for Job B are very scarce. Should the firm offer less pay to those who apply for Job A, or should the pay be equal?

2. Assume that the supply of electrical technicians is low so a firm hires a group of them at $18 per hour. Two years later, due to a recession, the supply of technicians is high so the market rate for them is now $15 per hour. Should the firm pay new hires $18 or $15? Should it lower the pay of existing technicians to $15?

3. Jim is given an extremely large raise because of his superb work record one year. As a result, he is currently earning $50,000 whereas others at the firm holding the same job are earning $45,000. Everyone expects Jim to continue to excel and enhance the entire unit's productivity. Unfortunately, Jim's performance drops off after the first year and is now just average. What should be done about his pay? Should it be reduced to reflect his current performance?

4. One year, Ethan's performance is truly spectacular (just as good as Jim's had been in the previous case). However, the company has no raise money available that year so no one, including Ethan, receives a merit raise. Is this appropriate?

5. Mary and Sue both work in the same department. Mary believes that Sue is being paid considerably more than she is. In fact, both employees are being paid about the same amount. Mary wants a pay raise and complains to her boss and the compensation manager. What should the compensation manager say, assuming the firm follows the policy of not revealing the pay of individual employees? Should Mary be told the amount of Sue's pay? Or, should Mary only be told that there is a "misunderstanding" and that her belief is incorrect? Or, should some other approach be taken?

6. When Mary was hired, she was told verbally that she would receive a raise when she finished her college degree and yet another raise when she was given additional responsibility. She accepted the job offer based on this understanding. However, during the next two years, the firm experienced slow sales and had to ask all factory employees to accept a 12 percent pay decrease. But Mary, who does not work in the factory, has finished college and has accepted more responsibility. Should she receive a raise?

7. Two firms in the chemical solvent industry decide to merge. Employees in the testing department of Firm A have enjoyed high pay for many years. However, Firm A is purchased by Firm B, which has a history of paying low wages. As a result, employees in Firm A's testing department earn on average $2.00 more per hour than those at Firm B. Upon completion of the merger, what wage levels should prevail? Should wages be cut for those who worked for Firm A? Or, should wages be increased for those in Firm B?

8. Sue is a 55-year-old employee of Company A. Her children are out of college and her parents have both died. Company A offers a child care program to all employees along with an elder care program. However, Sue, like many other employees, has no need for these services, neither now or in the future. Should the company retain these programs? Should alternative benefits for employees who have no use for such services be offered?

9. Helen works as an accountant for a firm in the textile industry. During non-working hours, she does extensive volunteer work for the American Red Cross, Meals on Wheels, and the American Heart Association. Helen's employer wants to maintain a favorable image in the community, so it wants every employee to donate money to the United Way. Should the employer pressure Helen to donate money? Keep in mind that if Helen does not donate money, other employees may not either, which could result in an unfavorable image in the community for the employer. On the other hand, Helen already donates time, which has a monetary value, and she may feel that it is unfair to be asked to donate even more.

10. Frank works 25 hours per week for a mail order firm in the packaging department. He receives no benefits other than those required by law. Frank does the same type of work as three other employees, all of whom work full time. These employees qualify for pensions, medical care, long-term disability, child care, etc. Is this a good business practice? Assume that Frank would like to work full time, really wants to receive benefits, and feels harmed because of his shortfall. On the other hand, the firm is not legally required to pay Frank benefits, Frank only works part time, and it would be expensive to pay benefits to all part-time employees, including Frank.

72   EXERCISE

Pay Inversion: Is It Practical and Ethical?

OVERVIEW

This exercise contains three different—but related—scenarios regarding pay inversion. Pay inversion is defined as "the hiring of new employees at a higher compensation level than that of current employees who have better skills and performance records." These scenarios examine the ethical and practical aspects of inversion from three different decision maker's perspectives.

I. OBJECTIVES

A. To familiarize students with the concept of pay inversion.

B. To examine different ethical approaches and how they may apply to pay inversion.

C. To examine the issue of whether an action is ethical irrespective of whether one is the beneficiary of an action, the victim of it, or a decision maker.

D. To familiarize students with the potential costs and benefits to a firm of inverting pay.

E. To examine alternatives to pay inversion.

II. OUT-OF-CLASS PREPARATION TIME: none, unless the instructor asks the class to read the exercise before class

III. IN-CLASS TIME SUGGESTED: 30 minutes

IV. PROCEDURES

To begin the exercise, the instructor will divide the class into groups of three to five students and ask each to select a spokesperson. Each group is to read Scenario I and answer the questions at the end. When all student groups have finished answering the scenario questions, the instructor will call on a representative from one or more groups to present the group's answers. The class will discuss the answers, and this same process will be followed for Scenarios II and III. The class will then develop conclusions based on the entire exercise.

In examining each of the scenarios, you will be asked to consider ethical aspects of pay inversion. In doing so, you may want to consider the following ethical philosophies:

1. Legalistic Approach. This approach argues that if an action is legal, then it is ethical.

2. Ethical Egoism. This approach contends that to be ethical, an action must be in the best interests of the decision maker. It argues that when making this determination, the decision maker need not take into consideration the effects the decision may have on others.

3. Utilitarianism. This approach argues that an action is ethical if it helps the most stakeholders and harms the least. This approach argues that decision makers need to do a cost/benefit analysis when making their decisions.

4. Distributive Justice. This approach contends that an action is ethical if it is fair. It argues that equals should be treated equally and unequals should be treated unequally.

5. Kant's Ethical Imperative Approach. This approach argues that an action is ethical if it shows respect for people. To be respectful, one needs to treat people only as they have freely consented to be treated beforehand.

6. Other Approaches (optional). As assigned by the instructor.

Scenario I—You have just graduated with a major that is in high demand. For example, you have an MS in biotechnology and are knowledgeable about mapping the human genome. You have been offered a very attractive job with a medium-sized firm. Your starting salary is at the current market wage for your major. A best friend who works for the same firm has told you that your starting salary is $3,000 more than experienced employees earn because your major is in high demand. They were hired by the firm before the current high demand for your type of skills materialized. Your friend tells you that your co-workers are very productive and skilled and they will train and mentor you. Assuming that this is your best job offer, would you accept it? Would it be ethical for you to do so?

Scenario II—You accepted the job and have been with the firm for three years. You have received excellent annual evaluations and significant merit raises. In fact, your supervisor said you will likely be promoted within the next few years. Recently, the firm's business has improved dramatically, and your department needs to hire a new employee. Given the shortage of applicants, the current average market wage has increased, and your boss offered a new graduate from your alma mater $3,000 more than you are receiving. Given your superior skills, you will be asked to train and mentor the new hire. Do you agree that the firm should pay the market rate? Would it be ethical for the firm to do so?

Scenario III—Based on your skills, performance, and years with the firm, you have recently been promoted to manager and given a significant pay raise. Because business continues to improve, you must hire one additional person. You return to your alma mater. Unfortunately, the supply of applicants is still small, and the demand is still large, so the market average starting salary is $3,000 more than the salary of any of the more highly qualified employees you supervise. Would you offer that amount to a new employee? Would it be ethical for you to do so? What are the costs and benefits to the firm of paying the higher salary? Are there any alternatives to paying higher salaries?

Contributed by Myron Glassman, Old Dominion University

73 INCIDENT

Merit Increases

Dr. Carl Jones is chairperson of the Department of Management in the College of Business Administration at a large state university in the East. He has been a member of the department for 14 years and a full professor for five years. Last summer he was asked to assume the chair after a screening committee conducted interviews and reviewed his resume and the resumes of three other candidates.

Dr. Jones was very excited about the new challenges and has begun several innovative projects to enhance faculty research and consulting. The teaching function in the department has always been first-rate while research has been somewhat weaker. Dr. Jones has continued to be very productive as a scholar, publishing three articles, two book chapters, and one proceedings article over the past year. He also made considerable progress on a management text of which he was a co-author. Finally, he remained active in his professional association, the Academy of Management, where he served as chair of one of the professional divisions.

The university's policy is that all salary increases are based only on merit. Dr. Jones had developed a very sophisticated performance appraisal system for his faculty to help him quantify salary recommendations. His point system considers and weighs different items in the areas of teaching, research, and service. Teaching and research are weighted 40 percent each and service is weighted 20 percent. For the coming academic year, his recommended salary increases averaged four percent and ranged from one to seven percent. Dr. Jones felt he had good documentation for all his recommendations.

Dr. Jones submitted his recommendations to Dean Edmund Smith and was pleased when all these recommendations were accepted. He then proceeded to schedule appointments to meet with each faculty member to discuss his recommendation, the reasons for the recommendation, and goals for the coming year. While a few of the faculty receiving lower increases indicated dissatisfaction with his weighting system, particularly the emphasis on research, these meetings generally went well.

Dr. Jones then submitted his own annual report detailing his accomplishments as chair as well as his more personal accomplishments. From his perspective, he felt he deserved at least a 6 percent increase since his department had made major strides in a number of areas while the other departments had been standing still. Moreover, none of the other chairs were professionally active on the national level and none had published in the past year. His teaching evaluations were also in the top 15 percent of faculty in the college.

Dean Smith sent out letters to all the department chairs in August. Dr. Jones was shocked to learn that his salary increase was just 4 percent. Information he received through the "grapevine" was that all the chairs had received the 4 percent increase. He also learned from one of the other chairs that the dean always gave the chairs equal percentage increases each year. Contrary to the official university policy, there were no distinctions based on merit. Dr. Jones was visibly upset about what he considered to be a major inequity. He then called the dean's secretary to schedule an appointment to discuss the situation with Dean Smith.

QUESTIONS

1. Describe the nature and causes of the compensation problem described in this incident.

2. Are "merit" salary increases always based on "merit"? Why or why not?

3. Why has Dean Smith had a policy of equal percentage salary increases for all department chairs despite the stated university policy? Are all the chairs equally meritorious?

4. How do you think Dean Smith's "merit" increases will affect Dr. Jones and his performance as department chair and faculty member? Why? What can Dean Smith do to motivate him if a large differential pay increase based on performance is out of the question?

5. What are the long-range benefits of a true "merit" program? What are the problems associated with the lack of such a "merit" system for department chairs?

74 SKILL BUILDER

You Be the Judge: Is This Job Exempt?

I. OBJECTIVES

    A. To help you understand the application of the Fair Labor Standards Act (FLSA).

    B. To help you understand how the law is applied in determining whether jobs are exempt or non-exempt under FLSA.

II. OUT-OF-CLASS PREPARATION TIME: 60 minutes

III. IN-CLASS TIME SUGGESTED: 45 minutes

IV. PROCEDURES

    A. Read the exercise and review the Fair Labor Standards Act excerpt pertaining to exempt status (see Exhibit 4.5).

    B. The class should be divided into groups of four students.

    C. Each group should read each of the incidents that follow and answer these questions:

        1. Analyze each case with respect to the tests that must be considered for determination of exempt status of executive, professional, or administrative jobs.

        2. If you were the judge, how would you rule? Is the job exempt or non-exempt? Why or why not?

Case 1 Harry Phipps, Senior Professional Sales Representative

Harry Phipps was employed by K & K Pharmaceutical Company as a senior professional sales representative. Phipps' position required him to travel across doctors' offices and hospitals where he promoted the benefit of K & K's drug, Provita, to the prescribing doctors. K & K used this method in the hope that when doctors realized the benefit of Provita, they would prescribe the drug for their patients.

By law, Phipps could not sell the drug directly to doctors. The company provided Phipps with a list of target doctors, and he was expected to complete ten visits per day, and each doctor had to be visited at least once a quarter. K & K left the itinerary and method of achieving the targets up to Phipps. However, they did provide Phipps with a budget for the visits. He was also given pre-approved visual aids and had received training in basic "marketing" skills, a core message about the product, and how to gauge doctor interest in the product. Each representative was expected to develop a plan for how to handle his or her territory. Phipps had to complete post-visit reports and refer back to them in planning the next visit. Being successful in the job required some creativity since doctors were extremely busy each day with their patients. Phipps cultivated relationships with their staff and used this as a means to gain access to the doctors.

Phipps earned $66,000 annually but was not paid for overtime. He also had the use of a company car. K & K could award a bonus based on the number of actual prescriptions issued in Phipps' territory. After the completion of two months on the job, Phipps added up the time he spent in completing his work and found he was working more than 8 hours a day. He approached K & K and requested to be paid for overtime. The HR manager indicated that Phipps did not qualify for overtime because the job of senior professional sales representative is exempt under the Fair Labor Standards Act and that overtime is only available to

Exemptions

The FLSA requires that most employees in the United States be paid at least the federal minimum wage for all hours worked and overtime pay at time and one-half the regular rate of pay for all hours worked over 40 hours in a work week. However, Section 13(a) (1) of the FLSA provides an exemption from both minimum wage and overtime pay for employees employed as bona fide executive, administrative, professional, and outside sales employees. Section 13(a) (1) and Section 13(a) (17) also exempt certain computer employees. To qualify for exemption, employees generally must meet certain tests regarding their job duties and be paid on a salary basis at not less than $455 per week. Job titles do not determine exempt status. In order for an exemption to apply, an employee's specific job duties and salary must meet all the requirements of the Department's regulations. An employee will qualify for exemption if he or she meets all of the pertinent tests relating to duties, responsibilities, and salary as stipulated in the applicable section of Regulations, 29 C.R.F. Part 541.

Executive Exemption

To qualify for the executive employee exemption, all of the following tests must be met:

- The employee must be compensated on a salary basis (as defined in the regulations) at a rate not less than $455 per week (or $380 per week, if employed in American Samoa by an employer other than the Federal Government), exclusive of board, lodging, or other facilities; and

- The employee's primary duty must be managing the enterprise, or managing a customarily recognized department or subdivision of the enterprise;

- The employee must customarily and regularly direct the work of at least two or more other full-time employees or their equivalent; and

- The employee must have the authority to hire or fire other employees, or the employee's suggestions and recommendations as to the hiring, firing, advancement, promotion, or any other change of status of other employees must be given particular weight.

Administrative Exemption

To qualify for the administrative employee exemption, all of the following tests must be met:

- The employee must be compensated on a salary or fee basis (as defined in the regulations) at a rate not less than $455 (or $380 per week, if employed in American Samoa by an employer other than the Federal Government), exclusive of board, lodging, or other facilities; and

- The employee's primary duty must be the performance of office or non-manual work directly related to the management or general business operations of the employer or the employer's customers; and

- The employee's primary duty includes the exercise of discretion and independent judgment with respect to matters of significance.

Professional Exemption

To qualify for the professional employee exemption, all of the following tests must be met:

- The employee must be compensated on a salary or fee basis (as defined in the regulations) at a rate not less than $455 per week (or $380 per week, if employed in American Samoa by an employer other than the Federal Government), exclusive of board, lodging, or other facilities; and

- The employee's primary duty must be the performance of work requiring advanced knowledge in a field of science or learning customarily acquired by prolong course of specialized intellectual instruction; or

- Require invention, imagination, originality, or talent in a recognized field of artistic or creative endeavor.

Outside Salespeople

The regulations under the FLSA exempt outside salespeople from both the overtime and minimum wage provisions. To be exempt, the following requirements must be met:

1) The employee's primary duty is:
   a. Making sales within the meaning of Section 3(k)[1] of the Act, or
   b. Obtaining orders or contracts for services or for the use of facilities for which consideration will be paid by the client or customer; and

2) She/he is customarily and regularly engaged way form the employer's place or places of business in performing such primary duty.

(a) The term primary duty is defined at Section 541.700. In determining the primary duty of an outside sales employee, work performed incidental to and in conjunction with the employee's own outside sales or solicitations, including incidental deliveries and collections, shall be regarded as exempt outside sales work. Other work that furthers the employee's sales efforts also shall be regarded as exempt work including, for example, writing sales reports, updating or revising the employee's sales or display catalogue, planning itineraries, and attending sales conferences.

(b) The requirements of Subpart G (salary requirements) of this part do not apply to the outside sales employees described in this section.

---

[1] *Section 3(k) of the FLSA defines sale as including "any sale, exchange, contract to sell, consignment for sale, shipment for sale, or other disposition."*

Source: U.S. Department of Labor, Employment Standards Administration, Wage & Hour Division, Exemption for Executive, Administrative, Professional, Computer & Outside Sales Employees Under the Fair Labor Standards Act (FLSA). www.dol.gov./dol/allcfr/ESA/Title_29/Part_541/29CFR541.100.htm

---

non-exempt employees. Additionally, the HR manager pointed out that although a supervisor accompanied Phipps during his doctor visits on a few days each quarter, he was unsupervised 95 percent of the time. Phipps did not agree with this and argued that he had little discretion in doing his job because he had to follow company guidelines and was given a list of targeted doctors. Furthermore, since he did not work at the company's offices, he was technically an outside salesman. Phipps subsequently filed a class action suit on behalf of himself and the other senior professional sales representatives at K & K, arguing that their jobs were non-exempt.

Case 2 Cheryl Wiley, Auto Damage Adjuster

Cheryl Wiley was promoted from auto damage appraiser to auto damage adjuster after being employed with Auto Insurance for three years. In her former position as auto damage appraiser, she worked at one of Auto Insurance's drive-in locations inspecting damaged cars that remain in drivable condition. She performed this job under close supervision and all of her work had to be approved by the supervisor. The job was considered non-exempt and Wiley received overtime pay whenever she exceeded her required work hours.

In her new position as auto damage adjuster, Wiley had responsibility for "assessing, negotiating, and settling automobile damage claims." She spent a majority of her time appraising damaged vehicles and estimating repair costs, but also negotiating and settling claims with body shops over repair costs and with claimants over total loss vehicles. An auto damage adjuster had to determine how much Auto Insurance should pay to restore a vehicle to its pre-damage condition using the most economical parts available unless safety was a consideration. In assessing each vehicle, the adjuster used a software program to perform the analysis. While the software assisted with providing information on the cheapest parts and prices, the adjuster also had to make decisions not dictated by the software. For example, the adjuster had to figure out if there was pre-existing damage, interview claimants, negotiate with shops over repair times, and ensure claims were not fraudulent. All adjustors had set dollar limits on their negotiating authority. Wiley was a level 1 adjuster and had settlement authority up to $10,000. However, she could recommend settlements in excess of her authority, but they had to be approved by her supervisor. Auto damage adjusters report to supervisors who report to auto damage managers who in turn report to auto damage directors.

In the case of total loss vehicles, Wiley had to decide whether it was economically feasible to repair a vehicle or to pay the owner its value. These decisions were more time consuming because they involved thousands of dollars in additional liability for Auto Insurance. However, Auto Insurance had set standards for determining when to declare a vehicle a total loss. In her job as auto damage adjuster, Wiley handled on average more than 1,000 claims per year, totaling $2.5 million. About 20 percent of the yearly claims involved total loss vehicles. Wiley also worked under some supervision in the field one or two days a week at one of the drive-in locations. Wiley earned $41,000 per year in her new position but regularly worked in excess of 40 hours per week. When she asked about being paid for overtime, she was told that unlike her prior job, the auto damage adjuster position was non-exempt. Wiley did not agree and filed a lawsuit against Auto Insurance alleging she is entitled to overtime pay because her job is primarily administrative, using well-defined guidelines and policies.

Case 3 John Krauss and National Bank

John Krauss was employed by National Bank for two years as an underwriter. As an underwriter, Krauss evaluated whether to issue loans to individual loan applicants by referring to a set of guidelines, known as the Credit Guide, provided to him by the bank. The Guide specified how underwriters should determine loan applicant characteristics such as qualifying income and credit history. It also instructed underwriters to compare such data with criteria set out in the Guide. The Guide contained standards for what qualified a loan applicant for a particular loan product. National Bank also provided supplemental guidelines and product guidelines with information specific to individual loan products. Krauss was expected to evaluate the applications using the Credit Guide and approving the loan if it met the standards set. As such, he had no interactions with applicants since this was a back-office operation. Underwriters were evaluated not by whether the approved loans were paid back, but by measuring each underwriter's productivity in terms of average of total actions per day and assessing whether the underwriters' decisions met National's Credit Guide standards.

National Bank sometimes used incentive schemes based on number of decisions made to increase underwriter performance. Underwriters at National Bank earned a salary of $42,000 per year. To keep up with the number of applications he had to evaluate, Krauss regularly worked overtime. When he inquired about being paid for overtime, Krauss was told the underwriter position was exempt from the Fair Labor Standards Act. Krauss did not agree and felt that he was basically an administrative employee who performed work that was well-defined by the company. Subsequently, Krauss filed a lawsuit requesting that he be paid overtime for the hours he had worked in excess of the required forty for the past two years.

Developing a Wage Structure

I. OBJECTIVES

A. To familiarize you with how data obtained when using the point system approach to job evaluation can be used to develop a wage structure.

B. To give you practice in developing a wage structure.

II. TIME REQUIRED TO COMPLETE: 1 hour or less

III. INSTRUCTIONS

Examine the pay data below.

Pay Grade	Job Evaluation Points	Top of Grade	Position
1	100–200	$36,000	Control Operator I
2	201–300	$39,000	Control Operator II
3	301–400	$47,500	Control Operator III
4	401–500	$53,800	Control Operator IV

Exhibit 4.6 shows a partially completed pay structure for control operator positions. Your first task is to complete the chart for pay grades 2, 3, and 4. Construct pay steps for each of the remaining pay grades based on the following guidelines for "time in service" in each pay grade.

Pay Step Data

Entry wage: 65.5 percent of top for each pay grade

Step 1: After 1 year within the pay grade   70 percent of top

Step 2: After 3 years within the pay grade   75 percent of top

Step 3: After 5 years within the pay grade   82 percent of top

Step 4: After 8 years within the pay grade   90 percent of top

Top of grade: After 10 years within the pay grade

In addition, listed below are the names of employees in each pay grade and their current salaries. Your second task is to plot each one on Exhibit 4.7 and to determine which of the current salaries fall outside the appropriate pay grade.

Control Operator I:

Charles Hamilton—6 years' services—paid $30,218

Mary Richardson—10 years' service—paid $32,250

Control Operator II:

Jerry Smith—2 years' service—paid $29,250

Theresa Jones—5 years' service—paid $31,600

Control Operator III:

Alicia Wadsworth—5 years' service—paid $38,950

Connie Johnston—7 years' service—paid $40,380

Velda Prescott—1 years' service—paid $33,250

Control Operator IV:

Gloria Lopez—3 years' service—paid $40,350

Rosemary Jensen—5 years' service—paid $44,120

EXHIBIT 4.6 *Pay Structure for Office Staff Positions*

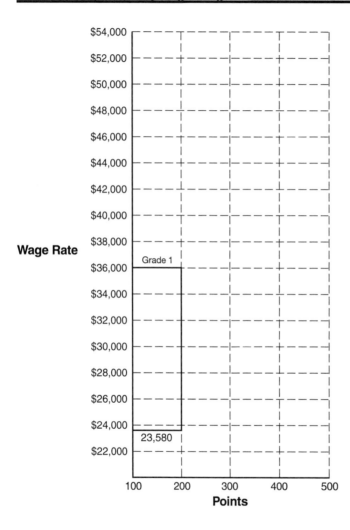

Managing Nonmonetary Compensation

Andrew Nelson supervised the respiratory therapy department at Dunesbury Medical Center in Owatonna and Waseca, Minnesota, towns of 16,000 and 2,000, respectively. Though he worked mainly at the local hospitals, he was employed by Breathing Care Associates (BCA), which was affiliated with St. Luke's Hospital in Rochester, Minnesota.

Nelson graduated from the Mayo Clinic Respiratory Therapy Program and earned a BS in Biology from a Minnesota state college. Before accepting this supervisory position three years ago, he had been a staff therapist at Mount Olympus Medical Center in Milwaukee, Wisconsin. A highly respected professional, Nelson tried to keep up with current developments in his field. He was well-liked by staff and patients and had a good sense of humor. If there was one thing Nelson lacked, it was formal management training. He now wished he had taken some business courses during college.

Nelson did not belong to a labor union. His parents had owned a trucking business and had dealt with teamsters. Stories about their shenanigans soured Nelson on union membership. However, therapists at St. Luke's Hospital who were employed by BCA were represented by a bargaining unit.

Nelson's supervisor, Matt Barnes, used to call or visit the Dunesbury Medical Center at Owatonna regularly to see how things were going or to bring supplies. Lately, Barnes's visits were less frequent. Months could go by before Nelson saw him.

Since 1963, Dunesbury Medical Center had operated another facility in Waseca, about 12 miles west of Owatonna. In 2009, Dunesbury's board of directors decided to close the Waseca facility on June 30th for economic reasons.

Exhibit 4.7 shows an organizational chart for the respiratory therapy department at Dunesbury Medical Center in January 2009.

Beginning January 3, 2009, Barb Johnson took a six-week paid maternity leave permitted under BCA's temporary disability program. At the end of January, Ramona Black had surgery and took a six-week medical leave. That left only Nelson, Pam Picha, and Lynn Owens to staff the two facilities.

Nelson was under pressure from BCA to cut labor costs. For about a month, he worked six days per week. The length of his workday varied from 8 to 12 hours or more. On the days Nelson worked, he also was on call. If a patient had breathing difficulties, Nelson was called to the hospital after normal working hours. Sometimes he would not get called in for several days. On other nights, he might get called in two or three times. If a doctor wanted a patient to be on an artificial breathing machine, called a respirator, Nelson had to provide staff at the hospital 24 hours a day.

Since he was an exempt employee, Nelson received no overtime pay. Originally he was not paid for on-call hours either. Then, he successfully negotiated with BCA to get $10.00 per hour on-call pay. In January and February 2009 combined, Nelson worked more than 140 hours beyond his normal scheduled work week. His salary was about $65,000.

In March, Pam Picha resigned to move to Texas. Lynn Owens gave two weeks' notice on April 2; she had accepted a position in a Minneapolis hospital. While Nelson attended a Minnesota Association of Respiratory Therapists' Convention in mid-April, Ramona Black quit without giving notice. Nelson left the conference early to fill in at the Owatonna facility.

EXHIBIT 4.7 *Dunesbury Medical Center Organizational Chart*

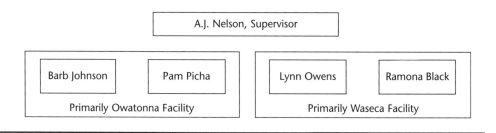

He began to feel he needed some time off from work as he was getting burned out with all of the overtime hours. Nelson's earned time account, which could be used for sick leave, vacation, holidays, and so on, had almost reached the 400-hour maximum. On April 21, Nelson asked Barnes if he could take a vacation from May 20–26. His wife had to attend a business meeting in New Orleans, and this would be a good chance for the family to spend a few extra days together sightseeing.

Upon receiving no reply from Barnes, Nelson sent him a note with the weekly payroll report of May 5 asking what decision had been made on his vacation request. In the meantime, Barb Johnson found out that Nelson was planning to take time off. She refused to work seven days in a row, which would have been necessary to provide adequate staffing in Nelson's absence. The previous summer, Nelson had worked seven days in a row so that she could take a vacation.

Finally, on May 12, Barnes called Nelson. "Good morning, Drew. Say about this vacation request. . . .. I really can't let you take off right now. I can't force Barb to work seven days in a row. Besides, if she did, I'd have to pay her overtime." Nelson swallowed hard, but before he could reply, Matt ended their conversation.

BCA's policy on earned time accrual and use is presented in Exhibit 4.8.

QUESTIONS

1. What are Andrew Nelson's alternatives?

2. What do you think Nelson should do? Justify your answer.

3. Does the hospital administration have any obligation to help alleviate Nelson's situation?

EXHIBIT 4.8 *BCA's Policy on Earned Time Accrual and Use*

Earned Time

Personal time off from the workplace is important in maintaining good health. Breathing Care Associates is introducing an innovative program for earned paid time off. The program is called Earned Time, and has been nicknamed "ET."

Earned Time combines traditional programs of paid vacation time, paid legal and personal holiday time, and paid sick time into one "bank" of paid benefit time off. For each hour you work—up to 80 per pay period—an amount of Earned Time is deposited into your personal Earned Time (ET) Account. Then, as you decide you want to schedule time off, the hours accumulated in your personal ET Account are yours to use.

You begin to earn time with your first hour of work at Breathing Care Associates. And for each hour you work—up to 80 per pay period—Earned Time continues to accrue. The amount of Earned Time you accrue depends on your length of continuous service at Breathing Care Associates, your exemption status (non-exempt or exempt), and the number of hours you work.

These are also the usual components for determining accrual rates for paid holiday, sick, and vacation time. With this new program, however, you have the flexibility to schedule time off for whatever purpose you choose.

Maximum Accumulation Amounts

The emphasis of Earned Time is to offer you scheduled time away from work for whatever purpose you choose. Full-time employees are strongly encouraged to take 15 days off each year. Because unused Earned Time can be forwarded from year to year, it is possible to reach your Account Maximum if you do not use enough Earned Time each year.

Your personal ET Account has a maximum accumulation amount of two times your annual accrual rate. When you near your account maximum, it is your responsibility to schedule Earned Time off. If the account maximum is reached, no ET will accrue beyond it.

Example of Maximum Accumulation Amounts

Years of Service	Annual Accrual	Maximum ET Accumulation
2–4	200 hours (25 days)	400 hours (50 days)
10	248 hours (31 days)	496 hours (62 days)

Scheduling ET

ET is available as you accrue it. However, requests for paid time off must be approved by your supervisor, who will consider staffing arrangements and departmental operations before granting your request. Schedule ET with your supervisor as far in advance as possible. Often, at least a two-week notice is required for a scheduled absence.

Contributed by Margaret Foegen Karsten, The University of Wisconsin, Platteville

Benefits

77 CASE
Controlling Employee Benefit Costs

John DeCarlo is President and CEO of Quality Auto Parts, an automotive parts equipment manufacturer and supplier in the Southwest. The company was started by DeCarlo and his father in 1988 and now employs 812 people at four different sites. Revenues and profits increased steadily from 1988 until 2001. Both revenues and profits were down in 2001 and 2002 and after recovering from 2003 to 2006, they were again down from 2007 to the present. As a result of declining auto sales, auto parts were also hit hard during the recent recession. In order to contain costs, the company has begun to examine its employee health benefits.

THE PROBLEM

DeCarlo recently met with his vice president for finance (David Schramm) and his vice president for human resources (Harriet Windham) to determine how costs could be cut so the company could price its products more competitively relative to foreign competitors. At this meeting, he learned that employee benefit costs had increased at approximately twice the rate of increase for wages alone (8 percent versus 2 percent yearly average increases) from 2000–2010. In particular, the total employee health insurance costs increased from $4,680 per employee per year in 2000 to $9,869 in 2010. DeCarlo expressed frustration at these increases and asked what could be done.

Windham and Schramm invited DeCarlo to a meeting of healthcare providers, insurers, and employers, sponsored by the area Chamber of Commerce and scheduled for the following week. The topic of the meeting is the implications of the healthcare reform legislation passed by Congress and signed by the President in spring of 2010. Most employers did not know the details of the legislation, and there was much uncertainty regarding the legal status of some of the provisions in the legislation. At this meeting, they learned that some of the provisions might be repealed in the future. However, they also learned that taxes on such benefits would be increased, thus making such benefits more expensive to employers. This legislation made it more imperative that Quality Auto Parts and other companies offering health insurance benefits find a way of controlling the costs of such benefits. If not controlled, some forecasters have predicted that health benefit costs will be equal to the total profits of all U.S. corporations by the year 2016.

They also learned more about the nature and causes of this problem. Many of the speakers at the conference cited large catastrophic-illness claims, increased use of mental health and substance abuse services, increased use of medical services, high-technology medicine, cost-shifting from government programs (Medicare and Medicaid) to private insurance, high physician fees, the AIDS crisis, the demographics of employees in the auto industry (i.e., a higher percentage of older employees), and recent premium increases by both traditional and managed care plans attempting to recoup recent losses. One speaker noted:

"If businesses in the private sector don't make a profit, they are not going to exist. The continuing escalation of healthcare costs is threatening the very survival of some companies, particularly small companies. Smaller businesses increasingly bear the brunt of the spiraling costs because they have no one else to whom they can shift their costs."

Several possible solutions were discussed although there was no consensus regarding their effectiveness or applicability to particular situations. Among the cost containment suggestions were self-insurance, utilization review, managed care (i.e., health maintenance organizations and preferred provider organizations), wellness programs, flexible benefits, cost-sharing (i.e., higher deductibles and co-insurance), pre-admission certification for surgery, financial incentives for outpatient services, use of retail clinics, development of employer health clinics, mail order prescription drug programs, health savings accounts, use of variable co-payments for different types of divisions, implementation of a disease management program, and audits of employee dependence to assess eligibility. Many speakers emphasized that the health reform legislation is not likely to contain employer costs but rather to increase such costs. When Congress has intervened in the past, it has usually made the cost problem worse as a result of mandates that raise costs for both insurance companies and employers.

THE CHALLENGE

DeCarlo came away from the conference with a greater appreciation of the complexity of the problem of increasing employee health insurance costs and a greater determination to do something about it. However, he wasn't sure about his next steps. He viewed his company as a "preferred employer" because it had always paid above the market wage rates and its benefits were always more liberal than those of other U.S. companies and particularly those of foreign competitors. DeCarlo did not want to do anything to jeopardize his company's advantage in attracting and retaining high-quality personnel. At the same time, he realized that if no changes were made, his health insurance premiums may be greater than his total projected company earnings by the year 2016.

Quality Auto Parts' present health insurance plan (Blue Cross-Blue Shield) is a traditional indemnity insurance plan. All employees have one plan, which makes no effort to control the health-care services provided. Employees select their own physicians, and the insurance company pays reimbursement for whatever services are provided at whatever price the particular provider charges. Neither physicians nor employees have a financial incentive to economize in the use of services or to seek out low-cost providers. Physician reimbursement is based upon the number of procedures they perform and the physician reimbursement rate for each procedure.

DeCarlo decided to establish an employee health benefits committee that would report to him in one month with recommendations for containing health benefit costs while minimizing adverse employee reaction. Membership on the committee consisted of Windham, Schramm, and two other employees. You have been asked to serve as an employee member of this committee. The committee has recommended that DeCarlo consider four general options for the future: 1) stay with the current traditional indemnity policy with an average cost of $10,465 per year; 2) offer an HMO option in addition to the current plan; 3) establish a special self-insurance fund and negotiate preferred provider arrangements (PPOs) with local providers (i.e., discounted prices in exchange for the directing of these employees to these providers); or 4) the combination of catastrophic health insurance plan for major medical expenses coupled with a Health Savings Account (HSA) for smaller, more routine healthcare expenses.

The committee members are split on the four options. The other employee wishes to continue with the current plan, Schramm wants to adopt the self-insurance option, and Windham wants to offer the HMO option. DeCarlo, the CEO, has previously expressed interest in the catastrophic plan coupled with an HSA. All four are looking to you to make a recommendation and help them reach a consensus.

QUESTIONS

1. Describe the nature and causes of the employee health insurance cost problem in this case.

2. What information should the employee health benefits committee gather before making any recommendations? Why?

3. Given the desire of most employees to protect themselves from high healthcare costs, is there any way for Quality Auto Parts to continue to attract the best employees while containing health benefit costs? Why or why not?

4. On the basis of what you know about Quality Auto Parts, which of the four specific proposals would you be likely to recommend? Can the company adopt some combination of the three options? What do you recommend and why?

78 CASE

Domestic Partner Benefits

Baptist Hospital is a 360-bed facility in a large facility in the southeastern United States. Recently, the human resource management director, Joan Collins, has noted a higher than average employee turnover among nurses and other clinical professionals such as occupational therapist, physical therapist, and laboratory technologist. She is concerned that Baptist Hospital is losing good employees to other hospitals in the metropolitan region that offer more liberal domestic partner benefits. In fact, the hospital does not recognize such partners and provides no health benefits to them.

Most large companies in the region do offer such domestic partner benefits. For their purposes, they typically define a "domestic partner" as a person over 18 who shares living quarters with another adult in an exclusive committed relationship in which the partners are responsible for each other's common welfare. A standard definition typically includes requirements concerning a minimum age, a requirement that the couples live together, financial interdependence, a committed relationship, and a non-blood relative. Before such benefits can be provided, these companies typically require a signed and notarized affidavit specifying these requirements must be signed by both domestic partners and witnessed by a notary.

Collins has also done some research that indicates that those companies providing domestic partner benefits experience lower health benefit costs. The reason is that many unmarried heterosexual partners or homosexual partners do not have children and therefore such unions utilize fewer health services. Her research also showed that as a result of ongoing lawsuits in this area, many more employers may be forced to offer domestic partner benefits in the future.

While Collins is convinced that such a change in health benefits would be advantageous to the company, particularly in terms of recruiting and retaining employees, she is concerned that the hospital's culture is socially conservative. Consequently, she feels that the CEO, the executive team, and the board of directors may be less enthusiastic about implementing such a change than she is. Collins is therefore uncertain as to how to proceed and has asked your instructor for advice. Your instructor has presented the case to the class but has changed the name of the institution so that students will not know the identity of the facility.

QUESTIONS

1. Would you recommend that Joan Collins bring this issue before the CEO and the board of directors and recommend implementation? Why or why not?

2. If you believe that Collins should recommend implementation of domestic partner health benefits, what are the potential benefits to Baptist Hospital, and how would she document these?

3. What are the potential disadvantages to the hospital, and what steps should she recommend to address these potential disadvantages?

4. Do you see any differences between heterosexual domestic partners and gay domestic partners in terms of the health benefits that should be provided? If so, how would you differentiate the two and why?

5. Are you aware of any companies that provide domestic partner health benefits and, if so, how effective have these programs been in attracting and retaining employees?

6. Is there any relevant research on the topic of domestic benefits and, if so, what does this research show?

79 EXERCISE

Flexible Benefit Plan Choices

I. OBJECTIVES

A. To familiarize you with how flexible benefit plans work.

B. To give you an understanding of some of the benefits offered in a flexible benefit plan.

C. To give you experience in selecting benefits.

D. To give you an understanding of the criteria individuals use in selecting benefits.

II. OUT-OF-CLASS PREPARATION TIME: 10 minutes to read the exercise and select benefits

III. IN-CLASS TIME SUGGESTED: 30–40 minutes

IV. PROCEDURES

Assume that you recently graduated from college and are just starting a new job at a large firm. You will be receiving a starting net pay (net of all taxes and mandatory deductions) of $30,000. Your task is to read the Benefit Policy described below and determine which benefits you would select. Keep in mind that any money you spend on additional benefits will reduce the $30,000 per year you can spend on other things such as housing, entertainment, and travel. After each student in the class has selected the benefits he or she would choose, the instructor will divide the class into groups of three to five. Then, each student will explain his/her selections to the rest of the group along with the rationale behind the decisions. After each student is finished, your group needs to prepare a list of criteria (reasons you would or would not want a benefit) that were used in making the benefit selections. These criteria will then be written on an overhead or blackboard for class discussion.

BENEFITS POLICY

Your company offers full-time employees the opportunity to participate in a broad range of programs to meet specific needs. Employees are responsible for selecting the benefits that best meet their needs.

PRE-TAX HEALTHCARE PREMIUM PAYMENTS

The firm offers employees a medical care program that includes doctor's visits, hospital services, emergency room visits, and diagnostic laboratory tests. Our program allows employees to pay a portion of their health insurance premiums through payroll deduction to receive a tax break by having the premiums deducted from their paychecks before taxes are calculated. New employees must opt into pre-tax within 31 days of employment to receive the benefit. The firm pays the remainder of your healthcare fees. However, if you choose this benefit, you will need to pay $65 per month for an employee-only policy, $137 per month for an employee plus one more family member policy, and $185 per month for total family coverage.

FLEXIBLE REIMBURSEMENT ACCOUNTS

Section 125 of the Internal Revenue Service's (IRS) Code allows employees to choose certain pre-tax benefits as an alternative to taxable monetary compensation. These include a medical and a dependent care reimbursement account.

MEDICAL REIMBURSEMENT ACCOUNT

This account allows an employee to set aside pre-tax dollars to pay for medical, dental, and vision care, or other eligible expenses not covered by the health plan. There is a $5,000 per plan year maximum and $10 is the minimum contribution per pay period. The employee must have maintained eligibility to participate in the healthcare plan described above for six or more continuous months to participate in the Medical Reimbursement Account.

DEPENDENT CARE REIMBURSEMENT ACCOUNT

This account allows you to set aside pre-tax dollars to pay for eligible dependent care expenses such as child care. You are eligible to enroll within 31 days of employment. Maximum amount during a plan year is:

$2,500–married and filing tax returns separately from spouse.

$5,000–single, or married and filing jointly.

$10 is the minimum contribution per pay period.

RETIREMENT

You will be automatically enrolled in our firm's retirement plan after 1,000 hours of service. Upon retirement or termination of service, you will receive 2 percent of your annual compensation for each year of service. Your pension is vested if you have three years of service with the firm. See your Benefits Office for more details.

EMPLOYEE STOCK PURCHASE PLAN

You are allowed to purchase common stock in this firm at a 15 percent discount off the fair market value through payroll deduction. Contributions are deducted on an after-tax basis. See the Benefits Office for details.

LIFE INSURANCE

Full-time employees of our firm have life insurance provided, effective the first day of employment, as a condition of employment. It provides two kinds of insurance—life and accidental death and dismemberment. The amount of insurance coverage is equal to the employee's annual salary rounded to the next highest thousand, and then doubled. An amount equal to four times the employee's salary is payable in the event of accidental death. Coverage is also provided for accidental blinding or dismemberment. Premiums are paid by the firm.

OPTIONAL LIFE INSURANCE

Additional optional life insurance is available and is administered by a large life insurance firm. It is available for employees and their spouses and dependents. Premiums are paid by the employee through payroll deduction. To receive up to $200,000 coverage without proving good health, you must request within 60 days of employment. Your cost will depend upon your age:

MONTHLY RATE PER $10,000 COVERAGE

Under 25	25–29	30–34	35–39	40–44	45–49
$0.40	$0.50	$0.70	$0.80	$1.30	$2.20

Price quotes are also available for those over 50. Check with the Benefits Office.

OPTIONAL LONG-TERM CARE INSURANCE

Long-term care insurance is offered to full-time employees, their spouses, parents, and parents-in-law. Employees enrolling within 31 days of hire do not have to complete a health care questionnaire. Long-term care is the care you need when you require assistance with day-to-day functions like dressing, eating, and getting into and out of bed due to medical problems caused by illness or accident. The cost of this insurance is dependent upon one's age and level of coverage. Check with the benefits office for specific costs.

OPTIONAL LONG-TERM DISABILITY

Long-term disability income insurance helps to protect your income when, due to a covered illness or injury, you are disabled. It has been designed to cover a disability sustained on or off the job. The plan provides up to 60 percent of your basic monthly earnings after 180 days of disability. The cost varies depending upon age and level of coverage.

PERSONAL ACCIDENT INSURANCE

Personal accident insurance is available for the employee, spouse, and dependent children and helps protect against losses due to accidents. A full benefit is paid for accidental loss of life; loss of use of both upper and lower limbs; loss of both hands, feet, or eyes; loss of speech; or loss of hearing in both ears. Partial benefits are paid in the event of loss of any one hand, foot, eye, both legs, or both arms. The firm pays all costs.

TRANSPORTATION REIMBURSEMENT ACCOUNT

You may contribute to a parking reimbursement account and/or a transportation account, which covers mass transit or vanpooling. These are two separate accounts. Contributions are pre-tax, deducted from your paycheck. You can contribute up to $185 per month for the parking account and $100 per month for the transportation account.

OPTIONAL PRE-PAID LEGAL PLAN

A pre-paid legal plan which, for a monthly payroll deduction of $19.20, provides legal services such as traffic court representation, first offense DUI court representation, will preparation, credit/warranty disputes, financial contract or lease review, uncontested divorce, uncontested adoption, and purchasing or selling a primary residence.

TUITION ASSISTANCE

Educational assistance is available for full-time employees with at least one year of service. Our firm will pay for a maximum of 15 credit hours for the year—six credit hours in the fall, six credit hours in the spring, and three credit hours in the summer. Courses must be work- or degree-related and taken at a fully accredited college or university.

80 EXERCISE

Executive Perks

I. **OBJECTIVES**

   A. To familiarize you with the wide variety of perks often given to top executives.

   B. To familiarize you with the arguments for and against various executive perks.

II. **OUT-OF-CLASS PREPARATION TIME:** none

III. **IN-CLASS TIME SUGGESTED:** 30–40 minutes

IV. **PROCEDURES**

At the start of class, your instructor will divide the class into groups of three to five. Your group is to assume that you are all members of the compensation committee for a large firm. Your committee is composed of independent members of the firm's board of directors. It is responsible for establishing annual and long-term performance goals for the firm's executives, for evaluating the performance of these officers, for setting the compensation of these officers, and for making recommendations to the board with respect to new compensation plans. The firm's current CEO has announced her retirement, so a new CEO will be chosen soon. Given the controversy regarding executive perks that arose after the 2009 federal bailout of the U.S. banking system, your committee has been asked by the board of directors to review the current CEO perks to determine if they should also be offered to the new CEO. You are to assume that the current CEO has a base salary of $863,000 and earned an additional $1 million from bonuses. Below is a list of the CEO's current perks. Your task is to evaluate each of the following in terms of whether it should be provided. So, for each item, circle "Y" or "N." Then, write below each item the reason behind your decision.

A. Physical Exams   Y or N

   Reason: _____

   Estimated Cost: $4,000–$8,000 per year

B. Personal Financial Counseling   Y or N

   Reason: _____

   Estimated Cost: $5,000–$10,000 per year

C. Company Car   Y or N

   Reason: _____

   Estimated Cost: $12,000 per year

D. Memberships in Country/Exercise Club(s)   Y or N

   Reason: _____

   Estimated Cost: $10,000 per year

E. First-class Air Travel for Overseas Travel   Y or N

   Reason: _____

   Estimated Cost: $40,000–$60,000 per year

F. Chartered Plane for U.S. Travel   Y or N

   Reason: _____

   Estimated Cost: $80,000–$100,000 per year

G. Personal Liability Insurance Protection Against Law Suits   Y or N
Reason: _____
Estimated Cost: $6,500 per year

H. Chauffeur Service to Meetings/Airport/Home   Y or N
Reason: _____
Estimated Cost: $18,000–$20,000 per year

I. Reserved Garage Parking   Y or N
Reason: _____
Estimated Cost: $5,000 per year

J. Clothing Allowance   Y or N
Reason: _____
Estimated Cost: $6,000 per year

K. Stock Options (allows executive to buy company stock in future years at favorable prices)   Y or N
Reason: _____
Estimated Cost: Up to $1,250,000 per year

L. Golden Parachute/Severance Pay (given if the executive's employment is terminated before end of contract)   Y or N
Reason: _____
Estimated Cost: $900,000 one-time payment

M. Guaranteed Pension   Y or N
Reason: _____
Estimated Cost: $600,000 per year for life

N. Bonuses   Y or N
Reason: _____
Estimated Cost: Up to $1,250,000 per year

81 INCIDENT

Retiree Health and Pension Benefits

Frank Sears was a blue-collar worker for a large chemical company in the Northeast for his entire career and retired in 2003 at age 60. Sears felt quite secure about his situation at the time of retirement. The union had negotiated very generous health insurance and pension benefits for its retirees. His home mortgage had been paid off in 1992, so his only household expenses were property taxes, repairs, and routine maintenance.

While their health and pension benefits have failed to keep up with inflation since 2003, Sears and his wife have adapted by eating out less often and postponing some needed home repairs. Since their pension benefits were not indexed to inflation, they had reconciled themselves to learning to live on less or to one or both of them going back to work. In conversations with other retirees from the same companies, they learned that others were also considering going back to work to augment their income. The only problem they faced was that unemployment in their area is currently 12.2 percent. Job opportunities at wage rates much above minimum wage are few and far between.

But their retiree health insurance premiums, purchased through Sears's former company, were a particular concern. Their premiums had increased 21 percent and 26 percent, respectively, for each of the past two years. Mrs. Sears called a number of other health insurance companies to determine how much it would cost to purchase insurance on their own directly from another insurer. To her amazement, she learned that direct purchase would cost them less.

After checking with two other retired couples who were insured with the original company, she learned they had switched a year ago when they found out that the original company had viewed retiree health insurance as a profit center and had charged accordingly. She promptly switched to a new insurer and felt their problem had been solved.

Yesterday, she received a letter from an executive of a company she had never heard of indicating that the new company had purchased the original company. The letter went on to say that, effective immediately, no more health or pension benefits would be paid to them or any other retiree. She was no longer concerned about the health insurance benefits, since these were paid directly out-of-pocket anyway. However, their ability to pay for the health insurance was dependent upon continued lifetime pension benefits as the union contract stipulated at the time of Sears's retirement.

QUESTIONS

1. Do companies have either a moral or legal obligation to honor all terms and conditions associated with an employee's retirement that were in effect at the time of that retirement? Why or why not?

2. Does the purchase of the original company by another company, or changing economic circumstances, obviate the employer's obligation concerning retiree benefits? Why or why not?

3. Could Mr. and Mrs. Sears expect to receive any retirement benefits as a result of ERISA?

The Educational Leave Problem

Rollermakers Corporation is a midwestern manufacturer of rollers used by most industrial firms to move products and packages from one location to another. For example, the U.S. Postal Service uses rollers to slide packages from one area of the post office to another, thereby minimizing the lifting of heavy parcels. Coal companies use rollers underneath conveyor belts to move coal from the mine to empty coal train cars. Rollers are usually made to customer specifications rather than mass produced. Typically, customers determine the type of rollers needed with the help of design engineers or Rollermakers's sales staff.

Rollermakers's staff consists of a production crew, inside sales force, outside sales force, and administration. Administration and the inside sales force work together to process quotes, orders, and invoices in the most efficient manner possible. The inside sales force is hired using a placement firm, and employees are trained internally. Administrative staff are usually hired from the same recruiting agency, with some exceptions. Purchasing managers and accounting positions are salaried and are filled through advertising and recruiters. In the recent past, the company has faced threats of racial discrimination lawsuits from former inside sales employees, and lawyers have contacted the firm on behalf of those who are issuing these threats. No lawsuits have been filed, but management has become more careful in all human resource matters.

The present purchasing manager was hired from another competitor a little over a year ago. At that time, the manager was also attending an evening MBA program at a local university and, as part of his compensation package, would be allowed tuition reimbursement and time off to attend classes with the understanding that the classes would not cause a major disruption to the daily work schedule. For the past year, this has worked well because classes do not start until 5:45 P.M.

With the new fall semester starting, two inside sales employees informed the inside sales manager of their intentions to return to college on a part-time basis. Jan Thornton, an African-American female, wanted to return to college to finish a degree in Accounting. She is a junior now and hopes to finish within the next two years. She is scheduled to take two Accounting classes, one on Tuesday and Thursday from 11:00 until 12:20, and the other on Monday, Wednesday, and Friday from 2:00 until 2:50. These are the only times the required classes are offered. The college is located about five minutes from work. Thornton has made it known that she will be leaving the company upon graduation. She has been with the company for 18 months and is well-liked and competent. She is one of the more efficient and accurate of the inside sales staff.

The second employee, Josephine Green, is a white female, starting community college after achieving a GED. She would like to take classes that meet from 2:00 until 2:50 and from 3:00 until 3:50 on Monday, Wednesday, and Friday. The community college is located within 20 minutes of work. She also plans to earn a degree or certificate in accounting and has stated that she wishes to stay with the company "for as long as they will have me." She wants to earn more money and was told if she obtained her degree she would be eligible to be promoted to an appropriate position. The current bookkeeper is planning on retiring in three years, and Green has her eye on this job. Green is also well-liked by most, but not all, of the inside sales force. Her error rate on specifications and pricing of specialty work is higher than most others.

Green submitted her class schedule to the inside sales manager as a request and had not registered or paid for classes. Thornton had registered and paid for her classes. The schedules chosen by the employees drastically conflicted with the regular business day. Nonetheless, both employees asked that their schedules be worked around and accommodated. They contended that the precedent set by the purchasing manager should apply to them. Rollermakers Corporation does not currently have any formal policy regarding educational leave. However, both employees were told when they were first hired that they were expected to be at work during business hours.

QUESTIONS

1. Should Rollermakers Corporation allow the two inside salespeople to miss work in order to attend classes? Should it pay for their tuition? Why?

2. Should the firm continue to allow the purchasing manager to attend the evening MBA program and to pay his tuition?

3. Should there be a formal policy regarding educational leave or should it remain informal? If the firm decides to formalize its policy, what provisions should it contain?

83 INCIDENT

The Lost Vacation Days

Ships, Inc. is a large shipbuilding company located in one of the eastern states. One September afternoon, the firm made the decision to shut down operations due to an approaching hurricane. This was based on the forecasted arrival of tropical storm force winds to the local area as early as noon on Wednesday. They made that decision at approximately 2:00 P.M. on a Tuesday afternoon, and some employees were told Tuesday by supervisors that the shutdown would occur beginning with the next morning's shift and that they were not to report to work. They were also told that the time they lost would be excused with pay.

By Tuesday evening, it was very clear that the hurricane would not hit the area until Thursday at the earliest. Nonetheless, the shipyard decided to maintain the decision to shut down on Wednesday. The emergency hotline message confirmed this information, but also said that missed time for salaried personnel would be charged against each employee's vacation bank.

By Wednesday evening, the emergency hotline message was updated to state that the shutdown would be continued through the first shift on Thursday, with normal operations commencing on the second shift. The hurricane subsequently hit the area Thursday night (during the second shift), leaving many roads littered with branches and debris.

On Friday morning, when all personnel reported for work again (many of them without electricity at home), they were hit with the fact that they had just lost two days of vacation—two days "gone with the wind." Hourly personnel had the option of charging the two days off to their vacation bank or taking time off without pay, but salaried personnel did not have a choice—they were required to charge the leave to their accrued vacation bank. This action was in line with the company's policy for complete shutdowns despite what some personnel were told prior to this shutdown.

Within a few days, many salaried employees became very upset with the way the company handled the situation and with the fact that they just lost two vacation days for no good reason. Why did the firm close down operations so soon instead of waiting for the storm to hit? Why didn't it close down operations on Thursday, the day the storm actually did arrive? Some employees had already scheduled vacation for the Thanksgiving and the Christmas holidays and now realized that they had insufficient vacation days left in their vacation bank. Those who had already paid for their airline and cruise tickets were particularly upset. Others were offended by the fact that they would now need to work uncompensated overtime to make up for the work missed, an action expected of all salaried employees.

The company's vacation policy states that salaried employees accrue vacation time based on length of service. Employees with less than five years' seniority receive one day per month, those with five to ten years' seniority earn one and one-half days per month, and those with more than ten years earn two days per month. Employees have the right to carry over unused vacation time to the next year. The policy also states that if the shipyard is shut down for any reason, the time lost by salaried employees will be charged to each person's vacation bank. Furthermore, the policy states that in the event of a partial shutdown, salaried employees who report to work and are then sent home will be paid for any time missed and will not be required to charge lost time to their vacation banks.

1. What, if anything, should Ships, Inc. do with regard to salaried personnel who have vacations planned later this year and now do not have enough vacation time?

2. What, if anything, should the firm do regarding the lost vacation time for all of the other employees, both salaried and hourly?

3. Should the firm change its current policy that requires salaried employees to charge their vacation bank whenever a shutdown occurs?

84 INCIDENT

The Medical Leave Problem (FMLA)

Maura Currier has been working for ComputerTech for four years as a lead supervisor. During the past two years, Currier's mother has needed frequent medical attention for her diabetes. Being the only child, Currier has helped her mother, Jane Currier, as often as her work schedule would allow. Unfortunately, during the past two years, her mother's condition has worsened.

With the passage of the Family and Medical Leave Act (FMLA), Currier asked the firm for, and was granted, an unpaid leave to care for her mother in accordance with company policy (see the policy in Exhibit 4.9). The agreement stated that Currier could miss work every Friday for 60 weeks rather than take off 12 straight weeks. At the end of 60 weeks, Currier returned to work full time and immediately began missing work to care for her mother until all of her allotted vacation and sick leave days were exhausted. She then asked that her Friday

---

EXHIBIT 4.9 *Family Medical Leave Policy*

Employees who have worked for at least one year and worked 1,250 hours during the 12-month period preceding the commencement of the leave year are eligible to take up to 12 weeks of unpaid job-protected leave during any 12-month period for one or more of the following reasons:

1. Because of the birth of a son or daughter of the employee and to care for such son or daughter;
2. Because of the placement of a son or daughter with the employee for adoption or foster care;
3. To care for the spouse, son, daughter, or parent of the employee, if such spouse, son, daughter, or parent has a serious health condition; or
4. Because of a serious health condition that makes the employee unable to perform the functions of the position of such employee.
5. For qualifying exigencies arising out of the fact that the employee's spouse, son, daughter, or parent is on active duty or call to active duty status as a member of the National Guard or Reserves in support of a contingency operation.

We will also grant an eligible employee who is a spouse, daughter, parent, or next of kin of a current member of the Armed Forces, including a member of the National Guard or Reserves, with a serious injury or illness, up to a total of 26 weeks of unpaid leave during a single 12-month period to care for the service member.

If two spouses are employed by us, they are limited in the amount of family leave they may take for the birth and care of a newborn child, placement of a child for adoption or foster care, or to care for a parent who has a serious health condition, to a combined total of 12 weeks (or 26 weeks if leave to care for a covered service member with a serious injury or illness is also used). Leave for birth and care, or placement for adoption or foster care, must conclude within 12 months of the birth or placement.

Under some circumstances, employees may take FMLA leave intermittently—taking leave in separate blocks of time for a single qualifying reason—or on a reduced leave schedule-reducing the employee's usual weekly or daily work schedule. When leave is needed for planned medical treatment, the employee must make a reasonable effort to schedule treatment so as not to unduly disrupt our operation. If FMLA leave is for birth or care, or placement for adoption or foster care, use of intermittent leave is subject to our approval.

Employees who wish to take advantage of this policy must fill out a Leave Request Form at least 30 days prior to the date they wish the leave to commence, or as soon as possible in cases where the reason for the leave (such as sudden illness) was unforeseeable. You will be entitled to return to your same job or an equivalent position as the one you held before, and all normal benefits will be restored. Eligible employees will also be entitled to maintain group healthcare coverage during the period of leave to the same extent as if they had continued to work during the leave period.

---

leave be extended indefinitely, because her mother's condition remained serious and she required ongoing assistance.

The firm's human resource director was uncertain what her response should be in this situation. ComputerTech needed Currier to be at work regularly because of the increasingly heavy workload, the fact that her job duties were critical, and because other supervisors and employees preferred not to have to cover for her. On the other hand, Currier was an excellent supervisor and had worked four years for ComputerTech. In addition, everyone was concerned about the welfare of both Currier and her mother and wanted to be supportive of them.

QUESTIONS

1. What are the advantages and disadvantages of extending Maura Currier's leave?

2. If you were the human resource director, would you grant her request? Explain your answer.

Safety Issues

85 CASE

Disaster Preparedness

Winston Hotels is a national hotel chain based in Orlando, Florida. The company employs 2,100 staff members in the United States, of which 118 are employed in the home office, 256 are employed in hotels in the Orlando area, and 1,726 are employed in hotels outside of Orlando. In 2004, Hurricane Charley blew through Central Florida and was followed by two other hurricanes within a 30-day period. During each of the three hurricanes, the two Orlando hotels were damaged by falling tree limbs and the accumulation of rainwater in some rooms.

The company required employees to work around the clock in these hotels even though the home office and the Orlando hotels lost power for one to three days during each hurricane. In addition, many telephone lines in Central Florida were down for various periods of time during these hurricanes. Some workers refused to work around the clock since they or family members had suffered major or minor damage to their homes and were attempting to arrange repairs or rebuilding. All of these employees were dismissed. One employee gained notoriety by appealing his dismissal based on his citizen's right to protect his home and property. He and his lawyer stated that this right superseded his employment contract.

In addition, some employees filed a lawsuit against the company because they were promised a higher pay scale for working continuously during the hurricanes. However, after the hurricanes, management decided either not to pay the employees for all of their extra hours or not to pay them overtime rates. Still other employees filed lawsuits because the company failed to provide adequate sleeping accommodations or food for those employees who remained on site.

George Baker is director of human resources for Winston Hotels. He has been told by lawyers representing the company that the lawsuits would be easier to defend if the company had a disaster preparedness plan in place to deal with extraordinary events such as hurricanes, floods, earthquakes, volcanoes, SARS, bird flu, bioterrorism, and other terrorism events. Baker knows that while the probability of any one of these occurring is very low, the company will function more smoothly during such events, recover more quickly, and be less vulnerable to lawsuits if it follows a clearly communicated disaster plan.

Up to this point, the company has had no disaster plan and managers "played it by ear" when the hurricanes struck. The only policy that existed was a general policy that each employee had to either report to work during his or her scheduled work hours or give adequate notice so a replacement could be scheduled. No possibility for extraordinary circumstances was provided in the policies.

Many of the lawsuits are still under appeal by the company and have not yet been resolved. Baker is very aware that the company is vulnerable to lawsuits and large financial losses as a result of not having a disaster plan. Yesterday he read in *The Wall Street Journal* that his company is not alone; 75 percent of all employers do not have a disaster plan. The article went on to say that the disaster plan needs to include policies and procedures for addressing employee absenteeism, operating with a reduced workforce, communicating with employees and customers, addressing payroll and employee benefits policies, addressing supply shortages, providing back-up electricity, maintaining information technology, maintaining security, assuring occupational health and safety, and minimizing litigation. In groups of two to four students, answer the questions below.

QUESTIONS

1. What policies and procedures do you suggest George Baker propose to his company to address each of the areas identified above in *The Wall Street Journal* (i.e., employee absenteeism, etc.)?

2. Given the central Florida location of Winston Hotels, what types of disaster threats are most likely to occur and why? Which disasters are most likely in your current location?

3. What are the components of today's corporate disaster plans with which you are familiar? Access company Web sites to determine the components of existing plans. Are these plans adequate to address the challenges of various kinds of disasters? If not, what additional policies or procedures would you suggest?

86 EXERCISE

Safety and Health Programs

I. **OBJECTIVES**

    A. To familiarize you with contemporary health and safety policies and procedures.

    B. To give you an understanding of the possible gaps that may develop between health and safety policies and procedures and actual practices on the job.

II. **OUT-OF-CLASS PREPARATION TIME:** 3 hours

III. **IN-CLASS TIME SUGGESTED:** 45 minutes

IV. **PROCEDURES**

    A. You or your group of three or four students (at the option of your instructor) select(s) one organization and obtain(s) its policies concerning health and safety. Examples might include workplace injuries, AIDS, employee assistance programs, and smoking. The information is often contained in the Employee Handbook.

    B. You or your group then interview(s) one person in the organization who is knowledgeable about these policies.

    C. You or your group then write(s) a brief report that answers the following questions:
        1. What safety and health policies/procedures currently exist? Are any changes in these policies contemplated for the near future? If so, why?

        2. What safety and health problems were the policies above designed to eliminate or minimize?

        3. To what extent do employees abide by these policies? How do employees feel about these policies? Why?

        4. Are these policies enforced and who is responsible for enforcement? If the policies are not enforced, why not?

        5. What impact does the Occupational Safety and Health Act (OSHA) (together with the agency) have on the organization?

        6. What future changes does the organization anticipate in the areas of health and safety?

    D. At the option of the instructor, you or your group report(s) the results of your study either to the class as a whole or to a small group.

    E. The reports are then turned in to the instructor.

The Safety Problem

Belcher Manufacturing Company employs 300 workers at its main plant in the upper Midwest. One of its major product lines is compressors for air conditioners. All compressors are tested when they come off the assembly line. Two years ago William Carlson was 28 years old, a high school graduate, and had been employed in the compressor division for five years. His job was to test each compressor using a standard procedure. Each inspector goes through an extensive training program where proper procedures for testing compressors are explained and demonstrated. In addition, inspectors are required to follow the detailed procedures for testing each unit specified in the company manual. No deviations from those procedures are permitted by company policy.

Two years ago Carlson was testing a compressor when it exploded and he was killed on the spot. The Belcher Manufacturing Company expressed sympathy to the family but also indicated that the company had provided proper training, proper clothing, proper warnings, and proper procedures. It reiterated its commitment to employee safety and implied that the cause of the explosion was probably due to improper employee testing procedures, which were neither known nor approved by the company.

Carlson's family hired an attorney on a contingency basis to pursue a lawsuit against the Belcher Manufacturing Company. Recently, the case was heard in federal district court. During court testimony it was revealed that most of the inspectors, including Carlson, had developed various "shortcuts" to reduce the time required to test each compressor. Some continued to use the shortcuts even after the accident. The plaintiff's lawyer argued that it was not clear that Carlson had violated procedures, but if he did, the company had an obligation to know about the deviations and take steps to bring inspectors back to the proper testing procedures. In addition, he argued the company was responsible for providing training, periodically reinforcing proper procedures, and monitoring practices to assure conformity to proper procedures. The jury then retired to consider a verdict and, if the company was found guilty of safety violations, to assess appropriate penalties.

Belcher Manufacturing then brought in an attorney from corporate headquarters to defend the company. Thomas King had a law degree from Northwestern University School of Law and had been practicing law for 27 years, and 12 of those years he had been counselor for Belcher Manufacturing with an excellent track record of defending the company in areas of safety and health. King had focused his law practice in the area of health and safety and was always up-to-date with information regarding data and trends in this field. For example, he knew the following:

- There are approximately 4.3 million injuries per year among private sector firms.

- Each year the cost of occupational injuries and illness total more than $165 billion.

- In any year, approximately 80 million working days are lost because of on-the-job injuries.

- In the most recent year, 6,480 employees died from work accidents.

King knew that Congress passed the Occupational Safety and Health Act (OSHA) in 1970 to ensure the safety and health of American workers by setting and enforcing standards;

providing training, outreach and education; establishing partnerships; and encouraging continual improvements in workplace safety and health. The most recent fatality numbers were only about one-third of the number of worker deaths reported in the late 1960s. Consequently, most observers believed the Act has been effective in reducing workplace injuries.

King was also aware that a supervisor at another company's construction site was charged with criminal negligence because he had failed to take "reasonable steps to prevent bodily harm" that caused a worker's death on his watch. Five years ago the supervisor pleaded guilty to eight counts of failing to ensure compliance under OSHA and received a $50,000 fine. Subsequently, the same company was charged with criminal negligence for causing another death related to failure to correctly package cement blocks on pallets. The company subsequently pleaded guilty and paid another fine of $110,000 dollars. King knew he needed to prove to the jury that Belcher Manufacturing had done everything they could to develop safety policies, communicate these policies to all employees, and train new and current employees periodically regarding safety procedures.

QUESTIONS

1. In this particular case, was the Belcher Manufacturing Company guilty or innocent of safety violations that resulted in the death of William Carlson?

2. Irrespective of the jury's decision in this case, what should the company do now to avoid a similar incident in the future?

5

Enhancing
Employee
Relations:
Discipline,
Motivation, and
Labor Relations

Discipline

CASE

The Drug Testing Problem at Standard Chemical

Standard Chemical Company's Camden Division processes volatile toxic chemicals that are sold for commercial use. The division consists of 500 employees, and approximately half are in the bargaining unit of the Machinists and Aerospace Workers Union at the Division. Safety is a critical issue at the plant because of the potential for environmental hazards resulting from accidents.

Vicky Jacobson, the human resource manager, had attended a seminar on drug abuse in the workforce and was concerned that some of the job-related accidents in the Camden Division might be due to drug use. As a result of Jacobson's concerns and the concerns of management at the other plants, the company decided to implement a Drug and Alcohol Program.

Notification was sent to the president of the local union. When Jacobson met with union representatives at the plant, she found little opposition to the policy. However, there was concern about how the policy would be enforced. Bob James, union representative, was concerned that the policy would be used by supervisors in a "witch hunt" to get rid of people they did not like. Jacobson assured him that there would be checks and balances so that the program would be administered even-handedly. She further assured the union that the emphasis would be on rehabilitation, not termination.

NOTIFICATION OF THE PROGRAM

The program was presented to employees during a series of group meetings. Jacobson read a prepared statement at each meeting to be certain that the policy was presented uniformly to all employees:

> *Standard Chemical is implementing a company-wide Alcohol and Drug Abuse Program effective January 1. We do not believe we have a serious problem with drug or alcohol abuse at Standard. However, we are committed to maintaining high standards of job performance and to protecting the safety of our employees, our community, and our environment. Therefore, we have implemented a policy that will significantly reduce the possibility that our employees or our environment might be harmed through alcohol or drug use of any individual employed at Standard Chemical. Please familiarize yourself with the policy as described to you in the brochure.*
>
> *(Brochures were distributed to each employee at the group meetings. See Exhibit 5.1 for a description of the brochure's contents.)*

SUSPENSION UNDER THE PROGRAM

During the time in which the policy has been in effect, Jacobson has, in practice, enforced the policy by suspending employees when there was reasonable suspicion of drug use. Suspended employees were then given three options regarding drug testing:

1. Refusing to undergo drug testing which resulted in immediate termination.

Standard Chemical Alcohol and Drug Abuse Policy

1. Use or abuse of any substance that may have an adverse effect on job performance or safety is a violation of Company policy.

2. Reporting to work or working while under the influence of alcohol or unauthorized drugs is a violation of Company policy.

3. Unauthorized drugs are any drugs that cannot be obtained legally or have been illegally obtained. Prescription drugs obtained without a prescription, or over-the-counter drugs used other than as instructed, are considered to be unauthorized drugs.

4. Drug testing is required as a condition of employment when there is reasonable suspicion of drug or alcohol use.

5. Reasonable suspicion is a basis for drug testing when, in the opinion of management, a job-related accident may have been caused by human error that may be drug or alcohol-related.

6. Employees who test positive may, if circumstances warrant, be permitted to continue employment provided they agree to undergo periodic drug/alcohol screening and participate in the Company-approved Employee Assistance Program (EAP).

2. Taking the drug test. If the drug test was negative, back pay was awarded for the time on suspension. If the drug test was positive, the employee was given the opportunity to participate in the Employee Assistance Program (EAP).

3. Enrolling directly in the EAP's drug and alcohol program in lieu of submitting to a drug test.

On March 7, Jacobson was in her office when John Martin, the company's security guard, asked to speak to her. "Ms. Jacobson, I thought I better report this to you. The forklift driver on the last shift must have been out of it when he parked that machine. The blade was driven through the crack between the concrete floor and the outer steel wall. The next shift driver is out there and he's having a heck of a time getting it out." The guard also told Jacobson that other employees had commented that "It was probably that 'pothead' Peter Carpenter."

When Jacobson and the guard walked over to the forklift, she noticed that the lower portion of the steel wall had buckled. During that day, she talked to several employees who had information about the accident. She discovered that Peter Carpenter was the driver of the forklift and that he had been seen driving the lift too fast around the corner at the end of his shift. Carpenter had worked for Standard Chemical for five-and-a-half years.

Jacobson met with Carpenter, his supervisors, and union representatives and questioned him about the forklift accident. According to Jacobson, the following conversations took place.

"Look, Ms. Jacobson, I admit that I parked that forklift there, but I had no idea I had parked so close to the wall."

Jacobson responded, "Mr. Carpenter, I have worked in this plant for 23 years and have seen my share of accidents. The blade of the forklift was wedged in the crack between the wall and the floor with enough force to buckle the steel wall. In my opinion, this accident is evidence enough for reasonable suspicion of drug or alcohol abuse."

After talking to Carpenter's supervisors and conferring with the plant manager, Jacobson met again with Carpenter and told him, "Mr. Carpenter, you are suspended effective immediately, based on reasonable suspicion of drug or alcohol use on the job. Company policy requires that you submit to a drug test or be terminated, effective immediately. If your

Contributed by Dr. Susan Corriher

drug test is negative, you will be paid for the time of your suspension. If it is positive, then you must enroll in the Employee Assistance Program and demonstrate a sincere commitment to the treatment program. You do have the option of enrolling directly into the EAP's alcohol and drug program. If you choose that option, you can forego the drug test at this time."

"Ms. Jacobson, I'd like to go ahead and get some help. I'll go on and get started with the EAP," replied Carpenter.

In Jacobson's presence, he then signed the company's EAP consent form which included the following statement:

> If I fail to meet my obligation to the EAP program, I will be subject to disciplinary action, including termination of employment.

After Carpenter signed the form, Jacobson telephoned the EAP (conducted by the local Alcoholism Council). Carpenter was given an appointment the next evening, March 8. Carpenter kept this scheduled appointment. During that first meeting with the counselor, he signed a Release of Information form authorizing the EAP to release information about his participation in the program, including keeping appointments, following EAP suggestions, and reporting to the designated lab for drug testing. He refused to give the EAP counselor permission to release the results of his drug tests to Standard Chemical.

REPORT FROM THE COUNSELOR

Robert Johnson, the EAP counselor, telephoned Jacobson to confirm that Carpenter had kept his appointment and explained that he had not given permission for the EAP to disclose results of the drug testing. Johnson also recommended that Carpenter be allowed to return to work while attending counseling sessions on an outpatient basis.

On March 13, Jacobson sent Carpenter a letter stating that his discharge was "held in abeyance" while he received counseling sessions. The letter further stated that Carpenter must attend counseling sessions and follow the guidelines of the program and submit to urine testing if instructed to do so by his EAP counselor. The letter also included the following statement:

> Any incident in the future, which indicates failure to comply with the EAP program, will result in disciplinary action up to and including termination of employment.

Carpenter attended EAP sessions regularly for the next eight weeks. Reports to Jacobson from his supervisors during that time period were extremely positive. His job performance was excellent and he had no safety violations.

On May 9, Johnson, the EAP counselor, called Sarah Green, the plant nurse, to discuss several EAP-related matters. They specifically discussed Carpenter's case because of Johnson's concerns about him. He noted that while Carpenter had attended every session and his supervisors reported that he had been an exemplary employee, his lab tests showed ascending levels of cannabinoids (marijuana metabolites). Johnson intimated that he was not sure that the EAP counseling sessions would be successful.

Green called Jacobson and reported that Carpenter's lab reports were positive. Jacobson telephoned Johnson and confirmed what had been said to the plant nurse. She also telephoned the company's medical department and was told that cannabinoids normally stay in a person's system for 35–45 days.

Later that same day, Jacobson met with Carpenter and the union representatives and confronted him with the information she had received about his drug tests. Carpenter argued with Jacobson and said that he did not understand why she was questioning him. He told her that he had attended every counseling session and felt like the sessions were helping him. Carpenter told her that his performance and his safety record had been great since he started the program. Carpenter further told her that he knew that his supervisors had reported his excellent work record to her. He also told her that he had stopped smoking marijuana. Jacobson then asked him to submit to a urine sample test. She told him that if he refused he would be terminated in compliance with company policy. Carpenter agreed to take the drug tests.*

On May 17, the lab reported that the results of both drug tests were positive. Later that same day, Jacobson met with Carpenter and informed him that he was fired. Carpenter immediately filed a grievance.

On May 26, the union recommended that Carpenter take another drug test. Standard Chemical agreed to take into consideration the results. Later that same day, Carpenter took the drug test.*

On May 30, Standard Chemical received the lab report that was negative for cannabinoids. On June 21 and July 12, Carpenter's drug tests were again negative for cannabinoids. Ten months later, Carpenter took another drug test that was also negative.

QUESTIONS

1. Was Peter Carpenter's suspension justified?

2. Was his termination justified?

3. Evaluate the adequacy of the Standard Chemical Company's drug and alcohol abuse policy. Are there any components that need improvement?

4. Were Carpenter's privacy rights protected?

---

*The company uses two tests: the enzyme-multiplied immunoassay technique (EMIT) and gas chromatography/mass spectrometry.

Violence at Work

Eastern State University is a state school with about 15,000 students. Half of the student population are commuters, and the rest live in university dormitories, apartments, or fraternity/ sorority houses. The university does not have high admissions standards, believing that students should be given a chance to prove themselves academically. About half of the freshman class needs to take either remedial English or math. The business school at the university often attracts students who could not succeed academically in other fields such as engineering or chemistry.

Because the university wants to improve its graduation rate, faculty in the business school are encouraged to work with students so that they do not fail and drop out. Nonetheless, grading standards are high, and it not unusual for 30–40 percent of the students to get a "D" or "F" in Introductory Economics or Accounting classes. Students who get low grades are rarely asked to leave the university. Rather, they are allowed to take the class again and substitute the new grade for the original one. Nonetheless, many students drop out, realizing they will never graduate.

In recent years, the university has experienced a serious increase in student misbehavior, ranging from swearing at faculty members to not leaving class when asked. Some of the faculty blame this on the university's admission and retention policies. Several times each semester, a faculty member has needed to ask a security officer to come to class and escort out one or more students. Fortunately, no student has ever physically harmed a faculty member.

One of the professors at the university, Roy Morris, has taught Marketing and Public Relations courses for over ten years. He is known for being a hard but fair grader, and his student evaluations are always high. He expects a lot from the class and is a stickler for meeting assigned deadlines. Morris rarely gives make-up exams and expects all papers to be turned in on time with no exceptions. He includes his expectations in his syllabus and repeats them orally throughout the semester.

Usually, Professor Morris is a happy, upbeat individual, but one December day he appeared very upset when he walked into the faculty lunchroom. Everyone there saw the expression on his face and knew that something serious had occurred. Morris sat down in a chair and exclaimed, "You will not believe what the chief of security and the dean of student affairs have just told me!"

Professor Morris further explained that after his Principles of Marketing class had ended earlier that morning, he had gone back to his office and was confronted by a student, Paul Lewis. Lewis was an older student who had served in the U.S. Marines prior to returning to school. He was majoring in Marketing, and most of the faculty knew him because he was so outspoken. He was at best a "C" student and liked to argue with other students during class discussion. Lewis was six feet, five inches tall and had an intimidating physical appearance.

Lewis told Professor Morris that he was unable to turn in a term paper due that day because he had been sick recently. He said he knew that Professor Morris had stated repeatedly when the paper was due and that no late papers would be accepted, but he wanted an exception in his case. The paper accounted for 10 percent of the course grade, and Lewis said he did not want to receive an "F" on it. Professor Morris said that he was sorry, but

Lewis had had 13 weeks to complete the paper and that, in fairness to all of the other students, he could not grant an exception.

Lewis argued vehemently that the policy was completely unfair, that he could not help it if he got sick, and demanded that an exception be made. Again, Professor Morris told him he was sorry, but if he made an exception for him, he would have to do it for all of the other students in the class. At this point, Lewis exploded and said in a loud voice, "This issue isn't over until I say it's over. You will regret your decision!!!" Shaking his fist at Professor Morris, Lewis walked out of the office and slammed the door behind him.

Professor Morris stated that he was dumbfounded by Lewis's actions. He was not sure what to do, so he called the campus chief of security. The chief told him there was nothing he could do about Lewis now, but that if further problems arose, and it got more serious, to call back and a guard would come to his office or classroom. Unhappy with this response, Professor Morris called the dean of student affairs, explained what had happened, and asked the dean to suspend Lewis from the university. He told the dean that he did not take Lewis's threat lightly and that he also feared for his safety. The dean's response was that he could remove Lewis from Professor Morris's class but not from his other classes. He would give Lewis an "I" in the class and allow him to take it again next semester without charging him tuition. The dean told Professor Morris that if any further problems occurred with Lewis, he should call security.

After Professor Morris finished talking, the faculty members in attendance looked at each other in amazement. "What kind of solution is that?" they asked each other. Several of those present also had Lewis in their classes, and as he was not performing well, they were worried about their own safety. What might Lewis do to them, particularly if they did not grant him an exception or gave him a failing grade? The faculty members agreed that they wanted Lewis permanently removed from the university. One professor reminded the others that violence on campus was increasing all over the country and pointed out that over 30 students and teachers were killed at Virginia Tech in 2007 by one disgruntled student. She added that calling security would not have prevented this massacre. She would not want to see Lewis in her Business Policy class the next semester. Another professor agreed by saying that calling security would definitely be "too little too late" and stated that he would henceforth lock his classroom door once class began, spend less time in his office, and keep his office door shut when he was there. He also said he would keep a watchful eye out for Lewis and suggested that the others do the same.

QUESTIONS

1. What action do you believe Eastern State University should have taken with regard to Paul Lewis? Do you agree with the dean's solution to the problem? Why or why not?

2. If you were Professor Morris, what preventive action would you take to insure your safety and prevent Lewis from harming you?

3. What steps should the university take to insure the safety of faculty?

████████   *Surfing the Internet on Company Time*

Helen Barnett was shocked by what she was seeing on the computer screen at the desk of James Erskine. On the screen was a picture depicting a sexual act! The picture appeared on a porn Web site that Erskine had evidently visited. Helen supervises 15 customer service representatives for National Insurance, a company specializing in home insurance. The job of a customer service representative is to assist clients with claims, insurance quotes, and other queries. Each customer service representative works in a cubicle furnished with a computer, a desk, and a phone headset. Only Barnett has a personal office. National Insurance prides itself in its efforts to make greater use of electronic technology in servicing its clients. Quotes for insurance and even samples of policies are often sent to clients via the computer. Most of the information representatives need to answer customer queries is available at their fingertips.

Erskine had been employed with National Insurance for the last six months. His 90-day performance review had been satisfactory. Lorraine Smalls, a co-worker who sat in a cubicle close to Erskine, had inadvertently discovered the pornographic picture. When her computer malfunctioned, Smalls had gone to Erskine's cubicle to quickly retrieve some data to respond to a customer's query. It was not unusual for representatives to use another staff member's computer. Erskine was out to lunch and his computer screen was in standby mode. When Smalls hit the enter key, the picture appeared and its graphic nature disturbed her greatly. She immediately called Barnett over to the workstation. When Barnett checked Erskine's browser, it seemed that he had visited the Web site more than a dozen times that morning. She felt that she needed to confront him about using company time in such an unproductive manner.

When Erskine returned from lunch, Barnett told him about her discovery. He was irate with her. Erskine told her that he had visited the site on his break time, not on company time. Furthermore, he felt that it was an invasion of his privacy that both a co-worker and Barnett had gained access to his computer. Barnett told Erskine she had no recourse but to report his behavior to the human resource manager. After he left Barnett's office, Erskine himself went to the human resource manager, Dale Gibbons. Erskine believed that the supervisor's actions violated his constitutional rights to privacy. Gibbons told him, "Even though the company does not have a written policy prohibiting visiting Web sites, all employees are expected to use their computers for work-related purposes. Unnecessary surfing ties up our ISDN line capacity and could impact service delivery. In addition, you exposed two of your fellow employees to pornography." He went on to say, "National Insurance operates on a trust basis in all its relationships with employees."

Two days later, Erskine was suspended for using the company's computer system for nonproductive, personal purposes. When he received his suspension notification, Erskine told Gibbons that he would sue National Insurance for violating his right to privacy. He also told Gibbons that he knew of many other employees who surfed the Internet and used the company's e-mail for personal purposes.

QUESTIONS

1. Did Helen Barnett's actions invade James Erskine's right to privacy?

2. Was National Insurance justified in suspending Erskine?

3. What should be the key elements of an employee computer and Web use policy?

91 EXERCISE

▰▰▰▰▰▰ *Developing an Employee Dress Code*

I. OBJECTIVES

A. To improve your skills in developing a new dress code.

B. To familiarize you with the reasons why firms develop dress codes.

C. To familiarize you with the content of different dress code policies.

II. OUT-OF-CLASS PREPARATION TIME: 1–3 hours

III. IN-CLASS TIME SUGGESTED: 30–45 minutes

IV. PROCEDURES

At the end of the class prior to the beginning of this exercise, your instructor will divide the class into small groups of two or three. Each group will meet outside of class and write up a dress code policy for one specific job at a firm. The instructor will assign each group a job from the list provided below or from his or her own list. The exercise begins by having each group state the job they were assigned and presenting their dress code policy to the class. This will be followed by a critique of the policy by class members and the instructor. The exercise ends when the last group finishes its presentation.

In writing a policy, keep in mind that firms typically develop dress policies for one or more of three major reasons:

1. To provide employees with a safe and healthy workplace as required under the Occupational Safety and Health Act (OSHA). For example, those working on construction sites may need to wear hard hats, ear protection, eye protection, and/or hard tip shoes.

2. To meet health ordinances and laws. For example, employees who handle food may be required to wear hair nets and plastic gloves to reduce the spread of germs and disease.

3. To enhance a legitimate business interest. For example, some firms state in their policies that they do not allow employees to wear any clothing that others might find highly offensive such as shirt with a swastika, a Confederate battle flag, a nude person, or a religious slur such as "God is Dead."

More commonly, many firms state in their dress policy the type of clothing they want employees to wear in order to create a favorable impression or specific image of the firm. For example, a firm that sells imported clothing from Scotland may legitimately ask employees to wear kilts while waiting on customers. Likewise, Walt Disney theme parks can legitimately ask employees to wear costumes that portray Mickey Mouse and Donald Duck.

It is important to note that dress policies should not be based on the personal whims of management. Firms have the burden of proof to show that their dress code enhances the firm's success. Keep in mind also that the policy must not be discriminatory and violate federal or state discrimination laws.

In writing a dress code policy, the following items need to be addressed:

1. What clothing is the employee required to wear and/or not wear on your assigned job? Hats? Shirts/blouses? Pants? Footwear? Safety or health attire? Company uniform? Name tag? Other?

2. Are there any requirements for your assigned job regarding hair style, length, or color? Are mustaches and beards permitted?

3. Does the dress code for your job need to include provisions that address items such as lipstick, false eyelashes, perfume, after-shave lotions, and false fingernails, and/or polish?

4. Should the dress code for your assigned job address the wearing of jewelry such as bracelets, rings, necklaces, ear/nose jewelry?

5. Should the policy for your assigned job address personal hygiene issues such as using deodorant, wearing clean clothes, or taking baths/showers?

6. Should the dress code for your job be the same for men and women? If not, how should they differ?

7. What disciplinary or other action will be taken if someone violates the policy?

Listed below are possible jobs for which your group could write a dress policy:

1. A horseback trip leader at a guest dude ranch.

2. A chain saw operator working for a logging firm.

3. A cook at a large expensive restaurant.

4. A salesclerk working at a retail store that sells clothing, apparel, and shoes that appeal to pop culture customers.

5. A barber or hair stylist.

6. A student at your college.

7. A bank vice president who makes loans to large corporations.

8. A life guard at a country club swimming pool.

9. A personal trainer working at a fitness center.

10. A nurse working at a hospital emergency room.

11. An exterminator who sprays chemicals around homes.

12. A pharmaceutical sales representative calling on doctors.

13. A TV weather announcer.

14. A realtor who shows houses to clients.

15. A hostess at a popular chain restaurant.

16. A professor at your college.

92 INCIDENT

Facebook Posting: I Hate My Stupid Boss

Shanti Williams, HR manager at a large retailer received a Facebook friend invitation from Marisa Hernandez, a senior clerk in the company's finance department. She and Hernandez had attended the same high school several years ago and had only recently discovered they were employed at the same company. During high school, they had been in several classes together, and Williams readily remembered Hernandez. She had met Hernandez again at one of the retailer's training programs she had launched about three weeks ago. When Williams saw the Facebook request, she quickly accepted it.

A few months later, she saw a Facebook posting from Hernandez to her friends that read:

"I hate my stupid boss. My new boss is a total jerk and makes each day a big pain in the xxx. He treats us finance clerks like we are his slaves. I can't wait to leave this job because I would rather eat beans than spend another day working for a moron! Help!"

That evening after reading the posting, Williams did not sleep very well. She wondered what action she should take as HR manager against Hernandez, if any, about what she had read in the Facebook posting.

QUESTIONS

1. What issues does this Facebook incident raise about social media and the workplace: (a) from the perspective of an employee, (2) from the perspective of management/managers, and (3) from a legal perspective?

2. Should Shanti Williams have accepted the friend invitation? Why or why not?

3. If you were in Williams's position, what would you do now? Why?

93 INCIDENT

Can He Wear an Earring at Work?

Peter Wood was hired as a personal services representative at South Town Bank, a small bank serving South Town for over 30 years. The bank had a reputation for being one of the more conservative places of employment in town. Because it offered good wages and benefits, the bank had no problems finding employees.

Personal service representatives sat at desks in the wood panel lobby of the bank to assist bank customers with account queries and other problems. All bank personnel were required to dress according to company rules. Men were expected to wear dress shirts and ties, while women were required to wear dresses or skirts. Recently the bank instituted "Casual Friday" on the last Friday of each month. On that Friday, employees could wear business casual clothes. Men could wear golf shirts or other shirts with collars. Women could wear slacks with appropriate blouses and/or sweaters. No jeans, shorts, halter tops, or t-shirts were allowed. Employees with tattoos were required to wear clothes that would cover tattoos.

When Wood reported for his first day at South Town Bank, he came dressed appropriately in a shirt and tie. He also had a discreet, but noticeable gold loop earring in his left earlobe. When the branch manager saw the earring, he told Wood to remove the earring since it was not consistent with the bank's employee dress policy. Wood became upset and pointed out that no one had told him during the employment interview that he could not wear an earring to work. The branch manager pointed out that if Wood had worn the earring during the job interview, he probably would not have been hired. He further stated that, because of the earring, Wood did not present the professional image the bank desired for its personal service representatives. Wood pointed out that female personal service representatives were allowed to wear earrings at work. The branch manager said it was customary in society for women to wear earrings but not men. He again asked Wood to remove the earring. When he refused, Wood was fired.

Wood felt that he had been discriminated against and vowed that he would take legal action against. The following statement regarding earrings appeared in the employee handbook: "Visible jewelry must be small and tasteful as determined by management. Jewelry must not interfere with job performance."

QUESTIONS

1. Is Peter Wood a victim of discrimination?

2. Evaluate the branch manager's comment that Wood would not have been hired had he worn the earring during the employment interview.

3. Evaluate South Town Bank's dress policy. Is it clear? Is it appropriate? Is it legal?

Spiked Milk

A reputable northeastern construction company employs six experienced construction supervisors for its various construction jobs. These supervisors have the overall responsibility of hiring and firing and seeing that the construction proceeds as close to time and cost schedules as possible. They also have the responsibility of overall quality control of the construction.

Larry Werst, age 55, has been a supervisor for this company for many years. He is never absent and has established a reputation for getting the job done right and close to schedule. He has supervised the construction of several prominent buildings and is now supervising the construction of a college fraternity house. Werst's approach to handling his employees is firm and sometimes harsh. He does not allow any back talk, and everyone who works for him usually earns his or her pay or is not on the job for very long.

The owner and manager of the company had become concerned about Werst because rumors were circulating that he was an alcoholic and that he drank on the job. The owner knew that Werst drank a lot and had a stormy home life, but he did not know whether he was drinking on the job.

One day, when the manager was talking with Werst, he smelled alcohol on his breath. This had happened on several occasions when office and storeroom employees noticed the odor when they talked to him. Also, the storeroom clerk noticed that almost every day Werst would come into the store, buy two Cokes, and then leave in his company truck, presumably to go back to his job site.

The manager decided to talk to Werst about this situation. When he confronted Werst with the rumors, his alcoholic breath, and the purchasing of two Cokes at a time, Werst denied that he was drinking on the job. He replied that the rumors were just that and that the two Cokes were for himself and his carpenter supervisor. The manager told him that he would have to let him go if he were caught drinking on the job. He reminded Werst that the firm's progressive discipline system included a rule that states, "No employee is permitted to go on duty or remain on duty if he or she possesses, is under the influence of, or is consuming an alcoholic beverage. Violation of this policy will result in dismissal."

About a year later, when the construction season was again in full swing, stories began circulating about Werst's drinking. His fellow employees now pondered over the quart of milk he drank every day. They wondered if he spiked the milk and/or used it to cover his alcoholic breath. Sometimes his speech seemed slurred, but Werst was gravel-voiced and had sloppy speech habits anyway. The workers were amused by the stories he would tell about things that had happened to him. They were just stories, of course, but lately they were becoming pathetically farfetched and made no sense at all.

The manager soon heard about some of the new rumors about Werst, and he wondered what he should do about the situation again. Werst still had never actually been caught drinking on the job. His construction project was proceeding satisfactorily, but it was a little behind schedule due to the inability to hire good carpenters and laborers at the beginning of the construction season. And worker turnover was perhaps somewhat higher on this project than the average turnover.

1. What course of action should the owner-manager follow? Why?

2. To what extent should the owner-manager go to try to catch Larry Werst drinking on the job?

3. What action, if any, should the owner-manager take if Werst confesses to being an alcoholic?

4. Does the owner-manager presently have sufficient proof that Werst is working under the influence of alcohol?

5. Critique the construction company's alcoholism rule.

Contributed by Arno F. Knapper, School of Business, The University of Kansas

Caught in the Act: Immoral Behavior at Work

It was about 1:30 in the morning when Mike Morrison, night supervisor at HITEC Corporation, a West Coast manufacturer of computer software, finally returned to his office to finish up a report. As he began writing, he heard a strange noise coming from the quality control lab down the hall. He knew that no one was assigned to work in the lab at that time, so he walked down to investigate. After knocking, he opened the door and was stunned to see two of his lead employees. Jim Harris, a lead maintenance supervisor, had his back turned to the door and was pulling up his pants. Mary Bridge, a lead production line supervisor, was next to an inspection bench and was likewise pulling up her pants. Morrison quickly shut the door and returned to his office, aghast at what he had just witnessed. Given the embarrassing nature of the situation, he decided to take no action.

Two weeks later, Teya Simpson, the human resource director, was talking to another lead supervisor when she heard about the incident. Apparently, everyone in the plant knew the story, except top management, because both Harris and Bridge had spread the word that they were "caught in the act" by Morrison.

Simpson immediately called Wayne Purdy, plant manager, to see what action, if any, should be taken. Both recognized that the firm had no work rule that specifically covered sexual relationships on the job and that the offense had occurred two weeks ago. On the other hand, both believed that the employees' behavior was highly unprofessional and noted that both managers had left their work areas unattended. Furthermore, they were concerned about the effect that this incident might have on future employee behavior if no disciplinary action was forthcoming.

QUESTIONS

1. What action should HITEC Corporation take, if any, with regard to Jim Arnold and Mary Bridge? Justify your answer.

2. What action should the firm take, if any, with respect to Mike Morrison? Why?

Motivation

INCIDENT

Motivating and Maintaining Morale during Downsizing

The Rutledge Company is an organization involved in the retail industry, operating more than 100 retail stores. The company's headquarters is going through what is termed "modernization." A new information system, which will completely alter the way the firm does business, is being implemented. In addition, the new system will affect the staffing required by the company. The company began implementing the new software last year, and it is projected that at least another year is required before the rollout will be complete. All personnel within the corporate office, including the large clerical staff, attended a four-day, comprehensive computer training program and were told to immediately incorporate the new software into daily use.

The completion of the rollout will primarily affect the clerical staff. It is the company's objective to eliminate the majority of these individuals. The technology of the new software will enable all management-level personnel to perform their jobs efficiently without the need for clerical support. The Rutledge Company has informed its large clerical staff that most, but not all, of their jobs will disappear once the rollout is complete. The prospect of future unemployment, along with the uncertainty regarding when their jobs will be terminated, has greatly affected the staff morale. Complacency, lack of initiative, and complaints all have accompanied the loss of morale.

The firm has another problem: some of the clerical staff are long-term employees who are accustomed to how the company operated ten years ago. These employees have not adapted to the new software or to the other new programs that have been implemented. Thus, these employees do not provide the full clerical support needed by management. Rather, they perform only those aspects of their jobs that existed prior to the introduction of the new software plus other menial jobs sufficient to keep them busy.

Individual managers must determine how to motivate all of the clerical support staff for the remaining time that they will be employed and must also determine how to motivate some employees to use the new software. It must also be determined which clerical help should be retained once modernization is complete. The firm would like to retain all of its clerical staff until that time.

QUESTIONS

1. What actions should be taken in order to increase the morale and motivation level of the clerical staff at the Rutledge Company?

2. What actions can be taken to motivate those employees who are not using the new technology required of their job?

3. What criteria should be used to determine which clerical employees should be retained?

4. Should the firm attempt to solve its motivational problems by conducting further training?

Motivating Employees during a Buyout

Radio, Inc. is a holding company for over 20 radio stations located throughout the West Coast. At its headquarters, the company employs approximately 65 media professionals. The firm has been in the news lately with speculations of a buyout, and both Wall Street analysts and news broadcasts indicate that the company is for sale. These statements have been circulating for a month now, and insiders know that they are not unfounded. Radio, Inc. is viewed as a "cash cow" and has been coveted by many outsiders for years because of its large listening audience.

Earlier this week, Radio, Inc. was visited by the president of a large firm. As he toured the facility, everyone recognized him and rumors reached a feverish pace. Accountants were asked to prepare current financial statements which added fuel to the rumors. Officially, this has all been "hush-hush," but staff members at headquarters had worked many overtime hours to provide the needed financial information. Employee morale is at an all-time low and most employees are fearful about their jobs and their future.

Meanwhile, the performance improvement and awards committee is finalizing plans for the second-quarter meeting. This committee was created several years ago to promote continuous improvement, reward individuals for performance excellence, and plan an off-site quarterly meeting. The first-quarter meeting was a huge success. Awards were presented with great fanfare and specific accomplishments of every recipient were cited. Slides of employees at work and play, gathered over the previous six months, were shown. The meeting boosted employee morale and provided incentives to improve performance with hopes of gaining recognition at the next quarterly meeting. The committee has created numerous awards that employees cherish. These include:

- People's Choice Award—given to the employee who has an infectiously positive influence on the company and on co-workers. This person is nominated by peers, voted on by management, and ultimately selected by the committee.

- Fiscal Responsibility Award—given to an employee who implements a program that saves the company the most money. The recipient is nominated by department heads or middle/senior management and is ultimately selected by the committee.

- Winning Attitude Award—given to the employee who performs both routine and special job tasks with a cheerful, can-do attitude.

- Extra Effort Award—given to an employee who gives extra effort, goes the extra mile, and contributes more than 100 percent to accomplish his or her job.

- Technical Achievement Award—given to the employee who invents and implements a new program or process that uses technology and results in improvements for internal/external customers.

- Out-of-the-Box Award—given to the employee who thinks of innovative, new ways of accomplishing his/her job, or contributes fresh ideas that focus on continuous improvement, or coordinates department efforts that enhance the change process.

Since March, the committee has prepared for the second-quarter event. They have scheduled the Shark Room at a local marine science aquarium for the afternoon, put together a great slide show, ordered sandwiches from a well-known catering firm, solicited senior and middle management for award nominations, and purchased gifts for the award recipients.

The quarterly awards meeting is scheduled to be held on Friday. However, on the preceding Wednesday, the president of Radio, Inc. receives an attractive buyout offer that she knows the firm's board of directors will accept. The details of the sale are expected to be finalized and announced on the same day as the awards banquet. The announcement cannot be postponed due to the risk of having confidential information leak out to the public. The president is now faced with the issue of whether the awards meeting should be held.

QUESTIONS

1. Should the awards banquet be held as scheduled or should it be canceled or postponed?

2. Assuming that Radio, Inc. is bought, what can the firm do to retain desirable employees and to enhance employee motivation and morale?

Labor Relations

98 CASE

Union Organizing at SGA Industries

INTRODUCTION

President White sat in his office at SGA Industries thinking about the union election taking place at the plant auditorium. He felt that the company had waged a successful campaign to persuade workers that their best interests would be served only if the company remained union-free. As he awaited the election results, his mind began to wander back to the events leading up to today's election.

BACKGROUND

SGA Industries is known as the world's largest producer of women's hosiery and employs approximately 6,500 people at ten plants in five communities in Georgia and South Carolina. The company's headquarters is located in Anderson, Georgia. The company's sales subsidiary, SGA Inc., has 12 offices in major market areas throughout the United States and sells its products directly to distributors around the world. The company's strategy of strong identification with the customer has made SGA one of the most recognized names in the entire hosiery industry.

SGA was founded in 1907 by Sam Gerome Anderson. Anderson built the company, and the surrounding community was named after him in 1910. Ever since, the fortunes of Anderson residents have been interwoven with those of SGA. Over the years the company supported the community, donating land and money for churches, schools, and hospitals, and providing jobs for nearly a third of the town's residents. As the years passed, further expansion and product diversification occurred, and the company gained a reputation as an industry leader in the design, production, and marketing of women's and men's hosiery and undergarments.

After the death of the last Anderson family member, SGA was managed by four chief executive officers in less than a dozen years. Then, the company was purchased for $550 million by Jack Phillips who is a well-known Atlanta entrepreneur and business leader. Soon after the purchase, Phillips appointed Ted White as president of SGA.

LABOR-MANAGEMENT RELATIONS

Over the years, SGA enjoyed a reputation as a steady job provider in an unstable industry. The company provided for its workers and treated them like family members. Many believe that the company's generosity to both its employees and the town of Anderson helped to defeat an earlier union organizing drive by the Textile Workers of America, by a vote of 3,937 to 1,782. At the time of the vote, the chairman called it "an expression of confidence by employees." The SGA vote was viewed as a severe blow to union organizing efforts in the South.

Contributed by Dr. Gerald Calvasina, Southern Utah University

When Phillips purchased SGA, he announced that his major goals would be to improve the community and to improve the quality of life for SGA employees and their families. Phillips invested over $100 million to reach these goals. The total included funds for pay increases; new job benefits; capital improvements, including the use of robots on the production line; community improvements; and other contributions. These improvements were also accompanied by a shift in management philosophy. The theme of the new philosophy was self-sufficiency, and it signaled an end to the benevolent paternalism that had so long characterized employee relations at SGA. Greater emphasis was henceforth placed on employee performance and productivity.

During the mid-1980s, the entire hosiery industry experienced major problems. Growing foreign competition and imports had a negative impact on domestic hosiery manufacturers. Many manufacturers attempted to reverse the impact by intensive capital investments in new technology, by the reorganization and downsizing of plants, and by instituting programs to improve employee productivity and efficiency. SGA was not spared from this competition. Its international sales fell dramatically from $26 million to $10 million. Faced with increasing imports and weak consumer sales, the company was forced to lay off 1,500 employees, reduce pay scales, and rescind many of the perks that the workers had enjoyed under the Anderson family. Many of these changes drew worker protests and created a good deal of tension between workers and management.

Wages in the industry had been rising steadily but were still lower than wages in the manufacturing sector in general. On a regional basis, the differential was still quite wide, with a study showing that wages ranged from $10.56 per hour in South Carolina to $14.90 in Michigan. In addition, as technology advanced, more skilled operatives were required, thus increasing the cost of turnover to companies. Employers in the industry also were becoming increasingly more dependent on women and minorities for employees. At SGA, 40 percent of the employees were women and 35 percent of the total workforce were minorities. Minorities and women made up less than 2 percent of the management staff.

THE ELECTION CAMPAIGN

Despite its earlier defeat, the Amalgamated Clothing and Textile Workers Union (ACTWU) was back in Anderson, armed and ready for an organizing effort that would divert the attention of SGA management for several long, tense months.

While many employers learn of union organizing efforts by their employees only after the National Labor Relations Board informs them, the ACTWU's efforts to organize SGA employees were clearly out in the open a full nine months before the election. With a union office in downtown Anderson and a healthy budget, the ACTWU, led by Chris Balog, engaged in one of the most sophisticated union organizing efforts ever seen in the area. Using computerized direct mailing to stay in touch with workers, as well as extensive radio and television advertising, the union effort at SGA attracted wide attention. Many observers felt that the outcome of ACTWU's drive would have significant implications for the ability of labor unions to make inroads into traditionally nonunion regions of the country.

UNION'S CAMPAIGN

The campaign issues developed and communicated to workers were, for the most part, predictable. Job security was brought to the front early and was easily introduced to the campaign in the wake of over 1,500 layoffs and selective plant closings by SGA management. In addition, in an attempt to become more competitive in the face of increasing foreign competition, increased workloads and reduced wage rates were key issues raised by the union. The union repeatedly accused Phillips of engaging in unfair labor practices by threatening to sell or close the company if the union were to win bargaining rights for SGA workers. To a certain extent, the union did expand on the traditional wage, hour, and working condition issues typically raised in organizing efforts. As the campaign progressed, Phillips became a focal point of union rhetoric, and the union attempted to portray Phillips as a greedy and ruthless city slicker from Atlanta who was not interested in the long-term survival of SGA and its employees.

MANAGEMENT'S CAMPAIGN

While Phillips became a focal point of union criticism as the campaign wore on, his role in management's response to the organizing efforts was critical throughout the months preceding the election. With President White leading the anti-union campaign, backed by a sophisticated strategy developed by an Atlanta law firm specializing in anti-union campaigns, SGA was able to quickly respond to every issue raised by the union.

The SGA strategy to defeat the union organizing effort included extensive meetings with community, business, and religious leaders in an attempt to influence workers' views about the union. Viewing anti-union films was required for workers on company time. Letters sent to workers' homes by President White and Phillips emphasized the need for team spirit, not only to keep the union out, but to overcome the threat created by hosiery imports. President White put it this way:

"We intend to do everything that is proper and legal in this campaign to defeat the union. This is essential if we are to remain competitive in the hosiery business. Every day, we are facing more foreign competition. Not only do our workers understand this, but I think the public does also. We have been able to communicate with our workers in the past, and we don't need a third party voice. We all must work together as a team. The only way SGA can beat the encroaching foreign competition is to streamline and consolidate our operations."

White and Phillips made repeated visits to plants to shake hands and listen to workers' concerns. The weekly employee newsletter was filled with anti-union letters written by workers and community members. Late in the campaign, a letter was sent to SGA workers from Jack Phillips explaining why they should vote against the union (see Exhibit 5.2). In response to the union claim that Phillips was attempting to sell the company, Phillips told the workers that "SGA is not for sale, but if I determine that the company cannot operate competitively, I can and I will cease to operate SGA. This is entirely up to me and nobody can stop me—including this union."

EMPLOYEES' VIEWS

The employees were divided over the union organizing campaign. Several employees formed an Anti-Union Committee, which organized an SGA Loyalty Day. At one rally sponsored by the Anti-Union Committee, "No Union" badges, "Be Wise—Don't Unionize" t-shirts, and "Vote No" hats were worn by several hundred employees. A statement by Terry Floyd, a shift leader, summed up the view expressed by some employees:

"We, as employees of SGA, do not feel that it is in the best interest of our company and its employees to be represented by ACTWU. Many generations of the same families have worked at this plant; part of our strength is family heritage. I'm afraid a union will destroy that strength. We feel that a union is not needed and that we can work with management as a team."

EXHIBIT 5.2 *Letter to SGA Employees*

To All SGA Employees:

It is only fair for you to know SGA's policy on unions. Our policy is quite simple. We are absolutely opposed to a union at any of our plants. We intend to use every legal and proper means to stay nonunion.

As you know, the hosiery industry has been under great pressure and competition from foreign firms. Sales in the industry have dwindled over the past few years, and we are in a poor profit position. Our government has done little to protect your jobs and stop the imports from eroding our sales. Only you and I can save this company and your jobs.

Our whole industry has been forced to modernize our production process to make it more efficient. In fact, you know that many firms have merged together to strengthen their market position. Our company, too, will have to explore the possible advantages of pooling resources and products. In the long run, such strategy can only benefit employees and management alike. I know bringing in the ACTWU at this time will only drive up our operating expenses and jeopardize our chances of making such arrangements. Only management has the right to decide how to operate this company. If we find we cannot operate this company profitably, we may be forced to consider other options.

We are convinced that unions have the tendency to create an adversarial relationship between employees and management. Cooperation and teamwork cannot exist in such a hostile environment. It is only through cooperation and teamwork that we will get through the crisis.

No SGA employee is ever going to need a union to keep his/her job. We know that ACTWU cannot help this company or you and will probably cause us to lose even more of our market and threaten your job security. I urge you—do not vote for the union. Let's all pull together and remember the goodwill of the Anderson family and how it has stood behind you all of these years.

Sincerely,

Jack Phillips

Jack Phillips
Chief Executive Officer

Others workers expressed support for the union. One worker stated, "We need a union for protection. At least it would give us a voice. Supervisors can be too arbitrary." Others pointed to pay increases and bonuses for top management in the wake of wage cuts and layoffs for plant workers. Many older employees, who remembered the generosity of the Anderson family, also expressed bitterness toward SGA and worried about their pensions.

QUESTIONS

1. What was the impetus for the Amalgamated Clothing and Textile Workers Union (ACTWU) organizing effort at SGA Industries?

2. Discuss SGA's strategy in managing the representation campaign.

3. Discuss any potential unfair labor practice charges SGA management might face as a result of their campaign strategy.

99 CASE

████████ *The Give Back: A Case of Union Busting*

Three years ago, Local 974 of the United Tireworkers of America made significant contract concessions to the North American Tire plant in Bailey, Georgia. The union concessions were made for the company's economic survival and for the plant to remain open. Now, as the U.S. economy was struggling to recover from what some had called the worst recession since the Great Depression, North American Tire and its union was back at the bargaining table. While the U.S. economy had shown some signs of recovery, the union was not looking to give back again but to recover some of what was given up in previous negotiations. The union's position was that its previous concessions had facilitated North American Tire's survival and that it had already done its part to ensure the company's viability. However, the company had other goals for negotiations.

The company's initial proposals did not satisfy the union's negotiating team, a strike resulted, and both sides indicated their resolve was strong. While picket lines and demonstrations at the plant were rather uneventful, a war of words was fought in the media. On the one hand, full-page ads appeared in the local papers condemning the company for going back on their word to make up for the givebacks of the past. On the other hand, the company claimed it needed to maintain its competitive position in an industry undergoing a shakeout of underperforming competitors. North American Tire's parent company, Swiss Financial, of Alpsland, Switzerland, reported that operating profit rose 20 percent to $68 million on sales of $1.1 billion in the most recent quarter. North American's other nonunion plants were operating at capacity, and the company recently announced the purchase of Mexico's largest tire maker.

Negotiations broke down when the union rejected what management called its best offer. The company stated that the contract proposal was well above average for the Bailey, Georgia area. However, the union countered that it was well below industry standards. In addition, the union filed unfair labor practice charges with the National Labor Relations Board (NLRB). The union alleged that the strike was caused by unfair labor practices including the company's refusal to bargain over medical insurance or to bring its decision makers to the bargaining table.

Supervisors and clerical employees kept the North American Tire plant in Bailey operating at less than 30 percent of capacity, and plans were made by management to hire strike replacements. Striking employees were invited to return to work, but only a small percentage returned. The company began to advertise, interview, and hire strike replacements. Although the labor market was tight and Bailey's unemployment rate was less than 3 percent, there was no shortage of applicants. The company increased production at the Bailey plant, and production was also stepped up at its nonunion plants. While the union cried foul, the company continued to increase production. A federal mediator was appointed to get both sides back to the bargaining table to resume negotiations.

QUESTIONS

1. What are the pros and cons of North American Tire's strategy of hiring replacement workers? How ethical is the behavior of management?

2. Assuming that the firm's goal is to break Local 974 of United Tireworkers of America, what are the advantages and disadvantages of this strategy?

3. What standard should the firm use in setting wage rates (industry or geographic)?

Contributed by Gerald E. Calvasina, Southern Utah University and Joyce M. Beggs, University of North Carolina at Charlotte

100 EXERCISE

■■■■■■ *Applying the NLRA*

I. OBJECTIVES

A. To help you understand the application of the National Labor Relations Act (NLRA).

B. To help you understand the court's interpretation of the NLRA.

C. To help you understand the meaning of the terms "decertification election," "union salting," "strike replacements," "Excelsior List," and the rights of supervisors under the NLRA.

II. OUT-OF-CLASS PREPARATION TIME: 60 minutes

III. IN-CLASS TIME SUGGESTED: 45 minutes

IV. PROCEDURES

A. Read the exercise, review the National Labor Relations Act, and complete any additional reading assigned by the instructor.

B. The class should be divided into groups of four.

C. Each group should read each of the case incidents that follow and develop responses to each situation.

1. You are finishing up some paperwork at the end of a hard day. As the human resources manager, you have been involved in the company's negotiations with the union regarding the truck drivers' new contract with your firm. The negotiations have not been going well and all signs indicate that a strike will be called in a matter of days. As you are preparing to leave your office, three long-time truck drivers ask to have a word with you in private. They inform you that they are not happy with their union and that a number of the other drivers feel the same way. They ask you to help them get rid of the union.

2. You have been interviewing an applicant for a production line opening. The applicant seems to have all of the necessary KSAs to do the job. You feel certain that he will be one of the three candidates you recall for a second interview with the production manager. As you are about to close the interview, the applicant informs you that if he is hired, he intends to encourage his co-workers to form a union.

3. The negotiations between your company and the union representing the 110 production workers in your firm have reached a dead end. Union members have already voted to go on strike. At a meeting of the key managers involved in running the company, the production manager suggests utilizing the remaining clerical, accounting, and managerial staff as replacements to keep the plant running. She also suggests contacting a temporary employment agency to help fill any remaining critical positions while the union members are on strike. As the human resources manager, how would you respond to this suggestion?

4. You are the human resources manager of a 150-employee retail establishment. The mix of employees in the store is 50 full-time sales associates, 50 part-time sales

associates, 20 full-time shipping and receiving employees, and 30 supervisory/managerial employees. You receive a call from the regional office of the National Labor Relations Board (NLRB) informing you that a petition for a representation election has been filed by your sales associates. Three weeks later, the NLRB informs you that an election has been ordered. The NLRB representative calls again and asks you to send him a copy of your current payroll complete with names and addresses of the employees in the potential bargaining unit. This list, you are told, will be turned over to the local union seeking to organize your employees.

5. You are the store manager for a regional supermarket chain. Your store is nonunion. When a local union attempts to organize your employees, you receive orders to terminate those employees of your store who have signed union authorization cards. Your regional manager also orders you to prepare termination slips for each of the fired employees detailing false reasons for their termination.

Contributed by Dr. Gerald Calvasina, Southern Utah University

101 EXERCISE
Labor Arbitration

I. OBJECTIVES

A. To familiarize you with the arbitration process.

B. To give you practice in presenting a case before others.

C. To examine issues relating to contract administration.

II. OUT-OF-CLASS PREPARATION TIME: 40–50 minutes

III. PROCEDURES

Either at the beginning of or before class, each student should read the exercise. To start the exercise, the instructor will divide the class into the following three groups:

A. Union representatives (approximately five individuals)

B. Company representatives (approximately five individuals)

C. Arbitrators (all remaining participants, divided into groups of three to five members)

The union representatives should meet together and carefully examine "The Union Position" and prepare to argue and defend this position. The company representatives should do the same with reference to "The Company Position." Meanwhile, the arbitrators should read both positions and discuss among themselves the arguments for and against each position.

After both the union and company representatives have prepared their position statements, each should present their case to the arbitrators. Each group will be allowed five minutes for their presentation, and then an additional five minutes to counter the other group's position.

After all presentations are complete, each group of arbitrators will be given ten minutes to discuss the case and reach a decision. These decisions should be presented, along with the reasoning behind them, to all participants. Finally, the instructor may (optionally) present the arbitrator's actual decision in this case.

THE ISSUE

Was the grievant discharged for just cause? The company claimed the employee's negligence of duty resulted in the discharge, and the union claimed poor performance was the issue. If the union is right, what should be the remedy?

PERTINENT PROVISIONS OF THE UNION AGREEMENT

Article I. Purpose of the Agreement

1.3 The management of the company and the direction of the working force, including the right to plan, direct, and control operations, the right to hire, suspend, transfer, or discharge for just and sufficient cause, to relieve employees from duties because of lack of work or for other legitimate business reasons, and the right to introduce new or improved methods or facilities of production, is vested exclusively in the company; provided, however, that such rights shall not be exercised for the purpose of discriminating against any employee, and such rights shall not conflict with the provisions of this agreement.

Contributed by Dr. Gerald Calvasina, Southern Utah University

Article 33. Discipline and Discharge

33.1 In cases of poor job performance, the following procedure dealing with discipline will be accomplished with written notification to the union:

a. Formal written warning in the first instance with copy to the employee.

b. In subsequent instances, formal written warning and/or suspension without pay for a period not to exceed five working days.

c. In the event three or more instances occur, one of which results in a suspension, within any two-year period, discharge for just cause will be accomplished.

33.1.1 For purposes of this article, job performance shall include consideration of the following factors:

a. Attendance record, including absenteeism, tardiness, and proven abuse of sick leave.

b. Adherence to industrial safety rules.

c. Adherence to company house rules.

d. Ability to perform assigned tasks satisfactorily.

33.2 In cases of personal misconduct, the disciplinary action taken, including discharge, will be consistent with the gravity of the offense.

BACKGROUND

The grievant was employed as a service technician for the ABC Petroleum/Gas Company from August 2003 to April 2009. On January 26, 2009, grievant was dispatched to a customer who reported a strong odor of gas. Grievant's service report showed that he spent 26 minutes on the call, that no leaks were found, and that no repairs were made. The grievant did not take a pressure/manometer test.

Later that same day, in response to a second call, another technician was sent to the customer's home. The second technician checked the gas tank and gauge readings, added some gas, used the track, and did the pressure/manometer test. He tested the lines and isolated the source of the gas odor at a leak in the heater connector after the shutoff valve on the heater. The leak was located less than two feet from the pilot light on the water heater, which was lit. The technician replaced the heater connector and put the old one in the back of his truck. Subsequently, the grievant's immediate supervisor talked with the second technician and examined the damaged heater connector.

On January 28, 2009, the supervisor met with the grievant and informed him that he was being suspended, pending an investigation. The reason for the suspension was "Negligent in responding to report of gas odor on January 26, failure to perform leak investigation according to company procedures, leaving party with hazardous condition." By letter on April 16, 2009, grievant was notified that he was being terminated based on the company's findings indicating that "the incident was of such serious nature that we would be remiss in continuing your employment as a technician."

THE COMPANY'S POSITION

The company contends that the grievant failed to follow normal procedures necessary to determine whether there was a gas leak, and that leaving the customer in a hazardous condition constituted just cause for discharge. The grievant's failure to find or repair the gas leak was not poor performance but negligence of duty. The company defined poor performance as involving a lack of skills or intelligence and that the grievant's behavior was not caused by a lack of skills or innate inability. The company specifically refers to Article 1.3 that permits the company to discharge an employee for "just cause" and that, under Article 1.3, no prior warnings are required. The company also noted in its presentation that the employee was previously suspended for five days in 2004, and that he has been reprimanded on numerous occasions for various infractions.

THE UNION'S POSITION

The union contends that the grievant should have been disciplined under Section 33.1 for poor job performance. The union contends that grievant performed three of the four tests usually performed and that, at worst, used poor judgment in not pressure testing the system. Further, the union contends that the company failed to give grievant adequate notice of the rule or the consequences of his action. The grievant did not have knowledge that he could be discharged for negligence in performance of his duties. Further, the union claimed that the company did not conduct a proper investigation and relied solely on the report of the second technician sent to the customer's home. The company made no attempt to visit the job site to determine firsthand if grievant had followed company rules.

Employee Communications during Union Campaigns

I. OBJECTIVES

    A. To give you practice in preparing an effective company communication during a union campaign.

    B. To help you understand the practical application of the National Labor Relations Act.

II. TIME REQUIRED TO COMPLETE: 1 hour

III. INSTRUCTIONS

Your company, Fruit Canners, Inc., has recently become aware that the United Food and Commercial Workers Union is attempting to convince employees in your plant to sign authorization cards. Management is somewhat surprised by the campaign because employee relations have generally been good. Prepare a one-page letter to be sent to all plant employees stating the company's position on the union drive and the company's desire to remain nonunion. Be certain that the content of your letter does not violate the provisions of the National Labor Relations Act.

Contributed by Dr. Gerald Calvasina, Southern Utah University

6

International HR and Term Project

International HR Issues

103 CASE

Selecting a Manager for a Nigerian Facility

Victoria Oilfield Equipment is a supplier of drilling equipment for oil and gas exploration. It is headquartered near Houston, Texas. The company has seven offices and warehousing facilities near potential markets for its equipment. Only 30 percent of Victoria's profits come from selling equipment; the rest comes from leasing the equipment. Within the company's leasing operations, half the profit comes from supplying operators for the equipment. Victoria has over 25 years of experience in Texas and Louisiana, and 10 years of experience in several Latin American countries. Most of its customers are large multinational oil companies. However, approximately 20 percent of its contracts are with small, independent exploration companies.

Victoria has just completed construction of a new facility near Port Harcourt, Nigeria—its first venture into Africa. Nigeria is the most populous country in Africa and has one of the fastest growing economies in the world and is the 12th largest oil producer. During the past few years, several armed militant gangs have disrupted life and commerce in the city. These gangs claim to fight for the interest of the indigenous people and ask for a share of Nigeria's oil wealth. However, they are mostly known for random and targeted killings, arson, bombings, and kidnappings of both foreign workers and indigenous people.

The machinery, trucks, and equipment to operate this facility are to arrive within the next three months. You are the assistant human resource officer for Victoria Oilfield Equipment and have been instructed to review the records of the three leading candidates for manager of this new facility. You must recommend one of the three to your boss, the human resources director.

Before you examine the records, you make a list of personnel and political factors that you believe should be taken into consideration:

1. The general criteria for this position are education, experience, job knowledge, desire, and stability.

2. The Nigerian facility will be in the start-up phase.

3. Victoria wants to develop some of its current managers in international operations.

4. Few Nigerians have experience in the technical aspects of drilling for oil, yet Victoria has built its reputation on the expertise of its managers and customer acceptance of its managers as knowledgeable professionals.

5. Although some of Victoria's managers have had experience in Latin America, none have had experience in Africa.

6. Political power within the Nigerian government shifts periodically, and many of those with whom Victoria negotiated its move into Nigeria are no longer in the government.

7. The supply of trained oil-drilling equipment operators in Nigeria is much less than the demand.

The three candidates are:

Henry Smith: Age 34, United States citizen, graduate of Texas A & M, served three years in the Army and then joined Victoria Oilfield Equipment. In his ten years with Victoria, his record has been outstanding, and it is often said that he will be president of Victoria someday. He has never been outside of the United States.

Juan Lopez: Age 46, Venezuelan citizen, has been with Victoria for 21 years and worked his way up in several offices in Latin America. He spent two years in company headquarters planning operations in Latin America and is well respected throughout the company. He currently manages Victoria's facility in Ecuador.

Matthew Ohwueme: Age 52, Nigerian citizen, educated in England, member of the Ibo ethnic group. He is the owner/manager of the largest Honda dealership in Lagos but has had no experience with oilfield equipment.

QUESTIONS

1. Would it be best for Victoria Oilfield Equipment to select a manager who is a local (citizen of Nigeria), a home-country national (citizen of the United States), or a third-country national (citizen of some country other than Nigeria or the United States)? Why?

2. Which of the factors to be considered would favor the selection of Henry Smith? Juan Lopez? Matthew Ohwueme?

3. Which candidate would you recommend? Why?

Contributed by Sam C. Holliday, formerly with the University of Southern California

Outsourcing Jobs to India

Argus Publishers Inc. is a New York City–based publisher specializing in college textbooks in the Social Sciences and Business. One of their best-selling texts is *Cases and Exercises in Marketing Management*, now in its seventh edition. This book is the fourth best-selling text in the field of marketing. Two of the authors are based in the southeastern United States (Professors John Sexton and Bruce Nystrom), and the third author is currently teaching at a British university (Professor Donna James).

Six months ago, the authors agreed to prepare an eighth edition to their text and deleted some cases and exercises while adding some new ones based on reviewer comments. The reviewers were faculty members who had used the seventh edition of the book. Their comments reflected what they liked and disliked as well as case or exercise topics they would find useful in the eighth edition of the text.

For the first seven editions over the previous 23 years, the authors had worked with various editors in the United States to whom the publisher had outsourced the editorial work. After finishing the revision for the new edition, the authors sent the manuscript to the publisher and waited for the edited manuscript, which they would proofread. It was agreed that each author would receive edited manuscript only for his or her chapters. In addition, the edited manuscript always came with detailed instructions from the editor indicating what they needed from each author and by what date.

This time, however, all three authors received hundreds of pages of manuscript from an editor, a Mr. Reddy, who was based in India, with no instructions at all. Each author received all parts of the revised text including those written by his/her co-authors. They also noted that some of the sentences and paragraphs were in red type within these manuscripts, but no explanation for the red type was provided. The three authors then called each other and tried to figure out what Reddy, the editor, wanted from them since no instructions were provided with the manuscript. Reddy was then replaced by two new editors at various points who also e-mailed large quantities of edited manuscript without instructions. In each case, the new editor indicated that the previous editor had left the company or was on vacation. Continuity of the editorial staff seemed to be nonexistent.

The three authors then e-mailed the managing editor, Sarah Shelly, that they had no clue what was going on with their revision, what the editors wanted from them, and what they should do with the hundreds of manuscript pages each had been sent. Shelly told them they had been sent the edited Parts I and II of the text and that five other Parts would be sent later to them. However, she was unclear as to what the Indian editors were asking of the authors. She further noted that a corporate decision had been made to outsource all editorial work to India for cost control reasons.

Further e-mail communications between the authors and the editors continued to be muddled. The authors could never get the editors to clearly communicate what they wanted from them and by what date. So each author downloaded the electronic manuscript files that had been sent to them, opened only those that they had authored, and proceeded to make their own edits and comments. This was frustrating since the authors had specifically indicated to everyone on the editorial team which author was responsible for which materials.

All three authors commented to the managing editor that they wished they could go back to the previous system where the text had been edited by U.S. citizens.

1. What are the advantages and disadvantages of publishers and other employers outsourcing editorial work or other activities to Third World countries?

2. What changes, if any, would you suggest for the publisher to better serve their authors during the editorial process? Why?

Fred Bailey: An Innocent Abroad

Fred Bailey gazed out the window of his 24th floor office at the tranquil beauty of the Imperial Palace and its gardens amidst the hustle and bustle of downtown Tokyo. Only six months ago, Bailey had arrived with his wife and two children for this three-year assignment as the director of Kline & Associates' Tokyo office. Kline & Associates is a large, multinational consulting firm with offices in 19 countries worldwide. Bailey was now trying to decide if he should pack up and tell the home office that he was returning home, or whether he should somehow try to convince his wife (and himself) that they should stay and finish the assignment. Given how excited Bailey thought they all were about the assignment originally, it was a mystery as to how things had gotten to this point. As he watched the swans glide across the water in the moat that surrounds the Imperial Palace, Bailey reflected upon the past seven months.

Seven months ago, the managing partner of the main office in Boston, Dave Steiner, asked Bailey to lunch to discuss business. To Bailey's surprise, the "business" was not the major project that he and his team had just finished, but was instead a very big promotion and career move. Bailey was offered the position of managing director of the firm's relatively new Tokyo office which had a staff of 40, including seven Americans. Most of the Americans in the Tokyo office were either associate consultants or research analysts. As managing director, Bailey would be in charge of the entire office and would report to a senior partner who was in charge of the Asian region. It was implied to Bailey that if this assignment went as well as his past ones, it would be the last step before becoming a partner in the company.

When Bailey told Jenny, his wife, about the unbelievable opportunity, he was shocked at her less-than-enthusiastic response. She thought that it would be difficult for their children to live and go to school in a foreign country for three years, especially when Christine, the oldest, would be starting middle school next year. Besides, now that the children were in school, she was considering going back to work—at least part-time. Jenny Bailey had a degree in fashion merchandising from a well-known private university and had previously worked as an assistant buyer for a large women's clothing store.

Her husband explained that the career opportunity was just too good to pass and that the company's overseas package was generous enough to allow for a relatively luxurious lifestyle. The company would pay all the expenses to move whatever belongings the Baileys wanted to take with them. The company had a beautiful and spacious house located in an expensive district of Tokyo that would be provided to them rent-free, and the company would rent their house in Boston during their absence. Also, the company would provide a car and driver, education expenses for the children to attend private schools, and a cost-of-living adjustment and overseas compensation that would nearly triple Bailey's gross annual salary. After two days of consideration and discussion, Bailey told the managing partner, Dave Steiner, that he would accept the assignment.

The previous managing director was a partner in the company, but had only been in the new Tokyo office for less than a year when he was transferred to head a long-established office in England. Because the transfer to England was presently taking place, the Baileys were given about three weeks to prepare for the move. Between getting things at the office transferred to Bob Newcome, who was being promoted to Bailey's position, and the logistical hassles of getting furniture and other belongings ready to be moved, the Baileys did not have much time to find out much about Japan and its culture.

When the Baileys arrived in Japan, they were greeted at the airport by one of the young Japanese associate consultants and the senior American expatriate. They were all tired from the long flight, and the two-hour limousine ride back to Tokyo was a quiet one. After a few days of becoming familiar with the new environs, Bailey spent his first day at the office.

Bailey's first order of business was to have a general meeting with all the employees of associate consultant rank and higher. Although he was not aware of this at first, the Japanese staff always sat apart from the American staff. After Bailey introduced both himself and his general ideas about the potential and future direction of the Tokyo office, he asked a few individuals for ideas about how their responsibilities would likely fit into his overall plan. From the American staff, Bailey received a mixture of opinions with specific reasons about why certain ideas might or might not fit well. From the Japanese staff, he only received vague answers and no outright opinions. When Bailey asked for more specific information, he was surprised to find that some of the Japanese staff made a sucking sound as they breathed and said that it was "difficult to say." Bailey sensed the meeting was not entirely fulfilling his objectives, so he thanked everyone for attending and said he looked forward to everyone working together to make the Tokyo office the fastest growing office in the company.

After they had been in Japan about a month, Fred's wife complained to him about the difficulty she had finding some everyday products like maple syrup, peanut butter, and quality cuts of beef. She said that when she could find these items at one of the specialty stores they cost three to four times what they would cost in the United States. She also complained that the washer and dryer were too small and that she had to spend extra money by sending clothes out to be dry-cleaned. Additionally, unless she went to the American Club in downtown Tokyo, she was never able to enjoy the company of English-speaking adults. After all, her husband was at the office 10 to 16 hours a day and their children were at school most of the day. Unfortunately, at the time of this discussion with his wife, Bailey was preoccupied with a big upcoming meeting between his company and a significant prospective client—a well-respected Japanese multinational company.

The next day, Bailey, along with the lead American consultant for the potential contract, Ralph Webster, and one of the Japanese associate consultants, Kenichi Kurokawa, who spoke perfect English, met with a team from the Japanese company. The Japanese team consisted of four members—the VP of administration, the director of international personnel, and two staff specialists. After shaking hands and a few awkward bows, Bailey said that he knew the Japanese team was busy and he did not want to waste their time, so he would get right to the point. Bailey then asked Webster to lay out their company's proposal for the project to include project costs. After the presentation, Bailey asked the Japanese clients for their reaction to the proposal. The Japanese did not respond immediately and so Bailey quickly launched into his summary version of the proposal, thinking that the translation might have been insufficient. But, again, the Japanese team had only the vaguest of responses to his direct questions.

His recollection of the frustration of that initial business meeting was enough to shake Bailey back to the reality of the situation. The reality was that, in the five months since that first meeting, little progress had been made and the contract between the companies had yet to be signed. "I can never seem to get a direct response from a Japanese person," he thought to himself. This feeling of frustration led him to remember a related incident that happened about a month after his first meeting with the Japanese client.

Bailey reasoned that little progress had been made because he and his group did not know enough about the client to package the proposal in a way that was appealing to them. Consequently, he called in the senior American associated with the proposal, Ralph Webster, and asked him to develop a research report on the client so the proposal could be reevaluated and tailored to better meet their needs. Jointly, they decided that one of the more promising Japanese research associates, Tashiro Watanabe, would be the best employee to take the lead on this report. To impress upon Watanabe the importance of this task and the great potential they saw in him, Bailey and Webster decided to have the young Japanese associate meet with them. During the meeting, they presented the nature and importance of the task. At that point, Bailey said to Watanabe, "You can see that this is an important assignment and that we are placing a lot of confidence in you by giving you this assignment. We need the report this time next week so that we can revise and re-present our proposal. Can you handle this?" After a somewhat pregnant pause, Watanabe responded hesitantly, "I'm not sure what to say." Bailey smiled, got up from his chair, and walked over to the young Japanese associate, extended his hand, and said, "Hey, there's nothing to say. We're just giving you the opportunity you deserve."

The day before the report was due, Bailey asked Webster how the research report was coming along. Webster said that since he had heard nothing from Watanabe, he assumed that everything was under control, but that he would double-check with him. Webster later met one of the American research associates, John Maynard, in the office hallway. He knew that Maynard was hired for the Tokyo office because of his Japanese language ability and that, unlike any of the other Americans, he often went out after work with some of the Japanese research associates, including Watanabe.

Webster asked Maynard if he knew how Watanabe was progressing on the report. Maynard then recounted that, last night at the office, Watanabe had asked if Americans sometimes fired employees for being late with reports. He had sensed that this was more than a hypothetical question and asked Watanabe why he wanted to know. Watanabe did not respond immediately and, since it was 8:30 in the evening, Maynard suggested they go out for a drink. At first Watanabe resisted, but then Maynard assured him that they could have a quick drink at a nearby bar and come right back to the office. At the bar, Maynard got Watanabe to express his concerns.

Watanabe explained the nature of the research report that he had been requested to produce. He went on to say that even though he had already worked many hours to complete the report, he found the task to be impossible; he had doubted from the beginning whether he could complete the report in a week.

At this point, Webster asked Maynard, "Why the hell didn't he say something in the first place?" Webster did not wait to hear whether Maynard had an answer to his question and headed to Watanabe's office. The incident then escalated as Webster lashed out at Watanabe and then went to Bailey explaining that the report would not be ready and that Watanabe did not think it could have been from the start. "Then why didn't he say something to us during the meeting?" Bailey demanded. No one had any clear answers, and the entire incident left everyone involved more suspect and uncomfortable with each other.

There were other incidents, big and small, that had made the last two months in Tokyo especially frustrating, but Bailey was too tired to remember them all. It seemed as if there was too much of a language and cultural gap between the Americans and the Japanese to overcome. Bailey felt that he could not communicate with his Japanese colleagues and that he could not figure out what they were thinking. This drove him crazy and made him feel as if he was not a success in his new position.

Then, on top of all the work-related problems, his wife had laid a bombshell on him last evening. She wanted to go home, and yesterday was not soon enough. Even though the children seemed to be enjoying their stay in Tokyo, his wife was tired of being stared at, of not understanding anybody or being understood, of not being able to find what she wanted at the store, of not being able to drive and read the road signs, of not having anything to watch on TV, and of not being involved in anything. Because of her feelings of isolation, she wanted to return to the United States and to their previous life. She reasoned that they owed nothing to the company because the company had led them to believe this was just another assignment, like the two enjoyable years they had spent in San Francisco, and it was anything but that!

Bailey looked out the window of his office once more, wishing that somehow all the problems could be solved or that time could be turned back. Down below, the traffic was backed up in the always crowded Tokyo streets. Though the traffic lights changed, the cars and trucks did not seem to be moving. Fortunately, in the ground below the streets, one of the world's most advanced, efficient, and clean subway systems moved hundreds of thousands of people to their destinations about the city.

QUESTIONS

1. What factors (individual, work, and organizational) contributed to Fred and Jenny Baileys' lack of adjustment to Japan?

2. What mistakes did Bailey make at work because of his lack of understanding of the Japanese culture?

3. What criteria would be important in selecting employees for overseas assignments?

4. What special training and development programs might have been beneficial to Fred Bailey and his family prior to his assignment in Tokyo?

5. Imagine that you are Dave Steiner and you receive a telephone call from Bailey in which he talks about his difficulties adjusting to life in Tokyo. How would you respond? What should be done now?

Contributed by J. Stewart Black, Insead

A Clash of Cultures in the Workplace: German Managers in South Africa

Dr. Christa Kriek was preparing for a lecture on cultural intelligence to her International Human Resource Management elective class when her cell phone rang. It was a call from a former student, Johan Coetzee, a quality manager in the Logistics Division of German Auto Manufacturer, Inc. (GAM). GAM had recently resumed business in South Africa after having left in response to the international boycotts against firms doing business in a country that practiced apartheid.* Its plants in the country assembled luxury cars for the domestic market and neighboring countries in southern Africa. Coetzee asked her if she would be able to assist the Division with morale and motivation problems among their associates by giving a motivational talk to staff. Coetzee said he was calling because his boss, Walter Koch (Division Head) had complained about low staff morale and motivation, especially among associates. Dr. Kriek asked if she could meet with Coetzee to hear more about the problem. At their meeting a week later, he provided her with additional details about the structure of the Division and its current personnel problems.

THE SITUATION AT LOGISTICS DIVISION

The Logistics Division was responsible for the supply of parts, subassemblies, and other items to the production line. This Division employed 425 people including a management staff of eight. The management team was culturally diverse and consisted of four German nationals, one of whom was Walter Koch, a British expatriate who had been in South Africa for two years, a black South African, and two white South Africans. In the GAM human resource management system, all shop floor employees were referred to as associates, and this is a practice they followed in their South African operations. The shop floor staff consisted primarily of black South Africans with different ethnicities, but were largely Sotho-speaking as they came from the surrounding townships located about 20 to 25 miles from the Division. Many of them relied on the taxis that operated daily from the townships to business areas for transport to and from the plant as few, if any, of them, owned cars. Management staff, however, were provided with company cars as part of their compensation package.

When the Logistics Division started operations six months ago, Koch, an engineer by training, had been appointed Division Head. He had never worked in South Africa before but had been successful in previous company assignments throughout Europe. GAM's human resource approach to expatriate assignments was to rotate managers every three years at different international sites. Maureen Kaiser, vice president of Global Human Resources, explains,

> "Our approach to international assignments complements our international business strategy. We believe our brand is known in the automobile market for its uncompromising quality and precision. Therefore, we want uniform standards across the globe, no matter where we operate. Thus, we assign our managers to three-year rotations so that they learn how to install our values and goals in any context."

---

*Apartheid was based on a system of legislated racial categorization and separation dividing the population into different racial groups. This separation governed every sphere of life, from education to employment, and resulted in legislating discriminatory practices by minority whites toward the black majority.

GAM believed this approach was the best way for their managers to develop the skills and knowledge to be effective in international assignments. In line with this philosophy, managers assigned to an international site were expected to draw upon their previous experiences to perform well. No country training was done prior to the assignments other than a review of management's strategy for operations in the country. Koch confessed to his fellow managers that he knew little about South Africa prior to arriving, but had believed that the company's well-defined strategy and performance culture would ensure success during his assignment.

When Koch arrived at the Logistics Division, he promptly put a strategic plan in place that was aligned to the company's goal to make sure all world-wide operations were "world class" no matter in which country they did business. Within the company, this goal was referred to as "Keeping the Rhythm." In line with the plan, performance metrics were set within a performance management system that covered all employees from management to associates.

Coetzee described the culture as both task-oriented and performance-driven. People were rewarded based on how well they performed in respect to the set targets. Each month, Koch held a communications session with employees to inform them about progress toward performance goals. These sessions were held in a large auditorium with the management team sitting behind a table at the front of the room and employees seated theatre-style in the spacious auditorium. Typically, Koch would make a 15-minute PowerPoint presentation with graphs and brief everyone on operations and progress toward goals. Generally, none of the other managers or team leaders made presentations. Once Koch finished his presentation, he would ask if there were any questions. In the five months he had been conducting these communications sessions, no one had asked a single question. Koch had told Coetzee on more than one occasion that he really believed all staff, including associates, really understood what needed to be achieved at the Division.

Yet, all was not going well. There was high absenteeism among shop floor employees as well as a problem with lateness in some of the departments. The team leaders who had been appointed by the management team complained of uncooperative workers and discipline problems. Additionally, in recent months they had experienced incidents of theft from the stores. All of these problems began to be reflected in the Division's performance on key metrics, and recently there had been an increase in complaints from the Production Division about delays in receiving parts. Koch was quite concerned because he had aspirations for one day becoming part of the top management team at GAM. He had two very successful international assignments under his belt and wanted this one to be just as successful.

Koch called a meeting of his management team to discuss what was transpiring at the Division. During the meeting, the South African managers were mostly quiet. Typical of his leadership style, Koch seemed to have the problem all figured out. He believed the problem was a lack of motivation among the workers. In his previous assignments in Belgium and the United Kingdom, workers had always responded well to tasks and set goals. He thought a "motivational" talk from a local expert might help to motivate the staff. He had then asked Coetzee for his assistance in finding a good speaker on motivation.

DR. KRIEK'S INTERVENTION

Dr. Kriek, an experienced human resources consultant, convinced Koch and the rest of the management team that she needed to do a survey of staff to really find out more about "the motivational problems." Koch agreed as long as Dr. Kriek ensured them that she would get to the "bottom" of the problem. She decided to survey a random sample of 50 percent of the staff as well as conduct 30-minute interviews with management. The original idea of surveying the shop floor associates was not feasible because of the insufficient literacy of most of them. Instead, Dr, Kriek held focus group discussions with the associates about the climate and culture of the Division.

The results of the interviews and focus group discussions revealed a huge gap between the perceptions and feelings of associates and management. Exhibit 6.1 contains what Dr. Kriek heard from each side. The majority of associates said they do not understand the behavior of the Germans. One associate expressed a view that most had agreed with during the focus group sessions: "They act strangely, including Mr. Koch. They have no manners. They come into the shop floor in the morning but they do not greet us. They just wave at us with their hands. What is this kind of behavior? We work for them every day." Another associate stated, "I do not think they really care about us. They rush everything, including the monthly meetings held in the big auditorium. We have been working here for almost seven months, and they do not know our names. But we know their names."

Another issue raised by the associates was about how the team leaders had been appointed. John Dube, who appeared to be a spokesperson for the associates in his focus group session said, "Team leaders were appointed by the Germans without consulting us. They are not our natural leaders, and we do not really trust them." When Dr. Kriek asked the associates what they expected from management, they readily offered a number of suggestions. Exhibit 6.2 contains a copy of what she wrote on a flip chart during the sessions.

The interviews with the management team presented a very different view of the problems. There was also a difference in the views of the local South African managers and the German nationals. Koch and the other German managers expressed the view that the workers were lazy and not willing to work hard. They felt the monthly forums were an excellent form of communication and did not understand why the associates never asked questions. Koch had stated during his interview that

> I feel like I have really done everything by the book in bringing staff up to speed on 'Keeping the Rhythm.' I also believe in keeping an eye on the shop floor, and I make it a regular task to walk through the departments each morning.

EXHIBIT 6.1 *Perceptions of Associates and Management Collected from Interviews and Focus Groups*

Perceptions of Associates	Perceptions of German Managers	Perceptions of South African Managers
■ German managers are cold and do not communicate with us ■ German managers do not greet us properly ■ Feeling of not belonging ■ Not recognized ■ Not important ■ Lower class ■ Hate being called an associate ■ Us versus Them ■ We feel invisible ■ Early and late shifts cause serious transport problems	■ We are good communicators ■ This is a business and work comes first ■ Associates are here to work and meet goals ■ Being on time is very important ■ We care about associates ■ We have a good bonus system based on performance ■ Performance management system works well ■ The division will be successful if associates work harder and are more motivated	■ German managers are arrogant ■ They do not listen to us ■ The focus is on reaching goals ■ German managers don't understand the South African culture or how to motivate associates

EXHIBIT 6.2 *Focus Group Notes*

✔ We want the Germans to treat us with respect by calling us by our real names.

✔ They must greet us properly and show courtesy by asking how we are feeling.

✔ In our culture, it is important that people are respectfully acknowledged.

✔ Do not just give us facts and figures at the monthly communication forums, there should be more dialogue.

✔ Let us have input in selecting the team leaders because we know who our leaders are in the community and who people will respect and respond to.

✔ Don't divide us by giving individuals bonuses instead of a group bonus.

✔ We are willing to work hard but do not feel we are really part of the company.

✔ Stop calling us associates and use our names instead.

He went on further to state:

> The workplace is about delivery and performance. It is not about making people feel good. Our company has been successful because of the precision and quality of our automobiles. That only happens when there is strict adherence to world-class standards.

When Dr. Kriek asked the German managers what they expected of staff, their list was rather straightforward. They expected everyone to work hard, be on time, and meet the performance goals set for the Division.

The South African managers had a different view about the situation than their German colleagues. They felt the Germans were arrogant and did not solicit their knowledge of local realities. Pieter Smit, warehouse manager, put it this way:

> They tell us what to do and do not ask for our opinions. There is a very formal, impersonal style of interaction which we South Africans are just not used to. We don't think the Germans really understood the culture among the shop floor employees.

After compiling these results, Dr. Kriek decided to share what she had heard from the associates and the non-German managers with Koch. Koch was shocked and could not understand how they could hold such views. Koch told her:

> Of course, we care about all the staff, especially the associates. I have made every effort to communicate the goals and the challenges of supply parts and subassemblies in a just-in-time production process. I thought everyone was clear that we are to produce and that the expectations of employees are high. Why haven't they ever told me these things at the forums we hold monthly?

DR. KRIEK'S PROPOSED SOLUTION

Based on what she had heard during her sessions with staff and management, Dr. Kriek decided a motivational talk was not going to adequately address these issues. Instead, she proposed a two-day cultural awareness and sensitivity workshop for the management team to address what she saw as primarily a clash of cultures— German versus South African. Exhibit 6.3 contains Dr. Kriek's proposal for the workshops and the topics that she planned to present and discuss. When she shared the proposal with Koch, he was doubtful that it would address the real problem with the Division. He told Dr. Kriek:

> I really don't understand this culture business. We have been successful wherever we have operated by applying our world-class standards and ways of doing business. But, you are the expert so I am willing to give the workshops a chance but things have to improve soon or our Division is in trouble.

EXHIBIT 6.3 *Cultural Awareness and Sensitivity Workshop*

Objectives of the Workshop

The objective of this workshop is to provide participants with an opportunity to:

- Understand how national cultures differ
- Understand how cultural differences impact organizations
- Develop leadership skills for managing cultural diversity
- Develop their cultural intelligence

Proposed Content

1. What is culture?
2. How cultures of countries differ in terms of:
   - Power Distance
   - Uncertainty avoidance
   - Individualism/Collectivism
   - Universalistic versus Particularistic
   - Masculinity versus Femininity
   - Long-term versus Short-term Orientation
   - Monochronic versus Polychronic Time
3. How culture shapes and influences approaches to management
4. Cross-Cultural Communication Skills
   - Communicating in Low-context Cultures
   - Communicating in High-context Cultures
5. Becoming a Culturally Intelligent Manager
   - Developing Self-Awareness of One's Own Culture
   - Social Awareness of Other Cultures
   - Adapting Behavior in Cross-Cultural Situations

QUESTIONS

1. Why are the views of the German managers and associates so different? What are the underlying cultural values that may be causing the differences?

2. Do you agree with the GAM's view that the best preparation for an international assignment is "learning on the job" instead of formal training programs?

3. What are the human resource problems associated with a multinational company adopting a global human resource management strategy rather than a local strategy for operations outside its home base?

4. Evaluate Dr. Kriek's approach and actions. Do you agree with the approach she took? Why or why not?

5. Evaluate her proposal for the cultural awareness and sensitivity workshop for management. What are its strengths and weaknesses? What effect do you think it will have on the managers?

Case was prepared by Professor Yvonne du Plessis, Department of Human Resource Management, University of Pretoria (South Africa)

Term Project

107   TERM PROJECT

Human Resource System or Subsystem Evaluation

I. OBJECTIVE   To help a student group of two to four students critically analyze a human resource management system or subsystem, identify problems, and recommend constructive improvements.

II. OUT-OF-CLASS PREPARATION TIME: 30–40 hours per group (10–15 hours per individual student) for a total human resource system evaluation and 20–25 hours (5–10 hours per student) for a subsystem evaluation.

III. IN-CLASS TIME SUGGESTED: None, unless an oral report is required by the instructor. In that case, each group will make a 15–20 minute presentation to the class.

IV. PROCEDURES

Option 1: Students will self-select or be assigned into groups of two to four students, identify a real organization, and receive permission from either the CEO or the human resources director to study the organization's human resource system. Once permission is received, the group should arrange to interview as many of the following as possible: the human resources director, other human resources department employees, and employees performing different functions at different levels in the organization. As an option to completing the entire Human Resource System Evaluation outlined here, the instructor could assign only specific sections to a given student group. In that case, all groups would complete Sections I and VII and then be assigned Section II, III, IV, V, or VI.

Option 2: Same as above except student groups select an organization and study information available on its Web site in order to answer questions and analyze that organization's human resources system or subsystem.

V. GENERAL PURPOSE

The study will focus upon the selected organization's human resources and employee relations objectives, structures, policies, practices, and selected administrative problems or challenges. It will give you the opportunity to learn firsthand about the management of human resource systems in actual organizations. It will also provide you with the opportunity to develop field research methodologies and evaluation skills that should prove beneficial in future academic and professional assignments. Finally, for the organization cooperating with each of the student projects, the results of these studies may prove helpful in future efforts to improve the efficiency and effectiveness of their human resource systems.

The final reports of both the in-person and the Web site evaluations may be turned in to the organization at the discretion of the instructor. The final product of this study will be a comprehensive written report to be submitted on the date determined by the instructor. Each student should assume the stance of an outside consultant who has been called in to evaluate the human resource system or subsystem of the particular organization. At a minimum, the paper should reflect the items contained in the Evaluation Guide as a whole in Sections I and VII, as well as one other part of the Evaluation Guide that follows.

EVALUATION GUIDE

I. *The Organization and Its Mission* (This section to be completed with both options.)

A. When and why was this organization established?

1. Under what statutory or legal authority was it created?

2. What are the principal needs and objectives that the organization is designed to fulfill?

B. What budgetary constraints confront the organization?

1. What are the sources of revenue for this company?

a. for capital expenditures?

b. for operating expenditures?

2. What changes have occurred in the organization's budget in recent years?

a. Have there been any noticeable increases or decreases in revenues?

b. Have there been any new sources of funding?

c. Have any old sources of funding been reduced or eliminated?

d. How have these trends affected management of the organization?

C. What is the total employment complement of the organization?

1. How are these employees distributed throughout the organization?

a. by department or operational function?

b. by skill, e.g., managerial, professional, technical, clerical, skilled craftsperson, semi-skilled operatives, unskilled laborers, etc.?

2. What have been some of the noticeable employment trends in recent years?

3. Does the organization operate overseas? If so, do you employ Americans or foreign nationals overseas?

D. What are the major strategic threats and opportunities confronting this organization?

1. Does the organization have a strategic management plan including goals, objectives, and timetables?

2. What strategies have you been pursuing and with what degree of success in order to address these challenges?

II. *The Human Resource Function, Diversity, and Legal Issues*

A. Does this organization have a formal and identifiable human resource function or department?

1. When was this department or function formally established and why?

2. How is the human resource function or department organized to carry out the objectives of the organization?

3. How many individuals are directly associated with the human resource function or department?

4. What are the academic and employment backgrounds of those involved in the function or department?

B. To what degree is human resource management centralized of decentralized?

C. To what degree has the human resource function used information technology to manage information?

D. How have shifting workforce demographics impacted the human resource function?

E. What is the perceived importance of the human resource function or department relative to other functional operations of the organization?

F. Does the human resource function provide support in foreign countries? What problems or challenges does this present?

G. To what degree has the human resource function been involved in any organizational restructuring (i.e., mergers, outsourcing to other companies or countries, etc.)?

H. To what degree and how does the organization support a goal of diversity in the workplace?

I. To what degree is the human resource function achieving diversity goals for professional and managerial positions?

J. What legal challenges (if any) is the human resource function currently addressing?

K. What recommendations do you have (if any) for reorganizing the human resource function? Why?

III. *Meeting Human Resource Requirements: Job Analysis, Planning, Recruitment, and Selection*

A. To what degree is human resources management integrated into the strategic management of the organization? How?

B. Who is responsible for human resource planning and forecasting for the organization?

1. What methods are used to determine staffing needs?

2. Does the organization focus primarily upon short-term or long-term human resource needs, or both?

3. Are job analyses and job descriptions made for each position in the organization? To what degree are they updated periodically?

4. Is any human resource planning done?

- How is it being done?
- If not, why not?
- Has the lack of human resource planning had any negative impact? Explain.

5. Does the organization provide career planning and career counseling for employees? Why or why not? If yes, how is this done and how effective is it?

C. Once staffing needs are established, what procedures are utilized for filling job vacancies?

1. Who is responsible for staffing the organization—the human resource department or the respective functional departments?

2. What methods are used to recruit new employees?

3. What methods and criteria are used for evaluating and selecting job applicants? Have these methods been validated? How?

4. Have you used employee recruitment through social network sites and through the Internet? How effective are these?

5. To what extent are new employee recruitment, evaluation, and selection procedures aided or restricted by

    a. established policies or practices of the organization?

    b. provisions contained in employment laws?

    c. factors associated with local labor markets?

6. To what degree does the organization seek to fill existing job vacancies from among present employees or by recruiting new employees, and why?

7. What selection processes and criteria do you use to select employees?

8. How have these criteria been validated?

9. What options do you provide for flexible employee work schedules?

10. To what degree does the staffing reflect the skills, knowledge, and abilities necessary to successfully implement the strategic goals of the organization?

11. What does the organization do to enhance the work and family interface?

D. To what degree has the organization outsourced or downsized positions?

E. What specific problems have been encountered in the employment staffing process?

1. To what can these be attributed?

2. What are the major alternatives for resolving these problems?

3. Which solutions are most feasible, and why?

IV. *Developing Effectiveness in Human Resources: Training, Career Development, and Performance Appraisal*

A. Has the organization supported programs for employee training and development? Why or why not?

1. What kinds of programs have been established? Have they been oriented toward

    a. job skills?

    b. supervisory and leadership skills?

    c. basic educational skills?

    d. knowledge, skills, and abilities necessary for strategic goal attainment?

    e. orientation of new employees?

2. How do these programs relate to the organization's strategic and operational objectives?

3. Does the organization maintain its own training staff or are outside organizations used for training purposes?

4. What proportions of employees have participated in training (in both general and specific job categories) and development programs supported by the organization?

5. Are training and development offered in-house, outside the organization, or both?

6. How has the effectiveness of employee training and development been evaluated?

B. To what extent have the organization's programs of employee training and development been used in making decisions related to promotions and transfers within the organization?

C. What processes and programs, if any, do you offer for employee career development?

D. What options, if any, do you provide for flexible employee work schedules?

E. What problems, if any, have been encountered in the administration of employee training and development programs within the organization? What suggestions for improvement can you make? Why?

F. What methods are used for evaluating employees for the purpose of determining their effectiveness and any merited salary increases?

a. What methods of appraising employee performance are currently being used?

b. Do employee performance appraisal systems actually reflect job performance? Why or why not?

c. How adequate or inadequate are the performance appraisal methods currently being used? Why?

d. Do they reflect the knowledge, skills, and abilities needed to successfully implement the particular organization's strategic goals?

e. What factors other than job performance influence employee performance appraisal outcomes? Explain.

V. *Implementing Compensation Systems and Security*

A. How are wage and salary levels and annual improvements determined?

1. Does the organization conduct periodic internal and external wage surveys?

2. Are salary levels adequate to enable the organization to attract and maintain an effective work force? Why or why not?

3. Do differentials in salary grades appropriately reflect differentials in skills and responsibilities?

4. How do salary levels compare with those of other comparable organizations for the same or similar occupational and experience groupings?

5. Does the current reward system adequately reward employees with the requisite knowledge, skills, and abilities necessary to implement the strategic plan?

6. What trends have taken place in salary levels over the past few years?

7. To what degree is merit pay and incentive compensation used and in what areas? How effective are they in achieving high levels of employee performance?

8. Do you provide bonuses for executives? If so, how are these bonuses determined? Do they reflect individual and/or organizational performance?

B. How adequate are non-wage fringe benefits?

1. How are they determined?

2. How do they compare with those of other organizations?

3. How have they changed in recent years and how will they change in the future?

4. Do you provide domestic partner benefits? If so, please describe.

5. Do you provide for family and medical leave? If so, please describe.

C. Does the organization provide employee health insurance coverage? If so, how have their benefits changed over time and how are they likely to change in the future as a result of healthcare reform?

D. Has the organization introduced any special programs or activities to improve health and safety conditions on the job (i.e., violence in the workplace)?

E. Has the organization developed, periodically reviewed, and implemented a disaster preparedness plan? If so, please describe.

F. What efforts, if any, are utilized to maintain employee morale and job satisfaction?

G. Does the organization provide for flexible work options such as telecommuting or job sharing? Please provide details.

H. What retirement pension benefits are currently offered and how are they expected to change in the future?

I. What improvements in compensation, employee motivation, and health and safety should be made? Why?

VI. *Enhancing Employee Relations: Employee Discipline and Labor Relations*

A. What methods and procedures are available for resolving employee complaints and grievances?

1. Have there been large numbers of such grievances? Why?

2. Has the volume of grievances been growing or declining? Why?

3. What are the problems eliciting the majority of employee grievances?

B. Have there been many employee discipline problems?

1. Are there clearly spelled-out formal procedures within the organization for handling discipline cases? What are they?

2. How often are employees disciplined or discharged?

a. What are the major causes of such problems?

b. How have these been dealt with by the organization?

c. Do you have any serious problems with employee violence or use of controlled substances in the workplace? How have these been addressed?

C. To what extent have employee tardiness, absenteeism, and turnover been problems?

1. Have these problems been studied to determine their most likely causes? What are they?

2. What steps have been taken to resolve these problems, if they exist? What steps should have been taken? Why?

D. What employee restrictions (if any) does the organization impose on employee free speech, surfing the Internet, and unhealthy behavior (smoking or drug use) on or off the job?

E. Have any of the employees sought to join labor organizations for the purpose of engaging in collective bargaining over wages, hours, and working conditions? Explain.

1. Why have, or have not, such organizing activities taken place?

2. What is the official position of the organization toward acceptance or rejection of unionism for its employees?

3. If a labor union exists in this organization, what effect has the union had upon

   a. overall decision-making within the organization?

   b. the efficiency and productivity of the organization?

   c. the administration of the human resources function?

   d. the relations between the managers of the organization and its non-managerial personnel?

   e. the interpersonal relationships among non-supervisory employees?

F. What has been the relationship between management and union leaders (e.g., cooperative, neutral, cold, hostile)?

1. Have there been any noticeable changes in the nature of this relationship in the recent past? Why or why not?

2. Have there been any work stoppages among employees in order to pressure management into agreeing to union demands?

   a. What were the issue(s)?

   b. Why did the dispute occur?

   c. How was it resolved?

   d. What has been its subsequent impact upon

      i. the operation of the company?

      ii. employee performance?

      iii. the work environment?

      iv. the decision-making process involved in personnel matters?

G. What suggestions would you make for minimizing employee grievances and improving the labor relations climate (if applicable)? Why?

VII. *Summary and Evaluation* (This section is to be completed with both options.)

A. How effectively is the human resource function of this organization contributing to the fulfillment of its mission, objectives, and strategic plan?

B. What are some of the problems of human resources management that have been adequately solved or are now in the process of being solved by the organization?

C. What are some of the major human resource problems that remain to be confronted and solved?

D. What would appear to be among the most desirable solutions to these problems? Provide specific detail and justifications for your recommendations.

Business Etiquette

Business Etiquette Business Etiquette Business Etiquette Business Etiquette Business Etiquette Business Etiquette Business Etiquette Business Etiquette Business Etiquette

Carol Bennet

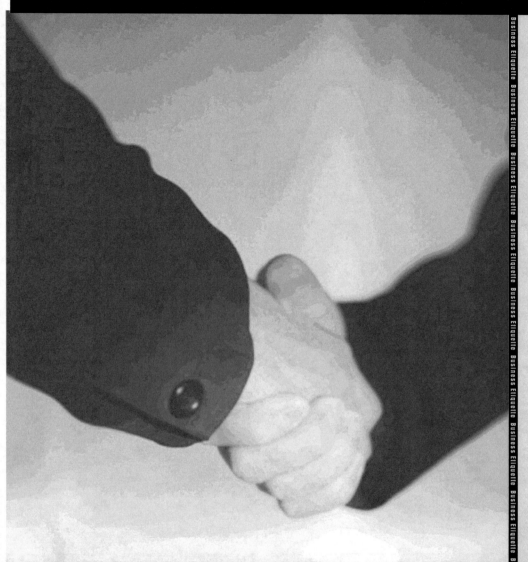

Business Etiquette Business Etiquette Business Etiquette Business Etiquette Business Etiquette Business Etiquette Business Etiquette Business Etiquette Business Etiquette Business Etiquette Business Etiquette

The Adaptable Courseware Program consists of products and additions to existing Cengage Learning products that are produced from camera-ready copy. Peer review, class testing, and accuracy are primarily the responsibility of the author(s). For more information, please contact Custom Solutions, a part of Cengage Learning, 5191 Natorp Boulevard, Mason, OH 45040. Or you can visit our Internet site at custom.cengage.com. Business Etiquette/Carol Bennet/ Book ISBN 10: 0-324-62761-0/Book ISBN 13: 978-0-324-62761-9

BUSINESS ETIQUETTE: THE BASICS

AT THE CORE
This topic examines:

- Rationale for learning business etiquette

- Common courtesies to opening office doors for others

- Common courtesies to opening car doors for others

- Courtesies when walking with others on a sidewalk

- Appropriate times to give up a seat in a public setting

- Why inappropriate behavior can be costly to business

- How perception equates to confidence and competitiveness

The first rule of etiquette is that the other person feels comfortable. This applies to all settings and social situations. The way for all of us to feel more comfortable in any type of corporate environment is to understand and have a pragmatic knowledge of basic business etiquette. Once we know the rules of etiquette and are comfortable using them, we can make our own choices regarding their application. We can gain a level of confidence knowing the basic rules of etiquette. This level of confidence transfers to our ability to relate to all kinds of business environments. This confidence also enhances our value as individuals as well as our value as employers and employees. We will begin by discussing common courtesy outside the office environment.

❖ Opening Office Doors

First of all, consider opening doors. If you are a woman and a man wants to open the door for you, allow him to do so. Consider it a gesture of courtesy to you as another person. Do not think of it as an act that is condescending. In contrast, however, if you are a man and a woman wants to open the door, allow her to do so. Consider it a gesture of assertiveness in the business world rather than one of gender assertiveness. Traditionally a man opens the door for a woman, an elder, or a senior in authority. A woman traditionally opens a door for either an elder or a senior in authority.

© Digital Vision

As a woman, slow your gait as you approach a door. When walking with a man who is older, give him a comfortable opportunity to open the door. If he doesn't, just open it yourself. When walking with people your age or younger, take turns opening the doors for each other as you progress through a building.

As a man, make an attempt to open the door for a woman, an elder, or a person of senior authority. Do not make a big show of it, however. If you are a man, think ahead and try to position yourself to open the door easily. Consider the individuals involved and the cultural environment. And remember that common courtesy is genderless.

❖ Opening Car Doors

Traditionally men open car doors for women, and men do the driving. However, these are not the roles observed in the business world today. Often women do the driving, and there are both men and women passengers. It is correct for the driver (the one with the keys) to at least unlock the passenger door before walking around to the driver's side. If the driver is a man, he should first open the door for the passengers. If the driver is a woman, she also can open the passenger door prior to walking to the driver's side.

Newer vehicles with remote door-unlocking devices almost make this issue moot. Sometimes passengers are not aware that all doors are unlocked, and they patiently wait for the door to be opened. A courtesy might be to announce that all the doors are unlocked.

If it is raining, the driver (whether man or woman) should offer to walk to the car and drive it back to where the sheltered passengers are waiting. In this case, the driver should unlock all the doors before arriving for the passengers. If two equivalent individuals go together in a car, the passenger should not consider it rude to have to wait while the driver opens his or her door first then unlocks the passenger door from the inside.

❖ Walking on Sidewalks

Traditional etiquette rules state that when walking on a sidewalk, the man always walks on the outside, or curbside, of a woman. Many mature men still feel more comfortable walking on the outside. The traditional rule was developed when streets were muddy and vehicles often splashed mud onto individuals walking down the street. The gallant man was supposed to take the brunt of the mess. Today's fast-paced business climate does not always expect this traditional rule to be followed. People walk together down a sidewalk without much regard for positioning.

Today's police departments and self-defense classes teach us that the common threats or dangers to a pedestrian in contemporary society are in and around the dark alcoves of buildings. Using that logic, a man today should walk on the inside of the sidewalk (away from the curb), thus protecting a woman from a would-be assailant.

© Digital Vision

❖ Giving Up Seats

If you are riding public transit or seated in a waiting room with limited seating, be conscious of those around you. If someone appears less fit than you, be polite and offer him or her your seat. Someone less fit might include an older person, a person who appears out of breath or tired, a person who does not have good balance inside a moving vehicle (bus), a person burdened with parcels, or a person who appears to be disabled. It is common courtesy for both men and women to give up their seats if the situation presents itself.

If you are standing and someone offers you a seat and you feel it is not justified, simply say "Thank you, but I'm fine. Perhaps someone else would like to sit down."

ON THE SCENE

In a large meeting room with a shortage of chairs, it is appropriate for a woman wearing pants to give up her seat for another woman wearing a skirt or dress. Obviously, it would be easier for me as a woman in pants to sit on the floor or stairs. Common sense is usually synonymous with common courtesy.

❖ The Corporate Culture

A recent tour of Cisco Systems, a large and fast-growing high-tech corporation, revealed a diverse nature of employees. In the employee cafeteria, there were men and women of different ethnicities and ages. To further the diversification, a few employees were dressed rather conservatively, yet most were dressed in casual work attire.

Most of the time we adapt quite readily to a working environment. There are times, however, when employees are asked to represent their company in a foreign or unfamiliar environment. Representing oneself or one's company in an unfamiliar business environment can present some challenges. Sometimes local habits and customs cause others to be uncomfortable, focusing attention on the "insiders" and excluding the "outsiders." In the way a formal environment can make us feel uncomfortable, a less-formal environment can make us feel uneasy.

Therefore, the rationale for taking this course is to be aware of and understand the correct rules of business etiquette. Whether you choose to follow them or not is your decision. Confidence comes with being cognizant of the rules and making conscious decisions whether or not to adhere to them.

❖ Manners are Cost Effective

More than just allowing you to gain personal confidence, "good manners are cost effective. They increase the quality of life in the workplace, contribute to optimum employee morale, embellish the company image, and hence play a major role in generating profit. On the other hand, negative behavior, whether based on selfishness, carelessness, or ignorance, can cost a person a promotion, even a job."[1]

"Up to 90 percent of unhappy customers never complain about discourtesy, and up to 91 percent will never again do business with the company that offended them. In addition, the average unhappy customer will tell the story to at least nine other people, and 13 percent of unhappy customers will tell more than twenty people."[2]

ON THE SCENE

© Digital Vision

Typically, a round dining table at a conference might serve eight to ten people. It can be almost humorous—and definitely predictable—to watch the anxiety developing on the faces of a few people around the table. Everyone is seated at approximately the same time. The panic sets in when people look at the overwhelming number of eating utensils, glasses, and plates in front of them. Adrift on a sea of silverware, they do not know which belongs to them or where to begin. It is fun to watch the eyes of the people around the table. Some have an air of confidence and know exactly what to do. Others sit anxiously with their hands in their laps waiting for someone else to make the first move. Actually, this is a smart thing to do if you are not sure of yourself. But think about how much more confident you could be if you knew exactly what to do. People gain a new level of respect for their "socially aware" colleagues who act with an air of confident ease at a social setting in the business world.

Try imagining what goes through the minds of people in such settings. They might be thinking, "Oh, my gosh! I know my parents used to tell me rules of etiquette, but I never thought I would have to remember to use them. I should have listened to what they were saying!"

We are moving up the corporate ladder because of our intelligence, our talent, and our creative abilities. Admittedly, we are a bit rusty when it comes to business etiquette.

Success Tip

Keep in mind that there is a vast difference between those who break the rules through choice and those who break the rules through ignorance. It shows!

❖ Competitive Edge

Corporate America is a fast-moving culture, and competition is an inherent factor. Corporations and businesses compete, and divisions within corporations compete against each other. Departments within divisions compete, and individuals within departments are competitive. Having knowledge of business etiquette can be one more tool to provide you with a competitive edge over others. It can be *the* tool that gives you the promotion you well deserve.

Repeatedly there are stories of individuals who have not been hired or who have not been promoted because of an inadvertent social *faux pas*. They may never have received feedback that an etiquette error was their problem. They may never have known why they were overlooked for the position. Could this ever have happened to you? Think about this question as you work your way through the module.

❖ Perception Is Essential

Think about the individuals who seem to know exactly what to do and when to do it and are always able to execute it with grace and style. Whether you like them or not, don't you secretly admire them? Don't you tend to think they probably have attended some special training program that you have not had access to?

Remember that correct behavior is learned behavior. If you commit yourself to practice the information in this module, you can generate the perception that you also have had that special training program. Practice in all settings, especially the most comfortable settings (such as at home), so that proper etiquette will become second nature to you in the work environment.

RECAP OF KEY CONCEPTS

- The first rule of etiquette is that the other person feels comfortable.

- Knowing the rules of etiquette helps builds confidence, which can improve competition in the business world.

- Traditionally a man walks on the outside of a sidewalk, a man drives the car, and a man opens the doors; these roles have changed with today's business climate.

- Positive behavior reflecting good manners to others is cost effective for business.

CORPORATE DRESS AND PRESENTATION

AT THE CORE
This topic examines:

- Today's corporate attire

- How to treat clients and/or visitors courteously

- The use of effective eye contact with others

- The effect that smiling has on others

- The importance of leaving an employer with a positive feeling

There is a general statement "You never have a second chance to make a first impression." How you package yourself and present yourself to the public is important to you personally for career advancement; it is also important to your employer and to the image of the company.

❖ Dress and Presentation

There was a plethora of books written in the 1980s about dressing for success—both for men and women. The "uniform" for success was at its peak during that time. This section will explore today's attitudes toward professional dress.

There has been a quiet rebellion against the dress-for-success rigidity within many corporations, especially in the high-tech world. Today's clothing guidelines are definitely more relaxed. However, there are still some basic rules. Remember that the way you dress reflects your personal marketing strategy; it is your "packaging." Many corporations have changed to "business casual," which consists of comfortable clothes that could be considered "dress casual."

The first rule, no matter where you work, is to learn the corporate climate. Basically, be alert. What are your bosses wearing? What is the attire of those employees who have gained a great deal of respect? A general guide is to wear clothes that are somewhat similar to those who are one step above you. You can dress for the job you want while dressing appropriately for the job you have.

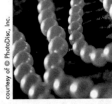

courtesy of © PhotoDisc, Inc.

General Guidelines for Dress and Presentation:

Rule: Do not mix styles. If one day you are dressing with a preppy look, then be consistently preppy from head to toe. If you are dressing with a European look, then be consistent with that look, too.

Rule: If you are color blind, get help. Have retail salespeople help you coordinate your clothes; then organize them in your closet so you remember what goes together. You do not need to make a fashion statement—just be sure your clothes and accessories match.

Rule: Avoid clothing that is too tight. Buy your clothes just a bit larger than you need to, to present a more flowing and stylish look. This is especially true for men's shirts and women's blouses.

Rule: Keep your shoes in good condition. Nothing ruins a "look" like unpolished shoes, run down heels, or holey soles. Unkempt shoes can detract from one's overall appearance.

Rule: Keep jewelry simple. In the business environment, modesty is the general rule with jewelry. If you wear three sets of earrings in each ear at home, wear just one pair to the office.

Rule: Avoid risqué clothing. It is not appropriate for the office. This is true for both men and women. It is unprofessional to see a man's chest, biceps, or belly peeking out from a shirt. Likewise, it is totally unprofessional to see a woman's cleavage or bare shoulders or too much bare leg. It may get attention—but not the kind of attention for long-term professional respect. Leave some aspects of your personal life (like overly casual or revealing attire) separate from your work life.

courtesy of © PhotoDisc, Inc.

❖ Casual Days

If your job requires you to dress casually on designated days, then do so. But remember that your professionalism needs to transcend your casual attire. If you deal directly with the public, try to maintain the image you project every other day—customers appreciate it. If you plan to go somewhere after work that requires more casual attire, bring clothes and change at the end of the day.

❖ Office Visitors

When someone takes the time to come to your office to see you, give your whole attention to that person. Make solid eye contact. Do not shuffle papers or talk on the telephone. If you are busy, say so.

You do not have to give away your precious time to visitors, however. There are ways to control your time. For example, while glancing at the clock, say "I've got an appointment at 2 p.m., so I have about four minutes for a quick chat. What's going on?" Then give your undivided attention. Make people feel welcome. Outside visitors should never be considered an interruption of your work.

If you are in a service organization (which probably applies to most workers), consider everyone who comes your way to be a potential

© Digital Vision

customer. You should never be too busy to share a kind word, to give quick directions, or to answer a question.

If a talkative coworker comes by, stand up when that person arrives, and stay standing. Do not invite him or her to sit down. Say "Where are you headed this morning? I'll walk in that direction with you." Then walk together out of the building, go in separate directions, and return alone.

❖ Eye Contact

Depending on the size of the community, there is a big difference in how strangers make eye contact. In big cities, strangers rarely make eye contact with others in public. Conversely, in small towns, you are expected to make eye contact with strangers on the street. In fact, you would be considered rude if you did not also smile and say "Good morning," "Hello," or at least "Hi."

If you live in a small town and visit large cities, you may have to remind yourself to curtail your customary small-town friendliness. You want to appear confident and alert, but people might misinterpret your intentions.

Direct eye contact between professionals is considered excellent business practice. Older traditional manners encouraged women *not* to make direct eye contact. In today's American business culture, however, eye contact is a positive means of projecting confidence, honesty, and good intentions. Lack of direct eye contact (especially in conversations between two people) can be offensive or perceived as deceitful.

ON THE SCENE

During a recent networking reception at a conference, I was feeling very uncomfortable. Whenever I started a conversation, the person with whom I was speaking would look over my shoulder. I had the impression the person was looking for someone else to talk to (obviously someone who was more important than I). I know this is just perception, but it does not leave a good impression. I am always impressed when someone of authority takes time to give me his or her undivided attention. I am especially impressed when I know there may be many others around who also want to talk to this person and that my partner in conversation is not distracted. The benefit of habitually giving your undivided attention is that you will earn the reputation of being a good listener.

❖ Smile

We all know how wonderful it is to have someone smile at us, and this is especially true in the work environment. A simple smile can positively enhance your work environment by altering a negative mood, nurturing camaraderie, and reinforcing self-esteem.

Smile when you see people. Smile when you meet people. Smile when you talk to people. Smile even when you talk to people on the telephone. Did you know that people actually *hear* a smile?

ON THE SCENE

In a former job, I passed rows of office workers on the way to my office. I always made a point to smile and acknowledge them personally as members of our work team. One day a woman I barely knew came into my office. "Do you have a minute?" she said. "I want you to know how much I appreciate working around you. You've been so pleasant and uplifting. I've been going through some personally trying times. The only nice part of my day has been coming to work and seeing your lovely smile. I've always wanted to thank you for helping me through this difficult time." This experience taught me that you never know how your attitude might affect another person. One courteous act communicates volumes.

❖ Leaving a Job

When you plan to leave a place of employment, be pleasant during your remaining time. No matter how you feel, do not "bad mouth" the place of employment. You never know when your bad actions will come back to haunt you. Remember that these are the people who provided you with a paycheck.

When you apply for a job, reference checks will be made. People talk to people they know; they do not call just the people you have listed on the application. It is amazing what you can learn about people in casual conversation. "Hey, Tom. You used to work for XYZ, didn't you? I thought so. Did you ever know someone named Susan Jones who worked in data processing?" That's how the *real* reference checks happen. Often people don't even realize they are supplying a reference check when they take part in such a conversation.

ON THE SCENE

Recently, I left a fabulous job. The people I left actually felt hurt and rejected. I could feel it when I informed them I was leaving. "Didn't you enjoy your job? What did we do to make you want to leave?" Such responses made me feel I had to give a reason for my departure. I made sure I expressed my sadness in leaving and that my decision was based on the necessity to live closer to my family and on my desire to return to teaching.

◆ One of the basic rules of appropriate professional attire is to learn the corporate climate.

◆ When someone comes to your work area, give him or her your undivided attention so he or she feels welcome.

◆ Eye contact between the listener and the one who is talking is necessary for effective communication.

◆ Smile when you see people; it is contagious.

◆ If you plan to leave a place of employment, do not talk negatively about your employer or the company's product or service; doing so could come back to haunt you.

INTERACTING WITH PEOPLE

Quality management practices recognize that all people are our "clients." Outside visitors to our company, of course, are potential clients, but people within our own organization should also be considered our clients.

❖ Making Introductions

When you introduce two people, look first to the person you consider to be more important. Say that person's name first, followed by "I would like you to meet . . ." Then look at the person being introduced, and reverse the order. How you make the introductions of people infers who you consider to be more important.

It helps to add a pertinent comment about the person to get the conversation going. Note in the following examples how the brief comments are added to the end of each introductory line. This provides a starting point for conversation between the individuals being introduced.

Introducing your boss to your visiting sister: "Dr. Smith, I would like you to meet my sister Jan Edwards, who is going to have lunch with me today. Jan, this is the president of our college, Dr. Marie Smith."

When individuals appear to be fairly equal in authority, you can choose who is "more special." If your guest, for instance, is a personal friend who is visiting you at work, you would probably begin with Joe Howard, the vice president: "Mr. Howard, I'd like you to meet my friend Carla Miller, who is going to lunch with me today. Carla, this is Joe Howard, our vice president." However, if you were providing a tour of the company to a special guest, you

courtesy of © PhotoDisc, Inc.

might chose to begin with him: "Carla, I'd like you to meet our vice president, Joe Howard. Joe, this is Carla Miller. She's my special guest today from Intel® Corporation and is touring our facility."

Introducing a younger person to an older person: "Mrs. Alomar, I want you to meet Bill Bromwell, who is responsible for organizing the event today. Bill, this is Mrs. Alomar; she's an active member of our Foundation."

❖ Repeating Names

As soon as someone has been introduced to you, make an attempt to repeat his or her name. This is a technique reinforced by Dale Carnegie[3] in his books and nationally recognized seminars and has been taught to salespersons for years. The other person feels recognized when you repeat his or her name. Additionally, repeating the name helps you better remember it. Here are some examples:

- "Exactly how do you spell your last name, John?"

- "I have a cousin who also has the name Barbara."

- "Dr. Mason, where do you live?"

- "Senator Barberi, would you like some refreshments?"

- "The name Hans sounds German. Is it?"

❖ Forgetting Names

When meeting a lot of people on a daily basis, it can be difficult to remember names. However, some people are offended if you don't remember their names.

ON THE SCENE

I have often moved to new communities, changed careers, and changed work environments. Each time a change is made, I must become acquainted with hundreds of new faces. For the person who stays in one job for, say, 40 years, the difficulty of remembering all those new faces may go unappreciated. It is easier being in one place and learning just the names of a few new people over the course of time.

Be tolerant of people who are new to your environment. Try hard to remember others' names, but do not be harsh if others cannot remember yours. Some people will use nicknames rather than real names: "Hi, buddy." "Hello, partner." "Hey, friend." This may be a way to get by if they do not remember names very well. The friendliness of the greeting is at least a start.

It may be better to be honest if you cannot remember someone's name. Say something such as, "I can't believe it! I've gone blank again. Please tell me your name one more time."

❖ Shaking Hands

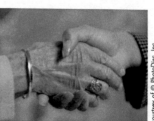

Shaking hands is very much an American custom. If you are not comfortable shaking hands, you are missing a wonderful opportunity to connect with other people.

Take time to practice shaking hands with a few close friends. Ask them what your handshake feels like. Practice until you have a firm "vertical" handshake. In other words, don't turn your knuckles, forcing the other person to give a "curtsy" handshake. Your hands should meet on an equal basis. Men should not shake hands with a woman any differently than they would with another man.

A handshake should not be a bone crusher, keeping in mind that a person wearing rings may feel pain if a handshake is too strong. Conversely, a handshake should not be limp. Some people are offended by a limp handshake, as the perception is one of being frail. People prefer a firm, friendly handshake.

When you know you are going to be introduced to others, be sure your right hand is free. If you are a woman, carry a bag over your shoulder. If you are at a social event, carry your plate or glass with your left hand so your right hand is free.

Three shakes seem to be about right. A lingering handshake is not necessary. Letting go prematurely, however, may indicate you are not comfortable with the person. Rely on your best sense of social timing.

When meeting someone new, try waiting for the other person to release your hand first. This might appear trivial, but you can tell he or she, appreciates it (along with, of course, a nice smile and direct eye contact).

If you are at work sitting behind your desk or on the other side of a table when a visitor comes by, walk around your desk so you are next to your visitor when you shake hands. This effort shows a sincere interest on your part in greeting the other person.

The days of women staying seated while men shake hands are long gone. In the business environment, all people should stand, recognize each other, and shake hands with each other. Women who are uncomfortable with this role should practice being more assertive and shaking hands until they become more comfortable.

❖ Making Small Talk

Some people dread social events because they are uncomfortable with small talk. You do not have to be a victim. You can learn to take control of conversation. You can make a social situation as interesting as you want it to be.

One of the big secrets to good conversation is to ask questions. Learn to ask questions that are open-ended, not closed. A closed question is one that begs only a one-word response. Here are some examples of dead-end closed questions that do nothing to enhance good conversation.

- "How are you today?"

- "Are you having a good time?"

- "Did you come in the same vehicle as the Browns?"
- "Which class did you decide to take for your staff development requirement?"

Do you get the idea? The short answers, respectively, would be as follows:

- "Fine, thank you."
- "Yes."
- "No, I came with Alice."
- "The Internet class."

If you seek information asking open-ended questions, you will get more meaningful answers. You actually will be able to lead conversations. You will not have to do much of the talking unless you want to, and you will learn a great deal about other people. Here are examples of open-ended questions to use when asking for information.

- "Tell me about the highlight of your day."
- "Who have you talked to, and what did you learn?"
- "How did you get here?"
- "What have you learned in the course you chose to take for staff development?"

If you ask questions like these, you will have lively verbal interaction that will be of interest to you and the other person. In addition, people will think you are the life of the party. Try it.

❖ The Art of Conversation

At social gatherings, people are generally most comfortable around people they know. They will group together, appearing to exclude others. The intent is not to be exclusive, but an outsider or new person may find it a challenge to join into conversation with such an established group. In this section, we will explore techniques you can use to reach out to new people.

Entering a Room. A room full of people can be a daunting experience if you do not have a plan of action. Preparing a plan before you enter a room will give you more confidence than just wandering into the room and hoping for the best.

First, consider what you want to accomplish, and focus on that. Are you there to celebrate a friend's achievement? Are you there to network and meet new people? Are you there to see friends and perhaps meet a couple of new people? Are you there to meet the love of your life? Again, keep the focus on why you are there. Set realistic goals, so they will be easier to accomplish. Making six new friends may not be too realistic. It may be easier to meet one new person with whom you have something in common. You will feel a sense of accomplishment and not be too disappointed in yourself if you set realistic goals.

Next, settle yourself and gain a sense of the whole room. After you first enter, stand off to one side, and survey the room. Breathe deeply a few times, and gain your composure. Check for people you recognize; then continue surveying the room. Look for interesting people you may want to meet. If you do find some people you know, walk over to them and acknowledge them, but do not stay with them the entire time. Make a point of getting to know new people. Keep in mind your original plan.

Starting a Conversation. Do not expect people to come up to you and begin a conversation. If you do, you may be alone for quite a while. Look for someone who is also alone. It is much easier to walk up to an individual and start a conversation than it is to walk up to a group of people. Find an individual who is not with anyone and start your conversation there.

Introduce yourself to the person. "Hello. My name is . . . What's yours?" Offer your hand in greeting. Give a little information about yourself; then ask some questions to start the conversation. Prepare ahead of time, especially if you are shy. Here are some suggested comments with open-ended questions.

- "I'm new here and don't know anybody. Do you know any of these people?"

- "I'm a bit shy when it comes to these kinds of things. What usually happens?"

- "This is my first time to one of these events. Have you attended before? What's is it like?"

- "I believe I saw you at the last meeting. What did you think of it?"

- "I'm a new hire as of last week. What do you do here at the company?"

- "I'm here at the wedding from out of town. How do you know the bride and groom?"

ON THE SCENE

When I first moved to the community of Santa Rosa, California, I knew only a few people. I attended one of my first parties at a private residence, but none of the few people I knew had arrived yet. I had no one to talk to. I saw a man off by himself, leaning next to the refrigerator. I began asking him some open-ended questions. He beamed when I began making conversation with him, and we both enjoyed our conversation off to the side of the crowd. I later learned that I had been talking to Charles Shultz, the creator of Peanuts, who was known to be a shy person and not one comfortable with conversation. We established an acquaintance that continued for years.

In the book *How to Start a Conversation and Make Friends*[4], the authors suggest that you remember the acronym *SOFTEN*, which will remind you of certain actions to take.

- Smile

- Open posture

- Forward lean of your body
- Touch with a nice handshake
- Eye contact
- Nod in affirmation

A genuine smile with a twinkle in your eye is a powerful way to communicate your willingness to meet another person. Just smile and say "hello." You will have someone to talk to in no time at all.

Negative body language can turn people away as quickly as a smile can engage them. Slouching, folding arms over your body, or leaning with legs crossed are all considered negative, or closed, postures. On the other hand, standing is always more approachable than sitting. Standing tall with an alert posture is positive. Plant both feet on the ground, supporting yourself in an upright manner. Communicate to others by your body language that you are willing to be engaged in conversation.

When you begin a conversation with another person, lean forward slightly toward the person. Tilting your head forward provides the same gesture. Consider people from Japan, who actually bend at the waist and bow when meeting someone. Americans nod slightly or lean forward, which may be a holdover from days gone by of bowing and curtsies. The reverse of this is to lean backward or lift the chin, which communicates the notion of being repulsed by someone.

❖ Keeping Promises

Do not trust your memory. Have a follow-up system ready so you remember to keep the promises you make. Carry a note pad, for instance, so you can write down even the smallest commitment you make.

You actually provide a compliment to people and impress them when you remember seemingly unimportant things. "Norman, here's that article on Harley-Davidson® I was telling to you about." "Sonja, here's my doctor's name and phone number I promised to share with you." "Joe, here's that web site we were talking about."

Use the calendar program on your computer to make notes to yourself. "Marie goes to Washington tomorrow. Call to see if she needs anything." "Henry's mother has surgery today. Send her a card." "Al's daughter graduates with an M.A. degree next week. Buy her a gift." You will be perceived as a compassionate person if you reach out to people and remember special events in their lives. Your awareness (and thoughtfulness) will work to your advantage.

❖ Exchanging Business Cards

Having personal business card enables you to network with people in the business world. You can exchange business cards at professional meetings and other events where you practice your conversation skills.

Your personal business card should have all pertinent information—your name, address, and phone number. Items such as e-mail address, fax number, logo, or motto are helpful additions. If you do not yet have a job or if you work out of your home, you may want to think twice about putting your home address on a business card. Consider obtaining a post office box for your official address. Or your phone number and e-mail address may be sufficient. Be sure the card is not cluttered and looks professional.

Microsoft Publisher® has an easy-to-follow Wizard that takes you through the process of designing a business card. Many formats are available that will give your card a professional appearance. You can buy plain business card stock from a stationery store to use in printing out your cards. At first, print just one page of ten cards. Hand out some cards to people, and observe their reactions. Evaluate the information on the card before printing more. Ask your friends and colleagues for their input. Your business card is a personal statement, so you want it to be right.

After meeting new people and talking with them, you may want to ask for their business cards. Then you can politely ask "Would you care to have my business card?" But keep in mind that exchanging business cards should follow a conversation of some substance.

Organize the business cards you collect from people. You may want to jot a few notes directly on the card that will jog your memory later. (For example, "He is interested in talking to me after I graduate.")

RECAP OF KEY CONCEPTS

◆ When introducing one person to another, take into consideration who the "senior" person is or the one of higher rank; that is the person to whom the other person should be presented.

◆ When introducing someone, include a sentence about the person that will invite conversation between the two people being introduced.

◆ When you are introduced to someone, repeat that person's name as soon as possible so it will be easier to remember.

◆ An American handshake is firm but not crushing; combine it with sincere conversation.

◆ Small talk is more interesting if you use open-ended questions that invite more than one-word responses as answers.

◆ Conversation can be aided greatly if you have a plan of action before entering a room.

◆ Carry a pen and paper to write notes to yourself so you can follow up on any promises you make.

◆ Always carry a professional business card ready to exchange with others at a business networking event.

OFFICE ETIQUETTE

To give your work life the quality of your personal life, you need to apply many of the same energies and skills. Be punctual. Be discreet. Empathize. Offer privacy. See the big picture. Dress to match the occasion. Behave honorably. The Golden Rule finds no better expression than in the workplace.

❖ The Work Day

Managers become annoyed with employees who appear to watch the clock. Managers especially resent those who spend 15 or 20 minutes preparing to leave for the day. These same people are the ones who arrive on time, yet spend 15 or 20 minutes getting ready to start their work day. If your day begins at 8:30 a.m., you should be in the office (with your coat hung up and your coffee poured) at your desk at 8:30. Likewise, if your day ends at 5 p.m., then 5 p.m. is the time to begin packing up your belongings for your departure. If you have an hour for lunch, that does not mean you leave 15 minutes before the hour and return 15 minutes after the hour. Keep in mind that you are being paid to work a certain number of hours. You owe it to your employer to give that amount of time in actual work.

© EyeWire

If you are a salaried employee, you have more of an obligation to accomplish your assignments. In American culture, salaried persons often work more hours during the week than the office staff, including the lunch break. Actually, lunch is an excellent time to accomplish a good deal of work. At lunch, you are away from the usual interruptions. The pleasant atmosphere in a restaurant sets a different mood. If you are in a position to do work during lunch, take a pad of paper so you can jot down notes or plan strategies.

Take time to have lunch with all of your coworkers—people you work with at all levels. About 15 minutes before lunch, walk into an office and say "Anybody here who does not have lunch plans? I don't have any plans today and would love to join someone." Even if you receive no offers (and feel a bit rejected), you will have spread some good will around the office.

❖ Respecting Others

There is a motto that says "Everyone needs and deserves to be treated with dignity and respect." This does make sense. Make sure you treat everyone at your workplace with respect.

You often spend more hours of your "awake life" with those at work than you do with members of your own family. This should make you stop and consider how many times a day you choose to criticize rather than empathize. It is important to nurture your relationships at work, as they can be vitally important to your personal happiness. There are ways to sustain a positive and healthy working relationship with your coworkers. First, treat everyone with respect.

ON THE SCENE

I know an office assistant who rolls her eyes and uses a contemptuous tone when speaking of her boss in his absence. If someone is looking for him and he happens to be at a meeting, she says "Who knows where he is? It's after 3, and he's rarely here this late." Instead, she should say, "You missed him again. He's so busy with various meetings that I can hardly keep up with him. Let me have your number so he can call you for an appointment."

Try to avoid the habit of using possessive pronouns when describing coworkers. For example, instead of saying "This is *my* assistant Mary," say "This is Mary who works in the Research Department." Another version would be "This is Mary who works with me in the Research Department." Leave it to Mary to explain her role and what she does. After all, the two of you are working together for the same end.

❖ Making or Not Making Coffee

Making coffee for the boss is frequently perceived as a demeaning chore for an assistant. Bosses may think that since they are paying the salary, they should be able to ask their staff to do anything. The whole issue comes down to courtesy and respect for each other.

The task of making coffee can be shared, which makes it much less demeaning. For instance, a boss can say to an administrative assistant, "Toni, I'm going down to the staff lounge. Would you like a cup of fresh coffee?" Toni will be more amenable later when her boss asks "This afternoon I'm having some special guests come into the office. Would you mind bringing us coffee then? I sure would appreciate it."

❖ "Not in My Job Description"

One of the most annoying sentences in the workplace is "That's not in my job description." Employers cringe when they hear employees say those words or express the attitude behind the words.

Many offices today follow quality management practices. With this in mind, the customer (client, student, patient) deserves the utmost respect. Everyone should try to accommodate the customer's needs. Many times that customer is internal. For instance, a manager can be the customer to the Payroll Department.

As employees, we should consider how we can all work together to get the job done as well as to provide the utmost service to our clients. Even if we are asked to do something outside of our job description, we should never respond with the sentence "It's not in my job description." Instead, we could say "I'm not the most knowledgeable person on that subject. Michael has more experience. Let me take you over to his office." Or "You really need to be talking to Joanna, who's in charge of our employee fitness program. Let me give her a ring and see if she's available."

❖ Complaining Effectively

Most managers spend a good portion of their time solving problems. This part of their job may not be pleasant. It is certainly important to be honest about job concerns, especially those that affect productivity and overall effectiveness. A healthy way to complain, however, is to be as objective as possible and present realistic solutions over which you can be directly responsible.

Do not just register a complaint: "I have a real problem with Fred's unwillingness to do work outside of what he considers his job description."

Do not bother to register a complaint accompanied by a solution over which you have no control: "I have a real problem with Fred's unwillingness to do work outside of what he considers his job description. Why don't you tell him that he should change his attitude."

Do register a complaint with a solution over which you have some control: "I have a real problem with Fred's unwillingness to do work outside of what he considers his job description. I was wondering if both he and I could attend the upcoming quality workshop. I'd be glad to be his study partner. Maybe he'll open up more with his self-imposed job parameters."

❖ Making Others Look Good

Try to give away more credit than you feel is actually due. Some people may not agree with this, but in the long run, you will be rewarded for doing so.

If coworkers contribute on a project, put their names in print as participants. When giving a speech, say "And we couldn't have accomplished this project without all the help provided by . . ." In actuality, their input may have been quite limited. So what. They will always appreciate the fact that you mentioned their names.

Workers resent an individual who takes credit for a project on which he or she had barely any input. People will be glad to work on your team knowing that you do not take all the credit yourself and that you share it with others.

Try to support the decisions of others, especially if you are working in a participatory decision-making environment. If a team works together to make a decision that isn't exactly in line with your thinking, support the decision anyway. As long as the decision is not life threatening or totally misguided, go along with it. Support it and think of the long-term picture of developing a productive team of co-workers.

❖ Telephone

Organizations spend an incredible amount of money on marketing to gain the attention of potential clients. The first point of contact for most new clients is a telephone call. This is the first impression a potential client will have of your company.

If you are in a position to answer telephones for your organization, consider how important it is to make a good impression.

When you answer the telephone, identify yourself using your first and last name. Identifying yourself properly saves time and confusion. Generally, it is unprofessional in many situations to identify yourself only by your first name. Women are particularly guilty of this. "Health Center, this is Kay."

© Digital Vision

ON THE SCENE

I do not think some of my friends realize how frustrating it is when they call my voice mail and say "This is Bill. I need to schedule a meeting. Call me back." I must know at least seven different men named Bill!

When using the telephone, don't forget to smile. People actually hear a smile! Your tone of voice on the telephone sets the tone of the business transaction to follow. Answer every telephone call as if it were the first one of the day, and there is a million dollars pending that call!

Professional use of the telephone includes returning calls. Not returning telephone calls sends a negative message. If you don't actually want to talk to an individual, call when he or she will not be available (such as during the lunch hour) and leave a message. At least you will have returned the call.

❖ Leaving Messages

Almost everyone today has voice mail. Do not get into the "loop" of playing telephone tag. Try to be as succinct as possible. Give some idea of why you are calling, and leave any pertinent information. Often business can be taken care of by leaving a quick message. You can eliminate hours of wasted time by becoming a practiced message leaver and receiver.

An example might be "Hello. This is Keisha Jaders in the Accounting Department. There appears to be an error on your purchase order #0137 for the scanner you ordered. The quantity is two, but the price total is for three items. Could you please clarify this? My extension is 4473." This is a much better way to use voice mail than saying, "Hello. This is Keisha Jaders. Please call me on extension 4473. It's urgent."

And the answer to this problem probably can be solved with one quick reply on the telephone, perhaps to Keisha's voice mail.

Slow down when leaving your telephone number. Many people leave a very clear message but speed up when they get to their phone number. Remember to slow down.

❖ Getting Attention

An old sales trick works well when you are calling busy people. Ask, "Do you have a minute?" A positive response to the question commits them psychologically to focus on your telephone call. "Hi, Jose. I'm glad I caught you. I need to talk to you about our annual budget. Do you have a minute?"

It does work. People then focus on what you have to say even if they have a distraction at hand. They have made the commitment to listen to you.

❖ Ending the Telephone Conversation

End your conversation on a positive note whether in person or on the phone. Leave people thinking positive thoughts about you as you sign off. Force yourself, if necessary, to think of something positive to say to others. This list of sentences can be used when ending a meeting or telephone call.

- "I always enjoy talking with you; you're so enthusiastic."

- "I always enjoy working with you; you're such a visionary person."

- "I always enjoy our conversation; you keep me very well informed about changes that are taking place."

- "Thank you for the information; you're such an upbeat and pleasant person."

RECAP OF KEY CONCEPTS

- ◆ Business etiquette means being respectful of your employer by working the number of hours for which you are paid.

- ◆ Treat everyone with dignity and respect.

- ◆ Provide the best service possible to customers and clients; do not be guilty of saying "That's not in my job description."

- ◆ If you have a complaint about someone or something, offer it along with a solution over which you have some control.

♦ Give others more credit that you think they deserve; you will generally be rewarded for it later.

♦ Always answer the telephone with a smile; answer each telephone call as if it were of the utmost importance.

♦ Leave telephone messages with some substance so people will not get caught in a telephone message "loop."

❖ Notes